Abraham Lincoln
THE WAR YEARS
IN FOUR VOLUMES

Volume 4

The worn but lighted Abraham Lincoln. One of a series of photographs by Alexandei Gardnei,
April 10, '65

From the Meserve collection

ABRAHAM LINCOLN

The War Years

BY CARL SANDBURG

WITH 426 HALF-TONES OF PHOTOGRAPHS, AND
244 CUTS OF CARTOONS, LETTERS, DOCUMENTS

Volume Four

HARCOURT, BRACE & COMPANY
NEW YORK

Typography by Robert Josephy

CONTENTS

tives and possible incitements – "Habiliments of mourning" – "A stricken people came to their altars"

LIST OF ILLUSTRATIONS

Abraham Lincoln
THE WAR YEARS

CHAPTER 61

"FOREVER FREE"—THE THIRTEENTH AMENDMENT

A NEWLY freed Negro was quoted: "When I was a slave, if I fell off a boat they would stop and pick me up and put me by a fire to dry. I was worth money. Now if I fall off a boat they calls out, 'It's only a damned nigger—let him go under.' "

More than 1,300,000 slaves had been freed "by the Lincoln Administration or by the events of the war," indicated a statistical table in the *Philadelphia North American* in November of '64. Of slaves when the war began one out of three now was free—under the Emancipation Proclamation of "military necessity." The Federal Constitution however still held these slaves to be property, except in Missouri and Maryland, two States which had legalized emancipation.

Journals of wide circulation published many incidents touching a changed Negro. *Leslie's Weekly* reported a Negro who took a hand in a guerrilla fight: "We fit 'em, we whopt 'em, and we kotched ten uv 'em." *Harper's Monthly* told of Confederate prisoners at Rock Island, Illinois, under Negro guards—and one guard, suddenly seeing his old master, the man who once owned him, cried out, "Hullo, massa! *bottom rail top!*"

Around this reversal surged the revolution. Soldiers and home folks now sang the mocking, triumphant laughter of Henry C. Work's "Kingdom Coming" and "Babylon Is Fallen." In the first the plantation master has seen the smoke up the river "whar de Linkum gunboats lay; he took his hat an' lef berry sudden." The overseer is locked in the smokehouse cellar, the key thrown in the well. "De whip is lost, de handcuff broken, but de massa'll hab his pay." From their slave cabins the Negroes move into the Big House parlor, enjoy the master's wine and cider, waiting "till de Linkum sojers come." The verses had pomp and circumstance, with a chorus ending "It must be now de kingdom comin', An de year ob Jubilo." The other song was meant for the Negro soldier. Thunder over the cornfields said Babylon is fallen, "And we's agwine to occupy de land." Their master, "de kernel in de rebel army, dey take him pris'ner tudder day." And now? "We will be de massa, He will be de sarvant—Try him how he like it for

3

BY THE PRESIDENT OF THE UNITED STATES OF AMERICA.

A Proclamation.

Whereas, on the twenty-second day of September, in the year of our Lord one thousand eight hundred and sixty-two, a proclamation was issued by the President of the United States, containing, among other things, the following, to wit:

"That on the first day of January, in the year of our Lord one thousand eight hundred and sixty-three, all persons held as slaves within any State or designated part of a State, the people whereof shall then be in rebellion against the United States, shall be then, thenceforward, and forever, free; and the Executive government of the United States, including the military and naval authority thereof, will recognize and maintain the freedom of such persons, and will do no act or acts to repress such persons, or any of them, in any efforts they may make for their actual freedom.

"That the Executive will, on the first day of January aforesaid, by proclamation, designate the States and parts of States, if any, in which the people thereof, respectively, shall then be in rebellion against the United States; and the fact that any State, or the people thereof, shall on that day be in good faith represented in the Congress of the United States, by members chosen thereto at elections wherein a majority of the qualified voters of such State shall have participated, shall, in the absence of strong countervailing testimony, be deemed conclusive evidence that such State, and the people thereof, are not then in rebellion against the United States."

Now, therefore, I, ABRAHAM LINCOLN, PRESIDENT OF THE UNITED STATES, by virtue of the power in me vested as commander-in-chief of the army and navy of the United States, in time of actual armed rebellion against the authority and government of the United States, and as a fit and necessary war measure for suppressing said rebellion, do, on this first day of January, in the year of our Lord one thousand eight hundred and sixty-three, and in accordance with my purpose so to do, publicly proclaimed for the full period of one hundred days from the day first above mentioned, order and designate as the States and parts of States wherein the people thereof, respectively, are this day in rebellion against the United States, the following, to wit: ARKANSAS, TEXAS, LOUISIANA, (except the Parishes of St. Bernard, Plaquemines, Jefferson, St. John, St. Charles, St. James, Ascension, Assumption, Terre Bonne, Lafourche, St. Mary, St. Martin, and Orleans, including the City of New Orleans,) MISSISSIPPI, ALABAMA, FLORIDA, GEORGIA, SOUTH CAROLINA, NORTH CAROLINA, AND VIRGINIA, (except the forty-eight counties designated as West Virginia, and also the counties of Berkeley, Accomac, Northampton, Elizabeth City, York, Princess Ann, and Norfolk, including the cities of Norfolk and Portsmouth,) and which excepted parts are for the present left precisely as if this proclamation were not issued.

And by virtue of the power and for the purpose aforesaid, I do order and declare that all persons held as slaves within said designated States and parts of States are, and henceforward shall be free; and that the Executive government of the United States, including the military and naval authorities thereof, will recognize and maintain the freedom of said persons.

And I hereby enjoin upon the people so declared to be free to abstain from all violence, unless in necessary self-defence; and I recommend to them that, in all cases when allowed, they labor faithfully for reasonable wages.

And I further declare and make known that such persons, of suitable condition, will be received into the armed service of the United States, to garrison forts, positions, stations, and other places, and to man vessels of all sorts in said service.

And upon this act, sincerely believed to be an act of justice warranted by the Constitution upon military necessity, I invoke the considerate judgment of mankind and the gracious favor of Almighty God.

In witness whereof I have hereunto set my hand and caused the seal of the United States to be affixed.

[L. S.] Done at the CITY OF WASHINGTON this first day of January, in the year of our Lord one thousand eight hundred and sixty-three, and of the Independence of the United States of America the eighty-seventh.

By the President: *Abraham Lincoln*

William H Seward Secretary of State.

A true copy with the autograph signatures of the President and the Secretary of State.

Jno G Nicolay
Priv. Sec. to the President.

John Murray Forbes, the wealthy abolitionist merchant of Boston, causes one million copies of this document to be printed and distributed in the South. From the Lincoln Library of the University of Chicago.

a spell." Reckless revolutionary passion sang here. A fighting Negro emerged from long despair into a new future.

Early in the war Congress declared slaves free when used by the enemy for military work. Later it was enacted that officers who returned fugitive slaves to owners should be dismissed from service; freedom beckoned slaves who made their way to the Union Army lines. In sight of the Capitol dome all bondmen of the District of Columbia had their freedom purchased by the Federal Government. Also in the District now colored persons on trial for crime had the same rights as white persons; Negroes could be put on the witness stand the same as whites; the law said Negro children should have school funds on the same basis as the whites; on street-railway cars it was unlawful to throw a person off because he was a Negro. In the Territories the Negro was declared free forever. All slaves arriving in Union Army lines, if the property of slaveowners aiding the enemy, were declared free. The President was authorized to receive into the military service "persons of African descent," and such person, his mother, wife, and children, "owing service to any person giving aid to the rebellion," were declared free. All fugitive-slave acts had been repealed, the idea being to offer freedom to any Negro willing to take it by running away.

These and like measures had resulted in 1,000,000 and more slaves, possibly a third of the total, having won a freedom not clear in the law.

To clear the air on this, to make all Negroes free under the law and the Constitution, Lincoln in his December message pointed to the last session of Congress. Then "a proposed amendment of the Constitution, abolishing slavery throughout the United States, passed the Senate, but failed for lack of the requisite two-thirds vote in the House of Representatives." He would not question "the wisdom or patriotism of those who stood in opposition," while venturing to recommend reconsideration and passage of the measure at the present session. "Of course the abstract question is not changed, but an intervening election shows, almost certainly, that the next Congress will pass the measure if this does not. Hence there is only a question of time as to when the proposed amendment will go to the States for their action. And as it is to so go, at all events, may we not agree that the sooner the better?"

The President would not claim that the November election had imposed a duty on members to change their views or their votes any further than, as an additional element to be considered, their judgment might be affected by "the voice of the people," for the first time endorsing a party whose platform declared for abolition of slavery. "In a great national crisis like ours, unanimity of action among those seeking a common end is very desirable—almost indispensable. And yet no approach to such unanimity is attainable unless some deference shall be paid to the will of the majority, simply because it is the will of the majority." Slavery as an institution unless abolished was certain to threaten the Union. Lincoln's closing appeal still placed the Union cause foremost. "In this case the common end is the maintenance of the Union, and among the means to secure that end, such will [of the majority], through the election, is most clearly declared in favor of such constitutional amendment."

The Senate, it was known, had more than the requisite two-thirds of votes for this proposed Constitutional Amendment. Its 36 Republicans were joined by two Democrats, Reverdy Johnson of Maryland and James W. Nesmith of Oregon, leaving an opposition of but 7 Democrats and 5 conditional Unionists; this was the poll in March of '64. With the November election it would show an increase of Yea votes. Senator John B. Henderson of Missouri had in January of '64 brought before the Senate a joint resolution proposing a Constitutional Amendment that slavery shall not exist in the United States; this went to the Judiciary Committee. A few weeks later Senator Sumner put in another joint resolution to the same effect, to be referred to the Committee on Slavery, of which Sumner was chairman. Sumner wished a more emphatic style, phrasing his proposed Amendment to the Constitution to read that "everywhere within the limits of the United States, and of each State or Territory thereof, all persons are equal before the law, so that no person can hold another as a slave." Chairman Lyman Trumbull of the Judiciary Committee reported back a substitute for the Henderson and Sumner proposals. This was the one finally voted on. Numbered as Article XIII of the Constitution, it read:

Section 1. Neither slavery nor involuntary servitude, except as a punishment for crime whereof the party shall have been duly convicted, shall exist within the United States, or any place subject to their jurisdiction.

Section 2. Congress shall have power to enforce this article by appropriate legislation.

In the House Ashley of Ohio and Wilson of Iowa had introduced this resolution. In June of '64 it failed of the required two-thirds vote. The Yeas were 93, Nays 65, absent or not voting 23. Democrats only voted Nay, while 4 Democrats joined the 87 Republican Yeas.

The question now in January of '65 was how the House would vote under the new and changed conditions. Since the failure to get a two-thirds vote in June of '64, the National Union party had endorsed the amendment in its Baltimore platform, which swept the country by a majority of 411,000 in November.

This the President stressed in his December message, predicting time was on the side of the Amendment. "The next Congress will pass the measure if this does not." No unanimity of action toward maintenance of the Union was possible "unless some deference shall be paid to the will of the majority."

Now what? The Senate was safe. Thirteen Democrats there had joined the 4 who voted with the Republicans the year before.

But what of the House? It looked doubtful. No one was sure. Up to noon of that January 31, when the vote was taken, "the pro-slavery party are said to have been confident of defeating the amendment," ran the report of a special committee of the Union League Club of New York. "One of the most earnest advocates of the measure said, ' 'Tis the toss of a copper.' "

For more than a year Lincoln had foreseen this narrow margin. Toward this day he planned when he instigated the admission into the Union of Nevada with her added votes, when he called in Charles A. Dana and arranged for patronage gifts that would have raised a high and noisy scandal if known to the opposition. Again toward this crisis Lincoln had looked when one day only two votes were needed to make a two-thirds in the House. These votes, according to Representative John B. Alley, Lincoln said "must be procured." Alley wrote an account of how they were procured:

Two members of the House were sent for and Mr. Lincoln said that those two votes must be procured. When asked, "How?" he remarked: "I am President of the United States, clothed with great power. The abolition of slavery by constitutional provision settles the fate, for all coming time, not only of the millions now in bondage, but of unborn millions to come—a measure of such importance that *those two votes must be procured*. I leave it to you to determine how it shall be done; but remember that I am President of the United States, clothed with immense power, and I expect you to procure those votes." These gentlemen understood the significance of the remark. The votes were procured.

Three constructions were later put on the incident as told by Alley. One was that Lincoln gave the two Congressmen about whatever they asked for in the way of offices. The second was that friends or kinsfolk of these Congressmen were in prison and were let out in exchange for two votes in the House on a measure imperative to Lincoln's plans. The third was that two Congressmen who favored the bill were empowered by the President to go about as far as they liked in any patronage promises they chose to make, in behalf of the President, to secure two more votes in the House.

Alley's reserve in giving this incident, his lack of detail, might mean that he had further particulars of a sort he did not care to mention. Alley had free entry to the White House. A very practical man was Alley, his hide and leather trade in Lynn, Massachusetts, his other business interests, not suffering through his political dealings; it was possible he was one of the two Congressmen who served Lincoln in this hour when very practical methods were required. In writing of this affair, Alley did not live up to the characterization of him by the newspaper correspondent George Alfred Townsend, who wrote, possibly with extravagance: "Alley is a short, demure, white-headed man, and has an endless tongue, which testifies all manner of hearsay, and covers time with space, to the exclusion of information, and to the prejudice of more modest and less doubtful evidence."

Now it was well that Lincoln had held to his genuine friendships among Border State men. Had he traveled with the radicals he could not now have made appeals and won results among certain House members. These included one of the largest slaveholders in Missouri, James S. Rollins. Several times Rollins consulted with the President about the proposed Constitutional Amendment. Rollins heard the President in early January speak "deep anxiety" over whether it could be passed in the House. "He and others had repeatedly counted votes," wrote Rollins. "He was doubtful about its passing, and some ten days before it came up for consideration in the House, I received a note from him, written in pencil on a card, stating that he wished to see me, and asking that I call on him at the White House."

The next morning at nine Rollins found him alone in his office. "Rollins, I have been wanting to talk to you." "Well, I am here and ready to talk." "You and I were old Whigs," continued Lincoln—both of them followers of Henry Clay in old days. Lincoln then urged that "those fellows down South" were relying on the Border States for help, but if enough Representatives from those States would join in passing the Thirteenth Amendment, "they would soon see that they could not expect much help from that quarter, and be willing to give up their opposition and quit their war upon the Government; this is my chief hope and main reliance to bring the war to a speedy close, and I have sent for you as an old Whig friend to come and see me, that I might make an appeal for you to vote for this amendment. It is going to be very close. A few votes one way or the other will decide it."

Rollins's response was quick. The President didn't need to send for him on this matter. "Although I represent perhaps the strongest slave district in Missouri, and have the misfortune to be one of the largest slave-owners in the county where I reside, I had already determined to vote for the thirteenth amendment." Then, as Rollins told it, "He arose from his chair, and grasping me by the hand, gave it a hearty shake, and said, 'I am most delighted to hear that.'" The President then named various Missouri Representatives and asked how they stood. Rollins named those he knew to be for or against the bill. And on Rollins saying he was "on easy terms" with the entire Missouri delegation, Lincoln asked him if he wouldn't "talk with those who might be persuaded to vote for the amendment," and to report soon what was the prospect. Rollins agreed with pleasure to do this, adding, "When I was a young man, in 1848, I was the Whig competitor of Representative Austin A. King for governor of Missouri, and as he beat me very badly, I think now he should pay me back by voting as I desire on this important question." The President urged, "I would like you to talk to *all* the border State men whom you can approach properly, and tell them of my anxiety to have the measure pass; let me know the prospect of the border State vote." Then soberly, even solemnly: "The passage of this amendment will clinch the whole subject. It will bring the war, I have no doubt, rapidly to a close."

In one of the many House debates on the bill during January, Rollins stood up to say that a telegram had just come to him. It told him that Missouri, by amending its constitution, had given immediate emancipation to all the slaves in the State. "I am," said Rollins, "no longer the owner of a slave, and I thank God for it. . . . To restore peace and preserve this

Union, if I had owned a thousand slaves, they would most cheerfully have been given up. I say with all my heart, Let them go, but let them not go without a sense of feeling and a proper regard on my part for the future of themselves and their offspring." Rollins mourned "the wickedness and folly" of the friends of slavery who by concessions could have kept the control of the Federal Government which they had held so long. Rollins spoke regrets over having joined three years before with those who rejected President Lincoln's proposals for gradual compensated emancipation. "If ever a people made a mistake on earth, it was the men of Kentucky, by whom I was somewhat governed myself, when three years ago, they rejected the offer of the President of the United States, who, wiser than we were, seeing the difficulties before us, but seeing the bow of promise set in the sky, and knowing what was to come, proposed to us to sweep the institution of slavery from the border States, offering the assistance of the United States to aid in compensating the loyal men of those States for their losses in labor and property."

As day followed day in January the fate of the bill hung by an eye-lash. Representative George W. Julian of Indiana, a wheel-horse abolitionist, wrote of success seeming "very doubtful," how it "depended upon certain negotiations the result of which was not fully assured, and the particulars of which never reached the public." Nicolay wrote a memorandum of one attempt at negotiation with the President. This connected with Senator Sumner on the warpath against the "odious usurpations" and "intolerable pretensions" of an incorporated $27,000,000 monopoly organized in the State of New Jersey, undertaking, according to Sumner, "to levy a toll on the commerce, the passengers, the mails, and the troops of the Union in their transit" between New York and Philadelphia. Sumner had introduced bills to curb what he termed a usurped power of taxation in New Jersey. Railroad interests affected were seeking to get Sumner to drop these bills, for the time, in exchange for Democratic Representatives of New Jersey voting for the Constitutional Amendment to abolish slavery. Nicolay's memorandum indicated the desperate tactics being used to gather a few more needed votes. It also indicated that Lincoln shrank from any interference with the rights of states beyond immediate necessity. The memorandum of Nicolay read:

I went to the President this afternoon at the request of Mr. Ashley, on a matter connecting itself with the pending amendment of the Constitution. The Camden and Amboy Railroad interest promised Mr. Ashley that if he would help postpone the Raritan railroad bill over this session they would in return make the New Jersey Democrats help about the amendment, either by their votes or absence.

Sumner being the Senate champion of the Raritan bill, Ashley went to him to ask him to drop it for this session. Sumner, however, showed reluctance to adopt Mr. Ashley's suggestion, saying that he hoped the amendment would pass anyhow, etc. Ashley thought he discerned in Sumner's manner two reasons: (1) That if the present Senate resolution were not adopted by the House, the Senate would send them another in which they would most likely adopt Sumner's own phraseology and thereby gratify his ambition; and (2) that Sumner thinks the defeat of the Camden and Amboy monopoly would establish a principle by legislative enactment which would effectually crush out the last lingering relics of the States rights dogma. Ashley therefore desired the President to send for Sumner, and urge him to be practical and secure the passage of the amendment in the manner suggested by Mr. Ashley.

I stated these points to the President, who replied at once: "I can do nothing with Mr. Sumner in these matters. While Mr. Sumner is very cordial with me, he is making his history in an issue with me on this very point. He hopes to succeed in beating the President so as to change this Government from its original form and make it a strong centralized power." Then calling Mr. Ashley into the room, the President said to him, "I think I understand Mr. Sumner; and I think he would be all the more resolute in his persistence on the points which Mr. Nicolay has mentioned to me if he supposed I were at all watching his course on this matter."

This was January 18. On the thirty-first at noon the galleries of the House were filled to overflowing, notables from government departments being present, many House members wearing anxious faces, in the air a subdued hum of excitement.

After formal preliminaries, the joint resolution for a Constitutional Amendment to outlaw "slavery or involuntary servitude," except for crimes, was up for final decision.

Ashley yielded the floor to a Democrat, Archibald McAllister of Pennsylvania, who announced he would change his vote of Nay last June to Yea. "In voting for the present measure I cast my vote against the cornerstone of the southern confederacy, and declare eternal war against the enemies of my country." Applause from the Republican side.

Ashley again yields the floor to a Democrat, Alexander H. Coffroth of Pennsylvania, who says the Constitution has been amended before and he favors amending it now by removing slavery as a cause of future strife. Though other Democrats may condemn him, says Coffroth, "If by my action to-day I dig my political grave, I will descend into it without a murmur." Coffroth makes it clear that he has a home to go to where "one dear, devoted, and loved being" will not shed tears over his political grave "but will strew it with beautiful flowers." His wife would just as soon he quit politics; he is not vague about that. At a later time, his speech concludes, the Democratic party will approve of those today voting for this amendment measure, and then "it will be the desire of our hearts to open our arms for your reception and shelter you as the hen shelters her brood." Applause on the Republican side.

Ashley now yields the remainder of his time to Herrick of New York, whereupon Johnson of Pennsylvania protests the proceeding is getting arbitrary. "One gentleman occupies the floor and farms it out to whoever he pleases." Speaker Colfax upholds Ashley and reads the rules. Herrick gives five minutes of his time to Miller of Pennsylvania. Miller says, in the main, that his oath will not permit him so far to forget himself as to violate the word and letter of the Constitution, that the proposed Amendment is "a broad farce," that the President and the House have been long enough violating the Constitution. "Abolish slavery, and no man . . . has pretended to show what we are to do with the freedmen, except that, as good Christians, it will become our duty to feed and clothe them. The true philanthropists and taxpayers of the country are equally interested in knowing what is to be done with the elephant when we get him."

Herrick of the Ninth District of New York, a Democrat who had voted against the bill in June of '64, now explains that the "tone of the public mind" has changed. "Events which will now govern my action have superseded the arguments which influenced the vote I recorded last year." The November verdict at the polls is sufficient. The next Congress will be more extreme in slavery measures than the present. Why raise a useless opposition to the inevitable? If this Congress refuses to pass this bill the President will call an extra session of the new Congress in March.

A Wisconsin Democrat, James S. Brown, speaks, commenting: "Whatever may be the personal wishes of the President, he is so committed to the radicals on this question that he must call a special session of Congress." And, continues Brown, "A session of Congress unsettles all the business interests of the country." He offers a substitute measure: (1) forbidding sale or transfer of slaves; (2) releasing "all females, such as are usually termed slaves," from service obligations to freedom; (3) fixing January 1, 1880, as the date for all slaves, except a few minor categories, to be set free; (4) providing compensation by the Federal Government to "loyal citizens of the United States" for loss or damage to property through operation of the law. This more moderate measure, urges Brown, will prevent an "industrial revolution" from destroying the South.

A Kentucky Democrat, Aaron Harding, rises to rebuke two Kentucky colleagues who have changed their minds since the vote of June in '64. One of them, Green Clay Smith, comes from a district which in the late election decided against Mr. Lincoln by a majority of 2,537 votes, says Harding. In the district of his other colleague, George H. Yeaman, "the majority against this measure, against President Lincoln and the abolition policy of his Administration," was 4,615. Harding says he will not bemoan these turncoats. "When a man puts on a borrowed coat it never fits exactly, and he feels inclined to change just as often as he can borrow." The borrowed principles of the new converts mean no real change. "On the contrary, some gentlemen must be changed to keep them from changing. [Laughter.] They must be regenerated and born again, or they will exhibit such changes." Harding inquires why, if the Emancipation Proclamation was issued under pressure of military necessity, as the President had declared, it is now to become an Amendment to the Constitution as a moral principle. After which he proceeds to justify slavery by familiar and conventional arguments.

Martin Kalbfleisch, a Democrat from Brooklyn, New York, stands up and reads twenty-two sheets of heavy words meaning nothing much except that he has the words. The clock says Three. Speaker Colfax announces that the hour for voting has arrived. Kalbfleisch says he has only six more pages to read. Speaker Colfax lets him drone on. The proposed Amendment, "as if it were in truth an amendment," proceeds Kalbfleisch, "I regard as subversive of the spirit of that instrument [the Constitution]." Thirty years he has been a Democrat, says Kalbfleisch, and now as ever before he must vote against "gentlemen . . . clamorous . . . so urgent and pertinacious in seeking to lay sacrilegious hands upon that venerated and almost sacred instrument, our glorious Constitution."

Kalbfleisch finishes. The speeches are over. Not a Republican has made an argument. They are there to vote. The Democrats for and against have had their day. It is time for voting. There have been oceans of debate, thirty years of snarling controversy, till words lost meaning and language was a vapor, and the two contestants had to fall back on the oratory of dumb cannon and the persuasions of steel fangs named bayonets. Kalbfleisch is a woodenhead unaware of the political reality that on this day only roll calls count.

Two roll calls are taken. The House refuses to table, refuses to reconsider. A Kentucky Democrat, Robert Mallory, tries to stave off the coming momentous roll call. At a fixed hour "to-morrow" he would have it. Why? Because "gentlemen belonging to this side of the House . . . can be here to-morrow, but are not here to-day." Ashley replies it has been a "universal understanding" the vote is to be taken today.

The hour of the final vote comes nearer. The galleries fill till standing room is gone. Crowded to the doors are the corridors and lobbies, faces beyond faces peering toward this long-awaited climax, wondering if the two-thirds vote will be there—or not. Into the reporters' gallery sweep "a mob of well-dressed women," as Noah Brooks describes them. Do the well-dressed women stand? No, with "good grace" the press writers give up their seats to the crinoline girls. One lives only once, and there has never been anything like this. The Senate, to the *New York Tribune* man, seems to have come over in a body to stand on the House floor and see what they will see. Secretary Fessenden, Postmaster General Dennison, Monty Blair, have stepped in to look on. Grave spectators are four Associate Justices of the Supreme Court and the highly tensed Chief Justice Salmon Portland Chase, enough of the Court perhaps to make or break the measure if it should pass.

The Yeas and Nays are ordered. Alley, Allison, Ames, Anderson, and so on. These are all Republicans, their Yeas expected. Comes the name of James E. English, a Connecticut Democrat. He shouts "Aye!" A long roll of applause bursts from the gallery and Republican House members. The Speaker hammers with his gavel. The tumult goes down. Again the voice of the clerk can be heard. For the Republican Ayes as the roll call goes on there is quiet. But with each Democrat shooting his vocal Aye at the calling of his name there is another tumult of handclapping, cheers, laughter, the noisemaking of pent-up emotion let loose. Eleven Democrats answer Aye, including Anson Herrick, William Radford, Homer A. Nelson, John B. Steele, and John Ganson of New York; A. H. Coffroth and Archibald McAllister of Pennsylvania; Wells A. Hutchins of Ohio; and Augustus C. Baldwin of Michigan. The roll call goes on. A surprising proportion of Democrats answer Aye. Noah Brooks sees a group of Democratic Senators cluster around George Pendleton, McClellan's running mate of '64, "looking gloomy, black, and sour." How could John Ganson and other good Peace Democrats have so changed?

The roll call reaches the W's and Y's, where the Wood brothers Ben and Fernando of New York City vote for slavery and Yeaman of Kentucky for freedom. Speaker Colfax now does the unusual and asks that his name be called, to which he answers Aye amid applause.

Swift pencils add up the lists. The clerk whispers the result to the Speaker. He announces that the question is decided in the affirmative—Yeas 119, Nays 56, not voting 8. The *Congressional Globe* had it: "So, the two thirds required by the Constitution of the United States having voted in favor thereof, the joint resolution was passed."

Or as the *New York Tribune* man wrote it: "The Speaker announces to the House what the audience quickly interpreted to be *the mighty fact that the XXXVIIth American Congress had abolished American slavery*," wherefore "the tumult of joy that broke out was vast, thundering, and uncontrollable." Wherefore "God Bless the XXXVIIth Congress!"

Three Yea votes changed to Nay would have lost the bill. Victory came by the margin of three men voting Yea.

One hush of silence follows the Speaker's words, his pronouncing of the figures "one hundred and nineteen" and "fifty-six." Then a mass of still faces break shining and lighting. Emotions explode into a storm of cheers. Men in tears throw their arms around each other. The crowds stand up, many mounting their seats, to shout their glee. Man after man goes handshaking and backslapping. A cloud of women's handkerchiefs wave and float. Ten minutes go by before this hurricane of feeling lets down.

Representative Ebon C. Ingersoll, brother of Bob Ingersoll of Peoria, Illinois, moves adjournment "in honor of this immortal and sublime event." The Maryland Democrat B. G. Harris, as a poor loser, calls for the Yeas and Nays on this motion—but most of his own crowd are out of the chamber before their names are called.

Outside is thunder. The air is torn. Someone has ordered three batteries of regular artillery on Capitol Hill to cry joy with a salute of one hundred guns.

Eight Democrats stayed away from this House session. Had they been present, all voting with their party, there would have been no men in tears hugging each other that day, no panels of women waving handkerchiefs, no salute of a hundred guns. They also serve who stay away and wait. Something was due these eight Democrats, absent, noted Nicolay and Hay, "not altogether by accident." Noah Brooks wrote of them it was fair to assume they were not unwilling slavery should be wrecked, but were not willing to be on record in a divided party vote.

News coming next day that Illinois had ratified the Amendment, starting the line-up of three-fourths of the States necessary to amend the Constitution, Lincoln smiled. "This ends the job. I feel proud that Illinois is a little ahead." To the White House that night came a crowd with a brass band, serenaders shouting for the President. At a window they saw standing in half-lights and shadows the solemn central figure of the drama of emancipation. His exact words were given to the press in a third-person report. To the country and to the whole world, he remarked, the occasion was one of congratulation. "But there is a task yet before us—to go forward and have consummated by the votes of the States that which Congress had so nobly begun yesterday. [Applause and cries, "They will do it."]" Illinois had already done the work. Maryland was about half through.

To the shadowy faces of the torchlighted crowd he sent the impressions he considered most important to stress at this hour. "He thought this measure was a very fitting if not an indispensable adjunct to the winding up of the great difficulty. He wished the reunion of all the States perfected, and so effected as to remove all causes of disturbances in the future; and, to attain this end, it was necessary that the original disturbing cause should, if possible, be rooted out. He thought all would bear him witness that he had never shrunk from doing all that he could to eradicate slavery, by issuing an emancipation proclamation. But that proclamation falls far short of what the amendment will be when fully consummated. A question might be raised whether the proclamation was legally valid. It might be urged, that it only aided those that came into our lines, and that it was inoperative as to those who did not give themselves up; or that it would have no effect upon the children of slaves born hereafter; in fact, it would be urged that it did not meet the evil. But this amendment is a king's cure-all for all evils. It winds the whole thing up. He would repeat that it was the fitting if not the indispensable adjunct to the consummation of the great game we are playing. He could not but congratulate all present—himself, the country, and the whole world—upon this great moral victory."

He could have mentioned, to no immediate use at all, that only four years ago, in the desperate hope of averting war, Congress had passed an act for the States to amend the Constitution. It provided that no Amendment to the Constitution could be made which would authorize Congress or give it the power to abolish or interfere with slavery. President Buchanan signed the bill. Then the howling winds of war blew it into the region of oblivion and forgotten things.

The solemn figure at the shadowy window could also have mentioned, to no immediate use in particular, that this latest and formidable act of Congress was only an empty mouthing of phrases unless the bayonets of Grant and Sherman had given an awful meaning to the seizure without compensation of property sanctioned by the Constitution and once valued at $3,000,000,000. That property was now ashes in the wind.

A popular cartoon now portrayed a Negro laughing—"Now I'm nobody's nigger but my own."

Not again were radicals to hold a public bonfire in Boston burning

Thomas Nast in *Harper's Weekly* sees a Lincoln triumph in the act to amend the Constitution, abolishing slavery

the Constitution of the United States because it sanctioned chattel slavery and involuntary servitude. Not again were satirists and critics to hold it against Lincoln that he proclaimed freedom for slaves only where the Union Army bayonets had not penetrated. Now the President had what he termed "the fitting if not the indispensable adjunct" to his emancipation edict. He hoped to see further adjuncts he considered indispensable. He hoped—and he was weary—but he hoped on.

William Lloyd Garrison believed that Lincoln, more than any other one man, managed the parliamentary victory by which the abolition of slavery was to be made constitutional. Garrison had pleaded with the radical opponents of Lincoln that they were wrong. He had told them the Chief Magistrate was always just a little ahead of events, always doing the best that could be done for emancipation at any given moment. On February 4 at a Boston Music Hall meeting called for rejoicing over passage of the Thirteenth Amendment, Garrison made his public acknowledgments, printed them in the *Liberator:* "To whom is the country more immediately indebted for this vital and saving amendment of the Constitution than, perhaps, to any other man? I believe I may confidently answer—to the humble railsplitter of Illinois—to the Presidential chainbreaker for millions of the oppressed—to Abraham Lincoln! [Immense and long-continued applause, ending with three cheers for the President.] I understand that it was by his wish and influence that that plank was made a part of the Baltimore platform; and taking his position unflinchingly upon that platform, the people have overwhelmingly sustained both him and it, in ushering in the year of jubilee."

Nearly four years had passed since the *Delta* of New Orleans spoke for some of the silent men of the South, "Is it just to hold the negro in bondage?" and proceeded to ask why so many statesmen past and present refused to face realities involved in Negro freedom. What necessities of industry, social stability, art and civilization would be served, for the moment forgetting politics and its easy drifting passions? The answer of the *Delta* to its own sternly realistic questions:

"The truth is, we are in the midst of facts having a philosophy of their own which we must master for ourselves, leaving dead men to take care of the dead past. The Sphinx which is now propounding its riddles to us the dead knew nothing about; consequently no voice from the grave can tell us how to get rid of the monster."

CHAPTER 62

HEAVY SMOKE—DARK SMOKE

A SOCIAL revolution moved toward its final collapses and shadows. The Southern planter class read a handwriting on the wall of fate. Not yet did the letters spell out the shape of their doom—but doom enough had already come to make it a dark story.

For thirty years this class had kept its hands on the economic controls of the South, managed its main political decisions, developed and spread as a necessity the doctrines of States' Rights, secession, the sanctity of the institution of slavery not to be compromised, modified, nor in any essential touched.

From this class came enough spokesmen and influence in the Confederate Congress at Richmond this fourth winter of the war to overcome the proposals of Davis, Lee, and others that Negro slaves be freed to fight alongside their masters for Southern independence. That Lincoln had blocked European recognition of the Confederacy by an Emancipation Proclamation revealed nothing to these die-hards. That they might have won recognition, supplies, funds, fresh replacements of black troops, had they changed front and with a wide gesture abolished slavery—this never dawned on them. To Davis and Lee there seemed this winter a last hope of holding out against the North by giving freedom to blacks who would fight. To the extremist slaveowning element this had no appeal, seemed near treason to the Confederate cause.

The London *Times* only added to confusion when in behalf of the Southern slaveholders it gave the world a nugget of thought: "The man who would submit without a murmur to the impressment of his horses or his crops, may very likely shrink back with a superstitious horror from the attempt of his own Government [at Richmond] to deprive him of those very slaves for whom he has already fought a long and desperate war."

Into Richmond came Lee one day to speak for the underfed, ragged Army of Northern Virginia, a valiant and proved army. To and fro in his own home he paced after dinner, tramping with his hands behind him, grave, troubled, as his son Custis later told it. Suddenly he stopped before Custis seated by the fire.

"Well," said General Lee . . . "I have been up to see the Congress and they do not seem to be able to do anything except to eat peanuts and chew tobacco, while my army is starving. I told them the condition the men were in, and that something must be done at once, but I can't get them to do anything, or they are unable to do anything." Bitter was General

Lee's tone of voice. He paced to and fro again. He stopped and spoke again to his son. "Mr. Custis, when this war began I was opposed to it, bitterly opposed to it, and I told these people that unless every man should do his whole duty, they would repent it, and now"—pausing as if for emphasis—"they will repent."

At the Confederate White House, members of the Congress advised General Lee to "cheer up," one saying, "We have done good work for you today," in passing a bill "to raise an additional 15,000 men for you." Lee bowed. "Yes, passing resolutions is kindly meant, but getting the men is another matter." He hesitated a moment, then with flashing eyes, "Yet, if I had 15,000 fresh troops, things would look very different."

So the hour seemed at hand when the Confederacy had put into use its last white man—and the efforts of Davis and Lee to put black men in fighting service were blocked by an element afraid of it as a departure from traditions of the white race and from long-sanctioned property rights.

In the coming April the war would have lasted four years. This four-year period of fierce, open, and declared war had suddenly issued from a thirty-year minor storm, preparatory weather filled with angry debate, tumults and threatenings, open and covert violence.

Entanglements and obstacles not foreseen by the secessionists when they launched their revolution in '61 stood now more clear. At the start they had to erect a government, starting "from scratch" without practice in administration of such a government. They were outnumbered to begin with and while the war went on the North grew further in numbers. The rumor ran across the South in January of '65 that Lincoln was raising a final army of 1,000,000 men. It was troublesome even where it was discredited—because it was nearly half true. The blockade had tightened. The partial isolation of the South was becoming complete. In munitions, supplies, transport, the South began with handicaps and now made a desperate comparison with the North steadily reaching new production peaks. The agricultural South was losing to the industrial North. Haunting in January of '65 was that prediction of William Tecumseh Sherman to future Confederate generals in January of '61: "You are rushing into war with one of the most powerful, ingeniously mechanical and determined people on earth—right at your doors. You are bound to fail." The South had correctly forecast that New England would furnish abolitionist cohorts to fight with passion for Negro freedom—and guessed completely wrong on the depth of the Union sentiment of Northwest, Midwest, and Border States. Elemental passion underlay Congressman John A. Logan's saying in '61 that if the South attempted to close the Mississippi River "the men of the Northwest would hew their way to the Gulf with their swords."

Sherman's men now at Savannah-by-the-Sea felt themselves perhaps intruders but no aliens there—they saw themselves fighting for the inherent right of Iowa, bounded by two muddy rivers, to ship its corn and cattle freely at any port on the two coasts of the United States. In inland South Carolina Sherman's men were to feel themselves somewhat alien, believing that soil a grower of treasons, and they were preparing to treat its people and cities with a vengeance they had not let loose in Georgia. And from "the mother-country," as the *Charleston Mercury* formerly so often termed England, had come help but no recognition, no British fleet to relieve Southern ports—this because the instigators of secession in '61 had guessed wrong on world sentiment regarding slavery, on an immense humanity

FRANK LESLIE'S ILLUSTRATED NEWSPAPER.

JAN. 28, 1865.

THE LAST SUGGESTION FROM RICHMOND.

GHOST OF THE CONFEDERACY—"*I propose to throw myself under your protection—either joint-ly or separately.*"

BOTH—"*We don't see it. While you were a live person we might—but now you are a mere skeleton-nary—no—no.*"

Leslie's cartoons John Bull and Napoleon III in final and complete desertion of the Confederacy shaken with feeling that the buying and selling of human beings, even if black-skinned and primitive, should be outlawed—wherefore the aged and crafty Palmerston, the bespangled and imperial Napoleon the Third, kept hands off—and the Vatican withheld moral approval.

Those blaming Jefferson Davis for Southern failure were in part hunting a scapegoat, as he was not to blame for the basic handicaps of the Confederacy. He personified the Southern planter class in its pride, its aristocratic feudal outlook on life and people, its agrarian isolation barred from understanding that fraction of the North which held the Union of States a dream worth sacrifice; in its lack of touch with an almost world-wide abhorrence of slavery as distinguished from what was called "nigger-loving."

Among these limitations the most serious was the aristocratic feudal outlook on life and people. The Clausewitz theory, that the military fronts must closely interweave with the civilian populations, had little practice in the methods of Davis. The War Office clerk J. B. Jones for more than a year had been writing in his diary of "speculators and extortioners" having their way beyond all human decency in Richmond itself—and of favors and privileges granted to the propertied though untitled nobles of the planter class. The war years rolled on and Davis failed to become either an idol or a name and a figure of faith—like Robert E. Lee. Yet Lee had never been such a spokesman of the Confederate cause as Davis. On the death of his wife's mother in 1862 Lee emancipated the slaves to which his family fell heir. Privately Lee spoke of slavery as a sinister, insidious, menacing institution—the view of his high exemplar George Washington. As a voice of States' Rights and secession Lee had no reputation at all; he was a Virginian, a trained man of war, a born fighting man, loyal to Virginia even after Virginia seceded and moved, against his wish, out of the Union. In his very silence about why the war was being fought, in the wide and deep love for him because while keeping silence he fought so magnificently—in this was some clue to the human dignity of a certain remnant of the Confederacy ready for sacrifice rather than submit to those they termed invaders.

As the pressure became fiercer in early '65 Lee consented, in perfect accord with Davis, to take chief command of all the Confederate armies. As a first move he appointed General Joseph E. Johnston to head an army, made from various fragments, to block the path of Sherman from Savannah up across the Carolinas. This reflected Lee's judgment that Davis had been mistaken in his abrupt dismissal of Johnston.

"If a surgeon is within call, and not too busy," said Johnston once in battle as he reeled in his saddle from a bullet shot, "at his convenience, perfect convenience—he might as well look me over." Johnston had what they called "the iron bearing of the soldier," though, said one of his staff, it would surprise many to hear "that we never met or parted, for any length of time, that he did not, if we were alone, throw his arms about me and kiss me, and that such was his habit in parting from or greeting his male relatives and most cherished friends." The wife of General Pickett

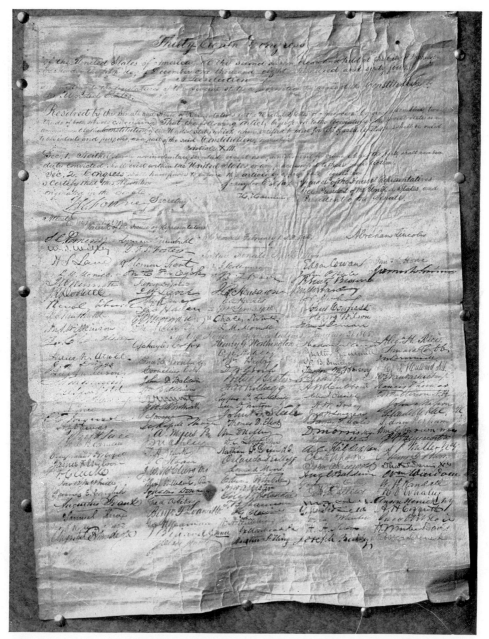

The President, the Vice-President, and Senate and House members sign the engrossed parchment of an act for the Constitutional Amendment for the abolishment of slavery, passed on January 31, '65

Original in the Barrett collection

The Confederate White House

From the Barrett collection

Varina Howell Davis, "the perfect wife of a difficult husband"

Joseph Eggleston Johnston (*above*). The later Jefferson Davis (*in corner at top*)

From the Meserve collection

regarded Lee as "a great general and a good man" but nevertheless, she said, "I never wanted to put my arms round his neck as I used to want to to Joe Johnston." With this commander Davis had kept up a running quarrel throughout the war. With Nathan Bedford Forrest, Davis had not so much of a quarrel, though he refused to agree with those who held Forrest the full equal of Stonewall Jackson in daring, mobility, strategy—the Forrest who, Sherman admitted, gave him more trouble than any Confederate commander on the horizon.

A host of personal matters such as the foregoing were covered in a *Charleston Mercury* editorial of January 10, 1865, drawing a deadly parallel between Davis and Lincoln. The contrast was appalling, sickening, noted the *Mercury*. In all departments, military, foreign, political, everywhere in the Confederate Government reigned "a pandemonium of imbecility, laxness, laxity, weakness, failure." Brave and able men were not lacking in the army. "We have an abundance of both. But they are so circumscribed and controlled as to produce weakness throughout." Abroad had been sent "commissioners" to crawl at the feet of Palmerston and Russell. In the home Government were "tools and sycophants, men subservient to Mr. Davis' will and whims and dictations . . . whilst the country reels and staggers under the fearful burden of their helpless counsels, and their imbecile actions."

The *Mercury* spoke for the faction which brought chief command to Lee. Hands with an iron will must be lifted toward the executive authority, with the earnest words "Do as we command, or vacate your position." This editorial was probably the most shrill and tragic cry of despair—and the most inequitable assessment of justice—that had as yet been raised in the Confederacy against the Davis regime in Richmond. It presented the Confederate Army as the most "lamentable and fatal" exhibit. "It is there where hatreds on the one hand, and favoritism on the other, strike deepest their roots, and poison most fatally the well-springs of our military actions. It is there where the fuming passions of Executive petty tyranny strike most directly at the heart of the Confederacy, by a corrupt and unscrupulous exercise of delegated power, in proscribing and ejecting from position. or forcing entirely out of the service, the very foremost military men in America; whilst men notoriously incompetent are made the pivots of our destinies. Nor are these remarks applicable alone to the leaders of armies; but on every side we see petty favorites lifted up to promotions and pushed into positions of importance, whilst men of magnificent gallantry and accomplished minds are suffered to fight on in the ranks, or to fall in some position of inferior command.

"Political tools are rewarded with commissions as Brigadier and Major-Generals, whilst their friends, relations and acquaintances generally fill up the lower grades of promotion. Not soldiers to lead armies are sought, but creatures to whine at the foot of the Executive; or else, honest, but incompetent men are made use of, as sticks to lay over the heads of some personal pet hatred. As an inevitable consequence, laxity and inefficiency prevail everywhere in the army. Imbeciles and good-for-naughts hold high commissions and low commissions—there is no responsibility anywhere—no discipline is enforced—men straggle and desert—even officers do the same. But favorites cannot be shot, or cashiered, and it would not do for 'Uncle Jeff' to make himself unpopular with the men, by allowing the penalties of military law to be executed. Thus contempt of officers and official sentences amongst the men, and contempt of law and order amongst the officers is spread broad-cast throughout our armies. More gallant men never stood in the ranks—a more inefficient organization never disgraced the science of war. Never was a cause more enthusiastically loved by a soldiery—never was so much power, in numbers, in enthusiasm, in endurance, in courage, so frittered away, so broken down, so misapplied, so utterly disorganized, by an ineradicable vice of unscrupulous administration."

This outburst came in '65 from the newspaper which in '61 was head bugler of the first seceded State. Thousands of young men in '61 read it as an exposition and a testament of true national faith; now in '65 they lay in graves from Savannah to Gettysburg. In those four years the *Charleston Mercury* changed its mind about Lincoln. The President at Washington was not less wicked, not less fanatic, than they thought him in '61, but in performance he had shown unexpected form. Now in January of '65 the *Mercury* set forth:

"When ABRAHAM LINCOLN took the chair of the Presidency of the United States, he promised in his flat-boat lingo, to 'run the machine as he found it.' Whether he has strictly kept his promise, those may doubt who choose to consider the subject. It is enough for us to know, that whether 'running his machine' in the pathway of his predecessors, or not, he has run it with a stern, inflexible purpose, a bold, steady hand, a vigilant, active eye, a sleepless energy, a fanatic spirit, and an eye single to his end—conquest—emancipation. He has called around him, in counsel, the ablest and most earnest men of his country. Where he has lacked in individual ability, learning, experience, or statesmanship, he has sought it, and has found it in the able men about him, whose assistance he unhesitatingly accepted, whose powers he applies to the advancement of the cause he has undertaken. In the cabinet and in the field he has consistently and fearlessly pressed on the search for men who could advance his cause, and has as unhesitatingly cut off all those who clogged it with weakness, timidity, imbecility, or failure. Force, energy, brains, earnestness, he has collected around him in every department. Blackguard and buffoon as he is, he has pursued his end with an energy as untiring as an Indian, and a singleness of purpose that might almost be called patriotic. If he were not an unscrupulous knave in his end, and a fanatic in his political views, he would undoubtedly command our respect as a ruler, so far as we are concerned. Abroad and at home, he has exercised alike the same ceaseless energy and circumspection."

Thus in the leading newspaper of the first city to repudiate him as President, Lincoln was credited with qualities seldom ascribed to him by Northern critics in and out of his party. One familiar with the files of the

Charleston Mercury would understand that newspaper as sincere and consistent in the estimate. Also one familiar with the short distance between Charleston and Savannah, where Sherman's army was resting before starting northward, would understand why the *Mercury* felt the need for some quick turn of the war—else they couldn't get out the paper as usual for the constant reader.

Late on the night of January 15, after three days' bombardment by a fleet under Admiral Porter, and desperate hand-to-hand fighting between the garrison and the assaulting infantry under General Alfred H. Terry, Fort Fisher fell. Wilmington, the last open port of the Confederacy, was closed to incoming supplies and outgoing cotton.

The *Richmond Enquirer* dismissed the event with "Nothing from abroad is indispensable to a brave and determined people." The *Richmond Whig* had seen New Orleans lost, the Mississippi River lost, Savannah lost, and each time the Confederacy had survived. "Therefore, we can stand the loss of Fort Fisher." One thing the Confederacy could not survive, "loss of spirit and determination," continued the *Whig*. "Let the people be firm, let them show determination to resist to the last dollar and the last man, and the capture of all our seaports will be of no moment whatsoever."

To no one was the taking of Fort Fisher more galling news than to Major General Benjamin F. Butler. Practically every move in the capture of the fort had been the same as when Butler advanced on it in December— except that instead of returning the troops to the transports and saying the job was impossible, as in December under Butler, General Terry sent the troops in and they took the fort, losing in round numbers of 600 as against the same for the garrison.

Of course, nothing could really embarrass Ben Butler, but now in January of '65 he was possibly nearer to hiding his face than at any time in his career as lawyer, politician, and general. This because Grant and Lincoln jointly and deliberately and with no reservations sent him away from his army to await further orders.

Butler was removed. Political and military circles were nothing short of amazed at the news telegraphed from Washington on January 13 saying it was "now specifically stated that on January 6 Lieutenant-General Grant indicated to President Lincoln his earnest wish that Major-General Butler be forthwith relieved of his command," and on the next day the President directed the Adjutant General to issue the order deposing Butler and ordering him to report at Lowell, Massachusetts, his home.

On January 4 Grant wrote the Secretary of War requesting the removal of Butler from command of the Department of Virginia and North Carolina, saying: "I do this with reluctance, but the good of the service requires it. In my absence, General Butler necessarily commands, and there is a lack of confidence felt in his military ability, making him an unsafe commander for a large army. His administration of the affairs of his Department is also objectionable." On learning that Stanton had gone to Savannah to visit Sherman, Grant on January 6 telegraphed the President asking that prompt action be taken in the matter. The order was made on January 7. The next day Colonels Porter and Babcock under Grant's direction went to Butler's headquarters. In Butler's tent they handed him an envelope. "He opened the communication, read the order, and was silent for a minute," noted Porter. "Then he began to manifest considerable nervousness, and turning to his desk, wrote 'Received' on the envelope, dated it 1864 instead of 1865, and handed it back. It was the custom in the army to return envelope receipts in case of communications delivered by enlisted men, but this was omitted when the instructions were transmitted by staff-officers. He was politely reminded that a written receipt was not necessary. Thereupon, in a somewhat confused manner, he uttered a word or two of apology for offering it."

To his army Butler issued a farewell address. "I have refused to order useless sacrifice of the lives of such soldiers, and I am relieved of command." Next Butler appeared in Washington, in citizen clothes, "manifestly in a warlike frame of mind," noted press accounts, arranging for a hearing by the Committee on the Conduct of the War. Weeks were to pass and Grant and others heard as witnesses under examination. In the end Butler's rating as a general and an administrator sank lower. "I wonder," wrote John C. Gray to his mother, "if people will ever be convinced in Butler's case that impudence is not ability." More gently, for its public *Harper's Weekly* held Butler "unjust" to himself and the Government "to utter such an insinuation" as that lives were sacrificed uselessly at Fort Fisher. "In all the record of his military career he is the man who always best knew how not to do it," said the *Richmond Examiner*. "Now that he is actually shelved for his failure at Wilmington, one begins to feel a certain partizan regard for him as against Lincoln." Had Butler waited ashore there on that bare spit of sand behind Fort Fisher, the furious North Carolina brigades would have hanged him had they caught him. "Does Mr. Lincoln please to recollect that General Butler was outlawed among Confederates, and that the first soldier who could catch him would never send him to the rear, nor report him as a prisoner, nor embarrass the Government in knotty controversies on his account, but simply kill him like a mad dog? Would Lincoln himself have come ashore that day upon such a footing?" The *New York World* notified readers, "This flinging Butler overboard is to our liking," and furthermore was the "best emancipation proclamation Mr. Lincoln has yet made." The *World* claimed a curious circumstance: "In this war north and south, every prominent politician and lawyer has failed to achieve reputation as a general. Cobb, Toombs, Pillow, Wise and Floyd on the one side, and Banks, Wallace, Sickles, Stanton, Lincoln and Butler on the other." Savagely the *World* referred to how Butler had blundered in not wearing on the beach at Fort Fisher "those ostrich feathers which he wore in the streets of New York, brandishing his puissant horse-pistols, and fixing on Fort Fisher the terrors of his revolving orb."

Thus amid hue and cry and guess and gossip, Grant and Lincoln got rid of the one man in the Union armies who stood foremost as a potential dictator. "A revolutionary chieftain," noted Goldwin Smith after interviewing Butler. The one major general around whose headquarters incessantly ran rumors of questionable commercial, financial, and trading transactions. The one figure about whom John Hay had spoken to Lincoln as dangerous and treacherous, with an eye on personal power and the audacity to seize it, Lincoln replying, "Yes, he is like Jim Jett's brother." The one commander who, under conceivable circumstances, which Hay had in mind, would not have hesitated at marching an army to Washington, taking over the Government, and issuing regulations to the country. Grant and Lincoln handled him "with tongs." A political trickster of dramatic daring, of occasional delicacy in sensing public issues, Butler was dazzled by the fertility of his own mind and seemed to have expected that little fighting would be needed to take Fort Fisher. The explosion of the powder boat would rock the earth, blast the fort, and leave no garrison to surrender it. Grant's report for the court of inquiry in the matter mentioned his not being aware that Butler was to command personally the Fort Fisher expedition and then, with mixed sarcasm and humor not at all on the surface: "I had rather formed the idea that General Butler was actuated by a desire to witness the effect of the explosion of the powder-boat."

In the summer of '64 Grant and Lincoln could have told the country during those gloom months that Richmond stood untaken because Butler had miserably blundered. Such an explanation, however true, would have brought scorn and blame heaped on Grant and Lincoln for letting Butler blunder, for keeping in command of the Army of the James a politician "who could strut sitting down," who with all the many chances given him was on record a failure. Then why was Butler not removed in the summer of '64? One widespread rumor held that Butler possessed some secret information through which he controlled Grant, "had Grant under his thumb," and Grant was afraid to remove him. Had this been true, Butler would have used this dominance in January to stop his removal or after his removal would have spread his alleged secret information over the whole country—that was his way. Then again and still more pertinent was the question of why Grant did not let Butler out in the summer of '64. The reason was plain, tacitly understood between Grant and Lincoln. Butler had a national political following. Shifting, as the war rolled on, from his former loyalty to the proslavery wing of the Democratic party, he turned radical on the slavery issue, radical enough so that Wendell Phillips publicly and repeatedly wished Butler were President instead of Lincoln. In the delicate political adjustments of the 1864 presidential campaign, only worse confusion could have resulted from a dismissal of Butler, raising the cry that it was the Frémont story over again, that a radical antislavery man was barred from leading troops against the slaveholders. So Grant and Lincoln had bided their time, and now with the Fort Fisher fiasco added to the others of Butler, he still had friends who resented his removal. But they could not muster any evidence in his favor. One common definite opinion ran with that of *Harper's Weekly:* "Of the patriotism, ability and energy of General Butler there can be no doubt. But of the fact that, from Great Bethel to Wilmington, the purely military movements which he has directed have not been successful, there is also no doubt."

Not in the slightest embarrassed, with as bland a face and as swaggering an assurance as ever, Butler circulated over Washington spinning designs from his fertile and wily brain, writing later: "Although I had no command in the army assigned me and had not asked for any, I retained the full confidence of the President, and from time to time when I happened to be in Washington, where indeed I was much of the time, he talked with me very freely. In these conversations I assured him that it was only a matter of months, if not of weeks, when the question would be before him on what terms a peace could be concluded." This in a benevolent and helpful tone, as though the point and the idea had not occurred to the President until he, Butler, laid it before him. One project he elaborated for Lincoln with all the details that could be asked for; in fact on paper it looked too good, too easy, just like the Fort Fisher powder-boat explosion. Butler would have the Government buy a thirty-mile strip of land across the Isthmus of Panama and then put Butler in charge of 150,000 Negro soldiers of the Union armies; he would see that an interoceanic canal was dug by those soldiers. Butler quoted Lincoln as saying that the matter might affect foreign relations, that Seward should be consulted, and "There is no special hurry, however. I will think it over, but nothing had better be said upon it which will get outside."

In the House Lewis W. Ross of Illinois demanded the previous question on a resolution "that the thanks of Congress and of the country are due, and are hereby tendered, to his Excellency Abraham Lincoln, President of the United States, for relieving from service Major General Benjamin F. Butler." Grinnell moved to lay it on the table. Washburne, Grant's home-town friend, wanted a discussion and hoped the previous question would not be seconded. The Speaker ruled they must vote on Grinnell's motion to table. The roll call gave 97 for and 43 against tabling. And the matter could be read in several lights, chiefly that the House, like Grant and Lincoln, chose to handle Butler "with tongs." Washburne, could he have secured a discussion, probably intended to register the point that Grant had initiated the Butler removal and if any thanking was to be done Grant should be included.

The Butler removal in the main passed off smoothly. The effort by Representative Blaine and others to make Sherman a lieutenant general of equal rank with Grant also failed to raise any dispute, since Sherman notified Grant and his brother Senator Sherman that he would stand for no folly that looked toward jealousy between him and Grant.

Disputes over how to run the war rose less often now. The war machine ran with fewer blowups. To Lincoln's desk came fewer tangled military matters for his final decision. During many sessions of House and Senate the war was scarcely mentioned. Discussions ran as though no war at all was on, almost as though peace had settled on the country and the call now was to build the Pacific railway, improve rivers and harbors, dig canals, make land grants to railroads and homesteaders, perfect coast surveys, ease commerce between the States, resettle Indian tribes. The Secretary of the Interior reported on some 4,250,000 acres of public land sold and granted, railroads and homesteaders moving toward a future of expected booms. Speaking for a bill to establish ocean mail-steamship service between California and China, Representative Alley of Massachusetts said the scheme, with the Pacific railway completed, would put New York twelve or fifteen days nearer Hong Kong than London, and as a result, "We can direct and control in great degree the commerce of the world." A vast Oriental trade with 500,000,000 potential Asiatic customers beckoned on the horizon, said Cole of California. That the United States was soon to bid strong for its share of world trade was evident.

The *Congressional Globe* was sprinkled here and there with paragraphs reading, "A message from the President of the United States, by Mr. Nicolay, his Secretary, announced that he had approved and signed the following bills and joint resolutions." The measures signed ran into hundreds, and whatever of conflict there was between the President and Congress had to be gathered elsewhere. In such matters as fund appropriations, the Pacific railway, land grants, commerce between the States, he was giving Congress everything it asked, while he concentrated on peace terms and "remolding society" shattered by the war.

The draft now had stiffer enforcement, less resistance and evasion. Deserters met less mercy. On Governor's Island a large crowd saw the hanging of a bounty-jumper who had three times pocketed his money and three times deserted. Near City Point with elaborate military ritual thousands of troops formed in a square and saw a firing squad shoot a soldier who had deserted, received pardon, returned to his regiment, and deserted again. Over the country went the story of it, with crayon sketches by artists who caught its horror.

In late January the outcry about Northern men languishing in Southern prisons reached the point where Grant decided to relent. In October of '64 he had asked Lee whether the Confederate Government would deliver in exchange colored troops "the same as white soldiers," Lee rejoining that "negroes belonging to our citizens are not considered subjects of exchange." On January 24 of '65, however, when the Confederate Government again offered to exchange man for man, Grant accepted the offer without mention of color.

On the point of information service Grant now had the advantage of Lee. Deserters each month by thousands, tired of short rations and hard fare in the Confederate Army, crossed the picket lines, nightly expected and welcomed by the Union forces. Always some of them would talk. Another related matter in Richmond was "certain youths, alleged to have received passports to Europe." The Confederate Congress by a resolution of January

4 called on Secretary of War Seddon for information about these youths. They were chiefly the creation of rumors, in tone with rumors that Davis, Benjamin, and others had sent chests of gold to Europe and that before the Confederacy fell they would be safe abroad with their stolen treasure— rumors later found to be lies, or fantasies of fear, or talk intended by war-weary people to undermine their Government. "Many fear," wrote J. B. Jones, "the high members of the government have turned brokers and speculators, and are robbing the country." Entries now from day to day in the diary of Jones told of people sick of the war. "It is the policy now," he wrote on January 18, "not to *agitate* the matter of disloyalty, but rather to wink at it, and let it die out—if it will."

On the day before Jones noted the *Richmond Examiner* openly calling for the removal of President Davis, and "Mentioning to R. Tyler the fact that many of the clerks, etc. of the War Department favored revolution and the overthrow of the President, he replied that it was a known fact, and that some of them would be hung soon." So Jones was not surprised one morning of this month on entering his chief's office to see the Secretary of War sitting before the fireplace, "his head between his knees."

In this Richmond atmosphere on January 14 Jones saw riding in an open carriage in the Confederate capital none other than Old Man Blair, Francis P. Blair, Sr. The newspapers said Blair had dined with President Davis and they were having long talks. "It is . . . published in the papers," wrote Jones in his diary, "that Mrs. Davis threw her arms around Mr. Blair and embraced him. This, too, is injurious to the President."

In the press North and South for two weeks now in January "the Blair mission" to Richmond held the front pages. There was a fury of guess and gossip about Old Man Blair. "What is he doing in Richmond?" One of his sons in Lincoln's Cabinet more than three years, another son a corps commander with Sherman—whom did Blair speak for in Richmond, and to whom? Were Lincoln and Davis getting together on a peace, and would the armies soon come home?

The one-time intimate adviser of Andrew Jackson, later a counselor of Lincoln, had gone to Richmond under peculiar conditions. In December a long letter from Horace Greeley awakened a motive that had lain sleeping in Blair. Greeley said it was time now to undertake openly peace negotiations with the Confederates. Mr. Lincoln in his inaugural had shown a spirit of wanting to avoid war, but, wrote Greeley, "I regret to find no exhibition of the same spirit in his later manifestoes." At least the South should be put in the position of refusing peace, insisted Greeley, and why should not Blair, an able publicist, "the counsellor and trusted adviser of men high in authority," consider the suggestion that he move toward peace? Blair replied that madmen had made the war, wise men would end it, and he, Blair, had months ago written to President Lincoln that Greeley's Niagara negotiations should be transferred to Richmond. Now, wrote Blair, he had a scheme, "benevolent as well as radical," and, "I think I will hint it to Mr. Lincoln."

Blair went to Lincoln, dazzled and ambitious with hopes of what he might show the world could be done by proper management of a peace cause. This was mid-December of '64. "Come to me after Savannah falls," said Lincoln.

And three days after Savannah fell Blair was on hand and Lincoln wrote one sentence on a card: "Allow the bearer, F. P. Blair, Sr., to pass our lines, go South, and return."

Then from Grant's headquarters Blair wrote a note addressed to "Jefferson Davis, President, etc., etc.," the et cetera abbreviation meaning that Blair considered Davis President of something, though it was not diplomatic to put it in any document likely to be made public. This note said Blair wished to visit Richmond to seek some title papers which "may have been taken by some persons who had access to my house when General Early's army were in possession of my place." Enclosed was a second and longer note to Davis saying he wished to "confidentially unbosom my heart frankly and without reserve," while the first note would serve to answer any inquiries as to why he was in Richmond. Davis replied in his own formal style telling Blair to come on, but this reply miscarried somehow and was delayed, so that Blair, disappointed, went back to Washington. The *New York Herald* had already noticed in Greeley's newspaper the editor's jubilation about Blair's mission and now jibed that President Lincoln had probably given Blair an official sanction and then dictated a telegram to Grant that Blair "had better be stopped." This would be perfectly like the sly and diplomatic President, garrulously insisted the *Herald*. "The President realizes the absurdity of these amateur attempts. . . . Our benevolent friend Greeley seems to be affected with a monomania for peace missions. . . . The President has learned to regard them with suspicion . . . has learned that we can only gain peace by whipping the Rebels, and that our only terms are unconditional surrender, and our best missionaries Grant, Sherman, Thomas, Sheridan, Farragut and Porter." The *Herald* in this was having its fling at Greeley, while the *New York World* hoped Greeley would be able to persuade the President to send Blair to Davis with peace overtures.

The delayed Davis reply came to Blair, who went back to the James River headquarters of Grant, took a naval boat from City Point to Richmond. At the Confederate White House Blair dined with Davis, fraternized with old cronies of days agone in the Democratic party, noticed with surprise how many able-bodied men were walking the streets, men he would have expected to be in Lee's army. In the *Richmond Examiner* Blair could read that the public would like to know "what particular piece of Yankee villainy and treachery lurks under the unofficial visit of Blair senior." Davis was too free about granting audiences to peace-palavering Yankees such as Gilmore and Jaquess last summer, and now Blair. The *Examiner* could picture Blair telling President Davis that "Lincoln is full of loving kindness and compassion, having no pleasure even in the death of rebels." The *Examiner* was not all wrong to be suspicious of Blair. The old man thrust at Confederate morale in telling Colonel Robert Ould, in charge of prisoner exchanges, that the waning Confederate armies could not long stand against the enlarging Union forces, in telling R. M. T. Hunter, president pro tempore of the Confederate Senate, and some of the Confederate Congressmen that President Lincoln would win the war if he had to employ foreigners in his armies.

Finally on January 12, closeted with the Confederate President for a secret interview, Blair spilled his various proposals, kept from the outside world till long afterward. Blair wrote for Lincoln a report of this interview, of how he told Davis of his relations with Lincoln, that he had no instructions at all from Lincoln, that before Savannah fell Lincoln had stopped him from outlining any peace designs, that after Savannah Lincoln "shunned an interview with me, until I perceived that he did not wish to hear me, but desired I should go without any explanation of my object." This made clear to begin with, Blair asked Davis in precise diplomatic style whether Davis was tied up in any way to any European powers that would stop him from doing what he might want to do with the Government of the United States. Davis answered he was tied in no way and would "die a free man." Blair then drew out a paper, saying that before he read it he wished Davis to know it was "somewhat after the manner of an editorial and was not of a diplomatic character." Davis then wished Blair to know that he gave Blair "full confidence," believed Blair an honest man, and in the words of Blair's report, "he [Davis] was under great obligations to my family for kindnesses rendered to his, that he would never forget them, and that even when dying they would be remembered in his prayers."

The paper Blair then read to Davis might have been translated from its long words and its weasel evasions into a few points in simple words; in the delicate tangle of issues these would have sounded out of order and too blunt. Such a translation could run: "You can all come back into the Union any time you are ready to take the Lincoln oath that you are back. Go ahead now and put the Negroes into your armies and slavery will be at an end. Then if the North and the South want peace, nothing but soldiers from foreign countries can stop peace. If any of the States that went out of the Union should try to stay out on account of slavery, the only way they could do it would be by getting foreign armies to help them. That would mean some king or emperor across the ocean would be running them. Can you think that the people anywhere would stand for it? In this connection look at Mexico. There the French emperor Louis Napoleon has put an Austrian archduke, Maximilian, on the throne and made a republic into a monarchy. There the grand old Monroe Doctrine, that Europe must keep its hands off this half of the earth, has been knocked into a cocked hat and kicked to pieces, and the North and the South have done nothing about it. Why can't we get together on this? Why not drop this war of brothers, and the two of us, North and South, join what we've got and go down

there and throw Louis Napoleon's puppet off the throne and set up the
Mexican republic again and get back our self-respect and put the Monroe
Doctrine in operation again? Who would be the one man to head those
armies for this cleanout in Mexico? Why, Jefferson Davis."

Or to use words of Blair which he read from the paper to Davis: "Jefferson Davis is the fortunate man who now holds the commanding position to
encounter this formidable scheme of conquest, and whose fiat can at the
same time deliver his country from the bloody agony now covering it with
mourning. He can drive Maximilian from his American throne, and baffle
the designs of Napoleon to subject our Southern people to the 'Latin race.'
With a breath he can blow away all pretense for proscription, conscription,
or confiscation in the Southern States, restore their fields to luxuriant culti-
vation, their ports to the commerce of the world," and so on. There was
much more, many details, such as that the Mexican Minister at Washington,
Romero, favored the plan and believed that the fugitive Mexican President,
Juarez, would be willing if necessary that Mexico have a dictatorship headed
by Jefferson Davis. The man who would expel the European despotism
from "our Southern flank" would "ally his name with those of Washington
and Jackson." Furthermore, Blair read on to the listening Davis: "If in delivering Mexico he should model its States in form and principle to adapt
them to our Union and add a new Southern constellation to its benignant
sky while rounding off our possession on the continent at the Isthmus, and
opening the way to blending the waters of the Atlantic and Pacific, thus
embracing our Republic in the arms of the ocean, he would complete the
work of Jefferson . . . restore the equipoise between the Northern and
Southern States—if indeed such sectional distinctions could be recognized
after the peculiar institution which created them had ceased to exist."

This was the end of the paper which Blair read to Davis. This was the
offer with its supporting argument. And Blair would have denied that he
was a rainbow-chaser. He would more likely have urged that he was hoping
to make a rainbow-chaser of Jefferson Davis. His later written report to
Lincoln continued:

"I then said to him, 'There is my problem, Mr. Davis; do you think it
possible to be solved?' After consideration he said, 'I think so.' " Blair returned to the point that a divided country at war usually brought monarchy.
Davis agreed, added that he favored "popular government," said that unity
of the two sections at war was hindered through "the excessive vindictive-
ness produced by outrages perpetrated in the invaded States during the war,"
reconcilement depending "upon time and events"; that Europe hoped to see
the two sections destroy each other; that no circumstance would sooner restore better feeling than the two sections joined in a war on a foreign power.
Blair told Davis this was encouraging.

Changing the subject, Davis asked, "What, Mr. Blair, do you think of
Mr. Seward?" Blair was ready on this. Seward was a pleasant companion
but "would betray any man" who stood in the way of "his selfish and ambitious schemes." But Seward would have no hand in this matter, which was

military and depended on the Commander in Chief, Mr. Lincoln. "Now I know," continued Blair to the listening Davis in the Confederate White House, "that Mr. Lincoln is capable of great personal sacrifices—of sacrificing the strongest feelings of his heart, of sacrificing a friend when he thinks it necessary for the good of the country; and you may rely upon it, if he plights his faith to any man in a transaction for which he is responsible as an officer or a man, he will maintain his word inviolably." Of this little speech Blair noted: "Mr. Davis said he was glad to hear me say so. He did not know Mr. Lincoln; but he was sure I did, and therefore my declaration gave him the highest satisfaction. As to Mr. Seward he had no confidence in him himself, and he did not know any man or party in the South that had any."

Davis now suggested he was willing to send men to some conference; there must be communication, and the men he would appoint could be relied on by Mr. Lincoln. And on Blair's drifting again into the rainbow dream of the fame that would come to Davis from extending the United States down to the Isthmus of Panama, Davis said what his name might be in history he cared not; his country's welfare was the aim of his being; death would end his cares.

Thus the interview in the Confederate White House closed. A memorandum of it written later by Davis ran parallel in the main to the report Blair handed Lincoln. A letter dated this same day was written by Davis for Blair to carry back to Lincoln. In the opening sentence Davis showed that his eye had caught the point where Blair in his letters used the expression "Jefferson Davis, President, etc. etc.," and he returned the compliment by writing "President Lincoln, etc., etc." The letter read:

F. P. Blair, Esq.   Richmond, Virginia, January 12, 1865
Sir:

I have deemed it proper, and probably desirable to you, to give you, in this form, the substance of remarks made by me, to be repeated by you to President Lincoln, etc., etc.

I have no disposition to find obstacles in forms, and am willing, now as heretofore, to enter into negotiations for the restoration of peace; am ready to send a commission whenever I have reason to suppose it will be received, or to receive a commission, if the United States Government shall choose to send one. That, notwithstanding the rejection of our former offers, I would, if you could promise that a commissioner, minister, or other agent would be received, appoint one immediately, and renew the effort to enter into conference, with a view to secure peace to the two countries.

                              Yours, etc.,
                                          Jefferson Davis

Arriving in Washington, Blair told a *New York Tribune* reporter that the people of Richmond were for peace, the working classes had an aching demand for peace, and the war might end in two months. So said the *Tribune*, which hoped it was true. Aside from this Blair gave it out that he had no news except that he was to see the President.

Blair at the White House now made known to Lincoln his Mexican offer to Davis. This was news to the President. He had, according to Nicolay and Hay, not the slightest interest in it, considered more seriously "the low morale of the Confederate leaders" noted by Blair and the revelations of the letter from Davis. Lincoln now wrote a little one-sentence letter to Davis via Blair:

F. P. Blair, Esq.　　　　　　　　　　　　　　　　Washington, January 18, 1865
Sir:
　　You having shown me Mr. Davis's letter to you of the 12th instant, you may say to him that I have constantly been, am now, and shall continue ready to receive any agent whom he, or any other influential person now resisting the national authority, may informally send to me, with the view of securing peace to the people of our one common country.
　　　　　　　　　　　　　　　　Yours, etc.,
　　　　　　　　　　　　　　　　　　　　A. Lincoln

Thus the Davis letter ending with the words "the two countries" had Lincoln's letter in reply ending with the phrase "our one common country." And where Davis had referred to Lincoln as President of "etc." Lincoln now alluded to "Mr." Davis as though whatever Davis might be President of he was definitely a "Mr." The score was about even.

Excitement rose higher over the country as news came that again Blair was in Richmond and again Blair was holding confidential talks with Davis in the Confederate White House. In the first of these talks Blair made excuses about the Mexican offer. Davis saw that either Blair had made the offer without Lincoln's knowing about it or else there was a trick. Davis leaned however toward accepting Blair's excuses, writing later of how Blair "unfolded to me the embarrassment of Mr. Lincoln on account of the extreme men in Congress and elsewhere, who wished to drive him into harsher measures than he was inclined to adopt."

Blair and Davis soon reached the point where there was nothing more to say. Blair went back to Washington. Davis had the letter of Lincoln to Blair and proceeded to act on it. While Davis so acted Richmond newspapers in effect held up Davis as something near to a traitor, who dined "foreign enemies," welcomed a "murderer" to the Confederate White House —so possibly Davis should take up his abode north of the Potomac.

Now for the first time since the Confederate capital had been moved to Richmond, Jefferson Davis asked his Vice-President Alexander Stephens to meet him in conference. Also Davis called his Cabinet on the matter of sending commissioners to Lincoln to negotiate over peace. Stephens argued that Davis should meet Lincoln at City Point in an absolutely secret conference. Losing on this, Stephens suggested the names of three commissioners. Davis agreed with one of the names, John A. Campbell, Assistant Secretary of War and former United States Supreme Court Justice, added R. M. T. Hunter, Senator and ex-Secretary of State, and Stephens himself. These were all three "peace men" or "submissionists" rather than uncompromising 'ast-ditchers. And though Lincoln's letter for Davis through Blair had said distinctly that he would receive agents from Davis for a conference on peace for "our one common country," the instruction carried by the commissioners said they were going to Washington seeking peace "to the two countries." The instruction read:

Richmond, January 28, 1865

In conformity with the letter of Mr. Lincoln, of which the foregoing is a copy, you are requested to proceed to Washington City for informal conference with him upon the issues involved in the existing war, and for the purpose of securing peace to the two countries.

Your obedient servant,

Jefferson Davis

By now excitement neared fever heat in some circles of the North, over what Lincoln, Blair, and Davis might be up to. On January 21 press items ran that Monty Blair was saying his father in a navy boat had gone to Richmond to resume informal peace negotiations with Jefferson Davis. On the next day press dispatches said Blair with authority from Lincoln was giving Jefferson Davis safe-conducts for peace commissioners to Washington. It was baffling and exasperating to those suspicious of Lincoln. Henry Ward Beecher packed up, left Brooklyn for Washington, and in behalf of himself and others went to the White House.

"We were all very much excited," wrote Beecher of this hour. "The war lasted so long, and I was afraid Lincoln would be so anxious for peace, and I was afraid he would accept something that would be of advantage to the South, so I went to Washington and called upon him. We were alone in his receiving room. His hair was 'every way for Sunday.' It looked as though it was an abandoned stubble field. He had on slippers, and his vest was what was called 'going free.' He looked wearied, and when he sat down in a chair, looked as though every limb wanted to drop off his body." Beecher told Lincoln that if public interest permitted he would like an explanation of these latest peace maneuvers. Lincoln listened patiently. looked up at the ceiling a few moments, then: "Well, I am almost of a mind to show you all the documents." Beecher said he would like to see them if it was proper.

Lincoln stepped to a desk, took out and handed to Beecher a little card "as long as my finger and an inch wide," noted Beecher as he handled it. It was the little one-sentence pass that had taken Blair through the lines to Richmond and back. "There," said Lincoln, "is all there is of it. Now Blair thinks something can be done, but I don't, but I have no objection to have him try his hand." Beecher now had his answer and said a great burden had been lifted off his mind.

The short, stubby, deep-chested man Ulysses S. Grant sat writing before an open fire in a log cabin lighted by a sputtering kerosene lamp. Another short man, at first shadowy and elusive to look at, having a wax-white face with burning eyes, the frail Alexander H. Stephens, sat watching Grant work. No guards nor aides were around, noticed Stephens, who had expected more show-off in the headquarters of the General in Chief of the United States armies. The two men just naturally liked each other, they found out. It was easy for them to talk. Both were old Steve Douglas Democrats. Both hoped for peace soon. But peace how?

With his two fellow commissioners Stephens had come to the Union Army lines on the evening of January 29, claiming that an understanding existed with General Grant to pass them on their way to Washington. On this being telegraphed to Washington, Lincoln at once sent Major Eckert of the war telegraph office with written directions to let the commissioners in with safe-conduct if they would say in writing that they were ready to talk peace on the basis of the President's note of January 18, peace for "our one common country." Before Eckert arrived with this message the commissioners applied by a written note to General Grant for permission "to proceed to Washington to hold a conference with President Lincoln upon the subject of the existing war, and with a view of ascertaining upon what terms it may be terminated." On reading this Grant had them conveyed to his headquarters. "Our relations were pleasant and I found them all very agreeable gentlemen," ran Grant's later account. "I . . . knew them well by reputation and through their public services, and I had been a particular admirer of Mr. Stephens." Stephens's account was in like tone regarding Grant: "Nothing in his appearance or surroundings . . . indicated his official rank. . . . He furnished us with comfortable quarters on board one of his dispatch boats. The more I became acquainted with him, the more I became thoroughly impressed with the very extraordinary combination of rare elements of character which he exhibited. . . . He met us frequently and conversed freely upon various subjects, not much upon our mission. I saw, however, very clearly that he was very anxious for the proposed conference to take place."

On receiving their note to him at dusk of evening Grant at once telegraphed it to Stanton and Lincoln. Lincoln decided he would not personally meet the commissioners. Instead he sent Seward to meet them at Fortress Monroe, giving Seward written instructions that he was to make known to them three things as indispensable to peace: "1. The restoration of the national authority throughout all the States. 2. No receding by the executive of the United States on the slavery question from the position assumed thereon in the late annual message to Congress, and in preceding documents. 3. No cessation of hostilities short of an end of the war, and the disbanding of all forces hostile to the government." All propositions of theirs, not inconsistent with these points, would be considered in a spirit of sincere liberality. "You," Seward was instructed, "will hear all they may choose to say, and report it to me. You will not assume to definitely consummate anything."

With this in his pocket Seward started February 1, while Lincoln telegraphed Grant to let the war go on while peace was talked. "Let nothing which is transpiring change, hinder, or delay your military movements or plans." Grant promised in reply there would be no armistice, that troops were "kept in readiness to move at the shortest notice."

On this first of February General Meade wrote to his wife that on the evening before he had "talked very freely" with the Confederate commissioners. They did not consider the slavery question so difficult as protection for their States "in case of other questions arising to produce strife." Meade half agreed with them when they said "they thought it a pity this matter [of slavery] could not be left to the generals on each side, and taken out of the hands of politicians." On the armistice they sought and on States' Rights he saw no chance for peace. "Still," wrote Meade, "I hope Mr. Lincoln will receive them and listen to all they have to say, for if it can be shown that their terms are impracticable, the country will be united for the further prosecution of the war." Emphasizing to his wife that this was all strictly confidential, Meade closed his letter by telling her that when the Confederate commissioners came within the Union lines "our men cheered loudly, and the soldiers on both sides cried out lustily, 'Peace! peace!'" This was meant as "a compliment" to the Confederate agents, and, believed Meade, "was so taken by them."

On this same day of February 1, however, Major Eckert arrived at City Point, and acting under Lincoln's instructions went alone to meet the three Confederate commissioners. "Grant wanted to be a party to the conference," ran Eckert's account. "I told him no. I said, 'You are the commanding general of the army. If you make a failure or say anything that would be subject to criticism it would be very bad. If I make a mistake I am nothing but a common business man and it will go for naught. I am going to take the responsibility, and I advise you not to go to the conference.' He finally said, 'Decency would compel me to go and see them.' I said that for the purpose of introduction I should be pleased to have him go with me but not until after I had first met the gentlemen. Grant was vexed with me because I would not tell him exactly what my mission was."

So Eckert alone went out on the dispatch boat, told the commissioners all proceedings must be in writing, gave them a copy of his instructions from President Lincoln, and left them studying those instructions. "Grant went with me on my second visit a few hours later," ran Eckert's account, "and after he was introduced, one of the commissioners, I am sure it was Hunter, said to Grant, 'We do not seem to get on very rapidly with Major Eckert. We are very anxious to go to Washington, and Mr. Lincoln has promised to see us there.' General Grant started to make reply when I interrupted him . . . 'Excuse me, General Grant, you are not permitted to say anything officially at this time,' and I stopped him right there. I added, 'If you will read the instructions under which I am acting you will see that I am right.' After listening a while to what the commissioners were saying Grant got up and went out. He was angry with me for years afterward."

The three commissioners had been considering the very explicit instructions from the President of the United States that they must agree in writing to no peace talk except on the basis of the President's note to Blair of January 18, peace for "our one common country." Their answer was a refusal. They would only go so far in writing as to say that they carried instructions from Jefferson Davis ending "the two countries," writing out a copy of those instructions, adding that they had an earnest desire for a just and honorable peace and were prepared "to receive or to submit propositions which may, possibly, lead to the attainment of that end." They also made clear that their instructions contemplated "a personal interview between President Lincoln and ourselves at Washington" but they were ready to meet any person or persons that President Lincoln might appoint, at such place as he might designate.

So their mission seemed at an end. They might as well go back to Richmond. So it seemed. Eckert telegraphed Lincoln that their reply was "not satisfactory" and notified the commissioners they could not proceed. The time was half-past nine on the night of February 1. They would stay overnight on a comfortable river steamer and see what tomorrow would bring. One of them, Hunter, explained afterward that they stayed on partly in the hope of gently leading Grant to see that an armistice between him and Lee would be the quickest way to end the war.

About an hour after their refusal to meet Lincoln's terms, Grant sent a long telegram to the Secretary of War, stating "confidentially, but not officially—to become a matter of record" that he was convinced on conversation with Messrs. Hunter and Stephens "that their intentions are good and their desire sincere to restore peace and union." Grant admitted he was in "an awkward position," fearing a bad influence from the commissioners going away with no results. He saw the difficulties of receiving them and did not know what to recommend. "Their letter to me was all that the President's instructions contemplated to secure their safe-conduct." And the Grant so shrewd in management of men put the high point of his letter in one sentence: "I am sorry, however, that Mr. Lincoln cannot have an interview with the two named in this despatch [Stephens and Hunter], if not all three now within our lines."

Lincoln the next morning walked over to the War Office, read Major Eckert's report, was framing a telegram to call Seward back, when Grant's long telegram of the night before was put in his hands. "This despatch," wrote Lincoln later . . . "changed my purpose." It spoke to him.

He at once wired Grant: "Say to the gentlemen I will meet them personally at Fortress Monroe as soon as I can get there."

The President went away from the White House, from all arranged Washington programs and appointments for public business, in a hurry and with secrecy. Not even the trustworthy Nicolay's ears were troubled with sudden information by the President as to where he was going. So it seemed from the account of a White House guest, Chaplain Edward D. Neill of the 1st Minnesota Infantry:

On the morning of the 2nd of February, 1865, between nine and ten o'clock, as I was ascending the stairs to the second story, to reach my room, I met Forbes, an intelligent servant, descending with a small valise in his hand, and I asked, "Where are you going?" Looking up to see that no one was near, he whispered, "Fortress Monroe," and hurried on. When I reached the upper hall I met the President with his overcoat, and going to my room, looked out of the window, and saw him quietly walking around the curved pavement which leads to Pennsylvania Avenue, while Forbes was following, at a distance of two or three hundred feet, as his valet. Waiting for some time, I then crossed the hall to the room of the principal secretary, Mr. John G. Nicolay, and quietly said, "The President has left the city." "What do you mean?" he asked; and I replied, "Just what I have said." Rising quickly, he opened the door which communicated with the President's room, and was astonished to find the chair of Mr. Lincoln vacant.

The news leaked from several sources. Welles in his diary grumbled over it. "None of the Cabinet were advised of this move, and without exception, I think, it struck them unfavorably that the Chief Magistrate should have gone on such a mission." To Eckert, Stanton confided his fear "that Lincoln's great kindness of heart and his desire to end the war might lead him to make some admission which the astute Southerners would wilfully misconstrue and twist to serve their purpose . . . throw the burden of failure upon the President."

Meantime down the Potomac on a naval vessel to Hampton Roads alongside Fortress Monroe, his personal guard a White House valet or footman carrying his traveling bag, Lincoln journeyed to meet a former United States Senator from Virginia, a former Associate Justice of the Supreme Court of the United States, and a former Georgia member of the United States House of Representatives who had once so moved Lincoln with a speech on the grandeur and misery of war that he wrote his law partner: "A little, slim, pale-faced, consumptive man . . . has just concluded the very best speech of an hour's length I ever heard. My old withered dry eyes are full of tears yet." Now the two of them were to meet, older and more withered.

"On the night of the 2d [of February]," ran Lincoln's account, "I reached Hampton Roads, found the Secretary of State and Major Eckert on a steamer anchored offshore, and learned of them that the Richmond gentlemen were on another steamer also anchored offshore, in the Roads; and that the Secretary of State had not yet seen or communicated with them. . . . On the morning of the 3d, the three gentlemen, Messrs. Stephens, Hunter, and Campbell, came aboard of our steamer, and had an interview with the Secretary of State and myself, of several hours' duration. No question of preliminaries to the meeting was then and there made or mentioned. No other person was present; no papers were exchanged or produced; and it was, in advance, agreed that the conversation was to be informal and be verbal merely." The instructions which the President had written for Seward were insisted on. "By the other party, it was not said that in any event or on any condition, they ever would consent to reunion; and yet they equally omitted to declare that they never would so consent. They seemed to desire a postponement of that question [of reunion of the States], and the adoption of some other course first which, as some of them seemed to argue, might or might not lead to reunion; but which course, we thought, would amount to an indefinite postponement. The conference ended without result."

Five astute men of politics and law talked four hours in a steamboat saloon. At the outset Lincoln's instructions to Seward marked off three areas where there could be no discussion. The three Confederate commissioners made many approaches trying to get a foot or a toe into some one of these areas. The Federal President and Secretary of State always ruled they were out of bounds, said discussion was impossible. What went on in the minds of the five men, the tangled cross-purposes underlying the words of their mouths, no onlooker could have caught and reported.

As between drinking men Seward on his arrival had sent the commissioners three bottles of whisky, though aware that Stephens never took more than a teaspoon of it at a time. Hunter, who had spent most of his life in Washington, genially asked Seward: "Governor, how is the Capitol? Is it finished?" Whereupon Seward described the new dome and the great brass door.

Stephens's account ran that greetings were cordial between those who had met before, that Lincoln and he spoke as old friends and at once asked about acquaintances of the Mexican War days when Lincoln and Stephens were in Congress together. There was good feeling and harmony between the States and sections then, Stephens suggested, with a query, "Mr. President, is there no way of putting an end to the present trouble?" Lincoln replied to the Confederate Vice-President that he knew of only one way and that was for those who were resisting the laws of the Union to cease that resistance.

There might be a "continental question" on which they could adjust the strife, Stephens once led off, Lincoln rejoining that Mr. Blair in Richmond on matters in Mexico had spoken with no authority from him. Often the talk ranged around States' Rights and slavery, courteously, respectfully, even-tempered—with deep chasms of disagreement. At one point, according to Stephens, Lincoln said it was not his intention in the beginning to interfere with slavery; necessity had compelled it; he had interfered only when driven to it; he had favored no extension of slavery into the Territories but did not think that the Federal Government had power over slavery in the States except as a war measure; he had always been in favor of emancipation, but not immediate emancipation, even by the States.

The people of the North were as responsible for slavery as the people of the South (as Stephens heard Lincoln say it) and "He knew some [in the North] who were in favor of an appropriation as high as four hundred millions of dollars for this purpose [of paying owners for the loss of their slaves]. 'I could mention persons,' said he, 'whose names would astonish you, who are willing to do this if the war shall now cease.'"

On Hunter's saying it seemed that Lincoln's terms forced the Confederate people to choose nothing else than unconditional surrender and submission, Seward with quiet dignity insisted that "no words like unconditional submission had been used" nor any harsh phrases meaning degradation or humiliation. With peace, said Seward, the Southern people would again be under the Constitution "with all their rights secured thereby."

Campbell had a feeling that Stephens along with Davis was "duped" by Blair into hopes of somehow using Mexico. "I was incredulous," wrote Campbell. "Mr. Hunter did not have faith. Mr. Stephens supposed Blair to be 'the mentor of the Administration and the Republican party.' " Of course Campbell, as a man of no vivid streaks and whimsical blends such as ran through Stephens, failed to credit Stephens with using the only prop and lever allowed them by Davis's instructions. The opening query of the conference had come from Stephens to Lincoln: "Well, Mr. President, is there no way of putting an end to the present trouble . . . existing between the different States and sections of *the country?*" In this Stephens did not go so far as Lincoln's term "our one common country," but he did with intention and meaning as his first stroke at the conference abandon the Davis phrase "two countries." Could Davis have listened in, he would have suspected the Stephens motive.

Stripping the discussions of the language of diplomacy and briefing it, Stephens in effect asked why not stop fighting among ourselves and take on a war in Mexico together? Lincoln answered in effect that we would take on another war only after the question of Union was settled. Campbell raised questions of how the Confederates might return armies to peace, of what would be done about the new freedom of the slaves, of Senators and Congressmen elected to go to Washington from seceded States returning to the Union, of Virginia now divided into two States, of claims for Southern property taken or wrecked in the war. Lincoln and Seward answered that some of these points were covered in the President's December message to Congress, other points would have to go to the courts, and Congress might be liberal in handling property claims after the war fever had cooled down. West Virginia would stay as a separate State. The new freedom of the Negroes would be passed on by courts; the Emancipation Proclamation would stand with no change from Lincoln. And it was news to the Confederate commissioners that the United States Congress on January 31 had passed the Thirteenth Amendment to the Constitution and when this should also pass three-fourths of the State legislatures, it would outlaw and abolish slavery.

Lincoln often had to make it clear that as the Executive he might personally wish to do some things, but under the Constitution those things would have to go to Congress or the courts or the States. Once he stressed the point that even if the Confederate States should consider coming back into the Union, he could not make any bargains with armed forces making war on his Government; until the war was over some things could not begin to commence.

At this Hunter reached back into history for a parallel. Hunter pointed to King Charles I of England and how that monarch bargained with people

A page from John A. Campbell's notes on the Hampton Roads conference. Original in the Barrett collection.

in arms against his Government. Hunter's argument was long and elaborate, insisting that peace could come through Lincoln's recognizing the right of Davis to make a treaty.

"Mr. Lincoln's face," ran a later newspaper account by Stephens, "then wore that indescribable expression which generally preceded his hardest hits, and he remarked: 'Upon questions of history I must refer you to Mr. Seward, for he is posted in such things, and I don't pretend to be bright. My only distinct recollection of the matter is that Charles lost his head.' That settled Mr. Hunter for a while."

Another account by Stephens had Lincoln replying: "I do not profess to be posted in history. On all such matters I will turn you over to Seward. All I distinctly recollect about the case of Charles I. is that he lost his head in the end."

Lamon later gathered this, possibly from Lincoln: "On the question of history I must refer you to Mr. Seward, who is posted in such matters. I don't pretend to be; but I have a tolerably distinct recollection, in the case you refer to, that Charles lost his head, and I have no head to spare."

How could Campbell at such a time and place tell Lincoln and Seward that in the first five minutes of the conference he saw that Davis had been under a "delusion" and fooled by Blair's Mexican moonshine, that there was no hope of peace except through the gate of agreement to "our one common country," that Davis's stipulation of "two countries" had the conference sunk at the start?

How could Little Aleck chime in with a footnote for Lincoln about how before the war began he said No when they came offering him place as President of the Confederate States of America if he would merely pledge himself to "strike the first blow"? Or how could "the little pale star from Georgia" shed light on his actions toward impeaching Davis? Or how could Lincoln in such a gathering tell the Confederates that they had millions of sympathizers in the North, that his own party leaders had wanted someone else for President of the United States, that they were heaping scorn on him now because he was not joining their cries for retaliation, punishment of the Southern leaders, wholesale hangings?

Hunter was to go away and report to a Richmond mass meeting, "Mr. Lincoln told us, told me, that while we could send representatives to the Yankee Congress, yet it rested with that Congress to say whether they would receive them or not." This was correct. "Thus," proceeded Hunter, "we would cast every thing away, and go to them as a subdued, subjugated and degraded people, to be held in subjection by their soldiery." That this was the spirit of Congress and not the animus of Lincoln and Seward during the conference failed to get into Hunter's report. None of the three commissioners reported to their people that Lincoln had said he could mention "persons whose names would astonish you" who favored a $400,000,000 appropriation for compensation to the South for its lost slave property. Stephens, according to the *Augusta Chronicle*, "thought he was doing a favor to Mr. Lincoln" in not publishing this matter of compensation, "for it would be used to the injury of Mr. Lincoln."

No good would have come to the commissioners from publishing part of the informal proceedings which came to Lamon's ear, it seemed, from Lincoln himself. A hush fell over the conference at one point where Lincoln found himself required to contradict gravely and directly remarks made by the Confederate commissioners. His words were measured and sounded like doom, for he was saying that the conduct of certain rebel leaders had been such that they had plainly forfeited all right to immunity from punishment for the highest crime known to law. He had come to the brink of saying they should be strung up for treason, hang high and lonesome as traitors.

There was a hush and a pause. Hunter gave Lincoln a steady, searching look, and then very deliberately: "Mr. President, if we understand you correctly, you think that we of the Confederacy have committed treason; that we are traitors to your government; that we have forfeited our rights, and are proper subjects for the hangman. Is not that about what your words imply?"

"Yes," rejoined Lincoln. "You have stated the proposition better than I did. That is about the size of it!"

Another hush and a somewhat painful pause, then Hunter with a pleasant smile: "Well, Mr. Lincoln, we have about concluded that we shall not be hanged as long as you are President—if we behave ourselves."

The painter Carpenter shortly after the confabulations at Hampton Roads asked Lincoln about the *New York Herald* account with its reference to his telling "a little story" amid the solemnities. "Why," said he, as Carpenter later wrote it down, "has it leaked out? I was in hopes nothing would be said about *that*, lest some over-sensitive people should imagine there was a degree of levity in the intercourse between us. You see, we had reached and were discussing the *slavery* question. Mr. Hunter said, substantially, that the slaves, always accustomed to an overseer, and to work upon compulsion, suddenly freed, as they would be if the South should consent to peace on the basis of the 'Emancipation Proclamation,' would precipitate not only themselves but the entire Southern society into irremediable ruin. No work would be done, nothing would be cultivated, and both blacks and whites would *starve!*

"I waited for Seward to answer that argument, but as he was silent, I at length said: 'Mr. Hunter, *you* ought to know a great deal better about this matter than *I*, for you have always lived under the slave system. I can only say, in reply to your statement of the case, that it reminds me of a man out in Illinois, by the name of Case, who undertook, a few years ago, to raise a very large herd of hogs. It was a great trouble to *feed* them, and how to get around this was a puzzle to him. At length he hit on the plan of planting an immense field of potatoes, and, when they were sufficiently grown, he turned the whole herd into the field, and let them have full swing, thus saving not only the labor of feeding the hogs, but also that of digging the potatoes. Charmed with his sagacity, he stood one day leaning against the fence, counting his hogs, when a neighbor came along. "Well, well," said he, "Mr. Case, this is all very fine. Your hogs are doing very well just now, but you know out here in Illinois the frost comes early, and the ground freezes a foot deep. Then what are they going to do?" This was a view of the matter Mr. Case had not taken into account. Butchering-time for hogs was 'way on in December or January. He scratched his head, and at length stammered, "Well, it may come pretty hard on their *snouts*, but I don't see but that it will be 'root, hog, or die!' " ' "

To Lamon also Lincoln told this fable, Lamon writing it somewhat different, ending: "Well, it will be a leetle hard on their snouts, I reckon; but them shoats will have to root, hog, or die." Then, according to Lamon, Lincoln drew the moral of his fable: "And so, in the dire contingency you name, whites and black alike will have to look out for themselves; and I have an abiding faith that they will go about it in a fashion that will undeceive you in a very agreeable way."

Thus Lincoln told the matter to Lamon. To his Secretary of the Interior, he gave it in shorter form. Usher noted that "from his manner in repeating this scene he seemed to appreciate the compliment highly." Hunter was the one Confederate conferee who stirred smoldering fire in Lincoln. An *Augusta* (Georgia) *Chronicle* interview with Stephens later related: "Hunter declared that he had never entertained any fears for his person or life from so mild a government as that of the United States. To which Mr. Lincoln retorted that he, also, had felt easy as to the Rebels, but not always so easy about the lamp-posts around Washington City,—a hint that he had already done more favors for the Rebels than was exactly popular with the radical men of his own party. Mr. Lincoln's manner had now grown more positive. He suggested that it would be better for the Rebel States to return at once than to risk the chances of continuing the war, and the increasing bitterness of feeling in Congress. The time might come, he said, when they would not be considered as an erring people invited back to citizenship, but would be looked upon as enemies to be exterminated or ruined. During the conference, the amendment to the Federal Constitution, which has just been adopted by Congress, was read, providing that neither slavery nor involuntary servitude, except for crime, should exist within the United States, or any place within its jurisdiction, and Congress should have power to enforce the amendment by appropriate legislation."

A fellowship resting on thin fire, in a far cavern of gloom, seemed to have renewal between Lincoln and Stephens. Stephens came aboard the steamer wearing a coarse gray woolen overcoat of newly improvised Southern manufacture. The thick cloth of this garment came down nearly to his feet and he looked almost like an average-sized man, though his weight was only ninety pounds. Lincoln, a foot taller than Stephens and nearly twice his weight, had come into the steamer saloon and stood watching the dwarfish Georgian shake loose and step out of his huge overcoat, unwinding a long wool muffler and several shawls. Lincoln moved toward Little Aleck.

whom he had not seen in sixteen years, and with a smiling handshake: "Never have I seen so small a nubbin come out of so much husk."

That was the way Stephens remembered and told it. As Lamon noted it from Lincoln himself the remark ran: "Was there ever such a nubbin after so much shucking?" And Grant was interested that Lincoln should ask him if he had seen that overcoat of Stephens's. Grant had noticed it very particularly. "Well, did you see him take it off?" Grant had. "Well, didn't you think it was the biggest shuck and the littlest ear that ever you did see?"

Once during the conference someone spoke of an Illinois Congressman who had gone to the Mexican War. This drew from Stephens a story touching on how in a House session the Illinois members themselves could not agree on how to pronounce the name of their State. Some insisted it was "Illi-*noy*" others that it was "Illi-*nois*." One of them appealed to the venerable John Quincy Adams, who with a malicious smile thrust out: "If one were to judge from the character of the representatives in this Congress from that State, I should decide unhesitatingly that the proper pronunciation was 'All noise!' " Thus Stephens's anecdote was relayed by Lincoln to Carpenter as a piece of brightness worth passing on.

Lincoln tried free straightaway peace talk on Stephens only—as though they might be alone on the wide heaving Atlantic and no listener but a gray sea as melancholy as their own two worn hearts. Lincoln spoke his personal judgments about immediate emancipation. "Many evils attending this appeared to him," wrote Stephens. A gradual emancipation across perhaps a five-year period would better enable the two races to work out their codes and designs for living together than emancipation at one sweep. Stephens wrote of this mood and what followed, that after pausing for some time, his head rather bent down, as if in deep reflection, while all were silent, Lincoln rose and used these words, almost, if not quite, exactly:

"Stephens, if I were in Georgia, and entertained the sentiments I do— though, I suppose, I should not be permitted to stay there long with them; but if I resided in Georgia, with my present sentiments, I'll tell you what I would do, if I were in your place: I would go home and get the Governor of the State to call the Legislature together, and get them to recall all the State troops from the war; elect Senators and Members to Congress, and ratify this Constitutional Amendment [outlawing and abolishing slavery] *prospectively*, so as to take effect—say in five years. Such a ratification would be valid in my opinion. I have looked into the subject, and think such a prospective ratification would be valid. Whatever may have been the views of your people before the war, they must be convinced now, that Slavery is doomed. It cannot last long in any event, and the best course, it seems to me, for your public men to pursue, would be to adopt such a policy as will avoid, as far as possible, the evils of immediate emancipation. This would be my course, if I were in your place."

Lincoln spoke this as though Stephens had a genius for suffering that might gather and use an appeal to suffer more yet. The two men had a like melancholy, Stephens once recording: "Sometimes I have thought that of all men I was most miserable; that I was especially doomed to misfortune, to melancholy, to grief. . . . The misery, the deep agony of spirit I have suffered, no mortal knows, nor ever will. . . . The torture of body is severe; I have had my share of that. . . . But all these are slight when compared with the pangs of an offended or wounded spirit. The heart alone knoweth its own sorrow. I have borne it these many years. I have borne it all my life." Lincoln knew deeply the same mood. They were the two most somber figures at this five-man conference. And by paradox they laughed more through the discussions than any two of the five.

Now came the friendly handshakings of saying good-by, of ending the Hampton Roads conference, a world of nations and people watching, a horde of journalists and politicians puzzling. Stephens again asked Lincoln to reconsider Blair's stalking horse, the plan of an armistice on the basis of a Mexican expedition commanded by Jeff Davis. Lincoln: "Well, Stephens, I will reconsider it; but I do not think my mind will change."

Nothing more seemed worth saying. The President of the United States said to the Vice-President of the Confederacy: "Well, Stephens, there has been nothing we could do for our country. Is there anything I can do for you personally?"

"Nothing." Then Little Aleck's pale face brightened. "Unless you can send me my nephew who has been for twenty months a prisoner on Johnson's Island."

Lincoln's face too brightened. "I shall be glad to do it. Let me have his name." And he wrote it down in a notebook.

After handshakings all round the Confederate commissioners were put in a rowboat and taken to their steamer for return to their own army lines. They were getting ready to steam away when they saw a rowboat with a Negro at the oars heading for their steamer. He reached their deck with a basket of champagne and a note with the compliments of Mr. Seward. The commissioners read the note, waved their handkerchiefs in acknowledgment. Then they saw Mr. Seward, speaking through a boatswain's trumpet. The words of the Secretary of State came clear. He was saying, *"Keep the champagne, but return the negro!"* Thus ran the final informal words of the Hampton Roads conference, which was quite informal but not at all final.

"To-day they returned to Richmond," wrote General Meade to his wife, "but what was the result of their visit no one knows. At the present moment, 8 P.M., the artillery on our lines is in full blast, clearly proving that at this moment there is no peace."

In company with Major Eckert, with Robert S. Chew, Seward's private secretary, and with Forbes, who carried Lincoln's traveling-bag, Lincoln and Seward rode a steamer up Chesapeake Bay for Annapolis. They had finished a hard day's work with a wide world wondering what of it. In Washington was curiosity and fury. In New York the stock market was nervous and wavering. The gold speculators were crazy to go but couldn't figure which way. A crowd was on hand at Annapolis to see the President. Newspapermen failed to wring anything definite from Lincoln, Seward, or Eckert.

But Eckert was staggered at what happened to him. On the railway station platform he saw a man he knew, an acquaintance, who drew him one side and talked fast, saying it was all strictly confidential, asking him for straight inside information on what had been done at Hampton Roads, at the same time putting in Eckert's hands an envelope which he said would pay Eckert for his trouble. Eckert put the man off with excuses, went to Lincoln's railway coach and, standing before Lincoln, opened the sealed envelope and showed Lincoln a certified check for $100,000, telling Lincoln how it had come into his hands. Lincoln asked Eckert who gave it to him. Eckert replied, "I am not at liberty to say, but when the train is ready to leave, I will be on the platform, and hand the envelop to the man from whom I received it, so that you can see who he is." This was done, Eckert telling the man that he was obliged to decline the offer and could give him no news at all about what had been done at the Hampton Roads conference. Thus David Homer Bates had the matter from Eckert, Bates writing that on the station platform "Lincoln saw the transaction, and recognized the man as one prominent in political affairs . . . who had held a responsible official position in one of the western States. Upon returning to the car, Lincoln remained silent for a long time, but afterward, when he and Eckert could converse together without attracting Seward's special attention, or that of Robert S. Chew, his private secretary, the only other occupants of the car, it was agreed that neither should disclose the incident to any one excepting only Secretary Stanton, Eckert contending that the effect on public opinion generally . . . would be very injurious at a time of such extreme tension."

At the White House that evening Eckert and Lincoln met Stanton, told him the peace-conference news, gave him the details about the certified check and the name of the man who let Eckert have it for a few minutes. In the many days to come the incident was kept secret, along with the man's name and why a little reliable inside information about what was done at Hampton Roads would be worth $100,000 to whatever unknown interests he served as a go-between.

The next day, February 4, not a Cabinet member was missing at the noon meeting. They heard from Lincoln and Seward that the conference of the day before won no results and the exchanges had been "pleasant and without acrimony." Seward, suspected Welles, would like in such affairs to manage the President. A jealous Cabinet, a peculiar array of counselors it was, in view of what happened the next day of February 5 at an evening session. Not one of the chosen advisers, not one of the seven executive department heads, neither Seward nor Welles of the first 1861 Cabinet, nor Stanton who had been there three years, nor Usher, Fessenden, Dennison, Speed, not one ranged himself alongside the President in one of the boldest constructive proposals he had ever laid before them. All were Christian churchmen, though each one withheld himself from joining Lincoln in an act for which an argument could be made that it was laden and shining with the spirit of the Sermon on the Mount.

Lincoln called the session for an evening. During this day of February 5 he spent most of his time on a message and proclamation from the President to go to the Senate and House, asking those "honorable bodies" to resolve that the President of the United States be empowered, in his discretion, to pay $400,000,000 to various Southern States, which were named. Six per cent Government bonds would form the payment, "to be distributed among said States *pro rata* on their respective slave populations as shown by the census of 1860, and no part of said sum to be paid unless all resistance to the National authority shall be abandoned and cease, on or before the first day of April next." The adoption of such a resolution was sought with a view to embody it, with other propositions, "in a proclamation looking to peace and reunion." The proclamation would read:

"Now therefore, I, Abraham Lincoln, President of the United States, do proclaim, declare, and make known, that on the conditions therein stated, the power conferred on the Executive in and by said joint resolution will be fully exercised; that war will cease and armies be reduced to a basis of peace; that all political offenses will be pardoned; that all property, except slaves, liable to confiscation or forfeiture, will be released therefrom, except in cases of intervening interests of third parties; and that liberality will be recommended to Congress upon all points not lying within Executive control."

This document Lincoln confidentially laid before his Cabinet. Did they consider it wise or expedient? not so bad or not so good? "It would appear," wrote Nicolay and Hay, "that there was but little discussion of the proposition. The President's evident earnestness on the one side, and the unanimous dissent of the Cabinet on the other, probably created an awkward situation which could be best relieved by silence on each hand."

Usher wrote of the President somewhat surprised at all the Cabinet being opposed, and asking, "How long will the war last?" No one answered, so the President took it on himself: "A hundred days. We are spending now in carrying on the war three millions a day, which will amount to all this money, besides all the lives." With a deep sigh, noted Usher, he added, "But you are all opposed to me, and I will not send the message."

On the back of the manuscript of this proposed message, under the date of February 5, 1865, Lincoln wrote: "Today these papers, which explain themselves, were drawn up and submitted to the Cabinet and unanimously disapproved by them." He signed his name as though it was history and should be of record.

Welles in his diary sketched it as "a scheme which he [Lincoln] hoped would be successful in promoting peace." Summarizing it, Welles wrote, "This in few words was the scheme." The best word Welles could find for it was "scheme." With his colleagues he saw the President in this a schemer rather than a solid statesman. "It did not meet with favor, but was dropped. The earnest desire of the President to conciliate and effect peace was manifest, but there may be such a thing as so overdoing as to cause a distrust or adverse feeling."

In the present temper of Congress, judged Welles, "the proposed measure, if a wise one, could not be carried through successfully. I do not think the scheme could accomplish any good results. The Rebels would misconstrue it if the offer were made. If attempted and defeated it would do harm."

Welles, whose judgment probably reflected that of most of the Cabinet, believed his guess was better than that of Lincoln on how the South would take the proposal. Also Welles looked toward Congress and the Lincoln opposition there rather than toward the country and the people, the forces by which Lincoln the year before had overcome the almost unanimous array of politicians in Congress opposed to him. Furthermore, Welles doubted whether the measure was "a wise one" but in case it could be proved wise, then it "could not be carried through successfully."

So the war would go on. The majestic and incalculably dynamic gesture Lincoln asked for, was out. A policy of nonretaliation, of "molding society for durability in the Union," as he hoped in the December message, would have to come slowly. Could an Executive tame and gentle in degree the savagery of a coming chaos? Far more often than his Cabinet during the war he had correctly fathomed the country and the people. The same vast audience one with him on the House Divided speech, on the Gettysburg Address, on the letter to Mrs. Bixby, would respond to the freehanded proposals of the proclamation on which the Cabinet now turned thumbs down— so he believed. His confidential advisers were thinking of Washington and Congress and politics; he was thinking of the great everyday masses of people North and South. The Cabinet was correct in feeling that the present controlling Southern politicians would hoot his proposed proclamation. But beyond might be a mass of Southern people moving and acting when those politicians were discredited as prophets and bankrupt as statesmen. As Lincoln laid aside the memorandum vetoed by his Cabinet, he looked forward, Nicolay and Hay were agreed, "to a not distant day when, in the new term of the Presidency to which he was already elected, the Cabinet would respond more charitably to his own generous impulses." Much was to happen before those now wishing to correct him would have any inklings of what he meant by "molding society for durability in the Union."

When the Confederate commissioners came back with their report, Richmond was turned upside down humanly, with high-noon processions, no less than twenty government orators joined by ministers in churches and theatres and at speaking stands where crowds gathered. "Lincoln has confessed," said Judah P. Benjamin at a midday church meeting, "that without 200,000 negroes which he stole from us, he would be compelled to give up the contest." "If anything was wanted to stir the blood," said Hunter the third day after he had been at Hampton Roads, at this midday church meeting, "it was furnished when we were told that the United States could not consent to entertain any proposition coming from us as a people. Lincoln might have offered something." In a speech that fascinated his audience with unexpected strength and passion Jefferson Davis spoke. In word and tone was a magnificent contempt of any death or humiliation that could be forced on him, and either of these he would prefer "sooner than we should ever be united again." With curled lips of scorn he referred to the archantagonist "His Majesty Abraham the First." He swept himself along in a rushing prophecy that the Confederacy would yet "compel the Yankees, in less than twelve months, to petition us for peace on our own terms."

Little Aleck Stephens sat listening, said afterward that as oratory it was bold, lofty, undaunted, and he could understand those who considered it superb. Some, noted the Georgian, compared Davis of this hour to Demosthenes, but for himself he was reminded of the charge of the Light Brigade at Balaklava and the Frenchman who summarized its useless sacrifice: "It is brilliant; it is grand; but it is not war." A few days proved that in effect the effort to rouse the Confederacy to new fighting spirit was the same as beating a half-starved horse. In the immediate neighborhood of the Confederate Government a new flame rose for a moment and then sputtered out. On the long line from Richmond, Virginia, to Corpus Christi, Texas, rose no fresh torches of hope. Lee got no troops, his wagons no corn nor fodder, from the oratory.

The Rhett faction was now saying in the *Charleston Mercury*, February 2, 1865, they would see "all our blood poured out for worse than nothing" unless the Confederacy held out for independence—and slavery. "If [the Confederate] Congress will perform its duties fearlessly even to the impeachment of Mr. Davis, if need be—reform the Government from turret to foundation stone—and the States will stand firm on the slavery platform—we may continue the struggle, and reasonably hope to succeed—not otherwise. Let us brace ourselves to the task."

"Perhaps . . . WAR will rage with greater fury than ever," wrote J. B. Jones in his diary, February 6. He hoped so. In the next sentence he wrote, "Mr. Stephens will go into Georgia, and reanimate his people." So it was said. But it was not so. They had asked him to join in the oratory at a Capitol Square meeting. "I declined," ran Stephens's explanation, "because I could not undertake to impress upon the minds of the people the idea that they could do what I believed to be impossible." He knew they were too far shattered in men and resources and leadership to hold out against the massive and growing Northern war strength.

After his refusal to join the orators the Vice-President of the Confederacy called on its President. "He inquired what it was my purpose to do. I told him it was to go home and remain there. I should neither make any speech, nor even make known to the public in any way my views of the general condition of affairs, but quietly abide the issue of fortune." Stephens parted from Davis, he noted, "in the same friendship which had on all occasions marked our personal intercourse." He was leaving Richmond in no ill humor, "but because I could not sanction a policy which I thought would certainly end in disaster, and I did not wish to be where my opinions might, by possibility, be the cause of divisions and dissensions." He left Richmond on February 9, reached his home at Crawfordsville, Georgia, on February 20, where, as he said, "I remained in perfect retirement." Stephens was too far committed, by word of mouth and by instinct of heart, to the States' Rights theory to go as far as Lincoln advised him to. On the other hand his conscience did allow him to go home, stay there, keep silence, and watch a tragic drama where his voice lacked authority draw to a close.

Lincoln in Washington sent a telegram to Johnson's Island, in Lake Erie north of Ohio, resulting in an officer entering the building which held a mass of Confederate prisoners, and calling out: "Lieutenant John A. Stephens of Georgia!" The Lieutenant thought he was called out to be shot. He had been captured at Vicksburg and after five months in a New Orleans doghouse transferred far north, he had heard nothing and seen nothing to help him imagine why his name now was called. Through some mistake they wanted him and were going to stand him before a firing squad. That was his main impression.

So Lieutenant Stephens was pleased to hear at headquarters that President Lincoln wanted to see him. They put him on a sleigh, a cutter, and to the jingle of merry bells in bitter winter weather he was driven twenty miles across the ice on Lake Erie to Sandusky. Transportation was handed him. He rode the railroad cars to Washington, called at the White House and sent in his name.

At once he was ushered into Lincoln's office, found the President half sitting and half slouched on a table, talking with Seward. Mr. Lincoln rose, shook his hand warmly and with a smile: "I saw your uncle, the Honorable Alexander H. Stephens, recently at Hampton Roads." The Lieutenant had seen no newspapers on Johnson's Island and this was even the first news he had that his uncle was still alive. Mr. Lincoln continued: "I told your uncle I would send you to him, Lieutenant." The Lieutenant was deeply moved and grateful. And he was just a little dizzy over the next words from the President: "You have the freedom of the city as long as you please to remain here. When you want to go home, let me know, and I will pass you through the lines." Mr. Lincoln went on talking pleasantly, telling him about Hampton Roads, asking him many questions, and making the hour one to remember. Two weeks the Lieutenant stayed in Washington, finding old friends of his own and his uncle's who entertained him. He put on weight, gained strength.

When he went to Mr. Lincoln and told him he was ready to go to Richmond, Mr. Lincoln gave him a letter he was to carry to his uncle. It read: "According to our agreement, your nephew, Lieutenant Stephens, goes to you, bearing this note. Please, in return, to select and send to me that officer of the same rank at Richmond, whose physical condition most urgently requires his release." He signed a pass through the Union Army lines for the lieutenant and then did a sentimental thing never done before in the White House. He handed the Confederate lieutenant a photograph of himself with the remark: "You had better take that along. It is considered quite a curiosity down your way, I believe." Why did Mr. Lincoln do this? He wanted to help Mr. Stephens remember what an old laughing friend looked like—was that it?

During the weeks of the Blair mission, the Hampton Roads conference, and its aftermath in Congress another affair progressed, little of it known to the public. One General J. W. Singleton arrived in Richmond on the return trip of the boat that had taken Blair away from his first visit to Richmond. Brief items in Northern newspapers about Singleton said he was an Illinois member of the Sons of Liberty, that he registered at the Spotswood Hotel, that he had earnest and cordial talks with many ladies and gentlemen who respected a Northern sympathizer with the South, that he interviewed General Lee and President Davis, that he then returned to Washington and reported to the President his conviction that the South would not make peace without independence. Under whatever open mission Singleton went to Richmond, it was mainly a false pretense. His real errand was a secret kept in a small circle, as told in a diary entry of Browning:

Thursday Jany 5 The President sent me word last night that he wished to see me this morning I had previously talked with him about permitting Singleton to go South to buy Cotton, tobacco &c. a scheme out of which he, Singleton, Judge Hughes of the Court of Claims, Senator Morgan myself and some others, hope to make some money, and do the Country some service. He wished to see me upon this subject now. We talked it all over, and before leaving him he gave me two cards for Singleton as follows

"Allow the bearer, James W Singleton, to pass our lines with ordinary baggage, and go South.
"Jany 5, 1865.   A Lincoln"

"Allow the bearer, James W Singleton to pass our lines, with any Southern products, and go to any of our trading posts, there to be subject to the regulations of the Treasury Department
"Jany 5, 1865   A Lincoln"

He gave me another paper for Hughes securing him and his agents, protection and transportation when we shall get the products on this side the line

He gave me a history of two of the half sisters of Mrs Lincoln who are rebels. Mrs Helm and Mrs White and wished some of us to see Mrs Helm, and make some arrangement with her about 600 bales of cotton she claims to have somewhere in the South.

Again Lincoln had favored friends, giving them the highly prized trading permits. Again there were complications. On January 30 Browning wrote of interviewing General Singleton just arrived from Richmond. "He brought back contracts for seven millions dollars worth of Cotton, Tobacco, Rosin and Turpentine, which will make us rich if we can only get it out." Two nights later "Singleton & I went to the Presidents, and had a talk about public affairs—Singleton reporting who he saw, and what was said in Richmond. He then showed him [the President] his contracts, and told him he only wanted protection in getting out what he had bought—the whole to be paid for in Green backs. He expressed himself pleased with what was done—said he wanted to get out all he could, and send in all the Green backs he could in exchange, and that he would do for us all that he could."

On February 7, noted Browning, Singleton left Washington "for New

At Grant's City Point headquarters: John Aaron Rawlins, Ulysses Simpson Grant, Theodore Shelton Bowers

Philip Henry Sheridan

From the Chicago Historical Society

Pup tents—the halt of marching troops

From the Chicago Historical Society

The war President, probably early '65, sits for a stereoscopic photograph (made by a two-eyed camera) probably by Brady—one of only two known stereoscopic prints of Lincoln

Original in the Library of Congress

York to make his financial arrangements for cotton, tobacco, &c." Two nights later the President gave Browning a letter dated February 7 for Singleton to deliver to General Grant. This letter threw all future decisions as to Singleton, and his war fortunes, into the hands of Grant. It read:

General Singleton, who bears you this, claims that he already has arrangements made, if you consent, to bring a large amount of Southern produce through your lines. For its bearing on our finances, I would be glad for this to be done, if it can be, without injuriously disturbing your military operations, or supplying the enemy. I wish you to be judge and master on these points. Please see and hear him fully, and decide whether anything, and, if anything, what, can be done in the premises.

A month later newspapers reported 200,000 pounds of tobacco bought by General Singleton as seized and burned by Grant's troops. Browning hurried with Judge Hughes to the White House. "There was a crowd of people in waiting," wrote Browning, "but we were admitted soon after we got there. The President at once showed us despatches from Genl Grant to Mr Stanton . . . saying substantially that General Singleton and Judge Hughes were at Richmond engaged in a stupendous scheme to make millions of dollars by buying produce of the rebels and giving them supplies in exchange—that they were willing to sacrifice the interests of the Country to the accomplishment of their purpose, and that they ought to be recalled and their permits taken away from them. He [Grant] said he got his information from our friends in Richmond of whom we had many. This astonished me greatly. . . . The President seemed troubled and perplexed, and distressed that the tobacco had been destroyed, and manifested a desire to keep faith, and save Singleton from ruin if he could, but at the same time gave me the impression that he was afraid to take the responsibility. I thought he was afraid of Secretary Stanton, although he said Stanton had always been in favor of getting out products. I suggested that I would see, and converse, with Mr Stanton upon the subject, and he urged me to do so. He also thought that Judge Hughes ought to go down and see Grant, saying he would give him a pass to go, and also wrote a letter to Grant."

In this interview on March 11 Lincoln felt that Browning was not entitled to know of a letter written to Grant three days before. Grant's wrathy telegrams to Stanton, about Singleton and Hughes fortune-hunting in Richmond, had been laid before him by Stanton, the President wrote to Grant. "As to Singleton and Hughes, I think they are not in Richmond by any authority, unless it be from you. I remember nothing from me which could aid them in getting there, except a letter to you." Here Lincoln inserted a copy of his letter to Grant February 7, adding: "I believe I gave Hughes a card putting him with Singleton on the same letter. However this may be, I now authorize you to get Singleton and Hughes away from Richmond, if you choose, and can. I also authorize you, by an order, or in what form you choose, to suspend all operations on the Treasury-trade permits, in all places southeastward of the Alleghanies."

This letter and the information in it the President withheld from

Browning. As in similar intricate paths, the President was keeping a record of it. On hearing from Browning that Singleton had bought options on $7,000,000 worth of commodities in Richmond, he instructed Grant on February 7 to do whatever Grant chose to do with the fortune-hunters. Grant was on the ground. Grant could decide whether to let them go to Richmond. Or Grant could stop them. "I wish you to be judge and master on these points." Of this he did not tell Browning. A month passed and Browning came in grief over news of Grant seizing and burning 200,000 pounds of tobacco, the grief not helped by the President showing Grant's anger over "a stupendous scheme to make millions of dollars." Browning saw the President "troubled and perplexed" but unwilling to overrule Grant's authority, Browning unaware that the President had three days before repeated with increased emphasis his point that Grant must be "judge and master on these points." It would have amazed Browning that the President that week distinctly wrote to Grant, "I now authorize you to get Singleton and Hughes away from Richmond, if you choose, and can."

On Sunday, March 12, Browning wrote in his diary, "At Church in the morning—At night went to Mr Stanton's and had a long talk with him about Singleton's affairs." Browning heard Stanton say "every man who went through the lines to buy cotton ought to be shot—that it was trading in the blood of our soldiers, and sacrificing the interests of the Country to enable mercenary scoundrels to amass large fortunes &c." Stanton was "gratified" at 200,000 pounds of Singleton's cotton being destroyed. Then Stanton was surprised at Browning producing a "paper Grant had given to Singleton." It looked as though Grant had given approval to Singleton's trading. Stanton said Grant's letter needed explanation. "If he [Grant] had given such a guaranty he would never have destroyed the produce afterward." Stanton asked Browning for a copy of the letter, which Browning promised to furnish the next day.

Four days later Browning saw the President, said it would be an outrage to ruin Singleton as he feared Stanton, now down at Grant's headquarters, might ruthlessly do. The President: "O, no, Stanton is not going to do anything desperate. He has always heretofore been as much in favor of the trade as I am."

The affair had many angles and phases. On February 7 Lincoln decided Singleton was perhaps a fisher in muddy waters. Grant, nearer Richmond, should have the complete say-so on whether Singleton could go to Richmond. So Lincoln wrote Grant to that effect. A few weeks passed and Grant too decided Singleton was a peculiar operator and the day might come when it would not look well that Grant had given him approval. So Grant sent wrathy telegrams to the War Department, excoriating Singleton. This timed with a story that flared in the newspapers, of Singleton's 200,000 pounds of cotton seized and destroyed. To that story Browning referred in his diary entry March 21: "Mr Stanton returned on yesterday from Genl Grant's head Quarters. I met [him] this morning in the War Department. He took my arm—said he was going to the Presidents, and asked me to walk with him. I did walk with him to the front portico of the White House. As we walked he looked at me, laughing, and said 'That was not Singletons tobacco that was seized at Fredericksburg after all—Strange what stories get in circulation' " To Browning's point that Singleton was acting "in perfect good faith," toward benefit of the Government, and that he should hate to see Singleton ruined, Stanton replied, "We'll not ruin him bad." Browning said he was sorry anything had been undertaken "which does not meet your approbation," wished that Stanton had been consulted in the beginning. This brought from Stanton words rare and remarkable, coming from him: "I am as liable to be mistaken as any body else—I may be wrong."

On March 25 Singleton was back in Washington from his second trip to Richmond, and Browning noted: "He has contracted for a large amount of produce, and we hope ultimately to be able to save it and get it out. Mrs. Helm and Miss Breeden came with him. I called on them at the Metropolitan in the afternoon. Mrs Helm claims to have 600 bales of cotton in the South, which the President is anxious for her to get out, and Genl Grant has given her an order for its protection."

There, for the time, this matter rested. Lincoln hoped that his wife's sister would be able to salvage her cotton. Singleton knew that he was under suspicion and whatever contracts he put through with profits would be with watch and scrutiny on him.

Very little came before the Cabinet meeting of February 7, noted Welles. "The President, when I entered the room, was reading with much enjoyment certain portions of Petroleum V. Nasby to Dennison and Speed. The book is a broad burlesque on modern Democratic party men. Fessenden, who came in just after me, evidently thought it hardly a proper subject for the occasion, and the President hastily dropped it."

In the Senate that day Wilson of Massachusetts sought to discredit the President, saying that Grant would have won the war by now if three months ago he could have had a reinforcement of 50,000 or 75,000 men to which he was entitled. "Why did we not have it? . . . We have had all sorts of interference." Committees representing draft-evaders had come to Washington to ask the President, the Secretary of War, or the Provost Marshal General "to do what none of them had any right to do." On so grave a matter Senator Wilson lacked particulars and offered rumors to support his allegations. "There is a report in circulation that a large percentage of the number called for from one of the States has been remitted by the President, who has no more right to do it than I have." On the basis of "a report in circulation" Wilson would like to convict the President of failing to get Grant troops needed to end the war. Well understood was it, among those who sought motives, that draft enrollment was a minor affair and Wilson was taking part in a concerted move to drag down the executive and raise up the legislative end of the Government.

In the same week Ben Wade tore into the President's "pretensions" in

Louisiana, saying of Lincoln's ten-per-cent plan that it was "the most absurd and impracticable that ever haunted the imagination of a statesman." He pictured Lincoln as a military autocrat setting up in Louisiana a semblance, a counterfeit State government. In the campaign of the year before, said Wade of Lincoln, "if it had taken these semblances, these counterfeits, to make out his title to the Presidency, before God I would not have consented to receive them."

An artist in vocal discourse and a superb debater, Wade could hit hard, if not always clean. Perfect courtesy in Chesterfieldian style got mixed with a smooth-flowing insolence in short words. Doolittle of Wisconsin undertook a defense of the President and came off a bad second. "If he wants to make it appear that he is the peculiar defender of the President of the United States," said Wade, "and that the President cannot stand alone anywhere unless braced up . . . allow me to say that he has a much poorer opinion of the President than I have. [Laughter.] . . . I care nothing for the Senator's attacks. Why wake up Rip Van Winkle? . . . I have done nothing to stir up the Senator's malice that I know of. I have not spoken of him or about him or thought of him. He was not even in my thoughts or in my mind. I care nothing about him any more than I do about anybody else. I bear him no malice, and very little good-will. [Laughter.] . . . As I said before, he will not provoke a reply from me. Perhaps I ought not to say a word in reply, as I did not before. I care nothing for what he has said; I even bear him no malice for anything he can say, for I have never had anything to do with him and never want to have. [Laughter.] . . . What fine statesmanship for a 'friend' of the President here, instead of undertaking to make peace and conciliation in this great council of the United States, to descend to the lowest depths of demagogism in order to provoke a controversy."

This clash began over a resolution of Sumner that the President "be requested, if in his opinion not incompatible with the public interest, to furnish to the Senate any information in his possession concerning recent conversations or communications with certain rebels." Sumner said he believed the President was ready to make a full and frank communication. "Perhaps I might say that he desires to do it." Sherman of Ohio doubted whether the President should be called on for information. What happened at Hampton Roads, Sherman surmised, "will probably never be disclosed, or at least not for some time. . . . The President of the United States ought to exercise his entire pleasure in the matter, and he ought not to communicate this information merely to satisfy the curiosity of the Senate and the country unless he thinks it will tend to quiet the public mind."

Doolittle stepped in with a heavy and lumbering defense of the President. His intentions good enough, what Doolittle had to say made no impression except to later draw a fierce fire from Wade. "Although he [the President] may not have displayed as much genius as some men possess," said Doolittle, "in the end he has displayed a wisdom and a sagacity which entitle him to the confidence of the country." And as though he might be speaking for the President, and certainly aware that it could be so construed, Doolittle advised that a request to the President for a peace conference report was "unwise," and in fact was "an attack substantially upon the President." Morrill of Maine joined Sumner in the point that Doolittle was jumpy and oversolicitous in his role of the President's friend. Doolittle rejoined that they were trying to cross-examine the President with impudent queries: "What have you been doing? Render us an account of yourself." Morrill returned to the fray, holding Doolittle's speech "obnoxious" and "offensive" in assuming a tone "as if there were a body of radical men in this Senate against whom the President of the United States needed to be defended." Doolittle insisted he was misunderstood, but he would quote the Senator from Ohio, meaning Mr. Wade, as having said: "Your Executive lacks blood; he has not got the nerve to carry out and perform his duties as he ought."

Wade had sniffed the battle from afar. He now arose, opened new issues and old sores of discussion, and in the course of several thousand words sowed about as many seeds of discord and bad feeling between the executive and legislative ends of the Government as one man might hope to in a day's work. First as to Doolittle: "I fear the President will fare very hard unless he has better support; but I care nothing about that; it is between him and the President." Then as to the President: "I do not think that it always consists with the honor even of the President that we should be his mere servants, obeying everything that we may ascertain to be his wish and will, because he is not always wiser than the whole of us or a majority of us. . . . I wish to God that the President had taken a different view from that by which he seems to have been actuated. I wish the President had conceived it incompatible with the high position he holds as the President of the United States to . . . meet the emissaries of the rebel chief. I think it was a condescension not very honorable to the nation, on his part. . . . I think the President ought to tell us what propositions he made to these scoundrels, and what they rejected, that the whole country may know how we stand related to them."

In the House session of the same day of February 8 Stevens put through a resolution, much like Sumner's in the Senate, requesting the President to report on Hampton Roads. In the House however it was managed with no show of what they liked to call "acrimony."

Many Senate and House members nursed a sullen mistrust of Lincoln's latest errand. With more than a few it was a baffled and inarticulate hate of the President. One hater and belittler was Representative George W. Julian of Indiana. He embodied the viewpoint known as radical. He spoke for associates. They agreed with Julian that the return of Lincoln from Hampton Roads was a proper moment for a statement of their case against the President. The atmosphere was there. When Lincoln had followed Seward to Hampton Roads and the completely unexpected news of it went forth over Washington, the undercurrents of excitement and frustration raged and whirled, wrote Noah Brooks. "The Peace Democrats went about the corridors of the hotels and the Capitol, saying that Lincoln had at last come to their way of thinking, and had gone to Hampton Roads to open peace negotiations. The radicals were in a fury of rage. They bitterly complained that the President was about to give up the political fruits which had been already gathered from the long and exhausting military struggle." The moderate Republicans of unshaken faith in Lincoln were in a minority; they failed to convince the radicals that Lincoln would not give ground on emancipation. Forney's morning *Chronicle* had blazed with claptrap editorials "which sought to prepare the public mind for the sacrifice of something vaguely dreadful and dreadfully vague." These, wrote Brooks, were "telegraphed all over the country, and indorsed by thoughtless men as the outgivings of President Lincoln. They were read by astonished and indignant thousands, were flouted and scouted by the followers of Wade and Davis, and they filled with alarm and dejection the minds of multitudes of readers not conversant with the facts." Brooks, as newspaperman and as a partial confidant of Lincoln, wrote of motives: "The war upon President Lincoln for his alleged slowness in regard to the slavery question having no longer that excuse . . . the ultra-radicals had flown to negro suffrage and a more vigorous system of retaliation upon rebel prisoners as convenient weapons in a new aggressiveness; and when it was confidently stated that Lincoln had gone to Hampton Roads because he feared that Seward would not make his terms 'liberal enough,' the excitement in and around the Capitol rose to fever heat."

Thad Stevens among the bitterest, according to Brooks, was saying "that if the country were to vote over again for President of the United States, Benjamin F. Butler, and not Abraham Lincoln, would be their choice." And for the first time since Lincoln had been President a faction of his own political party, ruthless men of no hesitations about extreme methods when necessary, mentioned the final and desperate weapon they might use against him. "Others," wrote Brooks, "of the same uncompromising and unreasonable stripe [as Stevens] actually hinted at impeachment and trial."

Certainly the February 7 speech of Representative George W. Julian set the frame and laid the scene for a possible impeachment of Lincoln. In case the radicals should find that his report on Hampton Roads was considered by them a betrayal of their cause, Julian had opened the course with a first blast. In some ten thousand words Julian reviewed the war as a procession of mistakes, chiefly by the Administration and its head. A mediocre speech in phrase, in direct utterance, in perspective or proportion, it lacked the passion of Wade, wanted the incisive color of Stevens. Nevertheless Julian gave it in a tone as though he hoped to be taken for a Domesday Book scribe. He would be the muse of History. "I shall not shrink from . . . it." He would bring out "the contrast between Radicalism and Conservatism" for Posterity to read in the *Congressional Globe* and to understand. "Justice to public men is as certain as that truth is omnipotent."

The war in the beginning lacked hate in the North, ran Julian's sketch.

A major general early in the war told him "we did not adequately hate," urging him to breathe into loyal people "a spirit of righteous indignation and wrath toward the rebels." This "sickly policy of an inoffensive war" was in part the result of the President in July, 1861, disavowing a policy "of coercing the revolted States." Under McClellan, a proslavery commander sanctioned by the President, the enemy was referred to as "our misguided fellow-citizens," "our erring southern brethren," "our wayward sisters." It was the radicals who insisted on violence, on blood and money being poured out, for the purpose of "*subjugation*." The time of "brotherly love toward rebels" had gone by. "Both the people and our armies, under this new dispensation, have been learning how to hate rebels as Christian patriots ought to have done from the beginning."

The radicals refused to go along with the Government and its head in a persuasion that "The rebellion was the work of chance; a stupendous accident, leaping into life full-grown, without father or mother. . . . Hence it was that the President, instead of striking at slavery as a military necessity, and while rebuking that policy in his dealings with Hunter and Frémont, was at the same time so earnestly espousing chimerical projects for the colonization of negroes, coupled with the policy of gradual and compensated emancipation, which should take place sometime before the year 1900, if the slaveholders should be willing." Hence the Administration gave four-fifths of the offices in the army and navy, in the government departments, to Confederate sympathizers and to men hostile to the principles of the Republican party of 1860.

The war moved on, continued Julian's picture, till the President saw slavery as its cause. No longer did the President recoil from "radical and extreme measures." No longer did the President mention fears of "a remorseless revolutionary conflict." Now "he at last marched up to the full height of the national emergency," though it was after "much hesitation and apparent reluctance . . . great deliberation, and many misgivings" that he issued his proclamation of freedom. "Months afterward he doubted its wisdom; but it was a grand step forward, which at once severed his relations with his old conservative friends, and linked his fortunes thenceforward to those of the men of ideas and of progress." It was the radicals who had "saved our nation from . . . political damnation."

Now that hate as a motive had been generated and was winning the war, it was no time for "tenderness" toward the "rebels" by a faltering Administration, warned Julian. The people had "little faith in the early policy of Mr. Lincoln," and he would better not return to it. The people voted in November "not that Abraham Lincoln can save the country, but that *they* can save it, with him as their servant." In seven presidential elections had Julian participated, and "I remember none in which the element of personal enthusiasm had a smaller share." Lightly and easily Julian dismissed the personality of Lincoln as any influential factor in the 1864 campaign. "Should the President now place himself in the people's way, by reviving the old policy of tenderness to the rebels . . . the loyal men of the country will abandon his policy."

Julian outlined the immediate demands of the radicals. They expected Congress to reconstruct the rebellious States with a guarantee of republican government in each of those States, with "complete enfranchisement of the negro; and they will not approve of any executive interference with the people's will as deliberately expressed by Congress." Congress would parcel out forfeited and confiscated lands of "rebels" in small homesteads among soldiers and seamen of the war. Julian indicated that Negroes as well as white men of Union Army service would get farms "as a fit reward for their valor and a security against the ruinous monopoly of the soil in the South." Should this measure fail through fault of Congress or the Executive, prophesied Julian, there would be disappointment. Expected also was "just retaliation" for outrages on Union prisoners. On these demands and expectations, forecast Julian, there would be steady and unrelenting pressure in Congress and on the President. The radicals, he assumed, had won the war and would dictate the terms of peace and reconstruction.

The negative, sickly, and awkward policies of the Administration, hoped Julian, would not be resumed. Having learned under the guidance of the radicals to treat the "rebels" as public enemies, the Administration must not again make its bed with slaveholders. "Clothed with solemn official authority, and intrusted by the nation with the sworn duty of serving it in such a crisis, it [the Administration] had no right to become the foot-ball of events." This of course was a direct reference to Lincoln's saying in April of '64, "I have been controlled by events."

In molding and shaping public opinion and feeling, the Government held immense power. When the President revoked Frémont's first emancipation proclamation it "chilled the heart of every earnest loyalist in the land, and came like a trumpet-call to the pro-slavery hosts to rally and stand together." From that event dated the birth of organized Copperhead Democracy. "The rebels of the South and their sympathizers in the North felt that they had gained an ally in the President." Had his official name and sanction been as often given to the radicals as they were to the conservatives, military victory would have come sooner.

This document uttered by an Indiana Congressman for Posterity closed with the shibboleths and worn platitudes of the second-rate abolitionist orators. It sounded a little as though Julian had heard and rehearsed the points of his speech so many times that he hoped for an era wherein he would not have to repeat it. It failed of the precisions, sonorous lines, dramatic human touches, of Garrison and Phillips. Garrison would have disagreed with the speech in all its main tones and trends. The President would, with his advisers and generals, be "weighed in the balance by the people and the generations to come," offered Julian toward the finish. He relented for a moment to say, "Much will be forgiven or excused on the score of the surpassing magnitude and difficulty of their work," returning to indicate again that Lincoln would not escape record of "the blunders proceeding from a feeble, timid, ambidextrous policy, resulting in great sacrifices of life and treasure, and periling the priceless interests at stake."

Outdoors on this day snow was falling, the nation's capital lay blanketed white. Hour on hour all day, on the just and on the unjust, came the snowfall.

This was on the same day, February 7, that Welles found Lincoln waiting for the Cabinet to come in, "reading with much enjoyment certain portions of Petroleum V. Nasby." When in the chaos of human events reason tottered on its proud throne, it seemed that Lincoln took shelter under the jibes and drolleries of the latest from Nasby, reading in part: "Cussid be Sherman, for he took Atlanta. And he marcht thro the Confedrisy, and respected not the feelins of ennybody. And the people of the South lift up their voisis and weep, becoz their niggers are not. And he took Savanner, and cotton enuff 2 hev satisfide Bookannon's cabbynet. And he turns his eyes toward Charleston, and is serusly thinkin uv Richmond. The wind bloweth where it listeth—he listeth where he goeth. Who will save us from the fury uv this Sherman? who will deliver us from his hand? Johnston he beat, Hood he fooled, and Wheeler he flogged. So he cavorts ez he wills, like a yearlin mule with a chestnut burr under his tale. Bitter in the mouth uv a Dimokrat is qwinine, bitter is gall, but more bitter is Fedral victrys. The Dimokrasy uv this sekshun [is] Hart-sick, weery, alone, bustid. Gone-up, flayed, skind, hung out. Smashed, pulverized, shivered, scattered. Physikt, puked, bled, blistered. Sich is Dimokrasy!" Perhaps it was there Fessenden came in and the President "hastily dropped" the reading of Nasby.

It may have been that someone from Capitol Hill brought Lincoln word that the radicals were getting ready "to skin him alive," a phrase in use by ruthless politicians, and Lincoln chose Dennison and Speed to listen to his reading of Nasby because they happened to be in the room and not because those very serious gentlemen had any notion that Petroleum V. Nasby was lightening the burden of war grief for many people by such folly as: "Dreems is unsubstanshel, and result, 9 cases out uv 10, from aboose uv the stummick. I am no bleever in gosts or dreems, or sich, nor never wuz. Ef the tyrant Linkin (which is a ape) shood draft me, and I shood be dragged to the tentid feeld, a unwilling marter, I know I shood much prefer meetin the gost uv a rebel soljer, wich is a shadder, than 2 enkounter wun in the flesh, with a muskit and baynet, wich is no shadder."

One rumor now gaining headway and credence was that Lincoln at Hampton Roads had taken a sheet of paper, written at the top the one word "Union," and shoving it across the table toward Stephens, had said, "Let me have that one condition and you can write below it whatever peace terms you choose." This reported repudiation of the Emancipation Proclamation was to the radicals a hair-raising piece of news.

Lincoln's trip to Fortress Monroe and the rumors about it had "produced a veritable panic among the Radicals who are preparing to attack the President if he makes the slightest concession to the South," wrote the Russian Minister, Baron Edward de Stoeckl, to his Government in St. Petersburg. "Already a certain coolness exists between the President and the ultras of his party who fear that Mr. Lincoln, now that he has been reëlected, will try to free himself from their influence." The Russian Minister quoted one of "the ultras" as saying to him: "We did not reëlect Mr. Lincoln because of his ability, but only because he obeys the party orders to the letter. He must accept our views, whatever they are, or we will find means to ruin him. We want to subjugate the South completely, and reduce it to a territory governed by the North."

On February 10 the tension began to let down. The House had been dealing with a new bridge over the Ohio River at Cincinnati, Pacific railway, national currency, pension laws, mileage of members, and was taking up a resolution to punish by fines a large number of members who were spending too much time elsewhere in Washington, absenting themselves from business of the House. In the midst of this the clerk announced "A message in writing received from the President of the United States, by Mr. Nicolay, his Private Secretary."

All other business was suspended. They wanted to hear about Hampton Roads.

The clerk began reading what the President had the honor to state pursuant to their resolution of the eighth instant. Documents, letters, dispatches, poured forth in a long stream. It seemed almost as though Lincoln had awaited this hour and knew it was coming during every moment when he made the slightest record of any transaction since Old Man Blair had come to him in December. The pass written for Blair to Richmond, the letter of Davis to Blair which Blair carried to Lincoln, the reply of Lincoln to Blair meant for Blair to carry to Richmond and show to Davis, the rise of the phrases "our one common country" and "the two countries," the documents passing between the Confederate commissioners showing at Grant's army lines and what passed between them and Grant, the further transactions between Eckert and the commissioners, the Lincoln letter of instructions to Seward with its three "indispensable" points, the dispatch to Grant to keep the war going no matter what he heard about peace, Grant's reply that he would sure keep the war going, the Eckert telegram in cipher to Lincoln which for the moment wrecked all chance of a conference, the long telegram of Grant to Stanton with Lincoln's brief comment that "this despatch . . . changed my purpose," the meeting at Hampton Roads and the reading of the commissioners' instruction from Davis that they were there "for the purpose of securing peace to the two countries," the breakdown of the negotiations ending with no result. The foregoing, "containing as is believed all the information sought," was respectfully submitted.

Pressmen from their gallery noted "absolute silence" from first to last during the reading of this message. Looking over the hall at the hundreds seated or standing, one might say, wrote Noah Brooks, they "had been suddenly turned to stone." They strained to hear, as a story unfolded document by document, fascinated by what important and mysterious end it might have. "For a little space at least no man so much as stirred his hand. Even the hurrying pages, who usually bustled about the aisles . . . were struck silent and motionless." At the President's final instruction to Seward, "You will not assume to definitely consummate anything," came a ripple of mirth from the many who suspected Seward's sinister influence over President Lincoln. Soon House members began exchanging smiles and glances of meaning. The President had never for a moment lost footing, had gone into a winding labyrinth where anything could happen and had come out without a flaw in the many delicate moments of diplomatic sharpshooting involved.

"When the reading was over," noted Brooks and the full name of "Abraham Lincoln" signed to the communication was read by the clerk with a certain grandiloquence, Brooks heard "an instant and irrepressible storm of applause, begun by members on the floor, and taken up by the people in the gallery." Speaker Colfax made only a pretense at stopping the disorder. "It was like a burst of refreshing rain after a long and heart-breaking drought."

Washburne moved that 20,000 extra copies of the message be printed. "The entire loyal people of this country" would approve the "wisdom and discretion in the President of the United States" shown in this matter, believed Washburne. Not so the Democratic Congressman from New York, James Brooks. He saw the "petty intricacies" of a President responsive to "fanatics." It was not a pointless speech Brooks made. He could see Abraham Lincoln and Jefferson Davis each helpless to "hush the storm they have raised," each limited by "wild men" as to peace terms.

Thad Stevens wished to correct Representative Brooks. Who but Brooks and his associate Democrats had a month ago been crying out loud for President Lincoln to send ambassadors or agents to hear what the South would say about peace? "But the President," continued Stevens, "has thought it was best to make the effort, and he has done it in such a masterly style, upon such a firm basis and principle, that I believe even those who thought his mission was unwise will accord to him sagacity and patriotism, and applaud his action." Stevens now read from a Richmond newspaper part of a Davis speech sarcastic and denunciatory of Lincoln, along with a mass-meeting resolution: "That we spurn with indignation the grossly insulting terms which the President of the United States has proffered." Stevens proceeded with a surmise that the war would last six to twelve months before those who had "concocted without the least cause the vastest and the foulest rebellion" would be subjugated. After their armies were crushed he looked for a year or two of guerrilla warfare.

Cox of Ohio, Democrat, wished to emphasize that Grant had tele-graphed Lincoln of the good intentions and sincere desires of two Con-federate commissioners for peace, wherefore "the thanks of this Congress and the thanks of the country are due to President Lincoln for this effort to negotiate." Cox could see peace coming sooner "if the President is not

HARPER'S WEEKLY.　　　　FEBRUARY 18, 1865.

THE PEACE COMMISSION.
Flying to ABRAHAM'S Bosom.

broken down in his laudable efforts by the fierce onslaughts of his radical adherents. God help him."

The high surprise, for those who listened to the reading of the stream of documents from Lincoln that day, perhaps was in the revelation that Grant had changed the President's purpose, that Grant's judgment had brought on the conference. Those who gossiped so freely that the wily

Seward was leading Lincoln into pitfalls were lost for excuses. They were, wrote Noah Brooks, "greatly chagrined when they ascertained that it was General Grant, the idol of the hour, who had influenced Lincoln" to go to Hampton Roads. Grant truly stood "the idol of the hour," and three days later on February 11 was to enter the House of Representatives, receive a lavish introduction—and make a low grave bow and leave without giving them a speech. For the first time in the years of war a Union general had so achieved that the House of Representatives considered it an honor to have him come in, show himself, and depart, so that they could say they had seen him and knew what he looked like.

To the Senate the President sent no such marshaled array of documents as he gave the House. To that graver and more sedate body, empowered to ratify treaties and conduct foreign affairs, went a copy of a long note written by the Secretary of State to Minister Adams at London, reciting the Hampton Roads negotiations. Saulsbury of Delaware, on hearing it read, said it was the most important message ever delivered to the Senate and moved to refer it to a select committee of five. To Senator Sherman it seemed it should lie over. Sumner thought it would be enough to order it printed. Sherman interposed that it better lie on the table. Sumner moved it be both printed and lie on the table. Saulsbury served notice he would move as he first indicated. This seesaw went on till the presiding officer ruled that a motion to lay on the table took precedence of all others; it was agreed to, and there would be no select committee of five and no printing of the message. The Senate was not impressed by the very dull, formal letter Seward wrote to the London Minister. When later the Senators learned that the whole array of storytelling documents had gone that day to the House they murmured that the President had slighted the upper body.

On February 15 the body of Senator Thomas Holliday Hicks of Maryland lay in state in the Senate chamber, the President, Senate, and House attending. The ritual of the Order of Knights Templar, with responses by Knights, was performed. At memorial ceremonies the next day extraordinary tributes were pronounced on the man who as Governor of Maryland stood as a loyal Unionist in the late winter of '61, seeming to waver when armed secessionists seized his State capital, then taking action that "secured" the presidential inauguration of March 4.

An old order was passing. What of the new? Now in the Supreme Court chambers where the Dred Scott decision had gone forth, for the first time a Negro was admitted to practice before that high tribunal: John S. Rock, an attorney of ability and good name in the city of Boston.

In House and Senate bills the American scene in varied lights passed before the President. Should Commodore Cornelius Vanderbilt receive from Congress a $3,000 medal in appreciation of his having donated to the Federal Government a $500,000 steamer? Two Californians rose in the House to say Vanderbilt was a monopolist and an extortioner; they had to travel on his boats and hated his exactions and pretensions. Brooks of New York and Stevens of Pennsylvania rebuked the West Coast men, and the medal was voted by a liberal margin. The five living veterans of the Revolutionary War, their ages from ninety-four to one hundred and one years, were voted pensions of $300 a year. Representative Henry L. Dawes brought up the case of Major David H. Hastings, convicted of forgeries and embezzlement of $26,000, Judge Advocate Joseph Holt recommending that the findings and sentence be disapproved. Dawes contrasted Holt's leniency with the treatment of a common private soldier getting five years in the Dry Tortugas for having while drunk insulted an officer. Dawes's motion was agreed to; all documents in the Hastings case should be printed, thus leaving Judge Holt's action a matter of record. A bill "to drop unemployed generals" failed to pass the Senate, Schenck in the House speaking in behalf of hundreds of colonels commanding brigades without brigadier pay. A bill authorizing payment of $25,000 to William H. Powell for a painting on the Capitol staircase "illustrative of some naval victory" passed the Senate after rejection of several Sumner substitutes and amid banter and laughter at Sumner's lectures on art and the beautiful. For more than five months hundreds of thousands of soldiers had failed to receive their $16-a-month pay, ran Senator Wilson's reminder as to government spending. Garfield in the House wished something could be done about brokers selling and buying substitute soldiers for the armies, holding them little less infamous than slave-traders. Chandler said these "depraved speculators in human flesh throng to New York."

Those echoing "the tyranny of Lincoln," raising a cry against military courts and their dealings with political prisoners, would be found other than loyal Union men, protested Senator Henry S. Lane of Indiana. "Whatever else Abraham Lincoln may be, he is to-day one of the kindest and most amiable gentlemen upon earth, having a sense of justice equal to any man who ever lived." Such bouquets in the printed record of the *Congressional Globe* were few and far between. Yet the old-time lamentations about an "imbecile Administration" came not so often now.

The race issue writhed and snarled again in debates over the proposed Bureau for the Relief of Freedmen and Refugees. Even with slavery abolished by the Thirteenth Amendment, the race issue was to persist, the color line be heard of. Politicians and journalists on both sides for a long time were to keep it alive, often for their own personal ends. The bill gave the President power to appoint commissioners to control the bureau, with authority to distribute "abandoned lands" among the Negroes, to pay out money and supplies. Senator Powell of Kentucky charged that these "bureaucratic overseers of freedmen" would give the Negroes "the care that the wolf does the lamb," Powell crying as he gazed at Sumner, "In the name of God, sir, do you want one half the people of this country to become salaried officers?" Powell was playacting, but not entirely.

Representative Joseph K. Edgerton of Indiana spoke of reconstruction and Lincoln's pocket veto at the close of the last session of Congress in

July of '64. "The President's will undid the work of his friends. . . . The majority in Congress kissed the hand that smote them." This again was chiefly playacting.

Motives on both sides of the Senate were honorable enough, said Senator Thomas Hendricks of Indiana. The strife between the Senators was not personal. It ranged around the question "What is to be done with the four million negroes when they are set free?" Hendricks would reply for his party that they were a unit in one sentiment: "This Government was made by white men for white men. . . . Let the controversy go on." Harris of Maryland, however, was less helpful than Hendricks, Harris alleging that Sumner and his associates "have contracted the disease called 'nigger on the brain.'" Sumner spoke his fear that by evasions and devices the whites of the South would bring back slavery "under a new alias." Sumner believed a bureau for freedmen could be set up to protect the rights of Negroes and to give them land.

By joint resolution Congress threw out the Electoral College votes of seceded States and set forth its constitutional powers to so do. Returning this joint resolution to Congress with his signature, Lincoln attached a curious little message. The Executive, he noted, signed it "in deference to the view of Congress implied in its passage and presentation to him." The Executive, "In his own view, however," held that the two houses of Congress had complete power to exclude from the count "all electoral votes deemed by them to be illegal"; and it was not competent for the Executive to defeat or obstruct that power by a veto. The preamble of the joint resolution, however, might be taken as having certain implications. These he was not signing. And to be safe against any such implications being brought up in the future, he took his own way of saying that he would not be responsible for them, writing of the Executive: "He disclaims all right of the executive to interfere in any way in the matter of canvassing or counting electoral votes; and he also disclaims that, by signing said resolution, he has expressed any opinion on the recitals of the preamble, or any judgment of his own upon the subject of the resolution."

This was "a very extraordinary course for the President to pursue," it seemed to Senator Reverdy Johnson of Maryland. "It is, in my judgment, a reflection upon the Senate and upon Congress, although not so designed." Johnson continued at length to say that the President ought either to approve or disapprove. "He reads us a lecture, virtually, in this paper." It savored of the pocket veto of last July, believed Johnson, speaking with deference. "Of course, I do not call in question his sincerity." No other Senators had comment, and the message was laid on the table.

Overshadowing all other discussions across February were those on bills for recognizing as "legitimate" the government set up in Louisiana a year earlier under the guidance of President Lincoln and the military commander of the department, General Banks. The election of State officers ordered by Banks for February 22, 1864, covered an area of about one-third of the

State. The voters were 11,411 white men, each having taken the oath required by the President, and they made a total of more than one-fifth of the entire vote of the State of Louisiana in 1860. They had elected three Congressmen and a governor. At a later election they had chosen delegates to a constitutional convention, which met in New Orleans in April. This convention, as such bodies go, was neither drab nor brilliant but rather ordinary as an instrument of democratic procedure. It abolished slavery in Louisiana "forever" by a vote of 72 to 13. It gave the ballot to white males only, yet it empowered the legislature to give the ballot to Negro soldiers of service in the Union Army and to Negroes who could read and write, meeting the qualifications Lincoln had suggested in his letter to Governor Hahn. The new State constitution was adopted by 66 to 16—though in the election by which the people ratified it only 8,400 votes were cast.

Of course these very human procedures in a scene of much chaos had many lapses, faults, contradictions, seized on for criticism of the President in House and Senate. What he saw he was up against in his preliminary attempts to bring a peaceable rebuilding of the wrecked State governments, the President recorded in both public and private writings. The new State governments he had guided were "shadows" and not "realities," according to the opposition. For himself he wished to regard them as "important," as "earnestly struggling," as admittedly "short of complete success." This was his view in his December message to Congress, relating: "Important movements have occurred during the year to the effect of *molding society for durability in the Union.* [Italics added.] Although short of complete success, it is much in the right direction that 12,000 citizens in each of the States of Arkansas and Louisiana have organized loyal State governments, with free constitutions, and are earnestly struggling to maintain and administer them."

Wade, Sumner, Julian, and other friends of the Negro did not like it that Lincoln in his Louisiana policy had the complete and unreserved endorsement of William Lloyd Garrison. If Garrison was not the friend of the Negro, who was? What other man had more often been hatefully termed "nigger-lover"? Yet here was the ascetic old agitator speaking Lincoln's case as though he had rehearsed it with the President in the White House and had it letter-perfect. "When was it ever known that liberation from bondage was accompanied by a recognition of political equality?" wrote Garrison in reply to an English abolitionist. "Chattels personal may be instantly translated from the auction-block into freemen; but when were they ever taken at the same time to the ballot-box and invested with all its rights and immunities? According to the laws and development of progress, it is not practicable. To denounce or complain of President Lincoln for not disregarding public sentiment, and not flying in the face of these laws, is hardly just."

And who could say the Federal Executive had the right to dictate who in Louisiana should vote or not vote? Garrison doubted that any Federal authority, executive or legislative, had that right. "Ever since this government was organized, the right of suffrage has been determined by each State in the Union for itself, so that there is no uniformity in regard to it. In some free States, colored citizens are allowed to vote; in others, they are not. It is always a State, never a National matter."

Suppose "by Presidential fiat" the freed blacks were given the ballot. Garrison could not see "any permanent advantage likely to be secured by it." At first it would be submitted to as a necessity, but later, "the white population, with their superior intelligence, wealth, and power, would unquestionably alter the franchise in accordance with their prejudices. . . . Coercion would gain nothing . . . universal suffrage will be hard to win and to hold without general preparation of feeling and sentiment. But it will come . . . yet only by a struggle *on the part of the disfranchised*, and a growing conviction of its justice, 'in the good time coming.' With the abolition of slavery in the South, prejudice or 'colorphobia,' the natural product of the system, will gradually disappear. . . . Black men will win their way to wealth, distinction, eminence, and official station. I ask only a charitable judgment of President Lincoln respecting this matter, whether in Louisiana or any other State."

Not to the public of this hour could Lincoln have given the painful details and sorry embarrassments which he confessed in peremptory letters to Union generals who were wrecking his work. On November 14, 1864, he began a letter to General S. A. Hurlbut, successor to Banks in command at New Orleans: "Few things since I have been here [that is, since he had been in the White House as President] have impressed me more painfully than what, for four or five months past, has appeared as bitter military opposition to the new State government of Louisiana." He had hoped he was mistaken as to the facts, but having seen copies of letters exchanged between Generals Hurlbut and E. R. S. Canby, the hope was gone. He sketched for Hurlbut, a fellow Illinois lawyer, what had been done. "A very fair proportion of the people of Louisiana have inaugurated a new State government, making an excellent new constitution—better for the poor black man than we have in Illinois. This was done under military protection, directed by me, in the belief, still sincerely entertained, that with such a nucleus around which to build we could get the State into position again sooner than otherwise." That two of his generals should join with secessionists in trying to undo his work was "incomprehensible"—and if continued would not be overlooked. This was the admonition in the closing part of this long letter, reading in part:

During the formation of the new government and constitution they [the nucleus] were supported by nearly every loyal person, and opposed by every secessionist. And this support and this opposition, from the respective standpoints of the parties, was perfectly consistent and logical. Every Unionist ought to wish the new government to succeed; and every disunionist must desire it to fail. Its failure would gladden the heart of Slidell in Europe, and of every enemy of the old flag in the world. Every advocate of slavery naturally desires to see blasted and crushed the liberty promised the black man by the new Constitution. But why General Canby and General Hurlbut should join on the same side is to me incomprehensible.

Of course, in the condition of things at New Orleans, the military must not be thwarted by the civil authority; but when the Constitutional Convention, for what it deems a breach of privilege, arrests an editor in no way connected with the military, the military necessity for insulting the Convention and forcibly discharging the editor is difficult to perceive. Neither is the military necessity for protecting the people against paying large salaries fixed by a legislature of their own choosing very apparent. Equally difficult to perceive is the military necessity for forcibly interposing to prevent a bank from loaning its own money to the State. These things, if they have occurred, are, at the best, no better than gratuitous hostility. I wish I could hope that they may be shown to not have occurred. To make assurance against misunderstanding, I repeat that in the existing condition of things in Louisiana, the military must not be thwarted by the civil authority; and I add that on points of difference the commanding general must be judge and master. But I also add that in the exercise of this judgment and control, a purpose, obvious, and scarcely unavowed, to transcend all military necessity, in order to crush out the civil government, will not be overlooked.

To General E. R. S. Canby, commanding in West Mississippi, the President wrote a month later humbly and pleadingly of the new State government of Louisiana. "Most certainly there is no worthy object in getting up a piece of machinery merely to pay salaries and give political consideration to certain men. But it is a worthy object to again get Louisiana into proper relations with the nation, and we can never finish this if we never begin it. Much good work is already done, and surely nothing can be gained by throwing it away."

Without losing cordial relations with Senator Sumner, Lincoln had held many talks with that Senator, who wrote to John Bright on January 1: "The President is exerting every force to bring Congress to receive Louisiana under the Banks government. . . . I have discussed it with the President, and have tried to impress on him the necessity of having no break between him and Congress on such questions."

Banks at this time was "very sore" at Sumner over his opposition to the Louisiana plan, so Sumner wrote to Franz Lieber. Also it was near fantasy at this time that Mrs. Lincoln was writing notes to Sumner asking him to use his influence to prevent Banks's appointment to the Cabinet, which she feared might take place.

Undoubtedly Lincoln in his discussions with Sumner advanced such points as he had written in December of '63 to a Louisiana man. "The strongest wish I have, not already publicly expressed," ran part of this letter, "is that in Louisiana and elsewhere all sincere Union men would stoutly eschew cliquism, and, each yielding something in minor matters, all work together. Nothing is likely to be so baleful in the great work before us as stepping aside from the main object to consider who will get the offices if a small matter shall go thus, and who else will get them if it shall go otherwise."

On December 18 the President had met Monty Blair and General Banks in a White House hall and called them into his office. "They immediately began to talk about Ashley's bill," wrote Hay in his diary. The bill included recognition of the new State government of Louisiana. "The President had been reading it carefully & said that he liked it with the exception of one or two things which he thought rather calculated to conceal a feature which might be objectionable to some. The first was that under the provisions of that bill negroes would be made jurors & voters under the temporary governments." Banks observed: "Yes, that is to be stricken out, and the qualification 'white mail [male] citizens of the U. S.' is to be restored. What you refer to would be a fatal objection to the Bill. It would simply throw the Government into the hands of the blacks, as the white people under that arrangement would refuse to vote." This of course was in substance the same view that Banks in Louisiana a year before had written to Lincoln.

Banks and Lincoln agreed the bill did not lay down "any castiron policy." It left the way clear for a different approach in other States. Blair, noted Hay, talked more than Lincoln and Banks, accusing the radicals in House and Senate of interested motives and of hostility to Lincoln.

The President said to Blair: "It is much better not to be led from the region of reason into that of hot blood, by imputing to public men motives which they do not avow."

For weeks across January and February Ashley's bill was debated and taken back to committee for revisions and modifications. Five times it was redrafted, always fixing cast-iron requirements to be followed in letting the seceded States come back into the Union. The uneasiness of the President and of many House members was spoken by Dawes of Massachusetts: "No form can be prescribed, no law laid down here, no unbending iron rule fixed by the central Government, for the governing of that people, or prescribing the method in which they shall make their organic law. Each of them shall work out that problem for itself and in its own way. That form and system . . . best adapted to Louisiana and Arkansas is quite different from that ultimately to be adopted in South Carolina and Georgia." Henry Winter Davis on February 21 spoke his fear that "the will of the President" since the November election had affected in the House "some minds prone to act upon the winking of authority." Suppose men came from Louisiana seeking seats in the House and Senate at Washington. They would be merely "the representatives of the bayonets of General Banks and the will of the President." The President stood for "anarchy." He, Davis of Maryland, favored legal rule. Davis closed his speech with the antique convention "Sir, I have done." He meant he was through. His forty-five minutes were up. As an actor and a wavy-haired orator the House always enjoyed him. It was the kind of fine public speaking that convinced nobody of anything particular to be done. Ashley arose in the same hour to say he was "pretty sure" that the bill with all its amendments and substitutes would fail of a majority. "It is very clear to my mind," ventured Ashley, "that no bill providing for the reorganization of loyal State governments in the rebel States can pass this Congress." He proved correct. On the final vote it failed by 80 to 65, with 37 members not voting.

In the Senate, reconstruction acts ran a different course. There Trumbull of Illinois reported from the Judiciary Committee a joint resolution declaring that the United States recognized the Louisiana government "inaugurated under and by the convention which assembled on the 6th day of April, A.D., 1864, at the city of New Orleans, as the legitimate government of the said State, entitled to the guarantees and all other rights of a State government, under the Constitution of the United States." Senators Sumner, Wade, and Howard spoke amazement and scorn that their former associate in opposition to the President now acted in behalf of the President's most earnest wishes. Serene and without a flicker of resentment, Trumbull led a parliamentary fight that had his old allies sore and desperate.

As the Senate debate rolled along in late February it was seen that most of the Democrats would vote against recognizing the new Louisiana State government. It was again the familiar Lincoln "military despotism," said Garrett Davis of Kentucky, a horse-thief Government which had illegally run off with some of the best horseflesh in Kentucky, impressed for Union Army cavalry. In his State of Delaware, urged Saulsbury, "the armed soldiery sent by the President of the United States" had in 1863 ruled at the polls, where voters walked "under crossed bayonets" to drop their ballots, in the event they had not been "run into the swamps, compelled to lay out in the night in the snow." The outspoken fear of other Democrats was that a military rule directed by a Republican administration at Washington would favor the Negroes. On the other hand the outspoken fear of the five Republican Senators who joined the Democratic opposition was that under the new State government of Louisiana, if it should be recognized, the whites would control and refuse the ballot to the Negroes. Therefore these five Republicans sought to put a rider on the bill which would insure the Negro the right to vote in Louisiana, this to be a precedent imperative on all other reorganized States.

Pomeroy of Kansas was for the bill. He replied to Saulsbury that Kansas had seen what Democrats could do with armed soldiery at the polls, saying, "Sometimes we could not get near enough to it [the ballot box] to shoot a ballot into it with a revolver. [Laughter.]" Patriotic and loyal men of every State should have the right to vote, continued Pomeroy. "I do not think that rebels should vote. I do not know that they have any rights that white men are bound to respect. [Laughter.]"

Ben Wade now picked his javelins with care and flung them with high scorn. "When the foundation of this Government is sought to be swept away by executive usurpation, it will not do to turn around to me and say that this comes from a President whom I helped elect, or that the measure is supported generally by my own party." Of the elected Louisiana men now in Washington and seeking seats in Congress: "If the President of the United States, operating through his major generals, can initiate a State government, and can bring it here and force us, compel us, to receive as associates on this floor these mere mockeries, these men of straw who represent nobody, your Republic is at an end." Of Lincoln's "ten-per-cent principle" Wade would say, "A more absurd, monarchical, and anti-American principle was never announced on God's earth."

There was nothing halfway about Wade's style. It was the same Ben Wade who in the old days had sent word to Bob Toombs that he was willing to fight a duel and shoot it out instead of arguing. Now he thundered: "Sir, I have as much respect for the President of the United States as anybody else has. I helped to elect him; I labored hard to do it; but I never did, and God knows I never will, sanction such fatal heresies as these. What, sir, the President of the United States attempt by a military order to initiate a State government! It is a dangerous precedent; and if it be submitted to here with our consent, it will reduce this great Republic of ours to a mere military despotism. If the President may do that in Louisiana, he may do it in any other State, and our associates on this floor may be the mere creatures of the President of the United States, representing nothing but his military power. . . . Are unwashed rebels to be brought in here, men who have not taken the oath, and who, without perjuring themselves to the lowest hell, cannot take it? . . . The Senator [Trumbull] says that two thirds of the people there were so conditioned that they could vote for or against the constitution. I do not believe a word of it; but suppose it was so, will you permit one third of the people of Louisiana to be under military duress while the other two thirds make a constitution for the whole? . . . Sir, you can never do it; it is not in the power of the President and Congress to set up a republican form of government in a State whose people are deliberately opposed to republican government. The Senator has well said that a military government is all you really have."

And what presentations had come from Senator Trumbull to rouse Ben Wade to such anger and denunciation? Trumbull had offered the figures on the Louisiana case. He gave the first complete details, the statistics and computations, showing that in the Louisiana polls the so-called "Lincoln's ten per cent" was nearer 20 per cent and more. The facts were dry, yet somewhat luminous—and certainly specific. They were as follows, the very sober and somewhat austere Trumbull said:

At the first election for State officers in Louisiana, which was held in February, 1864, 11,411 votes were cast. Some of the Senators say that is very few votes for Louisiana, when she cast 50,000 votes before the rebellion.

What if she did? She never but once in her whole history cast 50,000 votes. The vote of Louisiana has usually been exceedingly small; and will the Senator from Ohio be astonished when I tell him that at the gubernatorial election of 1853 only 22,000 and some odd votes were cast? More than half as many votes were cast for Governor at this election a year ago last February as were cast in 1853, when there was no disturbance in the State—22,000 then cast and 11,000 cast at this election.

And will the Senate be astonished when I tell them that even in 1859, at the last State election held in Louisiana before the rebellion, only 37,000 and some odd votes were cast? About one third as many votes were polled at the election held in February,

1864, as were cast for Governor in 1859, when there was no rebellion. Taking all the elections for ten years prior to that of 1864, and the average vote of the State was only 34,000.

You have about one third of all the voters in the State voting at this time, and some allowance must be made for the number of persons that have gone out of the State. Every Senator knows that hundreds and thousands of the voters of Louisiana went into the rebel army; many have died, many have fled the State, some are in our Army; and is it any wonder that the vote should not have been as large in 1864 as formerly? It is not then, you will see, a mere fraction of the people who voted at this election.

Again, on the ratification of this constitution 8,402 votes were cast. I heard some Senators stating that 6,000 voted for the constitution. Six thousand and odd voted for the constitution, and some one or two thousand voted against the constitution. Are not the men who voted against it just as much bound as those who voted for it? You must take the whole vote; and at that very election, when only 8,402 votes were cast on the ratification of the constitution, 9,024 persons took part in the election and voted on other questions. They did not all vote either one way or the other on the constitution. Its ratification was not seriously contested; it was conceded that it would be adopted.

In the State of Louisiana there are forty-eight parishes. Twenty of these parishes cast votes on the ratification of the constitution, and they are the large parishes, the most populous ones. I have had prepared a table showing exactly the population which was represented in the convention which framed this constitution; and the population of the twenty parishes which sent delegates to the convention, and which voted on the ratification of the constitution was, in 1860, 463,855, while the population of the State at the same time was only 708,002. These figures are from the census of 1860. So it will be observed that about two thirds of the population of the State took part in the formation and ratification of the constitution.

How different is that from the statements that have been made in the Senate! About two thirds of the entire population of the State was represented in this convention and took part in the adoption of this constitution, the entire population of the State being only some seven hundred thousand, and four hundred and sixty-three thousand of that population taking part in the organization of this State government.

Again, sir, the convention, which I believe was fairly apportioned through the State according to population, was made to consist of one hundred and fifty delegates. If every parish in Louisiana had sent a delegation to the convention according to population, there would have been present one hundred and fifty delegates. How many were there? Ninety-eight were elected and served, and seventy-nine signed the constitution which was adopted. To the State Legislature, which is made by the constitution to consist of thirty-six senators and one hundred and eighteen representatives, provided every part of the State was represented, twenty-seven senators and eighty-four representatives were elected and took their seats.

Thus you see that about two thirds of the population of Louisiana and about two thirds of the number of delegates if the whole State had been represented, and about two thirds of the members of the Senate and of the House of Representatives, if the whole State had been represented, have taken part in this new government.

What, then, does this show? It shows, in the opinion of the committee and according to the testimony that was before them, a clear case where a majority of all the people of Louisiana have expressed their preference for the State government which has been set up, whether it is considered upon the representative basis in the Legislature, upon the representative basis in the convention, or according to the population in the portions of the State represented. It is no answer to say that everybody did not vote. You could not expect as many voters there as before the rebellion.

Why, then, sir, not recognize this existing State government? The testimony was concurrent before our committee that a majority of the loyal people were represented in the convention and approved this government which had been set up. Under these circumstances, being desirous to remove the military government at the earliest practicable period, believing it would be better for the United States to recognize this government, and thinking it highly important at the earliest moment to have a government in Louisiana loyal to the United States around which the loyal men might rally, thinking it would add strength to the Government of the United States, we came to the conclusion under all the circumstances that it was best to recognize this State government. I think so now.

On this rested Lincoln's plea of urgency in Louisiana, no time to be lost, his friend Henderson of Missouri telling the Senate in words having a likeness to Lincoln's, "If we would have State governments we must begin somewhere and at some time."

How much of this array of allegations did Lincoln know to be true? Trumbull wanted to know about that. He had sent to Lincoln a paper on Louisiana conditions, submitted to the Senate Judiciary Committee by General Banks. In returning it to Trumbull on January 9 the President wrote: "The whole of it is in accordance with my general impression, and I believe it is true; but much the larger part is beyond my absolute knowledge, as in its nature it must be. All the statements which lie within the range of my knowledge are strictly true; and I think of nothing material which has been omitted." He made no mention of military force. The domineering genius of bayonets depicted by Senator Wade had a soft touch. This was the language Lincoln used in writing Trumbull about unhappy Louisiana:

Even before General Banks went to Louisiana I was anxious for the loyal people there to move for reorganization, and restoration of proper practical relations with the Union; and when he at last expressed his decided conviction that the thing was practicable, I directed him to give his official coöperation to effect it. On the subject I have sent and received many letters to and from General Banks and many other persons. These letters, as you remember, were shown to you yesterday, as they will be again if you desire.

If I shall neither take sides nor argue, will it be out of place for me to make what I think is the true statement of your question as to the proposed Louisiana senators?

"Can Louisiana be brought into proper practical relations with the Union sooner by admitting or by rejecting the proposed senators?"

Against the case made out by Trumbull, Wade hurled his barbed points and made no dent. Powell of Kentucky, a Democrat, alleged soldiers controlled the polls, alleged perjuries, alleged Northern soldiers had voted, alleged "the coercive finger of the military" operated, and went on with many allegations—and no particulars, nothing that shot a hole anywhere in Trumbull's case. Powell's style ran on like this: "Talk to me of freedom of election under such military orders! Why, sir, there was but one free man, in my opinion, in all Louisiana at that time, and that was Major-General Banks; and I do not know that he was free, for he was serving his master at the White House."

"There is no evidence to show that a single citizen of Louisiana was excluded from the right of voting," said the eminent Democrat Reverdy Johnson of Maryland. He pointed to the war taking away many voters from Louisiana. Thousands who had "forfeited their lives" on the battle-field, he was sure, would never vote again in Louisiana.

Leading all others in speeches of condemnation, in amendments, in motions to delay voting, was Sumner. In the Senate gallery from day to day sat one listener, one spectator, who charmed Sumner, fascinated him. She was to him the one woman in the world. He had fallen in love with her, Alice Mason Hooper, a niece of Jeremiah Mason of Boston, the widowed daughter-in-law of Sumner's friend and colleague Samuel Hooper. "His devotion [to her] had been marked and somewhat opposite to his usual stately ways," wrote Anna Laurens Dawes. "Among all the fascinating women of Washington she stood pre-eminent. Beauty, grace, a slender and stately form, a high-bred manner, and aristocratic reserve were all hers, and withal a special fascination, coming perhaps from the uncertain moods of an extremely variable temper—a temper which would pay its debts in the small coin of teasing or in the grand style, as fitted the mood of the hour." The match, the engagement to marry, came, wrote Miss Dawes, through "fascination and hope on the one side, fascination and ambition on the other." He was fifty-seven, a lifelong bachelor, and she at twenty-seven sat in the gallery watching him, she with "the habits at once of a belle and a spoiled child, looking forward eagerly to the new gayeties of a senator's wife, and contemplating a near future when she should be mistress of the White House."

For her now, besides his regular public, Sumner performed, not knowing that soon after their marriage, soon after moving into a house of their own, his pride and will would come into collision with hers, they would part soon, and he was to meditate suicide and never after refer to her except as "that person." Now in February of '65 he enjoyed it that his betrothed was there in the gallery watching him in a parliamentary fight that called to his blood.

On the Senate floor now Sumner rose to heights of stubborn granite and grandeur; also he sprawled in puddles of the ridiculous and the asinine. To brother Henry wrote Charles Francis Adams, Jr., "Sumner has run more than ever to seed, and now out-Sumners himself." Sumner argued that before he would recognize the new government of Louisiana the right of Negroes to citizenship must be therewith guaranteed. The difference of view between Sumner and the President in this was much the same as it had been with the Thirteenth Amendment, when Ashley had urged the President to send for Sumner and the President had replied: "I can do nothing with Mr.

Sumner in these matters. While Mr. Sumner is very cordial with me, he is making his history in an issue with me on this very point. He hopes to succeed in beating the President so as to change this Government from its original form and make it a strong centralized power." Oddly enough, according to this, it was States' Rights rather than Negro suffrage on which Sumner and Lincoln parted ways—and parted cordially, for Sumner in his many stubborn thrusts aimed to kill the joint resolution never hit at the President, never struck at Lincoln's motives.

Agreeing with others that the measure was perhaps the most important that ever had come before the present Senate body, Sumner said: "I shall regard its passage as a national calamity. It will be the political Bull Run of this Administration, sacrificing, as it will, a great cause, and the great destinies of this Republic." Trumbull spoke of Sumner as determined "to browbeat the Senate," as "associating himself with those whom he so often denounces, for the purpose of calling the yeas and nays and making dilatory motions." Sumner rejoined that the question between the Senator from Illinois and himself was simply this: "He wishes to pass the measure, and I do not wish to pass it. He thinks the measure innocent; I think it dangerous; and thinking it dangerous, I am justified in opposing it, and justified, too, in employing all the instruments I can find in the arsenal of parliamentary warfare." Doolittle of Wisconsin filed a verbal memorandum: "There are but five who usually act with the Administration who are making and voting for these dilatory motions, and there are eighteen of the friends of the Administration opposed to them."

Doolittle went farther. He pointed to Sumner as enjoying himself being wrongheaded and strongheaded, inconsistent, flighty, temperamental and huffy. This brought from Sumner one of the frequent little speeches which made Senators wonder how a man could be so completely unaware of his own fastidious postures. "Mr. President," began Sumner, "I do not like controversy. I am sorry always when I am engaged in it. [This from the most controversial man in the Senate, everyone knowing that controversy was his meat and drink.] I differ in that respect from the Senator from Wisconsin. [This being one of many forms in which Sumner could say "I am holier than thou."] He does like it. . . . He is perpetually alluding to me, and in an odious, I might say, almost vindictive spirit." After which Sumner dwelt farther on Doolittle as having "a monomania" for "attacking me." Near midnight of February 25 McDougall of California blamed Sumner for the lateness of the session, saying, "If volubility and wisdom are one, he is the wisest man in the world." Sumner on that day shared in a colloquy:

MR. SUMNER. . . . What I have to say now is simply to correct errors. I see the Senator from Maryland is reading a newspaper.

MR. JOHNSON. That is not unconstitutional, I hope. [Laughter.]

MR. SUMNER. The Senator says he hopes it is not unconstitutional. With his latitudinarianism in the construction of the Constitution, certainly it is not.

Never quick on his feet in debate, always preferring to write out his speeches elaborately beforehand, Sumner lost ground in several passages, one being prized by those who heard it or read it in the official *Globe*. Sumner had asked Senator Johnson whether in his opinion Northern States sliced out from the old Northwest Territory could override the slavery prohibition of the Territory's Ordinance.

> MR. JOHNSON. I certainly think they can, except so far as rights are vested.
>
> MR. SUMNER. The Senator, then, thinks Ohio can enslave a fellow-man?
>
> MR. JOHNSON. Just as much as Massachusetts can.
>
> MR. SUMNER. Massachusetts cannot.
>
> MR. JOHNSON. Why not?
>
> MR. SUMNER. Massachusetts cannot do an act of injustice.
>
> MR. JOHNSON. Oh, indeed! I did not know that. [Laughter.]

There was laughter again when Henderson inquired what had become of Sumner's "state suicide" theory. Was Louisiana in or out of the Union? Sumner: "It is in and it is not."

Others lingered toward the rear but Sumner pressed forward, saying toward the close of the debate: "The pretended State government in Louisiana is utterly indefensible whether you look at its origin or its character. To describe it, I must use plain language. It is a mere seven-months' abortion, begotten by the bayonet in criminal conjunction with the spirit of caste, and born before its time, rickety, unformed, unfinished—whose continued existence will be a burden, a reproach and a wrong. That is the whole case."

Allied with Sumner and Wade in this crusade were three other Republicans, B. Gratz Brown of Missouri, Jacob M. Howard and Zachariah Chandler of Michigan. These five voted together with 7 Democratic Senators on dilatory motions against from 18 to 20 Republicans who favored recognizing Louisiana. In some Yea and Nay votes 20 Senators, a majority of them Republicans, were silent. The Senate journal showed the measure on February 27 postponed by a vote of 34 to 12 "to to-morrow." This "to-morrow" never came. The session closed March 4 without a vote. Trumbull spoke his belief that there would have been a clear majority for the resolution had it not been fought by Sumner.

The central figure of the Senate, gazed at by all, Sumner in the last days of the session piled his desk high with documents, books, papers, notes, gave the word he was going to filibuster. There at his post, where once he had taken a merciless beating and come near death, there he would stand and speak and read—and read and speak—till the session officially ended. Thus he would kill three bills—a tax, a tariff, and an appropriation bill.

The Senate gave in. Sumner had his way. Louisiana was out. But for Sumner the first of the seceded States would have been invited back in the Union, with Senate approval of its constitution abolishing slavery, leaving to future action civil rights and the ballot for the Negro. Lincoln's foremost immediate project was lost, for the time. Another Congress, farther events, would pass on Louisiana.

Five Louisiana men claiming seats as Representatives had been in Washington since December 5. They now packed their bags and went home. Chairman Dawes of the Committee on Elections had reported in February that three of these Louisiana claimants were entitled to seats in the House. The House refused to seat them. Dawes reported a resolution that there be paid each of them $2,000 for compensation, expenses, mileage. They came not as adventurers but under what they supposed was the policy of the Government, said Dawes. The words "claimants for seats" troubled Thad Stevens. He asked to have the words stricken out. "I do not want to recognize the idea that anybody on earth thinks that these men are entitled to seats." The request however was denied, and the resolution adopted. Three like claimants from Arkansas were included in the compensation.

Of course it had not helped matters that A. P. Field, former judge of a circuit court in Louisiana, one of the claimants, had been in a high-toned restaurant one evening and following profane remarks which he directed at Representative William D. Kelley, had pulled a knife and inflicted a painful wound on Kelley, threatening that the next time he would have a gun and shoot Kelley. The House held a hearing and ordered that Judge Field be summoned for a reprimand at the bar of the House by the Speaker. The kindly and dignified reprimand of Colfax closed with the warning "Look not upon the wine when it is red, when it giveth its color in the cup; for at last it biteth like a serpent and stingeth like an adder."

Thus the tangled episode of Louisiana's political fate came to its climax and diminuendo. Heavy folios of narrative would be required to tell the entire story in all its chaotic and troubled lights. Passions—the same passions that had made the war—ran through all the breath of it. There were contemporary judgments. Sumner's behavior, wrote Samuel Bowles on March 12, was "perfectly unjustifiable" and "I shall henceforth always be intolerant of him." "Sumner," wrote Richard H. Dana on March 3 to Charles Francis Adams, "has been acting like a madman in the Louisiana question . . . not in the extreme course he took in defeating the majority by resort to delays—for that may be necessary and permissible in extreme cases, but in the positions he took, the arguments he advanced and the language he used to the twenty out of twenty-five Republican senators who differed with him. If I could hear that he was out of his head from opium or even New England rum, not indicating a habit, I should be relieved. . . . His answers to questions were boyish or crazy, I don't know which."

Yet Sumner in all his stubborn course of procedure had cast no aspersion on the President. And Lincoln in his turn had kept a perfect serenity toward Sumner. Each had stood by his sincere convictions as spoken to the other in early winter discussions. Anna Laurens Dawes, keenly sympathetic with both men, wrote of them in this latest chapter of their relations: "The phrases Sumner had been wont to hurl in the face of the slavemaster now did new duty for the policy of the President. This was a pet project with

Lincoln, and one upon which he built many hopes. The difficulty with Lincoln was his logic; more capable of an unprejudiced view than Sumner, he could not twist his law and his interpretations to suit his wishes. Thus in his theories he was the slave of his logic, but in practice he often freed himself from its bonds. Sumner, on the other hand, was above and beyond logic, and basing his action on what he believed ought to be true, he would not turn about or change that action."

It was about this time, according to an incident later related by Joseph G. Cannon of Danville, Illinois, that several Northern Congressmen in Lincoln's office were calling for retaliation. They wanted hangings of "rebel" leaders. A Pennsylvania Representative, James K. Moorhead, was making a second and more vitriolic attack than his first one when Lincoln leaned across his table, shot out an arm and pointed a long finger: "Mr. Moorhead, haven't you lived long enough to know that two men may honestly differ about a question and both be right?"

Along the hallways of the War Department building young Lieutenant G. S. Carpenter, an assistant of the adjutant general, had in the half-lights occasionally glimpsed a tall form which on second look he saw was President Lincoln. One day in the second week of February Lieutenant Carpenter had a few moments alone with Lincoln—and later wrote about it. The young assistant entered Major Eckert's large room on business, saw no one, and supposed the room to be empty. Suddenly he made out two men leaning in the deep angles and drapery of a big window where the daylight was good. They were scrutinizing and studying a yellow sheet of paper, a manifold copy of a telegram. Major Eckert saw Carpenter, came over for his message, then abruptly left for the telegraph room.

Carpenter saw the window drapery moving. Out of it slowly emerged the President, his tall silk hat on, his shoulders covered with a man's large tweed shawl. He slowly advanced, peering at the yellow manifold sheet, calling out in a high, strident voice, "Where is Salkehatchie?"

Carpenter had no idea where Salkehatchie was. It was the first he had ever heard of a Salkehatchie anywhere. He answered, "Major Eckert has gone out a moment, Mr. President, and I do not know, sir."

Still reading the dispatch, as though he could not be too sure about places named in it, the President said: "There is a map on the wall. It ought to be northwest from Savannah, in South Carolina."

Carpenter ran his young eyes over a large common map of the United States, hoping to find Salkehatchie, couldn't find it, had to tell the President so. As Lincoln came near, Carpenter noted the face mournful, anxious, "cross-lined with deep seams." His eye catching Carpenter's worriment, Lincoln lighted up with a smile.

Taking off his hat as if in salute, Lincoln remarked, "This is out of respect to General Sherman's despatch and"—hesitatingly—"my eyesight." The younger man was put at ease; it interested him that Lincoln too in searching the map couldn't find Salkehatchie.

Now Major Eckert returned, and soon brought out a large-scale war map of the region north of Savannah. "While I held one end, and the major the other," wrote Carpenter, "the President found the place, and with face abstracted and in deep anxiety studied for some time the whole region. From the occasional remarks that he dropped I gathered that this was the first intelligence from General Sherman in his progress northward, and it was still problematical whether his immediate objective was Charleston or Columbia; also, that he was then obstructed, foundering in swamps and streams with high water." On the President's face could be seen "distressful anxiety as he endeavored to trace the footsteps of the army."

Out of Savannah on February 1 Sherman had moved, his plan of campaign a secret, his lines of march baffling, the outside world unaware whether he was heading along the coast to Charleston or inland to Columbia. Now a dispatch had come through to Stanton and Lincoln that his route was inland, crossing the Salkehatchie River first, moving into Whippy Swamp. Before starting Sherman had said this march would be ten times as difficult, ten times more important, than the one from Atlanta to the sea. Able Confederate generals believed it impossible. Hardee at Charleston was sure that Sherman would not be so reckless. General Joseph E. Johnston, one of the supreme strategists of the war, waiting in North Carolina with 40,000 Confederate troops to meet Sherman, wrote that his engineers reported it was "absolutely impossible for any army to march across lower portions of the State in winter." To Johnston came a telegram from Hardee, "The Salk [short name for Salkehatchie] is impassable." Undoubtedly similar reports of a fearful area to traverse had come to Lincoln at Washington. His anxiety was deep. If Sherman now came through, the long war might be near its end.

In two columns with outriding cavalry Sherman's 60,000 men moved over the soil of the State that had led off in secession. Continuous winter rains had swollen all streams. Country not under water was mud and quagmire. They marched day on day with rain about two days out of three. They crossed five large navigable rivers, swollen torrents. From high waters near the Savannah River, they plunged into the swamps of the Combahee and the Edisto, negotiated the hills and rocks of the Santee, crossed flats of river land where Confederate cavalry with details of Negro laborers had cut down trees, burned bridges, and pulled out culverts. The advance pioneer corps performed heavy and skilled labor. At times every private in the army served as a pioneer, split saplings and carried fence rails for corduroy roads, laid pontoons, cleared entanglements. They waded streams, no time to bridge. Some forces worked for hours waist-deep in icy floodwaters. One captured Confederate trooper, seeing these exploits, told the 104th Illinois, "If your army goes to hell, it will corduroy the road." General Joseph E. Johnston said at a later time, "I made up my mind there had been no such army since the days of Julius Caesar."

The personnel of this army of Sherman had names that meant nothing beyond its picket lines, men who loved war as a game and were born to it.

These men knew each other—though to the outside world they were name-less shadows whose work and bravery in degree underlay the mighty name of Sherman. At the War Department or in the White House at Washington, as an instance, the name of Joseph Anthony Mower meant nothing in particular, a rather ordinary division or corps commander. Yet Mower was a phenomenon, one of the strangest personalities of the war. No West Pointer, a Mexican War volunteer private, in September of '61 commissioned a captain, he so fought and marched with his men that in August of '64 he was made major general of volunteers. A rough, irascible, hairy six-footer, swearing through his dark tawny whiskers, "you always had to look for him in the front line," said other officers. "He never spoke of himself," said Sherman, who added without reserve, "A better soldier or a braver man never lived." Over and again Grant and Sherman had used Mower as a smasher. They could count on him to bore in and crack an enemy line. He had a marvelous instinct for holding his men, letting the enemy dash himself to pieces against his rifle fire, then knew precisely the split second to yell "Charge!" The reports were monotonous: "General Mower drove the enemy two miles." He wrote few letters, seemed careless of distinction. Several successive sets of his staff officers had been killed in action while trying to keep pace with him. From a work of clearing Missouri of Confederate forces, on Sherman's request Mower had been ordered East, had hurried to join up for the march from Savannah. In the forefront, a terrific marcher of men, he led them through rain and mud, through icy hip-deep waters, taking the punishments of bad weather and outdoor sleeping with his troops. His fellow officers could hardly find words to describe how superbly he handled his men in the push through the Salkehatchie swamps. One of the greatest of American soldiers, he was also one of the many valorous, picturesque unknowns, a grim, silent man with a contempt of either death or fame.

Had Lincoln known Mower he would no more have worried about Salkehatchie than did Sherman, who emphasized as to Mower, "He never spoke of himself."

Confederate forces of about 15,000, chiefly under General Wade Hampton, made no headway in stopping the Northern invaders, who seemed to have saved their fury for South Carolina. Sherman wrote later of noticing that his men were determined to visit on South Carolina "the scourge of war in its worst form," and of his conclusion that "we would not be able to restrain our men as we had done in Georgia." Troops of the 2d Minnesota heard Kilpatrick, the cavalry head: "There'll be damn little for you infantrymen to destroy after I've passed through that hell-hole of secession." This from Kilpatrick just after the crossing of the Savannah River, when torpedoes mining the roadway had exploded, killing and wounding several soldiers.

Troops of the 15th Corps were heard to say, "Here is where treason began and, by God, here is where it shall end." General Howard heard Sherman laugh at Kilpatrick's having changed the name of a town from Barnwell to Burnwell. Officially Sherman's orders, as in Georgia, were against wanton violence and destruction, but they were not repeated now. He wanted terror and proceeded to achieve it. His theory was that South Carolina more than any other State had instigated the war, had welcomed it when it began, had asked for what it was now to get, "a bellyful of war." In Sherman's own words: "My aim then was to whip the rebels, to humble their pride, to follow them to their inmost recesses, and make them fear and dread us. 'Fear is the beginning of wisdom' . . . the soldiers and people of the South entertained an undue fear of our Western men and, like children, they invented such ghostlike stories of our prowess in Georgia, that they were scared by their own inventions."

Over the South arose a tradition that Sherman had raved in wrath, "I'm going to bring every Southern woman to the washtub." At the start of this march Sherman wrote to a lifelong friend, a Baltimore woman, "I will enter Carolina not as they say with a heart bent on desolation and destruction but to vindicate the just powers of a government which received terrible insults at the hands of the people of that State."

Undoubtedly his men went farther in robbery, violence, and vicious capers than he cared to have them, but their toils and marches, their readiness for hardship and fighting, were such that Sherman could not bring himself to penalize them. For himself he slept in a tree one night of flood, another night on a hard board church pew, living mostly as plain as any private. More than once he threatened to send the 8th Missouri to the rear for punishment, but knowing their valor over and again in battle, he said, "I would have pardoned them for anything short of treason."

Foragers stripped the country of many farm buildings, farm animals, fences, much property, and food of all descriptions. The railroads were torn up, and weather permitting, bridges burned, cotton bales set blazing, vacant dwellings and barns fired. Looters and bummers stole jewelry, watches, and silverware, smashed pianos and shattered mirrors, though the extent and the manner of these outrages became an issue of veracity as between Northern and Southern witnesses. Captain Daniel Oakey, 2d Massachusetts Volunteers, wrote of marching into the town of Cheraw with music and colors flying. The men stacked arms in the main street and made ready for a supper of cornmeal, sweet potatoes, and bacon brought in by foragers. "The railing of the town pump, and the remains of a buggy, said to belong to Mr. Lincoln's brother-in-law, Dr. Todd, were quickly reduced to kindling-wood to boil the coffee. The necessary destruction of property was quickly accomplished, and on we went."

The mansion of Wade Hampton's plantation was wrecked and burned. Not long afterward eighteen Union soldiers were found with papers fastened to them reading "Death to foragers," some throats slit from ear to ear. Kilpatrick came storming to Sherman about this; the order from Sherman was to "kill man for man" and to mark the bodies in the same style.

It was heartbreak time in South Carolina. The rains fell on the drooping Spanish moss of the live oaks, like Mrs. Chesnut at Columbia, "too dismal even for moaning." A letter from her husband warned her to make ready, "for the end had come," railroads all blown up, swamps impassable, new freshets daily, Negroes "utterly apathetic," no troops, $16,000 of Confederate bills traded for $300 in gold. "If I laugh at any mortal thing it is that I may not weep. Who dares hope?" In a little gathering someone prayed, "Grant us patience, good Lord," a youth rejoining profanely, "Not Ulysses Grant, good Lord." General Hood was staying at Mrs. Chesnut's house, speaking dreadful words about "my defeat and discomfiture, my army destroyed, my losses." The women told him their merriest stories. He seemed to hear nothing, sat staring into the fire, spots coming on his face, sweat on the forehead.

"Yes," whispered one woman to another, "he is going over some bitter scene; he sees Willie Preston with his heart shot away. He sees the panic at Nashville and the dead on the battlefield at Franklin." A young man spoke: "That agony on his face comes again and again. I can't keep him out of those absent fits." Came a telegram from General Beauregard to Mr. Chesnut. General Beauregard was unable to inform Mr. Chesnut whether Sherman's army would come by way of Branchville, Charleston, or Columbia. Soon then, said the women, Sherman, the destroyer, the Hun, the burner and killer, soon he might be in Columbia. Then what? They shuddered.

To Lincolnton, North Carolina, traveled Mrs. Chesnut, the last one to board the last railroad train of refugees fleeing Columbia. There at Lincolnton she was able to get a hotel room and meals of a sort for $240 for four days, in Confederate bills. Came a letter from her husband. He had been asleep on the morning of February 17 when the Yankees blew up the railroad depot and awakened him. On the streets he found that "nearly everybody had left Columbia," and the mayor had handed the city over to Sherman. "Mr. Chesnut" managed to get a horse, ride out of the city and overtake Hampton's command at Meek's Mill. "That night, from the hills where they encamped, they saw the fire, and knew the Yankees were burning the town, as we had every reason to expect they would."

The final dooms were weaving, Mrs. Chesnut writing February 22: "Charleston and Wilmington have surrendered. I have no further use for a newspaper. I never want to see another one as long as I live. . . . Shame, disgrace, beggary, all have come at once, and are hard to bear—the grand smash! Rain, rain, outside, and naught but drowning floods of tears inside." She couldn't bear it, and rushed downstairs and out through the rainstorm to the home of the Reverend Mr. Martin, who said, "Madam, Columbia is burned to the ground." Mrs. Chesnut bowed her head and sobbed aloud. "Stop that!" said the minister, trying to speak cheerfully, and, "Come here, wife," to Mrs. Martin. "This woman cries with her whole heart, just as she laughs." Then Mr. Martin began to break and his voice was hardly more calm than Mrs. Chesnut's.

Earlier that week she had spoken with friends of Lee possibly coming to help them. She wrote: "Lee could not save his own—how could he come to save us? Read the list of the dead in those last battles around Richmond and

Lincoln in early '65. Photograph by Brady.

Fringes of the throng that attended Lincoln's second inauguration despite heavy downpours of rain preceding the ceremonial.

From the Barrett collection

Thaddeus Stevens   Edwin Dennison Morgan   Jay Cooke

THE PEOPLE--AND VARIOUS PILLARS OF GOVERNMENT

From the Meserve collection

Lincoln at the table near the center of the picture (members of the Supreme Court seated at his left, military guards below him facing the crowd) reads his second inaugural address, March 4, '65

Petersburg if you want to break your heart." In bloody actions of February 5, 6, and 7 Grant had so struck at Lee that by no chance could Lee send any men toward Sherman.

In Washington on February 22 by order of the President there was a night illumination of the high domed building on the top of Capitol Hill— lights and singing bright windows in honor and celebration of victories re- sulting in Columbia, Charleston, Wilmington, and a fresh wide area coming again under the United States flag.

CHAPTER 63

THE SECOND INAUGURAL

FOUR years now this February since Abraham Lincoln under cover of secrecy and a slouch hat had set foot in Washington with his first inaugural address in an inside coat pocket, a few weeks later in the White House no mail nor telegrams arriving, no railroad trains running, wire communication cut off from Washington. To save his Government from going down and under, he had begun a war, though the Constitution said only Congress could declare war; and he had taken millions of dollars from the national treasury, and otherwise under what he considered imperative necessity had disregarded the Constitution, sponsoring arrests of scores of men without warrant and the holding of them without trial, slowly drifting into a war whose thunders echoed round the world. In the name of a Union of States he had called up through persuasion and force 1,000,000 men, 2,000,000, with guns. Out of fog and storm had come Grant and Sherman and the en- forcement of Federal authority with bayonets. Tightening his strong hand- shake with a volunteer of Company K, 57th Massachusetts regiment, at a White House reception, he said to young William D. Ordway: "I am pleased to shake hands with a soldier. It is the soldier who has made us what we are today." On Grant now menacing Lee before Richmond, on Sherman thrusting agony into the vitals of South Carolina—on these final struggles depended the length of the storm not yet spent. And on what the Chief Magistrate might have to say, on his words now, such had become his stature and place, depended much of the face of events and the character of what was to happen when the war was over. This no one understood more deeply and sensitively than Lincoln as he wrote his second inaugural address.

To the committee reporting to him that the Senate had canvassed the Electoral College votes and found him "duly elected President of the United States for four years, commencing on the fourth day of March, 1865," he had answered humbly, with an intricate humility. What might it foreshadow? He said: "With deep gratitude to my countrymen for this mark of their confidence; with a distrust of my own ability to perform the duty required under the most favorable circumstances, and now rendered doubly difficult by existing national perils; yet with a firm reliance on the strength of our free government, and the eventual loyalty of the people to the just principles upon which it is founded, and above all with an unshaken faith in the Supreme Ruler of Nations, I accept this trust. Be pleased to signify this to the respective Houses of Congress."

This he read to the committee, during informal talk afterward saying that his four years "in the depths of a great and yet unended national peril" had probably moved the public judgment "that I may better finish a difficult work in which I have labored from the first than could anyone less severely schooled to the task."

On the last Sunday evening in February Lincoln had come into his office holding in one hand a roll of manuscript. To the painter Carpenter and to a Congressman there by appointment he said: "Lots of wisdom in that document, I suspect. It is what will be called my 'second inaugural,' containing about six hundred words. I will put it away here in this drawer until I want it." Seating himself before the fireplace, in "a familiar and cheerful mood" he talked about old days in Illinois. Though now twice elected President, Carpenter heard him say that nothing had ever gratified him so much as the election just after his return from the Black Hawk War. In the township of New Salem he got 208 votes, his opponent only 3. Seldom had judgments on him been so nearly unanimous.

The program on March 4 set 12 noon as the hour for the Senate to swear in its new members and the new Vice-President, after which the President was to take his second oath of office outdoors on a platform at the east front of the Capitol. Hours before noon Lincoln's carriage brought him to his room in the Senate wing, where he considered and signed bills passed by Senate and House at the session to end at noon. Meantime a parade moved on Pennsylvania Avenue from the White House to the Capitol. The sky was gray, a light drizzle of rain falling, cold, gusty winds blowing. Two to three inches of muddy paste coated the sidewalks lined with spectators. Through a churned mud, in some places ten inches deep, moved four white horses, somewhat spattered, hauling a model of a navy monitor on wheels. The small cannon of its revolving turret blazed with salutes fired by grinning navy lads having a holiday. Civic and patriotic bodies with banners followed. A delegation of visiting firemen from Philadelphia were in line with their host, the Washington Fire Department. On one wagon platform printers from the Typographical Society, a labor union, ran a hand press and scattered programs of the day's events to the sidewalk public. For the first time in Washington a battalion of Negro troops in Union Army blue marched as inaugural guards, and in line with them the Negro Grand Lodge of Odd Fellows.

Missing from the parade was the expected White House carriage. Lieutenant George Ashmun of the White House guard gave the explanation.

His troop, ready for escort duty, drew up in front of the White House at nine in the morning, sat their horses while a rain poured down on their white gloves, polished boots, spick-and-span uniforms, saddles and glossy steeds. At eleven a carriage received Mrs. Lincoln, Robert Lincoln, and Senator Harlan, whose daughter was so rare a girl in Robert's eye that he was hoping to marry her. At the west gate they waited twenty minutes with no word from the tangled mass of troops, fire engines, marchers, where this distinguished White House vehicle of honor was to go. "Mrs. Lincoln became impatient," wrote Ashmun. "At last she inquired if a way could not be cleared for the carriage to pass out and on. Being assured that it could be done she gave the order to proceed at once, which was done at a gallop, and in spite of loud protests from marshals and aids, whose plans and efforts were thus demoralized. The carriage slackened its speed only when the Capitol was reached."

A holiday mood of the people disregarded the drab weather. Immense and impressive were the crowds "standing heroically on guard in front of the Capitol," wrote Noah Brooks. Before ten in the morning the throng reached beyond the approaches to the Capitol eastern portico. Toward noon flocks of women streamed around the Capitol, "in wretched plight, crinoline smashed, skirts bedaubed, and moiré antique, velvet, laces and such dry goods streaked with mud from end to end." And the women met their test of heroism, noted Brooks, keeping unfailing good nature though "such another dirty crowd probably never was seen." From the top flight of the marble steps came the bawlings of an officer in charge of a cordon of troops, while rain drizzled on the bonnets and velvets of a seething mass of women. Brooks and others managed to get word inside; "the epauleted popinjay" opened the doors, through which surged "a current of ladies, notables and newspaper men," enough to fill the corridors and all available floor space.

Later the doors of the galleries swung open. Women in wide crinoline drifted in, "filled the seats like a cloud," filled every gallery, not a man finding a seat. "All were in full dress, diamonds flashed, feathers nodded (damply), and bright faces gleamed everywhere, the noise of feminine tongues like a swarm of bees hovering over a blossoming apple-tree or a troop of zephyrs among riverside reeds." The ivory gavel of the presiding officer, Senator Foot of Vermont, came down rapping for order. "He might as well have talked to bees or zephyrs; the fair creatures *would not* stop; senators were mute before that rippling storm of small talk in the galleries, the women permitting their long-pent feelings to find vent in words."

The buzzing and clamor slowed down. Invited notables trod in to their reserved seats. General Joe Hooker, handsome, rosy, decked out as though for a corps review, strode in representing the army. From a side door stole a naval figure, women whispering "The dear old Admiral" as Farragut half slunk with modesty into his seat. From the press gallery young Noah Brooks enjoyed it as a show and wrote of it with occasional comic touches: "Mrs. Lincoln, attended by Senator Anthony, took a seat in the Diplomatic Gallery, where were many of the ladies and attachés of foreign embassies, who were greatly discomposed by one of the Ministers of a seven-by-nine European kingdom, whose legs got mixed up in his toggery so that he fell igno-miniously down stairs, whereat all of the spectators jumped up and looked disappointed because his embassadorial head did not break off on the railing and fall even into the Senatorial pit below. There was a buzz when the Justices of the Supreme Court came in, wearing their black robes of office, Chief Justice Chase looking very young, wearing a stove-pipe hat and a long black silk nightgown (so to speak), though it's all according to law, you know. A few stray Governors came in and took back seats; then filed in the Diplomatic Corps, gay birds every one, dressed in gold lace, feathers and unseasonable white pantaloons. One embassador was so stiff with gold lace that he could not sit down except with great difficulty, and had to unbutton himself before he could get his feet on the floor. These occupied the seats on the right of the chair, the Supreme Court being in front; behind were the members of the House, who came in procession at nocn. Next came the Cabinet, who occupied seats in the area on the left of the Chair, Seward leading off, and followed by Stanton, Welles, Speed and Dennison."

In the middle of the front row sat President Lincoln, his eyes turning with those of others as the clock struck twelve toward the main entrance, where Andrew Johnson, Vice-President-elect, came escorted by Senator Doolittle and arm in arm with Hannibal Hamlin, the outgoing Vice-President. Hamlin rose and spoke his farewell, "heartfelt and undissembled thanks" for kindness bestowed on him by every Senator, closing, "Is the Vice-President elect now ready to take and subscribe the oath of office?"

Andrew Johnson of Tennessee rose for his big moment, saying, "I am," and turning, "Senators, I am here today as the chosen Vice-President of the United States, and as such, by constitutional provision I am made the presiding officer of this body." This had a slight intimation that somebody might try to stop him from so serving. He continued, "I therefore present myself here in obedience to the high behests of the American people to discharge a constitutional duty, and not presumptuously to thrust myself in a position so exalted." This for an instant struck many of his hearers as more than an insinuation that Andy had been accused of presumptuously thrusting himself forward. What next? Andy went on, facing with no embarrassment what the *Congressional Globe* described as "a distinguished and brilliant assemblage," saying: "May I at this moment—it may not be irrelevant to the occasion—advert to the workings of our institutions under the Constitution which our fathers framed and George Washington approved, as exhibited by the position in which I stand before the American Senate, in the sight of the American people?" This was either too egregious or not quite coherent. He would proceed. "Deem me not vain or arrogant; yet I should be less than man if under such circumstances I were not proud of being an American citizen, for today one who claims no high descent, one who comes from the ranks of the people, stands, by the choice of a free constituency, in the second place in this Government. There may be those to whom such things are not pleasing, but those who have labored for the consummation of a free

Government will appreciate and cherish institutions which exclude none however obscure his origin from places of trust and distinction. The people, in short, are the source of all power."

No written papers in his hand, speaking impromptu, Andy became personal, saying to the Senators, then to the Supreme Court, that their power came from the mass of the people, and further, "You, Mr. Secretary Seward, Mr. Secretary Stanton, the Secretary of the Navy [he couldn't quite dig up the name of Welles], and the others who are your associates [why call the roll on the Cabinet?]—you know that you have my respect and my confidence—derive not your greatness and your power alone from President Lincoln." Andy was in a mood. They needed his instructions and he proceeded: "Humble as I am, plebeian as I may be deemed, permit me in the presence of this brilliant assemblage to enunciate the truth that courts and cabinets, the President and his advisers, derive their power and their greatness from the people. Such an assertion of the great principles of this Government may be considered out of place, and I will not consume the time of these intelligent people much longer; but I could not be insensible to these great truths when I, a plebeian, elected by the people the Vice President of these United States, am here to enter upon the discharge of my duties. For those duties I claim not the aptitude of my respected predecessor."

Part of this, of course, was Andrew Johnson's traditional stump speech with an ever sure-fire appeal to his Tennessee audiences. There was a shaking of fists and a tone of defiance, however, with nothing clear as to who was being defied and what about. He was coming to that, though first he must repeat, "I, though a plebeian boy, am authorized by the principles of the Government under which I live to feel proudly conscious that I am a man, and grave dignitaries are but men," which was true enough, but he had three times before said he was plebeian, and reporters noticed there was a general feeling he was overdoing the business of being a plebeian. Next, however, he spoke as one somewhat inarticulate, arrogant, and chaotic, fresh from the fiery furnace of reconstruction. Before all of them, high and mighty, he desired to proclaim "that Tennessee, whose representative I have been, is free." Today she stood redeemed. "She has bent the tyrant's rod, she has broken the yoke of slavery."

By now Hamlin had pulled at the coattails of the speaker and tried to coax him to quit, while the clerk of the Senate, John W. Forney, with whom Johnson had been drinking the evening before, whispered loud, hoped to catch Johnson's eye and flag him down. Johnson swept on into thanking God that Tennessee had never been out of the Union, and declaring flatly, "No State can go out of this Union; and moreover, Congress cannot eject a State from the Union." To this he added his promise that Tennessee was today electing her governor and legislature and would soon have her Senators and Representatives mingling with those of her sister States. Then Andrew Johnson took the oath of his new office, and Hamlin adjourned the Senate.

Rather sorry, and a little funny—but far more sorry than funny—was this performance—the sour note of the day. His face flushed, his voice hoarse, Johnson looked worn and sick. For weeks that winter he had been in bed with typhoid fever and a general exhaustion from heavy labors amid terrific excitement. He had written to Lincoln and to Forney inquiring whether by any precedents he could stay in Nashville and take his oath of office. Lincoln had wired a reply January 24 that while Johnson's wish was fully appreciated, "It is our unanimous conclusion that it is unsafe for you not to be here on the 4th of March. Be sure to reach here by that time." So Johnson had come on, had joined in a convivial party with Forney and others the night of March 3, and in Hamlin's room in the Senate building had required before going in to his inauguration that a bottle of whisky be brought him. "I am not fit to be here, and ought not to have left my home," said Johnson, "as I was slow recovering from an attack of typhoid fever. But Mr. Lincoln telegraphed me, as did other friends, that I must be here, and I came." He poured one tumbler of whisky and drank it down, and according to Hamlin, just before going into the overheated Senate chamber, drank another, saying, "I will take some more of the whiskey, as I need all the strength for the occasion I can have."

As Johnson had gotten well into his speech several Republican Senators bent their heads, unable to look at him, wishing themselves away. Sumner covered his face with his hands, and bowed his head down on the desk. "Seward," wrote Noah Brooks, "was as bland and serene as a summer day; Stanton appeared to be petrified; Welles's face was usually void of any expression; Speed sat with his eyes closed; Dennison was red and white by turns. Among Union senators Henry Wilson's face was flushed; Sumner wore a saturnine and sarcastic smile; and most of the others turned and twisted in their senatorial chairs as if in long-drawn agony. Of the Supreme Bench, Judge Nelson only was apparently moved, his lower jaw dropped clean down in blank horror. Chase was marble, adamant, granite in immobility until Johnson turned his back upon the Senate to take the oath, when he exchanged glances with Nelson, who then closed his mouth. When Johnson had repeated inaudibly the oath of office, his hand upon the Book, he turned and took the Bible in his hand, and facing the audience, said, with a loud, theatrical voice and gesture, 'I kiss this Book in the face of my nation of the United States.'"

Welles noted in his diary that Speed at his left whispered to him, "All this is in wretched bad taste," and later, "The man is certainly deranged." To Stanton on his right Welles said, "Johnson is either drunk or crazy," Stanton rejoining, "There is evidently something wrong." Seward said to Welles it was "emotion on returning and revisiting the Senate," Welles not concurring, though "I hope it is sickness."

At Lincoln's side during the scene sat the Senator who had escorted him to the Capitol, Henderson of Missouri. While the new Vice-President ranted, bellowed, and shook his fists, Henderson noticed Lincoln's head drooping in deep humiliation. A day or two later the new Secretary of the Treasury, Hugh McCulloch, spoke to Lincoln about alarm in some quarters. What would happen to the country if President Lincoln should be suddenly removed and Johnson replace him? Lincoln after a moment's hesitation and with unusual seriousness: "I have known Andy for many years. He made a bad slip the other day, but you need not be scared. Andy ain't a drunkard."

Andrew Johnson was important. A terrible importance gathered around him now. He might be a key figure. High men wondered about him. His political instincts told him this. He had tried to voice it, with a humility and courtesy of which he was capable, but his mind befuddled it and his tongue spoke mainly what he had been saying on the stump all of his life about all political power going back to the mass of people. To this in maudlin style he had joined words habitual to him in Tennessee, words that had cost him toil and suffering and for which he had risked his life. To the home of the Blairs at Silver Spring he now went for two weeks of rest while hullabaloo about his speech let down. Old Man Blair held Johnson was "all right"; he hadn't said anything "that was bad sense, only bad taste"; it wouldn't have been "nearly so much of a thing if Sumner hadn't been so exquisite about it."

As Senator Henderson offered his arm to Lincoln for taking their place in the march to the inaugural platform outside, Henderson heard Lincoln say to a marshal, "Do not let Johnson speak outside."

The procession formed and moved with the high figures of all branches of the United States Government, including the Supreme Court, the outgoing and incoming President in one person, members of the Senate, the diplomatic corps, heads of departments, governors of States and Territories, mayors of Washington and Georgetown. The drizzle of rain had stopped, and in the great plaza as they went out the Capitol door they looked on a sea of heads as far as the eye could reach, ending in scattered fringes of people near the buds and spring greenery of the grounds beyond. "A tremendous shout, prolonged and loud, arose from the surging ocean of humanity," wrote Noah Brooks. The President with invited notables took the platform. "Then the sergeant-at-arms of the Senate, the historic Brown, arose and bowed, with his shining black hat in hand, in dumb-show before the crowd, which thereupon became still, and Abraham Lincoln, rising tall and gaunt among the groups about him, stepped forward to read his inaugural address, printed in two broad columns upon a single page of large paper. As he advanced from his seat, a roar of applause shook the air, and, again and again repeated, finally died far away on the outer fringe of the throng, like a sweeping wave upon the shore. Just at that moment the sun, obscured all day, burst forth in its unclouded meridian splendor, and flooded the spectacle with glory and with light. Every heart beat quicker at the unexpected omen."

Many could not help remembering how different it was four years ago, with anxiety and gloom hung everywhere, sharpshooters with rifles lurking on watch at each of the near-by Capitol windows, and General Scott ready around the hill with troops and cannon. Then the unfitted sections of the great Capitol dome lay scattered in disorder near the inaugural stand—an unfinished job; the bronze figure of the matron Liberty lay abandoned on the ground; now she had been lifted to the supreme height of the Capitol, Walt Whitman writing of it, "I like to stand aside and look a long, long while, up at the dome; it comforts me somehow."

In a silence almost profound the audience now listened. Toward the edges of the crowd they listened but couldn't hear, so far off were they. "Every word was clear and audible as the ringing and somewhat shrill tones of Lincoln's voice sounded over the vast concourse," wrote Brooks. Seldom had a President been so short-spoken about the issues of so grave an hour. He read his carefully and deliberately prepared address:

"*Fellow-countrymen:* At this second appearing to take the oath of the presidential office, there is less occasion for an extended address than there was at the first. Then a statement, somewhat in detail, of a course to be pursued, seemed fitting and proper. Now, at the expiration of four years, during which public declarations have been constantly called forth on every point and phase of the great contest which still absorbs the attention and engrosses the energies of the nation, little that is new could be presented. The progress of our arms, upon which all else chiefly depends, is as well known to the public as to myself; and it is, I trust, reasonably satisfactory and encouraging to all. With high hope for the future, no prediction in regard to it is ventured.

"On the occasion corresponding to this four years ago, all thoughts were anxiously directed to an impending civil war. All dreaded it—all sought to avert it. While the inaugural address was being delivered from this place, devoted altogether to saving the Union without war, insurgent agents were in the city seeking to destroy it without war—seeking to dissolve the Union, and divide effects, by negotiation. Both parties deprecated war; but one of them would make war rather than let the nation survive; and the other would accept war rather than let it perish. And the war came.

"One-eighth of the whole population were colored slaves, not distributed generally over the Union, but localized in the Southern part of it. These slaves constituted a peculiar and powerful interest. All knew that this interest was, somehow, the cause of the war. To strengthen, perpetuate, and extend this interest was the object for which the insurgents would rend the Union, even by war; while the government claimed no right to do more than to restrict the territorial enlargement of it.

"Neither party expected for the war the magnitude or the duration which it has already attained. Neither anticipated that the cause of the conflict might cease with, or even before, the conflict itself should cease. Each looked for an easier triumph, and a result less fundamental and astounding. Both read the same Bible, and pray to the same God; and each invokes his aid against the other. It may seem strange that any men should dare to ask a just God's assistance in wringing their bread from the sweat of other men's faces; but let us judge not, that we be not judged. The prayers of both could not be answered—that of neither has been answered fully.

"The Almighty has his own purposes. 'Woe unto the world because of offenses! for it must needs be that offenses come; but woe to that man by

With malice toward none;

with charity for all; with firmness in the

right, as God gives us to see the right,

let us strive on to finish the work we

are in; to bind up the nation's wounds;

to care for him who shall have borne the bat:

the and for his widow, and his orphan—

to do all which may achieve and cherish a just

and a lasting peace, among ourselves, and with all nations

Lincoln writes words later to be recited and intoned by millions of people as a psalm of their nation—the softly human, closing paragraph of the second inaugural address

whom the offense cometh.' If we shall suppose that American slavery is one of those offenses which, in the providence of God, must needs come, but which, having continued through his appointed time, he now wills to re-move, and that he gives to both North and South this terrible war, as the woe due to those by whom the offense came, shall we discern therein any departure from those divine attributes which the believers in a living God always ascribe to him?

"Fondly do we hope—fervently do we pray—that this mighty scourge of war may speedily pass away. Yet, if God wills that it continue until all the wealth piled by the bondman's two hundred and fifty years of unrequited toil shall be sunk, and until every drop of blood drawn with the lash shall be paid by another drawn with the sword, as was said three thousand years ago, so still it must be said, 'The judgments of the Lord are true and righteous altogether.'

"With malice toward none; with charity for all; with firmness in the right, as God gives us to see the right, let us strive on to finish the work we are in; to bind up the nation's wounds; to care for him who shall have borne the battle and for his widow, and his orphan—to do all which may achieve and cherish a just and a lasting peace among ourselves, and with all nations."

Applause and cheers marked the sentence having the words "both parties deprecated war," so that Lincoln paused long before adding "And the war came." A subdued handclapping and occasional cheers punctuated other places in the address. Reporters noticed at the final paragraph many moist eyes and here and there tears coursing down faces unashamed of emotion.

Silence being restored after the last prolonged cheer, the President turned toward Chief Justice Chase, performing today the ritual conducted four years ago by Roger B. Taney. The Chief Justice with his right hand uplifted directed the clerk of the Supreme Court to bring forward the Bible. Then Lincoln, laying his right hand on an open page of the Book, repeated the oath of office after the Chief Justice: "I do solemnly swear that I will faith-fully execute the office of the President of the United States, and will, to the best of my ability, preserve, protect, and defend the Constitution of the United States—so help me God." Then Lincoln bent forward, kissed the Book, and arose to full height again, his authority complete to serve as Pres-ident of the United States for the next four years.

Cannon boomed, cheers rang on cheers. Lincoln turned bowing in vari-ous directions, then walked into the Capitol, at a basement entrance took his carriage, and was escorted back to the White House by a great proces-sion. To Noah Brooks he said: "Did you notice that sunburst? It made my heart jump." Another omen was noticed by several persons, Lieutenant Ash-mun of the cavalry escort back to the White House writing that some of his men looking skyward saw the star Venus shining clear and luminous about two o'clock in the afternoon, "the first and only time that most of us ever saw that star at that hour of the day." Accounts of the day mentioned at the close of the high ceremonial "a bright star visible in the heavens."

Chief Justice Chase noted the place where the President's lips touched the Bible page. Presenting the Book to Mrs. Lincoln, the Chief Justice pointed to the pencil-marked verses kissed by the President. They were the twenty-seventh and twenty-eighth verses of the fifth chapter of the Book of Isaiah, reading:

"None shall be weary nor stumble among them; none shall slumber nor sleep; neither shall the girdle of their loins be loosed, nor the latchet of their shoes be broken:

"Whose arrows are sharp, and all their bows bent, their horses' hoofs shall be counted like flint, their wheels like a whirlwind."

In the wide-flung comment on the second inaugural, the praise and blame ran somewhat like that given the Gettysburg speech. Journals keyed to the London *Times* agreed with its judgment that Lincoln wanted "fresh exertions and sacrifices" from his people, and "Mr. Lincoln, therefore, like a prudent statesman, conceals his own hopes, if he cherishes any, and bids the people, in effect, to make up their minds for another considerable term of fighting." On the whole, the *Times* would say, it revealed the Federal Magistrate "more completely than many of the verbose compositions which have proceeded from his predecessors." This left-handed compliment on brevity was a new one from the *Times*. E. L. Godkin, writing from America for his readers in the London *Daily News*, rebuked the "painfully absurd writers and orators in London" who chose to misinterpret. "Mr. Lincoln," wrote Godkin, "is perhaps the only man at the North who has never wavered, or doubted, or abated one jot of heart or hope. He has always been calm, confident, determined, the type and embodiment of the national will."

"Everyone likes a compliment," wrote Lincoln to Thurlow Weed with thanks for good words, and giving his own estimate of his second inaugural address. "I expect the latter [the address] to wear as well as—perhaps better than—anything I have produced; but I believe it is not immediately popular. Men are not flattered by being shown that there has been a difference of purpose between the Almighty and them. To deny it, however, in this case, is to deny that there is a God governing the world. It is a truth which I thought needed to be told, and, as whatever of humiliation there is in it falls most directly on myself, I thought others might afford for me to tell it."

Like the Gettysburg Address and more particularly the House Divided speech, the second inaugural took on varied meanings. To some it was a howl for vengeance, to others a benediction and a plea—with deep music. J. B. Jones in the Richmond war office wrote of it as a homily or sermon. "He 'quotes Scripture for the deed' quite as fluently as our President; and since both Presidents resort to religious justification, it may be feared the war is about to assume a more sanguinary aspect and a more cruel nature than ever before. God help us! The history of man, even in the Bible, is but a series of wars. It must be thus to make us appreciate the blessings of peace, and to bow in humble adoration of the great Father of all."

"What think you of the inaugural?" wrote Charles Francis Adams, Jr., to his father. "That rail-splitting lawyer is one of the wonders of the day.

Once at Gettysburg and now again on a greater occasion he has shown a capacity for rising to the demands of the hour which we should not expect from orators or men of the schools. This inaugural strikes me in its grand simplicity and directness as being for all time the historical keynote of this war; in it a people seemed to speak in the sublimely simple utterance of ruder times. What will Europe think of this utterance of the rude ruler, of whom they have nourished so lofty a contempt? Not a prince or minister in all Europe could have risen to such an equality with the occasion."

On the evening of March 4, people were massing and milling long before eight o'clock, when the doors of the White House were to open for the President's reception to the public. An insistent crowd it was, some having traveled from afar; they proposed to miss no numbers on the bill. "The platform in front of the entrance, the walks and drives back of the Avenue, were packed with people," noted Lieutenant Ashmun of the guards. He described the technical difficulties of policing this crush of mainly well-dressed humanity. "After consultation it was arranged that the district police, who were, of course, government officers, should manage the people inside the house, and the military force take care of them outside. In order to prevent a crush within it was decided to open the doors and let the house fill, then close them and keep them closed until the police had moved the people on and mostly out of a separate place of exit. The difficulties in this plan were to cut off the stream at the doorway long enough to close the doors, and then to pacify those kept in waiting for the next opening. Occasionally a lady would faint or become terrified and have to be rescued by taking her out of the mass over the heads of men, for they were packed so closely that they could not move or be moved to permit any other way of escape. From the midst of this compressed mass on that platform at the entrance I heard a voice and saw the hand of a tall naval officer waved toward me, with the call: 'Can't you get us out of this?' After a hard struggle he was reached and at his side a much shorter man in full uniform was standing, whom I had not seen until then, and who proved to be Admiral Farragut being released from a very uncomfortable position, to say nothing of the delay in reaching the President."

The hours from eight until eleven o'clock Lincoln spent in almost continuous handshaking. Newspapermen wrote that in these three hours he shook hands with more than six thousand persons. Among those who failed to make the grade for a handshake was Walt Whitman. "Never was such a compact jam in front of the White House," he wrote—"all the grounds fill'd, and away out to the spacious sidewalks. I was . . . in the rush inside with the crowd—surged along the passage-ways, the blue and other rooms, and through the great east room. Crowds of country people, some very funny. Fine music from the Marine band, off in a side place. I saw Mr. Lincoln, drest all in black, with white kid gloves and a claw-hammer coat, receiving, as in duty bound, shaking hands, looking very disconsolate, and as if he would give anything to be somewhere else."

Two policemen seized Frederick Douglass as he tried to walk through the entrance. They were mistaken, he told them; the President would order him admitted if the President knew about it. And with that Douglass flashed through the door, only to be taken by two inside policemen. They escorted him to a window and had him walking a plank that led outside. "This will not do, gentlemen," he said to the limbs of the law, and then called to a man passing by, "Be so kind as to say to Mr. Lincoln that Frederick Douglass is detained by officers at the door." Soon came word that the President invited Mr. Douglass into the East Room. He described the scene: "A perfect sea of beauty and elegance, too, it was. The ladies were in very fine attire, and Mrs. Lincoln was standing there. I could not have been more than ten feet from him when Mr. Lincoln saw me; his countenance lighted up, and he said in a voice which was heard all around: 'Here comes my friend Douglass.' As I approached him he reached out his hand, gave me a cordial shake, and said: 'Douglass, I saw you in the crowd to-day listening to my inaugural address. There is no man's opinion that I value more than yours: what do you think of it?' I said: 'Mr. Lincoln, I cannot stop here to talk with you, as there are thousands waiting to shake you by the hand;' but he said again: 'What did you think of it?' I said: 'Mr. Lincoln, it was a sacred effort,' and then I walked off. 'I am glad you liked it,' he said."

The crowds vanished and in the still midnight the White House looked, according to the guard Crook, "as if a regiment of rebel troops had been quartered there, with permission to forage." As a custom at these receptions there were odds and ends carried away as souvenirs, but the damage now seemed "monstrous." Mementoes were wanted. "A great piece of red brocade, a yard square almost, was cut from the window-hangings of the East Room, and another piece not quite so large, from a curtain in the Green Room. Flowers from the floral designs in the lace curtains were cut out, evidently for an ornament for the top of pincushions or something of the sort. Some arrests were made, after the reception, of persons concerned in the disgraceful business." The President, noted Crook, was "distressed greatly." Usually he was so calm about things, why should these acts of rowdyism impress him so painfully? Crook guessed it was "the senseless violence of it that puzzled him." Crook noted his saying, "Why should they do it? How can they?"

An American crowd, "a motley democratic crowd, such as could be seen in no royal country, and of which we are justly proud," thus ran the version of Adelaide W. Smith, an army nurse carrying a paper signed by General Grant ordering all guards, pickets, steamboats, and railroads to "pass Miss Ada W. Smith." With two friends she stood that afternoon on the rim of the crowd at the inaugural platform. Far off they managed to see a little pantomime ritual, catching not a sound of it. They saw Mr. Lincoln come forward, saw the robed Chief Justice open the Bible and

Mr. Lincoln bend and press his lips on a page. They stood while he spoke his second inaugural, hearing not a phrase nor a tone, so far off that, as Miss Smith said, "Not a word of that memorable address could we hear above the soughing, cold, gusty wind."

At the small hotel where she was staying she had met one Lieutenant Gosper. Their friendship was not ordinary. In a skirmish before Petersburg his right leg had been shot away and Miss Smith had been his nurse helping bring him back. "He manifested," she noted, "the usual cheerfulness of wounded men, while waiting to have an artificial limb adjusted, a free gift from the Government."

Would the Lieutenant go with Miss Smith and her friends to the President's reception in the evening? He positively declined. "It is no place for a cripple." Other arguments not moving him to go, Miss Smith said, "Well, Lieutenant, if you will not go with us I suppose I shall have to stay away also. Each of the other ladies has an escort, and, as every lady must be attended, I can not go alone."

"Would you go to a reception with a cripple on a crutch?" he half moaned.

"I would be proud of such an escort."

So, though he was not completely willing, they started, and soon found themselves in the frightful crush of folk jamming the White House grounds. "We quickly closed around the lieutenant," wrote Miss Smith, "fearing he might get under foot. Our party was carried bodily to the landing, where I found that my arm was quite badly bruised by the crutch. After getting breath and composing ourselves, we fell into the long procession of couples approaching the President, where the ushers went through the forms of taking our names and introducing us. In passing we saw a group of Cabinet officers and a number of ladies with Mrs. Lincoln, gowned in white satin with a deep black thread lace flounce over an expansive skirt, in the style of the day; and she wore her favorite head dress, a wreath of natural pink roses entirely around her plainly dressed hair."

Crowds of every grade passed before Miss Smith's eyes, "some in dashing uniforms, some in evidently fresh 'store clothes,' others in gorgeous costumes, and the good women from the country in sensible black—with ill-fitting gloves." Swept along in the seemingly endless procession, Miss Smith and Lieutenant Gosper on his crutch finally saw "the unmistakable form of Mr. Lincoln, his long arm and white-gloved hand reaching out to shake hands, and bowing in a mechanical manner, plainly showing that he wished this demand of the people was well over."

Then they saw the President suddenly straighten his tall form and look down the line. To their surprise he had detected the Lieutenant on the crutch and stepping out before the two of them, took the hand of Lieutenant Gosper, and in a tone of voice to them unforgettable, was saying, "God bless you, my boy!"

Owing to the Lieutenant's crutch, wrote Miss Smith, "I was obliged to take his left arm, which brought me on the outside away from the President. I attempted to pass with a bow, but he stood in my way, still holding out his large hand, until I released mine and gave it to him, receiving a warm sympathetic grasp. Then I saw that wonderful lighting of his beneficent grey eyes, that for a moment often beautified as with a halo that otherwise plain, sad face."

The two of them moved on. The Lieutenant was happy, even exulting. He was saying to Ada Smith, "Oh! I'd lose another leg for a man like that!"

CHAPTER 64

EXECUTIVE ROUTINE

AFTER one Cabinet meeting in March young Fred Seward heard Postmaster General Dennison say of the little old leather-covered chair at Lincoln's desk, "I should think the Presidential chair of the United States might be a better piece of furniture than that." Lincoln turned, let his eyes scan the worn, torn, battered leather, and "You think that's not a good chair, Governor," and with a half-quizzical, half-meditative look at it: "There are a great many people that want to sit in it, though. I'm sure I've often wished some of them had it instead of me!"

General Grenville M. Dodge came into the White House, a fresh scar on his head. Near Atlanta the previous August, ran his explanation of the scar, "The boys cautioned me, and said that if I wanted to see the enemy I could look through a peep-hole they had made under a log. I put my eye to this peep-hole, and the moment I did so I was shot in the head. I went down." He told Lincoln he had been at Grant's headquarters and simply stopped off in Washington to pay his respects. Dodge got up to leave, but Lincoln put out his hand, hoped Dodge wasn't in too much of a hurry, gradually emptied the room of callers, locked the door and the two of them were as alone as six years earlier when they stood on a hilltop at Council Bluffs, Iowa, and looked toward the West Coast and wondered together about how long the Pacific railway was to be a mere dream. Lincoln read Artemus Ward; it was Dodge's kind of humor and they laughed in unison.

They went to lunch and Lincoln's purpose in delaying Dodge came out. He suddenly was sending a series of questions on all that Dodge had seen and heard at Grant's headquarters, pointedly asked how Dodge estimated Grant and the plans to take Richmond. Dodge was sure that Grant would ultimately defeat Lee—and said so. And according to Dodge's account, Lincoln reached across the table, laid a hand on Dodge's, in a tone of deep feeling all but cried, "You don't know how glad I am to hear you say this."

Then Dodge had gone on to his birthplace at Danvers, Massachusetts, and on to a Faneuil Hall war meeting in Boston. Edward Everett saw Dodge in the audience, paid him tribute, and the crowd called for a speech. Dodge rose to his feet as a woman threw a large bouquet at him. The stem of a heavy rose hit him full in the forehead, opening the old wound so that blood trickled over his face. Amid crowd excitement General Dodge quietly wiped his face, stanched the red flow with a handkerchief, spoke briefly and calmly the same belief he had expressed to Lincoln—that he was sure Grant would defeat Lee.

Then Grant had consulted Lincoln about appointing Dodge commander of the Military Department of Missouri to replace Rosecrans, of whom Grant said to Stanton, "Rosecrans will do less harm doing nothing than on duty." Lincoln rated Rosecrans higher than did Grant, but he agreed to try still another man at the head of affairs in Missouri. Where Frémont, Schofield, Curtis, and Rosecrans had made no headway at calming Missouri, Dodge was to try his hand. More than any other State Missouri was seeing war civil rather than sectional, neighbors arrayed against neighbors, with roving guerrillas and bushwhackers, night riders, Confederate raiders, barn-burners, midnight shootings, Lincoln writing to Dodge January 15, "It is represented to me that there is so much irregular violence in northern Missouri as to be driving away the people and almost depopulating it." He suggested that Dodge should consider "an appeal to the people there to go to their homes and let one another alone," possible withdrawal of troops where they seemed an irritation, the President thus hoping to "restore peace and quiet, and returning prosperity."

Nothing came of this. The James brothers, Frank and Jesse, never would listen to appeals or let anyone alone when they believed they were wronged. Quantrell's guerrillas were a breed somewhat beyond Lincoln's grasp at Washington, many of them Confederate deserters or frontier desperadoes given added incitement by the chaotic morale of war civil and sectional. On February 20 Lincoln wrote to Governor Fletcher of Missouri that while no organized force of the enemy was operating in Missouri yet "destruction of property and life is rampant everywhere." Was not the cure for this in easy reach of the people themselves? "It cannot but be that every man not naturally a robber or cut-throat would gladly put an end to this state of things." Then Lincoln reasoned about the matter of peace and calm in Missouri, suggested steps he believed practical, voiced a faith in humanity not easy to apply in Missouri at that hour. One might almost read between the lines of this letter of Lincoln that he was weary of applying force and always force, that he cared little whether his proposals might seem ridiculous on the face of them. A curious, tender appeal it was, for the hour rather preposterous though nevertheless glowing in its faith in humanity, naïve in its hope of the human spirit of the hour working toward harmony and accord. He continued to Governor Fletcher:

"A large majority in every locality must feel alike upon this subject; and if so, they only need to reach an understanding, one with another.

Each leaving all others alone solves the problem; and surely each would do this but for his apprehension that others will not leave him alone. Cannot this mischievous distrust be removed?

"Let neighborhood meetings be everywhere called and held, of all entertaining a sincere purpose for mutual security in the future, whatever they may heretofore have thought, said, or done about the war, or about anything else. Let all such meet, and, waiving all else, pledge each to cease harassing others, and to make common cause against whoever persists in making, aiding, or encouraging further disturbance. The practical means they will best know how to adopt and apply. At such meetings old friendships will cross the memory, and honor and Christian charity will come in to help.

"Please consider whether it may not be well to suggest this to the now afflicted people of Missouri."

Governor Fletcher sent this letter on to General Dodge with the comment it was "passing strange" President Lincoln was "still unable to comprehend Missouri affairs." He would try the President's vague plan, though ready with troops to meet the consequence of its failure. "With your knowledge and mine of the real condition of the state," Fletcher wrote Dodge, "it is heart-sickening to be put off by such a policy." Grant agreed with Fletcher and Dodge that Lincoln's policy would not quiet Missouri, a State that had been half-slave and half-free, with "claybanks" and "charcoals" shooting at the drop of a hat, with thousands of individual hatreds that would burn till the flame of life went out. The Union authorities read Lincoln's point that at neighborhood meetings "old friendships will cross the memory," but felt sure that if such meetings could be arranged, in some cases those attending would bring guns and knives, savage old grudges would cross the memory, and there would be cries for blood. In some neighborhoods, the authorities were sure, it was best for the local boys not to meet; they had sworn to shoot on sight.

"Unless troops are kept in the Missouri River counties no loyal people can live there," Dodge replied to Lincoln. A form of county militia or citizenry police was organized, and county units holding the more peaceably inclined of Union and Confederate sympathizers--and in each county still another organization that offset the radicals on both sides and which had connections with the military: a blend of vigilante, civil, and military government which brought results. Dodge issued a general order that all guerrilla leaders must leave the State. A citizen hiding a guerrilla gang was taken by a Federal officer and shot to death. Appeals went to Lincoln to remove the ruthless Dodge. Besides the rural malcontents Dodge in St. Louis had to deal with cotton speculators, military attachés, and a variety of sophisticated leeches. They called him the worst of all the Lincoln dictators sent to Missouri. As Dodge drove from the Lindell Hotel to his headquarters one day an assassin fired at him, missed, and killed his Negro driver. In Dodge's possession was a copy of a newspaper published in Selma.

Alabama, sent to him by one of his spies at the time he was serving as intelligence chief for Grant. An advertisement in this newspaper read:

> ONE MILLION DOLLARS WANTED TO HAVE PEACE BY THE 1ST OF MARCH. If the citizens of the Southern Confederacy will furnish me with the cash, or good securities for the sum of one million dollars, I will cause the lives of Abraham Lincoln, William H. Seward and Andrew Johnson to be taken by the first of March next. This will give peace, and satisfy the world that cruel tyrants can not live in a land of liberty. If this is not accomplished, nothing will be claimed beyond the sum of fifty thousand dollars, in advance, which is supposed to be necessary to reach and slaughter the three villains.
>
> I will give one thousand dollars towards this patriotic purpose. Everyone wishing to contribute will address box X, Cabba, Alabama, December 1st, 1864.

At the top of his inauguration week letter to the *Sacramento Union* Noah Brooks quoted "Uneasy lies the head that wears a crown," Brooks being rather sure "Father Abraham lies uneasy o' nights, as he thinks of the sluice of office-hunting which may shortly be opened upon him by the cruel thoughtlessness of his friends (?), as they call themselves." From Lincoln himself Brooks had a point of view. "The President considers that as the people have voted to keep him in another term because the public good could best be served, he ought to make no changes in office which the public good does not demand; but politicians will not see it in that light, and will avail themselves of the excuse of a new term to have a new deal."

Under many a silk hat, and no less under many of the slouches, in the inaugural throng were hopes of connecting with favors at the hand of the President. As the day of his reinauguration drew near, Lincoln, according to Carpenter, had said to the New Hampshire Senator Clark: "Can't you and others start a public sentiment in favor of making no changes in offices except for good and sufficient cause? It seems as though the bare thought of going through again what I did the first year here, would *crush* me." To another he said, "I have made up my mind to make very few changes. . . . I think now that I will not remove a single man except for delinquency. To remove a man is very easy, but when I go to fill his place, there are *twenty* applicants, and of these I must make *nineteen* enemies." From a friend Carpenter heard now of how Lincoln's "natural charity for all often turned into an unwonted suspicion of the motives of men whose selfishness cost him so much wear of mind." To this friend, according to Carpenter, Lincoln just before reinauguration made the sorry commentary: "Sitting here, where all the avenues to public patronage seem to come together in a knot, it does seem to me that our people are fast approaching the point where it can be said that seven eighths of them are trying to find how to live at the expense of the other eighth."

Reporting to Lincoln of a visit to Grant's headquarters, Brooks heard a mocking query: "Did you meet any colonels who want to be brigadiers, or any brigadiers who wanted to be major-generals, or any major-generals who wanted to run things?" Brooks hadn't. "Happy man!" laughed Lincoln, putting out a hand in mock congratulation. "Happy man!"

Afterward Brooks recalled that an officer who had been attentive to him and his party at City Point did come to him complaining that he ought to be promoted and that his relationship to a distinguished general "kept him down." At this Lincoln went into high laughter and jumped up crying: "Keeps him down? Keeps him down? That's all that keeps him up!"

The President must put off granting a favor till nearer the end of the war, writing: "I know what our friend Corwin wants—He wants me to decide a matter in favor of his client, which I might possibly do if we were nearer the end of this war, but which, if driven to decide now, I should have to decide against him." Original in the Barrett collection.

To a group of men active in promoting the Bureau for the Employment of Disabled and Discharged Soldiers, Lincoln wrote March 1 of "hearty concurrence" with its purposes. "I shall at all times be ready to recognize the paramount claims of the soldiers of the nation in the disposition of public trusts. I shall be glad also to make these suggestions to the several heads of departments." For any vacant office the proven fighting man had first call. And it seemed that for any Senators or Congressmen whose co-operation Lincoln sought, he would go out of his way to grant them offices or favors. In the weeks following inauguration, according to one of Sumner's secretaries, "Mr. Lincoln bestowed more tokens of good-will on Sumner than on any other senator."

An old gentleman who said his sons had been killed in battle, now had come to Washington hoping to get work, Lincoln advising him that

Washington was the worst place in the country for anyone to seek to better his condition. "He wished," noted the listening editor of the *Baltimore American and Commercial Advertiser*, "some species of saffron tea could be administered to produce an eruption of those already in Washington and make this migration fever strike *out* instead of striking *in*." But the old gentleman hadn't railroad fare to leave Washington; he hoped to connect with some quartermaster. After thinking a minute the President wrote something on a piece of paper, and gave it to him, "when the old man's countenance brightened, and with profuse thanks he retired."

A wounded officer had a memorial from his home district saying he deserved an office. The President said he agreed with the memorial but must wait to hear from the member of Congress in that district. "He would be forever in hot water if he did not pay some deference to the wishes of members on these appointments." To a request that a soldier under age be discharged because a certain officer said the youth deserved such executive action, the President's immediate answer was: "Bring me his opinion to that effect in writing. His word will be sufficient for me. I will require no argument on the subject."

A young widow whose husband had been killed in battle asked for the postmastership of a small town in Orange County, New York. The President kindly told her to leave all the papers with him; he would go through them

Let this man take the oath of Dec. 8. 1863 & be discharged –

A. Lincoln

March 16. 1865.

One more pleasant little routine matter. Original in the Barrett collection.

carefully; if she would go home, he would attend to it as well as if she were staying in Washington. "I cannot act on it at once, for although I am President, you must remember that I am but one horse in the team, and if the others pull in a different direction, it will be a hard matter for me to outpull them." This one, in a series of cases, the editor of the *Baltimore American* watched the President handle. In the next the President said, "I don't know why it is that I am troubled with these cases, but if I were, by interfering, to make a hole through which a kitten might pass it would soon be large enough for the old cat to get through also."

At least once Lincoln sent a thorny rebuke to a man resigning an office, one Charles Gibson, solicitor of the United States in the court of claims at

St. Louis. In a letter through the clerk of the court Gibson had resigned, saying the Baltimore platform and the principles of the Lincoln Administration were repugnant to him. In a letter to the clerk of the court, John Hay replied that he had placed Mr. Gibson's letter in the hands of the President, who "says he was not aware that he was so much indebted to Mr. Gibson for having accepted the office at first, not remembering that he ever pressed him to do so." A one-sentence paragraph ended the letter of Hay, speaking for the President: "He thanks Mr. Gibson for his acknowledgment that he has been treated with personal kindness and consideration, and he says he knows of but two small drawbacks upon Mr. Gibson's right to still receive

Convinced by "this poor soldier," the President asks the Paymaster General to "please have him put on the right track to get his pay." Original in the Barrett collection.

such treatment, one of which is that he could never learn of his giving much attention to the duties of his office, and the other is this studied attempt of Mr. Gibson's to stab him." Bates wrote in his diary that the President was "incensed" and struck back in "bad taste" and blind "impetuosity."

In quite another mood six weeks before reinauguration the President, noted Welles, was "very happy" at one Cabinet meeting. "Says he is amused with the manners and views of some who address him, who tell him that he is now reëlected and can do just as he has a mind to, which means that he can do some unworthy thing that the person who addresses him has a mind to. There is very much of this."

During four years and one month of presidential appointive powers, Lincoln, according to a later estimate rather carefully based, removed 1,457 out of a possible 1,639 officials. In this period some offices were vacated two or three times. Naturally to begin with hundreds of open secessionists, or sympathizers with secession, had to go. In many responsible wartime positions the strictest of loyalty was a requirement; all under doubt had to go. Also there was the young growing Republican-party organization with a genuine minimum of demands beyond denial. So the Lincoln broom had swept wide with removals from office. And in the building of a loyalist

Government while meeting the calls, from both leaders and rank and file, of a young party seeking to keep its hold on the Government across a long future, Lincoln carried a heavy load and did a harassing work; in extent of cares and decisions the record stood beyond comparison with any President before his time.

Bitterly Lincoln spoke a straight refusal to an old friend, not fit for the office he was seeking, saying to Brooks, "I had rather resign my place and go away from here than refuse him, if I consulted only my personal feelings; but refuse him I must."

One F. J. Whipple of New York, seated in the hall opposite the President's office, saw a man come from the private part of the White House. He arose and said, "This is Mr. Lincoln, I believe."

"Yes. What can I do for you?"

"Nothing, sir. You have not an office I would accept."

Lincoln slapped him on the shoulder. "Is it possible? Come into my office. I want to look at you. It is a curiosity to see a man who does not want an office. You might as well try to dip the Potomac dry as to satisfy them all."

They talked. The President idled with a pencil and paper. The notable visitor who wanted no office departed with a warm handshake. And a few days later the guard Crook heard a Senator asking Lincoln what was the pencil sketch on the desk, and Lincoln: "It is the portrait of the one man who does not want an office."

Crook himself one day joined those seeking the President's name signed to a paper. He with other White House guards and Washington police department members had been drafted. "Frankly, I didn't want to go," wrote Crook. "I had served in the army already; I had a young wife and son at home to hold me. I couldn't afford to pay for a substitute." So on March 2 Crook stood for a time among those waiting to see the President. Then, remembering he was free to go anywhere over the White House, he went to seek the President. "I found him in his own room, in dressing-gown and slippers, asked him if he could do anything in my case and in that of Alexander Smith, my special friend on the force. He listened to my story as patiently as if he had not heard hundreds like it. Kindly he looked at me. When I had finished, he said: 'Well, I can't spare you. Come into my office.'" There Lincoln wrote and signed a small card to the Provost Marshal General: "These two of my men, Crook and Alexander [sic], are drafted, and I cannot spare them. P.M.G., please fix." This served its purpose. The other White House guards, noted Crook, "had their cases 'fixed' through Mrs. Lincoln."

Lincoln and Stanton, one day going over applications for commissions in the army, came to the last on the list. "This fellow hasn't any endorser," said Lincoln. He glanced at the letter, became interested. "It's a good, straightforward letter," Crook heard Lincoln say. "I'll be his endorser." And the young fellow got his shoulder straps.

Brooks gave a little list of good party men who had lost at the last election, each "like a lame duck, to be nursed into something else," as Brooks quoted the President, who managed to take care of some of the cripples. John P. Hale, after eighteen years in the Senate squeezed out by factional quarrels, was named Minister to Spain, at $12,000 a year. The few changes in foreign appointments were chiefly to benefit "lame-duck" Congressmen and Senators. Not in that category was John Bigelow, a journalist and diplomat of ability, named Minister to France. For the Paris consulate vacated by Bigelow, Lincoln's efficient and trusted private secretary John G. Nicolay was named, his service to begin in June.

The old and tried friend of true steel loyalty, Isaac N. Arnold, who had neglected his Chicago political fences while giving all he had for Lincoln in Washington, was out of his seat in Congress, but was staying on in Washington to write a biography of Lincoln and a history of the over-throw of slavery. To him Lincoln was offering a choice. Arnold could be United States District Attorney for the District of Columbia or Auditor of the Treasury for the Post Office Department. Arnold was thinking it over. The office of Solicitor of the Navy would have suited Arnold, but when Lincoln proposed to Secretary Welles that he should release its tried incumbent for a new one, Welles said that while he considered Arnold "worthy and estimable," he preferred to make no change.

Fessenden had resigned as Secretary of the Treasury and begun his third term as Senator from Maine. To this vacancy, inner circles were aware, Lincoln in February offered to appoint Edwin Dennison Morgan, former Governor of New York and United States Senator, associated with high financial and industrial interests. In fact, it would appear from a diary entry of Welles, Lincoln sent a messenger to the Senate with a batch of appointments just as Morgan called on the President and said he must decline. Lincoln at once sent another messenger to see that the Morgan appointment did not reach the Senate. Morgan's feelings about the office were probably surmised by John Bigelow, who from Paris wrote to Morgan, March 3: "As your friend I am glad you declined it. The country is not yet ready to enter upon a systematic reform and reorganization of our financial policy, and until then woe is the man who, like Judas, carries the bag for Uncle Sam. . . . I can conceive of no public position in the United States less desirable for a conscientious patriot or even for a man of honor-able ambition."

Welles thought Morgan made a big mistake in refusing to be Treasury head. Welles for an hour one Sunday evening urged Morgan to take the appointment, saying the country needed Morgan. But the New Yorker couldn't see it. Morgan said Thurlow Weed had been to see him that Sun-day morning and had spent several hours trying to persuade him to change his mind. Behind Weed, Morgan saw Seward. "What is Seward's object?" he asked Welles. "He never in such matters acts without a motive, and Weed would not have been called here except to gain an end." The nearest Morgan could figure it was that Seward wanted to be President and hoped to line up Morgan for him. So Welles wrote in his diary, noting that he heard Weed "expressed great dissatisfaction" that Morgan would not go along, adding: "The selection, I think, was the President's, not Seward's, though the latter readily fell in with it."

New England influence in particular and radicals in general favored John Andrew of Massachusetts for the vacant Cabinet place. The Maine Legislature recommended Hannibal Hamlin. So did Monty Blair, who suggested also that Seward should leave the Cabinet, that Sumner should take Seward's place, making way for John Andrew to fill Sumner's Senate seat. Leading Chicago bankers, many Western politicians, and the formidable Jay Cooke came to the front, sure that the most fit and able man was Hugh McCulloch, a Maine-born youth who in 1833 had settled in Fort Wayne, Indiana, and won his way to the top circles of banking. Solidly conservative, counted a "dependable" man, he had in May of '63 gone into the office of Comptroller of the Currency under Chase. McCulloch's hand perhaps more than that of any other in the Government had guided the organization and first operations of the newly created national banking system.

Lincoln a day or two after his inauguration sent a messenger asking McCulloch to call sometime during the day. In the afternoon McCulloch found Lincoln alone and, as they shook hands, saying, "I have sent for you, Mr. McCulloch, to let you know that I want you to be Secretary of the Treasury, and if you do not object to it, I shall send your name to the Senate." McCulloch wrote later that he was "taken all aback" at these sudden, unexpected words. "It was an office that I had not aspired to, and did not desire." His reply to Lincoln he recorded: "I thank you, Mr. President, heartily for this mark of confidence, and I should be glad to comply with your wishes if I did not distrust my ability to do what will be required of the Secretary of the Treasury in the existing financial condition of the Government." Then the President: "I will be responsible for that. I will be responsible for that, and so I reckon we will consider the matter settled." As McCulloch went away and thought about it he could not be sure whether "gratification or dread" moved him. The President he noted as "greatly careworn, but cheerful." The next day the Senate unanimously confirmed the appointment.

Not long afterward in connection with some current affair Lincoln confided to McCulloch: "I am here by the blunders of the Democrats. If instead of resolving that the war was a failure, they had resolved that I was a failure and denounced me for not more vigorously prosecuting it, I should not have been reëlected, and I reckon that you would not have been Secretary of the Treasury."

Now the Hoosier State had two Cabinet members. John P. Usher, Secretary of the Interior, formally notified Lincoln that to remove any possible embarrassment which might arise from Indiana having two members in the Cabinet, he was resigning. Lincoln endorsed the resignation: "Accepted, to take effect May 15, 1865." Later as a consulting attorney for the Union Pacific Railway Usher was to continue his interest and activity in the subject of public lands. To the Senate Lincoln sent the name of James Harlan, United States Senator from Iowa, to be Secretary of the Interior. The Senate confirmed this appointment of a frontier educator who had been superintendent of public instruction in Iowa in 1847, president of Iowa Wesleyan University in 1863, and during Senate service a member of the committees on agriculture, public lands, the Pacific railway.

The Cabinet existed for discussion rather than decisions, it seemed to Welles, who wrote that the President told the Cabinet he had held conversations with Usher about the necessity for Usher resigning because two in the Cabinet from Indiana were one too many. On the naming of McCulloch, wrote Welles, "So far as I know the President has not consulted the Cabinet." Welles serenely watched newspaper attacks, led by the *New York Herald*, aiming to get Welles out of the Cabinet. From a caller on Lincoln March 1 Welles learned that the President had said "great pressure had been made upon him to change" navy heads but that Welles "had his confidence." Two days later at Cabinet meeting, after saying that it was necessary to have only one Indiana man in the Cabinet, the President had remarked that "in regard to the other gentlemen of the Cabinet, he wished none of them to resign, at least for the present, for he contemplated no changes."

Across February and March Welles wrote in his diary of Chase stepping out of his judicial realm, spending an hour with the President on the evening of March 6 "urging upon him to exempt sundry counties in eastern Virginia from the insurrectionary proclamation," and going over old disputed points as to the legal status of the blockade. Welles noted, "He did not make his object explicit to the President, but most of the Cabinet came, I think, to the conclusion that there was an ulterior purpose not fully disclosed."

The President, along with his Attorney General and his War and Navy Secretaries, took no ease over what Chase had in mind. "I found the President and Attorney-General Speed," wrote Welles, February 21, "in consultation over an apprehended decision of Chief Justice Chase, whenever he could reach the question of the suspension of the writ of *habeas corpus*. Some intimation comes through Stanton, that His Honor the Chief Justice intends to make himself felt by the Administration when he can reach them. I shall not be surprised, for he is ambitious and able. Yet on that subject he is as much implicated as others." On the legal status of the blockade Speed asked the President some questions on March 7 when the President spoke of Chase having changed his mind, of Chase's original opinions having undergone a modification. Replying to Speed, the President said the matter "related to one of the early and most unpleasant differences we had ever had in the Cabinet."

Among oddest of rumors that had minor political and major social circles agog was one that Lincoln had offered James Gordon Bennett, publisher of the *New York Herald*, appointment as Minister to France. Though the rumor was "prevalent and generally believed," wrote Welles . . . "I discredit it." Monty Blair not only believed that the President had offered the French mission to Bennett, but Welles was surprised and sorry "to hear Blair speak approvingly of the appointment." And what was the fact? Blair's belief was nearer the fact than Welles's. Lincoln was keeping the promise he had made during the '64 campaign to an agent of Bennett, the agent writing to Bennett of Lincoln saying the matter was "shut pan," not to be mentioned, but the appointment would be made if he lived. This same agent of Bennett, W. O. Bartlett, Esq., New York, on January 23, 1865, had a telegram from Lincoln: "Please come and see me at once." And a biographer of Bennett was later to publish a note as having been written by Lincoln on February 20, 1865, to Bennett: "Dear Sir: I propose, at some convenient and not distant day, to nominate you to the United States Senate as Minister to France." Of such a proffer none of the Cabinet nor of Lincoln's secretaries had knowledge. It seemed, however, in keeping with a certain solidarity of interests for which Lincoln was striving. Thurlow Weed seemed to know who it was that had gone to Lincoln and arranged for his consent to naming a notorious journalistic profligate to represent the American people at a world capital. Weed wrote to John Bigelow: "I dare not tell all about the Bennett matter on paper. It was a curious complication for which two well-meaning friends were responsible. Seward knew nothing about it until the [November, 1864] election was over, when he sent for me. I was amazed at what had transpired." Thus the fox Weed. And the wolf Bennett? He sent word to Lincoln that he must respectfully decline to go to Paris as a spokesman for the American nation. So it seemed. And in the *New York Herald* its readers found no inkling of this news in the diplomatic field. The smooth and diabolical James Gordon Bennett was having more of his kind of fun.

Among some friends of Horace Greeley it was believed that he had during the fall campaign of '64 been promised the Postmaster-Generalship. It was also believed that the President would keep the promise and was merely awaiting the proper time to come through with an offer as genuine as the one made to Bennett—though it was considered far more certain that Greeley would accept, that he would really like to have the office once held by the earlier American figure to whom he had been likened, Benjamin Franklin.

At regular intervals the President had to say Yes or No about United States intervention in Mexico, where Napoleon III's puppet Emperor, Maximilian of Austria, was on a throne—and the Monroe Doctrine mocked at. Grant as the field commander of all the armies felt that he ought to know a little about how his country stood toward Mexico, but the questions he put to those who might be able to tell him brought him nothing. He wondered whether his country would do something about European interference in Mexico when there would be time to strike. "I often spoke of the matter to Mr. Lincoln and the Secretary of War," wrote Grant, "but never heard any special views from them to enable me to judge what they thought or felt about it." Seward wrote to Bigelow that the President's

United States Senate proposals to break off certain relations with Canada bring a *Punch* cartoon (February 18, 1865) with Lincoln saying: "Now, Uncle Sam [the eagle-faced biped], you're in a darned hurry to serve this here notice on John Bull. Now, it's my duty as your attorney, to tell you that you *may* drive him to go over to that cuss Davis"—one more of the needless, aimless, ineffectual drawings by Sir John Tenniel

foreign policy consisted of two propositions: "We shall attack nobody" and "We shall defend ourselves if assailed." Nor did the Secretary of State lack words about how any imaginable situation in foreign affairs would be met. He wrote to Bigelow, "All conjecture and collateral questions arising out of the war are left by us to the arbitrament of reason under the mutations of time." This came suitably from the only member of Lincoln's Cabinet having a gift for drollery.

In some British political and journalistic circles a war scare was on. Lincoln and Seward had their conferences over how to convey assurances to Britain that the United States was not preparing for violence overseas. The fighting prowess of the American nation under the Lincoln Administration had actually brought something like terror into the office of the *Times* of London. William H. ("Bull Run") Russell, an intimate of William F. A. Delane, publisher of the *Times*, wrote on March 8 to his good familiar John Bigelow: "I do not know what grounds Delane has for it, but he is quite sure Uncle Samuel is about to finish off the civil war by another war with us scarcely less horrible. . . . Someone has told him that Sherman declared he would not be satisfied till he pitched his tent in Hyde Park [London] and encamped his army there."

From possible foreign entanglements the President could turn to curious domestic involvements. He heard Seward, Speed, and Welles one day discuss the rights of courts or of Congress to go beyond public records and demand any papers whatsoever from any department of the Government. Seward pointed to the private, locked shelves of the President, saying, "They will demand those papers." "But those," said the President, according to Welles, "are private and confidential, a very different affair." "Call them what you please," said Seward, "you cannot retain them from Congress or the court if you concede the principle in this case [involving records of court-martial trials] . . . the Secretary of the Navy . . . must not furnish them copies nor must he testify." Without being convinced of Seward's points, the President was an attentive listener, and, wrote Welles, "I think his faith was somewhat shaken." The President said: "We will look into this matter fully and carefully. If the Secretary of State is right, we shall all of us be of his opinion, for this is a big thing, and this question must have been up and passed on before this day." He decided a legal opinion should come from the Attorney General with questions framed for him to answer. "The matter closed for the present," wrote Welles, "by the President instructing me not to give my evidence or copies till this question is decided." Seward during this conference had been not merely annoyed but angry. "He denied," wrote Welles, "that the public papers of any Department were to be subjected to private examination, and most emphatically denounced any idea of furnishing copies on the claim or demand of any State court or any court in a private suit. If it was conceded in a single instance, it must be in all."

An Indiana regiment on March 17 heard Lincoln speak of "the recent effort of 'our erring brethren,' sometimes so called, to employ the slaves in their armies." He had not written nor spoken on the subject "because that was their business, not mine." They were discussing whether the Negro, being put in the army, would fight for them. "They ought to know better than we. . . . I . . . having in my life heard many arguments . . . intended to show that the negro ought to be a slave—if he shall now really fight to keep himself a slave, it will be a far better argument why he should remain a slave than I have ever before heard. He, perhaps, ought to be a slave if he desires it ardently enough to fight for it. . . . I have always thought that all men should be free; but if any should be slaves, it should be first those who desire it for themselves, and secondly those who desire it for others." He did know the Negro could not fight and stay at home and make bread too. "And as one is about as important as the other to them, I don't care which they do." Referring to the Confederate Congress at Richmond, without naming it, he said they lacked one vote only for enrollment of Negro soldiers. "They have drawn upon their last branch of resources, and we can now see the bottom. I am glad to see the end so near at hand." Not a harsh nor a sour note ran through any part of the speech. For an immense audience he spoke as though he sat in a quiet corner and meditated alone—a way of speech not common in American politics then.

In a period of less than seven weeks Lincoln had guided the delicate legislative passage of the Thirteenth Amendment; had conducted the elaborate finesse of the Hampton Roads conference; had gone through the broils of the failure to secure recognition for Louisiana; had kept in touch with Grant and Sherman, naval affairs, the draft sending fresh replacements to the armies; had attended to a regular grist of courts-martial, arbitrary arrests, habeas corpus, pardons; had chosen two new Cabinet members, had written his second inaugural and taken oath for a second term; had passed on hundreds of applications for office—and on Tuesday, March 14, for the first time lay abed and held a Cabinet meeting, almost utterly worn, a man weary and haggard from emotional stress and overwork.

"The President was some indisposed . . . but not seriously ill," wrote Welles of this Cabinet meeting. While the President rested horizontal Seward brought up "a paper for excluding blockade-runners and persons in complicity with the Rebels from the country." The appointment of John P. Hale as Minister to Spain came up. Hale had been merciless and slashing in criticisms of the Navy Department. "Seward tried to gloss it over. Wanted Hale to call and see me," wrote Welles, "and make friends with Fox." Horizontal in bed the President, in a way, rested.

Eighteen days after reinauguration Brooks's news letter noted the President's health as "worn down by the constant pressure of office-seekers and legitimate business, so that for a few days he was obliged to deny himself to all comers." Since a new rule held to strictly, of closing the office doors at three o'clock in the afternoon, "receiving only those whom he prefers during the evening hours," the President was looking better.

Once after handling a grist of callers that included a Senator seeking to honor the Monroe Doctrine by a war with France, and a poor scrub-woman who wished merely the privilege of daily earning wages by shining the Treasury Building floors, Lincoln said to Brooks, "When I get through with such a day's work there is only one word that can express my condition, and that is—*flabbiness*." Again to Brooks he referred to "the tired spot which can't be got at."

Yet he had reserves of flesh and spirit, and once, speaking to Brooks of his own age and strength, he quoted an Old Testament passage: "His eye was not dim, nor his natural force abated." He would dwell on favorite Old Testament books, the simple style of Isaiah and the Psalms fixed in his memory, the wisdom of waiting for the developments of Providence, and the depth of meaning in that little sentence "The stars in their courses fought against Sisera."

Often to Brooks he said that the worst feature of the newspapers was that they were so sure to be "ahead of the hounds," outrunning events, and exciting expectations to be later dashed into disappointment. News of victory too often gave the public an impression the war was therefore to end soon. Nevertheless, noted Brooks, the patience of the American people the President thought something matchless and touching; he was never weary of commending it. "I have seen him shed tears when speaking of the cheerful sacrifice of the light and strength of so many happy homes throughout the land. His own patience was marvelous; and never crushed at defeat or unduly excited by success, his demeanor under both was an example for all men."

A profound believer in his own fixity of purpose, he took pride, according to Brooks, in saying that his long deliberations made it possible for him to stand by his own acts when they were once resolved upon. Acknowledging that he was slow in arriving at conclusions, he said he could not help that; but he believed that when he did arrive at conclusions they were clear and "stuck by." Brooks in looking back across four years felt this "slowness" of the President, so often criticized, was no weakness nor lack of decision. The trait was not vacillation but was rather a precious gift for sensing what *not* to do as well as what to do. The *Lexington* (Kentucky) *Observer and Reporter* quoted him: "I am a slow walker, but I never walk back."

For so long a time now in one crisis after another the President had seen the judgments of supposedly good minds, of some rated among "the best minds," so utterly wrong, so completely mistaken, so ready with advice that would have brought wreck and ruin beyond retrieving, that he had a deeper and surer feeling about his own reason and vision in the face of chaos. This feeling in some moods bordered on arrogance. Or if not arrogance a cold self-assurance, a refusal to say Yes to the proposals of even the so-called best minds until he had tested those proposals in the fire and the ice of his own mind and heart in long deliberations. Something of this phase of Lincoln moved him on the Sunday evening of January 15 of '65. Of that Sabbath Noah Brooks's news letter recorded that the President and his family had heard the chaplain of the House of Representatives preach in the hall of the House a sermon "with incidentally a glowing eulogium on the life and services of Edward Everett, no man present know‑ing that the distinguished orator was then no more in life."

Arriving at the White House after this sermon, Lincoln met the news that Everett was dead and ordered the Secretary of State to make public announcement of it to the people of the United States, and on the next day salutes to be fired and the department buildings, the Capitol, and the White House to be draped in mourning over the public loss of an American of world-wide distinction. All of this as a sincere gesture and mark of honor Lincoln saw as proper and fitting. His thought, however, ran that day to what in the long and lavishly praised career of Everett might be basic and enduring. To Brooks that evening he said, "Now, you are a loyal New Englander,—loyal to New England,—what great work of Everett's do you remember?" Brooks was forced to say he could not recall any. Lincoln persisted and wanted to know if Brooks couldn't recollect one great speech. And Brooks's later account proceeded:

Not receiving satisfaction, he said, looking around the room in his half-comical fashion, as if afraid of being overheard, "Now, do you know, I think Edward Everett was very much overrated. He hasn't left any enduring monument. But there was one speech in which, addressing a statue of John Adams and a picture of Washington, in Faneuil Hall, Boston, he apostrophized them and said, 'Teach us the love of liberty protected by law!' That was very fine, it seems to me. Still, it was only a good idea, introduced by noble language."

Continuing his discussion of Everett, he referred to his celebrated address on Washington, which was delivered through the South, as if in the hope that the rising storm of the rebellion might be quelled by this oratorical oil on the waters. Lincoln recalled a story told of Everett's manner. It was necessary, in his Washington oration, to relate an anecdote accompanied by the jingle of coin in the lecturer's pocket. This was done at each of the five hundred repetitions of the address, in the same manner, and with unvarying accuracy. When gold and silver disappeared from circulation, Mr. Everett procured and kept for this purpose a few coins with which, and a bunch of keys, the usual effect was produced. "And I am told," added Lincoln, "that whenever Mr. Everett delivered that lecture, he took along those things. They were what, I believe, the theatrical people would call his 'properties.'"

During the four years that the President had spoken so many confidences to Brooks, easing his mind freely to the young newspaper correspondent, their friendship had deepened. At no time in many delicate moments of tangled affairs had Brooks mistaken his place. So the quiet understanding was that probably next summer he was to be appointed private secretary to the President. He had the required gravity—and humor—with loyalty, affection, and sympathy, even though he had no special admiration for Nicolay and Hay, at one time early in the Administration writing a little paragraph for the *Sacramento Union* about the two secretaries being overly officious and self-important.

On the night after his re-election in November Lincoln had come into the White House parlor with a little roll of manuscript in his hand, saying to Brooks: "I know what you are thinking about. But there's no claptrap about me. And I am free to say that in the excitement of the moment I am sure to say something which I am sorry for when I see it in print. So I have it here in black and white, and there are no mistakes made. People attach too much importance to what I say anyhow." Of the mingled cheers, cries, noises, and applause of a crowd greeting his face and form, he had an almost morbid dread, noted Brooks. "A scene," he would call it. "The first sign of a cheer sobered him; he appeared sad and depressed, suspended conversation, looked out into vacancy, and when it was over resumed the conversation just where it was interrupted, with an obvious feeling of relief."

Again his eye and ear for plain duty, for the humble folk doing the best they knew how, was seen one January evening at the White House when five hundred members and guests of the United States Christian Commission met for fellowship and renewals of faith. To a banal and second-rate tune the singer Philip Phillips had sung "Your Mission" near the program opening. The verses took Lincoln. He sent a note to the chairman, "Near the close let us have 'Your Mission' repeated by Mr. Phillips. Don't say I called for it." Two of its six verses:

If you cannot, in the harvest,
   Gather up the richest sheaves,
Many a grain both ripe and golden,
   Oft the careless reaper leaves—
Go and glean among the briars
   Growing rank against the wall,
For it may be that their shadow
   Hides the heaviest wheat of all.

If you cannot in the conflict
   Prove yourself a soldier true,
If where fire and smoke are thickest,
   There's no work for you to do,
When the battlefield is silent,
   You can go with careful tread,
You can bear away the wounded,
   You can cover up the dead.

Brooks found it interesting that a member of the French Legation, an accomplished diplomat not so good with his English, having noticed and heard of Lincoln's poise, conscious strength, wit, and democratic instinct, should remark, "He seems to me one grand *gentilhomme* in disguise."

At the main door of the White House one morning an old woman pulled away at a doorbell just as the President happened to step out. What might she want? She answered, "Abraham the Second." This interested Lincoln. He asked who Abraham the First might be, if there was a second. The old woman: "Why, Lor' bless you! we read about the first Abraham in the Bible, and Abraham the Second is our President." Lincoln then told her that the President was not in his office at that time. "Then where is he?" was her query. The answer: "Here he is!" Nearly petrified with surprise, the old woman managed to tell her errand, was invited to come the next morning, when again she met kindness and care.

John M. Schofield, with his fair face and blond beard bronzed and tanned from service with Sherman's army, came in one January day to see Lincoln in their first meeting since a year before when the Senate was

Lincoln two days after his second inauguration

Photograph by a casual White House caller named Warren. Original in the Barrett collection.

The White House presidential carriage (barouche) with top folded down. Original carriage owned by the Studebaker Company, South Bend, Indiana. Two photographs of Lincoln (*upper left*) by Wenderoth & Taylor of Philadelphia, probably in '64. Photograph of Lincoln (*upper right*) by Brady, probably in late '63.

wrangling over the President naming him a major general. Lincoln's greeting: "Well, Schofield, I haven't heard anything against you for a year."

Often when someone would mention or begin quoting an unkind speech or remark to Lincoln, he would, according to Brooks, turn the talk and steer the indignation by a "judicious" story or by saying, "I guess we won't talk about that now." Of one virulent attack on his official conduct he mildly said that it was "ill-timed." Of one bitter political enemy: "I've been told that insanity is hereditary in his family, and I think we will admit the plea in his case." When reading some humorist like Artemus Ward to others he would at times "preserve his own gravity, though his auditors might be convulsed." To Brooks he quoted Sydney Smith in reference to one Cabinet member: "It required a surgical operation to get a joke into his head." Once he mentioned an old friend on the West Coast who wrote him letters —he used to read them; now he read no more of those letters; he had quit on an epistle that ran into seventy pages. His letter files, desk pigeonholes, accumulated copies, piled high now and Brooks asked why he didn't have a letter book and copying press. The reply: "A letter-book might be easily carried off, but that stack of filed letters would be a back-load." With unction and enjoyment he would recite from James Russell Lowell's "Hosea Bigelow," finding originality and impudence in the stanza:

> Ef you take a sword an' dror it,
>   An' go stick a feller thru,
> Gov'ment aint to answer for it,
>   God'll send the bill to you.

In a lecture in the hall of the House of Representatives Miss Anna Dickinson, in a mood more mellowed now toward the President, alluded to the sudden sunburst out of clouds as Lincoln stepped forward to take his oath of office. Miss Dickinson interpreted it as a happy omen. "The President," wrote Brooks, "sat directly in front of the speaker, and from the reporters' gallery, behind her, I had caught his eye, soon after he sat down. When Miss Dickinson referred to the sunbeam, he looked up to me, involuntarily, and I thought his eyes were suffused with moisture. Perhaps they were, but the next day he said, 'I wonder if Miss Dickinson saw me wink at you?'"

Saying good-by to Colonel James Grant Wilson, leaving for New Orleans, Lincoln gave him an autographed recent Brady photograph of himself, saying, "Now, my dear Colonel, perhaps you will value this after I am gone." Though Wilson saw a face careworn and haggard, it was a strong hand he felt encircling his. "Good-bye, Colonel, and a safe journey to New Orleans. *Au revoir!*" then with a laugh: "I hope my French pronunciation is correct. If not, how is this for German?—*Auf Wiedersehen!*" In his diary of March 15, 1865, Wilson wrote:

"Enjoyed a delightful afternoon drive with Mrs. S. A. Douglas. In the evening, at Grover's Theatre with the President, Mrs. Lincoln and Miss Harris, listening to the opera of 'The Magic Flute' and occupying a comfortable box. The President, alluding to the large feet of one of the leading female singers, which were also very flat, remarked, 'The beetles wouldn't have much of a chance there!' When asked by Mrs. Lincoln to go before the last act of the opera was concluded, he said: 'Oh, no, I want to see it out. It's best when you undertake a job, to finish it.' Among several 'good things,' the President told of a Southern Illinois preacher who, in the course of his sermon, asserted that the Saviour was the only perfect man who had ever appeared in this world; also, that there was no record in the Bible, or elsewhere, of any perfect woman having lived on the earth. Whereupon there arose in the rear of the church a persecuted-looking personage who, the parson having stopped speaking, said, '*I* know a perfect woman, and for the last six years.' 'Who was she?' asked the minister. 'My husband's first wife,' replied the afflicted female."

Some such anecdote was as near as Lincoln would go in reference to marriage as a comedy. That the White House couple were an oddly mated pair seemed to be generally assumed. When in January Mrs. Lincoln dismissed a doorkeeper who had held the post since the Jackson Administration, it was chronicled briefly in the newspapers. With more Union victories in sight and with her husband elected to four more years in the White House, there was less of malicious rumor published about her—though gossip still ran on, some of it not idle nor ill-meant. Smith Stimmel of the troop guard at the White House often saw the White House couple out the front door and into their carriage, never hearing their talk as anything but agreeable. Once he saw the President as completely accommodating to his wife, who was saying, "I will not drive past Seward's house. Let us take some other route." The President calmly ordered the coachman to drive along another street. When Mary Livermore invited the President to the Chicago Sanitary Fair and its immense crowds, he laughed. "What do you suppose my wife will say, at ten thousand ladies coming after me in that style?" Mrs. Livermore assured him that Mrs. Lincoln was included in the invitation. He hoped the war would shape up so that he could go to Chicago and perhaps Springfield again.

On the evening of the traditional national inaugural ball, March 6, the President with Speaker Colfax entered the long marble hall of the Patent Office. The leading lady of the grand march that ended at a dais arranged with blue and gold chairs of course was Mrs. Lincoln.

And could they believe their eyes? On whose arm was she leaning? They looked again to make sure. Yes, her escort was Senator Charles Sumner. Was not this the man who single-handed only a few days before had by a threatened filibuster wrecked the President's favorite reconstruction measure? Yes. And how had this come about? For such an affront the usual procedure for the President was to ignore his opponent and critic. What could it mean? It meant at least that they were on speaking terms, that cordial relations still held, that the President and his parliamentary foe were divided on principles but had not parted as personal friends. The gossip and the press items furnished no clues as to what had happened. It was not generally known that Mrs. Lincoln had a warm personal regard for Sumner. She sent him little notes, flowers from the White House Conservatory, kindly attentions. She seemed to admire him in about the degree she hated Seward. And what could Sumner do when to his surprise the President sent word asking

Executive Mansion
Washington, March 5/65
Hon. C. Sumner.
   My dear Sir
              I should be pleased
for you to accompany us to-mor-
row evening at ten o'clock, on
a visit of an half hour to the
Inaugeral ball; I inclose a
ticket. Our carriage will call
for you at half past nine —
                    Yours truly,
                        A. Lincoln

The President writes an irresistible invitation for a Senator to come to the inaugural ball. Original in the Barrett collection.

him to accompany Mrs. Lincoln to the inaugural ball in the President's own carriage? "You may imagine," said Sumner to a friend, "the kind of wonder which was excited when, with Mrs. Lincoln on my arm, I made my way through the throng and placed her in her selected seat."

A woman writer for the *New York Times* at this ball noted: "Mr. Lincoln was evidently trying to throw off care for the time; but with rather ill success, and looked very old; yet he seemed pleased and gratified, as he was greeted by the people. He wore a plain black suit and white gloves." Mrs. Lincoln's dress was of white satin covered by a tunic of point appliqué, with low corsage, a shawl of rich lace, "jewels of the rarest pearls, necklace, ear-rings, brooch and bracelets." Her hair, put back plainly from her face, was ornamented with trailing jessamine and clustering violets. "She looked exceedingly well with her soft white complexion, and her toilet was faultless. Her manners are very easy and affable. Mr. Robert Lincoln, a fine-looking young man, wearing the uniform of a Captain in the regular army, was also present." The bill of fare for the evening supper:

Oyster stews, terrapin stews, oysters pickled; beef—roast beef, filet de bœuf, beef à la mode, beef à l'anglais; veal—leg of veal, fricandeau, veal Malakoff; poultry—roast turkey, boned turkey, roast chicken; grouse—boned and roast; game—pheasant, quail, venison patés, paté of duck en gelée, paté de foie gras; smoked ham, tongue en gelée, tongue plain; salads, chicken, lobster; ornamental pyramids—nougat, orange, caramel with fancy cream candy, cocoanut, macaroon, croquant, chocolate; tree cakes—cakes and tarts, almond sponge, belle alliance, dame blanche, macaroon tart, tarte à la Nelson, tarte à l'Orleans, tarte à la Portugaise, tarte à la Vienne, pound cake, sponge cake, lady cake, fancy small cakes; jellies and creams—calf's foot and wine jelly, Charlotte à la Russe, Charlotte à la vanille, blanc mange, crème Néapolitaine, crème à la Nelson, crème Chateaubriand, crème à la Smyrna, crème à la Nesselrode, bombe à la vanille, ice cream, vanilla, lemon, white coffee, chocolate, burnt almond, maraschino; fruit ices, strawberry, orange, lemon; desert—grapes, almonds, raisins, &c., coffee and chocolate

Only three hundred at a time could be accommodated at the feast table. But there were five thousand guests. So there was disorder, "a crush," many like "one gentleman with a large plate of smoked tongue, requiring both hands to hold it, no place to sit down, and no way to eat it." In the men's hat room, however, not a hat was lost. The President left at midnight. The dancers in the East Room "threaded the mazes" till daybreak. Homeward in hacks, carriages and barouches went ladies, some of them to pillows of sleep whereon lay their heads of hair "frizzed, puffed, curled, powdered with diamond and gold dust."

Tenderly Mrs. Lincoln directed what was to be done one afternoon when a young woman arrived in the East Room with three children, one of them almost a baby. The President was in a Cabinet session and could not meet the visitor with three children. So she was told. Then the strange woman began talking about what she must do because there was nothing else to do. Placing her children on the floor of the East Room, she said she meant to leave them for the President. Her husband had been killed in the war, and what was she now to do with her children? The President was the head of the war. So why shouldn't he have her children? "The woman," noted the editor of the *Baltimore American*, on that day visiting the White House to interview the President, "was deranged by affliction. Mrs. Lincoln gave proper directions."

Indications were that Mrs. Lincoln chiefly shaped the military status of young Robert. The eldest son had been "very anxious to quit school and enter the army," according to the White House seamstress Elizabeth Keckley. "We have lost one son, and his loss is as much as I can bear," was the mother's argument. "His services are not required in the field, and the sacrifice would be a needless one." This was her feeling, as Mrs. Keckley noted it, about the father's urging, "But many a poor mother has given up all her sons, and our son is not more dear to us than the sons of other people are to their mothers."

These identical views were also heard in the White House by Mrs. Lincoln's sister, Emilie Todd Helm, widow of the Confederate general Ben Hardin Helm. In her diary in November of '63 Mrs. Helm wrote: "She [Mrs. Lincoln] is frightened about Robert going into the army. She said today to Brother Lincoln (I was reading in another part of the room but could not help overhearing the conversation): 'Of course, Mr. Lincoln, I know that Robert's plea to go into the army is manly and noble and I want him to go, but oh! I am so frightened he may never come back to us!' " From the father came the plea, as Mrs. Helm heard it, "Many a poor mother, Mary, has had to make this sacrifice and has given up every son she had and lost them all."

Not so easy was it for the widow of a Confederate general to live in the White House. She recorded a call from General Sickles and Senator Harris at the White House. Rather needless remarks from them about recent Northern victories brought a reply from her that angered them, and according to Mrs. Helm's diary: "Senator Harris turned to Mrs. Lincoln abruptly and said: 'Why isn't Robert in the army? He is old enough and strong enough to serve his country. He should have gone to the front some time ago.' Sister Mary's face turned white as death and I saw that she was making a desperate effort at self-control. She bit her lip, but answered quietly, 'Robert is making his preparations now to enter the Army, Senator Harris; he is not a shirker as you seem to imply for he has been anxious to go for a long time. If fault there be, it is mine, I have insisted that he should stay in college a little longer as I think an educated man can serve his country with more intelligent purpose than an ignoramus.' "

The mother had her wish. Her boy stayed on at Harvard and graduated, while the father of the boy enforced a draft law that he himself considered unjust because it failed of requiring universal service with no reservations, bounty money, or evasions. Had Lincoln been able to get passage through Congress of the enrollment law that he and Stanton and Schenck had sought, there would have been no basis for the saying "Lincoln keeps his own son out of the army while calling for new drafts of the sons of others." It was probably by agreement with Mrs. Lincoln, with her specific consent, that Lincoln on January 19, 1865, sent Grant a letter reading:

"Please read and answer this letter as though I was not President, but only a friend. My son, now in his twenty-second year, having graduated at Harvard, wishes to see something of the war before it ends. I do not wish to put him in the ranks, nor yet to give him a commission, to which those who have already served long are better entitled and better qualified to hold. Could he, without embarrassment to you or detriment to the service, go into your military family with some nominal rank, I, and not the public, furnishing his necessary means? If no, say so without the least hesitation, because I am as anxious and as deeply interested that you shall not be encumbered as you can be yourself."

Grant replied that he would be glad to have the son "in my military family in the manner you propose." What then followed in this delicate arrangement was reported by Grant's staff member Colonel Horace Porter: "The President replied that he would consent to this upon one condition: that his son should serve as a volunteer aide without pay or emoluments; but Grant dissuaded him from adhering to that determination, saying that it was due to the young man that he should be regularly commissioned, and put on an equal footing with other officers of the same grade. So it was finally settled that Robert should receive the rank of captain and assistant adjutant-general; and on February 23 he was attached to the staff of the general-in-chief. The new acquisition to the company at headquarters soon became exceedingly popular. He had inherited many of the genial traits of his father, and entered heartily into all the social pastimes at headquarters. He was always ready to perform his share of hard work, and never expected to be treated differently from any other officer on account of his being the son of the Chief Executive of the nation."

The fabricated stories of preceding years alleging that Robert had gathered a fortune in war contracts, alleging that the President had his salary paid in gold while others got greenbacks—the air seemed to have been cleared of these. Press reports of February gave the President's income-tax payment for the year at $1,279.13. Of curiosity around the query "How much is Mr. Lincoln worth in money?" there seemed to be little. The leading newspapers seemed to assume that his assets were few and not worth itemizing. His salary of $25,000 a year was the largest steady income he had ever had in his life. It was paid each month in Treasury Department warrants, with the income tax deducted. These payments Lincoln had invested in more than $75,000 worth of United States securities, of which more than $50,000 were "registered bonds bearing 6 per cent interest, payable in coin." He had come to Washington worth about $25,000 in real estate, farm lands, and collectible bills, loans to friends. One loan in November of '64 was $260 to "Mr. M. B. Church" of Springfield, Illinois, a piece of paper later to be marked as "worthless." In publishing a sketch of the Lincoln home in Springfield, *Leslie's Weekly* in December of '64 noted it as "indicative of the well-to-do country lawyer or retired farmer." Of the parlor pictured *Leslie's* said: "Such is the room to which, after his eight years sojourn in the White House, the President of the United States will retire to reflect on the most terrific epoch of his life."

The minor incident of O'Leary, a new doorman at Lincoln's office, came and was soon over. Hundreds of times now the President had turned Confederate soldiers out of their prisons by a signed and dated paper reading: "Let this man (or these men) take the oath of December 8, 1863, and be discharged." O'Leary noticed that the President asked few questions and was more than willing in nearly every case to issue such discharges. To friends and relatives who came seeking the release of prisoners O'Leary would give the whispered word that he could fix it for them, that instead of taking chances of having the President refuse them they should leave the matter with him—for a $10 bill he would smoothly and in a short time have their man out of military prison. And O'Leary won an undercover reputation and built up a thriving little business of selling these precious pieces of paper signed by the President. The bitterly anti-Lincoln Tennessee Congressman Emerson Etheridge handed some good money to O'Leary, got from O'Leary the discharges thus paid for, and then rushed into the *Washington Constitutional Union*, newspaper, with a loud swaggering exposure of this peculation and corruption right at the doorway of the President's office. "Etheridge preferred bribing a servant to accomplish what any man could do in the regular way," wrote Noah Brooks, "and then rushed his shame and disgrace into print, as if he had done a very fine thing. O'Leary was, of course, instantly dismissed from service when the President ascertained what had been done."

Representative Alexander H. Rice found Lincoln alone, weary, familiar with the case but not interested in action about Captain Henry S. Burrage of the 36th Massachusetts Volunteers. Captured and sent to Libby Prison, Burrage had been dismissed from the army service while in the hands of the enemy. General Meade had ordered no more exchanging of newspapers with the enemy, and Burrage's disobedience of this order brought his removal, the order being approved by the President. Friends of Burrage set forth that he was in hospital recovering from wounds when the order was issued and heard nothing of such an order. Lincoln told Representative Rice he could not attend to individual cases of this kind, though not doubting there were "a great many cases of peculiar hardship" in the Army of the Potomac, adding, "It is all I can do to hear cases in classes, and those belonging to each class must abide by the decision made for that class." Rice said he appreciated this view but believed the case of Burrage so peculiar it must stand alone.

Rice saw Lincoln lean back in his chair, cross his knees, and then: "Mr. Rice, go on." Rice went on in a plea for the exchange of his disgraced friend in prison at Richmond. "I ask, Mr. President, is it right to leave him there? Is this a fitting reward for more than two years of faithful service?"

"I wish," said the President, "you would go over to the War Department and state this case to General Hitchcock just as you have stated it to me, and say to him that if he can effect the exchange of this officer I desire that it shall be done."

Rice suggested that the Confederates might refuse to exchange a Union Army officer dismissed from the service. If General Hitchcock raised that point, replied the President, "Say to him that if he can take care of the exchange, I think I can take care of the rank."

Soon at the War Department Rice heard General Hitchcock saying, "If the President will restore this officer to his rank, I can effect his exchange." Rice asked Hitchcock to say this in a written note to the President. With such a note Rice returned to the White House, gave the note to John Hay, who read the name of Burrage and said: "I knew him in college. I will take this to the President at once." Shortly it was that Hay came to Rice saying the President had revoked the order of removal and restored Burrage to his rank, the War Department so announcing on February 7, 1865.

And there was the case of the Smith brothers of Boston, Benjamin G. and Franklin W. For almost a year now, in and out of the bureau offices, into the Senate and House anterooms, over into the Executive Mansion, up to Boston and back again over the same tortuous path, went the case of the more or less honest, the not entirely blameless, Smith brothers.

Late on the afternoon of March 17 Lincoln was about getting into his carriage for a drive when Sumner arrived with papers in the Smith case, his own written Opinion, and a demand for instant action. The Senator might come back the next day, suggested Lincoln. Sumner, in a finality of insistence that few dignitaries in Washington could equal, said the President "ought not to sleep on the case," urging that if Abraham Lincoln had suffered unjust imprisonment as a criminal, with degradation before his neighbors, an immense bill of expense, a trial by court-martial, and an unjust condemnation, he would cry out against the postponement of justice for a single day.

The President was impressed. This was no small-potato affair. He would go over the case, hear Sumner read his written Opinion, at eleven o'clock that evening. Eleven o'clock came and with it a thunderstorm and a wind that shook the chimneys. Sumner was on hand. The President stretched himself in a big chair. Sumner read his Opinion. The President listened, commented, spoke with sympathy. At twenty minutes past midnight the President said he would write his conclusion at once, and that Mr. Sumner must come and hear it the next morning, "when I open shop."

"And when do you open shop?"

"At nine o'clock."

And at that morning hour Sumner was again on hand, and the President came in almost on the run and read for Sumner what he had written. It was impressive. Sumner was delighted. He began writing an abstract of it to send on to the anxious Smith brothers. The President broke into a quotation from Petroleum V. Nasby. Sumner didn't get it. Lincoln: "I see I must initiate you," and he quoted for Sumner the message he had sent to Nasby: "For the genius to write these things I would gladly give up my office." From a near desk Lincoln brought out a pamphlet collection of Nasby papers and with enjoyment read aloud for the Massachusetts Senator and himself. "People is queer. Humanity, pertiklerly American humanity, vewd from a Dimekratik standpint, is a inscrootable mystery." And so on. "I ain't the rose uv Sharon, nor the lily uv the valley—I'm the last uv the Kopperheds! I bilt my polittikle howse on sand—it hez fell, and I'm under the rooins. Uv pollytix I wash my hands, I shake its dust orf my few remainin garmence." This reading went on for twenty minutes. It was morning. Out-

Workingmen (in war-supply industries in a Washington shop of the type often visited by Lincoln)

From the Meserve collection

James Speed, Attorney General   Hugh McCulloch, Secretary of the Treasury

James Harlan, Secretary of the Interior   John Palmer Usher, Secretary of the Interior

THE LATER CABINET MEMBERS

From the Meserve collection

side waited dignitaries. Sumner picked a moment of pause, said he must be going, thanked Lincoln for the morning lesson, opened the door to see some thirty or more persons, including Senators and Representatives, waiting to transact public business. Later that day of March 18 the President returned to Secretary Welles a Navy Department paper in the Smith brothers' case. On this paper the President had written out the points which he chose to stress, the points so highly welcome to Sumner. They read:

"I am unwilling for the sentence to stand, and be executed, to any extent in this case. In the absence of a more adequate motive than the evidence discloses, I am wholly unable to believe in the existence of criminal or fraudulent intent on the part of men of such well established good character. If the evidence went as far to establish a guilty profit or one or two hundred thousand dollars, as it does of one or two hundred dollars, the case would, on the question of guilt, bear a far different aspect. That on this contract, involving some twelve hundred thousand dollars, the contractors would plan, and attempt to execute a fraud, which, at the most, could profit them only one or two hundred, or even one thousand dollars, is to my mind beyond the power of rational belief. That they did not, in such a case, make far greater gains, proves that they did not, with guilty or fraudulent intent, make at all. The judgment and sentence are disapproved, and declared null, and the defendants are fully discharged."

Welles was sore about it. He wrote in his diary, "It is, I regret to say, a discreditable indorsement, and would, if made public, be likely to injure the President. He has, I know, been much importuned in this matter, as I have, and very skillful and persistent efforts have been pursued for months to procure this result. Senators and Representatives have interposed their influence to defeat the ends of justice, and shielded guilty men from punishment, and they have accomplished it. They have made the President the partisan of persons convicted and pronounced guilty of fraud upon the government. Of course, rascality will flourish. I regret all this on the President's account, as well as that of the ends of justice."

At the Cabinet meeting in Lincoln's bedroom four days earlier Welles had mentioned the case of the Smith brothers to the President, who had then promised, on Welles's requesting it, that he would hold a conference with him about it. The President had handed the Navy Department paper in the case to Sumner, he explained to Welles, and would see Welles about the case when Sumner returned the document. "Having got excited," noted Welles, "the President may have forgotten my request and his promise."

Two days later, however, Welles brought new phases of the Smith brothers' case before the President. Shoddy and inferior articles and materials, not up to contract specifications, had been passed by Navy Department employees in complicity with Ben Smith. What of them? "The President said if they had been remiss, Smith's pardon ought not to cover them." And on Welles citing other cases of contractors found guilty of fraud, who had confessed and made restitution, "The President was annoyed. . . . After some little talk, he wished me to get our solicitor to look into these cases, and call again. He has evidently acted without due consideration, on the suggestion and advice of Sumner, who is emotional, and under the pressure of Massachusetts politicians, who have been active to screen these parties regardless of their guilt."

Welles read in the *Boston Journal* a review of the case by Sumner, terming it "not a creditable document for Mr. Sumner in any aspect." Welles wrote of John Murray Forbes, a Boston businessman with a reputation for rather extraordinary integrity, saying to Sumner and two associates who spoke in high glee over the executive pardon they had won for the Smith brothers, that he, Forbes, believed it an executive error, and a greater error for Massachusetts Representatives to stop legal proceedings through their political influence. "Sumner spoke of the smallness of the amount involved. Forbes replied that if one of his servants was detected, and convicted of having stolen a silver spoon, though only a teaspoon, he would kick him out of the house and not trust him farther. Nor would he be persuaded to excuse and take the thief into favor because he had been trusted with all his silver and only stolen, or been detected in having stolen, one small spoon."

On Sumner's usual Saturday afternoon call on Welles March 25 he read to Welles from Boston newspapers high praise for his course in behalf of men "greatly, deeply wronged." Welles swept Sumner down from this high moral atmosphere with a series of questions about the facts and what of them. "I asked him what he had to say of the transaction of the Smiths in regard to anchors, an article in which they did not deal, but for which they had by some means and for some purpose got the contract; had them by collusion paid for in May; they were arrested on the 17th of June, when the articles, though paid for, were not all delivered. They had underlet the contract to Burns, who made the deliveries, and the anchors were many of them worthless, would not pass inspection; and the arrest before full and final delivery was plead as the excuse, although requisition had been issued in May. What of the files, machine-cut, instead of hand-cut as contracted? What of the combination with Henshaw not to bid, whereby they got a contract for a number of hundred tons of iron at $62.50, when other parties sold at the same time for $53? Sumner had not looked into these matters. He could not answer me. I showed him the correspondence of the Smiths with the Trenton Iron Company, expressly stipulating for inferior iron to be delivered to the navy yard, if it would pass inspection. After reading, he said he did not like the transaction. Evidently knew not the case in which he had interfered."

One angle of the case not covered in these points by Welles, and not touched by Lincoln in his endorsement and pardon, was that of naval operations and ship navigation as affected by shoddy materials. This phase of the affair burned deep in the Assistant Secretary of the Navy Gustavus Vasa Fox. One might overlook stealing, Fox held, but inferior tin, anchors unfit to weigh down a vessel, files machine-cut instead of hand-cut, these it was unjust to put on the men expected to move and fight on the sea.

Lincoln's motives in pardoning the Smiths? They were mixed. The amounts proved to be stolen were, as he noted, small as compared with the totals involved. There was a sniff of man-hunting about the affair. The detective Olcott, procurer of much of the evidence, was not fully trusted by Welles. In other matters Welles noted Olcott as overzealous, rash, reckless, wild, "in a certain sense I think honest." Olcott the man-hunter was out to get his man. Sumner was out to beat Olcott and the navy court-martial that had convicted and sentenced the Smiths. Welles was correct that Sumner had won the pardons from the President and that stiff political pressure in Massachusetts was moving Sumner. With Sumner out of the picture the President would probably not have been so sweeping and unique in his statement of the case. It was one of the instances Sumner's secretary had in mind in saying that in the weeks following inauguration "Mr. Lincoln bestowed more tokens of good-will on Sumner than on any [other] senator." By accommodating himself to the wishes of the one Senator cloaked in a peculiar fame for the moment, Lincoln had little or nothing to lose—and meantime he was holding together a variety of forces that he hoped to use, as he wrote, "to the effect of molding society for durability in the Union." Lincoln more than anyone else concerned had searched himself and knew where his feet were leading him every moment in the case of the more or less honest, the not quite blameless, the rather oily and possibly hypocritical Smith brothers.

Writing a card for Mrs. Harriet C. Bledsoe, January 16, 1865, "to pass our lines with ordinary baggage and go south," Lincoln knew he was doing this favor for the wife of the Assistant Secretary of War in Richmond. To Bishop Charles P. McIlvaine, who had requested the pass, Lincoln said, "Do not tell Stanton I gave it." It might have amused Lincoln had he heard that later Mrs. Bledsoe got from Jefferson Davis his autograph on the same card, this being one of the few documents on which those two signatures stood next to each other.

One such other document was brought to Lincoln by the Reverend Thomas C. Teasdale, D.D. He and Lincoln needed no introduction. Lincoln recognized and greeted him as a former Baptist minister in Springfield, Illinois. Now Teasdale was seeking to raise funds for the Orphans' Home of the State of Mississippi, devoted chiefly to the care of children whose fathers had been killed by Union soldiers. Lincoln smiled. "You ask me to give you relief in a case of distress, just such as we have been striving to produce." To this Lincoln added, according to Dr. Teasdale, "We want to bring you rebels into such straits that you will be willing to give up this wicked rebellion." Jefferson Davis had written on the petition of the Orphans' Home board his endorsement of it as a "praiseworthy effort." To this Lincoln added his written instruction to the Union military commander in the area where Dr. Teasdale was to operate. Dated March 18, 1865, it read: "Gen. Canby is authorized, but not ordered, to give Rev. Mr. Teasdale such facilities in the within matters, as he, in his discretion, may see fit."

Next Dr. Teasdale told the President he was traveling without a pass. Lincoln began writing a pass. Mr. Teasdale suggested he should like to take some baggage. Mr. Lincoln, pleasantly: "Now you bother me again. How much baggage would you like to take with you?" "Well, Mr. President, a good deal, sir. You folks have made some things rather scarce with us down South." "Oh, well," went on the Writer of Passes, "I will write this pass so as to suit you, I reckon." And it read: "Pass the Rev. Thomas Teasdale through our lines going South, with convenient baggage."

To General Ord, commanding a corps with Grant, went a telegram to watch about a man passing with a false name of Stanley, under arrest as a deserter. "He is," wrote Lincoln, "the son of so close a friend of mine that I must not let him be executed."

In mid-March came Senator John B. Henderson of Missouri with two lists of men and boys held in military prisons in his State or near by. All sorts of appeals had been coming to the Senator, and before leaving for home he wanted to clear up as many of these cases as he could. He laid before Lincoln first a list of those he considered fairly innocent. Lincoln looked it over. "Do you mean to tell me, Henderson, that you wish me to let loose all these people at once?" Henderson said Yes; the war was nearly

At the top of a long petition reciting cases of military prisoners the President writes an order for their discharge. Original in the Barrett collection.

over; the time had come to try generosity and kindness. "Do you really think so?" asked Lincoln. Henderson was sure he thought so; he was trying to slow down the guerrilla warfare of his torn and weary State. "I hope you are right," said Lincoln, "but I have no time to examine this evidence. If I sign this list as a whole, will you be responsible for the future good behavior of the men?" Henderson would. "Then I will take the risk and sign it," said Lincoln as he began writing the word "Pardoned" after each name of some man convicted by a military commission, finally writing a general order of release.

Henderson thanked the President. Then Henderson pulled out his second list. These were names of men maybe not so very innocent but maybe safe to take a chance on. "I hope," said Lincoln, according to Henderson's account, "you are not going to make me let loose another lot." Yes, Henderson thought it good policy, safer and better than holding them in jails. "Yes,"

> Executive Mansion
> Washington Feb. 24 1865
>
> To-day Hiram Hibbard calls
> voluntarily under apprehension
> of being punished as a deserter
> Now on condition that
> he faithfully serves out
> his term (as A, in 50th N
> Y. Engineers, he is fully
> pardoned for any supposed
> desertion
>
> A. Lincoln

The President fixes out Hiram Hibbard so he can go back to his company with a clean bill and a wide grin. Original in the Barrett collection.

said Lincoln, "but you know I am charged with making too many mistakes on the side of mercy." Henderson was sure he was right and said the President ought to sign out the whole batch.

"Well, I'll be durned if I don't," said the President, this being, noted Henderson, "the only time I ever heard Mr. Lincoln use a word which approached profanity." As he handed the list back, Lincoln said: "Now, Henderson, remember you are responsible to me for those men. If they do not behave, I shall have to put you in prison for their sins."

Early one evening Senator Hendricks came with an Indiana lawyer to ask stay of death sentence on conspirators found guilty by a military commission. Hendricks had believed it useless to go to the White House on such an errand. But they found Lincoln "cheerful and reminiscent." He kept his callers till almost eleven o'clock. He indicated certain errors in the papers of the case which would take time for official correction. Then to the Indiana lawyer: "You may go home and I'll send for you when the papers get back. But I apprehend and hope there will be such a jubilee over yonder"—putting a finger out of a near-by window toward the dark hills of Virginia just across the river—"we shall none of us want any more killing done."

Solidarity was wanted. For the Jewish chiropodist Zacharie, Stanton must arrange a pass to Savannah and let Zacharie bring back his father and sisters, if he so wished. Blumenberg, a Baltimore Jew, Lincoln wrote Stanton in the same letter, should have a hearing. Blumenberg had "raised troops—fought, and been wounded—He should not be dismissed in a way that disgraces and ruins him without a hearing." At Bardstown, Kentucky, ran a telegraphed order, "Let no depredation be committed upon the property or possessions of the Sisters of Charity of Nazareth Academy." And two orders addressed "To whom it may concern" specified that Sisters of Mercy in charge of military hospitals in Chicago or Washington should be furnished such provisions as they desired to purchase, "and charge same to the War Department."

The man-hunter approach as often as possible was to be avoided. Some such point of view seemed more and more to animate Lincoln in the latest war flares and shadows. Against Stanton's express wishes, and knowing well that Stanton would be furious should he hear of it, Lincoln took his own whimsical course with one of the three secession leaders who had commenced the war by starting the first shot and shell that in '61 battered Fort Sumter into fine fragments. This secessionist, a brigadier general, now was one of twelve Confederate prisoners in one vaulted chamber in Fort Lafayette; they slept on straw mats on the floor; the brigadier fried his own slender daily ration of meat on a grate; the brigadier daily took a bucket and went down into a cellar and brought up coal. His wife in Richmond had been selling her silk gowns, opera cloak, point-lace handkerchiefs. His wife had interested Washington McLean of the *Cincinnati Enquirer* to see Stanton about an exchange for her husband, General Roger A. Pryor. McLean in Washington in the old days had formed a friendship with Pryor. He found Stanton at home, holding a curly-headed daughter on his knee as McLean talked, Stanton at the mention of the name of Pryor pushing the child from his knee and thundering: "He shall be hanged! Damn him!"

McLean with a letter from Horace Greeley went to Lincoln, who listened, who recalled that even though Roger Pryor had been foremost of the fire-eaters who fomented the secession, Pryor also had a record for uniformly generous treatment of Union prisoners who had been in his custody. Lincoln issued an order on the Fort Lafayette commandant to "deliver

Roger A. Pryor into the custody of Colonel John W. Forney, Secretary of the Senate, to be produced by him whenever required." So McLean went to Fort Lafayette, took Pryor to Washington, put him in the home of Forney, who also in the old days had enjoyed the fiery and vivacious Pryor. Stanton, it was reported, got wind of where Pryor was and issued orders that he was to be arrested on sight, with the hope of hanging him. Forney managed to quiet Stanton's hunt for Pryor by having his secretary, John Russell Young, go to the newspaper offices and get an item published that Pryor had passed through Washington and under parole entered the Confederate Army lines. Grim Thad Stevens, however, knew where Pryor was, and every day for a short while asked his fellow Pennsylvanian: "How is your Democratic friend General Pryor? I hope you are both well."

One day with a queer gleam of eye the stern and uncompromising Stevens heard from Forney a request that Stevens sign an appeal to the President to pardon another fire-eating secessionist. Stevens amazed Forney by saying that he would sign any proposition for pardon that Forney might write. Forney then wrote an appeal painting the ex-fire-eater as a sort of hero. Stevens put his name to it without the slightest quiver. Later when Forney tried to tease Stevens about being inconsistent, Stevens said: "Oh, you need not be riled about it. I saw you were going heavily into the pardon business, and I thought I would take a hand in it myself." Forney in his frequent visits at the White House giving Lincoln the news and trading stories undoubtedly passed along to Lincoln these anecdotes and enjoyed seeing Lincoln's face light up about "going heavily into the pardon business."

"I am in a little perplexity," wrote Lincoln to Grant February 24. "I was induced to authorize a gentleman to bring Roger A. Pryor here with a view of effecting an exchange of him; but since then I have seen a despatch of yours showing that you specially object to his exchange. Meantime he has reached here and reported to me. It is an ungracious thing for me to send him back to prison, and yet inadmissible for him to remain here long. Cannot you help me out with it?"

Did Grant have a quiet chuckle over this confessed "little perplexity"? Over the possible humor of whether it would be "an ungracious thing" to send back to prison one of the three men who took the responsibility of firing the first shots of the war? Over the watchers like Stanton who made it "inadmissible" for a Confederate brigadier general to be the constant and jolly house guest of the Secretary of the Senate in Washington?

The next day Lincoln wrote: "Allow the bearer, Roger A. Pryor, to pass to General Grant, and report to him for exchange."

Before leaving, Pryor with Forney and Washington McLean called on the President at Pryor's earnest request that he might speak in behalf of his friend, his prison roommate, Captain John Y. Beall, under sentence of death. The answer came: The death penalty was harsh but in this case execution of the sentence was indispensable. After which Lincoln turned the talk to the Hampton Roads conference and its failure through Jefferson Davis's obstinate insistence that the war and bloodshed go on rather than his people should accept re-establishment of the Union and abolition of slavery. "On this topic," recorded Mrs. Pryor, "Mr. Lincoln dwelt so warmly and at such length that General Pryor inferred that he still hoped the people of the South would reverse Mr. Davis's action and renew negotiations for peace. . . . It was apparent to General Pryor that Mr. Lincoln desired him to sound leading men of the South on the subject. Accordingly on the General's return to Richmond, he did consult with Senator Hunter and other prominent men in the Confederacy, but with one voice they assured him that nothing could be done with Mr. Davis, and that the South had only to await the imminent and inevitable catastrophe."

In a pocketbook well taken care of Roger A. Pryor cherished a little visiting-card on which Lincoln had written his parole. In troublesome days to come he was to fish it out and see it command respect for his roof and family.

In the case of John Y. Beall, however, Lincoln decided he could go too far in the pardoning business. There was such a thing as being too soft. Carefully had Lincoln gone over the record of the trial. Convinced was he that the evidence proved Beall a spy, a pirate, and a privateersman, leading a band which had captured vessels on the Great Lakes, seized cargoes and money, scuttled one steamer, and failed in a plan to release the Confederate prisoners on Johnson's Island. At no time however during the four years of war had such a mass of formidable influence come forward seeking from the President a commutation of death sentence to life imprisonment. Money was poured out and a vast personal influence enlisted. James T. Brady of New York served as counsel for Beall. Also serving was Orville Hickman Browning, who called on his old friend in the White House with a delegation of important citizens from Baltimore. Again Browning called alone and was closeted with his old friend an hour on the Beall case. Again on February 17 came Browning with a petition signed by 85 members of the House and 6 members of the Senate. Other intercessors included the Librarian of Congress, the president of the Baltimore & Ohio Railroad, Thad Stevens, John Andrew, Monty Blair. Such an aggregate of influence for a pardon was a new thing. Over and again Lincoln and Major General John A. Dix, commanding the Department of the East, gave the same answers, Lincoln saying, "General Dix may dispose of the case as he pleases—I will not interfere!" General Dix saying, "All now rests with the President—as far as my action rests there is not a gleam of hope."

So the gallows was prepared and the platform drop tried out and the rope and the weights tested. And no word having come from Lincoln or Dix, Captain John Y. Beall of the Confederate Army on February 24, 1865, was hanged by the neck till he was dead, as duly required by law.

"I've had more questions of life and death to settle in four years than all the other men who ever sat in this chair put together," said Lincoln to Bromwell of Illinois, with Seward and others present. "No man knows the distress of my mind. Some of them I couldn't save. There are cases where the law must be executed. The case of Beall on the Lakes—there had to be an example. They tried me every way. They wouldn't give up. But I had to stand firm. I even had to turn away his poor sister when she came and begged for his life, and let him be executed, and he was executed, and I can't get the distress out of my mind yet." Bromwell noticed Lincoln's eyes moisten, and turned and saw other eyes in the room the same.

On March 11 went forth the President's proclamation that any and all deserters, wherever they might be and no matter what had happened to carry their feet away from the army, on return to their regiments or companies "shall be pardoned."

On this same day of March 11 the man-hunter Colonel La Fayette C. Baker at New York telegraphed Provost Marshal General Fry of the day before raiding bounty-jumpers and "capturing 590 of the most desperate villains unhung." Baker wanted to parade these prisoners down Broadway in irons, "in order that the people may have a sight of them." Fry's first telegram to Baker that day said there would be no objection. Fry's second telegram to Baker said representations held that Baker was arresting men without sufficient evidence and hereafter he must forward his evidence to Washington and have the arrests ordered from there. Personal liberty in measure was beginning to return. The hand and tone of the President were having effect. The third telegram of Fry that day Baker found abrupt and peremptory: "Do not march the deserters down Broadway, and do not iron them or any other men."

As an executive dispenser of patronage and offices, of favors and benefits, Lincoln had grown without ceasing in his instincts about where to give and where to withhold. As at no previous time, now in March of '65 observers and participants in the game of American politics hesitated at laughing over this or that appointment. They would look it over and study about it before they cared to say Lincoln didn't know what he was doing—so often had he fooled them. The classical instance was Grant. To Lamon, Lincoln once confided that "even Washburne, who has always claimed Grant as his by right of discovery," had once joined those who demanded Grant's removal. In that hour Lincoln said, according to Lamon, "I really believe I am the only friend Grant has left." Now in '65 he was saying to Lamon: "If I had done as my Washington friends, who fight battles with their tongues at a safe distance from the enemy, would have had me do, Grant, who proved himself so great a captain, would never have been heard of again."

Now again came a suggestion that Confederate prisoners who would take the oath and were willing to be put into Union Army uniforms should be enlisted for some such service as that of fighting Indians on the frontier. Lincoln telegraphed the Chicagoans thus interested that the War Department must handle the matter. "The Rock Island case referred to, was my individual enterprise, and it caused so much difficulty in so many ways that I promised to never undertake another."

In one War Department matter Lincoln wrote an intricate memorandum on a complaint of Governor Fenton of New York, that in draft credits "*one* three-years man is counted equal to *three* one-year men," while in a pending call for troops "each man is to count *one* and *only* one, whether he went for one, two or three years." To the Secretary of War he wrote of Fenton: "The Governor has a pretty good case. I feel sure he is more than half right. We don't want him to feel cross and we in the wrong. Try and fix it with him."

Lincoln in this memorandum took a supposed case. "The towns of A & B, before any enlisted, had each 100 men. On the late call A gave sixty-six *one* year men, leaving only 34 at home, while B gave 33 three-years men, leaving 67 at home. On the pending call each owes 100 men, subject to its credit. But while A gets credit for 66, it owes 34, taking the last man in it; while B gets credit for 99, owes one, and has sixty-six left quietly at home." Having gazed at this curiosity of justice in draft arithmetic, he decided: "This ugly conjunction . . . burthens the one class absolutely beyond their immediate power to bear."

Decisions—Yes or No—or a balance somewhere between the two. "Fix it with him." Unless fixed, into the White House doors it would come again. Life? It was a series of fixes, right ones and wrong. Or as in the case of Fenton "more than half right." And every day ugly conjunctions burthening men. Of his supposed case in the memorandum, seemingly fantastic, he noted, "I am told there are realities that are even stranger."

Of the President on March 16 leading the grand promenade of the inaugural ball the *Chicago Tribune* reporter wrote: "Mr. Lincoln was evidently trying to throw off care for the time, but with rather ill success, and he looked very old."

Harriet Beecher Stowe had called one winter evening. She asked if he did not feel a great relief over the prospect of the war soon coming to a close. She went away, and telling her brother Henry Ward Beecher about her question, said Lincoln had answered in a sad way: "No, Mrs. Stowe, I shall never live to see peace. This war is killing me."

In another mood he was not so gloomy, saying to Noah Brooks one day, "When we leave this place [the White House], we shall have enough, I think, to take care of us old people. The boys must look out for themselves. I guess mother will be satisfied with six months or so in Europe. After that, I should really like to go to California and take a look at the Pacific coast."

Eaton of the Freedmen's Bureau saw him in February "thinner than ever," face drawn with suffering and thought. A strange and great tenderness moved him, and according to Eaton, "He was like a man seeing visions, and even the 'little stories' of which he was always reminded, and the jokes in which he took such quaint enjoyment and consolation, had assumed a melancholy tone."

On some matter of no moment Greeley had a brief interview with Lincoln in early March and had a feeling Lincoln was worn down to his last physical reserves. "His face was haggard with care and seamed with thought and trouble. It looked care-ploughed, tempest-tossed and weather-beaten."

Most often this was the testimony. On many a day the man seemed almost gone—with phantom gleams about him. On March 21, however, the editor of the *Baltimore American and Commercial Advertiser* watched him an hour in the morning and an hour in the afternoon receiving many difficult visitors, the editor writing: "The President looked extremely well, seemed in excellent spirits, and bore none of those evidences of debility or failing health which the *New York Tribune* daily talks about. His form is lithe and elastic, his features firm and expressive of energy and vigorous thought, and his manner of receiving his visitors was indicative of all that kindness of heart for which he is so distinguished. Indeed, there is good reason to hope that he will not only live many years to witness the future of his restored country, but should the people so decide, retain the physical and mental ability to administer its Executive functions even beyond his present term of office."

This seemed to be the first published suggestion that after Lincoln had served his second term as President he might be well able to serve a third term.

In a special envelope Lincoln filed letters threatening him with death. On this envelope Charles A. Dana took notice of the word "Assassination" in Lincoln's handwriting.

In November Dana had brought the President two letters which General Dix had forwarded from New York. They had been picked up in a Third Avenue streetcar. One was believed genuine, in a woman's handwriting the salutation "Dearest Husband" and the query, "Why do you not come home?" The other seemed less genuine, overly theatrical, reading in part: "When you remember the fearful, solemn vow that was taken by us, you will feel there is no drawback—Abe must die, and now. You can choose your weapons. The cup, the knife, the bullet. The cup failed us once, and might again. Johnson, who will give this, has been like an enraged demon since the meeting, because it has not fallen upon him to rid the world of the monster."

On reading the letters Dana had at once taken them to the President. "He looked at them," wrote Dana, "but made no special remark, and, in fact, seemed to attach very little importance to them. I left them with him."

CHAPTER 65

LINCOLN VISITS GRANT'S ARMY

DOWN Pennsylvania Avenue one day, wrote Noah Brooks, moved "a Confederate regimental band which had deserted in a body with its instruments, and was allowed to march through the streets of the national capital playing Union airs."

During the month of March more than 3,000 Confederate deserters were received in Washington, thousands more at Fortress Monroe, Annapolis, and other points. Further thousands of Confederate soldiers, absent without leave, had gone home or joined guerrilla and bushwhacker outfits or had gone North and found jobs. Of the total of 600,000 Confederate troops in the field two years before it was believed at least half of those alive had left the service for home and were now deaf or indifferent to any calls for fighting men. They had seen enough.

For a listening world in March Jefferson Davis spoke to his people saying: "Our country is now environed with perils which it is our duty calmly to contemplate." Action might follow the duty of calm contemplation. It was like him. Northern journals seized on it. It had the breath of the unyielding Davis now become slightly trancelike.

Congressman Ashley, just from Grant's headquarters, reported to Lincoln of Grant saying, "For every three men of ours dead, five of theirs; for every three of our cattle dead, five of theirs." And picking up some paper from a table and crushing it in his hand, "Tell the President I have got them like that!" This sounded dramatic. Was Grant getting dramatic? No, he was in a confident mood. Ashley said, "It made the cold chills run over me."

Sheridan the destroyer had driven the last of Early's army out of the Shenandoah Valley and his report in late March listed 780 barns burned, 420,000 bushels of wheat taken, also 700,000 rounds of ammunition, 2,557 horses, 7,152 head of beef cattle. So often now the wagons of Lee went out for food and came back empty. In comparison Grant's military city, and its line of tents and huts along a forty-mile front south of Richmond, was rather snug and cozy. When it wanted food, clothing, supplies, guns, munitions, telegrams went north and by steam transport on land and water, the cargoes arrived. The besiegers had nearly everything requisite of material and supplies. In beleaguered Richmond was starvation and want. Mrs. Jefferson Davis sold her carriage horses. Jones the diarist saw many red flags out, the auction banners of those selling anything to get food. Flour on March 20 reached $1,500 a barrel. A Negro man slave brought $10,000 in Confederate money or $100 in gold.

At last after long bickering, and through the Confederate Senate reversing itself and by a majority of one voting to arm the slaves for defense, President Davis signing the bill—at last the Negro slave was to be put in the army to fight for his master. This was one final hope for more soldiers.

Apricot blossoms came out and the bright Judas tree, the redbud, again failed not this spring—but down the river the low roar of Grant's guns broke on the air. And Robert E. Lee took note of the Union Army having "an overwhelming superiority of numbers and resources."

Mary Boykin Chesnut in Chester, South Carolina, looked out the window and saw Confederate soldiers marching. But not like they used to. Now no songs, jokes, shouts—just glum plodding. Again she looked out and saw another butternut brigade. And they sang—heartbreak songs—but they sang. "They would have warmed the blood of an Icelander." She plucked up heart. And yet—were they going to surrender? The wind flapping a curtain of her room that night seemed to moan, "Too late." She wrote, "All this will end by making me a nervous lunatic."

Louis T. Wigfall spoke to Mrs. Chesnut, Wigfall the fire-eater from Texas who had helped start the bombardment of Fort Sumter and then gone on to Washington and held his seat in the United States Senate till expelled in July of '61, Wigfall who lashed with a loose tongue at Lincoln and the "Black Republicans," Wigfall the duelist and killer who was good in a private shooting affair but less effective at his post as a Confederate Army brigadier general—Wigfall was now saying to Mrs. Chesnut, "It is all over; the game is up." Now he had an idea. "He is on his way to Texas, and when the hanging begins he can step over into Mexico." He was not going to stick with Lee or Johnston to the last.

From Lee however had come to Mrs. Chesnut an impressive saying: "This is the people's war; when they tire, I stop." She wrote as though she believed in this hour Lee had said it. Yes, this was momentous. If the mass of Southern people had tired of the war, no longer seeing any use in its cost and sacrifice, then what?

When a certain order of passion, faith, and endurance goes down, its final extinction is miraculously swift, Mrs. Chesnut mused. It was like the snuffing out of a candle: "One moment white, then gone forever."

And in the long darkness of the lost cause afterward? Then an added woe. In its March appeal urging continued resistance, the Confederate Congress prophesied: "Failure will compel us to drink the cup of humiliation even to the bitter dregs of having the history of our struggle written by New England historians."

The rumor kept traveling that Sherman had said, "I will bring every Southern woman to the washtub." Sherman hadn't said it. But on March 12 Sherman was writing his wife: "The importance of this march exceeds that from Atlanta to Savannah. South Carolina has had a visit from the West that will cure her of her pride and boasting. . . . The same brags and boasts are kept up, but when I reach the path where the lion crouched I find him slinking away." In spreading terror, in sowing war weariness, in bringing the war to the homes, farms, towns of the deep South, Sherman's army as much as any other created the conditions that had Lee saying in effect: "This is the people's war; when they tire, I stop."

To one White House caller Lincoln gave his metaphor of the major strategy of recent weeks. "Grant has the bear by the hind leg while Sherman takes off the hide."

To another who asked one March day what was the news from Sherman, Lincoln said he couldn't tell just where Sherman was but he could make a pretty sure guess. Pointing with a forefinger on a map, he said that Sherman when last heard of had his cavalry, vanguard, and infantry columns here, there, and there, "expecting to bring them all together *here*." Then after a pause: "Now when he does that, he'll—but that reminds *me* of the horse-dealer in Kentucky who got baptized in the river. The ceremony once over he insisted on it a second time. The preacher hesitated but the horse-trader had his way. And when he came up from the second ducking he gasped, 'There now! Now I can tell the devil to go to hell!' "

The Richmond correspondent of the London *Times* had written March 4 that Sherman in a few weeks "may, by possibility, be autocrat of this continent." Whatever fear there was of the United States soon starting a war with Britain—and such fear found voice in high places in England—the Richmond correspondent did not forget. "Mr. Lincoln has found General Sherman hitherto a very valuable friend—it is possible that before the end comes he will find him a still more dangerous enemy." Much like Cromwell, the vain, eager, fanatical, gloomy, impulsive, talkative General Sherman, "by some regarded as half-mad when the fit is on him," had a character "of what great and mysterious actors in history are often made." This fantasy the London *Times* in a critical hour gave its readers.

Judging by some 487 Yankee prisoners sent to Richmond by General Wade Hampton, taking these shoeless, hatless, grimy captives as specimens, the *Richmond Examiner* saw Sherman's rank and file as "scabs, scavengers and scum of creation." Not since the war began "has such a crew of hell-born men, accursed and God-forsaken wretches polluted the air and defiled the highways of Richmond with the concentrated essence of all that is lecherous, hateful and despised." This was the "human fungi" Johnston's army must stop. "If he can not successfully resist them, God help Richmond and her citizens."

This from the *Richmond Examiner*, noted one journal in the North, again was "the voice of the chivalry shuddering at the approach of the shovelry."

Meantime Johnston on March 11 notified Lee that if a Federal force of some 20,000 moving from the seacoast and Wilmington should manage to join Sherman's 60,000, Johnston with his 40,000 would not be able to stop them from marching up into Virginia. Up across North Carolina marched Sherman to Fayetteville, then to Goldsboro, where he paused for rest. There at Goldsboro March 23 he met General Terry and the troops that had taken Fort Fisher and Wilmington.

Another Sherman campaign was over, this time with 80,000 men answering roll call.

Sherman's 60,000 had a right to a rest. Behind them toward Savannah lay four hundred and twenty-five miles of foraged and ravaged country, Sherman terming their exploit "one of the longest and most important marches ever made by an organized army in a civilized country." Their legs had performed. Add the hike from Atlanta to the sea, then add other footwork since raids in Mississippi in July of '63—and their mileage was colossal. They had come on their feet no less than 2,500 miles, fording ordinary streams and flooded rivers, through rains and hot sun, over mountains and plains, across marshes and swamps where day after day every private was a toiling unit of the engineer corps. On speared bayonets some now carried potatoes, others pigs. Many were ragged, their trousers half gone from tussling through underbrush. More than half had thrown away their worn-out shoes, some walking barefoot, others with feet wrapped in blanket pieces. They leaped and shouted as they slid into new issues of shoes, uniforms, overcoats, at Goldsboro.

They were mainly from the West, the Midwest, and the Northwest. Already was talk in the North about whether they were to go on and take Richmond and Lee's army, with the result that history would say Westerners won the war. But that was a small matter. It could wait. They had joyous legs. Spring shone with lilacs and apple blossoms. The new shoes and trousers felt good. Not much longer could the war last. Daylight was ahead and home folks, girls and women. They were human even though Mrs. Chesnut was writing in her diary of Sherman, "that ghoul, that hyena," she believing her home had been sacked, wrecked, and burned—which hadn't happened at all, as she was to soon find out.

These weeks in latter March and early April, Grant wrote later, were for him "the most anxious" of the whole war. Lee was hemmed in with food and supplies cut off to such an extent that Grant figured Lee must soon try to break through or swing around the Union lines. "I was afraid, every morning, that I would awake from my sleep to hear that Lee had gone, and that nothing was left but a picket line. He had his railroad by the way of Danville south, and I was afraid that he was running off his men and all stores and ordinance except such as it would be necessary to carry with him for his immediate defense. I knew he could move much more lightly and rapidly than I, and that, if he got the start, he would leave me behind so that we would have the same army to fight again farther south—and the war might be prolonged another year."

These possibilities occurred to Lincoln's mind too. He knew with Grant that the old ancient rule held: "In war you can't make the same mistake twice."

On the news that Sherman with 80,000 troops rested and waited in North Carolina not far from the Virginia line, Lincoln left Washington to visit with Grant, to stay with Grant's army he did not know how many days, perhaps a week or two. Grant on March 20 sent Lincoln as cordial an invitation as could be asked: "Can you not visit City Point for a day or two? I would like very much to see you, and I think the rest would do you good." By this visit Lincoln would serve two purposes. He would have a needed vacation, a breakaway from many pressures at Washington. And he might in various ways accomplish something around the question of what terms should end the war. Early in March this matter came to a head. Word from Lee to Grant then could be taken to mean that those two commanders might get together, agree to disband their armies, and end the war with confusion in the air. Wherefore on March 3 Lincoln wrote an order for Stanton to send to Grant.

This order indicated Grant's line of authority in dealing with any proposals for peace. The President wished him to have no conference with

General Lee unless it should be for the capitulation of Lee's army, or on some minor or purely military affair.

"He instructs me to say," ran the order Lincoln wrote for Stanton to sign, "that you are not to decide, discuss, or confer upon any political questions. Such questions the President holds in his own hands, and will submit them to no military conferences or conventions. Meantime you are to press to the utmost your military advantages."

The President had been taking on himself too many matters "that properly belong in the Departments," wrote Welles on March 23, and this, added to "the throng that is pressing upon him" had worn him down. "The more he yields, the greater the pressure upon him. It has now become such that he is compelled to flee." Of the second and possibly the more imperative reason Welles was aware, noting: "Besides he wishes the War terminated, and, to this end, that severe terms shall not be exacted of the Rebels." In thus writing in that very hour Welles had no shaded or modified opinion. The many conferences of recent months had sunk deep in Welles and others the definite impression that the President toiled actively toward an end "that severe terms shall not be exacted of the Rebels."

The President was to sail from Washington on the *Bat*, a fast, comfortable, well-armed dispatch boat. G. V. Fox and the captain of the *Bat*, John S. Barnes, called on Lincoln and heard him say he wanted ordinary comforts —what was good enough for the captain of the boat would be good enough for him—covering all points with, "I'm only a fresh-water sailor and I guess I'll have to trust to you salt-water folks when afloat."

Then came later orders for Captain Barnes to report at the White House, where in Lincoln's private room in the residence end, noted the Captain, "Mr. Lincoln received me with great cordiality, but with a certain kind of embarrassment, and a look of sadness which rather embarrassed me. After a few casual remarks he said that Mrs. Lincoln had decided that she would accompany him to City Point—could the *Bat* accommodate her and her maid-servant?" Barnes as delicately as he could managed to say that the *Bat* was in no respect "adapted to the private life of womankind, nor could she be made so."

"Well," said the President, "I understand but you will have to see mother."

Barnes was ushered into Mrs. Lincoln's presence, noting that "she received me very graciously, standing with arms folded." Her wishes: "I am going with the President to City Point, and I want you to arrange your ship to take me, my maid and my officer [or guard], as well as the President." Barnes was bothered. He went to Fox. They agreed the *Bat* couldn't be fixed over. Together they went to the White House. There "in very funny terms the President translated our difficulties." Fox promised another and better boat.

On the unarmed and less safe though more spacious *River Queen*, with the *Bat* as convoy, the Lincoln family made the trip, Tad sleeping in a stateroom with the guard Crook. Down the Potomac and up the James

Mary Todd Lincoln, a popular carte de visite

Lincoln and Tad (probably '61). A retouched Brady photograph—widely reproduced and much prized by admirers of the President

Robert Todd Lincoln, the Harvard graduate

Mrs. Lincoln in party attire; they always reported what she wore

THE LINCOLN FAMILY

From the Barrett collection

Lincoln in a slight change of expression in two photographs by Brady in late '64

From the Meserve collection

Lincoln in two photographs in a sitting for Brady, probably in '64. From the normal rugged-ness seen in this page of portraits the President moved into the months of early '65, when he was known to be thirty pounds underweight.

River they went on a holiday—and some very strict and secretive business.

They pulled away from the Sixth Street wharf in Washington at 1 P.M., March 23, and about nine o'clock the evening of the next day tied to the wharf at City Point, from the deck gazing off into the night and the grim quiet mystery lying just yonder where 130,000 well-fed, well-clad Union soldiers for ten months had been trying to trap 50,000 ill-fed, ill-clad Confederates.

The sun would rise in the morning and go down in the evening how many times, with how many men broken and mangled, before this drama of national agony would be over? This the whole world was asking. Here on this Virginia ground the immediate action, the fury and the grief, would take place.

Grant came aboard with greetings and the news. Any hour he expected the enemy, because of their forces dwindling through desertion, to make a desperate attempt to crash the Union lines and force a path toward joining Johnston in North Carolina. Such an attempt was preparing as he spoke, and came before daylight. Later Lincoln heard of what was happening to his darling Tad. "After General Grant had gone," wrote the guard Crook, "Taddie and I went ashore to take a look at the place by starlight. We did not get many steps from the steamer before we were halted by a sentinel. I explained who we were, but Taddie thought he would go back. He said he did not like the looks of things. He wasn't used to being halted by sentinels who didn't know who he was. We went back to the boat. Everybody was up until late. The President and Mrs. Lincoln talked of the trip; they were in very good spirits."

At breakfast on the twenty-fifth Lincoln ate very little, but was very jolly and pleasant, noticed Captain Barnes. On the day before the President had not looked so well, his system upset, he believed, by the drinking water furnished the *River Queen* at Washington. At Fortress Monroe Barnes had taken on board a supply of fresh water in demijohns for the President's special use.

Captain Robert Lincoln came in from Grant's headquarters, telling of a fight at dawn that morning and an assault repelled. At the breakfast table Lincoln wrote a dispatch to Stanton, "No war news," ending "Robert just now tells me there was a little rumpus up the line this morning, ending about where it began." Officers, including Admiral David D. Porter, came aboard to pay their respects. The party went ashore and walked to Grant's headquarters. Lincoln wanted to look over the scene of the morning fight. Grant said the President couldn't be exposed to fire. On later reports Grant said the President could go.

Behind a slow-going locomotive in a jolting coach over the military railroad from City Point toward the front Lincoln rode past scenery where in the first daylight hours that morning men were mowed down by fort guns and men had fought hand to hand with bayonet and clubbed musket. Confederate troops under General John B. Gordon had taken Fort

Stedman and pressed on with the aim of destroying a railroad and Union supply stores. Had they won through, Lee would have had an open road to Johnston in North Carolina. Grant expected an attempted break through his lines and made a close guess as to where it would come. At the embankment of the railroad which Gordon sought to destroy, the Union troops had rallied, had driven the enemy back and retaken Fort Stedman—and Lincoln's breakfast hour, as he wired Stanton, saw the fight "ending about where it began."

Lincoln's coach halted at the point on the railroad embankment where the Unionists began to regain lost ground. Barnes wrote of "the ground immediately about us still strewn with dead and wounded of both sides." This was where Lincoln first saw close up the results of desperate combat on more than a small scale. Reports gave Union losses at 500 killed and wounded, 500 captured; Confederate losses 800 killed and wounded, 1,800 captured.

While the President journeyed to the front via railway Mrs. Lincoln and Mrs. Grant rode in an ambulance over a muddy, rough corduroy road. They were to join the President and Meade's staff in reviewing Crawford's division. As the wagon rolled along Badeau, seated with his back to the horses and facing the ladies, did his best at conversation, mentioning that all the wives of officers at the army front had been ordered to the rear, a sure sign of big action soon to come. Not a lady had been allowed to stay at the front, continued Badeau, unaware of what he was getting into, not a lady except Mrs. Griffin, the wife of General Charles Griffin, she having a special permit from the President.

Swift as a cat leap, Mrs. Lincoln: "What do you mean by that, sir? Do you mean to say that she saw the President alone? Do you know that I never allow the President to see any woman alone?" Badeau saw the face of a woman boiling with rage. He tried smiling toward this face, to show there was no malice. Badeau's smile was timed wrong. "That's a very equivocal smile, sir," he now heard. "Let me out of this carriage at once. I will ask the President if he saw that woman alone."

Badeau and Mrs. Grant tried to smooth and quiet a woman later and definitely found to be insane. They failed. Mrs. Lincoln ordered Badeau to have the driver stop, and Badeau hesitating, she thrust her arms past him and took hold of the driver. By now however Mrs. Grant was able to coax Mrs. Lincoln to be still and to wait. As they alighted at the reviewing ground General Meade walked up, paid his respects to Mrs. Lincoln, escorted her away, later returning her with diplomatic skill, Mrs. Lincoln informing Badeau, "General Meade is a gentleman, sir. He says it was not the President who gave Mrs. Griffin the permit, but the Secretary of War." Thus ran Badeau's account.

Badeau and Mrs. Grant agreed "the whole affair was so distressing and mortifying that neither of us must ever mention it again." No inkling of it seemed to reach Meade, who wrote to his wife of her visit to his headquarters that week "it seems so like a dream I can hardly realize you have been here." The President had spoken of Mrs. Meade, "expressed regret that your visit should have been so abruptly terminated," while "Mrs. Lincoln spoke very handsomely of you and referred in feeling terms to our sad bereavement [the recent death of a child]."

It was a fine day, without wind, spring in the air, the earth awaking again after the winter sleep under changing rain, snow, and sleet. In his letter Meade epitomized for his wife a day of fine weather: "The President and party came about 1 P.M. We reviewed Crawford's Division, and then rode to the front line and saw the firing on Wright's front, at the fort where you were, where a pretty sharp fight was going on. Indeed Humphreys and Wright were fighting till eight o'clock with very good results, taking over

A bombproof at Petersburg

one thousand prisoners from the enemy, and inflicting heavy losses in killed and wounded. The day turned out to be a very successful one, we punishing the enemy severely, taking nearly three thousand prisoners and ten battle flags, besides the morale of frustrating and defeating his plans."

In company with General Meade, Lincoln rode to a high slope and viewed the landscape over which the Confederate thrust had swept forward, halted, broken. It interested Lincoln that an order of Grant circulated inside of the Confederate lines the autumn before had played a part. This order promised amnesty and pardon to Confederate deserters, and gave them the encouragement of pay for their arms. On the night of February 24 nine deserters had come in on this brigade front, and on the next night fourteen, including a commissioned officer. "On this occasion [March 25]," wrote George L. Kilmer of the 14th New York Heavy Artillery, "Confederates claiming to be deserters came in large numbers, and very soon overpowered the pickets and passed on to the first line of works." Or as Grant described it: "The Confederate general . . . sent his pickets, with their arms, creeping through to ours as if to desert. When they got to our lines they at once took possession and sent our pickets to the rear as prisoners. This plan was to have been executed and much damage done before daylight."

The entire action that day, of which Lincoln saw vividly a section, was later sketched by Grant in five sentences: "Parke threw a line around outside of the captured fort and batteries, and communication was once more established. The artillery fire was kept up so continuously that it was impossible for the Confederates to retreat, and equally impossible for reinforcements to join them. They all, therefore, fell captives into our hands. This effort of Lee's cost him about four thousand men, and resulted in their killing, wounding and capturing about two thousand of ours."

On the soil where Union countercharges began Lincoln saw the dead in blue and gray and butternut lying huddled and silent, here and there the wounded gasping and groaning. Burial squads were at work. Surgeons were doing their service and Sanitary Commission workers giving out water and food. Herded by their guards was a collection of prisoners taken that morning, a ragged and dusty crew. "Mr. Lincoln remarked on their sad condition," noted Barnes. "They had fought desperately and were glad to be at rest. Mr. Lincoln was quiet and observant, making few comments, and listened to explanations in a cool, collected manner, betraying no excitement; but his whole face showed sympathetic feeling for the scene before him." Before returning to the railroad train Lincoln saw a white flag of truce flying between the two army lines, Confederate ambulances and burying squads taking up their dead and wounded. On the train Lincoln saw the loading of the Union wounded. "Mr. Lincoln looked worn and haggard," noted Barnes. "He remarked that he had seen enough of the horrors of war, that he hoped this was the beginning of the end, and that there would be no more bloodshed." Wrote the guard Crook of this day, "I saw him [Lincoln] ride over the battlefields at Petersburg, the man with the hole in his forehead and the man with both arms shot away lying, accusing, before his eyes."

Barnes told Lincoln of a half-hour spent in carrying a canteen of water among the thirsty Confederate wounded. Lying on the ground was a little redheaded boy in butternut clothes, moaning, "Mother, mother." Barnes asked him where he was hurt. He looked up, turned toward Barnes the back of his head, where a bullet had plowed a ghastly furrow, then sank back white and still with death. "Mr. Lincoln's eyes filled with tears and his voice was choked as he repeated the familiar phrase 'robbing the cradle and the grave.' "

Beyond the immediate scene that Lincoln gazed on that day other fighting had gone on. The Union troops advanced along the whole of Lee's right, taking entrenched picket lines. The Union estimate put their own losses at 2,080 as against 4,800 to 5,000 Confederate. Lee the next day was writing President Davis, "I fear now it will be impossible to prevent a junction between Grant and Sherman." Johnston, Lee further informed Davis, reported only 13,500 infantry, a loss of 8,000 men, largely by desertion. The united armies of Grant and Sherman, Lee estimated, "would exceed ours by nearly one hundred thousand." It was seven weeks since Lee had notified the Secretary of War at Richmond, "You must not be surprised if calamity befalls us."

From the battlefield which Lincoln found truly and in fact crimson, where he had seen the altars of sacrifice wet and red, he rode on the jolting railroad coach back to City Point. To Stanton he wired that he had nothing to add to General Meade's reports "except that I have seen the prisoners myself and they look like there might be the number he states—1,600."

Lincoln sat for a while at the headquarters camp-fire, according to Colonel Horace Porter, "and as the smoke curled about his head during certain shiftings of the wind . . . he brushed it away from time to time by waving his right hand in front of his face." To Grant and staff men gathered around he talked. "At first his manner was grave and his language much more serious than usual." He spoke of "appalling difficulties" the Administration had met, field losses, troubles in finance and foreign affairs, how they had been overcome by the unswerving patriotism of the people, the devotion of the loyal North, and the superb fighting qualities of the troops. He drifted into a more cheerful vein, getting into his storytelling stride by way of the Trent Affair, and reeling off an elaborate version of the fable of the barber and his worried customer. Porter caught it as follows:

"England will live to regret her inimical attitude toward us. After the collapse of the rebellion John Bull will find that he has injured himself much more seriously than us. His action reminds me of a barber in Sangamon County in my State. He had just gone to bed when a stranger came along and said he must be shaved; that he had a four days' beard on his face, and was going to take a girl to a ball, and that beard must come off. Well, the barber got up reluctantly and dressed, and seated the man in a chair with a back so low that every time he bore down on him he came near dislocating his victim's neck. He began by lathering his face, including his nose, eyes, and ears, stropped his razor on his boot, and then made a drive at the man's countenance as if he had practised mowing in a stubble-field. He cut a bold swath across the right cheek, carrying away the beard, a pimple, and two warts. The man in the chair ventured to remark: 'You appear to make everything level as you go.' 'Yes,' said the barber; 'and if this handle don't break, I guess I'll get away with most of what's there.' The man's cheeks were so hollow that the barber couldn't get down into the valleys with the razor, and the ingenious idea occurred to him to stick his finger in the man's mouth and press out the cheeks. Finally he cut clear through the cheek and into his own finger. He pulled the finger out of the man's mouth, snapped the blood off it, glared at him, and cried: 'There, you lantern-jawed cuss, you've made me cut my finger!' And so England will discover that she has got the South into a pretty bad scrape by trying to administer to her, and in the end she will find that she has only cut her own finger."

The laugh following this subsided, and Grant asked, "Mr. President, did you at any time doubt the final success of the cause?" And Lincoln, leaning forward in his camp chair, with an emphatic right-hand gesture: "Never for a moment."

Whatever the dark slow storm of thought and feeling that moved Lincoln after his first battlefield visit where he saw the wounded writhing and moaning, whatever his outlook, he had already said part of it in the second inaugural. He was, according to Barnes, "overcome by the excitement and events of the day," boarded the *River Queen*, declined supper at Grant's headquarters, "saw no one again that evening." The next day Barnes "found Mr. Lincoln quite recovered," lamenting the loss of life, confident the war was ending. He read to Barnes dispatches from Stanton in anxiety lest he expose himself, drew contrasts between the duty of a "general" and a "president." He was pleased at news that Sheridan from the Shenandoah Valley had moved in a big swing around Lee's army to the north and arrived safe at Harrison's Landing to join Grant that day.

In the tent of Colonel Bowers of Grant's staff and the tent of Grant's cipher operator Beckwith, Lincoln gathered the news that morning. Horace Porter and others in Beckwith's tent saw him pull from his pocket a telegram and with a grin: "Well, the serious Stanton is actually becoming facetious. Just listen." And he read Stanton's reference to the battle of the previous day as a "scrimmage" after which "the rebel rooster looks a little the worse," closing with the admonition to the President: "I hope you will remember General Harrison's advice to his men at Tippecanoe, that they can 'see just as well a little farther off.' "

The President's eyes roved the floor of the telegraph hut. They caught on three tiny kittens, wandering, mewing as if lost. He picked up one and asked it, "Where is your mother?" Someone answered, "The mother is dead." And as he petted the little one: "Then she can't grieve as many a poor mother is grieving for a son lost in battle." Then, gathering the two others in his hands, he put them on his lap, stroked their fur, and according to Admiral Porter, meditated, "Kitties, thank God you are cats, and can't understand this terrible strife that is going on." Then more practically and immediately to the kittens, according to Colonel Horace Porter, "Poor little creatures, don't cry; you'll be taken good care of." And to Bowers, "Colonel, I hope you will see that these poor little motherless waifs are given plenty of milk and treated kindly." Bowers promised he would see that the mess cook did right by them. Several times later in the telegraph hut Horace Porter noticed Lincoln fondling these kittens. "He would wipe their eyes tenderly with his handkerchief, stroke their smooth coats, and listen to them purring their gratitude to him." A curious sight it was, thought Porter, "at an army headquarters, upon the eve of a great military crisis in the nation's history, to see the hand which had affixed the signature to the Emancipation Proclamation and had signed the commissions . . . from the general-in-chief to the lowest lieutenant, tenderly caressing three stray kittens."

The *River Queen* moved down the James River that morning and from her deck Lincoln saw the bank lined with men shouting, laughing, swimming, watering their horses—Sheridan's men getting the dust of the Shenandoah Valley out of their armpits. They spotted the President and sent him cheers. Then the *River Queen* turned, passed through a naval flotilla, ships dressed with flags, ranged in double line. The crews cheered the Commander in Chief, saw his tall frame in a long-tailed black frock coat, a cravat of black silk carelessly tied, topped by a silk hat. Barnes noted, "As he passed each vessel he waved his high hat, as if saluting friends in his native town, and seemed as happy as a school boy."

At an elaborate lunch on Admiral Porter's flagship *Malvern*, Lincoln enjoyed the quips and banter between army and navy officers. Colonel Horace Porter was lending his horse that day to the *River Queen* commander Barnes, a favor, said Porter, "usually accorded with some reluctance to naval officers when they came ashore; for these men of the ocean at times tried to board the animal on the starboard side, and often rolled in the saddle as if there was a heavy sea on." Porter told of a naval hero not long before on a borrowed horse. "When the officer could not succeed in making him shorten sail by hauling in on the reins, he took out his jack-knife and dug it in the animal's flanks, swearing that if he could not bring the craft to in any other way he would scuttle it." This horseplay was welcome to Lincoln, also retorts of navy men about army officers treating a rowboat as if it were a horse, expecting it to stop at the order "Whoa!" In the laughter of this noonday lunch, noted Barnes, "the moving spirit" was the President, who had "funny comments" contrasting army and navy life.

Up the James steamed the *River Queen* to Aiken's Landing. There horses and ambulances were put ashore to carry officers and ladies to a field review by the President of a part of the Army of the James. "In a more gloomy mood than usual" was the President on this boat trip, observed Horace Porter. "He spoke with much seriousness about the situation, and did not attempt to tell a single anecdote." Sheridan came aboard. The President shook hands with his commander whose name in the North had taken a shine like that of Stonewall Jackson to the South in the earlier years of the war. As the boat passed where Sheridan's cavalry was crossing a pontoon bridge Lincoln plied him with questions.

The greeting given Sheridan was remembered. The President ended his long-held handshake. "General Sheridan, when this peculiar war began I thought a cavalryman should be at least six feet four high, but"—still gazing down on the short General—"I have changed my mind—five feet four will do in a pinch."

On landing, Lincoln had a lavish though quiet gesture from Grant. The horse allowed him for the day's riding was one of Grant's favorites. Grant himself was riding Little Jeff, a black, shapely pony once owned by Mrs. Jefferson Davis and captured at Grand Gulf, Mississippi, in early '63. Lincoln was astride Grant's famous Kentucky thoroughbred chestnut gelding Cincinnati, a fast and gentle animal that had carried the General in Chief through some of the fiercest days of the Wilderness campaign. Ord on one side, Grant on the other, escorted the President over a rough corduroy road two miles to the reviewing ground. An ambulance followed bringing Mrs. Lincoln and Mrs. Grant in care of Colonel Horace Porter and Grant's secretary, Adam Badeau. Improved springs on the ambulance only served to toss the occupants higher, but Mrs. Lincoln in fear that they would miss the review asked Porter for more speed. The driver accommodated till the mud flew from the horses' heels, and the ladies' hats were jammed and heads bumped against the top of the wagon. "Mrs. Lincoln now insisted on getting out and walking," wrote Porter; "but as the mud was nearly hub-deep, Mrs. Grant and I persuaded her that we had better stick to the wagon as our only ark of refuge."

Meantime the President, with a squadron of twenty or more officers and orderlies, rode through woods and swamp, "in high spirits," noted Barnes, "laughing and chatting first to Grant and then to Ord." At the headquarters of Meade that general said he had a dispatch from General Parke to show. Lincoln pointed to the parade ground: "*There* is the best despatch you can show me from General Parke." Standing at "parade rest" the division had waited for hours. Grant asked Lincoln whether they should wait longer, for the arrival of Mrs. Lincoln and Mrs. Grant. "Mr. Lincoln," wrote Barnes, "exclaimed against any postponement, and in a few moments the review began; the President, with Grant and Ord leading, proceeded to the right of the line and passed in front, the bands playing, colors dipping, and the soldiers at 'present arms.'" The troops cheered the Chief Magistrate, noted Colonel Theodore Lyman, as he rode down the ranks "plucking off his hat gracefully by the hinder part of the brim." The review over, shellfire began on the enemy picket line in sight, heavy skirmishing lines moved forward, took the picket-line trenches, swelled the day's total of prisoners to 2,700, repulsed two fierce counterattacks, ending the day with Union losses of about 2,000 to 4,000 Confederate.

Colonel Theodore Lyman of Meade's staff at this review had his first look at Lincoln. In a letter to his wife that evening Lyman gave her his impression of what he believed he saw. An heir to an independent fortune, a Harvard graduate and a European traveler, a devotee of science who in his work under Agassiz had become a leading authority on the ophiurans (star-shaped and disklike relative of the sea urchin), now of nearly two years' loyal service in the field with Meade, Lyman wrote home a terse, frank appraisal of the President, a thumbnail portrait. It was meant for his wife to read. It was in confidence. It was what he would have answered her in their Brookline mansion if she over the breakfast coffee had asked him, "What was your impression of Lincoln as you saw him?" He wrote for her:

"The President is, I think, the ugliest man I ever put my eyes on; there is also an expression of plebeian vulgarity in his face that is offensive (you recognize the recounter of coarse stories). On the other hand, he has the look of sense and wonderful shrewdness, while the heavy eyelids give him a mark almost of genius. He strikes me, too, as a very honest and kindly man; and, with all his vulgarity, I see no trace of low passions in his face. On the whole, he is such a mixture of all sorts, as only America brings forth. He is as much like a highly intellectual and benevolent Satyr as anything I can think of. I never wish to see him again, but, as humanity runs, I am well content to have him at the head of affairs."

Mrs. Lincoln and Mrs. Grant had arrived late for the review but in time for Mrs. Lincoln to see Mrs. Ord riding near the President in the reviewing column, though equally near her husband, who was the immediate commander of the troops under review. Seeing the ambulance drive in on the parade line, Mrs. Ord excused herself with, "There come Mrs. Lincoln and Mrs. Grant—I think I had better join them." The accounts of Barnes, Porter, and Badeau as to what then happened agreed that there were embarrassing moments and bitterly pathetic exhibitions, Badeau's later recollections being more complete in detail, though having slight discrepancies. It seemed however that Mrs. Lincoln furiously exclaimed: "What does this woman mean by riding by the side of the President and ahead of me? Does she suppose that *he* wants *her* by the side of *him?*" She went into a frenzy that mingled extravagant rage and drab petulance. "All that Porter and I could do," wrote Badeau, "was to see that nothing worse than words occurred." They feared some wild scene of violence enacted before the troops so calmly standing at "present arms." One outburst flung itself at Mrs. Grant: "I suppose you think you'll get to the White House yourself, don't you?" Mrs. Grant kept cool, saying she was quite satisfied with her present position, that it was far greater than she had ever expected to attain. Mrs. Lincoln: "Oh! you had better take it if you can get it. 'Tis very nice." Then the slings of reproach were sent at Mrs. Ord, with Mrs. Grant quietly and at some risk defending her friend.

A nephew of Secretary Seward, a young major and a member of General Ord's staff, a joker, rode alongside and blurted out with a rich grin: "The President's horse is very gallant, Mrs. Lincoln. He insists on riding by the side of Mrs. Ord." This of course helped no one. Mrs. Lincoln cried, "What do you mean by that?" and young Major Seward at once had horse difficulties and shied away in a crazy gallop.

When the review had ended—and the troops were moving toward the enemy picket lines and death and wounds—Mrs. Lincoln in the presence of a group of officers, according to Badeau, hurled vile names at Mrs. Ord and again asked what Mrs. Ord meant by following the President. Enough of this sent Mrs. Ord into tears, into asking what in the world she had done. Mrs. Lincoln stormed till she spent her strength. A manner of silence ensued. Porter believed "Mrs. Lincoln had suffered so much from the fatigue and annoyances of her overland trip that she was not in a mood to derive much pleasure from the occasion." Badeau saw "everybody shocked and horrified." Barnes found Mrs. Grant silent and embarrassed. "It was a painful situation, from which the only escape was to retire. Mrs. Ord and myself with a few officers rode back to City Point."

On the return trip of the *River Queen*, "the President seemed to recover his spirits," according to Horace Porter, who thought perhaps the strength and fighting quality he witnessed that afternoon in the Army of the James "had served to cheer him up." Whatever his mood, whatever the trouble he might be disguising, he spoke to Colonel Porter of a prominent general, possibly Frémont being in mind, who had failed again and again in the numerous attempts of the President to make the officer a useful instrument of service to the country—and how finally he had under necessity relieved the general of all command. As Horace Porter gathered this long-spun anecdote Lincoln said:

"I was not more successful than the blacksmith in our town, in my boyhood days, when he tried to put to a useful purpose a big piece of wrought-iron that was in the shop. He heated it, put it on the anvil, and said: 'I'm going to make a sledge-hammer out of you.' After a while he stopped hammering it, looked at it, and remarked: 'Guess I've drawed you out a little too fine for a sledge-hammer; reckon I'd better make a clevis of you.' He stuck it in the fire, blew the bellows, got up a good heat, then began shaping the iron again on the anvil. Pretty soon he stopped, sized it up with his eye, and said: 'Guess I've drawed you out too thin for a clevis; suppose I better make a clevis-bolt of you.' He put it in the fire, bore down still harder on the bellows, drew out the iron, and went to work at it once more on the anvil. In a few minutes he stopped, took a look, and exclaimed: 'Well, now I've got you down a leetle too thin even to make a clevis-bolt out of you.' Then he rammed it in the fire again, threw his whole weight on the bellows, got up a white heat on the iron, jerked it out, carried it in the tongs to the water-barrel, held it over the barrel, and cried: 'I've tried to make a sledge-hammer of you, and failed; I've tried to make a clevis of you, and failed; I've tried to make a clevis-bolt of you, and failed; now, darn you, I'm going to make a fizzle of you'; and with that he soused it in the water and let it fizz."

Shortly afterward at City Point Grant heard from Lincoln either the same anecdote or another version of it, Grant's later recollection of it being different enough to make an interesting contrast. Grant took the President to see the works at the Dutch Gap Canal, explaining how in blasting one section of the excavations, the explosion threw material back into, and filled up, a part already completed. Lincoln turned and said, according to Grant's account:

"Grant, do you know what this reminds me of? Out in Springfield, Illinois, there was a blacksmith named ——. One day, when he did not have much to do, he took a piece of soft iron that had been in his shop for some time, and for which he had no special use, and, starting up his fire, began to heat it. When he got it hot he carried it to the anvil and began to hammer it, rather thinking he would weld it into an agricultural implement. He pounded away for some time until he got it fashioned into some shape, when he discovered that the iron would not hold out to complete the implement he had in mind. He then put it back into the forge, heated it up again, and recommenced hammering, with an ill-defined notion that he would make a claw-hammer, but after a time he came to the conclusion that there was more iron there than was needed to form a hammer. Again he heated it, and thought he would make an ax. After hammering and welding it into shape, knocking the oxidized iron off in flakes, he concluded there was not enough of the iron left to make an ax that would be of any use. He was now getting tired and a little disgusted at the result of his various essays. So he filled his forge full of coal, and, after placing the iron in the centre of the heap, took the bellows and worked up a tremendous blast, bringing the iron to a white heat. Then with his tongs he lifted it from the bed of coals, and thrusting it into a tub of water near by, exclaimed with an oath, 'Well, if I can't make anything else of you, I will make a fizzle anyhow.' "

Grant responded he was afraid that was just about what had been done in the blasting and filling at the Dutch Gap Canal.

Of what happened that evening of March 26 when the *River Queen* returned to her moorings at City Point perhaps the later recollections of Horace Porter were more correct than those of Adam Badeau, though Badeau as the military secretary of the General in Chief of the armies necessarily had some merits of accuracy. Badeau wrote: "That night the President and Mrs. Lincoln entertained General and Mrs. Grant and the General's staff at dinner on the steamer, and before us all Mrs. Lincoln berated General Ord to the President, and urged that he should be removed. He was unfit for his place, she said, to say nothing of his wife. General Grant sat next and defended his officer bravely." Possibly Badeau confused this occasion with some other, Colonel Horace Porter, who had merits of accuracy fully equal to Badeau, wrote: "It was nearly dark when the party returned to City Point. After dinner the band was brought down to the steamboat, and a dance was improvised. Several ladies were on board, and they and the officers danced till mid-night. Neither the President nor General Grant joined, even in a square dance, but sat in the after part of the boat conversing."

Lincoln and Grant had said good night on the *River Queen*. The officers had left their waltzing partners, wondering when again they might be dancing. Saloon and cabin lights were out. Up over was starlight. Below and around were camp lights, boat lights. With the war and more on his hands President Lincoln was not at ease. Out in the dark night along a forty-mile front 100,000 men and more lived hugging the dirt of the earth, some in tents but more in huts and shelters flung up somehow amid trenches, forts, rifle pits, embrasures, barricades, and the first frail works of far picket lines where lonesome squads spoke, if at all, in whispers. Soon they might go into the wildest, bloodiest battle of the whole war. This was quite possible. That would be a grief. Beyond a horror-dripping victory ending the war lay the solemn matter of what kind of a peace should be signed. President Lincoln was not at ease. Yet these problems had not engulfed him. A personal grief occupied him on this night. He sent off the ship an orderly who about eleven o'clock awakened Captain Barnes with a message that the President would like to see him.

Barnes stepped into his clothes in a hurry, boarded the *River Queen*, and found Mr. and Mrs. Lincoln awaiting him in the upper saloon. The President "seemed weary and greatly distressed," on his face an accentuated melancholy. What followed was to Barnes "a very unhappy experience, the particulars of which need not be gone into." A few essentials Captain Barnes would disclose, writing: "Mr. Lincoln took little part in the conversation which ensued, which evidently followed some previous discussion with Mrs.

Lincoln, who had objected very strenuously to the presence of other ladies at the review, and had thought that Mrs. Ord had been too prominent in it; that the troops were led to think she was the wife of the President, who had distinguished her with too much attention. Mr. Lincoln very gently suggested that he had hardly remarked her presence; but Mrs. Lincoln was not to be pacified, and appealed to me to support her views. Of course I could not umpire such a question, and could only state why Mrs. Ord and myself found ourselves in the reviewing column, and how immediately we withdrew from it upon the appearance of the ambulance with Mrs. Lincoln and Mrs. Grant. . . . I extricated myself as well as I could, but with difficulty, and asked permission to retire, the President bidding me good-night sadly and gently."

Barnes having refused to say that Mrs. Ord was to blame, "Mrs. Lincoln never forgave him," wrote Badeau. On this Barnes recorded nothing, though Badeau wrote of another day that week when Barnes went to speak to the President on some official business when Mrs. Lincoln and others were present. "The President's wife said something to him unusually offensive that all the company could hear. Lincoln was silent, but after a moment he went up to the young officer, and taking him by the arm led him into his own cabin, to show him a map or paper, he said. Lincoln made no remark, Barnes told me, upon what had occurred. He could not rebuke his wife; but he showed his regret, and his regard for the officer, with a touch of what seemed to me the most exquisite breeding imaginable."

On another occasion, of which Barnes did record in bare outline what he saw and heard, he had gone at Mrs. Grant's suggestion to where Mrs. Lincoln stood alone on the uncovered deck near the pilot house. He pushed out of a door a large upholstered armchair, bade Mrs. Lincoln good morning, and invited her to take the chair. She didn't wish a chair, thank you. "Finding my presence unwelcome," wrote Barnes of an incident seldom met by ship captains, "I returned to Mrs. Grant, who had witnessed my failure. Very soon Mrs. Lincoln beckoned to her, she joined Mrs. Lincoln and an animated conversation ensued between them; Mrs. Grant returned to the cabin and told me Mrs. Lincoln objected to my presence aboard the Queen and requested Mrs. Grant to so inform me. This made things rather uncomfortable." So Barnes managed to be put ashore at Point of Rocks, got him a horse, and rode back to City Point. When he next saw Lincoln it was in the stateroom office of the *River Queen*, and, "he made me sit down and we talked for a while—mainly, I could see, to put me at my ease. Tad was with him as usual hanging or half sitting on his father's knee."

Amid the scenes created by the disordered brain of a tragically afflicted woman, young Captain Barnes felt himself drawn to the one person he saw as writhing inwardly more than any other, writing, "I came to feel an affection for him that none other inspired." The melancholy of Lincoln he believed related in part to the torments Mrs. Lincoln was under. "I had the greatest sympathy for her and for Mr. Lincoln, who I am sure felt deep anxiety for her," Barnes noted. "His manner towards her was always that of the most affectionate solicitude, so marked, so gentle and unaffected that no one could see them together without being impressed by it." Though a common undertone phrase for her was "crazy woman," Barnes's more humanly decent description ran: "She was at no time well; the mental strain upon her was great, betrayed by extreme nervousness approaching hysteria, causing misapprehensions, extreme sensitiveness as to slights or want of politeness or consideration."

At intervals during this City Point visit, however, several credible observers without particular prejudice agreed in the main with Badeau's account that "Mrs. Lincoln repeatedly attacked her husband in the presence of officers because of Mrs. Griffin and Mrs. Ord." As for the head of the state, wrote Badeau, "he bore it as Christ might have done . . . with supreme calmness and dignity . . . he called her 'mother' . . . pleaded with eyes and tones, endeavored to explain or palliate the offenses of others, till she turned on him like a tigress; and then he walked away," hiding his face that others might not see it. When Mrs. Stanton had shortly before visited City Point, Badeau chanced to ask her something about the President's wife. "I do not visit Mrs. Lincoln," was the reply. Badeau believed he hadn't heard correctly. Surely, he said, the wife of the Secretary of War must visit the wife of the President. "Understand me, sir," repeated Mrs. Stanton. "I do not go to the White House. I do not visit Mrs. Lincoln." Toward Mrs. Grant, Mary Todd Lincoln showed no relenting, according to Badeau once rebuking the General's wife, "How dare you be seated until I invite you?"

Gunboats, monitors, transports, crowded the river. The dock to which the *River Queen* usually tied held piles of stores and munitions, with teamsters shouting to their horses and mules, roustabout crews yelling at each other, moving quartermaster supplies to the front. Now it happened in the shifting of boats for convenience and utility that several times the *Mary Martin*, on which Mrs. Grant and her family lived, tied up alongside the crowded wharf with her gangplank down, and the *River Queen* next to her. "It was sometimes a question of precedence as to which boat should lie next the dock—a question not raised by Mr. Lincoln," wrote Barnes. "But Mrs. Lincoln thought that the President's boat should have place, and declined to go ashore if she had to do so over the *Martin:* so several times the latter was pushed out and the *Queen* in, requiring some work and creating confusion, despite Mr. Lincoln's expostulations. The two craft came to be called 'Mrs. Lincoln's boat' and 'Mrs. Grant's boat,' and the open discussions between their respective skippers were sometimes warm. Of course neither Mr. Lincoln nor General Grant took notice of any such trivialities."

The army had terrible work ahead and Barnes noted "it was generally believed that General Grant was not particularly desirous of Mr. Lincoln's presence at City Point, and it was in fact, a somewhat embarrassing factor." However that may have been, "General Grant never for a moment manifested any impatience, but gave to the President every possible consideration." Grant was to write later: "Some of the cruel things said about President Lincoln, particularly in the North, used to pierce him to the heart, but never in my presence did he evince a revengeful disposition—and I saw a great deal of him at City Point, for he seemed glad to get away from the cares and anxieties of the capital."

On the morning after the tragicofarcical March 26 Barnes reported as usual to the President, received "marked kindness," and in a small state-room converted into an office heard the President read dispatches from Stanton and from the front, while Tad ran in and out, sometimes "clinging to his father and caressed affectionately by him." Barnes inquired about Mrs. Lincoln, hoping she had recovered from the fatigue of the previous day. "Mr. Lincoln said she was not well at all, and expressed the fear that the excitement of the surroundings was too great for her or for any woman." Then Lincoln and Barnes started afoot for Grant's headquarters.

In the roomy log cabin of Grant, a meeting-place where corps and division generals were often present to discuss the latest enemy moves and their own prospects, Lincoln spent the forenoon mainly in talk with Admiral David D. Porter, Grant a listener "in grim silence, or only answering direct questions from Mr. Lincoln" in monosyllables. The Admiral had storytelling gifts, some saying that even in his reporting of actual historic events he let his imagination ride too free. A Rabelaisian streak ran through him, and as he got going with various sea yarns of the war, Lincoln laughed. "I like your sea stories; I never heard them before." Porter could tell one of the seagoing classics about a Yankee skipper to whom came an admiral saying, "I seizes you as a bony fidy prize, a derilick without papers on the high seas." On the admiral's paying $40,000 for the impressed ship, the skipper said, "I offered to sell her for twelve thousand dollars, but they said she wasn't good for anything but fire-wood. An' here in the nick of time comes this navy feller and relieves me from all my difficulties." Then the skipper spoke of his ship: "You've done bruk my heart; me an' my old gal as has stuck together for thirty years must part. You'll get a flag-ship as is a flag-ship; her upper works is from fair to middlin', but she wants an entire new hull; her bilers were condemned eight years ago, and she can't carry only ten pounds of steam. Her shaft is broke in three places, but you can't see it for the putty. We keeps six siphon-pumps agoin' and the steam pipes all the time. Her steam-chist has busted thirty-six times in the last two years, and killed four men, and she's bin on fire twenty-two times. She's full of rats, cockroaches, and bedbugs, but if her cook can't make the best lobscouse and slapjacks in this country I'll eat him."

Someone mentioned a shooting affair in the direction of General Parke's corps one or two evenings before. Musket fire first rattled and then became the bang-bang of volley fire followed with a few cannon booms. It sounded like a battle opening. What had happened? Some raw recruit handled his gun careless and it went off. Other country boys got the idea something was in the air and they started firing at another part of the line. More and more troops began taking potshots at imaginary enemies, and when the cannoneers turned loose a couple of salvos, it became a disturbance that headquarters had to notice. and was soon stopped.

Lincoln was reminded of one night of a July third in Springfield, Illinois, when everybody had gone to sleep except a few prowling and frolicsome young fellows. A little after midnight one of them bet drinks for the party that inside of five minutes he could make every rooster in the whole town start crowing. This young fellow had practiced and reached perfection in his imitation of the chicken-cock crow. He leaped on a fence and, slapping his thighs with his open hands, elevated his mouth and gave forth a vociferous "Cock-a-doodle-do-o-o-o." In the stilly night this hell-bent bugle call of the rooster crossed over into every nook and corner of the town. But no answer came. Once more the young fellow let loose a rooster crow that seemed to break all records for piercing noises in the night. Now from some chicken roost on the edge of Springfield came a lone clear call. Soon this was taken up by others. Before the five-minute limit was up it seemed that every cock in the town was joined in the grand chorus. Then oddly enough the idea spread among the boys of the town, sleeping with one eye open. They believed the crowing meant Fourth of July had dawned. They leaped out of bed, jumped into their clothes, rushed pell-mell to the streets and began shooting firecrackers, pistols, squirrel rifles, Mexican War muskets, and toy cannon. "But," concluded Lincoln, "nobody was hurt any more than when Parke's roosters prematurely crowed the other evening."

In very good spirits that morning was Lincoln, thought Barnes. "Running his hands with an upward movement through his rumpled hair, his eyes glistening, his face expressing in every feature his keenest enjoyment, he would stretch himself out, and look at the listeners in turn as though for sympathy and appreciation." Grant, however, "seldom smiled." His sense of humor felt no urge. He was thinking about his armies, about moving out of the trenches and trying to take Lee. If Lee escaped the net now spread, the war might go another year or two—or longer.

Four years now the war had gone on, four years lacking not quite three weeks since Fort Sumter at Charleston crumbled. Now that fort was under repair, getting fixed over, and Stanton, Admiral Dahlgren, William Lloyd Garrison, Henry Ward Beecher, and Nicolay to represent the President were preparing to go down and hold a flag-raising ceremony of speeches and prayers, with the Union banner again floating from that citadel where the war began. A white-haired old man, feeble for his sixty years, living now on Fifth Avenue, New York, wearing a long military cape hiding his rank of major general when he walked the streets, proud of Sherman and saying of the man whose strategy had again brought Fort Sumter into Federal control, "He is one of my boys"—Robert Anderson on the retired list was to go to Charleston for the flag-raising over the ramparts where he had seen his flag shot away. Stanton queried Lincoln about this celebration, Lincoln had but one suggestion, which he wired March 27. He corrected Stanton as to a date, the date the war began. "I feel quite confident that Sumter fell on the 13th, and not on the 14th of April, as you have it. It fell on Saturday, the 13th; the first call for troops on our part was got up on Sunday, the 14th, and given date and issued on Monday, the 15th. Look up the old almanac and other data, and see if I am not right." Which Stanton did, and the new date was ordered, though again later changed to April 14.

Down in North Carolina that week Sherman in the hearing of a *New York Herald* man said: "I'm going up to see Grant for five minutes and have it all chalked out for me and then come back and pitch in. I only want to see him for five minutes and won't be gone but two or three days." A steamer put Sherman ashore at City Point late in the afternoon of this March 27. Grant was there waiting. They had parted just a year ago in Cincinnati —and the strategy they then talked had worked. As Sherman with long strides moved toward Grant, he heard, "How d'you do, Sherman!" answered, "How are you, Grant!" and the two of them locked hands in a long warm handshake and a laughter like two ticklish schoolboys. They walked to Grant's cabin. Sherman talked. They kept at him to talk. He had a big story to tell and they wanted to hear it. Colonel Lyman described the Ohio orphan boy as of this time: "He is a very remarkable-looking man, such as could not be grown out of America—the concentrated quintessence of Yankeedom. He is tall, spare, and sinewy . . . with lips that shut tightly together . . . a very homely man, with a regular nest of wrinkles in his face, which play and twist as he eagerly talks on each subject; but his expression is pleasant and kindly. But he believes in hard war. I heard him say: 'Columbia!—pretty much all burned; and burned *good*.' "

After nearly an hour Grant interrupted. "I'm sorry to break up this interesting conversation, but the President is aboard the *River Queen*, and I know he will be anxious to see you. Suppose we go and pay him a visit before dinner." "All right," said Sherman. They took Admiral Porter and soon the three found Lincoln alone in the after cabin of the steamer. Sherman and Lincoln after nearly four years again faced each other. Lincoln had then belittled Sherman's fears of a long war of horror with "I guess we'll manage to keep house," and Sherman had walked away with his brother calling damnation on all politicians, until recent months rating Lincoln as too slow and too political-minded.

"He remembered me perfectly," wrote Sherman later of this meeting, "and at once engaged in a most interesting conversation." Admiral Porter however wrote that Lincoln "did not remember" when he had seen Sherman before "until the general reminded him of the circumstances of their first meeting." Porter thought this "singular" of Lincoln. It would be. Senator John Sherman in April of '61 had called on Lincoln with reference to Ohio appointments, introducing to Lincoln his brother Colonel Sherman, who had just resigned as head of the State Military Academy of Louisiana. Lincoln had forgotten about that, according to Porter. But the forgetfulness of Lincoln didn't sink in with Sherman. He went away with the impression Lincoln *did* remember they had met before and there had been no necessity of his reminding Lincoln. "He remembered me perfectly."

Sherman found Lincoln "full of curiosity" about the marches, the "bummers," the foraging, along with anxiety about what might happen to the army while its commander was gone. Sherman explained that the army was snug in good camps at Goldsboro, that it would require some days to collect forage and food for another march, that General Schofield was competent to command in his absence. The conversation ranged wide from moments of laughter to solemnity, Lincoln reverting again and again to the safety of Sherman's army and the fear that Johnston would escape capture. Sherman's assurance that he had Johnston faded was complete.

After an hour or so Grant and Sherman returned to Grant's cabin, where Mrs. Grant after greetings had a question. Colonel Horace Porter heard her, in her womanly way, inquire of the two generals, "Did you see Mrs. Lincoln?"

GRANT. Oh, we went rather on a business errand, and I did not ask for Mrs. Lincoln.

SHERMAN. And I didn't even know she was aboard.

MRS. GRANT. Well, you are a pretty pair! I do not see how you could have been so neglectful.

GRANT. Well, Julia, we are going to pay another visit in the morning, and we'll take good care to make amends for our conduct to-day.

As Mrs. Grant fixed tea for four she said, "Perhaps you don't want me here listening to all your secrets." Sherman, with a shy glance at Mrs. Grant: "Do you think we can trust her, Grant?" Grant with a twinkle spoke of what one woman knows being known to everybody, and Sherman began putting Mrs. Grant through a mock examination. Mrs. Grant giving nice nonsensical answers, Sherman finally said with a wrinkled grin, "Well, Grant, I think we can trust her."

Next morning, March 28, the generals boarded the *River Queen*, where, wrote Sherman, "we were again received most courteously by the President, who conducted us to the after-cabin. After the general compliments, General Grant inquired after *Mrs.* Lincoln, when the President went to her state-room, returned, and begged us to excuse her, as she was not well."

Then came a conference of the three pivotal Northern men of the war, with Admiral Porter also present. Grant explained that at the very instant Sheridan was crossing the James River below City Point, that Sheridan had a large effective cavalry force for striking Lee's only remaining rail-road connections, that a crisis was drawing near, that his only apprehension was that Lee would not wait long enough. In case Lee did break through, or swing around, Grant was sure there would be hot pursuit.

Both Grant and Sherman supposed that one or the other of them would have to fight one more bloody battle, and that it would be the *last*. "Mr. Lincoln exclaimed, more than once," wrote Sherman, "that there had been blood enough shed, and asked us if another battle could not be avoided." The generals told Lincoln they could not control that event. That the war might be ended without another big dance of death and wholesale slaughter seemed a deep and constant hope with Lincoln. Sherman pictured his army as probably having a final big fight somewhere near Raleigh. Grant's picture depended on Lee. If Lee yet waited a few more days, he would be able to stop Lee from joining Johnston. Grant could only be sure that if Lee did get between him and Johnston he would be on Lee's heels and moving fast.

"Mr. Lincoln," wrote Sherman, "more than once expressed uneasiness that I was not with my army at Goldsboro', when I again assured him that General Schofield was fully competent to command in my absence; that I was going to start back that very day." Admiral Porter's account of this conference held that the President expressed fears that the Confederate general would escape south again by the railroads, that Sherman would have to chase Johnston anew, over the same ground, Sherman remarking: "I have him where he cannot move without breaking up his army, which, once disbanded, can never again be got together; and I have destroyed the Southern railroads, so that they cannot be used again for a long time." Grant interposed, "What is to prevent their laying the rails again?" Sherman: "Why, my bummers don't do things by halves. Every rail, after having been placed over a hot fire, has been twisted as crooked as a ram's-horn, and they never can be used again."

Sherman came now to a momentous point. For his army, the country North and South and the society to be molded in the immediate future, it was momentous. Sherman's account written years later, reported:

"I inquired of the President if he was all ready for the end of the war. What was to be done with the rebel armies when defeated? And what should be done with the political leaders, such as Jeff. Davis, etc.? Should we allow them to escape, etc.? He said he was all ready; all he wanted of us was to defeat the opposing armies, and to get the men composing the Confederate armies back to their homes, at work on their farms and in their shops. As to Jeff. Davis, he was hardly at liberty to speak his mind fully, but intimated that he ought to clear out, 'escape the country,' only it would not do for him to say so openly. As usual, he illustrated his meaning by a story: 'A man once had taken the total-abstinence pledge. When visiting a friend, he was invited to take a drink, but declined, on the score of his pledge; when his friend suggested lemonade, which was accepted. In preparing the lemonade, the friend pointed to the brandy-bottle, and said the lemonade would be more palatable if he were to pour in a little brandy; when his guest said, if he could do so "unbeknown" to him, he would not object.' From which illustration I inferred that Mr. Lincoln wanted Davis to escape, 'unbeknown' to him."

Lincoln was this day talking with two men like himself terribly intimate with awful authority, more personal power than any of them enjoyed handling. They hoped soon to be free from their daily arithmetic of slaughter, disease, hunger. They had, as foretold, ridden in blood up to the horses' bridles. Their smoke and its remembrance were to stay long. They were hammering out a national fate, not seeing at all in any clear detail the shape of things to come. Before them hazards and intricacies lay too vast to put on paper. Lincoln hesitated at outlining for his generals any peace terms or reconstruction policies beyond the few simple conditions he had named at Hampton Roads.

In Europe at that hour could be heard the prediction that Sherman would take over the Washington Government and run it. Delane of the London *Times* spoke fears of that event. In Europe so often it had happened that the brilliant and terroristic military conqueror, after marches and battles, by a few words and a turn of the hand through a coup d'état became dictator. Of this point in the conference of Lincoln, Grant, and Sherman, there seemed to have been no mention nor any slightest fear. They knew that McClellan in one hour was conceivable as a dictator had he possessed the audacity, the cunning, and the ruthlessness of Ben Butler, who in turn had never had a real army behind him ready to topple Lincoln and take over the Federal Government. For two years Lincoln and these two generals had been welding a strange partnership that worked, strange because it operated so smoothly and effectively. Amid malice, conspiracy, jealousies, amid crooked and crazy entanglements of human impulse and motive that made the war a dismal swamp-jungle affair, the three held together. A rare trust, a common understanding that had stood many a fierce test, a species of comradeship, had been created between these three men. Of each of them it had been graphically said that he was intensely American and could have been born and made nowhere but in the "U.S.A." They read each other now by signals, intentions, and hopes rather than by promises and stipulations that given circumstances of war could wreck and blow away.

So now Sherman asked about the end of the war, the crushed Confederate armies, the flying and fugitive Confederate political leaders. "I inquired," wrote Sherman. He was eager to hear any specific recommendations that might have occurred to the mind of the President. Always Sherman tried to look ahead and be ready for contingencies. Now what? Of the President's answers Sherman later wrote:

"Mr. Lincoln was full and frank in his conversation, assuring me that in his mind he was all ready for the civil reorganization of affairs at the South as soon as the war was over; and he distinctly authorized me to assure Governor Vance and the people of North Carolina that, as soon as the rebel armies laid down their arms, and resumed their civil pursuits, they would at once be guaranteed all their rights as citizens of a common country; and that to avoid anarchy the State governments then in existence, with their civil functionaries, would be recognized by him as the government *de facto* till Congress could provide others.

"I know, when I left him, that I was more than ever impressed by his kindly nature, his deep and earnest sympathy with the afflictions of the whole people, resulting from the war, and by the march of hostile armies through the South; and that his earnest desire seemed to be to end the war speedily, without more bloodshed or devastation, and to restore all the men of both sections to their homes. In the language of his second inaugural address, he seemed to have 'charity for all, malice toward none,' and, above all, an absolute faith in the courage, manliness, and integrity of the armies in the field. When at rest or listening, his legs and arms seemed to hang almost lifeless, and his face was care-worn and haggard; but, the moment he began to talk, his face lightened up, his tall form, as it were, unfolded, and he was the very impersonation of good-humor and fellowship. The last words I recall as addressed to me were that he would feel better when I was back at Goldsboro'.''

Those were the deep and abiding impressions of Sherman from this conference. A Frémont, a McClellan, a Butler, even a Sheridan, might in Lincoln's fathomings have required more specific instructions. On only two points did Lincoln throw misgivings and gloom toward Sherman. One was that there might be another needless big battle. The other was that Sherman's army was not safe outside of Sherman's hands. In the matter of disorder, civil tumults, violence, "anarchy," to ensue after peace and disbandment of the Confederate armies, the techniques of reconstruction, neither worried the other. Lincoln seemed aware that Sherman, one-time superintendent of the Louisiana State Military Academy, author of the remarkable letter from Black River sketching the Southern war scene, would be guided by conditions toward the same generous policy of which Lincoln had tried to persuade the Republican radicals in House and Senate. As to Grant, so near to Washington, Grant the Hammer of War who was nevertheless an old-time Douglas Democrat, there too Lincoln had little of gloom or misgiving, though on Grant too he repeatedly impressed his hope of avoiding another large-scale combat.

Porter claimed that after this conference he "jotted down" what he remembered of the conversation, later writing from these notes that the President "was then wrought up to a high state of excitement." This could be directly taken to mean that Lincoln's self-control was not so good, that he was not keeping cool, that he was more than grave of manner and more than deeply moved. This state of mind and nerves was not observed nor mentioned by Sherman and Grant. The President "wanted peace on almost any terms," ran the loosely framed opinion of Admiral Porter, "and there is no knowing what proposals he might have been willing to listen to." This to Nicolay and Hay seemed incompatible "with the very guarded language of Mr. Lincoln elsewhere." The secretaries judged it was "no doubt true that he spoke of his willingness to be liberal to the verge of prudence, and that he even gave them to understand that he would not be displeased at the escape from the country of Jefferson Davis and other principal rebel leaders."

The three Northern pivotal men were parting, Sherman to remember Lincoln in a most simple manner: "Sherman, do you know why I took a shine to Grant and you?"

"I don't know, Mr. Lincoln, you have been extremely kind to me, far more than my deserts."

"Well, you never found fault with me."

Lincoln and Sherman had done most of the talking, Grant not mentioning a matter which he later brought before Lincoln. "I told him that I had been very anxious to have the Eastern armies vanquish their old enemy,"

wrote Grant of this matter new to the President, the General in Chief pointing to the striding Western legions who had swept over an area from the
Mississippi River to the State of North Carolina and were now almost ready
to knock at the back door of Richmond. "I said to him that if the Western
armies should be even upon the field, operating against Richmond and Lee,
the credit would be given to them for the capture, by politicians and non-
combatants from the section of country which those troops hailed from.
. . . Western members [of Congress] might be throwing it up to the members of the East that . . . they were not able to capture an army, or to
accomplish much . . . but had to wait until the Western armies had conquered all the territory south and west of them, and then come on to help
them capture the only army they had been engaged with. Mr. Lincoln said
he saw that now, but had never thought of it before, because his anxiety
was so great that he did not care where the aid came from so the work was
done."

On the swift armed steamer the *Bat* Sherman started down the James
River that afternoon, pacing the deck with his brother Senator John Sherman of the Buckeye State. A knowing scribe was to write of the two
brothers and how dramatically time had reversed their characters. "John,
once the wild, bad boy of the Sherman family, was now watchdog of the
nation's finance, chairman of the Senate committee on expenditures, a man
already cold from the handling of money, public and private. Cump (the
family nick-name for William Tecumseh), the shy, gentle boy, had become
a man whose name symbolized devastation." To the shut-mouthed Senator
the General confided some of Lincoln's ideas and feelings spoken in the
morning, the Senator writing later, "I did not at the time agree with the
generous policy proposed by Mr. Lincoln."

Arriving at New Bern and hurrying toward his army, Sherman met his
army mailman and confidential messenger, Colonel Markland. At a candle-
lighted breakfast Markland learned that easy peace terms would be offered
Joe Johnston, and as to Davis and his Cabinet: "Said Mr. Lincoln, we will
leave the door open; let them go! We don't want to be bothered with them
in getting the Government to running smoothly." Markland noted: "I felt
then that General Sherman had really given me the terms suggested by
Mr. Lincoln to him."

To Lee that week Johnston telegraphed his summary of what he might
expect to do against his old antagonist: "I can no more than annoy him."

Back at City Point Lincoln kept close to Grant, whose company he
would lose in a day or two, when a big push was to begin and Grant would
live at the fighting front with his troops in motion. The newspaper correspondent Charles Carleton Coffin was at headquarters the day Sherman left
and Lincoln greeted him: "What news have you?"

"I have just arrived from Charleston and Savannah."

"Indeed! Well, I'm right glad to see you. How do the people like being
back in the Union again?"

"I think some of them are reconciled to it, if we may draw conclusions from the action of one planter, who, while I was there, came down the Savannah River with his whole family—wife, children, negro woman and her children, of whom he was father—and with his crop of cotton which he was anxious to sell at the highest price."

"Oh, yes, I see." Lincoln brightened with sparkling eyes. "I see; patriarchal times once more; Abraham, Sarah, Isaac, Hagar and Ishmael, all in one boat!" And with a chuckle: "I reckon they'll accept the situation now that they can sell their cotton."

From the deck of the *River Queen* that night as Sherman sped south on a steamer and Grant made ready to move his army out of camps, shelters, huts, and trenches they had occupied ten months, Lincoln could look out toward near-by hills and rolling land where he had seen ground torn and gashed, large spaces for miles naked of trees cut by shellfire or chopped down for fuel, trenches, forts, traverses, defenses, huts. On a wide front the army would move tomorrow. And for what? For another shambles and again burying squads and again the surgeons amputating till the arms and legs piled high for wagonloads?

That sword of Robert E. Lee—how it had vanished and come back and held its ground beyond prophecies! Could Lee and those valiant bayonets of his on which the Confederate Government had been carried for three years, could he again swing round and baffle pursuit, perhaps win to the mountains, fight guerrilla style till he could recruit a new army? This was the forecast among a few—not many—observers. It was a method that had won the War of the Revolution, carried through by Lee's hero and exemplar George Washington.

What did the night's darkness hold? In a few days, in a week, Lincoln would set foot in Richmond, the Southern capital in Northern hands—this was one prediction. And then what? Would Grant take Lee? If he did, then both the structure and the dream of a Confederate States of America was sunk with the fabrics of all shadows and dust. A republican Union of States cemented and welded with blood and iron would stand for a long time among World Power nations, committed to government of, by, and for the people. Only for the assurance of that reality had Lincoln cared to live these last four years of burdens and bitterness.

Beyond the screen and mist of the night lay what? Peach blooms and apricot blossoms had risen in the air the last few days in rare spots. April was so near. What of this April?

CHAPTER 66

GRANT BREAKS LEE'S LINE '65

AT eight-thirty on the morning of March 29, 1865, Lincoln went ashore from the *River Queen* to Grant's shanty. They were putting the horses aboard the railroad train that was to take Grant and his staff to the Petersburg front. Lincoln and Grant spoke of the devices daily proposed to them for destroying the enemy. The most recent plan offered, said Grant, "was to supply our men with bayonets just a foot longer than those of the enemy, and then charge them. When they met, our bayonets would go clear through the enemy, while theirs would not reach far enough to touch our men, and the war would be ended."

"Well, there is a good deal of terror in steel," rejoined Lincoln. "I had a chance to test it once myself." And the final anecdote they had time for before leaving Horace Porter gathered:

"When I was a young man, I was walking along a back street in Louisville one night about twelve o'clock, when a very tough-looking citizen sprang out of an alleyway, reached up to the back of his neck, pulled out a bowie-knife that seemed to my stimulated imagination about three feet long, and planted himself square across my path. For two or three minutes he flourished his weapon in front of my face, appearing to try to see just how near he could come to cutting my nose off without quite doing it. He could see in the moonlight that I was taking a good deal of interest in the proceeding, and finally he yelled out, as he steadied the knife close to my throat: 'Stranger, kin you lend me five dollars on that?' I never reached in my pocket and got out money so fast in all my life. I handed him a bank-note, and said: 'There's ten, neighbor; now put up your scythe.'"

Mrs. Grant stood by, her face pale and sorrowful. At the door Grant kissed her, over and again, joined Lincoln; the two walked down to the railroad platform. "Mr. Lincoln looked more serious than at any other time since he had visited headquarters," noted Horace Porter. "The lines in his face seemed deeper, and the rings under his eyes were of a darker hue. It was plain that the weight of responsibility was oppressing him." At the train the President gave a warm handshake to the General and to each member of the staff, and then stood near the rear end of the car while they went aboard. The train was ready to start. They all raised their hats in respect to the President. His hat went off to them and his voice was broken and he couldn't hide it as he called to them: "Good-by, gentlemen. God bless you all! Remember, your success is my success." The whistle sounded. The train moved. Grant was off to a campaign all hoped would be his last and the last of the war.

Lighting a cigar and amid smoke rings that wreathed him, Grant went over some of his plans with staff officers, detouring once to say: "The President is one of the few visitors I have had who has not attempted to extract from me a knowledge of my movements, although he is the only one who has a right to know them. He intends to remain at City Point for the present, and will be the most anxious man in the country to hear from us, his heart is so wrapped up in our success; but I think we can send him some good news in a day or two." Porter thought he had never seen Grant so cool and sure about results from the coming death-grapple.

The news that day and the next was rain. Over all was the rain. Fair weather of several days on the evening of March 29 gave way to torrents from the sky. On the two armies, on the just and the unjust, on Grant and Lee in the field, on the Davis home in Richmond, on the *River Queen* cabins sheltering the Lincoln family, the rain poured down all night of the twenty-ninth and all day on the thirtieth.

In dense underbrush and in swampy ground where troops were under orders to move, fields became beds of quicksand. Troops waded in mud above their ankles. Horses sank to their bellies and had to be pulled out with halters. Wagon wheels sank to the hubs and in some cases above the axles to the wagon box. Roads became sheets of water and Horace Porter heard that not a Grant but a Noah would be needed to save the army. Soldiers cried to officers, "I say, fetch along the pontoons," or "When are the gunboats coming up?" Marching on such a terrain was only worse than trying to sleep in wet blankets on soaked ground. On March 30 men's tempers showed. Some went in for profanity contests. At headquarters Rawlins gloomed and told his chief it might be better to fall back and later make a fresh start. Grant held that soon as the weather cleared up the roads the men would be gay again. Sheridan arrived on a white pacer and was all for action.

Lincoln on the evening of the thirtieth telegraphed Stanton his feeling that he ought to be in Washington, yet he disliked to leave without seeing nearer to the end of Grant's present movement. Grant had now been out "since yesterday morning and although he has not been diverted from his programme no considerable effort has yet been produced so far as we know here." What little action there was the President described: "Last night at 10:15 P.M. when it was dark as a rainy night without a moon could be, a furious cannonade soon joined in by a heavy musketry fire opened near Petersburg and lasted about two hours. The sound was very distinct here as also were the flashes of the guns up the clouds. It seemed to me a great battle, but the older hands here scarcely noticed it and sure enough this morning it was found that very little had been done."

On his maps Lincoln traced the troop dispositions ordered by Grant from right to left: Weitzel in front of Richmond, with a portion of the Army of the James, Parke and Wright holding Union works in front of Petersburg, Ord extending to the intersection of Hatcher's Run and the Vaughan Road, Humphreys stretching beyond Dabney's Mill, Warren on the extreme left reaching as far as the junction of the Vaughan Road and the Boydton Plank Road, and Sheridan at Dinwiddie Court House. For thousands of men each of these names came to have meanings of struggle, hardship, laughter, terror. Over mud and quicksand they built miles of corduroy road for the hauling of heavy artillery. At noon of the thirty-first Lincoln had a telegram from Grant: "There has been much hard fighting this morning. The enemy drove our left from near Dabney's house back well toward the Boydton plank road. We are now about to take the offensive at that point, and I hope will more than recover the lost ground." Before three o'clock came a second telegram from Grant: "Our troops, after being driven back to the Boydton plank road, turned and drove the enemy in turn, and took the White Oak road, which we now have. This gives us the ground occupied by the enemy this morning. I will send you a rebel flag captured by our troops in driving the enemy back. There have been four flags captured to-day."

Having studied his map, as Lincoln relayed these telegrams to Stanton he commented: "Judging by the two points from which General Grant telegraphs, I infer that he moved his headquarters about one mile since he sent the first of the two despatches."

Seward came down for a business visit. Lincoln on April 1 wired to Grant a correction of a mistaken impression that Stanton had come down to look and see. "I presume," wrote Lincoln, "the mistake comes of the fact that the Secretary of State was here. He started back to Washington this morning."

To Stanton, Lincoln wired at noon that dispatches from Grant had little additional news to that of the day before "except that Sheridan also had pretty hot work yesterday, that infantry was sent to his support during the night, and that he [Grant] has not since heard from Sheridan." To this Lincoln added the personal item that Mrs. Lincoln had started home for Washington, and he would thank Stanton "to see that our coachman is at the Arsenal wharf at eight o'clock to-morrow morning, there to wait until she arrives."

Sheridan had fallen back from Five Forks in good order before an attack conducted by Lee's nephew Fitzhugh Lee and General Pickett, the same commander who had led the famous charge at Gettysburg. In Sheridan's taking his troops back to wait for reinforcements, he "displayed great generalship," Grant officially reported. The next morning, noted Horace Porter, the 5th Corps of the Army of the Potomac "seemed eager once more to cross bayonets with their old antagonists." Sheridan chafed at delay in moving forward, struck the clenched fist of one hand into the palm of another, and fretted like a caged tiger, once saying, "This battle must be fought and won before the sun goes down." Skirmish lines followed by assaulting columns began their action on Pickett's entrenched line.

One skirmish line halted and seemed to waver. Sheridan put spurs to his black Rienzi, who had carried him from Winchester to Cedar Creek, and dashed along the front from regiment to regiment shouting cheer and counsel such as: "Come on, men! Go at 'em with a will! Move on at a clean jump or you'll not catch one of them. They're getting ready to run now, and if you don't get on to them in five minutes, they'll every one of them get away from you. Now go for them!" Thus Horace Porter, on the ground sending his messages every half-hour to Grant, saw and heard much that day of Sheridan. A man on the skirmish line was struck in the neck; the blood spurted as if the jugular vein had been cut. "I'm killed!" he cried, and dropped on the ground. "You're not hurt a bit!" cried Sheridan. "Pick up your gun, man, and move right on to the front." These words brought the man up, he snatched his musket, and rushed forward a dozen paces before he fell never to rise again. Over mud roads, swampy fields, and through dense undergrowth the spattered and foaming Rienzi carried Sheridan from point to point rallying his men.

Once where the lines had broken under a staggering fire, Sheridan rushed in. "Where is my battle flag?" And as the color sergeant rode up and handed him the crimson and white banner, the wild Irish commander waved it over his head, cheered the ranks on—while bullets hummed like swarming bees. One pierced the flag itself, another brought down the sergeant who had carried it; horses of two staff officers went down from the flying lead.

A regimental band mounted on gray horses, playing lively tunes, cheered the fighters on till a bullet went through the trombone horn and another split the snare drum, after which the band quit its music and took a hand in combat.

Sheridan went on dashing where the fire was most furious, waving his battle flag, praying, swearing, shaking his fist, yelling threats and blessings, a demon in the flesh dedicated to fighting. With fixed bayonets and a final rousing cheer, the Union columns under Ayres overran the enemy earthworks, swept everything before them, killed or captured in their immediate front every man whose legs had not saved him.

Rienzi with a leap carried Sheridan over the earthworks, landing amid a line of prisoners who had thrown down their muskets. Some called, "Whar do you want us-all to go to?" Sheridan's battle rage turned to humor. "Go right over there," pointing toward the rear. "Get right along, now. Oh, drop your guns; you'll never need them any more. You'll all be safe over there. Are there any more of you? We want every one of you fellows." Some 1,500 of the ragged and butternut-clad troops were escorted to the rear from this angle.

Lincoln while this battle raged did his best at picturing it from a dispatch sent by Grant. On the basis of this Lincoln wired Stanton at Washington and Seward at Fortress Monroe that "Sheridan, aided by Warren had at 2 P.M. pushed the enemy back so as to retake the five forks and bring his own headquarters up to I. [J.] Boisseans [Boisseau's]. The five forks were barricaded by the enemy and carried by Diven's [sic] division of cavalry. This part of the enemy seem to now be trying to work along the White Oak road to join the main force in front of Grant, while Sheridan and Warren are pressing them as closely as possible."

To Lieutenant General Grant, so designated, Lincoln wired appreciation of Sheridan's success, and "Having no great deal to do here, I am still sending the substance of your despatches to the Secretary of War." Then across the next two days Lincoln sent to Stanton a series of Grant's dispatches, relayed as Grant wrote them, and these the Secretary of War gave to the press. Thus millions of readers in the North had what they took as authentic information about the crumbling of Lee's lines around Richmond and the foreshadowing of the capture of Petersburg and the fall of Richmond.

From the afternoon of April 1 to the evening of April 2 this series of telegrams told the main story, chiefly in Grant's text as forwarded by Lincoln. Anxious Northern readers, including a horde of speculators and gamblers, saw in the public prints that Sheridan with his cavalry and the 5th Corps had captured three brigades of infantry, a train of wagons, several batteries, several thousand prisoners—that Grant on the morning of April 2 ordered an attack along the whole line—that Wright and Parke got through the enemy's lines, that on further breaking the enemy entrenched lines they had taken forts, guns, prisoners, that Wright was tearing up the Southside Railroad, that the 6th Corps alone took 3,000 prisoners, that the Union lines were enveloping Petersburg, Grant telegraphing at 4:30 P.M. of April 2 several details with assurances: "The whole captures since the army started out will not amount to less than 12,000 men, and probably fifty pieces of artillery. . . . All seems well with us, and everything is quiet just now."

In sending Mrs. Lincoln the gist of this last dispatch from Grant the President added: "He suggests that I shall go out and see him in the morning, which I think I will do. Tad and I are both well, and will be glad to see you and your party here at the time you name." And speaking as a President in the solemnity of a high action he telegraphed Grant: "Allow me to tender to you and all with you the nation's grateful thanks for this additional and magnificent success. At your kind suggestion I think I will visit you to-morrow."

To Sherman Grant telegraphed his pride over "this army" winning "a most decisive victory" after which it "followed the enemy," a point Grant would stress. "This is all that it ever wanted to make it as good an army as ever fought a battle."

Now Robert E. Lee was making his decision that his troops move out of Petersburg. This would give Richmond to Grant and Lincoln. Lee had stretched his line of men till it was too thin. It was thin because he had too few men, only 1,100 men to the mile, or a five-foot length for each soldier. Each of these soldiers, however, had the advantage of an elaborate system of zigzag approaches and crisscrossed connecting trenches, with bombproof shelters, batteries, rifle pits. As some of the assaulting Union troops gazed at sectors of the line they had taken that day they wondered how anyone could ever have gotten through. Possibly they wouldn't have gotten through had not hunger, desertion, dissension, and a confused and weakening Confederate morale cut down the number of Lee's effective troops. The prime factor perhaps was that Southern man power, in its total, had been steadily slashed from the first battle of Bull Run on through successions of bloody battles to Five Forks, till the list of brave men in gray killed, dead, or disabled from wounds or disease was of mournful extent. The dead Stonewall Jackson and J. E. B. Stuart, so precious to Lee, had been joined that morning of April 2 by General A. P. Hill, so long a reliable outrider with Lee.

Head Quarters Armies of the United States,

City-Point, April, 2, 8¼ P.M. 1865.

Lieut. General Grant.

Allow me to tender to you, and all with you, the nations grateful thanks for this additional, and magnificent success — At your kind suggestion, I think I will visit you to-morrow.

A. Lincoln

Lincoln thanks Grant and promises a visit. Original in the Barrett collection.

On a dapple-gray horse Hill had ridden out and on in a morning fog, suddenly encountering two Federals who answered the call of "Surrender!" with rifle shots. And A. P. Hill toppled out of his saddle. Tears came to Lee's eyes on hearing of it. "He is at rest now," murmured Lee, "and we who are left are the ones to suffer."

The eyes of Lee lighted on old comrades who had flirted with death, General Hunton returning from Five Forks with a scabbard bent double from some missile, three bullet holes through his clothes. Lee briskly greeted Hunton: "I wish you would sew those places up. I don't like to see them." Hunton: "General Lee, allow me to go back home and see my wife and I will have them sewed up." Lee toyed with this a moment. It gave him a ripple of light thought. "The idea of talking about going to see wives; it is perfectly ridiculous, sir."

On both sides hundreds of items of valor, Lyman writing of a redoubt where a Confederate captain told his men to surrender to nobody. "He himself fought to the last, and was killed with the butt-end of a musket, and most of his command were slain in the work. But we carried the works; neither ditches nor abatis could keep our men out that day!" Lyman was caught in an elation kindred to that of Sherman, who in the entrancement

of a hard-won performance once wrote to his wife of "the grand and beautiful game of war." Lyman shared this elation in writing to his wife Mimi of
the captain killed with the butt end of a musket, not entering into the gory
details of the slippery, dripping butt end nor of the look of a human head
having a hole stove in it by the impact of wood and metal driven only by
the muscle power of an assailant.

The human cost of breaking Lee's line, however, was less than it might
have been. It had not reached such a major conflict as Lincoln had feared.
At a lesser price than predicted Lee's army was cut off from Richmond,
and on the night of April 2 his troops, ordered out of Petersburg and other
points on the line, were reconcentrating to march west, aiming to move
around Grant and join with Johnston's army in North Carolina. This movement of Lee, Grant's preparations to head off Lee, the expected fall of Richmond, were the immediate items of war interest when Lincoln boarded a
railroad car at City Point for a ride to Petersburg.

Rear Admiral Porter on this ride was to accompany Lincoln, who had
moved his living quarters from the *River Queen* to Porter's flagship the
Malvern. On Porter's inquiring of the first night Lincoln said: "I slept well
but you can't put a long blade into a short scabbard. I was too long for
that berth." During the day, without Lincoln's being told of it, Porter had
carpenters take down the stateroom and rebuild it longer, also widening the
berth and mattress, Lincoln saying of the second night, "I shrunk six inches
in length and about a foot sideways." The guard Crook wrote of a man
asking to see the President, saying he was a Republican who had spent
money to elect the President and being now in trouble, must be admitted
for an interview. The name, he told Crook, was Smith. Lincoln refused to
see the man named Smith and merely Smith. Crook ordered "Smith" away
and the man left voicing vague threats. According to both Crook and Admiral Porter, Vice-President Andrew Johnson sent word he was aboard a
near-by vessel, Lincoln avoiding an interview with "I guess he can get along
without me."

According to Admiral Porter's somewhat fulsome account, not lacking
in discrepancies, he stood at the locked door of the car where the President
had entered and was seated for the ride to Petersburg when three nicely
enough dressed men came saying they must see the President. They kept insisting, two of them mounting to the rear platform where Porter, according
to Porter, with his bare fists sent them sprawling in the mud. The President
wished to know what Porter "would sell that trick for," and according to
Porter, added with a laugh, "I intend never to travel again unless you go
along."

At Petersburg Captain Robert Todd Lincoln was on hand with a
mounted escort and a horse for his father. Porter managed to get a soldier
to dismount and let him have a rawboned trotter and stumbler that disgusted
the Admiral. As they arrived at Grant's quarters Porter asked one of the
staff if he could buy the horse. Lincoln, on hearing the offer, according to

Porter, exclaimed: "Why in the name of all that's good do you want that horse, Admiral? Just look at him; his head is as big as a flour-barrel."

"That's the case with all horses' heads."

"Well, look at his knees; they're sprung. He's fourteen years old if he's a day; his hoofs will cover half an acre. He's spavined, and only has one eye. What do you want with him? You sailors don't know anything about a horse."

"But I want it for a particular purpose. I want to buy it and shoot it, so that no one will ever ride it again."

This pleased the President, and according to Porter he said it was "the best reason he had ever heard of for buying a horse." Undoubtedly there was some sort of horseplay between Admiral David D. Porter and the President on that day and other days, but the Admiral's later recital of it lacked the precision and persuasion to be found in the accounts of humor written by Colonel Horace Porter.

On the piazza of a house Grant and his staff were waiting, ready to go. They received the President, who spoke warm congratulations, Grant writing of their meeting, "About the first thing that Mr. Lincoln said to me . . . was: 'Do you know, general, that I have had a sort of a sneaking idea for some days that you intended to do something like this.' "

Except for Negroes, the town of Petersburg seemed abandoned. Grant had started all his troops out early in the morning; there were only his staff and a small cavalry escort left. Grant now felt himself more free to talk about his plans, which had worked out much as he had designed. He spoke also of how the record of the Eastern troops was such that between them and the Western soldiers there could be no ill feeling; only the politicians on that score could provoke any envy or bickering between sections.

The man at whose house this meeting was held, one Thomas Wallace, had been a friend of Lincoln in old Whig days. To a Sanitary Commission worker, C. C. Carpenter, Wallace told of his small boy seeing Lincoln dismount in front of the house, the boy muttering, "You are not going to let that man come into the house!" the father replying, "I think it would not do to try to stop a man from coming in who has fifty thousand men at his back." Lincoln after greetings as between old Whigs enjoyed hearing this from Wallace.

A little newssheet, *Grant's Petersburg Progress*, printed by Union soldiers, carried an item: "Some inquiries had been made about a possible renting of the beautiful brick mansion in which General Hartsuff has his headquarters. The President had heard of it and he had also seen the tearing effects of our shelling on the building. Said he, 'It is my opinion,' as if giving answer to the enquirer, 'our batteries have made *rent* enough here already.' The joke was, of course, perceived and enjoyed."

At City Point Lincoln wired Stanton at 5 P.M. this April 3: "Stayed with General Grant an hour and a half and returned here. It is certain now that Richmond is in our hands, and I think I will go there to-morrow." Stanton had again warned him about his personal safety and he assured the Secretary of War. "Thanks for your caution. . . . I will take care of myself." This solicitude of Stanton regarding the President's safety was continuous, though Stanton nevertheless had his satisfactions over the President's being away. Of a meeting of three Cabinet members on March 30 Welles wrote in his diary: "Stanton, who was present, remarked that it was quite as pleasant to have the President away, that he [Stanton] was much less annoyed. Neither Seward nor myself responded." Seward's departure for City Point that day Welles surmised was another "irregular proceeding" in connection with peace efforts. "Yet the President has much shrewdness and sagacity. He has been apprehensive that the military men are not very solicitous to close hostilities,—fears our generals will exact severe terms." This as a diary entry merely revealed that the Secretary of the Navy was vastly unaware of feeling in the armies about peace, and particularly the fact that the peace terms in the minds of Grant and Sherman much more nearly coincided with those of the President than did Welles's own views about the necessity for punishment of Confederate leaders.

As Lincoln visited the sick and wounded among avenues of hospital tents at City Point that week, Adelaide W. Smith, the nurse who had attended the inaugural evening reception at the White House with the soldier on crutches, saw the President but hesitated at pushing forward to speak to him. Miss Smith heard the camp talk that when the President's party came to one set of tents young Dr. Jerome Walker of the Sanitary Commission pointing at them said, "Mr. President, you do not want to go in there."

"Why not, my boy?"

"They are sick rebel prisoners."

"That is just where I do want to go," and he strode in and shook hands from cot to cot and spoke such words as came to him which he thought might comfort.

Shot-torn in both hips, in one ward the only Confederate among wounded Union officers, lay Colonel Harry L. Benbow of South Carolina, who had commanded three regiments at Five Forks. Down the long aisle between cots came the Union President, bowing and smiling "Good morning." And according to Colonel Benbow:

"He halted beside my bed and held out his hand. I was lying on my back, my knees drawn up, my hands folded across my breast. Looking him in the face, as he stood with extended hand, 'Mr. President,' I said, 'do you know to whom you offer your hand?' 'I do not,' he replied. 'Well,' said I, 'you offer it to a Confederate colonel who has fought you as hard as he could for four years.' 'Well,' said he, 'I hope a Confederate colonel will not refuse me his hand.' 'No, sir,' I replied, 'I will not,' and I clasped his hand in both of mine."

In a ward given entirely to sick and wounded Confederate officers, Lincoln spoke with several about old friends among their kinsfolk he had known, in one particular case a general whose brother had been with him in Congress in 1848. Between five and six thousand men of both sides were in these hospitals at City Point, and Lincoln, even when informed by the head surgeon of this number, insisted he must try and visit every last man of them. He did not find time, however, to make the complete rounds. His right arm lame from handshaking at the end of one afternoon, the surgeon said it certainly must ache. Lincoln smiled, mentioned "strong muscles," stepped out the door of the surgeon's shanty, took an ax, sent chips flying, then paused and slowly with his right arm raised the ax till he was holding it at full horizontal without a quiver. Before leaving the head surgeon he was offered what he might like by way of a drink. He took a glass of lemonade.

CHAPTER 67

LINCOLN SITS IN THE CONFEDERATE WHITE HOUSE

ON the Sabbath day of April 2, 1865, in Richmond, Virginia, the diarist Jones noted: "I met Judge Campbell in Ninth Street, talking rapidly to himself, with two books under his arm." What the Judge was talking about Jones couldn't hear. It was the kind of a day wherein if you talked to yourself you were sure of a listener.

Robert E. Lee by telegraph talked with Jefferson Davis that Sabbath. From the field out near Petersburg Lee was issuing orders that his men destroy many supplies and guns that could not be moved, with further orders that as the troops moved westward they were to wreck all bridges after the last Confederate forces had crossed. To President Davis, Lee dictated a telegram which was carried to Richmond. Then, a story goes:

In the Davis family pew of St. Paul's Episcopal Church, seated erect and calm under the chancel, Jefferson Davis was in attendance in a congregation chiefly of women in black and rusty black attire. Their menfolk in the main were keeping the Sabbath at battle and marching fronts. The Reverend Mr. Minnegerode intoned, "The Lord is in His holy temple; let all the earth keep silence before Him," and in the pause following, an adjutant, mud on his boots, a hard-riding man, holding his saber so it wouldn't clank or jingle, came up the aisle in a swift military stride and handed a paper to President Davis. It rustled as it unfolded. In quiet with everybody gazing at him and wondering what the news might be, Davis read the words General Lee had long delayed and sent at last when imperative: "I advise that all preparation be made for leaving Richmond tonight. I will advise you later, according to circumstances."

Taking his hat, President Davis arose, walked down the aisle, erect as ever, his face calm, white, marble-cold. Mrs. Davis had already departed southward. Going from the church to the War Department, Davis telegraphed to Lee that a move from Richmond that night would "involve the loss of many valuables, both for the want of time to pack and of transportation." Lee in the field on receiving this message, according to one of his staff men, tore it into bits, saying, "I am sure I gave him sufficient notice," and replying calmly by telegraph to Davis that it was "absolutely necessary" to abandon the position that night. Lee thought at the time that President Davis would go with the army and arranged to let Davis know the route of the army and to furnish him with a guide. Davis, however, after directing what should be done in the hurried removal of the government funds and archives, wrote of his departure and intentions that he "started for Danville [North Carolina], whither I supposed General Lee would proceed with his army."

On a Richmond & Danville Railroad train at eleven that Sabbath night, Davis with his Cabinet and other officials left their capital city, their Executive Mansion, their arsenals and remaining stores, arriving safely in Danville the next afternoon.

Word spread in Richmond this Sabbath that Lee's army, so long their shield and fortress, had taken its last man and gun out of Petersburg—and Richmond would fall next. On railroad trains, on wagons, carts, buggies, gigs, on horses piled with bundles and belongings, the Government and many citizens in flight had a moving day. "Dismay reigned supreme," wrote Captain Clement Sulivane, in charge of the evacuation, dismay meaning that some, like Judge Campbell, talked rapidly to themselves and knew what they were saying, while others spoke lines meaning in effect "We have never drilled or rehearsed for this day—what do we do?"

"It was a quiet night, with its millions of stars," noted Jones. That was overhead. Below in Richmond only the slothful and the utterly weary slept. Into food stores and vacated houses went little gangs of hungry people along with hoodlums and thieves. Captain Sulivane's men arrested a few ringleaders and their followers, but it was no time for law and order. The Captain's own men were being taken by department heads for transport and guarding of the archives. "Battalions melted away as fast as they were formed . . . partly, no doubt, from desertions," wrote the Captain.

Burning and dynamiting of bridges, arsenals, and warehouses went on through the night. Those who knew their Richmond tried to read the marching devastation by the booms they heard. One by one the bridges went. Before daylight only the one from Richmond to Manchester was standing. Three high arched bridges blazed with tall flames and lighted the two cities and the sparkling, snarling river between. Heavy smoke clouds rose from cotton warehouses, in one of them Gen. James W. Singleton losing his 200,000 pounds from which he had hoped to glean a fortune. Every now and then a powder magazine went into the air, a fountain of white smoke shooting to the sky, followed in an instant by a deafening roar and a quaking of the ground on which Richmond stood, in another instant hundreds of shells exploding in high air and sending down an iron spray—with a little aftermath of stores of ignited cartridges rattling with low thunder the same as volley fire of musketry on the battlefield. The theory was that the Confederacy must shoot these off now or later they might be shot at Confederate troops as the war went on. Fire began sweeping in wide paths over the city itself. "Either incendiaries, or (more probably) fragments of bombs from the arsenals, had fired various buildings," wrote Captain Sulivane, "and the two cities, Richmond and Manchester, were like a blaze of day amid the surrounding darkness." Near dawn a few thundering explosions downriver told Sulivane that some of the last gunboats of the Confederate Navy were sunk.

Also just after daylight on April 3 a crowd of thousands of men, women, and children swarmed at the doors of a commissary depot. They represented that part of the people of Richmond hardest hit by food scarcity and high prices. Many of them had not tasted a full, nourishing meal in months. Behind those depot doors they had heard—and heard correctly—were barrels of ham, bacon, whisky, flour, sugar, coffee. Why these had not been put into the hands of General Lee and his army weeks ago was a question for responsible officials to answer. The desperation of rampaging human animals heaved at those depot doors, so long guarded, no longer held by men with rifles. The doors went down. Crying, yelling, raging, laughing, snarling, the crowd surged in; men fought with each other over the best pickings. Later in the morning the city government ordered the stores in saloons and liquor shops to be wrecked and poured into the streets. Gutters ran whisky and kneeling men and women here and there lapped it up. Black and white women and boys were seen filling pitchers and buckets from the street gutters these few hours running with famous distilled Southern liquors.

The commissary looters scattered right and left as a final handful of Confederate cavalry came galloping to cross the only bridge standing. Their commander, General Gary of South Carolina, pointed at his last bunch of gray horsemen taking the bridge at headlong speed, touched his hat to Captain Sulivane and ordered: "All over, good-bye—blow her to hell."

Sulivane and an engineer officer walked slowly across the bridge setting fire to prepared combustibles. Soon the bridge sagged and went down in smoke and flame. Captain Sulivane and two companions at the other end of the bridge sat in their saddles a half-hour and watched strings of horsemen in blue taking over Richmond. They fired a few shots at Sulivane, but the shooting was what he called "random." Across the way he could see columns of blue infantry arriving and he heard a new sound floating on the air from across the river—cheers for the United States flag.

General Godfrey Weitzel received the surrender of Richmond that morning of April 3 at the city hall. By midafternoon his troops had stopped rioting and the main disorders, had begun issue of provisions to the needy, and blown up several city blocks of houses to check the fire.

In Washington, wrote David Homer Bates, "Lincoln's despatch from City Point gave us in the War Department the first news of the capture of Petersburg and Richmond." Shortly after that message, came over the wires the first one in four years from Richmond, General Weitzel saying: "We took Richmond at 8:15 this morning. . . . The city is on fire in two places." One of the cipher operators ran to a window and put his head out crying to passers-by, "Richmond has fallen!" The news spread fast. Press extras sent the excitement higher. Thousands crowded around the Secretary of War's office, called on Stanton for a speech. He spoke gratitude to Almighty God for deliverance, said thanks were due to the President, to the army and navy, to the great commanders, to officers and men, and the hour called for humility and goodwill. Stanton read a dispatch from Grant saying Richmond was on fire and asked the crowd what he should reply to Grant. The cries came, "Let her burn!" and "Burn it! burn it!" At other government buildings and in Willard's Hotel crowds heard speeches in the afternoon, and in the evening went with brass bands serenading public officials and calling for more speeches. Record-breaking crowds lined the saloon bars. Men habitually sober for years took this night as a summons of patriotic duty to drink hard and "get full" and let everybody know it. "A more liquorish crowd was never seen in Washington than on that night," wrote Noah Brooks. . . . "I saw one big, sedate Vermonter, chief of an executive bureau, standing on the corner of F and Fourteenth streets, with owlish gravity giving away fifty-cent 'shin-plasters' (fractional currency) to every colored person who came past him, brokenly saying with each gift, 'Babylon has fallen!'"

From the Capitol on to the White House and executive buildings, Pennsylvania Avenue took on bunting and banners. The national flag so held the air that it "seemed to burn," wrote Brooks. The sky was shaken by a salute of eight hundred guns, fired by order of the Secretary of War, three hundred for Petersburg, five hundred for Richmond. Houses wore special illuminations that night. In the streets people hugged each other, men made up old quarrels, marched singing and prankish and lit up with fellowship and flowing bowls. Washington went on a spree of happiness over the taking of its rival city with a rival government—and hopes of the end of the war.

Union Leaguers on parade waved their flags in front of the State Department and called for Secretary Seward. He was feeling good toward the whole world this day and let it come out. In writing his foreign dispatches now what should he tell the Emperor of China? "I shall thank him in your name for never having permitted a piratical flag to enter the harbors of the empire. [Applause.]" To the Sultan of Turkey he would give thanks for always having surrendered rebel insurgents taking refuge in that kingdom. [Cheers.] To the Emperor of the French he would say that "he can go tomorrow to Richmond and get his tobacco so long held under blockade there, provided the rebels have not used it up. [Laughter and cheers.]" To Lord John Russell he would say that British merchants would now find cotton legitimately exported cheaper than cotton from running the blockade. Furthermore, he would tell Lord Russell himself "that if Great Britain should only be just to the United States, Canada will remain undisturbed by us so long as she prefers the authority of the noble Queen to involuntary incorporation with the United States. [Cheers and exclamations of "That's the talk," "You're right."]" He would tell the King of Prussia "that the Germans have been faithful to the standard of the Union, as his excellent minister, Baron Gerolt, has been constant in his friendship to the United States during his long residence in this country. [Cheers.]" The Emperor of Austria had proved himself "a very wise man, for he told us in the beginning that he had no sympathy with rebellion anywhere."

The pleasant and quizzical Seward released a confession: "I do not doubt, fellow citizens, but that at least you accede to the theory by which I have governed myself during the war—namely, that the rebellion was to end in ninety days. [Laughter and cheers.] I have thought this the true theory, because I never knew a physician able to restore the patient to health unless he thought he could work a cure under the most unfavorable circumstances in ninety days. [Renewed laughter.]"

At City Point on the *Bat* lying near the *Malvern*, Captain Barnes on the night of April 3 saw where "heavy explosions lit up the sky—the blowing up of the rebel ironclads." On the *Malvern* Lincoln considered whether he should go to Richmond—and decided to go. Richmond was not only a place but a symbol. There might be a little business to transact—and his very act of setting foot in that city would be a sign and a ceremonial.

The next morning the *Malvern* steamed toward Richmond. The channel was reported clear of the many torpedoes once infesting it. Dead horses floated by, broken ordnance, wrecked boats—the river was not in good order. Nearing Richmond, the *Malvern* went aground. Admiral Porter ordered a twelve-oared barge to carry the President ashore. Lincoln, Tad, and the guard Crook sat amid the oarsmen. They had started that morning in a proud flagship, escorted by the *River Queen* and the *Bat*, which escorts they had lost. A gig holding Barnes and a few others now acted as escort. Lincoln was reminded of an anecdote, which ran, according to Admiral Porter: "A fellow once came to me to ask for an appointment as a minister abroad. Finding he could not get that, he came down to some more modest position. Finally, he asked to be made a tide-waiter. When he saw he could not get that, he asked me for an old pair of trousers. It is well to be humble."

On the edge of Richmond at a place called Rockett's the little barge landed the President of the United States. The receiving crowd ashore was, according to Porter and Crook, entirely of Negroes. By the grapevine some of them had heard here was Lincoln. One old-timer of sixty sprang forward crying: "Bress de Lawd, dere is de great Messiah! I knowed him as soon as I seed him. He's bin in my heart fo' long yeahs. Glory, hallelujah!" He fell on his knees and bowed at the President's feet. Other Negroes came likewise. The President: "Don't kneel to me. You must kneel to God only and thank him for your freedom." The old-timer had his excuse: "Yes, Massa, but after bein' so many years in de desert widout water, it's mighty pleasant to be lookin' at las' on our spring of life. 'Scuse us, sir, we means no disrespec' to Marse Linkum." The shouts of other black men came, as they reached hands toward him in greeting and salute. "Dar come Marse Linkum, de

Sabior ob de lan'—we so glad to see him." From corners that had seemed deserted suddenly sprang out black folk, some silent and awe-struck, others turning somersaults and yelling with joy as though their voices and bodies could never tell what they wanted to tell. The stories they had heard about being free, about being no longer slaves, now if Marse Linkum could come to Richmond with his soldiers, surely those stories must be true and no foolin', no make-up story. With a few of them Marse Linkum shook hands. Others saw him handshaking with Negroes. Who would have believed it?

This brief scene closed with twelve armed sailors forming a guard and escort for the President's more or less triumphal entry into the Confederate capital. At his left the President had Rear Admiral Porter and Captain Penrose, at his right Crook holding Tad by the hand, in the advance and the rear six sailor boys, each with the sawed-off rifle known as the carbine. This procession began its march. Just before they started Captain Barnes and one of his officers tried to push through a frantic and struggling crowd and warn the procession to wait. Barnes thought "nothing could have been easier than the destruction of the whole party." General Weitzel had expected to provide a proper escort and guard, but Porter had made a surprise landing with the leading figure. Barnes saw a lone cavalryman at a street corner and sent him galloping to Weitzel's headquarters with news of the slender presidential cohort marching across Richmond.

The pedestrian President and his seagoing footmen saw at first mostly Negroes. Then they came to streets alive with black and white spectators. "Wherever it was possible for a human being to find a foothold there was some man or woman or boy straining his eyes after the President," wrote Crook. "Every window was crowded with heads. Men were hanging from tree-boxes and telegraph-poles. But it was a silent crowd. There was something oppressive in those thousands of watchers without a sound, either of welcome or hatred. I think we would have welcomed a yell of defiance. I stole a look sideways at Mr. Lincoln. His face was set. It had the calm in it that comes over the face of a brave man when he is ready for whatever may come. In all Richmond the only sign of welcome I saw, after we left the negroes at the landing-place and until we reached our own men, was from a young lady who was on a sort of bridge that connected the Spottswood [sic] House with another hotel across the street. She had an American flag over her shoulders."

The later recollections of Crook also maintained that once in the line of march the blinds of a second-story window of a house on the left partly opened, and a man dressed in gray pointed something that looked like a gun directly at the President. "I dropped Tad's hand and stepped in front of Mr. Lincoln," wrote Crook. "I was sure he meant to shoot. Later Mr. Lincoln explained it otherwise. But we were all so aware of the danger . . . that our nerves were not steady."

Nearly two miles along dusty streets on a warm day this little presidential party marched from Rockett's landing to the center of Richmond. Not a soldier nor a citizen nor a horse nor a wagon had met them. The President could have said, "Wait." So could Admiral Porter. But they didn't. They moved as though they had an appointment to keep. "One cannot help wondering at the manifest imprudence of both Mr. Lincoln and Admiral Porter in the whole proceeding," commented Nicolay and Hay, who valued "the humbleness and simplicity" of such an entry of a conqueror but doubted its wisdom.

The President had stopped a moment to gaze at Libby Prison, according to Porter, and on someone calling, "Pull it down," he replied, "No, leave it as a monument." Once a man in shirt sleeves rushed out crying, "Abe Lincoln, God bless you!" and being pushed away by Porter when he sought a handshake, the man stood with arms folded and suddenly threw his hat in the air. A girl of perhaps seventeen, blooming and graceful, ran out with a bouquet of flowers which they let her hand to the President. One Union soldier called out, "Is that Old Abe?" One older Negro was heard to say, "Go 'way, dat ain' no Fadder Abraham. Why, dat man look lak a 'onery ol' famah [farmer], he do." Porter saw more cordiality than did Crook in the crowds lining the sidewalks and in the faces at the windows.

The cavalry escort arrived; those around the President breathed easier. The horse guards led them to the Confederate Executive Mansion, a two-story brick house of gray stucco fronted with tall Colonial pillars, the building now serving as the headquarters of General Weitzel and the temporary government, such as there was, of the City of Richmond and the State of Virginia. Into this house dedicated to the principle of States' Rights and secession, consecrated with the blood and sacrifice given to the Confederate cause, entered the archantagonist of that principle and cause. Dusty and sweating from a walk of nearly two miles amid sights of burned buildings, wreckage on the streets, and terror in the air, Lincoln sank into a chair at a long table, "pale and haggard, utterly worn out," noted Barnes, his first words, "I wonder if I could get a glass of water." It interested him to know that this was the chair in which Jefferson Davis had sat and over this table handled the high documents of the Confederate States of America. He asked for the housekeeper and was told she had left. Then shortly he went over the house guided by a Weitzel aide, Thomas Thatcher Graves, who said there was "a boyish manner" about Lincoln as he went through the rooms downstairs and up. Returning down the staircase, Graves saw the President's face lose its boyish expression as General Weitzel out of breath and in a hurry came through the front door. After greetings Lincoln probably asked about the same question he had telegraphed the General six days before: "What, if anything, have you observed on your front today?"

Crook in the meantime had found an old Negro manservant staying on in the house, telling Crook for one thing that Mrs. Jefferson Davis on leaving had ordered him to have the house in nice condition for the Yankees when they came. Her good-by to the old Negro had the words: "I am going out into the world a wanderer without a home." On Crook asking about it, the old Negro hunted out a long black bottle of rare old whisky. Passed around to Weitzel and the staff and the President and his party, everyone except Lincoln taking a long or short pull at it, the bottle came back empty.

The President had a little rest; there was a lunch and an informal reception, chiefly of Union officers. Then the President, with a cavalry escort under Weitzel, with Porter and others rode in a carriage over the city, seeing some of the seven hundred burned dwellings and stores, Libby Prison, Castle Thunder, thousands of homeless whites and Negroes, acres of them located with their few rescued belongings on the lawn of the capitol building. Into that now disordered building where the now fugitive Confederate Congress had held its sessions, Lincoln was ushered. And if he was reminded of any anecdote no one made a record of it—though it was said of that day his eyes often had a dreaminess in them.

At one street corner a Negro woman held up her sick child for a look at Lincoln, but the child kept turning its head away, the mother finally saying: "See yeah, honey, look at de Savior, and you'll git well. Touch de hem of his gahment, honey, and your pain will be done gone." At the Grace Street home of Burton Harrison, secretary to Jefferson Davis, Mrs. Harrison saw Lincoln ride past, and she thought of how that morning her uncle, an elderly physician, reading from an old-time prayer book, had without meaning to do so read out the petition and blessing for the President of the United States. The youngest daughter Edith, rising from her knees, cried out, "Oh! papa, you prayed for the President of the United States!" "Did I?" queried the old doctor, then blurted, "Devil fetch him!"

Weitzel's aide Graves went along on this ride, and of it wrote that he heard General Weitzel ask one very important question, namely, What should he, Weitzel, do in regard to this conquered people?

"President Lincoln replied," wrote Graves, "that he did not wish to give any orders on that subject, but, as he expressed it, 'If I were in your place, I'd let 'em up easy, let 'em up easy.' "

The wife of General George Pickett was to tell at a later time of a caller that day knocking at the door of their Richmond home, of how she stood with a baby on one arm and told the visitor Yes, it was General Pickett's home, "But he is not here."

The visitor said he knew General Pickett was not there. "I know where George Pickett is." She was a little shocked when the visitor rambled on about old days when he knew Pickett as a boy and a young man, and "I am Abe Lincoln," he told Mrs. Pickett. It was his law partner John Stuart who had gotten George Pickett's appointment to a West Point cadetship. They talked more. Lincoln kissed the baby and said good-by. Thus in brief ran Mrs. Pickett's later story, which may have been entirely correct in fact, though none of the companions and observers of Lincoln in Richmond afterward recalled his having taken out time to call at the Pickett home and kiss the baby.

To Roger Pryor, Lincoln sent word inviting a little conference. General Pryor excused himself on the ground that he was a paroled prisoner, that

General Lee was still in the field, and that he could hold no conference with the head of the opposing army.

Judge John A. Campbell, Confederate Assistant Secretary of War, the only prominent member of the Confederate Government remaining in Richmond, had reported to the Union military governor, General G. F. Shepley, and informed him of his "submission to the military authorities," so it was both a convenience and a pleasure for Lincoln to grant an interview to this Southern liberal and moderate whom he had last seen at Hampton Roads.

In the evening of this April 4 Judge Campbell called. He told Lincoln, according to his own version written later, that the war was virtually over, that General Lee could not hold his army together, that the public men of Virginia would help the President of the United States restore the Union, and that the President might rely on this. Judge Campbell urged moderation, quoting, "When lenity and cruelty play for a kingdom the gentler gamester is the soonest winner." The successful party in this war between communities in any event should make his success as little aggravating as possible to the other party. With reference to a new government in Virginia, observed Campbell of Alabama, "I speak for Virginia what would be more appropriate for a Virginian." To these various points Lincoln made no reply except to say he had concluded to stay over and would have another interview with Campbell the next morning.

The *New York Herald* man, William H. Merriam, in a signed dispatch from Richmond to his paper, wrote that Generals Weitzel and Shepley gave the President the substance of an interview they had held with "several prominent secessionists," including Campbell. "The President listened patiently, and indicated his sense of the magnitude of the propositions submitted for his consideration by great nervousness of manner, running his hands frequently through his hair and moving to and fro in the official chair of the late Jefferson Davis, in which he sat. The result of this interview may be summed up in the accompanying remark of Mr. Lincoln: 'Well, say to them that I will entertain their propositions, with the condition that I shall have one friend with the same liberty to them.' "

In an officers' ambulance Tad and his father rode to a wharf and a waiting rowboat. Porter and Crook heaved sighs of relief on getting the President aboard the *Malvern*, which had now been brought up-river. Any one of many kinds of fools could have taken a potshot at the President that day—they all knew that. And the one who had the least to say about it was the potential living target himself. There was ease of heart that the fallen Confederate capital had been the scene of no act against the President's person.

The next morning at ten Judge Campbell arrived in company with a Richmond attorney, G. A. Myers, and went into conference with Lincoln and General Weitzel. The talk ranged wide on how to again get local government going in the South. Lincoln brought out a memorandum he had written on peace terms. They were in effect the same as those he had stated at Hampton Roads, with perhaps added stress on the point that States in good faith withdrawing their troops from further resistance to the Govern-

Negro soldiers

A Union wagon train enters Petersburg

A dismantled locomotive in Richmond

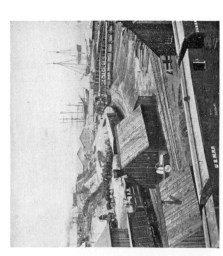

Rail and water transport at City Point

Bombproofs outlying Petersburg

From stereographs in the Barrett collection

The James River and Union ships

City Point and the James River—transports and supply landings for the Union Army in '65, about the time of Lincoln's visit

From the Meserve collection

ment would suffer less from property losses through confiscation and war. Campbell took this paper handed him by Lincoln and handed Lincoln a paper of his own. It was a legal device. Both men as lawyers knew that legal devices sometimes could be powerful. General Weitzel summarized this device as set forth in writing and conversation:

"Mr. Campbell and the other gentlemen assured Mr. Lincoln that if he would allow the Virginia Legislature to meet, it would at once repeal the ordinance of secession, and that then General Robert E. Lee and every other Virginian would submit; that this would amount to the virtual destruction of the Army of Northern Virginia, and eventually to the surrender of all the other rebel armies, and would insure perfect peace in the shortest possible time."

Mr. Lincoln considered this. He saw Virginia as a tenant torn between two contending landlords who should now transfer allegiance definitely to the contender who had established his right. He said that he had, wrote Campbell, "a government in northern Virginia but that its margin was small and that he did not desire to enlarge it." In effect, Campbell had the impression that Lincoln would discard his own "reconstructed" State government of Virginia if he could get the hitherto seceded and Confederate government of the State to do what he wanted. In this impression Campbell was only partly correct. He was to be mistaken eventually in the matter of precisely what it was that Lincoln wanted that legislature to do. Lincoln was still considering how he would put on paper what it was he wanted and told Judge Campbell he would send on such a paper from City Point. Campbell was rowed ashore from the *Malvern* feeling that in the morning's conversation there had been "no effort to mystify or overreach."

Merriam of the *New York Herald*, however, was slightly mystifying and overreaching in his signed dispatch to his paper intimating that he knew the details of this conference but could not disclose them. In the final sentence of the dispatch Merriam planted the word "suspicious" precisely where it would have on the reader an intriguing and mischievous effect, saying for his national audience: "It is entirely proper to add that suspicious results are known to be about to accrue from this most important conference at this exciting era in our national affairs."

Commander F. W. Cotton of the converted torpedo boat *Clinton* came aboard the *Malvern*. His crew were on short rations because in their work of clearing the river of torpedoes and other obstructions they had been "hailed at different points by Southern ladies destitute of food." Admiral Porter refused to sign requisitions for new stores of provisions, and according to Cotton, when the matter was referred to the President he made a gesture with both hands, and "Give them all the provisions they want; give them all they want." Porter then signed the paper. Cotton, a twenty-one-year-old from Dedham, Massachusetts, walked off with the paper, suppressing a smile and wearing a sober seagoing face.

Later that day came the seriocomic affair of Duff Green. What happened was fantastic, and in the later account of it by Admiral Porter it was made unbelievably so, the guard Crook more likely having the essentials. Lincoln had said Yes to Duff's coming aboard. In December of 1860 he had written Duff, with no results, a long letter hoping that Duff might make certain efforts toward thwarting what Lincoln termed "the dismemberment of the Union" then in process. Duff Green had been a free-going journalist, by turns Democrat and Whig, one of Washington's kitchen-cabinet powers supposed to be working behind the scenes of history. Now seventy-four years old, an ancient leaf blown out of the book of the past, he came aboard the *Malvern*, tall and gaunt, carrying a long Bible-times staff.

The President held out his hand. Green wouldn't take it. "I did not come to shake hands." With Weitzel, Porter, Crook, and others standing by, Duff Green started a wordy lambasting of the President, working up to a climax: "I do not know how God and your conscience will let you sleep at night after being guilty of the notorious crime of setting the niggers free."

Lincoln listened, kept cool, had no answers. Duff Green had a few more remarks and was near given out when he came to the point of his errand: "I would like, sir, to go to my friends." The President turned to Weitzel. "General, please give Mr. Green a pass to go to his friends." That was all. There was no more of a good-by handshake than there had been how-do-you-do. Duff Green was set ashore and not heard of again.

The *Malvern* steamed down-river for City Point. To Stanton, Lincoln had relayed information, from Weitzel about Richmond, from Grant about the pursuit of Lee's army. Into Weitzel's hands had fallen, because of the sudden and hurried evacuation of Richmond, 28 locomotives, 44 passenger and baggage cars, 106 freight cars. Sheridan had picked up 1,200 prisoners; 300 to 500 more had been gathered by other troops. In the wake of Lee's retreating army were abandoned artillery, ammunition, burned wagons, caissons, ambulances—and a country "full of stragglers." To Seward the President wired that he might stay away from Washington two days more and if that was too long a time for Seward's business to wait, then "come down." In a white nightgown that night Lincoln entered a stateroom and for a moment Crook thought he saw a ghost. But it was only Mr. Lincoln wanting to see if Tad was all right. He mentioned Duff Green to Crook as rather angry, "but I guess he will get over it." Then before closing the door, "Good-night, and a good night's rest, Crook." The two-day journey to and from Richmond was over. Yes, they had seen Richmond.

On the second night of these two days of chaos, of seeing acres of blackened timbers and blasted homes, on this night Lincoln might have had the dream of which Mrs. Lincoln later spoke to Bill Herndon. The fact was spare and the dream lacking detail in her short statement: "Mr. Lincoln had a dream when down the river at City Point, after Richmond was taken. He dreamed that the White House was burning up."

At noon of the next day of April 6 Lincoln telegraphed Grant that Seward had been thrown from his carriage, seriously injured, and this with other matters would take him to Washington soon. At Richmond, he wished Grant to know, he had met Judge Campbell and put in Campbell's hands "an informal paper" repeating the Hampton Roads peace conditions, "and adding that if the war be now further persisted in by the rebels, confiscated property shall at the least bear the additional cost, and that confiscation shall be remitted to the people of any State who will now promptly and in good faith withdraw its troops and other support from resistance to the government."

With the same guarded method he had used in the Hampton Roads affair, Lincoln was proceeding to get a vitally important matter, and the extent of his hand in it, into a proper and official record. He continued to Grant: "Judge Campbell thought it not impossible that the rebel legislature of Virginia would do the latter if permitted; and accordingly I addressed a private letter to General Weitzel, with permission to Judge Campbell to see it, telling him [General Weitzel] that if they attempt this, to permit and protect them, unless they attempt something hostile to the United States, in which case to give them notice and time to leave, and to arrest any remaining after such time."

The matter was delicate—but Lincoln was taking a chance. He was meeting fully and squarely any leanings toward the Union, any changed attitude, that might have developed among the Virginia legislative members. Once they had officially seceded their State from the Union. Now they could officially return if they chose. They were being given assurance that they were not regarded as outlaws, though they could construe for themselves the extent of dignity and authority accorded them by the President's telegram to Weitzel dated April 6 at City Point:

"It has been intimated to me that the gentlemen who have acted as the legislature of Virginia in support of the rebellion may now desire to assemble at Richmond and take measures to withdraw the Virginia troops and other support from resistance to the General Government. If they attempt it, give them permission and protection, until, if at all, they attempt some action hostile to the United States, in which case you will notify them, give them reasonable time to leave, and at the end of which time arrest any who remain. Allow Judge Campbell to see this, but do not make it public."

Of this attempt at results by legal device Lincoln wrote Grant he did not think it very probable anything would come of it, "but I have thought best to notify you so that if you should see signs you may understand them." From recent dispatches, he would have Grant know, "it seems that you are pretty effectually withdrawing the Virginia troops from opposition to the government." He was not touching in the slightest any decision or policy of Grant. "Nothing that I have done, or probably shall do, is to delay, hinder, or interfere with your work."

At noon Mrs. Lincoln arrived at City Point this April 6 in a party of important persons, including Senator Charles Sumner, Attorney General James Speed and his wife, the new Secretary of the Interior James B. Harlan and his wife, and Charles Adolphe Pineton, better known as the Marquis de Chambrun, an interesting young French diplomat and scholar, a special friend of Sumner. The President received them on board the *River Queen*, led them to the saloon where the Hampton Roads conference had been held, pointed to the chairs where the participants of the conference had sat, mentioning how not one of the five men drew pencil or paper or made any record of what was being said. The President read dispatches from Grant, rose to fetch his maps, returned and spread the maps on a table and put his finger on the locations of this and that army corps.

Young Chambrun, thirty-four years old, studied Lincoln. The father of the Marquis had been an intimate of Alexis de Tocqueville, whose book on American democracy was a standard work. As Lincoln over the maps and dispatches spoke of the war soon ending and his own armies winning, Chambrun was sure that victory had not gone to his head. "It was impossible to detect in him the slightest feeling of pride, much less of vanity." He seemed to accent modestly his satisfaction that military success ended certain terrible responsibilities. Wrote Chambrun: "He had visited Richmond, he said to us; the reception given him there did not seem to be of good omen; his only preoccupation appeared to be the necessity of wiping out the consequences of the civil war, and to drive the war from the memory of all, nay, even of the criminal instigators; far then, from feeling any resentment against the vanquished, he was rather inclined to place too much confidence in them."

Lincoln went ashore. The visitors boarded a boat that took them to Richmond, where they drove sightseeing with a cavalry escort. Sumner wished especially to see Crawford's statue of Washington—and of course saw it. At the capitol Sumner asked about archives, about his old acquaintance United States Senator Robert M. T. Hunter, and about the ivory gavel of the Congress. This gavel was the one relic interesting Sumner enough for him to put it in his pocket to carry away. The party stayed overnight on their steamer near Richmond on one side in darkness and Manchester on the other still sputtering with flame.

The next morning they rejoined Lincoln at City Point and on his invitation took a train for Petersburg. They seated themselves in the coach grouped around the President. Several army officers and guards hovered close and it was evident that added personal protection was being provided. "Curiosity," wrote Chambrun . . . "had induced the negro waiters of the River Queen to accompany us. The President, who was blinded by no prejudices against race or color, and who had not what can be termed false dignity, allowed them to sit quietly with us."

Along the route to Petersburg Lincoln indicated Fort Stedman, where the Confederate attempt to break through had failed. From the car windows they saw a gashed landscape, broken artillery wheels, and the signs of the fury of eight days ago now quiet. Petersburg seemed abandoned except for Negroes. While Lincoln interviewed the garrison commander the Senators and their wives went sightseeing. In the garden of a silent house whose master was away they saw peach trees abloom like clouds of pink mist, crocus, flowering quince, and a little riot of roses. Chambrun asked an escorting army officer who owned the place. In the officer's answer was a war hate. For him the war throve on hate. Chambrun later trying to remember the answer could only recall the officer saying, "These people were traitors."

On the road back to the train, riding in a carriage with Mrs. Lincoln, Sumner, and Chambrun, Lincoln's eye caught a tree worth a long look. He had the driver stop, let his eyes range further over the tree while he talked about it. What took Chambrun was Lincoln's absorption in a tree. Lincoln talked as though he might be some kind of a tree himself, and it was worth any man's time to hold communion with trees. This oak had a trunk with wide outrunning branches reminding him of tall trees in whose shadow he had spent his youth. He went into expert comparisons of trees and pointed to special features of this one, not talking as "an artist who seeks to idealize nature" but more strictly as "a man who seeks to see it as it really is." Chambrun couldn't see the tree for Lincoln, and noted: "That dissertation about a tree did not reveal an effort of imagination, but a remarkable precision of mind."

The carriage moved on, topics changed, the President spoke of Union commanders reporting as to Petersburg: "Animosity in the town is abating; the inhabitants now accept accomplished facts, the final downfall of the Confederacy, and the abolition of slavery. There still remains much for us to do, but every day brings new reason for confidence in the future."

At no time on this day was Lincoln's mind free from the near-by tense excitement of a military struggle directed by veteran masters. Any flaw or piece of bad luck was at cost. Off to the west, not many miles, horsemen and foot troops were harassing Lee's army in retreat. At Amelia Court House Lee's men found no food supplies as expected. The Confederate officials at Richmond in charge of this vital matter had either misunderstood General Lee's orders or in the hurry of flight had mismanaged. Anyhow at this point where they had hoped to eat was practically nothing to eat. The wagons went out and sought rations but came back practically empty. Not since the times of George Washington and Nathanael Greene had the troops of an important army marched and fought on such short rations as Lee's men this week. At the same time Grant was in top form, alive every hour to each move reported to him. Near midnight of April 6 Grant wired Lincoln a message from Sheridan which Lincoln relayed to Stanton at 8:35 A.M. of April 7. In this Sheridan reported captures of several thousand prisoners, including Custis Lee, the son of General Robert E. Lee, and Generals Ewell, Kershaw, Button, Corse, and Debray. Taken also in this sweep were many wagons and 14 cannon, Sheridan closing his dispatch, "If the thing is pressed I think that Lee will surrender." Lincoln thought about this and near noon wired Grant:

GENERAL SHERIDAN SAYS "IF THE THING IS PRESSED I THINK THAT LEE WILL SURRENDER." LET THE THING BE PRESSED.

On the *River Queen* in the evening Congressmen Elihu B. Washburne and James G. Blaine joined the party, the former seeing Lincoln "in perfect health and exuberant spirits," at ease and talking freely about the trip to Richmond, unfailing with anecdotes. "He never flagged during the whole evening." In the morning, said Washburne to the President, he was to go to the front and see Grant. "I believe I will drop Robert a line if you will take it," said Lincoln. "I will hand it to you in the morning before you start."

And another night closed in and the *River Queen* with a hundred other vessels, steamers, tugs, transports, gunboats, cruisers, floated the silent waters, and those on board wondered what news might come on the air in the week to follow this April 7, 1865. Some were high-keyed. And Lincoln had a dream which he was to tell of to his Cabinet friends in Washington.

The next morning Lincoln ashore gave Washburne the letter for Robert, they talked a little, and Washburne saw the President "erect and buoyant," never before looking quite so "grand." On this day Lincoln and his party visited tent hospitals for some five hours and he shook hands with several hundred sick and wounded soldiers, saying to Sumner when it was over that his arm was not tired. Chambrun on this day took note of the same thing that had so often impressed Walt Whitman in hospital visits, a thing that had its effect on Lincoln too—the marvel of what suffering and even torture many of these men and boys could stand without complaining. "The American," wrote Chambrun, "displays a sort of stoicism which has nothing of affectation. . . . Strange men they are, whom many approach and cannot understand, but who explain to him who does understand them the true greatness of their land."

On one cot Lincoln saw Captain Charles H. Houghton of the 14th New York Heavy Artillery. In the retaking of Fort Stedman Houghton had received two wounds early in the action, and a third later, staying with his men till they had re-established their lines, then being carried to hospital, where on recommendation of his superior officers for valor he received promotion by the President to the rank of brevet major. He had lost much blood in the amputation of the left leg above the knee and a secondary hemorrhage of an artery, surgeons and nurses taking a special interest, working until daylight to stanch the flowing blood, the query going the rounds the next day among cot occupants: "How is Houghton? Will he pull through?" Twenty-two years old, six feet tall, with black hair, large black eyes, he had more than a touch of romance about him as he lay white-faced and calm, prepared for what the day might bring. Lincoln stooped, put a hand lightly on Houghton's forehead, bent lower and kissed his boy on the cheek. The surgeon demurred to Lincoln's request to see the amputated leg. The sight might be too shocking, he suggested to the President, who insisted, so the covers were thrown back. The President saw the bare, mutilated stump. He bent down low and shook as he sobbed to the boy: "You must live! Poor boy, you must live!" And the young brevet major's whispered answer was, "I intend to, sir." And Houghton did come through, remembering the President's last words to him: "God bless you, my boy."

On one bed to which Lincoln came lay a dying man, a twenty-four-year-old captain, "noticed for bravery." One of two friends held his hand while another in low voice read a Bible passage. "Mr. Lincoln walked over to him," wrote Chambrun, "and took hold of his other hand, which rested on the bed. We formed a circle around him, and every one of us remained silent. Presently the dying man half-opened his eyes; a faint smile passed over his lips. It was then that his pulse ceased beating."

They came to a plainly dressed woman; a surgeon explained that she had left the comforts of one of the wealthiest families in Massachusetts for long trying hours of toil and care among the wounded. Chambrun spoke his admiration of her kind of heroism. She insisted that it was not peculiar and there were many women sharing the camp life of regiments and their wounded the same as she. Chambrun saw her as a type of the Puritan women of old, "who, in the performance of deeds most heroic, remain stiff and proud; who sustain themselves by efforts of stoical fortitude, and not by the more tender feelings of charity; who accomplish by a yearning of the mind what women of other countries would accomplish by a yearning of the heart; who aspire to command admiration, rather than to awaken gratitude; women, in short, whom the wounded must thank, but whom he cannot bless."

Chambrun thought Lincoln should meet this woman, spoke of her to him, and they went into the kitchen over which she was the director. Miss G——, as Chambrun wrote of her, "urged the President to enter into what she was pleased to call her room." It was a small room next the kitchen, her bed a plain soldier cot, her table resting on four rustic legs, and the chairs tree stumps. Miss G—— noticed Chambrun's curiosity in her well-worn Bible, so evidently often read, and she spoke of it to Lincoln, adding: "That is not my only book; here is another I found in the pocket of a German soldier who died a few days ago." Lincoln and Chambrun examined the book, also well-worn and often read, the title *How to Make One's Way in the World*.

From having heard Lincoln give the second inaugural, from published items and the talk of several circles in Washington, Chambrun had formed impressions of Lincoln. Now he was enjoying his close-up studies of the man, "for Mr. Lincoln would have scorned that sort of art which consists in showing one's self to a looker-on in a carefully-prepared light." None of the portraits or photographs of Lincoln reproduced "the complete expression of his face," and still more would there be failure at catching the interior contours of the man. So thought this keen young impressionable Frenchman. He sketched Lincoln in words as though he might be a graphic or plastic artist who hoped to experiment with the form and essence of this American character, now possibly in a niche among timeless world figures. "Carrying one shoulder higher than the other might at first sight make him seem slightly deformed . . . shoulders too sloping for his height. . . . But his arms were strong and his complexion sunburned . . . his gestures were vigorous and supple, revealing great physical strength and an extraordinary energy for resisting privation and fatigue." The war years had played on the face, wrought their invisible drama on it. To its decided lines, Chambrun felt, "Nothing seemed to lend harmony. . . . Yet his wide and high forehead, his gray-brown eyes sunken under thick eyebrows, and as though encircled by deep and dark wrinkles, his nose straight and pronounced, his lips at the same time thick and delicate, together with the furrows that ran across his cheeks and chin, formed an *ensemble* which, although strange, was certainly powerful," denoting "remarkable intelligence, great strength of penetration, tenacity of will, and elevated instincts."

The prairie years and rough usage of life had put its scrawny marks on the man now President of the United States who "made no efforts of bad taste to conceal what he had been under what he had become." This simplicity gave him ease of behavior, though lacking the manners of the general world, Chambrun finding "he was so perfectly natural that it would have been impossible I shall not say to be surprised at his manners, but to notice them at all."

Like many others Chambrun gathered an impression of vague and deep sadness always there. Rarely did one exchange even a few words with Mr. Lincoln and not feel something poignant. Could this impression be put on paper through words or ideas? Chambrun tried it but every time failed. "And, strange to say, Mr. Lincoln was quite humorous, although one could always detect a bit of irony in his humor. . . . He willingly laughed either at what was being said to him, or at what he said himself. But all of a sudden he would retire within himself; then he would close his eyes, and all his features would at once bespeak a kind of sadness as indescribable as it was deep. After a while, as though it were by an effort of his will, he would shake off this mysterious weight under which he seemed bowed; his generous and open disposition would again reappear. In one evening I happened to count over twenty of these alternations and contrasts."

Not pessimism nor melancholy as usually understood gave Lincoln these woe-struck moods of face. "No one more than he possessed that confident audacity so common among Americans, and which cannot be termed courage, because it is not the result of determination." Was it political care, war anxiety, the burden of heavy labor? These questions probably no one would ever answer.

Chambrun had many hours watching and listening to the now highly matured and intricately developed Lincoln—not the solitary man but the social creature, Lincoln the mixer in company letting his wit and talk roam free. Anyone hearing him then thinking aloud on great topics, or on the minor and incidental, would not be long in finding out how straight were his mental operations and what a sharpshooter's bead he could draw in one sentence. "I have heard him," wrote Chambrun, "give his opinion on statesmen, argue political problems, always with astounding precision and justice. I have heard him speak of a woman who was considered beautiful, discuss the particular character of her appearance, distinguish what was praiseworthy from what was open to criticism, all with the sagacity of an artist." To not many men was it given to see his definitions passing into daily proverbs of the people. Lincoln had, in Chambrun's estimate, better than anyone stamped the character of the war in his saying seven years ago: " 'A house divided against itself cannot stand' . . . this government cannot endure permanently half slave and half free."

In creative faculties Chambrun would not rate Lincoln as having high gifts. "He was not one of those rare and terrible geniuses who, being once possessed of an idea, apply it, curbing and sacrificing other men to the imperious instinct of their will. No; but, on the other hand, he knew better than anyone the exact will of the American people . . . he well understood that he was the people's agent . . . was well aware of that close union which must exist in a free democracy between the authority representing the nation and the nation itself. . . . The tendencies of his mind were all liberal . . . a nature . . . admirably constituted to direct through . . . an heroic struggle a people proud enough to prefer a guide to a chief, a man commissioned to execute its will to one who would enforce his own."

Chambrun was all the more impressed with a certain attitude and feeling he found in Lincoln because he was hearing on so many sides such shrilling as, for instance, came from Vice-President Andrew Johnson in a speech to an immense crowd in Washington on the day news arrived of Richmond taken. "Infamous in character, diabolical in motive," were those who had instigated the rebellion, said the Vice-President, and "If we had Andrew Jackson, he would hang them high as Haman. . . . When you ask me what I would do, my reply is, I would arrest them; I would try them; I would convict them, and I would hang them. . . . My notion, treason must be made odious; traitors must be punished and impoverished." Words such as these were in Chambrun's mind as he watched Lincoln this week in April, when he found "It was impossible to discover in Mr. Lincoln a single sentiment, I shall not say of revenge, but even of bitterness, in regard to the vanquished. Recall, as soon as possible, the Southern States into the Union, such was his chief preoccupation. When he encountered contrary opinion on that subject, when several of those who surrounded him insisted upon the necessity of exacting strong guarantees, at once on hearing them he would exhibit impatience. Although it was rare that such thoughts influenced his own, he nevertheless would evince, on hearing them expressed, a sort of fatigue and weariness, which he controlled, but was unable to dissimulate entirely." He seemed to have "irrevocably" made up his mind regarding the men who had taken a leading part in the rebellion. "Clemency never suggested itself more naturally to a victorious chieftain. The policy of pardon and forgiveness appeared to his mind an absolute necessity."

Chambrun took occasion to question the President several times about the attitude of the United States toward France, talk being common that the United States with its civil war over would begin another war on the French Government established in Mexico. He quoted Lincoln as replying more than once: "There has been war enough. I know what the American people want, but, thank God, I count for something, and during my second term there will be no more fighting."

Of what he heard his friend Sumner say, by contrast with Lincoln, on

pardons for the conquered enemies, Chambrun wrote nothing at all. He respected Sumner. Their friendship ran long and unbroken, though Chambrun's feeling seemed definite that Lincoln's instinct wove close with the
American people and with those of many soldiers. "The very words," wrote
Chambrun, "that fell from his lips [regarding pardon and forgiveness] I have
heard uttered at the bedside of the wounded; I have heard them expressed
by a Massachusetts colonel, who . . . had just gone through the amputation of one of his legs. Not only did he forgive, but he wished the United
States to forgive those who, five days before, in the affray of the Plank
Road, had shattered him with their bullets."

With a rare delicacy and reserve Chambrun withheld himself from any
slightest revelation of things he saw as a guest. "Certainly I have had a close
insight into Mr. Lincoln's family life; but when to a stranger is given the
privilege of lifting a corner of that sacred veil, he must, out of respect, let
it fall again, lest he be tempted to express that which he has been allowed
to see."

A Parisian and cosmopolite versed in style and address, also a man who
cared about world democracy, Chambrun tried to fathom Lincoln's genius
as a spokesman. Those "short and clear sentences" of Mr. Lincoln—why did
they reach out so far and "captivate" so many who read them? "His incisive
speech found its way to the very depths of the soul"—this because amid
the noisy confusion of discordant voices always heard in free countries at
moments of crises, Mr. Lincoln had "marvellous acuteness" in reading far
under the deeper and underlying public feeling and thought. The common
politicians subject to "popular caprice" tried to mislead him with "lamentable schemes," but he let himself be guided by his own more sure guesses
about what the public wanted.

An estimate of President Lincoln, partly as General Lee failed to see him,
came from a later commentator, an intimate of the documented Lee, a four-
volume biographer of Lee. This set forth Lincoln in the role of a spokesman, a sayer. "Lee's balancing of the ponderables on the military scales was
accurate," ran this picture. "He could not realize, and few even in Washington could see, that an imponderable was tipping the beam. That imponderable was the influence of President Lincoln. The Richmond government had discounted his every moderate utterance and had capitalized his
emancipation proclamation in order to stiffen Southern resistance. The Confederate people had mocked him, had despised him, and had hated him. Lee
himself, though he had avoided unworthy personal animosities and doubtless had included Mr. Lincoln in his prayers for all his enemies, had made
the most of the President's military blunders and fears. . . . He was much
more interested in the Federal field-commanders than in the commander-in-
chief. After the late winter of 1863-64, had Lee known all the facts, he
would have given as much care to the study of the mind of the Federal
President as to the analysis of the strategical methods of his immediate adversaries. For that remarkable man, who had never wavered in his purpose
to preserve the Union, had now mustered all his resources of patience and

of determination. Those who had sought cunningly to lead him, slowly found that he was leading them. His unconquerable spirit, in some mysterious manner, was being infused into the North as spring approached."

As spokesman of the Confederacy, Jefferson Davis was completely unaware of what Lincoln had in the way of style and human appeal. During the four years of many words Davis at no time tried for such public speech as in Lincoln's Gettysburg Address, where 190 of the 266 words had one syllable, 56 had two syllables, and only 20 ran to more than two syllables. As the war drew on Lincoln's role took on larger proportions. "Those who had sought cunningly to lead him, slowly found that he was leading them."

No Southern spokesman had framed in simple words a statement or a slogan that lasted, held strong, sank deep in the minds of people, as for instance the often quoted lines of Lincoln from his House Divided speech which Sumner asked him about at City Point. Sumner, the most widely labored student of oratory in the United States Congress, was curious as to whether Lincoln had changed or come to doubts about his 1858 declaration: "'A house divided against itself cannot stand.' I believe this government cannot endure permanently half slave and half free. I do not expect the Union to be dissolved—I do not expect the house to fall—but I do expect it will cease to be divided. It will become all one thing, or all the other." The fastidious Sumner considered this statement "memorable," having "insight," being "the true starting-point" of the political discussions that brought on the war. Had the President ever wavered about this declaration? He answered, according to Sumner: "Not in the least. It was clearly true, and time has justified me."

As utterance worth study for style Sumner would point to Lincoln's exposition seven years before of the Douglas doctrine of Popular Sovereignty as meaning simply "that if any one man chooses to enslave another, no third man shall be allowed to object." In this and like close-packed sentences Sumner said "there was fire as well as light in the words." Sumner's former regrets or tolerant amusement over the President's style of writing had changed. The two men had grown during the war years, Sumner in at least slight degree coming to favor short words that said as much as long ones. Even in the quality of humor Sumner had learned in some degree to let himself go in appreciation of the occasional eye-twinkle of Lincoln. Of the President saying "The United States Government must not undertake to run the churches" Sumner felt that "here wisdom and humor vie with each other."

Sumner saw Lincoln as lacking executive experience, lacking knowledge of history, on entering the White House, though "becoming more familiar with the place, his facility increased. He had 'learned the ropes,' so he said." The two men were now living on the same steamboat and getting along very well, each keeping silence on the one immediate deep point of difference, reconstruction in Louisiana. Of the President's course in this and similar issues Sumner had the view: "He did not see at once the just proportion of things. . . . Even in small matters, as well as great, there was in him a certain resistance to be overcome. Moments occurred when this delay excited impatience, and the transcendent question seemed to suffer."

Of their intimacy on the *River Queen* Sumner wrote to the Duchess of Argyll that those aboard were "breakfasting, lunching, and dining in one small family party." Conversation ran free with an air of happiness over the war soon coming to an end.

Sometimes, noted Sumner, Lincoln insisted that he had "no invention, only a good memory" for anecdotes. And Sumner, it seemed, cultivated a manner of keeping some actual sense of humor hidden, or he could not have managed one of the best metaphors ever coined about the way Lincoln used stories in place of argument or to support an argument.

"His ideas moved," noted Sumner, "as the beasts entered Noah's ark, in pairs."

And of Lincoln's humor operating with iron and without anecdote, Sumner had an instance of the President saying to him of a political antagonist indifferent to slavery: "I suppose the institution of slavery really looks small to him. He is so put up by nature, that a lash upon his back would hurt him, but a lash upon anybody else's back does not hurt him."

Fearful lashes on the back had been taken by Sumner, and any study of the relations of Lincoln and Sumner could not leave out Lincoln's awareness of the long-drawn-out suffering Sumner had borne. Lincoln possibly even suspected what Sumner's best friend Longfellow had written in a diary, that the spinal lacerations from the cane of Preston Brooks had not left the brain unaffected.

Out of their many interviews Sumner would say of Lincoln's face that while sad in repose "yet it lighted easily." Often they had been near what seemed the breaking-point, though not yet had Lincoln's face failed to light easily on greeting Sumner. In two respects Sumner found Lincoln different from any and all other characters he had met in the history books. One was Lincoln's state papers, "failing often in correctness," in weight and pith "suffused with a certain poetical color" recalling Bacon's *Essays,* having "unconscious power without form or apparent effort," arising from no model but springing directly from the man himself; in all his shelves of books Sumner could think of nothing past or present with which to compare Lincoln's public-affairs writings. "Nothing," wrote Sumner, "nothing similar can be found in state-papers."

The second point wherein Sumner found Lincoln out of any comparison was on looks. The President had "little resemblance to any historic portrait" unless he might seem to justify the epithet or nickname given to the early English King Edward the First also known as Longshanks. The very signature of Lincoln had an interest out of the ordinary for Sumner, the collector of etchings, art works, and historical relics. The same easy simplicity of his manner and conversation, "without form or ceremony beyond that among neighbors," Sumner saw in Lincoln's handwriting. "It was as clear as that of Washington, but less florid. Each had been surveyor, and was perhaps indebted to this experience. But the son of the western pioneer was more simple in nature, and the man appeared in the autograph."

A curious friendship it was between these two strong men, having as many differences and contrasts as the remarkable and continued affection between Robert Toombs and Alexander H. Stephens. Having said, "Sumner thinks he runs me," Lincoln had no fear of evil resulting from the Bostonian's so thinking, and even encouraged the thought. Very slowly had the President during '61 and '62 moved toward what Sumner urged at the beginning, emancipation of the slaves. To John Bright and to the Duke and Duchess of Argyll Sumner wrote that the President was slow, and conveyed the impression that under Sumner's steady prodding, which never ceased, the President in the end would take the right action. On the emancipation issue the two men had come through still on excellent speaking terms. Now they were at loggerheads over the question whether full civil rights should be guaranteed the freed Negroes before seceded States were readmitted to the Union. Under their surface cordiality, which was deeper than surface because each respected an integrity the other had, each hoped to win his purpose. The result on this issue was yet to be seen. Again perhaps those who sought cunningly to lead the President, slowly might find that he was leading them. Lincoln favored civil rights for the Negro as completely as Sumner—if and when the guarantees of such rights could be kept without race wars and government by bayonet.

The young Illinois Congressman Shelby M. Cullom was to write of his observation of the present and later scenes, "Mr. Lincoln was the only man living who ever managed Charles Sumner or could use him for his purpose."

The country liked it that Lincoln was at the front. He sensed that. Several of his telegrams to Stanton had been given to the press as war news. "Taught by experience," said the *New York Herald* of April 4, "Old Abe now takes the field again, succeeds in extinguishing Davis and is in at the death of the rebellion. His bulletins from City Point are so readable that we may offer him a situation on the *Herald,* after his present term expires, as a war correspondent in the grand struggle with Europe which is to follow the close of our civil contest. [Incessantly the *Herald* threw this war scare at Britain.] Should he accept he can have one hundred dollars a week, his rations and a fresh horse every six months."

On second thought the *Herald* believed the President could do better yet. So it made the suggestion that he might be in the running politically for a third term. "He has so far eclipsed all other politicians by his movements on both flanks and in front and rear that we should not wonder if he took the starch out of them all for the succession in 1868. Who can tell what will happen?"

Lincoln in Virginia relaxed a little, eased off the Washington burdens. It was the nearest approach to a vacation he had had since the war began. Of course it wasn't much of a holiday to look at the ruins of Richmond, nor an interval of sport to shake hands in tent hospitals with men whose abdominal tracts were traced with bullet paths. But Washington with its intrigue and smug satisfactions was worse. Grant and others thought they saw Lincoln's anxiety diminish in the City Point stay of fifteen days.

On Saturday, April 8, the *River Queen* was leaving for Washington. A military band came on board, and after several pieces, "Mr. Lincoln thought of the 'Marseillaise' and said to us that he had a great liking for that tune," wrote Chambrun. "He ordered it to be played. Delighted with it, he had it played a second time." To Chambrun he said with a twinkle of eye, "You must, however, come over to America to hear it." He then called for a playing of "Dixie," saying to Chambrun, "That tune is now Federal property." The musicians were surprised. And many an officer, sentinel, teamster, or sailor was surprised too that evening on hearing from the President's flagship on the James River the lively air of Dan Emmett's minstrel song with words beginning, "I wish I was in de land of cotton, Old times there am not forgotten, Look away, look away, Dixie Land!" The song had been learned by millions since Lincoln with Henry C. Whitney heard it at a minstrel show in Chicago. Composed by a Northerner and published as sheet music in the North, it was being taken up by singers North and South. Lincoln wanted it to be a goodwill song of the reunited States.

The *River Queen* steamed off. Mr. Lincoln stood a long while looking at the spot they were leaving. To the west beyond those shadowy hills two armies were in a race, some of the Union pursuers going it day and night, with little sleep. On that race, and who should win it, depended the length of the war. Mr. Lincoln gazed and had his thoughts, the others letting him alone with those thoughts. Whatever they were, they held him till long after the speed of the *River Queen* had put City Point and its hauling and mauling military supply depots, its tall river bluffs, its tent hospitals and men and boys with pale white faces, far behind in the deep river mist.

"Before leaving City Point," wrote Captain Barnes of the escorting *Bat*, "the Admiral [Porter] talked over the precautions and showed great uneasiness for the President's safety: so I caused two officers to be added to the *Bat*, with a guard of sailors, with minute instructions for guarding the President's person, day and night. The crew of the *River Queen* were examined, and their records taken." The next morning at Fortress Monroe Barnes spoke good-by to the President, not expecting to see him at the Washington landing that day. The President thanked Barnes for attentions and "good care," and made "jocular allusions to the comforts of navy men in war times."

On Sunday, April 9, steaming up the Potomac, wrote Chambrun: "That whole day the conversation dwelt upon literary subjects. Mr. Lincoln read to us for several hours passages . . . from Shakespeare. Most of these were from 'Macbeth,' and, in particular, the verses which follow *Duncan's* assassination." These relate how Macbeth becoming king after the murder of Duncan suffered torments of mind. "Mr. Lincoln paused here while reading, and began to explain to us how true a description of the murderer that one was; when, the dark deed achieved, its tortured perpetrator came to envy the sleep of his victim."

This scene Lincoln read aloud twice, holding what Sumner described as "a beautiful quarto Shakespeare in his hands." As if to test out further some dark magic not gathered in the first reading he gave again the lines:

> Duncan is in his grave;
> After life's fitful fever he sleeps well;
> Treason has done his worst; nor steel, nor poison,
> Malice domestic, foreign levy, nothing
> Can touch him further.

Politics and immediate affairs did for a moment arise this Sabbath steaming up the Potomac on the *River Queen.* Mrs. Lincoln, "one privileged to address him in that way," noted Sumner, spoke of Jefferson Davis: "Do not allow him to escape the law—he must be hanged!" The President replied calmly, "Judge not, that ye be not judged."

And by Sumner's account, when pressed again by the remark that the sight of Libby Prison made it impossible to pardon the Confederate chief, Lincoln repeated twice over the words, "Judge not, that ye be not judged."

Veiled in his own meditations as they steamed past the enshrined home of Washington, Chambrun said to him, "Mount Vernon and Springfield, the memories of Washington and your own, those of the revolutionary and civil wars; these are the spots and names America shall one day equally honor." Lincoln came out of himself. "Springfield! How happy, four years hence, will I be to return there in peace and tranquillity!"

The roofs of Washington came into view. Mrs. Lincoln in long silence looked at the city, turned to the Marquis. "That city is filled with our enemies." The President heard. He raised an arm and somewhat impatiently: "Enemies! we must never speak of that."

Sumner and Chambrun entered a carriage with the President and Mrs. Lincoln, drove with them to the White House, where the President expected in the morning to take up much business left unfinished while he had been at City Point.

One errand and duty, however, must be done this night. Straight to the home of William H. Seward he drove. Four days ago on a sunny spring afternoon Seward in a carriage for his customary daily drive, in company with his son and daughter and a young friend of the latter, had watched his fast team of young horses prance and go, had enjoyed it. Horses were his outdoor sport and pleasure; a team of Arabians he once owned won national reputation. Suddenly on this afternoon these carriage horses took fright and plunged into a wild runaway. Seward stood up, tried for a leap to the pavement, was thrown in the air, took a bad fall, and when a crowd gathered he was found unconscious. Taken to his home, physicians examined him to find the right shoulder badly dislocated, the jaw broken on both sides, his slow and partial return to consciousness coming with agonizing pain. On the third day his wife, who had journeyed from Auburn, New York, with heartache, saw his face so bruised, swollen, discolored, his voice so changed and hoarse, that he seemed a man she had never before looked at. At first he wandered in delirium, but on the third day was again in his right mind.

The gaslights in the house were turned low as Lincoln entered, the rooms quiet, everyone moving softly and speaking in whispers. On a bed in the center of his second-floor room lay the Secretary of State, swathed in bandages. To his now old and proven friend young Frederick Seward guided the President, who sat down on the side of the bed near the left arm of the sick and broken man. The wounded right arm was sensitive and at times crazy with pain. The face looked out from a steel frame that held the jaw for healing.

Lincoln spoke softly, solemnly, his greetings and sympathy. From the swollen tongue came with pain and effort the hoarse whisper, "You are back from Richmond?"

Then Lincoln leaned across the bed, rested on an elbow so as tc bring his face nearer to the face of his friend, and told of many things he had seen and heard on the trip to City Point. Seward listened, his mind eager.

"They were left together for a half hour or more," wrote the son Frederick. "Then the door opened softly, and Mr. Lincoln came out gently, intimating by a silent look and gesture that Seward had fallen into a feverish slumber and must not be disturbed."

CHAPTER 68

PALM SUNDAY OF '65

WHILE Lincoln traveled on the *River Queen* one night and one day, from City Point to Washington, the main prop and bulwark of the Confederacy fell and lay fallen beyond saving.

In the race westward to see whether Grant could stop Lee from heading south and joining Johnston, no one could be sure what was going to happen. On the Peninsula, at Fredericksburg and Chancellorsville, at Gettysburg and in the Wilderness and at Spotsylvania Court House, the traps had been set for the Army of Northern Virginia and it had broken through, at times handing bloody punishment to an enemy having twice as many troops. Now again Grant hoped to throw such a ring of men and steel around Lee that another escape would be impossible or too costly to think about.

In ten days of latter March and early April Lee lost 19,000 men to Grant as prisoners. In a series of desperate fights the total of Lee's killed and wounded ran high—and of effective troops he had none to spare. The race westward on parallel lines was clocked with running battles. The one day's stop at Amelia Court House instead of expected food supplies saw nothing at all. The rank and file of the army must march on slim rations, mainly of parched corn.

At a branch of the Appomattox River named Sayler's (or Sailor's) Creek enough of the Union Army had overtaken Lee to force a combat that resulted in Lee's saying to one of his officers, "General, that half of our army is destroyed."

Hunger was a helper of Grant—hunger counting more than guns and munitions. The cannon of Lee were on short rations as well as the foot soldiers and cavalry horses. The artillerists knew if they went into a straight frontal battle they wouldn't have shells to last through. For this the North had played, and Sherman and Sheridan had devastated and Grant had hammered and Lincoln had toiled and held on—for this, the exhaustion of the South—a whittling away and a wearing down till the Army of Northern Virginia was a spectral shadow of the body that not quite two years ago had invaded Pennsylvania and threatened Philadelphia and Baltimore.

Many were barefoot, many had toes and heels out from their shoes; hats and clothes testified to wear and weather, and their blanket rolls were thin and down to final necessities—in the kind of marching and fighting they had gone through every useless ounce of weight was left behind. Yet as troops they were proved and fast. Whatever General Lee asked they would give. The basic essential remnant of this army was ready for death or starvation or retreat to the mountains and guerrilla warfare till the last man was gone. They had fought, dug, pivoted, maneuvered, till they knew each other and had timing and concentration down to fine points.

Grant knew probably better than anyone that he could beat this army, smash pieces of it and send it recoiling in retreat. But he wouldn't swear he could capture it. To bag such an army of proved wit and flair—to take the whole of it and end the war—that was something else. Anything could happen. Of his own Army of the Potomac Grant was proud. Never, he was saying now, had it marched and fought with such fine co-ordination, commanders and men at times outdoing what he ordered and expected. The immediate objective however was immense—and might be lost—no one could tell beforehand.

So while Lincoln sailed down the James River and out on the Atlantic the night of April 8, Grant the iron man, Grant the cool and imperturbable, Grant the model of self-possession and personal control during heavy and fierce action, Grant in the rear of the Army of the Potomac pressing Lee's rear guard, stopped at a farmhouse with a sick headache. Grant spent the night bathing his feet in hot water and mustard, putting mustard plasters on his wrists and the back of his neck, moving restlessly on a sitting-room sofa trying to snatch a little sleep. He was a worn man, keeping his saddle day and night, living on scant and hurried meals, now at the rear and again at the farthest front, where troops seeing him said, "The old man is here—the fur is going to fly!"

His mind had concentrated intensely on notes he wrote to Lee and Lee's answers. Each of these great and adroit commanders was making deep guesses about what was going on in the mind of the other. Rawlins in one of his frank outbursts was telling Grant that Lee's latest note was "cunningly worded," false, and deserving of no reply, Grant quietly replying: "Some allowance must be made for the trying position in which General Lee is placed. . . . If I meet Lee he will surrender before I leave." Rawlins exploded farther: "You have no right to meet Lee, or anybody else, to arrange terms of peace. That is the prerogative [Rawlins was a lawyer back home in Galena, Illinois] of the President and the Senate. Your business is to capture or destroy Lee's army." Then Rawlins brought out the instructions which Lincoln had sent to Grant on March 3 saying Grant was held strictly to military matters and must not assume "to decide, discuss, or confer upon any political questions."

Grant however believed he knew the mind and feeling of Lincoln beyond these instructions. Their many talks at City Point made him sure of what he could offer Lee that would be as though from the President. So he refused to string along with Rawlins, and sent Lee another note to the effect that while he had "no authority to treat on the subject of peace," he would however state "that I am equally anxious for peace with yourself, and the whole North entertains the same feeling." Lee read the note as an invitation for him to meet Grant and discuss terms of surrender, this in line with Grant's hope "that all our difficulties may be settled without the loss of another life."

Whatever might be the communications of men at daybreak this morning of April 9, the earth spoke of peace. The oaks flung out fresh tassels. Trees leafed out pale green. Peach trees sang with blossoms. New grass and opening buds put the breath of spring on the air. Winter had said good-by a week or so before when troops had shaken a white frost off their blankets before the morning coffee. Now softer nights had come. Now it was Palm Sunday, April 9, 1865, a date to be encircled in red, white, and blue on calendars.

Across the path of Lee's army and blocking its way this morning stood the cavalry of Phil Sheridan. At five o'clock this morning General Lee on high ground studied the landscape and what it held. Through a fog he looked. What had arrived yonder? Was it Sheridan only, or did the horse have supporting foot troops? He would wait. He had seen his troops breakfast that morning on parched corn, men and horses having the same food. He had seen his officers breakfast on a gruel of meal and water. He had not been seen to eat any breakfast himself. He had put on his handsomest sword, coat, hat, boots and spurs looking new and fresh, the array topped with a sash of deep-red silk, saying when General Pendleton asked about this gay garb, "I have probably to be General Grant's prisoner and thought I must make my best appearance."

Eight o'clock came. Also came word that Sheridan's cavalry had fallen slowly back and widened out. Behind the cavalry and screened by woodland waited heavy bodies of infantry in blue; these were the troops of Ord and Griffin, who had made an almost incredible march of thirty miles the night and day before, coming up at daybreak to support Sheridan and invite battle. To the left, to the rear, were other Union lines. Their circle of campfires reflected on clouds the night before told of their surrounding the Army of Northern Virginia.

Robert E. Lee now had three choices. He could go into frontal battle, fight the last, bloody, forlorn conflict of the war. He could escape with a thin remnant to mountains lying westward and carry on guerrilla warfare. Or he could surrender.

He asked Longstreet and other generals whether the sacrifice of his army in battle would help the Confederate cause elsewhere. They said in effect that a battle lost now against overwhelming numbers and resources would be of no use. To General Alexander, Lee spoke of the lawless futility of bushwhacking and guerrilla fighting, which "would bring on a state of affairs it would take the country years to recover from."

Lee's staff officers heard him say, "There is nothing left me to do but to go and see General Grant, and I would rather die a thousand deaths."

"Oh, General," protested one, "what will history say of the surrender of the army in the field?"

"Yes, I know they will say hard things of us! They will not understand how we were overwhelmed by numbers. But that is not the question, Colonel: The question is, is it right to surrender this army. If it is right, then I will take all the responsibility."

He looked over the field at a lifting fog and spoke as though tempted to go out where, the war being still on, he would be one easy target. "How easily could I be rid of this, and be at rest! I have only to ride along the line and all will be over!" For a moment he seemed almost helpless, then recovered. "But it is our duty to live."

Lee wrote a note asking Grant for an interview "with reference to the surrender of this army." Grant on receiving it at once wrote Lee to name the place for their meeting. Grant riding toward the front said to Colonel Horace Porter, "The pain in my head seemed to leave me the moment I got Lee's letter."

And it became a folk tale and a school-reader story how at the McLean house on the edge of Appomattox village, ninety-five miles west of Richmond, the two great captains of men faced each other in a little room and Lee gave over his army to Grant, and the two men looked so different from each other. Lee tall and erect, Grant short and stoop-shouldered. Lee in a clean and dazzling military outfit, Grant in a rough-worn and dusty blouse telling his high rank only by the three stars on the shoulders, Grant apologizing to Lee that he had come direct from the field and hadn't time to change his uniform. Lee fifty-eight years old with silver hair, near the evening of life, Grant forty-two with black hair and unspent strength of youth yet in him.

Lee inside was writhing over the bitter ordeal, and Grant later admitted that he was embarrassed—though both of them wore grave, inscrutable faces and no one could have read the mixed feelings masked by the two commanders. Grant had never been a Republican, never voted for Lincoln till '64, never traveled with the abolitionists. Lee had never advised the secession of Virginia; had never been a slaveholder except by inheritance and had immediately sold the slaves; had never given to the Confederacy his first and deepest loyalty, which for him belonged to Virginia; had never said otherwise than that he would have stayed out of the war if Virginia had stayed out of the Confederacy; had never sought to devise a grand

The McLean house

strategy of the war based on the whole Confederacy; had never, so it seemed, in reality considered the Confederacy as a nation, but rather as a loose league of States, each one a sovereign nation.

Both saw slavery as a canker and an evil. Neither cared for war as a game for its own sake. Each loved horses, home life, wife and family. And Lee, though it would have been an insolent lie to call him a Union man, had some mysterious, indefinable instinct about a Union of States, one common country, if it could be effected with honor. The Jefferson Davis and Rhett-Yancey vision of a Confederate slave empire stretching from the Ohio River to the Isthmus of Panama, including the Island of Cuba, had never had mention or approval from Lee. And yet, what he was doing this day in the McLean house came hard, and was, as he said, worse than dying a thousand deaths.

"I met you once before, General Lee," began Grant in even voice, "while we were serving in Mexico. . . . I have always remembered your appearance, and I think I should have recognized you anywhere."

"Yes, I know I met you on that occasion, and I have often thought of it and tried to recollect how you looked, but I have never been able to recall a single feature."

Talk about Mexico ran into memories of that war when they both wore blue. Grant just about forgot why they were there, it seemed, or else the old and early bashfulness of Grant was working. Lee brought him to the point. "I suppose, General Grant, that the object of our present meeting is fully understood. I asked to see you to ascertain upon what terms you would receive the surrender of my army."

Not a shading of change crossed Grant's face. He went on as between two good neighbors. "The terms I propose are those stated substantially in my letter of yesterday—that is, the officers and men surrendered to be paroled and disqualified from taking up arms again until properly exchanged, and all arms, ammunition and supplies to be delivered up as captured property."

Lee nodded assent. This was what he had hoped for, though one of his generals had predicted that the army would be marched off to prison in shame and disgrace. "Those," said Lee to Grant, "are about the conditions I expected would be proposed."

Grant, seated at a table, put it in writing, his staff aides and corps commanders standing by, Lee seated with his aide Colonel Charles Marshall standing behind his chair. Grant rose, stepped over to Lee, and handed him the paper scrawled in pencil. Lee took out spectacles from a pocket, pulled out a handkerchief and wiped the glasses, crossed his legs, and read slowly and carefully the strangest and most consequential paper for him that had ever met his eyes.

At the words "until properly" he suggested that General Grant must have meant to add the word "exchanged."

"Why, yes," said Grant, "I thought I had put in the word 'exchanged.'"

Lee said that with Grant's permission he would mark where the word "exchanged" should be inserted. "Certainly," said Grant. Lee felt his pockets for a pencil and seemed that day to have no pencil. Colonel Horace Porter stepped forward with a pencil. Lee thanked him, put a caret where the word "exchanged" was to go in, read to the finish, and then with his first touch of warmth said to Grant, "This will have a very happy effect on my army."

Grant asked for any further suggestions. Lee had one. In his army the cavalrymen and artillerists owned their horses. He wanted these men who owned their mounts to have them on their farms for spring plowing. Grant said this subject was quite new to him. He hadn't known that private soldiers owned their horses. In his own army the rank and file had only government horses and mules. However, "I take it that most of the men in the ranks are small farmers, and as the country has been so raided by the two armies, it is doubtful whether they will be able to put in a crop to carry themselves and their families through the next winter without the aid of the horses they are now riding." So without changing the written terms he would instruct officers receiving paroles "to let all the men who claim to own a horse or mule take the animals home with them to work their little farms."

Lee showed relief. "This will have the best possible effect upon the men. It will be very gratifying and will do much toward conciliating our people."

Lee shook hands with some of Grant's generals who offered theirs, bowed, said little, was too heavy of heart to join in a pleasantry from one old West Point acquaintance, then turned to Grant saying that a thousand Union prisoners, including some officers, had been living the last few days on parched corn only; they required attention, and of provisions "I have,

Grant and Lee sign their names to a paper on a table in the McLean house

indeed, nothing for my own men." This was discussed briefly and Grant directed that 25,000 rations be sent to Lee's men.

Lee wrote an acceptance of Grant's terms, signed it, and at 3:45 in the afternoon of this Palm Sunday, April 9, 1865, the documents of surrendering an army were completed. There remained only such formalities as roll call and stacking of arms. Union gunners made ready to fire a salute of grand national triumph, but Grant forbade any signs of rejoicing over a broken enemy that he hoped hereafter would no longer be an enemy. Grant directed his men that no cheers, no howls of triumph, were wanted—and few were heard. The rank and file of these two armies, "bluebelly" and "butternut," had traded tobacco and coffee and newspapers on the picket lines enough to have a degree of fellowship and affection for each other. Too often this fraternizing on the front lines had troubled commanders who felt it was interfering with the war.

Lee rode among his men—who crowded around him crying, "We'll fight 'em yet"—and explained, with tears and in a choked voice, that they had fought the war together, he had done his best, and it was over. Many were dazed. Some wept. Others cursed and babbled. The army could die but never surrender, they had hoped. Yet they still worshiped Lee. They touched his hands, his uniform; they petted Traveller and smoothed his flanks with their hands. One man, throwing down his musket, cried to the blue heaven: "Blow, Gabriel, blow! My God, let him blow, I am ready to die!"

A gentleman fighter, in dirt and rags, reached up a hand saying: "General, I have had the honor of serving with this army since you took command. If I thought you were to blame for what has occurred today, I could not look you in the face. God bless you!" Another gripped the commander's hand with "Farewell, General Lee. . . . I wish for your sake and mine that every damned Yankee on earth was sunk ten miles in hell!"

Perhaps no man in either army did better at briefly sketching what had happened than Meade writing to his wife: "Lee's army was reduced to a force of less than ten thousand effective armed men. We had at least fifty thousand around him, so that nothing but madness would have justified resistance." This was more basic than Colonel Theodore Lyman exulting to his wife in a one-sentence message inked in large letters: "The rebellion has gone up!!"

For Grant it was one more odd day. Three times now he had bagged a whole army. Three times now—at Fort Donelson, at Vicksburg, at Appomattox—he had been the center figure of operations bringing in an entire army for surrender. But he admitted that he worried more before Appomattox than at Donelson or Vicksburg. He had kept his pledge to Lincoln that he would do his best to avoid a final bloody battle. He was in faith with Lincoln's spirit at City Point in his order to stop the firing of salutes: "The war is over; the rebels are our countrymen again; and the best sign of rejoicing after the victory will be to abstain from all demonstrations in the field."

The next day it rained. The paroles amounted to 28,231. Grant and Lee sat their horses between lines for a farewell talk. Grant said he was interested in peace and hoped to have soon the surrender of the other Confederate armies. Lee replied that the South was a large country and that the Federals might be compelled to march over it three or four times before the war was entirely ended, but the Federals could do this, he said, because the South could no longer resist. For his own part, he hoped there would be no further sacrifice of life. Grant said that not a man in the South had so great an influence with soldiers and people as General Lee, that if Lee would now advise the surrender of the other armies his advice would be followed. Lee said he could not do this without first consulting President Davis. And with no misunderstandings Grant and Lee said good-by.

Some of Grant's staff men asked permission to go over into the Confederate lines and visit "old friends." "They went over," wrote Grant, "had a very pleasant time with their old friends, and brought some of them back with them when they returned." Truly the war was beginning to be over. Lee, going back to camp, met a cavalcade of blue and a cheery good morning from a bearded man at the head of it who took off his cap to Lee. A second look told Lee it was George Gordon Meade of Gettysburg and other points North. "But what are you doing with all that gray in your beard?" quizzed Lee. Meade smiled to an old friend of kindlier days. "You have to answer for most of it!" Then as Lee and Meade rode together toward Confederate headquarters cheers and yells rose from Lee's rank-and-filers. Meade turned to his color-bearer and ordered him to unfurl the Stars and Stripes. And a proud though lean and famished trooper at the

Head Qr Army N Va
April 10th 1865

General Order No 9

After four years of arduous service, marked by unsurpassed courage and fortitude the Army of Northern Virginia has been compelled to yield to overwhelming numbers. I need not tell the survivors of so many hard fought battles who have remained steadfast to the last, that I have consented to this result from no distrust of them. But feeling that valor and devotion could accomplish nothing that would compensate the loss that would attend the continuance of the contest—I determined to avoid the useless sacrifice of those whose past services have endeared them to their countrymen. By the terms of the agreement Officers and men can return to their homes and remain until exchanged. You will take with you the satisfaction that proceeds from the consciousness of duty faithfully performed, and I earnestly pray that a merciful God will extend to you His blessing and protection—With unceasing admiration of your constancy and devotion to your Country, and a grateful remembrance of your kind and generous consideration of myself, I bid you an affectionate farewell

R E Lee
Genl

The South treasures the general order signed "R E Lee Gen," dated April 10, 1865, at "Head Qr Army N Va," reading: "After four years of arduous service, marked by unsurpassed courage and fortitude the Army of Northern Virginia has been compelled to yield to overwhelming numbers. I need not tell the survivors of so many hard fought battles who have remained steadfast to the last, that I have consented to this result from no distrust of them. But feeling that valor and devotion could accomplish nothing that would compensate the loss that would attend the continuance of the contest—I determined to avoid the useless sacrifice of those whose past services have endeared them to their countrymen. By the terms of the agreement officers and men can return to their homes and remain until exchanged. You will take with you the satisfaction that proceeds from the consciousness of duty faithfully performed, and I earnestly pray that a merciful God will extend to you His blessing and protection—With unceasing admiration of your constancy and devotion to your country, and a grateful remembrance of your kind and generous consideration of myself, I bid you an affectionate farewell[.]" Slightly reduced in size from the original in the Barrett collection.

roadside cried: "Damn your old rag! We are cheering General Lee." Here the war was still on. As Confederate Colonel Bryan Grimes shook hands in good-by to a North Carolinian he heard, "God bless you; we will go home, make three more crops and then try them again."

The giving up of ragged and shot-pierced battle flags came hard. Veterans wept as they stood them alongside surrendered muskets. In a few instances color-bearers hid the flags under their shirts and carried them home. Still other banners were torn into pieces and shared out among men who had heard shells and bullets singing around the old emblem. They understood General Lee's farewell order of that day saying they had been "compelled to yield to overwhelming numbers and resources," and though they were "steadfast to the last" they had arrived where "valor and devotion could accomplish nothing to compensate the loss . . . the useless sacrifice." Back to their homes and fields, toward the things that used to be, they started, in columns, in squads, as lone stragglers, some of them wondering what they might find where Sherman and Sheridan had been. On the war they were pretty well talked out. Later again they might talk about the war. Now it was home and the folks and girls and women and how to make a living—this they talked about—some with occasional blasphemy and eternal curses on Abe Lincoln, the one man on whom they blamed the war.

Sheridan paid $20 in gold for the table on which General Grant wrote the terms of surrender and presented it to the wife of his dashing, long-haired, Indian-fighter General Custer. Ord paid $40 for the table at which Lee sat and tried to give it to Mrs. Grant, who insisted that Mrs. Ord should have it. The chairs in which Lee and Grant sat, a stone inkstand, brass candlesticks, a child's doll—these and other articles in the surrender room were bought and carried away as relics of a scene that could never happen again. Later the land thereabouts was to be dedicated as Surrender Grounds.

Yes, it was to become a folk tale and a school-reader story, how at Appomattox Grant and Lee signed papers. For a vast living host the word Appomattox had magic and beauty. They sang the syllables "Ap-po-mat-tox" as a happy little carol of harvest and fields of peace and the sun going down with no shots in the night to follow.

One of the great Confederate combat leaders proven in the war, General John B. Gordon, had sat his horse and spoken farewell to his men. Some of them he had seen weeping as they folded burnt and shot-pierced battle flags and laid them on the stacked arms of surrender. As he told his troops of his own grief he tried to give them hope to rebuild out of the poverty and ashes to which many would return. While he spoke there drifted into his audience numbers of Union soldiers. They carried his remarks to Congressman Elihu Washburne, who came to General Gordon, made himself known, said he was pleased with the trend of Gordon's remarks, and made one emphatic statement which Gordon found "greatly encouraged" him.

Gordon wrote later that he could never forget the laconic answer to his inquiry, "Why do you think, Mr. Washburne, that the South will be generously dealt with by the Government?" The reply: "Because Abraham Lincoln is at its head." Gordon was one of those who in the rush and fury of the war had not had time to study Lincoln's words and policies.

"I knew something of Mr. Lincoln's past history," wrote Gordon, "but I had no knowledge whatever of any kindly sentiment entertained by him toward the South. The emphatic words of Mr. Washburne, his intimate friend and counsellor, greatly interested me. I was with Mr. Washburne for several succeeding days—we rode on horseback together from Appomattox toward Petersburg; and his description of Mr. Lincoln's character, of his genial and philanthropic nature, accompanied with illustrative anecdotes, was not only extremely entertaining, but was to me a revelation. . . . Mr. Washburne said . . . it would speedily be known to the Southern people that the President was deeply concerned for their welfare, that there would be no prosecutions and no discrimination, but that the States' governments would be promptly recognized, and every effort made to help the Southern people. These impressive assurances were adding strength to my hopes."

It was thirty months since Antietam and Gordon's message to General Lee that his men were still holding the shot-bitten center of the army, thirty months since Fanny Haralson Gordon, his wife, had come into a hospital to hear a man with a shattered jaw greeting her, "Mrs. Gordon, you have not a very handsome husband!"

Gordon could never forget a Kentucky father who lost two sons, one dying for the North, the other for the South. Over the two graves of his soldier boys the father set up a joint monument inscribed "God knows which was right."

CHAPTER 69

THE NORTH GOES WILD

HOW Lincoln slept that night of April 9 and whether dream shapes spoke to him—this would have interested many whose minds at once ran to him in connection with a telegram received at the War Department at nine o'clock that night.

From Appomattox Grant telegraphed Stanton at 4:30 that afternoon: "General Lee surrendered the Army of Northern Virginia this afternoon on terms proposed by myself. The accompanying additional correspondence will show the conditions fully."

The war was over. It would have various dying flares in a sunset sky. The costs and sacrifices could never be forgotten. There would be hates and rankling memories kept alive and lingering in a miasma of swamp mist. The war nevertheless had spent itself and gone now into a realm of memory and hallucination, a national ordeal and fever over and past.

The newsmen wrote their stories, put on the wires the glad tidings, and then went out and got drunk, or as Noah Brooks had it, "unbent themselves in a private and exclusive jollification." Cannon boomed out over Washington at dawn, a salute of five hundred guns ordered by the Secretary of War. Over muddy streets surged people singing and cheering. The government departments gave their clerks another holiday. Treasury employees gathered in the main corridor, sang "Praise God from whom all blessings flow," marched across to the White House and serenaded the President at breakfast with "The Star-spangled Banner." To Stanton Lincoln sent a note: "Tad wants some flags. Can he be accommodated [?]"

The forenoon wore on with the area in front of the White House filling with an enormous crowd. Howitzers dragged up from the navy yard growled in the street. Brass bands had their music interrupted by guns. Tad showed at the well-known window from which the President always spoke. The crowd roared as he waved a captured Confederate flag. Hats went in the air with volleys of yells as the President came out to look at a throng where hatless men were now throwing into the air other men's hats and crazy emotion poured out in screams that rose and curved in rockets. As the heaving surface of hats, faces, and arms quieted down, the President spoke brief congratulations on the occasion, said arrangements were made for a formal celebration and he would defer his remarks.

"We can't wait," came voices. He went on, "If there should be such a demonstration, I, of course, will have to respond to it. [A voice, "Bully for you."] And I will have nothing to say if you dribble it out of me now.

[Laughter and cries, "We want to hear you now."] I see you have a band. [Voices, "We have three of them."] I propose now closing up by requesting you to play a certain piece of music or a tune. I thought 'Dixie' one of the best tunes I ever heard. [Laughter.]"

A band started playing "Dixie" and quit on seeing the President had not finished his remarks. He was still talking about "Dixie." "I had heard that our adversaries over the way had attempted to appropriate it. I insisted yesterday that we had fairly captured it. [Cheers and laughter.] I presented the question to the Attorney-General, and he gave his opinion that it is our lawful prize. [Laughter and cheers.] I ask the band to give us a good turn upon

The President requests flags for Tad; above three officials add their memoranda.
Originals in the Barrett collection.

it." The band gave "Dixie." The crowd gave three cheers and a tiger. The band followed with "Yankee Doodle," the President then leading off, waving his hand, in three cheers for Grant and his officers and men, three more cheers for the navy—and the rollicking crowd moved away. Down Pennsylvania Avenue beflagged steam fire engines roared, their whistles screeching.

Over the North that day of April 10 everything done before in victory celebrations was again done—but longer, oftener, and with a complete and final enthusiasm. To the prowar celebrants were joined the antiwar people, the peace men and women who had always said the war was a cruel and costly failure; they too were glad now. Everybody threw in—everybody still alive and humanly registering. The day dedicated itself to humanity and the Union of States, to the importance of "Yankee Doodle" and the dazzling and inexplicable paradoxes of the American Dream. What would make a noise and proclaim joy? The shooting of cannon and shotguns? So they shot them, and there was booming and roaring. And bells? They would make a happy sound? Yes, church bells and college and school bells and farmhouse dinner bells and fire-wagon bells—the bong-bong and the clang-clang went on the air. Farmers heard the news and stepped out on the front porch with whatever shotgun or squirrel rifle there was and with a grin let the blast go and with a grin turned to the family to talk about how soon the boy with Grant or Sherman would be home for spring plowing. Between bells and salute shots the cry again and again: "The war is over! The war is over!" Too long had they wondered if it would ever end. Four years is a long time. So many, even so many of the loyal ones, had been heartsick about the way it dragged for four years beyond all first expectations. The Union had won the war. Lincoln had had his way. What was Lincoln doing? How did he feel today? Great God, but Lincoln must be thankful today. Hurrah for the Union! Hurrah for Lincoln! Hurrah for Grant and Sherman, the grand right and left arms of Lincoln! Get out the flags. Hang out every rag in the house that looks like a flag. Hang out red-white-and-blue bunting. Make a show. Great Jehovah, but we're glad the war's over!

Men on horseback rode up and down swinging cowbells and tooting horns. Men tied tin cans to sticks, to ropes, and stood on street corners rattling their noisemakers. Express-company wagons, freight trucks of wholesale houses, rumbled hither and yon with no destination, filled with men and boys singing, shouting, outblaring each other with tin horns, halting to take on board laughing apple-cheeked girls. A brass-foundry wagon loaded with men hammering away, each seeing who could bong the loudest on a big bell. Brewery wagons hauled by strapping big horses, with giants of men in leather aprons hoisting kegs of beer, stopping to draw free beer for thirsty crowds. The bells of two, six, twenty churches and cathedrals tolled without ceasing, occasionally joined by a screaming chorus of factory and river-boat whistles. Six-horse and eight-horse wagons loaded with noisemakers, sometimes pounding a row of anvils or a long steam boiler, merchants, doctors, lawyers, ministers, clerks, porters, roustabouts, all joined in hammering out joy over victory and better yet, joy over the war coming to an end. Nothing but flood or fire could have kept local drum majors with twirling batons, brass bands, fife-and-drum corps, and boy-zouave outfits from performing, from marching between jammed sidewalks and flags and red-white-and-blue bunting. In newspapers metropolitan and rural over and again the reporters writing, in effect, "Above the noise and jollification two names are on every lip, Lincoln and Grant."

Many a storekeeper shut his doors and went celebrating. It was a holiday. The night saw torches and transparencies, bonfires, songs and howling. Nobody could be too foolish this day. Men climbed lampposts, stood upright on bareback horses, invented ways to defy gravitation. Laughing men rode sober-faced mules, riding backward and brandishing the mule's tail at onlookers. Those who could turn somersaults and handsprings, those who could imitate roosters or tame or wild animals—they performed for those who wished they could walk on their hands or stand on their ears or go up in a chariot of fire like Elijah. The crazy and cruel dance of death called War had come to an end. No more one-legged, one-armed lads coming home, no more cripples and men broken in skirmish and charge and assault. For many there was nothing to do but get drunk. "Have annozer an' annozer—ish de biggesh day zish country ever saw." Shake hands once, shake hands again, put your arms around anybody, today we love everybody, the war is over, throw your hat on the windmill, throw your hat over the moon.

"The tidings were spread over the country during the night, and the nation seems delirious with joy," wrote the grave Gideon Welles in his diary. . . . "All, all are jubilant." For himself he was not delirious, though quietly jubilant. This would go for the President too on this day. Welles called on the President, found him "looking well and feeling well." Why not? This was his day. He had answers to prayer. His heart probably ran with that of his friend Professor James Russell Lowell writing that day to Professor Charles Eliot Norton: "The news, my dear Charles, is from Heaven. I felt a strange and tender exaltation. I wanted to laugh and I wanted to cry, and ended by holding my peace and feeling devoutly thankful. There is something magnificent in having a country to love." The journalist Edwin L. Godkin wrote that he had waited so long and so eagerly desired Lee's surrender that "it had taken the shape in my mind of a wild dream" and on now hearing the news, "I sat dumbfounded for an hour." In Willard's Hotel an elderly gentleman having had a few drinks, but not too many for the day, leaped up on the bar and led the crowd in singing "Praise God from whom all blessings flow." In the streets of New York City, on the Board of Trade, on the Stock Exchange floor, there too the old Doxology was one of the popular songs of the day, along with the other songs heard everywhere from the Biblical and the bibulous on this day: "John Brown's Body," "My Country, 'Tis of Thee," "Rally Round the Flag, Boys," "The Star-spangled Banner," and occasionally was heard the swaggering, savage merriment of the revolutionary "Jubilo" and the striding "Marching through Georgia."

Prevailing was hilarity, high jinks and headaches, with an undertow of humility and gratitude. Motley wrote of twenty thousand businessmen in New York City uncovering their heads and singing in unison the psalm of thanksgiving: "Praise God." Reports credited even the gold speculators and army-supply contractors as cheerful about the future. Trinity Church at a

midday service overflowed with worshipers, Manhattan "figures of distinction." The choir chanted the "Te Deum," a great pipe organ pealed, and
the congregation rose at word from the clergyman and sang the "Gloria in
Excelsis." New York, the financial capital and the cultural center of the
nation, from the beginning more half-hearted about the war than any other
large Northern city, New York voices sang the line "Glory be to God on
high, and on earth peace, good will towards men." To a far-stretching
throng on the White House lawn late that afternoon the President spoke
from the usual middle-front, second-story window facing Lafayette Park,
one press report giving his little address as follows:

"If the company had assembled by appointment, some mistake had crept
into their understanding. He had appeared before a larger audience than
this one to-day, and he would repeat what he then said—namely, he supposed
owing to the great good news there would be some demonstration. He
would prefer to-morrow evening, when he should be quite willing, and he
hoped ready, to say something. He desired to be particular, because everything he said got into print. Occupying the position he did, a mistake would
produce harm, and therefore he wanted to be careful not to make a mistake."

A transcript of the speech as taken down by a reporter and published in
several newspapers was more interesting, in its offhand manner somewhat
parallel with the various speeches he delivered when on his way to his first
inauguration. Then he was a butt of ridicule for having nothing to say in
a crisis, "a simple Susan." Now he had a right, it was assumed, to pleasant
banter about his responsibility. He was now also better aware of the length
of the shadow he threw, and he surpassed all of these former offhand
speeches to White House lawn crowds in telling them why they must wait
for what he had to say.

"I am informed," he began, "that you have assembled here this afternoon
under the impression that I had made an appointment to speak at this time."
They had, of course. He corrected them. "This is a mistake. I have made
no such appointment. More or less persons have been gathered here at different times during the day, and in the exuberance of their feeling, and for
all of which they are greatly justified, calling upon me to say something,
and I have, from time to time, been sending out what I suppose was proper
to disperse them for the present. [He hoped this was clear. He had tried to
"disperse" them but they kept coming back for more.] I said to a larger
audience this morning what I now desire to repeat. It is this: That I supposed, in consequence of the glorious news we have been receiving lately,
that there is to be some general demonstration, either on this or to-morrow
evening when I shall be expected, I presume, to say something. Just here I
will remark that I would much prefer having this demonstration take place
to-morrow evening, as I would then be much better prepared to say what
I have to say than I am now or can be this evening. I therefore say to you
that I shall be quite willing, and I hope ready, to say something then;
whereas, just now. I am not ready to say something that one in my position
ought to say."

And soberly and familiarly, in the style of the Father Abraham they had come to see: "Everything I say, you know, goes into print. [Laughter.] If I make a mistake it doesn't merely affect me, or you, but the country. I, therefore, ought at least try not to make mistakes. [A voice, "You haven't made any yet."] If, then, a general demonstration be made to-morrow evening, and it is agreeable, I will endeavor to say something, and not make a mistake, without at least trying carefully to avoid it. Thank you for the compliment of this call. I bid you good-evening." Of course they cheered. He had given them all that under the circumstances he could give, no oration, but the warmth and shine of his personality.

A North Carolina man who heard this speech wrote of it to the editor of *Harper's Monthly*. The crowd had persisted. The reluctant President finally made a speech that asked for more time. "He appeared somewhat younger and more offhand and vigorous than I should have expected. His bright, knowing, somewhat humorous look reminded me of a well-practiced country physician who had read men through till he understood them well. There was the humorous kindness of a good-natured doctor who had seen his patients through a most awful siege of sickness, till they were now fairly and fully convalescent, and who was disposed to let the past, whatever it had cost him or them, go by for the time, and have a little cheerful congratulation. His gestures and countenance had something of the harmless satisfaction of a young politician at a ratification meeting after his first election to the Legislature. He was happy, and glad to see others happy."

This gave the exterior Lincoln of that night of April 10. On the same night Ralph Waldo Emerson at Concord wrote in his journal a meditation on the inconceivably higher stature and reach that now attached to Lincoln, his words, gestures, even silences, counting far beyond the earlier expectations of him. "Why talk of President Lincoln's equality of manners to the elegant or titled men with whom Everett and others saw him? A sincerely upright and intelligent man as he was, placed in the Chair, has no need to think of his manners or appearance. His work day by day educates him rapidly and to the best."

Like many others, Emerson was being drawn into the orbit of Lincoln's influence. His doubts about Lincoln's style as an executive and a Leader of Men now resolved in the sentence: "He exerts the enormous power of this continent in every hour, in every conversation, in every act;—thinks and decides under this pressure, forced to see the vast and various bearings of the measures he adopts; *he* cannot palter, he cannot but carry a grace beyond his own, a dignity, by means of what he drops, e.g., all his pretension and trick, and arrives, of course, at a simplicity, which is the perfection of manners."

The editor of *Harper's Weekly* found in the *Northern Whig* of Belfast, Ireland, a sketch of Lincoln worth reprinting because an Irish editor arrived in his own way at the same estimate *Harper's* had continuously set forth. "An American statesman with a European varnish . . . Abraham Lincoln, with his genius for silence, and its correlative, occasional felicitous speech

View down Pennsylvania Avenue to the Capitol in '65

From an engraving in the Barrett collection

South front of the White House or Executive Mansion

From the Barrett collection

The Capitol in '65

From the Barrett collection

. . . the fine spirit in the rough garb . . . a deep religion, with a genuine, if homely humor . . . history will recognize one thing common to George Washington and Abraham Lincoln—a pure honesty devoid of all self-seeking. When the heats of party passion and international jealousy have abated, when detraction has spent its malice, and the scandalous gossip of the day goes the way of all lies, the place of Abraham Lincoln, in the grateful affection of his countrymen and in the respect of the world, will be second only, if it be second, to that of Washington himself."

In his speech of farewell to Springfield in '61 Lincoln had spoken of "a task before me greater than that which rested upon Washington." Occasionally now he heard of someone who placed him as the equal, at least, of Washington in national achievement. The eminent American actor universally conceded as foremost in Shakespearian roles, Edwin Booth, though Maryland-born, was not in agreement with his Southern kinsmen. According to the editor of *Harper's Weekly*, Edwin Booth the winter before had closed one conversational topic with saying to a friend: "Don't speak to me of politics, for we can not agree. Abraham Lincoln will be loved and honored hereafter not less than Washington."

Joshua Speed was shown into the President's office while Senators and Congressmen waited outside. Speed saw several visitors rapidly disposed of, the President turning to a final pair, a little "peevish" in tone, thought Speed, as he said, "Well, ladies, what can I do for you?" Both commenced talking at once. It came out they wanted releases for a batch of draft-resisters in Pennsylvania. The President sent for a War Department official, scanned the records, decided, "I believe I will turn out the whole flock," and signed an order. Then, as Speed later related to Herndon, the younger of the two women kneeled in thanks, and heard, "Get up, don't kneel to me, but thank God and go." The older one, tears in her eyes, took his hand. "Good-bye, Mr. Lincoln. I shall probably never see you again till we meet in heaven." He took her right hand in both of his and escorting her to the door: "I am afraid with all my troubles I shall never get to the resting-place you speak of; but if I do I am sure I shall find you. Good-bye."

Now he was alone with his old crony of tested loyalty in friendship, who was saying, "Lincoln, with my knowledge of your nervous sensibility, it is a wonder that such scenes as this don't kill you." Thoughtful a moment, then in a languid voice: "Yes, you are to a certain degree right. I ought not to undergo what I so often do. I am very unwell now; my feet and hands of late seem to be always cold, and I ought perhaps to be in bed; but things of the sort you have just seen don't hurt me, for, to tell you the truth, that scene is the only thing today that has made me forget my condition or given me any pleasure. I have, in that order, made two people happy and alleviated the distress of many a poor soul whom I never expect to see.

"That old lady," he continued, "was no counterfeit. The mother spoke out in all the features of her face. It is more than one can often say that in doing right one has made two people happy in one day. Speed, die when I may, I want it said of me by those who know me best, that I always plucked a thistle and planted a flower when I thought a flower would grow."

Joseph Gillespie of Illinois, on asking what was to happen in the South after the war, heard Lincoln say that some thought that certain heads ought to come off. "But if it was left to me, I could not tell where to draw the line between whose heads should come off, and whose heads should stay on." He had been reading of David's putting down a rebellion and David's nephew, Abishai, crying that a man ought not to be pardoned because he had cursed the Lord's anointed. David's reply came: "What have I to do with you, ye sons of Zeruiah, that you should this day be adversaries unto me? Shall there any man be put to death this day in Israel?"

CHAPTER 70

"NOT IN SORROW, BUT IN GLADNESS OF HEART"

UNDER date of April 11 the President issued a proclamation closing Southern ports, naming them from Richmond, Virginia, to Brownsville, Texas. "All right of importation, warehousing, and other privileges shall, in respect to the ports aforesaid, cease until they shall again have been opened by order of the President." Any ship or vessel from beyond the United States trying to enter these ports with articles subject to duties, "the same, together with its tackle, apparel, furniture, and cargo, shall be forfeited to the United States."

This was farewell to blockade-running profits, news of no second importance to the London *Times* and its maritime interests. Welles brought the proclamation to Lincoln, who signed it with no changes. "Seemed gratified," wrote Welles, "that Seward and myself were united in the measure, remembering, I think, without mentioning, the old difference."

Also of this date was a proclamation barring from all United States ports the war vessels of any foreign country whose ports refused equal privileges and immunities to war vessels of the United States. Whatever claims or pretenses might have heretofore shut out United States naval ships from harbors of other nations would now meet with retaliation—no port rights nor hospitalities for the naval craft of those nations.

The home war fading, the Union could risk challenging other countries. Welles had for months wished the President to issue this proclamation but Seward had not been willing. "Insolence of the petty officials of John Bull" would diminish now, Welles believed. "We shall assert now our rights and, I hope, maintain them."

The President spent his best working hours this day on his speech for the evening. In the afternoon he went to the war telegraph office. And according to the operator Charles A. Tinker, "Something reminded him of a story, and to illustrate the finale he gathered his coattails under his arms and, with about three long strides, crossed the room and passed out of the door with the last words of the story echoing from his lips." This, however, was a light interval in a very sober day.

The President was losing no time, was seizing the initiative, moving with the old sagacity and patience to set in motion his own reconstruction program. Not until next December would Congress meet, not unless he called a special session. And it was no more in his mind to call any special session now than it was in April, May, and June of '61, when during eighty terrific days he delayed summoning Congress. Between this mid-April and the next December when Congress met, the Executive would have a wide and free hand in a thousand immediate affairs and practical actions touching Louisiana, the other seceded States, and the terms on which they should come back into the Union. Already it was a result of the President's policy that Robert E. Lee was peacefully riding home to his Richmond house a free man. Had the President listened to those who wanted trial and hanging of Confederate leaders, he would have instructed Grant to hold Lee for punishment. The entire army of Lee was now footloose and free, Lincoln and Grant referring to them as "our countrymen." The terms of surrender which Grant gave Lee were about what Lincoln on the spot would have given. From their long talks Lincoln knew that Grant, the old Douglas Democrat, and Sherman, the former superintendent of the State Military Academy of Louisiana, agreed with him as against Sumner, Wade, Chandler, Thad Stevens, Julian, the sincere friends of the Negro seeking to give the black man full civil rights.

To question the sincerity of these extremists, to attack their motives—this Lincoln could not and would not do. His dispute with them was over method, over what to do next and how to do it. He intended to speak to the country so plainly that before next December, when Congress met, there would be no mistake that the overwhelming majority of the people were with him. His policy in the main would have behind it the word and weight of Grant, Sheridan, and Sherman, Logan, Meade, Frank Blair, most of the corps and division commanders, their immense personal influence. They were key men and idolized figures. Joined with them would be the mass of a million fighting men now in the field and a half-million troops more at home mustered out, crippled, sick, devoted to the Lincoln Administration, which had already begun its care of them and marked them for preferment. It was an immense political organization that would be responsive to Lincoln's reconstruction plan, an organization that was personal, devoted to the President because of the tests they had seen him pass through, because over and again during the war chaos so many of his judgments at first doubted had eventually won through. In the realm of ideas, as a national spokesman, no one else could get such a hearing, no one else had such a following of people inclined to say, "Maybe it will work—if Old Abe says so it's worth trying." There was, as some knew, an abolitionist remnant who wished for some other man, by some act of God, to replace Lincoln and carry through a program giving the Negro full civil rights. They were a small minority, and they lacked in their ranks the most exalted of abolitionists, those two steadfast friends of Lincoln, William Lloyd Garrison and Harriet Beecher Stowe.

Trailing with the Lincoln chariot of political reality were the tariff beneficiaries fairly well satisfied they would be taken care of, the homesteaders now located and many more in hopes, the Union Pacific Railway crowd with active and ramified prospects, several Old Masters of politics such as Simon Cameron and the Blairs, wild Jim Lane, and here and there such powerful factors as James Gordon Bennett and his *New York Herald*, a slithering chameleon that had changed its color to that of nearly every political and civic animal except the abolitionist extremist who demanded full civil rights for the Negro. In Ohio that zealous custodian of property rights, Senator John Sherman, might yet be compelled to move with an interparty faction to destroy Ben Wade and choose another for that senatorial mantle; the same wind that had blown out Henry Winter Davis in Maryland might rise in Ohio. Politics was conditioned on weather, and Lincoln had an eye for just such weather. In the South during the pangs and twists of reconstruction Lincoln, if he lived, would have with him, in his policy outlined in the speech he was writing this April 11, such varied Southerners as the idolized Robert E. Lee, the commanders Johnston and Longstreet, the former Vice-President of the Confederacy Alexander H. Stephens, and moderates who would include Judge John A. Campbell.

This loose, informal, nameless aggregate of political power responsive to Lincoln had grown, by fate and circumstance had come into existence with common understandings. It had no voice but Lincoln. No other voice could arise that might shape it as a force for remolding Southern society and politics toward peaceful resumption of their place as States in the old Union. For this unorganized but distinct array of political forces Lincoln was timing a speech for tonight. He knew his American people. There had been a genius of timing in his House Divided speech and its terrible foreshadowings. And again in his abrogations of the Frémont and Hunter abortive emancipation proclamations, in his slowly given preliminary and final edicts of Negro freedom "under military necessity," in the sweet note to Greeley about saving the Union with or without slavery, in his quizzical stump-speech letter to Conkling at Springfield after the Gettysburg and Vicksburg victories, in his tiny and tremendous dedicatory Gettysburg Address, in the letter of scorn and rebuke to Vallandigham and the Copperheads, in the letter to Hodges saying he had always hated slavery but was "controlled by events," in the proclamation pocket-vetoing the Wade-Davis reconstruction bill, in the clamps of complete silence during the fall campaign of '64 when only military victories counted, in the majestic second inaugural holding both terror and hope and charity—yes, he knew his American people and had a genius for timing what he had to say so that either it was nearly always what the people wanted for that hour or before long they were wanting it.

He had not forsaken the point he stressed years ago for Oglesby, that the people when rightly and fully trusted would return the trust. Nor had he changed from being the man he was when the Missouri-Kansas committee of radicals had called on him and the tears had coursed his face as he told them that though he lost all other friends there was one friend he had to keep, which was himself. He had a heart and a mind profound and intense enough to search deep for such human justice as could be had in the immediate facts. He would meditate aloud for the world to hear about it— and then let events operate. He would carry his case to the people, believing that the people would either now or in the near future, certainly before next December when Congress met, stand with him when they had heard what he had to say.

"He never misled me," ran the testimony of Senator Lyman Trumbull, once a sharp and incessant critic joined with Sumner and Wade, now the loyal coadjutor of Lincoln, the floor leader whose parliamentary fight for recognition of the new Louisiana government would have won Senate approval of the President's policy but for the abrupt, temperamental filibuster threat of Sumner. The deep undertows of political power were with Lincoln. He was anchored in deep hope that the opposition would crumble and vanish in the tides of thought and feeling whose flow he was nearer to than any other man in the American scene.

And his statements would be so exact, his appeals so free from accusations or prejudice, so detached from personal grounds, that those who opposed him might come to recognize that he too wanted full civil rights for the Negro and was taking the one course that would assure such civil rights as could not be easily swept away at sorry cost to the colored race. The factions and passions of a people at peace, though full of the ranklings and hates of the war coming to an end, were more natural to his skilled referee hand than the remorseless devastations required for war. What the Lee biographer was to note of the late winter of '64 now held pertinent and applicable because Lincoln had in him more of the born umpire and political genius than the natural warrior. "Those who had sought cunningly to lead him, slowly found that he was leading them. His spirit, in some mysterious manner, was being infused."

Panic, want, fanaticism, race hatred, cries for retribution, lust for big money and fortunes, these were spread over the country. Lincoln had his choice of going with those who, to win a complete and abstract justice for the Negro, would not hesitate about making the South a vast graveyard of slaughtered whites, with Negro State governments established and upheld by Northern white bayonets.

An argument could be made for this. Lincoln had implied in his second inaugural that there was Holy Writ to support this argument. For a long-continued monstrous injustice such as slavery there might naturally follow its sudden and violent abolition a weary and terrible period of slowly getting back to something nearer justice.

From this implied argument Lincoln receded, preferring "malice toward none," "charity for all." The supreme devastators Grant and Sherman were not politically joined to those, like Sumner, demanding a justice which would consist of Southern Negro State governments made and upheld by Northern white bayonets. The caldron of war hate still boiled under the surface rejoicing of April 10 over Appomattox. The passions of Sumner and Wade had become a habit. They rose to passion chiefly on the race ques· tion. As born haters they had difficulty adjusting themselves to the ways of Lincoln, the man of kaleidoscopic humor to whom justice, when found operating as a practical reality on earth, was a marvel and a phantom.

Who could say but future historians and commentators might hold that the war was a form of national insanity, its major participants the victims of hallucinations and sick imaginings? This had occurred to Lincoln. It was there in many a ringing laugh at some of his anecdotes of fools lighting their own way to dusty death.

The record of the "fiery ordeal" was being made. Time and generations to come would pass judgment on who were the hesitant knowers, doers, and sages as against those so deadly certain of their own righteousness. The word to Weitzel, "Let 'em up easy," the repeated and mournful "Judge not, that ye be not judged," might have a better sanction from time and the generations to come than counsels encouraging a prolonged race war in the South wherein the Negro could in the very nature of the sad and unchangeable facts maintain political supremacy over the white man only by the extermination and wholesale deaths of white men. Banks of Massachusetts, an antislavery moderate, had hoped this was not so when he went to Louisiana, but being witness on the ground that votes for all Negroes at once meant race war, with the whites refusing to participate in political government, Banks notified Lincoln that a thing he had believed would work he now saw was impossible. In long talks with Lincoln in Washington Banks had reinforced this position with regard to universal suffrage for the Negro. Senator Lyman Trumbull had swung round to this viewpoint in a way that shocked and amazed Wade and Sumner on the Senate floor. And William Lloyd Garrison, among supreme and tested friends of the colored race, stood fast on the same points, to which he had come slowly and inexorably. Many background considerations moved Lincoln as he wrote on April 11 his speech to be given that night. Those expecting grand rhetoric about victory were to be disappointed. Those hoping to hear that all was well with the world now that the South was prostrated and subjugated were to glean other tidings. Joseph Medill had said, "Lincoln is going to boss the reconstruction job." That job and the hard going as a boss—this was to be Lincoln's theme. He would refer to a good practical cause nerving the hearts of men and what should be done—"argue for it, and proselyte for it, and fight for it, and feed it, and grow it, and ripen it to a complete success." This, by direct implication, was his own purpose. The mood was one Zach

Chandler had once found him in, the Senator leaving the White House to say, "The war will now go on—Lincoln is mad!" Yet no man on the government lists and roll calls could be so cool and measured in his anger. It was past four years since Henry Adams had written from Washington to a brother: "No man is fit to take hold now who is not as cool as death." Now too that would stand. And the address prepared for reading, every sentence calculated yet flowing free and serene with involved meditation on an intricate tangle of fact, would be mindful of the close of the letter James Conkling read to the Springfield mass meeting in September of '63: "Let us be sober."

A "carefully written paper" rather than a speech the President held in waiting for the crowd, and in the estimate of Nicolay and Hay, it furnished "the shortest and clearest explanation of both his past and future intentions" on reconstruction.

A light mist floated in over Washington that night and around the illuminated public buildings hung its moving filament and gauze. From many miles away could be seen the dome of the Capitol hovering in the moist air with its curves of light. The windows of Arlington House, across the river, the old home of Robert E. Lee, shone with a brightness reaching Washington. Rockets and colored lights blazed from the lawn where a thousand freed slaves sang "The Year of Jubilee."

With bands of music and banners of freedom, with shouting and hoorah and hullabaloo, an immense throng poured into the area in front of the White House. This was the night set for Washington's formal celebration of the end of the war. Many were the surging calls and cries for the President.

Cheers, national songs, airs from brass bands and human throats, broke on the air, mingling with a concert of fireworks, curving rockets of red and yellow, bombs hissing skyward and exploding in bouquets and fountains. As Lincoln started from the lower floor for the second, an unusual yell mixed with the outside merriment and cheers. He paused and asked what that might be. The answer came with Tad tumbling down the stairs and bursting with anger. The boy, shaken with the excitement of the evening, had just been having one of his biggest life moments, leaning out of a second-story window waving a captured rebel flag and hearing a vast crowd howling wonder and delight. Then a watchful doorkeeper had plucked Tad by the seat of his breeches and drawn him back to safety. The father soothed the boy, straightened his face after his good laugh at Tad, went upstairs and out of the large open window over the main entrance, stepped to a balcony.

The crowd saw him. It was a signal. "There was something terrible," thought Noah Brooks, "in the enthusiasm with which the beloved Chief Magistrate was received. Cheers upon cheers, wave after wave of applause, rolled up, the President patiently standing quiet until it was all over."

He began to read his speech holding a candle in his left hand and the manuscript in the right. "Speedily becoming embarrassed with the difficulty of managing the candle and the speech," wrote Brooks, "he made a comical motion with his left foot and elbow, which I construed to mean that I should hold his candle for him, which I did." From behind a drapery Brooks held the candle and studied the near-by mass of faces caught clear in the high-lighted windows of the White House and then far away toward the street fading off into the blur of moist night air. "A silent, intent multitude," thought Brooks as the President spoke.

"Fellow Citizens," began the speaker of the evening, "we meet this eve-ning not in sorrow, but in gladness of heart. The evacuation of Petersburg and Richmond, and the surrender of the principal insurgent army, give hope of a righteous and speedy peace, whose joyous expression cannot be re-strained. In the midst of this, however, He from whom all blessings flow must not be forgotten.

"A call for a national thanksgiving is being prepared, and will be duly promulgated. Nor must those whose harder part give[s] us the cause of re-joicing be overlooked. Their honors must not be parceled out with others. I myself was near the front, and had the high pleasure of transmitting much of the good news to you; but no part of the honor for plan or execution is mine. To General Grant, his skilful officers and brave men, all belongs. The gallant navy stood ready, but was not in reach to take active part."

This to the crowd was in somewhat the expected tone. Then the subject shifted. The key changed. The crowd was "perhaps surprised," thought Brooks. The President read on, dropped to the floor each written page when read, and became aware that Tad was picking them up as they dropped. He could hear Tad, unseen to the crowd, calling for "another" and "another" of the fluttering sheets. He read on:

"By these recent successes the reinauguration of the national authority—reconstruction—which has had a large share of thought from the first, is pressed much more closely upon our attention. It is fraught with great diffi-culty. Unlike a case of war between independent nations, there is no author-ized organ for us to treat with—no one man has authority to give up the rebellion for any other man. We simply must begin with and mould from disorganized and discordant elements.

"Nor is it a small additional embarrassment that we, the loyal people, differ among ourselves as to the mode, manner, and measure of reconstruc-tion. As a general rule, I abstain from reading the reports of attacks upon myself, wishing not to be provoked by that to which I cannot properly offer an answer. In spite of this precaution, however, it comes to my knowl-edge that I am much censured for some supposed agency in setting up and seeking to sustain the new State government of Louisiana. In this I have done just so much and no more than the public knows."

There was no hoorah to this. Those of the crowd who had come for hoorah wondered how much more of it there would be. It was a little heavy, it seemed. Others knew he was talking not to the thousands on the White

House lawn but to the whole American and European world. He went on with the personal story of his hand in the matter of reconstruction:

"In the Annual Message of December, 1863, and in the accompanying proclamation, I presented a plan of reconstruction, as the phrase goes, which I promised, if adopted by any State, would be acceptable to and sustained by the Executive Government of the nation. I distinctly stated that this was not the only plan which might possibly be acceptable, and I also distinctly protested that the Executive claimed no right to say when or whether members should be admitted to seats in Congress from such States."

He would let them know how his Cabinet took this plan. They might be interested. It was pertinent. Many present knew the Cabinet well.

"This plan was in advance submitted to the then Cabinet, and approved by every member of it. One of them [meaning Chase, whom he did not name] suggested that I should then and in that connection apply the Emancipation Proclamation to the theretofore excepted parts of Virginia and Louisiana; that I should drop the suggestion about apprenticeship for freed people, and that I should omit the protest against my own power in regard to the admission of members of Congress. But even he approved every part and parcel of the plan which has since been employed or touched by the action in Louisiana. The new constitution of Louisiana, declaring emancipation for the whole State, practically applies the proclamation to the part previously excepted. It does not adopt apprenticeship for freed people, and is silent, as it could not well be otherwise, about the admission of members to Congress. So that, as it applied to Louisiana, every member of the Cabinet fully approved of the plan."

And what of Congress? Well, it seemed that Congress agreed with his Cabinet and favored the plan until it first got into motion. "The message went to Congress, and I received many commendations of the plan, written and verbal, and not a single objection to it from any professed emancipationist came to my knowledge until after the news reached Washington that the people of Louisiana had begun to move in accordance with it."

His special interest in Louisiana had started when New Orleans and several parishes of the State fell into Union hands. Three years ago that was. Three years he had been studying what to do about getting Louisiana properly back into the Union.

"From about July, 1862, I had corresponded with different persons supposed to be interested in seeking a reconstruction of a State government for Louisiana. When the message of 1863, with the plan before mentioned, reached New Orleans, General Banks wrote me that he was confident that the people, with his military coöperation, would reconstruct substantially on that plan. I wrote to him and some of them to try it. They tried it, and the result is known. Such has been my only agency in getting up the Louisiana government.

"As to sustaining it my promise is out, as before stated. But, as bad promises are better broken than kept, I shall treat this as a bad promise, and break

it whenever I shall be convinced that keeping it is adverse to the public interest; but I have not yet been so convinced."

He hoped he was not opening any old sores or egging anybody on to an
acrimonious quarrel. It would be easy to drop a phrase, a veiled hint carrying a vile thrust, laying him open to the practiced sarcasm he had heard
winter and summer. He would confess:

"I have been shown a letter on this subject, supposed to be an able one,
in which the writer expresses regret that my mind has not seemed to be
definitely fixed upon the question whether the seceded States, so called, are
in the Union or out of it. It would perhaps add astonishment to his regret
were he to learn that since I have found professed Union men endeavoring
to make that question, I have purposely forborne any public expression upon
it. As appears to me, that question has not been, nor yet is, a practically
material one, and that any discussion of it, while it thus remains practically immaterial, could have no effect other than the mischievous one of
dividing our friends. As yet, whatever it may become, that question is bad
as the basis of a controversy, and good for nothing at all—a merely pernicious
abstraction."

Off to the rubbish piles, off to the dustbins, he was throwing those many
learned and labored legal arguments in Congress that the seceded States
through the act of secession had "committed suicide" and thereby were no
longer States. "Good for nothing at all," he held this question. "A merely
pernicious abstraction." What would he offer? This reasoning:

"We all agree that the seceded States, so called, are out of their proper
relation with the Union, and that the sole object of the Government, civil
and military, in regard to those States, is to again get them into their proper
practical relation. I believe that it is not only possible, but in fact easier,
to do this without deciding or even considering whether those States have
ever been out of the Union, than with it. Finding themselves safely at home,
it would be utterly immaterial whether they had ever been abroad. Let us
all join in doing the acts necessary to restore the proper practical relations
between these States and the Union, and each forever after innocently indulge his own opinion whether in doing the acts he brought the States from
without into the Union, or only gave them proper assistance, they never
having been out of it."

Now he would turn to the much-discussed Louisiana State government
itself and the ever delicate shadings of the race issue.

"The amount of constituency, so to speak, on which the Louisiana government rests, would be more satisfactory to all if it contained 50,000 or
30,000, or even 20,000, instead of only 12,000, as it does. It is also unsatis-
factory to some that the elective franchise is not given to the colored man.
I would myself prefer that it were now conferred on the very intelligent,
and on those who serve our cause as soldiers. Still, the question is not
whether the Louisiana government, as it stands, is quite all that is desirable.
The question is, will it be wiser to take it as it is and help to improve it, or
to reject and disperse? Can Louisiana be brought into proper practical re-

lation with the Union sooner by sustaining or by discarding her new State government? Some twelve thousand voters in the heretofore Slave State of Louisiana have sworn allegiance to the Union, assumed to be the rightful political power of the State, held elections, organized a State government, adopted a Free State constitution, giving the benefit of public schools equally to black and white, and empowering the legislature to confer the elective franchise upon the colored man. Their legislature has already voted to ratify the constitutional amendment recently passed by Congress, abolishing slavery throughout the nation. These 12,000 persons are thus fully committed to the Union and to perpetuate freedom in the State—committed to the very things, and nearly all the things, the nation wants—and they ask the nation's recognition and its assistance to make good their committal. Now, if we reject and spurn them, we do our utmost to disorganize and disperse them."

What was being said and what might come of what was being said, by those against his plan, conjured up dark visions of the future to Lincoln. Out of the grandeur of the ending of the war he could picture a long involved misery to follow. He was sick of force, of government applied by force, and gave his forecast, spoke as a sad prophet, of what would follow from spurning the present Louisiana State government:

"We, in fact, say to the white man: You are worthless or worse; we will neither help you, nor be helped by you. To the blacks we say: This cup of liberty which these, your old masters, held to your lips we will dash from you, and leave you to the chances of gathering the spilled and scattered contents in some vague and undefined when, where, and how. If this course, discouraging and paralyzing both white and black, has any tendency to bring Louisiana into proper practical relations with the Union, I have so far been unable to perceive it." He would turn from these dark visions. "If, on the contrary, we recognize and sustain the new government of Louisiana, the converse of all this is made true. We encourage the hearts and nerve the arms of 12,000 to adhere to their work, and argue for it, and proselyte for it, and fight for it, and feed it, and grow it, and ripen it to a complete success.

"The colored man, too, in seeing all united for him, is inspired with vigilance, and energy, and daring, to the same end. Grant that he desires the elective franchise, will he not attain it sooner by saving the already advanced steps toward it than by running backward over them?

"Concede that the new government of Louisiana is only to what it should be as the egg is to the fowl, we shall sooner have the fowl by hatching the egg than by smashing it."

To the many who cared deeply about the Thirteenth Amendment to the Constitution, and its passage required by three-fourths of the State legislatures of the Union, the President addressed an argument that belonged in his case, that would leave its effect even on those who denied it.

"Again, if we reject Louisiana, we also reject one vote in favor of the proposed amendment to the National Constitution. To meet this proposition it has been argued that no more than three-fourths of those States which have not attempted secession are necessary to validly ratify the amendment.

I do not commit myself against this further than to say that such a ratifica
tion would be questionable, and sure to be persistently questioned, while a
ratification by three-fourths of all the States would be unquestioned and un-
questionable."

He came to his closing words. Beyond Louisiana he saw the other seceded States, one by one to be let in, or held out of, the Union.

"I repeat the question, Can Louisiana be brought into proper practical relation with the Union sooner by sustaining or by discarding her new
State government? What has been said of Louisiana will apply to other
States. And yet so great peculiarities pertain to each State, and such important and sudden changes occur in the same State, and withal so new and
unprecedented is the whole case that no exclusive and inflexible plan can be
prescribed as to details and collaterals. Such exclusive and inflexible plan
would surely become a new entanglement. Important principles may and
must be inflexible. In the present situation, as the phrase goes, it may be my
duty to make some new announcement to the people of the South. I am
considering, and shall not fail to act when satisfied that action will be
proper."

As he stood for a moment taking the plaudits of the crowd, he smiled
to the candle-bearer Brooks. "That was a pretty fair speech, I think, but
you threw some light on it."

There were applause and cheers, with no such uproar as had begun the
evening. The speech had been too long, too closely reasoned, to please a big
crowd. Yet the occasion was perfect, in Lincoln's view, for reminding the
country during its victory jubilees that victory could have grandeur plus
misery, that the aftermath of the war could not be as tragic as the war and
yet might be appalling. He would hear from the country about the speech.
What he heard would help guide him farther. And he had the opposition
worried. What was this "new announcement to the South" which he considered it might be his duty to make? His powers were vast. Before Congress
met in December he might put through a series of decisions and actions that
would channel and canal future policy for years, in accord with his outspoken designs of this evening.

The *New York Tribune* report of the speech held that it "fell dead,
wholly without effect on the audience," and furthermore, "it caused a great
disappointment and left a painful impression." Other newspapers noted frequent applause and "silent attention" between the punctuations of applause.
Sumner's friend and admirer Edward L. Pierce believed the President had
"Sumner's opposition in mind." Sumner was not present, but was called for
by the crowd, according to Pierce, who wrote his impression: "The speech
was not in keeping with what was in men's minds. The people had gathered,
from an instinctive impulse, to rejoice over a great and final victory; and
they listened with respect, but with no expressions of enthusiasm, except
that the quaint simile of 'the egg' drew applause. The more serious among
them felt that the President's utterances on the subject were untimely, and
that his insistence at such an hour on his favorite plan was not the harbinger

of peace among the loyal supporters of the government. Sumner was thoughtful and sad when the speech was reported to him; for he saw at hand another painful controversy with a President whom he respected, on a question where he felt it his duty to stand firm, whatever might be the odds against him."

To his friend and confidant Franz Lieber, Sumner wrote: "The President's speech and other things augur confusion and uncertainty in the future, with hot controversy. Alas! alas!"

Into the Senator's mailbox were to come letters reporting on the President's speech and advising in the tenor of A. P. Grunzer of Syracuse, New York: "Magnanimity is the great word with the disloyal who think to tickle the President's ear with it. Magnanimity is one thing and weakness is another. I know you are near the throne and you must guard its honor. . . . The Blacks are entitled to all the Rights that *white men are bound to Respect*. . . . A universal amnesty must not be granted. Never were men more guilty. The honor of the country requires a sacrifice and it cannot be dispensed with." R. F. Fuller of Boston wrote to Sumner his fear that the President's Louisiana policy was to be "wicked and blasphemous" in its betrayals through easy compromise. "No power but God ever has or could have forced him up to the work he has been instrumental of; and now we see the dregs of his backwardness."

On the calendars the day of April 11 was marked off. Midnight came. The lighted windows of the White House had darkened. The curves of light shining from the Capitol dome were gone. The moist air stayed on. Washington slept in the possession of a mist that crept everywhere, finespun, intangible, elusive.

CHAPTER 71

NEGOTIATIONS—AN OMINOUS DREAM

IN Richmond the Sunday before had been embarrassment about prayers to God Almighty, Ruler of Hosts. As in Norfolk, Savannah, New Orleans, Natchez, and other points, there was a conflicting viewpoint as to whether God should be implored on the one hand to rain down blessings on President Jefferson Davis or on the other hand to shower divine beneficence on President Abraham Lincoln.

General Weitzel inclined to let the churches open in Richmond and conduct services, on condition that no disloyalty be uttered and that the Episcopal clergymen should read the prayers for the President of the United States. Weitzel so told Dana, Assistant Secretary of War. Then General Shepley, Military Governor of Virginia, came to Dana asking that Weitzel's order be relaxed to permit services on condition that the clergy be required merely to omit the prayer for the fugitive President Jefferson Davis, though it was agreed that never in his life had Davis been in such dire need of prayers for his safety and personal freedom. Judge Campbell used his influence with Weitzel and Shepley to get them to consent that a loyal prayer in behalf of the President of the United States should not be exacted. Weitzel took this course, recalling Lincoln's remark to him: "Let 'em up easy; let 'em up easy."

Stanton telegraphed Weitzel a reprimand for allowing ritual services to be read without formal prayer for the President of the United States. Weitzel made a fair explanation of what he had done, but Stanton nevertheless insisted that Weitzel must order the Richmond clergy to read the petitions to Almighty God, Ruler of Nations, for the President of the United States. Weitzel in obedience to the Secretary of War then gave the order that the President of the United States must be prayed for. Following this a memorial to Lincoln was prepared by the clergy of the Episcopal churches, united in declaring with respect and dignity that they waited only the proper ecclesiastical sanction for changing the phraseology of the prayer for the President.

Out of this muddle Lincoln telegraphed Weitzel on April 12 that he had seen Weitzel's dispatch to Colonel Hardie about the matter of prayers. "I do not remember hearing prayers spoken of while I was in Richmond; but I have no doubt you have acted in what appeared to you to be the spirit and temper manifested by me while there."

And the President queried Weitzel: "Is there any sign of the rebel legislature coming together on the understanding of my letter to you? If there is any such sign, inform me what it is; if there is no such sign, you may withdraw the offer."

After he sent this telegram to Weitzel there arrived in Lincoln's hands a letter of Judge Campbell to Weitzel. This letter reported what Judge Campbell had been doing. He had called together a committee of some five of the members of the Virginia (seceded) Legislature, in a letter to this committee informing them that he had had two conversations with Mr. Lincoln, President of the United States, in "relation to the establishment of a government for Virginia," oaths of allegiance, and the terms of settlement with the United States. "With the concurrence and sanction of General Weitzel he [President Lincoln] assented to the application not to require oaths of allegiance from the citizens. He stated that he would send to General Weitzel his decision upon the question of a government for Virginia." The committee invited to conference by Judge Campbell was "to determine whether they will administer the laws in connection with the authorities of the United States. I understand from Mr. Lincoln, if this condition be fulfilled, that no attempt would be made to establish or sustain any other authority."

The text of this document Lincoln read in the war telegraph office, also a telegram from Weitzel saying passports had gone out to members of the Virginia (seceded) Legislature, "and it is common talk that they will come together." At once Lincoln saw he must act so decisively as to sweep away any misunderstanding that had arisen. Stanton and others were in a fury over what they feared had been an open recognition of the Virginia (seceded) Legislature by the Federal Executive. Before the incident could come to a boiling-point, Lincoln swept away all preparations with a telegram to Weitzel. From the operator Albert Chandler he borrowed a Gillott's small-barrel pen—No. 404—and, while standing, wrote:

I have just seen Judge Campbell's letter to you of the 7th. He assumes, as appears to me, that I have called the insurgent Legislature of Virginia together, as the rightful Legislature of the State, to settle all differences with the United States. I have no such thing. I spoke of them, not as a legislature, but as "the gentlemen who have acted as the legislature of Virginia in support of the rebellion." I did this on purpose to exclude the assumption that I was recognizing them as a rightful body. I deal with them as men having power *de facto* to do a specific thing, to wit: "To withdraw the Virginia troops and other support from resistance to the General Government," for which, in the paper handed Judge Campbell, I promised a specific equivalent, to wit: a remission to the people of the State, except in certain cases, of the confiscation of their property. I meant this, and no more. Inasmuch, however, as Judge Campbell misconstrues this, and is still pressing for an armistice, contrary to the explicit statement of the paper I gave him; and particularly as Gen. Grant has since captured the Virginia troops, so that giving a consideration for their withdrawal is no longer applicable, let my letter to you and the paper to Judge Campbell both be withdrawn, or countermanded, and he be notified of it. Do not now allow them to assemble; but if any have come, allow them safe-return to their homes.

That Lincoln telegraphed so clear-cut and peremptory a letter on April 12 made matters easier for General Weitzel. Lacking specific written instructions, Weitzel had been guided by the scant conversational line from Lincoln speaking in Richmond: "If I were in your place, I'd let 'em up easy; let 'em up easy." This was not a difficult nor complicated instruction to remember. "Let 'em up easy" was spoken twice. There was no forgetting it. Weitzel might forget his name and rank, but not that line "Let 'em up easy." So in case of doubt whether to be hard or easy he was easy. And being easy, he had permitted a procedure this day of April 12 and signed his name to it and it was published and at once put Lincoln in a bad light. To Sumner, Wade, Chandler, it looked suspiciously like an assumption of the President that he would yield to his own executive wishes, that he would play the game his own way without consulting Congress, that no one could guess what would be his secret collusions and open arrangements with "the subjugated slaveholders."

Friends and enemies of the President, certainly the President himself, were surprised—some of them amazed and dumfounded—to read in a newspaper, the *Richmond Whig* of April 12, an Address to the People of Virginia signed by a long array of members of the Virginia (seceded) Legislature, judges of courts, college presidents, the Mayor of Richmond, the editors of the *Richmond Examiner* and *Enquirer*. "An immediate meeting of the General Assembly of the State is called for by the exigencies of the situ-

Office U. S. Military Telegraph.

WAR DEPARTMENT,

Washington, D. C., April 12 1865.

Time

"Cypher"

Major General Weitzel
Richmond, Va

I have just seen Judge Campbell's letter to you of the 7th. He assumes, as appears to me, that I have called the insurgent legislature of Virginia, together; as the rightful legislature of the State, to settle the all differences with the United States. I have done no such thing. I spoke of them not as a

...end is still pressing for an armistice, confining to the explicit statement of the papers I send; and particularly as Gen. Grant has since captured the Virginia Troops, so that giving at consideration for their withdrawal is no longer applicable, let my letter to you, quote the papers to Judge Campbell to find he notified of it. Do not now allow them to assemble; but if any have come allow them days — returned to their homes.

A. Lincoln

This and the cut on the opposite page reproduce opening and closing parts of a telegram written by Lincoln when standing and using an unusual pen. Original in the Barrett collection.

ation," ran part of this address. "The consent of the military authorities of the United States to the session of the Legislature in Richmond . . . to their free deliberation upon public affairs . . . has been obtained. The United States authorities will afford transportation. . . . The matters to be submitted to the Legislature are the restoration of peace to the State of Virginia, and the adjustment of questions involving life, liberty and property that have arisen." Safe-conducts had already been granted, said the address, to Robert M. T. Hunter, William C. Rives, John Letcher—and others whose very names were a red rag of infuriation to ultraloyalist Union adherents. Signed to the address was the name of J. A. Campbell and the portentous added line "Approved for publication in the Richmond Whig and in hand-bill form. G. Weitzel, Major-General Commanding."

It helped none that the *Richmond Whig* in a news paragraph related: "It is understood that this invitation has been put forth in pursuance of the plan of proceeding assented to by President Lincoln." Nor was there balm in the intimation that Lincoln had commenced a complete and sweeping reconstruction of Virginia, all on his own. "It will be hailed by the great body of the people of Virginia as the first step toward the reinstatement of the 'Old Dominion' in the Union."

Those who wished to question Lincoln's motives gathered in little cliques and brandished this number of the *Richmond Whig*. Though Lincoln's long telegraphed order to Weitzel completely and peremptorily annulled the address, it was construed in opposition circles as a revelation that the President was carrying on his own reconstruction efforts as he pleased, that he would go as far as he could in thwarting those who demanded punishment and retaliation.

At a later time in a statement under oath Stanton gave the date of Lincoln's telegram of April 12 as April 13, said that he had an hour's talk on the subject with Lincoln and Speed at the White House and again another conversation with the President, who came over to the War Office. "After I repeated my reasons against allowing the rebel legislature to assemble, or the rebel organizations to have any participation whatever in the business of reorganization," ran this sworn statement of Stanton as to how he managed the President and saved the country, "he sat down at my desk, and wrote a telegram to General Weitzel and handed it to me, saying: 'There, I think that will suit you.' I told him no, it did not go far enough; that the members of the rebel legislature would probably come to Richmond and that General Weitzel ought to be directed to *prohibit* any such assembling. He took up his pen again and made the alteration and signed the telegram. He handed it to me. I said, *that*, I thought, was exactly right."

Stanton's secretary, Major A. E. H. Johnson, whose furtive manner Lincoln on occasion impersonated for the laughter of Western friends, wrote an amplified version of how Lincoln was managed by Stanton in this affair. "It was while sitting on the sofa in the Secretary's room looking towards my desk," wrote Johnson, "that Mr. Stanton told the President why." Then came Stanton's long argument having no points Lincoln had not had dinned into his ears before, and finally: "In pleading with the President—I can see the Secretary now, earnest and full of feeling and the President listening in profound thought, saying not a word—the Secretary's manner was not his usual manner; it was argumentative. The President had no story to illustrate his position or that of his Secretary."

Both of these statements assumed that Lincoln had taken a position and under pressure from Stanton reversed himself. They shrank under comparison with Lincoln's first short letter to Weitzel, regarding what Campbell might do in assembling that body which called itself the Virginia Legislature, and Lincoln's long telegram to Weitzel later explaining exactly what his short letter meant. The two dovetailed perfectly. The long telegram merely made clear that Campbell had misconstrued the short letter. The later sworn statement of Stanton assumed that Lincoln had instigated a meeting of the "rebel" Virginia Legislature, that Lincoln favored giving it full authority and did not recede from this position, that Lincoln did not know how to correct Weitzel and Campbell, that Lincoln wrote one telegram too mild for Stanton and on Stanton's bidding wrote a second dispatch which satisfied the War Secretary. A reader of motives could also consider the statement of the telegraph-office operator Albert Chandler that Lincoln stood alone amid the Morse code instruments and wrote of his own initiative the long telegram to Weitzel "with a Gillott's small barrel pen—No. 404." In one detail lay the pivotal explanation. Lincoln told Weitzel, "If I were in your place, I'd let 'em up easy; let 'em up easy." Such a phrase in a like moment would be alien to Stanton's lips.

Incorruptible by money, of demoniac energy, ruthless and of few scruples in working his own designs for power, Stanton was, wrote Grant, "a man who never questioned his own authority, and who always did in war time what he wanted to do." His communications this week to equally relentless members of House and Senate were private and confidential. His assurance that God walked with him and scorned Robert E. Lee's prayers was there in a transparency shining from the Capitol dome, visible from afar, with the words ordered by Stanton:

THIS IS THE LORD'S DOING
AND IT IS MARVELOUS
IN OUR EYES

A long memorandum from Chief Justice Chase came to the President on April 12, Chase admitting that he recognized himself as the correctly quoted Cabinet member referred to but not named in the President's Louisiana speech the evening before. Chase most earnestly wished that the President could have read the New Orleans newspapers in past months, in which case "your feelings of humanity and justice would not let you rest till all loyalists are made equal in the right of self-protection by suffrage." This followed a long letter of April 11 wherein Chase saw the unrestricted ballot for Negroes as the key to unlock the white doves of peace and justice and send them winging over the Southern landscapes. "Enrollment of the loyal citizens without regard to complexion, and encouragement and support to them . . . is recommended by its simplicity, facility, and, above all, justice." In Virginia, Louisiana, and Arkansas Chase was sure this would work. The new Chief Justice had read the New Orleans newspapers and wished the President had. He began his letter: "When all mankind are congratulating you, one voice, heard or not, is of little account; but I add mine." He closed in distinctive Chase manner: "I most respectfully but most earnestly commend these matters to your attention. God gives you a great place and a great opportunity. May He guide you in the use of them!"

It was told that Senator Harlan in a speech April 11 at the White House celebration had asked, "What shall we do with the rebels?" and a voice from the crowd came like a shot: "Hang them!" Tad playing with pens on his father's table looked up at his father's face and set up a clamor: "No, no, papa. Not hang them. Hang on to them!" The father, with jubilation: "That's it—Tad has got it. We must hang on to them!"

The *New York Herald* man sent his paper a story. Prominent rebels, probably Judge Campbell and R. M. T. Hunter, were soon expected in Washington "in connection with the business of restoration." With this straw plucked from the wind the *Herald* man did much, puffing it out into quite a balloon of large expectations. Lincoln in fact and reality did not expect any prominent "rebels" in Washington unless, like Roger Pryor, by accident or the mishaps of war; he had invited no prominent "rebels." The *Herald* man thought he would invite them and it would make "a whiz" of a story. In newspaper lingo of the day it was "a live item," though fabricated and laying a false stress on Lincoln's goodwill policy, which had not yet gone that far and could not for weeks or months reach that stage. A series of similar irresponsible stories added to the ferment of fear and unrest among those suspicious of Lincoln's motives.

To Welles the President said Stanton and others were "dissatisfied." Welles doubted any results to be had from the Virginia Legislature, saying that once recognized and convened, they would perhaps conspire. "He [the President] said he had no fear of that. They were too badly beaten, too much exhausted. His idea was, that the members of the legislature, comprising the prominent and influential men of their respective counties, had better come together and undo their own work. He felt assured they would do this, and the movement he believed a good one. Civil government must be reëstablished, he said, as soon as possible; there must be courts, and law, and order, or society would be broken up, the disbanded armies would turn into robber bands and guerrillas, which we must strive to prevent. These were the reasons why he wished prominent Virginians who had the confidence of the people to come together and turn themselves and their neighbors into good Union men. But as we all had taken a different view, he had perhaps made a mistake, and was ready to correct it if he had."

This careful diary entry of Welles indicated that the President strongly inclined to let the insurgent Virginia Legislature have wide powers, that he peremptorily stopped that legislature from convening because once more his Cabinet of select advisers was against him—and it was one of the cases where it was better to go along with them—and wait. The "so-called legislature," Welles told the President, "would be likely to propose terms which might seem reasonable, but which we could not accept." The President could make a better arrangement "with any one—the worst of them—than with all," thought Welles . . . "he might be embarrassed by recognizing and treating with them, when we were now in a position to prescribe what should be done."

Lincoln had sent a telegram April 10 addressed to "Governor Pierpoint [sic], Alexandria, Va." urging, "Please come up and see me at once." Of Francis H. Pierpont it was said that "for three years he carried the State Government of Virginia in his vest pocket." An honest, amiable Union man, he had helped carve out West Virginia as a separate State, and then conducted a puppet State government of Virginia with Alexandria as a sort of capital, while on Virginia soil the contending armies sought a stranglehold to decide who should govern Virginia. In his little talk with Lincoln the decision seemed to be that Pierpont should move his civil State government—it was not cumbrous, its archives no heavy load—to Richmond and see what could be done.

One minor transaction of the President on April 12, writing with a pen not flowing freely. Original in the Barrett collection.

To Pierpont, Lincoln made clear that Judge Campbell had for months pressed for a peace move inside the Confederate Government. Campbell had gone to Lee and heard from that commander that it was not part of his duty to propose or to make peace, for "that belonged to the President and Congress." From Davis, Campbell heard that the Confederate President believed he had been elected "to establish the government, not to abolish it." From members of the Confederate Congress Campbell heard that they were elected "to make laws and provide means" for the Confederacy, not to break it up. Then it occurred to Campbell that, according to the Confederate Constitution, the legislature of the State of Virginia had power and authority "to put an end to this war." Or, as Lincoln phrased it for Pierpont, "They [the Virginia Legislature] had put the army in the field, why not take it out and quit?" And, continued Lincoln, so carefully must the order be drawn authorizing General Weitzel to permit the Virginia Legislature to meet, for a single express purpose, that: "The drafting of that order, though so short, gave me more perplexity than any other paper I ever drew up." Thus Pierpont noted it.

They talked further. Lincoln wished for more light on what the Southern people wanted. "Was there any Union sentiment among the Southern people that had sufficient force to develop itself?" If so, what measures would give that sentiment a chance to function? Pierpont guessed there was "very little settled sentiment among the people," that as communications and a more normal life were restored, more could be known. "Be industrious," Lincoln counseled Pierpont, "and ascertain what Union sentiment there is in Virginia and keep me advised." He spoke to Pierpont "profound thankfulness" over the war ending—and of his many trials and perplexities declared: "Amid them all I have been angry but once since I came to the White House. Then, if I had encountered the man who caused my anger, I certainly would have hurt him." And for a moment Lincoln reminisced of early days: "When I had to measure my strength with that of other reputed strong men, I found I had great power in my arms."

Among those high in the Government persistently vocal for punishing the defeated Confederates was Vice-President Andrew Johnson. To Dana in Richmond he insisted "their sins had been enormous," and if they were let back into the Union without any punishment the effect would be very bad, raising dangers in the future. For fully twenty minutes Johnson gave Dana "an impassioned, earnest speech on the subject of punishing rebels." Dana suggested his remarks should be addressed to the President and to members of Congress, quoting Johnson as replying, "Mr. Dana, I feel it to be my duty to say these things to every man whom I meet, whom I know to have any influence. Any man whose thoughts are considered by others . . . I must speak to."

Seward was among those who mainly favored the President's policy of goodwill, of being generous and taking chances on double-dealing. Through different processes of thought, "we frequently arrived at the same conclusion," Seward described their joint operations; on the large questions "no knife sharp enough to divide us." In their four years together once only were they seriously at odds. "His 'colonization' scheme [for gradual emancipation of Negroes by purchase and sending the freed slaves to colonies removed from American soil] I opposed on the self-evident principle that all *natives* of a country have an *equal* right in its soil."

To Grant it came that Vice-President Johnson in Washington, in Richmond, had an "ever-ready" remark: "Treason is a crime and must be made odious." To Southern men who went to Johnson for assurances that they might begin some sort of rebuilding, he offered merely vehement denunciations. To Grant this was a sorry performance. Grant believing that the

Lincoln view had behind it "the great majority of the Northern people, and the soldiers unanimously," the Lincoln view favoring "a speedy reconstruction on terms that would be the least humiliating to the people who had rebelled against their government . . . being the mildest, it was also the wisest, policy. . . . The people who had been in rebellion . . . surely would not make good citizens if they felt that they had a yoke around their necks." Grant also agreed with Lincoln in a belief that a majority of the Northern people of the hour were not in favor of votes for the Negro. "They supposed that it would naturally follow the freedom of the negro, but that there would be a time of probation, in which the ex-slaves could prepare themselves for the privileges of citizenship before the full right would be conferred."

One outstanding impression in Grant's mind stayed on from the conference he and Sherman held with Lincoln at City Point. This was Lincoln's report to the two generals of what he had said to the Confederate peace commissioners at Hampton Roads. To Grant and Sherman in thinking about it afterward it seemed to have more guidance value to them for armistice terms than any other rules, if any, laid down by Lincoln. The matter was precisely one where Grant, usually meticulous in such a piece of testimony, though writing in the third person seemed to have kept some of the flavor of Lincoln's speech. "Mr. Lincoln said to the peace commissioners when he met them at Hampton Roads . . . that before he could enter into negotiations with them they would have to agree to two points: one being that the Union should be preserved, and the other that slavery should be abolished; and if they were ready to concede these two points he was almost ready to sign his name to a blank piece of paper and permit them to fill out the balance of the terms upon which we could live together."

Sherman's ideas about peace terms and reconstruction, it would be too easy to say, were identical with those of Grant; Sherman held torrents of thought and feeling that outran expression in words. The Union general who more than any other favored a war strategy of punishment and destruction of the South decidedly favored a mild and kindly peace policy. And opposing him he had a different case from Grant. Grant and Lee had respect for each other, with little or no affection. Between Sherman and Joe Johnston was not merely respect but a curious affection. They were two fighters who each knew that the other always fought fair and clean, each having admiration for the style of the other. Not often does it happen in war, but a curious fellowship had grown up between those two commanders. Neither Sherman nor Johnston had ever owned slaves. Both disliked Jefferson Davis. Grant knew Sherman would drive no hard bargain with the bald little leader who had written Lee that he "could no more than annoy" Sherman's army. Sherman had shown to Stanton, on the visit of the Secretary of War to Savannah, a letter to a Savannah man wherein Sherman wrote his belief "that according to Mr. Lincoln's Proclamation and Message, when the people of the South had laid down their arms and submitted to the lawful powers of the United States, *ipso facto*. the war was over as to them; and furthermore, that if any State in rebellion would conform to the Consti-tution of the United States, cease war, elect Senators and Representatives to Congress, if admitted (of which each House of Congress alone is the judge), that State becomes instanter as much in the Union as New York or Ohio."

All of which in this crowded hour of decision meant power beyond fathoming in Lincoln's hand. Had Frémont and Butler, who played con-tinuously a political game openly or covertly in opposition to Lincoln's "slow and vacillating" policies, proved themselves as commanders—that is, if it could be imagined that they now stood in the boots of Grant and Sherman heading victorious armies—Lincoln would have had no other course perhaps than to trail, in degree, with those crying for sacrifice and hang-ings. As events had turned out however, Lincoln, Grant, and Sherman were a triumvirate holding such actual power that if imperative they could set up a dictatorship. The historic point to be reckoned in the balances during early April was that the three high commanders and a million soldiers were, to use Grant's word, "unanimous" for ending the war on practically any terms that would bring a restored Union with slavery gone. To these two major conditions, high-lighted by Lincoln, all else was minor and could be threshed out in parliamentary debate and political battles in the old-fashioned Ameri-can way.

While Sumner was writing "Alas! alas!" to the necessity of dispute with the President over immediate universal Negro suffrage, Mrs. Chesnut noted her Negroes as unchanged in loyalty to their masters, plowing fields as be-fore the war, "not a single case of a negro who betrayed his master." Of one of her old slaves she wrote: "Ellen has had my diamonds to keep for a week or so. When the danger was over she handed them back to me with as little apparent interest in the matter as if they had been garden peas." Yet a change had come, the mistress of Mulberry Plantation in South Caro-lina saw. Behind the black masks of faces lay a new motive. Sherman heard them swear devotion; "just the same, the minute they see an opening to better themselves they will move on." This Negro mobility of course was but one new phase of a chaotic and devastated South, whereas thousands of former masters of wealth had now only fat wads of Confederate Govern-ment paper promises to pay. And many of the former masters could merely wonder whether any works of peace they might begin would be interrupted by Federal military police come to put them on trial for treason.

Grant was wishing luck to Jefferson Davis, hoping the fugitive would escape from the United States. This wish and hope he believed "Mr. Lincoln shared." Off in the immense areas of Texas or thereabouts in the trans-Mississippi region, Davis might set up a new, though shrunken, Confederacy with outfits of restless, unemployed young men drawn from the various abandoned Confederate armies. Besides this, believed Grant, Lincoln wanted Davis to escape because as the Federal President he did not wish to deal with the matter of punishment for the Confederate chieftain. Grant saw Lincoln as the best possible man to be in power as umpire during wrangling and bitterness to come. And Grant believed that an overwhelming majority of the Northern people, "and the soldiers unanimously," thus saw Lincoln in this hour that Grant traveled toward Washington for an interview with the President and a joining of counsels.

To Carpenter, to Dana, Brooks, and others, came an anecdote used by Lincoln when he was asked what he would do with Jefferson Davis when that marvelously stubborn and unrepentant Confederate leader was captured.

"There was a boy in Springfield," said Lincoln, "who saved up his money and bought a 'coon,' which, after the novelty wore off, became a great nuisance. He was one day leading him through the streets, and had his hands full to keep clear of the little vixen, who had torn his clothes half off of him. At length he sat down on the curb-stone, completely fagged out. A man passing was stopped by the lad's disconsolate appearance, and asked the matter. 'Oh,' was the reply, 'this coon is such a *trouble*, to me!' 'Why don't you get rid of him, then?' said the gentleman. 'Hush!' said the boy; 'don't you see he is gnawing his rope off? I am going to let him do it, and then I will go home and tell the folks *that he got away from me?*' "

Thus Carpenter wrote the anecdote as he believed it had been told to him. Ward Hill Lamon had another version, nearer to Lincoln's style and more pat as an illustration, Lincoln saying: "When I was a boy in Indiana, I went to a neighbor's house one morning and found a boy of my own size holding a coon by a string. I asked him what he had and what he was doing. He says, 'It's a coon. Dad cotched six last night, and killed all but this poor little cuss. Dad told me to hold him until he came back, and I'm afraid he's going to kill this one too; and oh, Abe, I do wish he would get away!' 'Well, why don't you let him loose?' 'That wouldn't be right; and if I let him go, Dad would give me hell. But if he would get away himself, it would be all right.' Now," said Mr. Lincoln, "if Jeff Davis and those other fellows will only get away, it will be all right. But if we should catch them, and I should let them go, 'Dad would give me hell.' "

If Lincoln had his wish, it was evident, Jeff Davis would skip the country and make a home in Mexico, Peru, London, Paris, anywhere beyond reach of the United States Government. As an exile Davis could do little harm. As a martyr buried after trial and hanging, his name betokening sacred ashes, the Confederate leader would throw a moving shadow. An example was the ghost of John Brown, his body a-moldering, his tongue alive. That line of hate sung by millions—"We'll hang Jeff Davis to a sour apple tree" —was good enough for war propaganda, for stirring the will to kill, but now Lincoln wanted that song line forgotten. It was not unpleasant for him to look back and consider that in all his speeches and papers no one could find a phrase of hate or personal evil wish against the head of the Confederate Government. Not until December of '64 had he belittled Davis, as a matter of record pointing to Davis's own people belittling their leader and no longer following him as they once did.

On scores of occasions in conversation Lincoln mentioned "Jeff Davis," but he never permitted the name of Davis to creep into any public address—as though the insurgent leader was nameless or anonymous.

Came on April 12 the instance of Lincoln holding the kindliest and most neighborly talk imaginable with a Confederate who was still a Confederate, Lincoln doing a valued personal favor for a businessman who had backed the Confederacy with money, property, and personal influence and now refused Lincoln's suggestion that he take the oath of allegiance to the Union. This was W. C. Bibb, Esq., of Montgomery, Alabama, with a note of in-

Lincoln signs such a card with easier assurance, the war being ended

troduction from the commander of the *Monitor* in her battle with the *Merrimac*, John L. Worden. Captain Worden vouched for Bibb as "a leading and influential citizen of Montgomery." In the first year of the war they had jailed Worden in that city, and General Bragg and others talked of hanging Worden as a spy. During which time, wrote Worden, Bibb "did me various kind and friendly acts, although at the time I was a stranger to him . . . in spite also of the fact that those citizens who treated me with kindness were looked upon with suspicion by officials, Mr. Bibb did me justice and extended to me attentions very grateful to my feelings."

Bibb had been to Seward, who from an early manhood residence in Georgia recalled knowing Bibb's father, also Bibb's uncle, who was a United States Senator from Georgia. Bibb tried to draw from Seward some inkling of whether he was radical or conservative toward the South, getting chiefly the dry observation "I was once a resident of Georgia and at times the idea occurs to me that if I had remained there I might possibly have prevented this war."

Bibb had been let into a prison for an interview with a Confederate captain captured in Grant's recent frontal attack on Lee's line, Bibb's son belonging to the same regiment, Bibb asking for news about his boy. The captain said the boy was taken prisoner just before the battle closed and he was sure that young Bibb on that day was safe and alive with the retreating regiment.

Bibb had consulted with Orville H. Browning, attorney-at-law, and with Attorney General Speed on the possible prospect of the President's taking early action with regard to 5,000,000 bales of cotton stored in the South and other large properties thrown into jeopardy and new legal risks in the war coming to an end. On the morning of April 12 this Confederate, ushered into Lincoln's office, met the President, who handed him a chair, asked him to be seated, and was so easily informal that Bibb was "struck with astonishment by the total absence of all effort to impress one with the fact that he was President of the United States." This President drew his own chair back from a table, slid in, threw a leg over one arm, and proceeded to read the Worden note handed him by Bibb. His face brightened as he read, and at the finish he put out his hand for a renewed acquaintance with a Southern man who had kept his sanity amid the uproar. Lincoln spoke of Mr. Browning as having mentioned W. C. Bibb's Kentucky relation, George M. Bibb. With George M., Lincoln was well acquainted.

Bibb asked about a proclamation of amnesty which Washington reports said would soon be issued. Would its terms extend to Confederate leaders? "Yes," Bibb quoted Lincoln as replying. "It is universal in its application. I have consented to withhold it from publication for a few days for special reasons which have been urged, but which I regard as of little force, but I thought it better to pay that respect to the opinion of others."

Lincoln continued: "I love the Southern people more than they love me. My desire is to restore the Union. I do not intend to hurt the hair of the head of a single man in the South if it can possibly be avoided."

"Mr. Lincoln, what will be required of the Southern States to allow them admission into the Union?"

"All that I ask is that they shall annul their ordinance of secession and send their delegates to fill the seats in Congress which are now vacant awaiting their occupation."

"Mr. Lincoln, what do you propose to do in relation to the slave property?"

"I am individually willing to grant either gradual emancipation, say running through twenty years, or compensated emancipation at the option of the Southern people; but there are certain amendments to the Constitution now before the people for their adoption or rejection, and I have no power to do anything at present; but if it should so happen that I could control it such would be my policy."

Their talk ran two hours, according to Bibb, who rose to say he was trespassing. Lincoln took hold of Bibb's coat lapels, asked him to again be seated, took up the Worden note, glanced over it, and "What can I do for you?" Bibb would be glad to have a passport to his home in Alabama.

Lincoln wrote two little documents for Bibb. He liked Bibb. That Worden note said much. The likes of Bibb would help the Union cause. Lincoln signed and dated one card: "Any military commander in whose way it may fall, will give protection to the bearer, W. C. Bibb, his family and property," and another card: "Allow the bearer, W. C. Bibb, to pass our lines with ordinary baggage and go south."

Bibb read these, spoke his gratitude, then: "I feel that it is due both to you and myself to tell you that I have not taken the oath of allegiance to the Federal Government and cannot do so until after the surrender of the Confederate armies." This, Bibb confessed afterward, he said "with trepidation."

Lincoln's eyes dropped, studied the carpet. Bibb thought a shadow crossed his face. Lincoln raised his eyes, looked into Bibb's:

"I respect your scruples. Probably under the same surroundings I should have entertained them myself."

Bibb asked if a cavalry raid had reached Selma, Alabama. Lincoln doubted it. Bibb wished to visit Baltimore and New York for a couple of days. "You will have no use for another pass," said Lincoln, "and if you return by way of Washington I shall be very glad to see you." Bibb went away a perplexed and rather happy man. His idea of Lincoln had been shaped mainly by Southern newspapers. He had come frankly with high prejudice and low hope. Now instead of a monstrous gawk he had met a man he saw as "homely and ungainly" but strangely wise, with a calm face masking a rare sensitivity.

The same Virginia-born go-between and observer that Lincoln had sent to Charleston in '61, just before the war broke, he now sent to Richmond. For Ward Hill Lamon he wrote on April 11 a pass to Richmond and return, the errand, as Lamon wrote, being "business for Mr. Lincoln connected with the call of a convention for reconstruction, about which there had arisen some complications." Before leaving Lamon urged Secretary Usher to persuade Mr. Lincoln to exercise extreme caution, "and to go out as little as possible while I was absent." They talked about this and decided the two of them should go to Lincoln.

Lamon asked Lincoln if he would make him a promise. Lincoln asked what it was and said that he thought he could venture to say he would. Lamon then asked the President to promise that he would not go out after nightfall while Lamon was gone, and particularly that the President would not go to the theatre.

Lincoln turned and said, according to Lamon: "Usher, this boy is a monomaniac on the subject of my safety. I can hear him or hear of his being around, at all times of the night, to prevent somebody from murdering me. He thinks I shall be killed; and we think he is going crazy." To this Lincoln added: "What does anybody want to assassinate me for? If anyone wants to do so, he can do it any day or night, if he is ready to give his life for mine. It is nonsense."

Usher then said: "Mr. Lincoln, it is well to listen and give heed to Lamon. He is thrown among people that give him opportunities to know more about such matters than we can know."

Lamon renewed his request for the promise, standing with his hat in his hand, ready to start for Richmond.

"Well," said Lincoln, "I promise to do the best I can towards it." Then, giving Lamon a warm handshake: "Good-bye. God bless you, Hill!"

To their old Illinois associate Orville H. Browning, Lamon had spoken more than once his fears about the President's safety, one diary sentence of Browning this week reading: "The Marshal W H Lamon has several times within the last two months told me that he believed the President would be assassinated."

Besides the written threats from enemies or cranks, which Lincoln filed, there were spoken warnings, advice as to plots and machinations afoot, some of them published and sent broadcast. Greeley in the *New York Tribune* had given the fullest publicity to the weird advertisement in an Alabama newspaper that was signed with a post-office box number for the communications of any and all who cared to raise $1,000,000, which sum would assure the death of Abraham Lincoln, the chief obstacle to the Southern cause.

On the morning of April 5 in Admiral Porter's cabin of the flagship *Malvern* Lincoln had received Brevet Brigadier General Edward H. Ripley. On a long cushioned seat running along the side of the ship behind a dining-table sat the President while Tad ran up and down the length of the sofa behind his father, leaping the father's back in passing. General Ripley, sitting opposite, explained his errand while "Mr. Lincoln let his head droop upon his hands as his elbows rested on the table, his hands supporting his chin, his eyes filling the cabin with mournful light." Outside and waiting, proceeded General Ripley, was a Confederate soldier in uniform, "a more than usually intelligent and fine-appearing man," who had come to believe with the capture of Richmond and Lee in retreat that the war was hopeless and not another life should be given to it; he was an enlisted man in "Rains's torpedo bureau," a Confederate secret-service organization carrying on an irregular warfare with explosives; the men detailed for an operation never knew what they were to do till they arrived at designated points and got their orders. This man had signed a sworn statement of his knowledge that the bureau had sent a party of men on a secret mission which he vaguely understood was aimed at "the head of the Yankee government," and though he could give no names or specific facts, he wished to put Mr. Lincoln on his guard, being convinced the President was in great danger. General Ripley read this statement to Lincoln, emphasized what he believed the good faith and integrity of the man.

"I begged the President to let me bring him in and talk," wrote General

Ripley, "but it was all to no purpose." He quoted Lincoln as slowly and sorrowfully replying: "No, General Ripley, it is impossible for me to adopt and follow your suggestions. I deeply appreciate the feeling which has led you to urge them on me—but I must go on in the course marked out for me, for I cannot bring myself to believe that any human being lives who would do me any harm."

The two men who most often warned Lincoln about his personal safety were Stanton and Lamon. To Stanton, Lincoln's response usually was serious, though in the earlier years of the cavalry escort and the posted sentinels the President had protested with sarcasm. To Lamon he had laughing retorts most often, though in their latest exchange he had for the first time offered the point that he would have no chance under any conditions against a would-be killer "if he is ready to give his life for mine." The envelope on which he had written "Assassination," wherein Lincoln filed threat letters, numbered eighty items in latter March when the painter Matthew Wilson was doing his portrait. John W. Forney wrote of Seward standing behind Lincoln's chair as Lincoln sat for the artist and as he opened a note saying, "Here is another of these letters," after reading it pointing to a pigeonhole: "In that place I have filed eighty just such things as this. I know I am in danger; but I am not going to worry over threats like these." Then, wrote Forney, he "resumed his usual animation" and the interested painter studied his face.

Lamon as he rode to Richmond took no ease about this matter and had less than ever about it this week because of a dream Lincoln told him. As Lincoln had gradually before Lamon's eyes become a world figure and a legend, he tried to analyze more closely Lincoln the dreamer. He saw Lincoln "believing, like the first Napoleon, that he was a man of destiny," and accepting "certain phases of the supernatural." What Lamon thought or surmised in this field had at least the value of the observation of an intimate. No one else plucked a banjo for Lincoln or answered to the wish "Hill, sing me a sad little song" in a concert for those two alone. No one else came nearer being a "boon companion," as the phrase goes. Out of moods and fragments of speech Lamon made his derivations as to Lincoln's inner life: "Assured as he undoubtedly was by omens which to his mind were conclusive that he would rise to greatness and power, he was as firmly convinced by the same tokens that he would be suddenly cut off at the height of his career and the fulness of his fame. He always believed that he would fall by the hand of an assassin; and yet with that appalling doom clouding his life,—a doom fixed and irreversible, as he was firmly convinced,—his courage never for a moment forsook him."

In astrology, horoscopes, prophecies, ghost lore, witcheries and divinations, Lincoln was no dabbler. Dreams and presentiments rested on natural laws, Lamon hearing him define Nature as "the workmanship of the Almighty." Often, wrote Lamon, he heard Lincoln repeat lines from "The Dream," a Byron poem:

> Sleep hath its own world,
> A boundary between the things misnamed
> Death and existence: Sleep hath its own world,
> And a wide realm of wild reality.
> And dreams in their development have breath,
> And tears, and tortures, and the touch of joy;
> They leave a weight upon our waking thoughts,
> They take a weight from off our waking toils,
> They do divide our being.

With the Rabelaisian Lamon, of valor and humor and conviviality compounded, Lincoln seemed during the war years to speak his dejection, his hilarity—or frailty—more easily and naturally than with any other man. To Lamon he spoke more than once of his failure to produce again the double image of himself in a looking-glass, which he saw in 1860 lying on a lounge in his own chamber in Springfield. One face held glow of life and breath, the other shone ghostly pale white. "It had worried him not a little . . . the mystery had its meaning, which was clear enough to him . . . the life-like image betokening a safe passage through his first term as President; the ghostly one, that death would overtake him before the close of the second, . . . With that firm conviction, which no philosophy could shake, Mr. Lincoln moved on through a maze of mighty events, calmly awaiting the inevitable hour." Three things, in Lamon's estimate, sustained and upheld him under the weight of this darkly foretold doom conveyed by an illusion in a mirror. "His sense of duty to his country; his belief that 'the inevitable' is right; and his innate and irrepressible humor."

Sternly practical and strictly logical man that Lincoln was, rigorous realist that he could be in given events, having in so many of his papers a scientific approach using relentless scrutiny of facts and spare derivations of absolutes from those facts, he nevertheless believed in dreams' having validity for himself and for others. According to Lamon's study, Lincoln held that any dream had a meaning if you could be wise enough to find it, your wisdom perhaps leading you at times into preposterous tricks and vagaries of the human mind and frame. When a dream came Lincoln sought clews from it. Once when Mrs. Lincoln and Tad were away he telegraphed her to put away a pistol Tad was carrying. "I had an ugly dream about him."

To Lamon it was charming and appropriate that Lincoln held the best dream-interpreters were the common people. "This accounts in large measure for the profound respect he always had for the collective wisdom of the plain people,—'the children of Nature,' he called them." Some basis of truth could be found, he believed, for whatever obtained general credence among these "children of Nature." The very superstitions of the people had roots of reality in natural occurrences. "He esteemed himself one of their number, having passed the greater part of his life among them."

Of the dream that came to Lincoln this second week of April, 1865, Lamon wrote that it was "the most startling incident" that had ever come to the man, of "deadly import," "amazingly real." Lincoln kept it to himself as his personal secret for a few days and one evening at the White House, with Mrs. Lincoln, Lamon, and one or two others present, he began talking about dreams and led himself into telling the late one that haunted him. Of Lamon's later written account of the evening, Lamon said, "I give it as nearly in his own words as I can, from notes which I made immediately after its recital."

Mrs. Lincoln had spoken of his face looking so solemn and his want of spirit. This seemed to rouse him. Lincoln began telling what was heavy on his mind:

"It seems strange how much there is in the Bible about dreams. There are, I think, some sixteen chapters in the Old Testament and four or five in the New in which dreams are mentioned; and there are many other passages scattered throughout the book which refer to visions. If we believe the Bible, we must accept the fact that in the old days God and His angels came to men in their sleep and made themselves known in dreams. Nowadays dreams are regarded as very foolish, and are seldom told, except by old women and by young men and maidens in love."

Mrs. Lincoln here remarked, "Why, you look dreadfully solemn; do *you* believe in dreams?"

"I can't say that I do," returned Mr. Lincoln; "but I had one the other night which has haunted me ever since. After it occurred, the first time I opened the Bible, strange as it may appear, it was at the twenty-eighth chapter of Genesis, which relates the wonderful dream Jacob had. I turned to other passages, and seemed to encounter a dream or a vision wherever I looked. I kept on turning the leaves of the old book, and everywhere my eye fell upon passages recording matters strangely in keeping with my own thoughts,—supernatural visitations, dreams, visions, etc."

He now looked so serious and disturbed that Mrs. Lincoln exclaimed: "You frighten me! What is the matter?"

"I am afraid," said Mr. Lincoln, seeing the effect his words had upon his wife, "that I have done wrong to mention the subject at all; but somehow the thing has got possession of me, and, like Banquo's ghost, it will not down."

This set on fire Mrs. Lincoln's curiosity. Though saying she didn't believe in dreams, she kept at him to tell what it was he had seen in his sleep that now had such a hold on him. He hesitated, waited a little, slowly began, his face in shadows of melancholy.

"About ten days ago," said he, "I retired very late. I had been up waiting for important dispatches from the front. I could not have been long in bed when I fell into a slumber, for I was weary. I soon began to dream. There seemed to be a death-like stillness about me. Then I heard subdued sobs, as if a number of people were weeping. I thought I left my bed and wandered downstairs. There the silence was broken by the same pitiful sobbing, but the mourners were invisible. I went from room to room; no living person was in sight, but the same mournful sounds of distress met me as I passed along. It was light in all the rooms; every object was familiar to me;

but where were all the people who were grieving as if their hearts would break? I was puzzled and alarmed. What could be the meaning of all this? Determined to find the cause of a state of things so mysterious and so shocking, I kept on until I arrived at the East Room, which I entered. There I met with a sickening surprise. Before me was a catafalque, on which rested a corpse wrapped in funeral vestments. Around it were stationed soldiers who were acting as guards; and there was a throng of people, some gazing mournfully upon the corpse, whose face was covered, others weeping pitifully. 'Who is dead in the White House?' I demanded of one of the soldiers. 'The President,' was his answer; 'he was killed by an assassin!' Then came a loud burst of grief from the crowd, which awoke me from my dream. I slept no more that night; and although it was only a dream, I have been strangely annoyed by it ever since."

"That is horrid!" said Mrs. Lincoln. "I wish you had not told it. I am glad I don't believe in dreams, or I should be in terror from this time forth."

"Well," responded Mr. Lincoln, thoughtfully, "it is only a dream, Mary. Let us say no more about it, and try to forget it."

The dream had shaken its dreamer to the depths, noted Lamon. As he had given the secret of it to others he was "grave, gloomy, and at times visibly pale, but perfectly calm." To Lamon afterward, in a reference to it Lincoln quoted from *Hamlet*, "To sleep; perchance to dream! ay, *there's the rub!*" —stressing the last three words.

Once again and with playful touches, bringing his sense of humor into use as though he might laugh off the dream, he said to Lamon: "Hill, your apprehension of harm to me from some hidden enemy is downright foolishness. For a long time you have been trying to keep somebody—the Lord knows who—from killing me. Don't you see how it will turn out? In this dream it was not me, but some other fellow, that was killed. It seems that this ghostly assassin tried his hand on someone else. And this reminds me of an old farmer in Illinois whose family were made sick by eating greens. Some poisonous herb had got into the mess, and members of the family were in danger of dying. There was a half-witted boy in the family called Jake; and always afterward when they had greens the old man would say, 'Now, afore we risk these greens, *let's try 'em on Jake. If he stands 'em,* we're all right.' Just so with me. As long as this imaginary assassin continues to exercise himself on others *I* can stand it." He then became serious and said: "Well, let it go. I think the Lord in His own good time and way will work this out all right. God knows what is best."

This last he gave with a sigh, and in a way as if talking to himself with no friend Lamon standing by.

Into the realm of sleep Lincoln carried part of his waking world. To such as Donn Piatt in a given moment he could say he slept the sleep of the just, he slept like a log, as a heavy sleeper he was a treasure and a model. The guard Crook knew otherwise. In his midnight and dawn patrol of the White House, near the door of the President's room he could hear the deep breathing. And the sober and loyal Crook, who had his moments of awareness beyond ordinary minions of the clock, wrote of Lincoln sometimes having a day of unusual anxiety and then in the night "I have heard him *moan* in his sleep." This gave Crook a queer feeling. He reasoned about it:

"While the expression of Mr. Lincoln's face was always sad when he was quiet, it gave one the assurance of calm. He never seemed to doubt the wisdom of an action when he had once decided on it. And so when he was in a way defenceless in his sleep it made me feel the pity that would have been almost an impertinence when he was awake. I would stand there and listen until a sort of panic stole over me. If he felt the weight of things so heavily, how much worse the situation of the country must be than any of us realized! At last I would walk softly away, feeling as if I had been listening at a keyhole."

CHAPTER 72

THE CALENDAR SAYS GOOD FRIDAY

The purple lilacs bloomed April the Fourteenth of the year Eighteen Sixty Five.
And the shining air held a balance of miracles good and evil.

Wrens on the White House lawn chattered a fast evil gossip soon forgotten.
Cardinals streaked in crimson curves and whistled happy landing on tall treetops.
A veery thrush and a brown thrush in a circle of bushes poured out a living waterfall of cool song.

The oaks and chestnuts stood grave and thoughtful.
From any window of the honorable Executive Mansion they were beyond reproach.
In mist or moonlight or noonday sun they kept their serene stature and measured men without praise or blame.
They seemed to stand waiting, in silence giving thanks for as much of life as had been given them.

The sidewalk passers-by glanced through the iron fence pickets to see how the White House looked this morning of April the Fourteenth.

Teamsters and horsemen rattling over the street cobble-stones took their look too at the famous old house where all the Presidents since Washington had made a home.

The smells on the air and the taste of spring made a smiling forenoon.

Like any other day of spring mystery and bloom—so it looked.

Not till afterward did they know they might have listened for deep sea bells calling and looked for a dreamship and studied over the fabrics of fate and the brotherhoods of dust and shadow.

Later they considered the moist earth gathering those long known as the Great Majority, the fogs forever haunting that deeply cloven line beyond which men say is the Other Shore.

Did any lover of trees have a daybreak dream of a Great Oak on a high hill under the flash of a lightning prong crashing down helpless, a loss for all time to the winds and sky who had loved it and not known how much they loved it?

Did any Negro preacher notify the world beforehand that the Almighty on the Great White Throne had spoken to the Angel on the Pale Horse saying:

"Go down now, go down to the United States, to Chesapeake Bay and the Potomac River, and find Washington, D.C., and find One Man for me there and touch him on the shoulder and tell him it's time for him to come, I'm wanting him here, his time is up today"?

Did any fortune-teller, any dealer in abracadabra, any reader of the mystic Crystal Ball, see that day a phantom horseman come riding on a phantom horse, a skeleton rider on a skeleton steed, a rider with a red rose in his teeth, a grim rider laughing softly as though he might be a bringer of Judgment Day, a keeper of a Domesday Book, singing "John Brown's Body Lies A-mouldering," singing "Go Down, Moses, Let My People Go," singing of the grapes of wrath trampled red and crushed scarlet and how in the beauty of the lilies Christ was born across the sea—a white-skulled rider with a flame-rose in his teeth?

Did any clairvoyant foreteller write a forecast that today, this April the Fourteenth, one man must hear a deep sea bell and a farewell gong and take a ride skyward swifter than Elijah in the chariot of fire?

Did any poet or genius of imagination picture the ancient crowded Hall of Valhalla alive with tumult over a newcome arrival who would stand before them only a trifle abashed drawling, "Well, this reminds me . . ."?

No, there seemed to be nothing foretold in essential particulars except to the Dreamer himself most concerned, who had it from a dream he accepted, though himself not in the slightest aware of the way, the method, the arrangements, the timing.

FROM mid-April of '61 to mid-April of '65 some 3,000,000 men North and South had seen war service—the young, the strong, the physically fit, carrying the heavy load and taking the agony. The fallen of them had seen Antietam, Murfreesboro, Fredericksburg, Chancellorsville, the Wilderness, Spotsylvania, Cold Harbor, each a shambles, a human slaughterhouse. In the burnt and blackened Shenandoah Valley were enough embers of barns and men to satisfy any prophet of doom.

From Malvern Hill and Gettysburg down to Chickamauga, Chattanooga, Island Number Ten, Vicksburg, the Red River and beyond, the burying-grounds deep and shallow held the consecrated dead—some of them lone white skeletons not yet accorded burial—fallen from flying lead and steel, from the reapers typhoid, dysentery, inflammations, prison starvation—thousands having crawled away to die alone without witnesses or extreme unction—tens of thousands buried in trenches with mass markers for the nameless and unidentified: UNKNOWN.

They were a host proven in valor and sacrifice—swept to the Great Beyond. No man who actually and passionately loved the cause of either flag could evade moments when he reproached himself for being alive. Robert E. Lee had those moments, well attested. So did Abraham Lincoln. His Gettysburg speech and his letter to Mrs. Bixby had an undeniable undertone of this reproach.

Killed in action or dead from wounds and disease were some 620,000 Americans, 360,000 from the North, 260,000 of the South—planted in the tomb of the earth, spectral and shadowy, blurred and discordant in their testimonies for posterity as to why they fought the war and cut each other down in the heyday of youth.

They were a host. They were phantoms never absent from Lincoln's thoughts. Possibly from that vanished host, rather than from the visible and living, Lincoln took his main direction and moved as though the word "reconciliation" could have supreme beauty if he could put it to work.

In Greensboro, North Carolina, at a rather ordinary house, in an upstairs room having a bed, a few small chairs, a table with pen and ink, Jefferson Davis, with four remaining Cabinet members and two veteran generals, held a final meeting over the affairs of the Confederate States of America, its government, its armies and prospects.

President Davis spoke to a man he had humiliated and quarreled with more than three years. "We should like to have your views, General Johnston."

With sharp intensity as if in anger, General Johnston: "My views are, sir, that our people are tired of the war, feel themselves whipped, and will not fight. . . . We cannot place another large army in the field. . . . My men are daily deserting in large numbers. . . . Since Lee's defeat they regard the war as at an end. . . . I shall expect to retain no man beyond the by-road or cow-path that leads to his house. . . . We may perhaps obtain terms that we ought to accept."

Davis sat unmoved. He had been calm throughout, having said: "Our late disasters are terrible, but I do not think we should regard them as fatal. I think we can whip the enemy yet, if our people turn out. . . . Whatever can be done must be done at once. We have not a day to lose." This Johnston had answered, as though to break the calm of the unruffled President Davis who still seemed to carry himself as the head and front of a powerful government, commander in chief of powerful armies that had not melted away, innocent of realities.

His eyes on the table, his fingers folding and refolding a piece of paper, Davis heard Johnston, waited, and suddenly in low easy tone: "What do you say, General Beauregard?" The reply: "I concur in all General Johnston has said."

They agreed a letter should be written to Sherman asking for terms. Johnston asked President Davis to write it—which he did. They parted.

The sunset of the Confederacy had shaded over into evening stars, into lasting memories of a Lost Cause.

In its Richmond capitol building the enemy pawed among remaining fragments of its archives.

In its earlier and first capitol building at Montgomery, Alabama, Union horsemen made merry.

In the sky its final embers of hope had flickered and sunk and the overhead constellations lighted tall candles for remembrance.

For millions of the struggling masses of Southern people the war had settled nothing in particular, and their lives centered around the same relentless question that guided them before the war began—"How do we earn a living?"

A battered and valiant remnant that feared neither torment in an afterworld nor hell on earth was to find joy in a song line, "I won't be reconstructed, And for the Union I don't give a damn."

Some would find welfare and kindness in the old Union. Two sections of the country fought a duel and came out with honors enough for both—this was the philosophy of some who really loved two flags--and why was a mystery—was their personal secret. Some who had starved and suffered and taken wounds in the rain and lived on the food of rats and lost everything except a name for valor and endurance—some of these could never repent or be sorry. They were to make a song of their hate against "the lying, thieving Yankees," their scorn of the Constitution, the Freedmen's Bureau, the Eagle, the Declaration of Independence, and furthermore:

Three hundred thousand Yankees	I can't take up my musket
Lie stiff in Southern dust;	And fight 'em now no more;
We got three hundred thousand	But I ain't a-going to love 'em,
Before they conquered us;	Now that is sartain sure;
They died of Southern fever	And I don't want no pardon,
And Southern steel and shot;	For what I was and am;
I wish it was three millions,	I won't be reconstructed,
Instead of what we got.	And I don't care a damn.

As a song and a viewpoint it represented little or nothing to be found in the counsels of Robert E. Lee, foremost of Southern cherished figures, who would take the oath of allegiance to the Union. It did however sing deep wishes incarnate in Jefferson Davis, who meant it when he said he would die before he would take an oath of loyalty to the United States.

On this April 14 Davis, still at Greensboro, wrote to his wife. Before her leaving Richmond he had given her a pistol, shown her how to use it, told her to be brave. Now he was to journey southward and join her. "One perfect bliss have I," Mrs. Davis was writing to Mrs. Chesnut: "The baby, who grows fat and is smiling always, is . . . not old enough to develop the world's vices."

"Dear Winnie," wrote the now fugitive President of the Confederate States of America on April 14, "I will come to you if I can. Everything is dark. You should prepare for the worst. . . . I have lingered on the road and labored to little purpose. My love to the children."

As Davis packed his kit for moving farther south he knew there were not a few at the North who wished to see him hang on a sour-apple tree, though he was unaware that the head of the Federal Government at Washington wished him Godspeed and good luck as a refugee, hoped he would cross the Rio Grande into Mexico or board some vessel that would take him beyond all United States Navy patrols—any news coming to Lincoln about Jeff Davis would be welcome except word of Davis's capture or the killing of him in combat or flight. Davis would have been interested that one report credited Lincoln with saying: "This talk about Mr. Davis tires me. I hope he will mount a fleet horse, reach the shores of the Gulf of Mexico, and ride so far into its waters that we shall never see him again." Something like that the mulatto doorkeeper Slade heard Lincoln say and told of it to Chaplain Neill. A vanished Davis was wanted. A living Davis would be an embarrassment, a dead Davis a reproach. It was a long time since the two of them as youths, Lincoln and Davis, had joined in a war on an Indian tribe and slaughtered its braves and crushed its power and taken its Chief Black Hawk a prisoner of war, in the custody of Lieutenant Jefferson Davis.

Peace was beginning to smile. "All serious, alarming difficulty," wrote E. L. Godkin, "is now over," whether military, political or financial.

Lincoln sat for a photograph by Alexander Gardner—and for the first time when facing a camera in the four years of his Administration permitted a smile to wreath his face. Until this camera register in the second week of April, 1865, he had most often been grave and somber. Now he smiled.

The hurricane was spent, the high storm winds gone down. Rough weather and choppy seas were ahead—but the worst was over and could not come again. He hoped for goodwill and mutual trust and let that hope shine on his face.

"I confess," wrote Godkin this week, echoing a rather common thought, "I should be very anxious about the terms of reconstruction, if Lincoln were not to be President for the next four years."

Emerson, in his wagon hitched to a star, feared this goodwill. "The high tragic historic justice" pounded out on the anvils of war he was afraid would "be softened and dissipated and toasted away at dinner-tables." What lay ahead was intricate and perplexing with "men very much at a loss as to the right action." The Concord Sage was suspicious of Grant's terms to Lee as "a little too easy." He questioned the wisdom of letting the Southern States back into Congress to join Northern Democrats "in thwarting the will of the Government." The Negro should have his right to vote—but perhaps only those Negroes who could read and write. It was confusing. Perhaps the brag of the South needed further humbling. Emerson recalled his neighbor George Minott, when urged to go to town meeting and vote, giving a Yankee answer over the garden wall: "Votes do no good. What is done so won't last. But what is done by bullets will stay put." The gentle seer and poet of Concord thought perhaps force and more force of some sort was needed in the South—but how turn it on and when and where? And how many times in his dazzling and provocative essays had Emerson not said with testamentary faith that force, as such, loses its purpose as often as it wins?

Senator Ben Wade had a wish as to force. "There is no doubt"—he framed this wish in a private letter not worth making public—"that if by an insurrection they [the colored people] could contrive to slay one half of their oppressors, the other half would hold them in the highest respect and no doubt treat them with justice."

Thus ran the hope of a white man of Ohio, where Negroes were few and far between, who wanted revolutionary Negro uprisings with wholesale slaughter of whites a thousand miles from his Ohio home in Gulf States where in some counties the Negroes outnumbered the whites.

Lincoln had flung his Emancipation Proclamation broadcast over the South knowing well and fearing deeply there might be slaughter and horrors of race war. In his every step toward abolishing slavery he had favored his own feelings, though guided mainly by public opinion at home and abroad. In his efforts to get compensation paid to the South for the freed slaves, however, he was consulting public opinion in the South as well as the equity given slave property by the Constitution. This would likewise apply to his neglect to use the authority given him by the Confiscation Act; under that law he had taken so little Southern property that Ben Wade was disgusted about it.

Lincoln knew that now as truly as at any time during the war his course to some bystanders seemed crooked, his conduct a riddle, for he was seeking a social stability that concerned public opinion as related to property. Public opinion at bottom settled every question, he had told an audience in Hartford, Connecticut, in March of 1860, and in that process, "The property basis will have its weight. The love of property and a consciousness of right or wrong have conflicting places in our organization, which often make a man's course seem crooked, his conduct a riddle."

He had spoken prophecy seven years ago, saying it sadly as if it were wrenched from the depths of him and he could say nothing else because no other words for him so epitomized the national fate to come. Yet his speech had been taken by many as a terrible wish. They read him as wanting war and a crimson river of hell with blood to the bridles of the horses. "In my opinion," he had said then, "agitation will not cease until a crisis shall have been reached and passed. 'A house divided against itself cannot stand.' I believe this government cannot endure permanently half slave and half free. I do not expect the Union to be dissolved—I do not expect the house to fall—but I do expect it will cease to be divided." That day seven years ago it was a phantom chance and a far gamble that he should be the one man chosen to make the high decisions, frame the controlling issues, steer the course through a bedlam of babblers, through crazy tornadoes and equally cruel doldrums of monotony and weariness.

The wild hammers of war had broken keys, had pounded out of shape and flung off as scrap iron a series of keys. The head hammerman had spoken eight years ago of those keys, the pity and shame of them. "To aid in making the bondage of the negro universal and eternal" the once sacred Declaration of Independence was "assailed and sneered at and construed, and hawked at and torn, till, if its framers could rise from their graves, they could not at all recognize it." He named the powers of earth combined against the black man. "Mammon is after him, ambition follows, philosophy follows, and the theology of the day is fast joining the cry. They have him in his prison-house; they have searched his person, and left no prying instrument with him. One after another they have closed the heavy iron doors upon him; and now they have him, as it were, bolted in with a lock of a hundred keys, which can never be unlocked without the concurrence of every key—the keys in the hands of a hundred different men, and they scattered to a hundred different and distant places; and they stand musing as to what invention, in all the dominions of mind and matter, can be produced to make the impossibility of his escape more complete than it is."

Step by step the keys locking the Negro into bondage had been broken. And now among those who had destroyed the property status of the black man, no longer now a chattel bought and sold, there was dispute and a hate

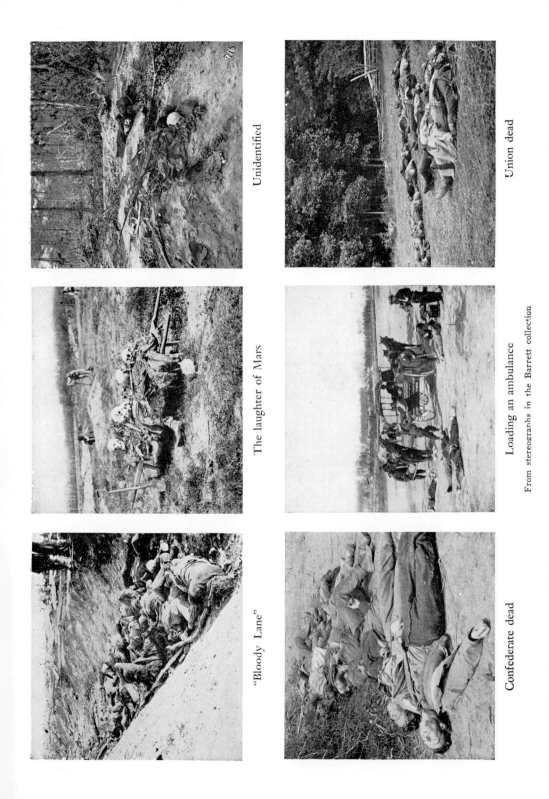

Unidentified

Union dead

The laughter of Mars

Loading an ambulance

From stereographs in the Barrett collection

"Bloody Lane"

Confederate dead

Wounded and convalescent soldiers in Carver Hospital, Washington, often visited by Lincoln (*right*)

From the U.S Army Signal Corps

Confederate prisoners shortly after capture, ready for northward transfer under Union guards. (*below*)

Photograph by Gardner, from the Barrett collection

harsh and sure, bringing a new conflict over whether the keys to complete political freedom should be given the Negro now—or later.

Slimmer than a single cobweb thread was the hope that the President would call an extra session of Congress and let the legislative end of the Government dictate the reconstruction. Speaker Colfax had seen the President about it and heard the President say he "should put it off as long as possible," merely promising that if he did call an extra session he would give the due "sixty days' notice." Congressman George Julian was trying to be polite and practice understatement in saying that Mr. Lincoln's "well-known views on reconstruction" were discussed in cloakrooms and "were as distasteful as possible to radical Republicans." Wendell Phillips still estimated the President "a first-rate second-rate man," slow and obstructive, needing attention. His fear was that the President might carry through a reconstruction program withholding the ballot from all Negroes except those who could read and write and those who had fought in the Union armies. Sumner studied a cheering letter from Wendell Phillips on what they might do together to block the President. "My point is," wrote Phillips, "there's ample public opinion to sustain your course. It only needs a reputable spirited leader to make this evident. . . . Accept if offered, an opportunity to sound one bugle note . . . & set the tone for the summer. We have six months to work in (barring the extra session) & if you'll begin an agitation—we will see that it reaches the Senate room by December."

This opposition to Lincoln would have considered themselves sunk had they been merely politicians. They were crusaders not entirely wrong in believing they had been instrumental in bringing on a war for freedom. Nor were they completely mistaken in their belief that they and the John Brown song had won the war. Their fellow crusaders, however, William Lloyd Garrison, Harriet Beecher Stowe, and Frederick Douglass, would argue that Lincoln, Grant, Sherman, various unexpected matter-of-fact circumstances of fate, had won the war.

This crusader opposition to the President saw a long hard fight ahead. They would have to break the President's control of his party. They would have to pry loose from him several powerful Northern economic factors that had not suffered loss at his hands and expected favors to come. They had not yet been able to solve the political genius by which he had so repeatedly foiled those seeking to unhorse him. Their agitation would have to undermine the deep-rooted popularity of a President regarded by millions as a familiar and homely neighbor who was also a terrible fighter, the master mind that had won the war.

Phillips, Sumner, Wade, Stevens, were not sure what strategy would overcome the odds against them. But they were sure the fight must be made; the Executive must somehow be shorn of his power, at least to the extent that he should not dictate the terms of reconstruction. They saw themselves standing at a momentous and historic crossroads where they were figures of the American conscience and makers of justice through law. Among the mediocrities who trailed after the leaders was Senatoı Morrill of Maine, who was to find it "truly most difficult to speak candidly of the elements of Lincoln's character without offending public sense." Another was Julian, whose February speech had reached nowhere with its analysis of Lincoln as lacking decision, intelligence, and possibly honor. Still others, such as Schenck of Ohio, had no real color as crusaders and might languish in the cause if the right plums of patronage were handed them.

A careful reading of his many speeches would show that Wade held some natural scorn of Lincoln and spat on what he read as Lincoln's motives. Sumner kept himself on higher ground; he still respected the sincerity of Lincoln, which Lincoln returned in kind; he would stick to principles and avoid personalities probably, as he had done in his February and March parliamentary battling. Thad Stevens—who could fathom the heart caverns of that wit and realist, genius of retribution, reader of Blackstone and Dante, groper after justice, hater of all Pharaohs, kinsman of the malformed and the crippled, the utterly forsaken, the lowly who suffer and wait and hope?

One prize chameleon had joined the radicals. That foremost of turn-coats, Ben Butler, was lending his wily brain to the movement, confident that his political torpedoes would wreak more havoc with the Lincoln leadership than the powder boat he had exploded at Fort Fisher with no result except a loud noise. Thus far he had been instrumental in planting spicily malicious stories about Lincoln, printed in the *New York Tribune*. Greeley too was in the radical line-up—though his next shift as usual was beyond prediction. In time he was to befriend Jefferson Davis so loyally that he would hear a song line "We'll hang Horace Greeley to a sour-apple tree." The same George G. Hoskins (according to an almost too circumstantial story) who had brought Greeley the word directly from Lincoln in September of '64 that the President intended, "if I am reëlected and reinaugurated," to appoint Greeley Postmaster General, this same Hoskins was now speaker of the New York State Assembly and often meeting Greeley. On this day of April 14 he saw Greeley and heard the editor refer to himself as forgotten in the Lincoln Cabinet changes, bursting out, "Hoskins, didn't I tell you that was a lie?" Hoskins promised to take a night train to Washington and on the next day of April 15 to interview the President about the pledge of last September that Greeley would be appointed Postmaster General.

By some mischance, or more likely by the wish and intention of Greeley, his letter to Lincoln the summer before regarding the Niagara Falls conference, urging peace for our "bleeding, bankrupt, ruined country," was in late March published in England. Lincoln had been willing to let all the letters they exchanged be published if Greeley would merely cross out the words "bleeding, bankrupt, ruined." Greeley refused to do this. And now the English press had "scooped" the American newspapers in the printing of Greeley's opinion that in the summer of '64 the United States was "bleeding, bankrupt, ruined." Welles, as a Hartford, Connecticut, editor, thought it strange this letter should have first publication abroad. "I should have preferred its appearance at home in the first instance," he wrote. "Poor Greeley is nearly played out. He has a morbid appetite for notoriety. Wishes to be noted and forward in all shows. . . . Has been scolding and urging forward hostile operations. Suddenly is for peace, and ready to pay the Rebels four hundred millions or more to get it. . . . I doubt his honesty. . . . He is a greedy office-hunter." In the main this judgment of Greeley by Welles would prove up. Greeley did wish the President would appoint him Postmaster General. More than that, he thought he would make a great President. He would run for that office when the chance came.

The radical faction now had Greeley with them. He would stay till the mood and whim took him away. Just now he was more heard than any of the radical voices in speaking suspicion of Lincoln. So sharply and peculiarly hostile was the tone of Greeley's newspaper to Lincoln at this time that *Harper's Weekly* editorially rebuked Greeley for indulging in petty and needless outbursts. According to a statement which the eminent Unitarian clergyman Edward Everett Hale said he had from the *New York Tribune* managing editor, Sidney Howard Gay, Greeley on this day of April 14 handed to Gay an editorial he had written, "a brutal, bitter, sarcastic, personal attack" on the President. Gay handed it to the composing-room foreman. Proofs came back to Gay. He read it again, decided to hold it over, told the foreman to lock up the type and tell no one about it. For the first time Gay overstepped his authority and of his own will on April 14 kept out of the April 15 issue an editorial from his chief verbally trying to tear Lincoln to pieces.

In the three days since the President had made his speech on Louisiana reconstruction and a restricted ballot for the freed Negroes, the attacks and the censure preceding that speech had definitely increased. His cool approach and perfectly dispassionate manner toward his critics then had more than annoyed some of them. "As a general rule," he had said, "I abstain from reading the reports of attacks upon myself, wishing not to be provoked by that to which I cannot properly offer an answer. In spite of this precaution, however, it comes to my knowledge that I am much censured for some supposed agency in setting up and seeking to sustain the new State government of Louisiana." He was accusing no one, naming nobody; they could guess who was meant. He was not "provoked," that was clear. And there was a playful touch about saying he had heard much censure of himself in spite of his "precaution"—his abstinence in not reading reports of attacks on him.

Probably some of Lincoln's own definite feeling on April 14 about his political opposition in his own party—and doubtless some of the fact and viewpoint he considered essential on that day—were written by Noah Brooks in a news letter to the *Sacramento Union* dated April 14. In June, it was planned, Brooks was to replace Nicolay as private secretary to the President. As a friend and intimate he could not be far wrong on fact or viewpoint in the White House. Heading his news letter "A Bone of Contention,"

Brooks above his pen signature of Castine wrote from Washington to his West Coast readers:

The views of the President concerning reconstruction, as enunciated in his speech of the 11th April, are very animatedly discussed and meet with widely different comments from different people. It is, of course, acceptable to the conservative element of the Union party, largely dominant, that the President shall have insisted upon the views which he was known to have entertained on the policy of reconstruction, especially as applied to Louisiana, as a sample or instance of the working of that policy. But the radicals, so called, are as virulent and bitter as ever, and they have gladly seized upon this occasion to attempt to reorganize the faction which fought against Lincoln's nomination, very much as Sydney Smith's Mrs. Partington fought with her broom against the rising tide.

These men were the bitter opponents of new Louisiana in the last Congress, and they are enraged that the President should dare to utter his sentiments as antagonistic to theirs. They thought that Louisiana was killed off, and now they nose out "Executive interference with legislative prerogatives"; they discern conservative policy afar off, and see an unconditional amnesty to all rebels in the signs of the times. Among these men are Benjamin F. Butler, who is here endeavoring to make all the mischief he can and get up a radical organization with himself and Caleb Cushing (*par nobile fratrum!*) at the head; he has an ally in R. C. Schenck of Ohio, who it is supposed will be the "medium" and organ of Henry Winter Davis in the next Congress. Still, these men and their associates form but an inconsiderable portion of the great mass of the loyal people.

Butler, I hear, is very much disgusted at the slow response of the people to his incendiary appeals, and at their obvious reluctance to rally round his flag. One of his *claqueurs* has been sending sensational telegrams from Washington to the *Tribune*. Anent "great satisfaction of the people"; "Lee's parole a bribe for a surrender"; "split in the party that elected Lincoln," etc., etc., all of which appears in ludicrous contrast with the pro-conservative views concerning amnesty, which Greeley affects of late. Of course, the Opposition press will seize upon this small diversion as a sign of the dissolution of the Union organization, forgetting or ignoring the fact that the only reports of this suppositious quarrel which have appeared in any journal are those of a single individual, responsible to nobody for his truthfulness, his candor, or his intelligence.

Whatever aspect the question may now wear to the great mass of the people, they have an implicit and trustful faith in Lincoln, which is almost unreasonable and unreasoning; he has so often proved himself wiser than his critics and advisers that many truly wise men say that they have done with contending against his better judgment, while "the simple people" say, "Oh, well, Old Abe will come out all right—he always does, you know."

Any man who looks over the political history of the four past years will be surprised to see how often adverse, though friendly, criticisms of the President's acts and opinions have been made foolishness by the development of events.

Of like color was a *New York Herald* editorial in its issue of the day before. The President's reconstruction speech had been "very generally canvassed," said the *Herald*, "and meets with approbation from a large majority of the people." It saw however "a very active minority of the more radical of the Republicans much chagrined at the indications of a disposition to heal up existing difficulties." Though comparatively few in number, they included "prominent and influential members of the dominant party" and would "try to complicate matters as much as possible." And the *Herald* put out a hand of understanding in saying: "The President relies upon the good sense of the people, and their desire to secure lasting peace and quiet as speedily and with as little difficulty as possible, to carry him successfully through the new ordeal to which he is about to be subjected."

Whatever might have been the discussions and proceedings of the malcontent Republicans in Washington since Lincoln's speech of April 11 giving them added offense, those sharing in a movement to block Lincoln's executive designs sealed their lips with the discretion of model mummies. To one seeking revelations Wade later said, "There is no use telling what we know unless we tell the whole truth, and if I tell the whole truth I shall blast too many reputations." A biographer of Zach Chandler was to be sure that a lifting of the veil over these days would let loose "startling revelations" and "shed light on the hidden springs of actions of vast moment."

On the calendar it was Holy Week and April the Fourteenth was Good Friday. Some were to say they had never before this week seen such a shine of beneficence, such a kindling glow, on Lincoln's face. He was down to lean flesh and bone, thirty pounds underweight, his cheeks haggard, yet the inside of him moved to a music of peace on earth and goodwill to men. He let it come out in the photograph Alexander Gardner made this Holy Week.

The schedule for this day as outlined beforehand seemed much the same as scores of other days at the White House: office business till eight o'clock; breakfast and then interviews till the Cabinet meeting at eleven o'clock; luncheon, more interviews, a late afternoon drive with Mrs. Lincoln; an informal meeting with old Illinois friends; during the day and evening one or more trips to the War Department; another interview, then to the theatre with Mrs. Lincoln and a small party. Such was the prepared docket for this Good Friday.

The city of Washington outside the White House kept on being gay. Flags and bunting still flew across streets and up and down building fronts in riots of red-white-and-blue. Window illuminations, fireworks, impromptu processions with brass bands and serenades, kept going the night of April 13. Churchgoers in large numbers filled the pews, joined in responses and hymns, heard Good Friday sermons of the Prince of Peace having brought unutterable blessings to the country.

The distinctive national event planned for this day of April 14 took place at Charleston, South Carolina. With formal ceremonies and amid thundering guns of the Dahlgren fleet and Federal land artillery, the flag was again raised over the fort. The Reverend Henry Ward Beecher spoke, blamed the war on a small ruling class of the South, predicted that the common people North and South would join and rule the country, praised the army and navy, the members of the Federal Government, the loyal citizens of the North, offering to the President of the United States "our solemn congratulations that God has sustained his life and health under the unparalleled burdens and sufferings of four bloody years, and permitted him to behold this auspicious confirmation of that national unity for which he has waited with so much patience and fortitude, and for which he has labored with such disinterested wisdom." Psalms of thanksgiving were read, the assemblage intoning: "The Lord hath done great things for us; whereof we are glad. . . . Some trust in chariots, and some in horses: but we will remember the name of the Lord our God."

No idle phrases were these in the mouth of one present who uncovered his bald head and stood reverently with lights of jubilee in his eyes. The South had set a price on his head and Charleston thirty years before hanged and burned him in effigy, William Lloyd Garrison, the Agitator who had publicly burned to ashes the Constitution of the United States as a document infamous in its sanction of slave property. Now a fleet, guns, armies, and the Federal Government upheld his doctrine that the Constitution must outlaw slave property. The shattered Fort Sumter walls, the outlying captured forts, the speakers and singers, the bands and booming guns of the warships, the hundred flagpoles flying Union colors, the wide beautiful harbor itself, made a scene with plenty to think about or dream over. An epic poem glittered in the lights and shadows, the implications and foreshadowings, present in the action. The high moment came when ship bells rang the noon hour. Major General Robert Anderson, "Bob Anderson, my beau," the loser and image of defeat four years ago to a day, stood at the flagpole. His own hands hauling at a rope sent up a flag, the same flame-licked and shot-pierced United States flag he had brought down when he surrendered Fort Sumter on April 14 of '61. Then voices, horns, drums, guns, joined in a grand acclamation to the restored banner of the fort which the President of the United States had said must be "repossessed."

In Washington General Grant had arrived from the front, heard shouts of welcome, and in trying to walk from his hotel to the War Department had to call on the police to help make a path through the curious, cheering throngs. The Secretary of War had announced that after "consultation with the lieutenant-general," it was decided to stop all drafting and recruiting, curtail supply purchases, reduce the number of officers, and lift regulations toward helping trade and business as far as consistent with public safety. This good news reaching the country on April 14 cleared the air in several quarters. Though the war contractors would have to seek new outlets and the gold speculators hunt fresh fields, ordinary businessmen breathed easier, and deserters, draft-evaders, and skedaddlers felt safer about telling their real names.

At breakfast with Robert the President heard his son tell of life at the front, and he probably did, as one story ran, take up a portrait of Robert E. Lee which his son had brought him, after placing it on the table scan it long, saying: "It is a good face. I am glad the war is over at last."

After breakfast came Speaker Colfax. They discussed government policy. Possibly they mentioned the future of Colfax. Four years ago Lincoln had written to Colfax that the young Hoosier was Cabinet timber, that he was not refused appointment as Secretary of the Interior because in 1858 Colfax was understood to have favored Douglas's re-election. Politician anxious for high place, rather than crusader, was Colfax. Nor was he indifferent to money. As Speaker of the House he was important. He had leaned toward the radicals, in the winter of '64 considering it necessary to deny publicly that he was quoted correctly in favor of a second term for Lincoln. Lincoln was paying him attention. Perhaps a Cabinet place was mentioned this morning. That would have been Lincoln's method with one who was politician first and crusader if it paid. If Colfax went away from the interview unconvinced as to Lincoln's reconstruction policy, it was not because Lincoln had failed to present matters aimed at the personal material interest of Colfax as well as the larger cause of the country.

Other callers included Congressman Cornelius Cole of California, a Grand Rapids, Michigan, lawyer, W. A. Howard, and the "lame-duck" Senator John P. Hale of New Hampshire, appointed by the President to be Minister to Spain, his many slashing attacks on the Administration now forgotten. Lincoln was quoted as saying in some interviews that he trusted an "era of good feeling" had returned. No one, it seemed, on this day of April 14 came away from a White House visit having heard the President say they must be on guard against new conspiracies of Southern traitors who planned to thwart the Government. That point was sufficiently stressed elsewhere. The President emphasized restoration of goodwill between the two sections whose war had ended.

John A. J. Creswell came, one of the Union men who kept Maryland out of secession, on the death of United States Senator Thomas H. Hicks elected to fill the vacancy. He quoted Lincoln's greeting: "Creswell, old fellow, everything is bright this morning. The war is over. It has been a tough time, but we have lived it out—or some of us have," the voice dropping on those last five words. "But it is over. We are going to have good times now, and a united country."

Creswell made known his errand. An old friend had drifted South, got into the Confederate Army, fallen into Federal hands, and was now a prisoner. Creswell offered affidavits bearing on character and circumstances, adding: "I know the man acted like a fool, but he is my friend and a good fellow. Let him out, give him to me, and I will be responsible for him."

"Creswell," said Lincoln, "you make me think of a lot of young folks who once started out Maying. To reach their destination they had to cross a shallow stream, and did so by means of an old flat boat. When they came to return, they found to their dismay that the old scow had disappeared. They were in sore trouble, and thought over all manner of devices for getting over the water, but without avail. After a time one of the boys proposed that each fellow should pick up the girl he liked the best and wade over with her. The masterly proposition was carried out, until all that were left upon the island was a little short chap and a great, long, gothic-built elderly lady. Now, Creswell, you are trying to leave me in the same predicament. You fellows are all getting your own friends out of this scrape, and you will succeed in carrying off one after another until nobody but Jeff Davis and myself will be left on the island, and then I won't know what to do. How should I feel? How should I look lugging him over? I guess the way to avoid such an embarrassing situation is to let them all out at once."

Others came seeking pardons, releases, discharges, which Lincoln wrote with an easier hand than he could while the war was on. He also wrote out minor appointments, notes referring persons to officials and departments, and a card for two Southerners who wanted passes to Richmond: "No pass is necessary now to authorize anyone to go to and return from Petersburg and Richmond. People go and return as they did before the war."

The President's policy now in filling Federal offices in the South was noted by Edward D. Neill, the Minnesota infantry chaplain briefly resident in the White House at this time. From John W. Forney, secretary of the Senate and owner-editor of the *Washington Chronicle* and the *Philadelphia Press*, Chaplain Neill had it that Lincoln sent for Forney and suggested that Forney should go to Richmond and other Southern cities and urge on editors and leading men their support of Federal Government measures. "By this method he [the President] hoped that enough at least would be persuaded to rally around the flag, so as to obviate the necessity of appointing as postmasters, collectors of revenue, and judges of courts those not native of the South, with no permanent interest in its welfare, who would leave as soon as the emoluments of office ceased." That is, within five days after Lee's surrender Lincoln had sped away southward an emissary of Southern sympathies, a confidential political agent, in agreement with his own views looking toward the South, whose purpose was to arrange if practicable that Southern communities should have the least possible number of Northern outsiders holding Federal offices.

A fever of a bright new time coming possessed many this day. "Washington was a little delirious," wrote Crook. "Everybody was celebrating. The kind of celebration depended on the kind of person. It was merely a question of whether the intoxication was mental or physical. A stream of callers came to congratulate the President, to tell how loyal they had been, and how they had always been sure he would be victorious. The city became disorderly with the men who were celebrating too hilariously. Those about the President lost somewhat of the feeling, usually present, that his life was not safe. It did not seem possible, now that the war was over . . . after President Lincoln had offered himself a target for Southern bullets in the streets of Richmond and had come out unscathed, there could be danger. For my part, I had drawn a full breath of relief after we got out of Richmond, and had forgotten to be anxious since."

To General Van Alen, who seemed to have written some warning, the President wrote this day, "I intend to adopt the advice of my friends and use due precaution." And he wrote further to Van Alen a warm and pulsing sentiment, rather richly colored, probably in tone with what he had instructed Forney to convey southward. "I thank you for the assurance you give me that I shall be supported by conservative men like yourself, in the efforts I may make to restore the Union, so as to make it, to use your language, a Union of hearts and hands as well as of States."

The evening was to be set apart for a theatre party planned by Mrs. Lincoln. A third-rate drama, *Our American Cousin*, which the star Laura Keene had carried to popularity was showing at Ford's Theatre. Lincoln was disinclined to go, but Mrs. Lincoln had set her heart on it. On his suggestion she invited General and Mrs. Grant to join their party—and General Grant accepted. The newspapers were so announcing. "Honor to Our Soldiers," a new patriotic song by H. B. Phillips with music by Professor W. Withers, Jr., "will be sung this evening by the entire company to do honor to Lieutenant-General Grant and President Lincoln and Lady, who visit the theatre in compliment to Miss Laura Keene, whose benefit and last appearance is announced," ran one item in the *Washington Evening Star*. Three advertisements in different places in the *Star* whetted the interest of those who might not care about the play but were keen to look at America's two foremost political and military stars.

At Grover's Theatre they had expected until the morning of April 14 that the President would attend the performance there of *Aladdin, or The Wonderful Lamp* with Miss Effie Germon in the leading role. "Mr. Lincoln had reserved a box at my theatre that night," wrote Grover, "and it should be noted that up to that time he had never attended Mr. Ford's theatre. . . . John T. Ford was an amiable gentleman, whose political proclivities differed little from mine. He was a stanch member of the Union party, which elected him to office as President of the Board of Aldermen, and acting Mayor of the City of Baltimore. Doubtless his personal sympathies were with his State and with that portion of the country in which he was born and reared, as mine were with my own native section. But he was as chary of expressing them as I was. . . . From no actions or expressions of Mr. Ford (for he was seldom in attendance at his Washington theatre), there had gradually come about a separation and widening of the theatrical clans, until Ford's Theatre had been regarded as the accepted House of the Bourbons. I have sometimes thought that the motive which prompted Mr. Lincoln to visit Ford's that night was in furtherance of his general purpose, to extend the hand of conciliation." Also Grover heard in this connection that "some time during the day Mrs. Lincoln learned that Laura Keene was to have a benefit and a last appearance at Ford's and she requested Mr. Lincoln to change his destination."

Grant however had changed his mind about going. Mrs. Grant, in all probability, had told the General that she would enjoy accommodating the President, but the more she thought about it, the more it seemed impossible that she could endure an evening with the unfortunate woman she had last seen in such outbursts of temper and rages of jealousy at City Point. The

General himself, anyone who knew him would testify, could see no fun ahead in such an evening. A little more than a year ago he had peremptorily refused to stay on in Washington for a dinner and reception suggested by Mrs. Lincoln, leaving for his army with a remark that he was tired of the "show business." He had not yet learned how to be pawed over and acclaimed by crowds.

Stanton told both Lincoln and Grant that from his secret-service agents and other sources he had heard of threats and conspiracies of such a character that it would not be safe for the two eminent leaders to put themselves on view before a large crowd that might have "evil-disposed persons." Stanton, according to David Homer Bates, urged Grant not to go, "and, if possible, to dissuade Lincoln from going." Stanton in this was taking the same course he had continuously held for more than three years. Against Lincoln's open wishes he had thrown cavalry, foot guards, and plain-clothes attendants around the President. Grant agreed with Stanton that the theatre party was unwise, "and said he only wanted an excuse not to go," wrote Bates. So Grant informed Lincoln that Mrs. Grant had left the city for their home in Burlington, New Jersey, and he himself was starting in the afternoon to see his children and have a long-delayed family reunion. Lincoln's further action and humor in preparing to see a play that evening—and to be seen by many who took him as part of the show—were in the account written by David Homer Bates:

On the morning of the 14th, Lincoln made his usual visit to the War Department and told Stanton that Grant had cancelled his engagement for that evening. The stern and cautious Secretary again urged the President to give up the theater-party, and, when he found that he was set on going, told him he ought to have a competent guard. Lincoln said: "Stanton, do you know that Eckert can break a poker over his arm?"

Stanton, not knowing what was coming, looked around in surprise and answered: "No; why do you ask such a question?" Lincoln said: "Well, Stanton, I have seen Eckert break five pokers, one after the other, over his arm, and I am thinking he would be the kind of man to go with me this evening. May I take him?"

Stanton, still unwilling to encourage the theater project, said that he had some important work for Eckert that evening, and could not spare him. Lincoln replied: "Well, I will ask the Major myself, and he can do your work to-morrow." He then went into the cipher-room, told Eckert of his plans for the evening, and said he wanted him to be one of the party, but that Stanton said he could not spare him. "Now, Major," he added, "come along. You can do Stanton's work to-morrow, and Mrs. Lincoln and I want you with us."

Eckert thanked the President but, knowing Stanton's views, and that Grant had been induced to decline, told the President he could not accept because the work which the Secretary referred to must be done that evening, and could not be put off.

"Very well," Lincoln then said, "I shall take Major Rathbone along, because Stanton insists upon having someone to protect me; but I should much rather have you, Major, since I know you can break a poker over your arm."

Grant sat that morning in his first session with a President and a Cabinet. One subject, wrote Welles, was "the relations of the Rebels, the communications, the trade, etc.," how to again set trade moving smoothly. "Stanton proposed that intercourse should be opened by *his* issuing an order, that the Treasury would give permits to all who wished them to trade, excluding contraband, and he, Stanton, was to order the vessels to be received into any port." Welles saw Stanton in this as having too wide a hand over the navy. "I suggested that it would be better that the President should issue a proclamation stating and enjoining the course to be pursued by the several Departments."

Those war-zone travelers known as "Treasury agents" came up for discussion as to what should be done with them. "McCulloch," wrote Welles, "expressed a willingness to be relieved of the Treasury agents. General Grant expressed himself very decidedly against them; thought them demoralizing, etc. The President said we, *i.e.* the Secretaries of the Treasury, War, and Navy, had given the subject more attention than he had, and he would be satisfied with any conclusion we would unite upon."

Stanton requested the Cabinet to hear a plan he had drafted, "after a great deal of reflection, for reconstruction in the Rebel States." The first section dealt with assertion of Federal authority in Virginia. Welles favored it with slight changes. The second section, for re-establishing a State government, was not so good, in Welles's view, being "in conflict with the principles of self-government which I deem essential." Little was said on this. "The understanding was that we should each be furnished with a copy for criticism and suggestion, and in the mean time we were requested by the President to deliberate and carefully consider the proposition."

Noted Welles of the President as to this point of State self-government: "He remarked that this was the great question now before us, and we must soon begin to act. Was glad Congress was not in session."

Then came three interesting paragraphs in Welles's diary of this day. Welles gave the Cabinet his candid views about reconstruction in Virginia. And with these views the President agreed. And Dennison and Stanton agreed on one essential, and implied they agreed in the main, with what the President wanted in Virginia. Of the other Cabinet members Welles recorded nothing, which would in all probability mean that no one spoke any opposition, that the President had a Cabinet in harmony with him on the outlines of his immediate projects. He had seen his Cabinet divided against him so often, had seen it unanimously reject his February proposal of $400,000,000 for compensation to slaveholders, that this unity was heart-warming. Welles recorded:

"I objected that Virginia occupied a different position from that of any other State in rebellion; that while regular State governments were to be established in other States, whose Secession governments were nullities and would not be recognized, Virginia had a skeleton organization which she had maintained through the War, which government we had recognized and still recognized; that we to-day acknowledged Pierpont as the legitimate Governor of Virginia. He had been elected by only a few border counties, it was true; had never been able to enforce his authority over but a small portion of the territory or population; nevertheless we had recognized and sustained him.

"The President said the point was well taken. Governor Dennison said he thought we should experience little difficulty from Pierpont. Stanton said none whatever.

"I remarked the fact was not to be controverted that we had treated with the existing government and could not ignore our own acts. The President and a portion of the Cabinet had, in establishing the new State of West Virginia, recognized the validity of the government of Virginia and of Pierpont's administration, which had given its assent to that division. Without that consent no division could legally have taken place. I had differed with others in that matter, but consistency and the validity of our own act required us to continue to acknowledge the existing government. It was proper we should enforce the Federal authority, and it was proper we should aid Governor Pierpont, whose government was recognized and established. In North Carolina a legal government was now to be organized and the State reëstablished in her proper relations to the Union."

What Welles wrote in his diary of this Cabinet-room scene he later amplified in a magazine article. Nicolay and Hay, so rigidly scrupulous about accuracy in quoting the President, found this account of the day's conversation "candid and trustworthy." The President's comment on Stanton's plan for re-establishing law and order and new State governments in the South led off by saying that the plan embodied substantially, though not wholly, the result of frequent discussions in the Cabinet. Changing Welles's report from the third person to the first, Lincoln said:

"I think it providential that this great rebellion is crushed just as Congress has adjourned and there are none of the disturbing elements of that body to hinder and embarrass us. If we are wise and discreet we shall reanimate the States and get their governments in successful operation, with order prevailing and the Union reëstablished before Congress comes together in December. . . .

"I hope there will be no persecution, no bloody work after the war is over. No one need expect me to take any part in hanging or killing those men, even the worst of them.

"Frighten them out of the country, open the gates, let down the bars, scare them off"—throwing up his hands as if scaring sheep. "Enough lives have been sacrificed.

"We must extinguish our resentments if we expect harmony and reunion. There is too much of a desire on the part of some of our very good friends to be masters, to interfere with and dictate to those States, to treat the people not as fellow-citizens; there is too little respect for their rights."

He regretted that suffrage, under proper arrangement, had not been given to Negroes in Louisiana, but he held that her constitution was in the main a good one. He was averse to the exercise of arbitrary powers by the Executive or by Congress. Congress had the power to receive or reject members; the Executive had no control in this; but the Executive could do very much to restore order in the States, and their practical relations with the Government, before Congress came together.

After Welles and Dennison had opposed Stanton's proposal to unite the States of Virginia and North Carolina under one government, the President closed the session by saying the same objection had occurred to him, directing Stanton to revise the document and report separate plans for the government of the two States. He did not wish the autonomy nor the individuality of the States destroyed. He commended the whole subject to the most earnest and careful consideration of the Cabinet; it was to be resumed on the following Tuesday; it was, he said, the great question pending—they must now begin to act in the interest of peace.

Early in this Good Friday session of the Cabinet curiosity was sharp about army news and particularly, "Has anything been heard from Sherman?" Stanton had not arrived. Grant said he was hourly expecting to hear from Sherman. Came a response from Lincoln. He had no news. But he had a dream. He contributed his dream as having significance. Wrote Welles:

"The President remarked it would, he had no doubt, come soon, and come favorable, for he had last night the usual dream which he had preceding nearly every great and important event of the War. Generally the news had been favorable which succeeded this dream, and the dream itself was always the same. I inquired what this remarkable dream could be. He said it related to your (my) element, the water; that he seemed to be in some singular, indescribable vessel, and that he was moving with great rapidity towards an indefinite shore; that he had this dream preceding Sumter, Bull Run, Antietam, Gettysburg, Stone River, Vicksburg, Wilmington, etc. General Grant said Stone River was certainly no victory, and he knew of no great results which followed from it. The President said however that might be, his dream preceded that fight.

" 'I had,' the President remarked, 'this strange dream again last night, and we shall, judging from the past, have great news very soon. I think it must be from Sherman. My thoughts are in that direction, as are most of yours.' "

Young Frederick Seward attended this Cabinet meeting as Acting Secretary of State in place of his father, who still lay abed with a broken jaw and his face in a steel frame. Young Seward's account of the session agreed basically with that of Welles, though adding details that escaped Welles. "Visible relief and content" was on the President's face as he sat by a south window while the members were arriving, chatting over "the great news" from which none had as yet recovered. Curiosity was spoken about the "rebel" leaders. Would they escape? Would they be caught and tried, and if so, what would be the penalties? "All those present thought that, for the sake of general amity and good will, it was desirable to have as few judicial proceedings as possible. Yet would it be wise to let the leaders in treason go entirely unpunished?" Mr. Speed remarked that it would be a difficult problem if it should occur.

"I suppose, Mr. President," said Postmaster General Dennison, "you would not be sorry to have them escape out of the country?"

"Well," came a slow answer, "I should not be sorry to have them out of the country; but I should be for following them up pretty close, to make sure of their going."

Young Seward wrote of Lincoln describing a phenomenon during sleep. "Mr. Lincoln remarked that a peculiar dream of the previous night was one that had occurred several times in his life,—a vague sense of floating—floating away on some vast and indistinct expanse, toward an unknown shore. The dream itself was not so strange as the coincidence that each of its previous occurrences had been followed by some important event or disaster, which he mentioned."

There were comments. One thought it merely coincidence. Another laughed. "At any rate it cannot presage a victory or defeat this time, for the war is over."

Young Seward suggested, "Perhaps at each of these periods there were possibilities of great change or disaster, and the vague feeling of uncertainty may have led to the dim vision in sleep."

"Perhaps," said Lincoln thoughtfully, "perhaps that is the explanation."

After Grant had arrived and heard welcomes and congratulations, he told briefly the incidents of Lee's surrender. Seward quoted the President asking, "What terms did you make for the common soldiers?" Grant: "I told them to go back to their homes and families, and they would not be molested, if they did nothing more."

Several tangled questions arose as to various details of any new State government, Seward hearing the President remark: "We can't undertake to run State governments in all these Southern States. Their people must do that—though I reckon that at first some of them may do it badly."

Young Seward's picture of reconstruction, what he took to be the general impression of the main work ahead as gathered from the outline drafted by Stanton and read to the Cabinet, actually was a sketch of the colossal hydra-headed United States Government reversing its war functions and stepping in on a peace job of vast ramifications. Seward wrote:

"In substance it was, that the Treasury Department should take possession of the custom houses, and proceed to collect the revenues; that the War Department should garrison or destroy the forts; that the Navy Department should, in like manner, occupy the harbours, take possession of navy yards, ships, and ordnance; that the Interior Department should send out its surveyors, land, pension, and Indian agents and set them at work; that the Postmaster-General should reopen his post-offices and re-establish his mail routes; that the Attorney-General should look after the re-establishment of the Federal courts, with their judges, marshals, and attorneys: in short, that the machinery of the United States Government should be set in motion; that its laws should be faithfully observed and enforced; that anything like domestic violence or insurrection should be repressed; but that public authorities and private citizens should remain unmolested, if not found in actual hostility to the Government of the Union."

In this two-hour Cabinet session, wrote Seward, were no rifts in the lute, not one sour note, pitch and tempo excellent. "Kindly feeling toward the vanquished, and hearty desire to restore peace and safety at the South, with as little harm as possible to the feelings or property of the inhabitants, pervaded the whole discussion."

So the Cabinet session of Friday, April 14, came to an end with the expectation that four days would pass and on Tuesday, April 18, again they would meet and resume discussion of how to bind up the nation's wounds, of how "to do all which may achieve and cherish a just and lasting peace among ourselves, and with all nations."

Bidding good-by to Hugh McCulloch leaving the White House, the President said, "We must look to you, Mr. Secretary, for the money to pay off the soldiers." McCulloch said he should look to the people. "They have not failed us thus far, and I don't think they will now."

A new British Minister, Sir Frederick Bruce, had arrived in Washington and was awaiting presentation to the President. Young Seward mentioned it. At what time the next day would it be convenient? Lincoln paused a moment, then: "Tomorrow at two o'clock?" Seward supposed it would be in the Blue Room. "Yes, in the Blue Room," said Lincoln, who seemed to picture himself reading to the new British Minister the stilted formal address handed him by the State Department to vocalize on such an occasion, adding with a wrinkle of comedy: "Don't forget to send up the speeches beforehand. I would like to look them over."

Chaplain Neill came to Lincoln's office with a Vermont colonel seeking a brigadier general's commission Lincoln had signed. The President had not returned from lunch. Neill was looking among papers on the President's desk. The President came in eating an apple. "I told him for what I was looking," wrote Neill of this, "and as I talked he placed his hand on the bell-pull, when I said, 'For whom are you going to ring?' Placing his hand upon my coat, he spoke but two words,—'Andrew Johnson.' Then I said, 'I will come in again.' As I was leaving the room the Vice-President had been ushered in, and the President advanced and took him by the hand." Seldom had Lincoln and Johnson met. Few were their communications. Definitely Lincoln had on several occasions avoided a conference sought by Johnson. Flauntingly on their inaugural day Johnson had put stress on himself as a plebeian as though Lincoln were not equally plebeian, log-cabin, mudsill, poor white. Now they consulted. Before Johnson left Lincoln would have sounded and fathomed him on immediate issues.

To one caller President Lincoln "expressed himself warmly" toward his Vice President, reported the *New York Evening Post*, quoting Lincoln as saying of Johnson, "He is too much of a man for the American people to cast him off for a single error."

A black woman faint from hunger and a five-mile walk arrived at the

White House gate, where the guards queried with a grin, "Business with the President?" and heard her grimly: "Befo' Gawd, yes."

"Let her pass—they'll stop her further on," she heard one guard say as she took a deep breath and went on. The main-entrance guard stopped her: "No further, madam. Against orders." In a flash she darted under his arm and went straight to the guard at the farther door.

"Fo' Gawd's sake, please lemme see Mistah Lincoln."

"Madam, the President is busy. He can not see you."

Either a cry she gave or the little tumult of her coming had reached in-side the White House, because, as she afterward related: "All of a sudden de do' open, and Mistah Lincoln hissef stood lookin' at me. I knowed him, fo' dar wuz a whimsy smile on his blessed face, an' he wuz a sayin' deep and sof'-like, 'There is time for all who need me. Let the good woman come in.'"

He heard Nancy Bushrod tell of her life with her husband Tom, how they were slaves on the old Harwood plantation near Richmond till the Emancipation Proclamation brought them to Washington. Tom joined a regiment with the Army of the Potomac, leaving Nancy with twin boys and a baby girl. At first his pay kept coming every month. Then it stopped. The soldiers were behind in pay from the Government. She had tramped seeking work but Washington was overrun with Negro help. Could the President help her get Tom's pay?

He heard her through and, according to Nancy, told her: "You are en-titled to your soldier-husband's pay. Come this time tomorrow and the papers will be signed and ready for you." And as Nancy told it, "I couldn't open my mouf to tell him how I'se gwine 'membah him fo'evah fer dem words, an' I couldn't see him kase de tears wuz fallin'."

He called her back. "My good woman, perhaps you'll see many a day when all the food in the house is a single loaf of bread. Even so, give every child a slice and send your children off to school." With that, the President bowed "lak I wuz a natchral bawn lady."

Assistant Secretary of War Dana called. He had a report from the Pro-vost Marshal of Portland, Maine, saying that Jacob Thompson, the Confed-erate commissioner in Canada who had fomented raids, explosions, and vari-ous disorders in the Great Lakes region, was to arrive in Portland this night of April 14 for the purpose of taking a steamer for Liverpool. Dana had carried the telegram to Stanton, who said promptly, "Arrest him!" Dana was leaving the room when Stanton called him back and said, "No, wait; better go over and see the President." It was now between four and five o'clock in the afternoon, regular business at the White House completed for the day. Dana found Lincoln with his coat off in a closet attached to the office, washing his hands.

"Halloo, Dana!" said the President as Dana opened the closet door. "What is it now?"

"Well, sir, here is the Provost Marshal of Portland, who reports that Jacob Thompson is to be in that town to-night, and inquires what orders we have to give."

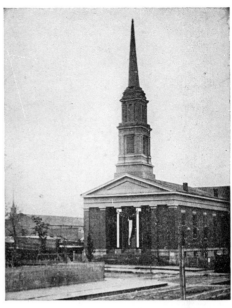

New York Avenue Presbyterian Church

Phineas Densmore Gurley, pastor of the New York Avenue Presbyterian Church, where Lincoln regularly attended services and had a family pew

Lincoln, probably early '65. Photograph by a Treasury Department official, F. H. Walker.

The mistress of the White House, often termed "The First Lady of the Land"

Autographed daguerreotype of Junius Brutus Booth, thirty years America's pre-eminent
Shakespearean actor

Original in the Barrett collection

"What does Stanton say?"

"Arrest him."

"Well," continued Lincoln, drawling the words, "no, I rather think not. When you have an elephant by the hind leg, and he's trying to run away, it's best to let him run."

This answer Dana carried back to the War Department, which on Stanton's wish sent no instructions at all to Portland. No reply was sent this day to the Provost Marshal's anxious inquiry. If the Marshal on his own initiative should make the arrest, Stanton would have Thompson where he wanted him—without having ordered the arrest.

A long carriage drive this afternoon made an interlude away from the incessant White House pressure. Mrs. Lincoln told Crook, Arnold, and others later of her query whether some friends should be invited for this drive and Lincoln saying No, he wanted "just ourselves." As the carriage rolled along he talked about the next four years in Washington, how he hoped afterward perhaps for a trip abroad, then a return to Springfield, perhaps law practice and a prairie farm on the banks of the Sangamon. Mrs. Lincoln spoke too of a happiness moving him, a happiness so strange and unusual that she could not read it, and it troubled her. She quoted him as saying, "I never felt so happy in my life," and a fear crossing her as she replied, "Don't you remember feeling just so before our little boy died?"

Walking over to the War Department late this afternoon of April 14, Lincoln did one thing he was rarely known to do. It was perhaps the first time he ever did this thing. Always, it seemed, others brought up the matter of possible harm to come to him—and he laughed them off or promised to take care. In this instance it was Lincoln who first mentioned it, according to Crook's account.

They passed some drunken men, profane, violent, irresponsible. And Lincoln turned, saying, "Crook, do you know, I believe there are men who want to take my life?" And after a pause, half to himself, "And I have no doubt they will do it."

Crook wanted to protest, but Lincoln's tone was so calm and sure that Crook found himself saying, "Why do you think so, Mr. President?"

"Other men have been assassinated"—this still in the manner of half talking to himself.

"I hope you are mistaken, Mr. President," offered Crook. And after a few paces in silence, Lincoln in a more ordinary tone: "I have perfect confidence in those who are around me—in every one of you men. I know no one could do it and escape alive. But if it is to be done, it is impossible to prevent it."

After a short conference in Stanton's office Lincoln came out, Crook noticing that the "depression" or "intense seriousness" had passed. "He talked to me as usual." Of the theatre party planned by Mrs. Lincoln for the evening he said: "It has been advertised that we will be there, and I cannot disappoint the people. Otherwise I would not go. I do not want to go." This surprised Crook, who knew well the ease and enjoyment Lincoln usually found at the theatre. So Crook meditated, "It seems unusual to hear him say he does not want to go tonight." At the White House door he stood facing his guard a moment and then, "Good-bye, Crook." This puzzled Crook somewhat. Until then it had always been "Good-night, Crook."

At the White House Congressman Samuel Shellabarger of Ohio pleasantly asked that one of his constituents might be appointed to a staff position in the army. Lincoln pleasantly said he was reminded of when he was a young man in Illinois and a woman in the neighborhood made shirts. "An Irishman went to her and ordered a white shirt for some special function. The woman made it, and laundered it and sent it to her customer. When he got it the Irishman found the shirt had been starched all the way around, instead of only in the bosom, and he returned it with the remark that he didn't want a shirt that was all collar. The trouble with you, Shellabarger, is that you want the army all staff and no army." Thus Shellabarger told it to his Buckeye friend J. Warren Keifer.

Dick Oglesby, the new Governor of Illinois, and Dick Yates, the new United States Senator from Illinois, had an evening hour at the White House with Lincoln. They were home folks. Oglesby was salty and Yates convivial. Lincoln read to them, horseplay humor, from the latest outpouring of Petroleum Vesuvius Nasby, said Oglesby, perhaps including a letter dated April 10 wherein the satirist took his fling as follows: "I survived the defeet uv Micklellan (who wuz, trooly, the nashen's hope and pride likewise), becoz I felt assoored that the rane uv the Goriller Linkin wood be a short wun; that in a few months, at furthest, Ginral Lee wood capcher Washinton, depose the ape, and set up there a constooshnal guverment, based upon the great and immutable trooth that a white man is better than a nigger." The Confederates had "consentratid" and lost their capital. "Linkin rides into Richmond! A Illinois rale-splitter, a buffoon, a ape, a goriller, a smutty joker, sets hisself down in President Davis's cheer, and rites dispatchis! . . . This ends the chapter. The Confederasy hez at last consentratid its last consentrate. It's ded. It's gathered up its feet, sed its last words, and deceest. . . . Linkin will serve his term out—the tax on whisky won't be repeeled—our leaders will die off uv chagrin, and delirium tremens and inability to live so long out uv offis, and the sheep will be skattered. Farewell, vane world." This extravaganza rested Lincoln. It had the flavor Oglesby liked. And Yates could take it.

After dinner Speaker Colfax called by appointment. He asked whether the President intended to call an extra session of Congress during the summer. The President assured him he had no such intention. This left Colfax free for a trip to the West Coast. Lincoln gave him a message to the mountain regions that their gold and silver mines must count in a coming peace prosperity.

Colfax spoke of how uneasy all had been over his going to Richmond and taking risks amid the tumult there. "He replied," noted Colfax, "pleasantly and with a smile (I quote his exact words), 'Why, if anyone else had been President and gone to Richmond, I would have been alarmed too; but I was not scared about myself a bit.' "

Congressman George Ashmun of Massachusetts waited below, said a card brought in. A loyal party man, presiding chairman of the 1860 convention that had nominated Lincoln for President, he was entitled to a hearing. One published report assumed to give concretely the gist of their interview. Ashmun spoke for a client of his who had a cotton claim against the Government and he desired a "commission" appointed to examine and decide on the merits of the case. Lincoln was quoted as replying rather warmly: "I have done with 'commissions.' I believe they are contrivances to cheat the Government out of every pound of cotton they can lay their hands on." Ashmun's face flushed. He answered that he hoped the President meant no personal imputation. Lincoln saw that his sudden and sharp comment on such "commissions" had been taken as personal and he had wounded a good friend, instantly saying: "You did not understand me, Ashmun. I did not mean what you inferred. I take it all back." He would see Ashmun first of all callers on the docket the next morning, and taking a card, wrote:

> April 14, 1865.
> Allow Mr. Ashmun
> & friend to come in
> at 9 A.M. tomor-
> row—
> A. Lincoln

They joined Colfax, Mrs. Lincoln, and Noah Brooks. Lincoln mentioned to Colfax the gavel of the Confederate Congress at Richmond which Sumner had taken to hand to the Secretary of War. "I insisted then that he must give it to you. You tell him for me to hand it over."

The President, ran Brooks's impression, had no enthusiasm about the play for the evening, felt "inclined to give up the whole thing," Brooks quoted him, but hearing that the party had been advertised, consented to go "rather than that people should be disappointed." He was unusually cheerful, thought Brooks, "never more hopeful and buoyant concerning the condition of the country, full of fun and anecdotes." The party stepped out on the White House portico, Lincoln going toward the carriage, saying, "Grant thinks we can reduce the cost of the army establishment at least a half million a day, which, with the reduction of expenditures of the navy, will soon bring down our national debt to something like decent proportions, and bring our national paper up to a par, or nearly so, with gold—at least so they think."

Good old Isaac N. Arnold of Chicago came along, mentioned his errand as Lincoln was stepping into the carriage, and was answered, "Excuse me now. I am going to the theater. Come and see me in the morning."

From the carriage window as they drove away Lincoln had a final casual glance at the White House where he had lived four years and forty-one days.

CHAPTER 73

BLOOD ON THE MOON

And I looked, and behold a pale horse:
and his name that sat on him was Death.
REVELATION 6:8

IN the carriage into which the President and his wife stepped was a be-trothed couple. Henry Reed Rathbone, assigned by Stanton to accompany the President, had brought along his fiancée, Miss Clara Harris. For them the future was bright this evening. He was twenty-eight years old, of a well-to-do clan of Rathbones at Albany, New York, a major of volunteers since November of '62, a trusted War Office attaché. His sweetheart was the daughter of Judge Ira Harris of Albany, since 1861 United States Senator from New York, a lecturer on law in the Columbian College of Washington, D.C., and an officer of the American Baptist Missionary Union and other religious bodies.

The bodyguard in whose line of duty it fell to be with the President this evening was John F. Parker. He was one of four officers detailed from the Metropolitan Police Force of the city for White House duty in watch-ing the President—or rather in staying close to the President and keeping a sharp eye on the hands, the possibly wayward hands, of anyone who might have designs on the life and person of the President. Of these four guards only one, it afterward appeared, had a questionable record—and he was John F. Parker. On this evening he was thirty-five years old lacking one month; born in Frederick County, Virginia, he had worked at the carpenter's trade in Washington, enlisted in the army as a three-months man, in '61 joining the Metropolitan Police as a patrolman. At his home on 750 L Street he had then a wife and three children. Thus far the known record showed good behavior. On October 14 of '62 he was put on trial, the Police Board finding he had been profane and insolent to the owner of a grocery store who com-plained of patrolmen loafing in front of his place of business, had used "dis-respectful" language to a superior officer in a way that if continued "must lead to insubordination." For this he was reprimanded and transferred to another precinct.

In March and April of '63 John F. Parker was on trial on various charges: of being found asleep on a streetcar when he should have been patrolling his beat; of conduct unbecoming an officer through five weeks of residence in a house of prostitution, where it was alleged he had been drunk, had been put to bed, had fired a revolver through a window; the board found he was "at a house of ill fame with no other excuse than that he was sent for by the Keeper (Miss Annie Wilson)," although there was "no evidence that there was any robbery there or disturbance of the peace or quiet of that neighborhood." And though in addition Parker was charged with willful violation of the police rules and regulations, having again used highly offensive language toward a superior officer, the board took no action—and within three months heard testimony that he had used insulting language to a lady who complained of the conduct of Negroes in her neighborhood as disorderly. The list of trials, the repeated similar charges against Parker, the board's own language about his conduct, and the findings in the evidence did not merely indicate but showed conclusively that he was slack rather than vigilant, of loose habits rather than a steady reliable man, a cheap and slipshod specimen of a police officer rather than a sober and dependable operative for highly responsible work.

How Parker found his way into the White House to begin with was not clear in the records. On April 3, however, when he was drafted for army service, Mrs. Lincoln on Executive Mansion stationery had written to the District of Columbia Provost Marshal, James R. O'Beirne, a certificate "that John F. Parker . . . has been detailed for duty at the Executive Mansion by order of [signed] Mrs. Lincoln."

This was the drab, well-meaning, lackadaisical, muddle-headed wanderer who was to have a role this evening of April 14, enacting the part of a strange cipher—a weird and elusive Mr. Nobody-at-All—a player of a negation. For this night he would distinguish himself as the world's foremost and vacant-minded Naught. He had eyes to see not, ears to hear not—and political pull.

Tom Pendel, who had been advanced from guard to doorkeeper, noted of this time when the President's carriage was about to leave for the theatre: "Previous to starting, I said to John Parker, who had taken my place, to accompany Mr. Lincoln, 'John, are you prepared?' I meant by this to ask if he had his revolver and everything all ready to protect the President in case of an assault. Alfonso Dunn, my companion at the door, spoke up and said, 'Oh, Tommy, there is no danger.' I said, 'Dunn, you don't know what might happen. Parker, now you start down to the theater, to be ready for the President when he reaches there. And you see him safe inside.' He started off immediately."

Cold, raw weather, gusty and changeable, met those who stepped from indoor comfort the afternoon and evening of this April 14. A ceiling of clouds hung low, mist and fog held the streets, and occasional showers had put a chill and a pervasive damp on the air. In the daytime hours no one could throw a shadow from the sun and in the nighttime away from street lamps the walking men became blurred humps. The evening lighted windows and the corner gas jets formed vague lumps of light, dim agglutinates of light; the world between sky and ground lacked firm ceiling and had an uncertain floor. Oblongs of yellow stretching from home windows soon lost their cubical angles and merged into black and gray nothings of night, into a cavern of vague footings. Had there been a full golden moon streaming down with a spacious flow into a clear air, doorways and doorknobs would have been more clear-cut, less noncommittal and secretive, not so much like faces wearing a blank look of nothing to say, nothing worth telling. Whether at mansion of brick with its tall windows and glass chandeliers of victory illumination or among huddled alleyway huts and shanties where they economized on candles, the covering shawl of night was anonymous and indecisive. The moving shapes of the moist nocturne lacked edge and clarity of line in man and horse, wagon and wheels, roving patrols, and Pennsylvania Avenue's two blurred zigzag paths of lighted gas lamps and the dark ghost of the illuminated Capitol dome.

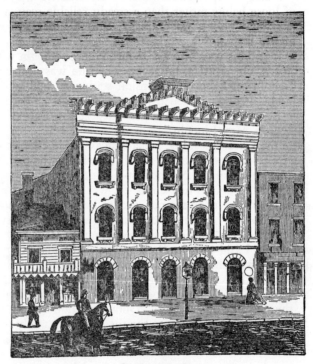

Ford's Theatre

The carriage left the White House with its four occupants, with the coachman Francis Burns holding the reins, and alongside him the footman and valet Charles Forbes. Burns spoke to the horses. They moved off. No sudden news came. No circumstance delayed or hindered. Out of the gates of the White House grounds they rode. No telegram of commanding importance suddenly found itself in the President's hands. No imperative word arrived that might have held him at the Executive Mansion where his immediate decision was required. Nothing happened to cancel the theatre date of the evening. News that a fire had swept away the whole block where Ford's Theatre stood—no such news came. Out of the gates they drove. And the horses obeyed the reins and took the vehicle over the cobblestones and accepted the evening as one having oats and harness duty: they did not take the bits in their teeth and crash the carriage in imitation of Seward's blooded steeds nine days before.

Through the carriage window before they turned one corner Lincoln by leaning forward could see the mystic Capitol dome in a haze of light, a floating mid-air symbol of the Union of States.

On Tenth Street between E Street and F, at Ford's Theatre, Burns pulled up his horses. Forbes swung down to the sidewalk and opened the carriage door. The President and his wife stepped out, followed by Major Rathbone

Ford's Opera House!

JOHN T. FORD, PROPRIETOR.

ADMISSION TICKET 50 C.

HANZSCHE & C? PRINT

Ticket used on the night of April 14, 1865. From the Barrett collection.

and Miss Harris. The guard John F. Parker was at hand. The party walked into the theatre at about nine o'clock. An usher led them toward their box. The audience in their one thousand seats saw or heard that the President had arrived. They applauded with handclapping. Many rose from their seats. Some cheered. The President paused and nodded his acknowledgments of their welcome to him.

As the President and his party had entered, Miss Keene as the English cousin Florence Trenchard, and the slow-witted Lord Dundreary had spoken lines about a window-*draught*, a doctor's prescription or *draught* which cured a cold, and a check or *draft* paid the doctor, Florence saying: "Good gracious! what a number of draughts. You have almost a game of draughts."

DUNDREARY. Ha! ha! ha!
FLORENCE. What's the matter?
DUNDREARY. That wath a joke, that wath.

About here Miss Keene interpolated, "The draft has been suspended," and while Dundreary was saying he couldn't see the joke, Miss Keene's eye caught sight of the President and she flung out the impromptu, "Well, anybody can see that!" The audience approved the grace and readiness of this. It made a nice punctuation and signal for the applause given to the President and his party, who went up a stair, through the dress-circle aisle and the little hallway, before entering their box.

They are entering the box about where Lord Dundreary has seen through a joke again and is screaming, "Ha! ha! ha!"

ALL. What's the matter?
DUNDREARY. Why, that wath a joke, that wath.
FLORENCE. Where was the joke?
DUNDREARY. Especially, ha! ha!

Major Rathbone and Miss Harris, seated toward the front of the box, are in view of the larger part of the audience. Mrs. Lincoln, seated farther back, is seen by less of the audience. The President, slouched back in comfort in a roomy haircloth rocking chair with arm rests, has at his left a part of a wall and a curtain. These hide him from almost the entire audience.

On the stage proceeds a play written fourteen years before by the English dramatist Tom Taylor, who decided on rehearsal that it was not for the British public. Later Taylor had sent it to the New York producer Lester Wallack, who had told Laura Keene it would fit her. She had put it on, but after a fairly good run it has about reached its limit. Lincoln from his roomy armchair shortly after being seated, if listening, is probably mildly interested in these lines:

DUNDREARY. Miss Florence, will you be kind enough to tell Miss Georgina all about that American relative of yours.
FLORENCE. Oh, about my American cousin; certainly. (*Aside to* HARRY.) Let's have some fun. Well, he's about seventeen feet high.
DUNDREARY. Good gracious! Seventeen feet high!
FLORENCE. They are all seventeen feet high in America, ain't they, Mr. Vernon?
VERNON. Yes, that's about the average height.
FLORENCE. And they have long black hair that reaches down to their heels; they have dark copper-colored skin, and they fight with— What do they fight with, Mr. Vernon?
VERNON. Tomahawks and scalping knives.
FLORENCE. Yes; and you'd better take care, Miss Georgina, or he'll take his toma-hawk and scalping knife and scalp you immediately.
[GEORGINA *screams and faints.*]
DUNDREARY. Here, somebody get something and throw over her; a pail of water; no, not that, she's pale enough already. (*Fans her with handkerchief.*) Georgina, don't be afraid. Dundreary's by your side, he will protect you.
FLORENCE. Don't be frightened, Georgina. He will never harm you while Dundreary is about. Why, he could get three scalps here. (*Pulls* DUNDREARY'S *whiskers.* GEORGINA *screams.*)
DUNDREARY. Don't scream. I won't lose my whiskers. I know what I'll do for my own safety. I will take this handkerchief and tie the roof of my head on. (*Ties it on.*)
FLORENCE (*pretending to cry*). Good-bye, Dundreary. I'll never see you again in all your glory.
DUNDREARY. Don't cry, Miss Florence, I'm ready for Mr. Tommy Hawk.

In a later scene the newly arrived Asa Trenchard meets his English cousin at her house, has called the servant Binny "this darned old shoat," and ordered him, "Hurry up, old hoss."

BINNY. He calls me a 'oss, Miss, I suppose I shall be a hox next, or perhaps an 'og

ASA. Wal, darn me, if you ain't the consarnedest old shoat I ever did see since I was baptized Asa Trenchard.

FLORENCE. Ah! then it is our American cousin. Glad to see you—my brother told us to expect you.

ASA. Wal, yes, I guess you do b'long to my family. I'm Asa Trenchard, born in Vermont, suckled on the banks of Muddy Creek, about the tallest gunner, the slickest dancer, and generally the loudest critter in the state. You're my cousin, be you? Wal, I ain't got no objections to kiss you, as one cousin ought to kiss another.

VERNON. Sir, how dare you?

ASA. Are you one of the family? Cause if you ain't, you've got no right to interfere, and if you be, you needn't be alarmed, I ain't going to kiss you.

The play proceeds, not unpleasant, often stupid, sprinkled with silly puns, drab and aimless dialogue, forced humor, characters neither truly English nor truly American nor fetching as caricatures. The story centers around the Yankee lighting his cigar with an old will, burning the document to ashes and thereby throwing a fortune of $400,000 away from himself into the hands of an English cousin. The mediocre comedy is somewhat redeemed by the way the players are doing it. The audience agrees it is not bad. The applause and laughter say the audience is having a good time.

Mrs. Lincoln sits close to her husband, at one moment leaning on him fondly, suddenly realizing they are not alone, saying with humor, "What will Miss Harris think of my hanging on to you so?" and hearing his: "She won't think anything about it."

From the upholstered rocking armchair in which Lincoln sits he can see only the persons in the box with him, the players on the stage, and any persons offstage on the left. The box on the opposite side of the theatre is empty. With the box wall at his back and the closely woven lace curtains at his left arm, he is screened from the audience at his back and from the musicians in the orchestra pit, which is below and partly behind him.

The box has two doors. Sometimes by a movable cross partition it is converted into two boxes, each having its door. The door forward is locked. For this evening the President's party has the roominess and convenience of double space, extra armchairs, side chairs, a small sofa. In the privacy achieved he is in sight only of his chosen companions, the actors he has come to see render a play, and the few people who may be offstage to the left.

This privacy however has a flaw. It is not as complete as it seems. A few feet behind the President is the box door, the only entry to the box unless by a climb from the stage. In this door is a small hole, bored that afternoon to serve as a peephole—from the outside. Through this peephole it is the intention of the Outsider who made it with a gimlet to stand and watch the President, then at a chosen moment to enter the box. This door opens from the box on a narrow hallway that leads to another door which opens on the balcony of the theatre.

Through these two doors the Outsider must pass in order to enter the President's box. Close to the door connecting with the balcony two inches of plaster have been cut from the brick wall of the narrow hallway. The intention of the Outsider is that a bar placed in this cut-away wall niche and then braced against the panel of the door will hold that door against intruders, will serve to stop anyone from interference with the Outsider while making his observations of the President through the gimleted hole in the box door.

At either of these doors, the one to the box or the one to the hallway, it is the assigned duty and expected responsibility of John F. Parker to stand or sit constantly and without fail. A Ward Lamon or an Eckert on this duty would probably have noticed the gimleted hole, the newly made wall niche, and been doubly watchful. If Lincoln believes what he told Crook that afternoon, that he trusted the men assigned to guard him, then as he sits in the upholstered rocking armchair in the box he believes that John F. Parker in steady fidelity is just outside the box door, in plain clothes ready with the revolver Pendel at the White House had told him to be sure to have with him.

In such a trust Lincoln is mistaken. Whatever dim fog of thought or duty may move John F. Parker in his best moments is not operating tonight. His life habit of never letting trouble trouble him is on him this night; his motive is to have no motive. He has always got along somehow. Why care about anything, why really care? He can always find good liquor and bad women. You take your fun as you find it. He can never be a somebody, so he will enjoy himself as a nobody—though he can't imagine how perfect a cipher, how completely the little end of nothing, one John F. Parker may appear as the result of one slack easygoing hour.

"The guard . . . acting as my substitute," wrote the faithful Crook later, "took his position at the rear of the box, close to an entrance leading into the box. . . . His orders were to stand there, fully armed, and to permit no unauthorized person to pass into the box. His orders were to stand there and protect the President at all hazards. From the spot where he was thus stationed, this guard could not see the stage or the actors; but he could hear the words the actors spoke, and he became so interested in them that, incredible as it may seem, he quietly deserted his post of duty, and walking down the dimly-lighted side aisle, deliberately took a seat."

The custom was for a chair to be placed in the narrow hallway for the guard to sit in. The doorkeeper Buckingham told Crook that such a chair was provided this evening for the accommodation of the guard. "Whether Parker occupied it at all, I do not know," wrote Crook. "Mr. Buckingham is of the impression that he did. If he did, he left it almost immediately, for he confessed to me the next day that he went to a seat, so that he could see the play." The door to the President's box is shut. It is not kept open so that the box occupants can see the guard on duty.

Either between acts or at some time when the play was not lively enough to suit him or because of an urge for a pony of whisky under his belt, John F. Parker leaves his seat in the balcony and goes down to the street and joins companions in a little whiff of liquor—this on the basis of a statement of the coachman Burns, who declared he stayed outside on the street with his carriage and horses, except for one interlude when "the special police officer [meaning John F. Parker] and the footman of the President [Forbes] came up to him and asked him to take a drink with them; which he did."

Thus circumstance favors the lurking and vigilant Outsider who in the afternoon gimleted a hole in the door of the President's box and cut a two-inch niche in a wall to brace a bar against a door panel and hold it against interference while he should operate.

The play goes on. The evening and the drama are much like many other evenings when the acting is pleasant enough, the play mediocre and so-so, the audience having no thrills of great performance but enjoying itself. The most excited man in the house, with little doubt, is the orchestra leader, Withers. He has left the pit and gone backstage, where, as he related, "I was giving the stage manager a piece of my mind. I had written a song for Laura Keene to sing. When she left it out I was mad. We had no cue, and the music was thrown out of gear. So I hurried round on the stage on my left to see what it was done for."

And of what is Abraham Lincoln thinking? As he leans back in this easy rocking chair, where does he roam in thought? If it is life he is thinking about, no one could fathom the subtle speculations and hazy reveries resulting from his fifty-six years of adventures drab and dazzling in life. Who had gone farther on so little to begin with? Who else as a living figure of republican government, of democracy, in practice, as a symbol touching freedom for all men—who else had gone farther over America, over the world? If it is death he is thinking about, who better than himself might interpret his dream that he lay in winding sheets on a catafalque in the White House and people were wringing their hands and crying "The President is dead!" —who could make clear this dream better than himself? Furthermore if it is death he is thinking about, has he not philosophized about it and dreamed about it and considered himself as a mark and a target until no one is better prepared than he for any sudden deed? Has he not a thousand times said to himself, and several times to friends and intimates, that he must accommodate himself to the thought of sudden death? Has he not wearied of the constructions placed on his secret night ride through Baltimore to escape a plot aimed at his death? Has he not laughed to the overhead night stars at a hole shot in his hat by a hidden marksman he never mentioned even to his boon companion Hill Lamon? And who can say but that Death is a friend, and who else should be more a familiar of Death than a man who has been the central figure of the bloodiest war ever known to the Human Family— who else should more appropriately and decently walk with Death? And who can say but Death is a friend and a nurse and a lover and a benefactor bringing peace and lasting reconciliation? The play tonight is stupid. Shake-speare would be better. "Duncan is in his grave . . . he sleeps well."

Yes, of what is Abraham Lincoln thinking? Draped before him in salute is a silk flag of the Union, a banner of the same design as the one at Inde-pendence Hall in Philadelphia in February of '61 which he pulled aloft say-ing, "I would rather be assassinated on this spot than surrender it," saying the flag in its very origins "gave promise that in due time the weights would be lifted from the shoulders of all men, and that all should have an equal chance." Possibly his mind recurs for a fleeting instant to that one line in his letter to a Boston widow woman: "the solemn pride that must be yours to have laid so costly a sacrifice upon the altar of freedom." Or a phrase from the Gettysburg speech: "we here highly resolve that these dead shall not have died in vain."

Out in a main-floor seat enjoying the show is one Julia Adelaide Shep-hard, who wrote a letter to her father about this Good Friday evening at the theatre. "Cousin Julia has just told me," she reported, "that the Presi-dent is in yonder upper right hand private box so handsomely decked with silken flags festooned over a picture of George Washington. The young and lovely daughter of Senator Harris is the only one of his party we see as the flags hide the rest. But we know Father Abraham is there like a Father watching what interests his children, for their pleasure rather than his own. It had been announced in the papers he would be there. How sociable it seems like one family sitting around their parlor fire. Everyone has been so jubilant for days that they laugh and shout at every clownish witticism such is the excited state of the public mind. One of the actresses whose part is that of a very delicate young lady talks about wishing to avoid the draft when her lover tells her not to be alarmed 'for there is to be no more draft' at which the applause is loud and long. The American cousin has just been making love to a young lady who says she'll never marry but for love but when her mother and herself find out that he has lost his property they retreat in disgust at the left hand of the stage while the American cousin goes out at the right. We are waiting for the next scene."

And the next scene?

The next scene is to crash and blare and flare as one of the wildest, one of the most inconceivably fateful and chaotic, that ever stunned and shocked a world that heard the story.

The moment of high fate was not seen by the theatre audience. Only one man saw that moment. He was the Outsider. He was the one who had waited and lurked and made his preparations, planning and plotting that he should be the single and lone spectator of what happened. He had come through the outer door into the little hallway, fastened the strong though slender bar into the two-inch niche in the brick wall, and braced it against the door panel. He had moved softly to the box door and through the little hole he had gimleted that afternoon he had studied the box occupants and his Human Target seated in an upholstered rocking armchair. Softly he had opened the door and stepped toward his prey, in his right hand a one-shot brass derringer pistol, a little eight-ounce vest-pocket weapon winged for death, in his left hand a steel dagger. He was cool and precise and timed his every move. He raised the derringer, lengthened his right arm, ran his eye along the barrel in a line with the head of his victim less than five feet away—and pulled the trigger.

A lead ball somewhat less than a half-inch in diameter crashed into the left side of the head of the Human Target, into the back of the head, in a line with and three inches from the left ear. "The course of the ball was obliquely forward toward the right eye, crossing the brain in an oblique manner and lodging a few inches behind that eye. In the track of the wound were found fragments of bone, which had been driven forward by the ball, which was embedded in the anterior lobe of the left hemisphere of the brain."

For Abraham Lincoln it was lights out, good night, farewell and a long farewell to the good earth and its trees, its enjoyable companions, and the Union of States and the world Family of Man he had loved. He was not dead yet. He was to linger in dying. But the living man could never again speak nor see nor hear nor awaken into conscious being.

Near the prompt desk offstage stands W. J. Ferguson, an actor. He looks in the direction of a shot he hears, and sees "Mr. Lincoln lean back in his rocking chair, his head coming to rest against the wall which stood between him and the audience . . . well inside the curtains"—no struggle or move "save in the slight backward sway."

Of this the audience in their one thousand seats know nothing.

Major Rathbone leaps from his chair. Rushing at him with a knife is a strange human creature, terribly alive, a lithe wild animal, a tiger for speed, a wildcat of a man bareheaded, raven-haired—a smooth sinister face with glaring eyeballs. He wears a dark sack suit. He stabs straight at the heart of Rathbone, a fast and ugly lunge. Rathbone parries it with his upper right arm, which gets a deep slash of the dagger. Rathbone is staggered, reels back. The tigerish stranger mounts the box railing. Rathbone recovers, leaps again for the stranger, who feels the hand of Rathbone holding him back, slashes again at Rathbone, then leaps for the stage.

This is the moment the audience wonders whether something unusual is happening—or is it part of the play?

From the box railing the Strange Man leaps for the stage, perhaps a ten-foot fall. His leap is slightly interrupted. On this slight interruption the Strange Man in his fine calculations had not figured. The draped Union flag of silk reaches out and tangles itself in a spur of one riding-boot, throwing him out of control. He falls to the stage landing on his left leg, breaking the shinbone a little above the instep.

Of what he has done the audience as yet knows nothing. They wonder what this swift, raven-haired, wild-eyed Strange Man portends. They see him rush across the stage, three feet to a stride, and vanish. Some have heard Rathbone's cry "Stop that man!" Many have seen a man leap from a front seat up on the stage and chase after the weird Stranger, crying "Stop that man!"

It is a peculiar night, an odd evening, a little weird, says the audience to itself. The action is fast. It is less than half a minute since the Strange Man mounted the box railing, made the stage, and strode off.

Offstage between Laura Keene and W. J. Ferguson he dashes at break-neck speed, out of an entrance, forty feet to a little door opening on an alley. There stands a fast bay horse, a slow-witted chore boy nicknamed John Peanuts holding the reins. He kicks the boy, mounts the mare; hoofs on the cobblestones are heard but a few moments. In all it is maybe sixty or seventy seconds since he loosed the one shot of his eight-ounce brass der-ringer.

Whether the Strange Man now riding away on a fast bay horse had paused a moment on the stage and shouted a dramatic line of speech, there was disagreement afterward. Some said he ran off as though every second of time counted and his one purpose was escape. Others said he faced the audience a moment, brandished a dagger still bloody from slashing Rath-bone, and shouted the State motto of Virginia, the slogan of Brutus as he drove the assassin's knife into imperial Caesar: *"Sic semper tyrannis"*—"Thus be it ever to tyrants." Miss Shephard and others believed they heard him shriek as he brandished the dagger: "The South is avenged!" Others: "The South shall be free!" "Revenge!" "Freedom!"

Some said the lights went out in the theatre, others adding the detail that the assassin had stabbed the gasman and pulled the lever, throwing the house into darkness. Others a thousand miles from the theatre said they saw the moon come out from behind clouds blood-red. It is a night of many eye-witnesses, shaken and moaning eyewitnesses.

The audience is up and out of its one thousand seats, standing, moving. Panic is in the air, fear over what may happen next. Many merely stand up from their seats, fixed and motionless, waiting to hear what has happened, waiting to see what further is to happen. The question is spoken quietly or is murmured anxiously—"What is it? What has happened?" The question is bawled with anger, is yelled with anguish—"For God's sake, what is it? What has happened?"

A woman's scream pierces the air. Some say afterward it was Mrs. Lin-coln. The scream carries a shock and a creeping shiver to many hearing it. "He has shot the President!" Miss Shephard looks from the main floor to-ward the box and sees "Miss Harris wringing her hands and calling for water." There are moanings. "No, for God's sake, it can't be true—no! no! for God's sake!"

Men are swarming up to the edge of the stage, over the gas-jet footlights onto the stage. The aisles fill with people not sure where to go; to leave would be safe, but they want to know what has happened, what else they may see this wild night. Men are asking whether some God-damned fool has for sure tried to shoot the President. Others take it as true. The man who ran across the stage did it. There are cries: "Kill him! Shoot him!" On the stage now are policemen, army officers, soldiers, besides actors and actresses in make-up and costume. Cries for "Water! water!" Cries for "A surgeon! a surgeon!" Someone brings water. It is passed up to the box.

An army surgeon climbs to the stage and is lifted up and clambers over the railing into the box. Some two hundred soldiers arrive to clear the theatre. The wailing and the crazy chaos let down in the emptying play-house—and flare up again in the street outside, where some man is accused of saying he is glad it happened, a sudden little mob dragging him to a lamp-post with a ready rope to hang him when six policemen with clubs and drawn revolvers manage to get him away and put him in jail for safekeeping.

Mrs. Lincoln in the box has turned from the railing, has turned from where she saw the wild-eyed raven-haired man vanish off the stage, sees her husband seated in the rocking chair, his head slumped forward. Never before has she seen her husband so completely helpless, so strangely not himself. With little moaning cries she springs toward him and with her hands keeps him from tumbling to the floor. Major Rathbone has shouted for a surgeon, has run out of the box into the narrow hallway, and with one arm bleeding and burning with pain he fumbles to unfasten the bar between wall and door panel. An usher from the outside tries to help him. They get the bar loose. Back of the usher is a jam of people. He holds them back, allowing only one man to enter.

This is a young-looking man, twenty-three years old, with mustache and sideburns, Charles A. Leale, assistant surgeon, United States Volunteers, who had left the army General Hospital at Armory Square, where he was in charge of the wounded commissioned officers' ward, saying he would be gone only a short time. Rathbone shows Dr. Leale his bleeding arm, "be-seeching me to attend to his wound," related Leale later. "I placed my hand under his chin, looking into his eyes an almost instantaneous glance revealed the fact that he was in no immediate danger, and in response to appeals from Mrs. Lincoln and Miss Harris, who were standing by the high-backed arm-chair in which President Lincoln sat, I went immediately to their assistance, saying I was a United States army surgeon."

Leale holds Mrs. Lincoln's outstretched hand while she cries piteously: "Oh, Doctor! Is he dead? Can he recover? Will you take charge of him? Do what you can for him. Oh, my dear husband! my dear husband!" He soothes her a little, telling her he will do all that can possibly be done.

The body in the chair at first scrutiny seems to be that of a dead man, eyes closed, no certainty it is breathing. Dr. Leale with help from others lifts the body from the chair and moves it to a lying position on the floor. He holds the head and shoulders while doing this, his hand meeting a clot of blood near the left shoulder. Dr. Leale recalls seeing a dagger flashed by the assassin on the stage and the knife wound of Rathbone, and now sup-poses the President has a stab wound. He has the coat and shirt slit open, thinking to check perhaps a hemorrhage. He finds no wounds. He lifts the eyelids and sees evidence of a brain injury. He rapidly passes the separated fingers of both hands through the blood-matted hair of the head, finding a

wound and removing a clot of blood, which relieves pressure on the brain
and brings shallow breathing and a weak pulse. "The assassin," Leale commented later . . . "had evidently planned to shoot to produce instant death,
as the wound he made was situated within two inches of the physiological
point of selection, when instant death is desired."

RESERVED

TAKEN.

Cards found on the floor of Lincoln's box, having bloodstains which engraving craft
could not reproduce. From the Barrett collection.

Dr. Leale bends over, puts a knee at each side of the body, and tries to
start the breathing apparatus, attempts to stimulate respiration by putting
his two fingers into the throat and pressing down and out on the base of the
tongue to free the larynx of secretion. Dr. Charles Sabin Taft, the army
surgeon lifted from the stage into the box, now arrives. Another physician,
Dr. Albert F. A. King, arrives. Leale asks them each to manipulate an arm
while he presses upward on the diaphragm and elsewhere to stimulate heart
action. The body responds with an improvement in the pulse and the irregular breathing.

Dr. Leale is sure, however, that with the shock and prostration the body
has undergone, more must now be done to keep life going. And as he told
it later: "I leaned forcibly forward directly over his body, thorax to thorax,
face to face, and several times drew in a long breath, then forcibly breathed
directly into his mouth and nostrils, which expanded his lungs and improved
his respirations. After waiting a moment I placed my ear over his thorax and
found the action of the heart improving. I arose to the erect kneeling pos-
ture, then watched for a short time and saw that the President could continue independent breathing and that instant death would not occur. I then
pronounced my diagnosis and prognosis: 'His wound is mortal; it is impossible for him to recover.'"

Brandy and water arrive. Dr. Leale slowly pours a small quantity into
the President's mouth. It is swallowed and retained.

More bystanders arrive. They are kindly and thoughtful. No one suggests anything or interferes in the slightest. Mrs. Lincoln sits near by in

Ford's Theatre

Alley and rear of
Ford's Theatre

The Outsider

The President's box, Ford's Theatre, on the
night of April 14, '65

From the Meserve collection

The President's
chair in the box
at the left

Edward Otho
Cresap Ord
and family
(*above*)

Julia Dent
Grant (Mrs.
Ulysses Simpson)
(*above*)

Henry Reed
Rathbone and
his fiancée,
Clara Harris
(*right*)

Edwin Booth, "America's foremost
Shakespearean actor"

Laura Keene, costumed for *Our American Cousin*

From the Meserve collection

quiet. Someone asking whether there is hope, Dr. Leale repeats "His wound is mortal; it is impossible for him to recover."

Dr. Leale speaks to the other physicians his desire that the President may be moved to the nearest house on the opposite side of the street. Several ask if the President cannot be taken to the White House. Dr. Leale replies, "If it is attempted the President will die long before we reach there." While they are waiting for the President to gain strength, wrote Leale later, Laura Keene "appealed to me to allow her to hold the President's head. I granted this request, and she sat on the floor of the box and held his head in her lap. We decided that the President could now be moved to a house where we might place him on a bed in safety."

Four soldiers from Thompson's Independent Battery C, Pennsylvania Light Artillery, lift the body by the trunk and legs, Dr. Taft carrying the right shoulder, Dr. King the left shoulder, Dr. Leale the head. They come to the door of the box. Dr. Leale sees the passageway packed with people. He calls out twice, "Guards, clear the passage!" A captain goes into action with troopers. They show muskets, bayonets, sabers. "Clear out!" rings the repeated order. "Clear out!" they cry to the curiosity-seekers, and to some who hesitate and still insist on blocking passage. "Clear out, you sons of bitches!"

Then the solemn little group with their precious freight carried head-first moves slowly through a space lined by protecting soldiers. At the stair head they shift so the feet are carried first. Two more soldiers join the original four in holding the body and moving it. As they go out of the door of the theatre Dr. Leale is again asked if the President can be taken to the White House and answers, "No, the President would die on the way."

Overhead is night sky. Clouds of dark gray unfold and unroll and show a blazing white moon and fold and roll and cover it again.

On Tenth Street between E Street and F in Washington humanity swirls and wonders and wants to know. "Is that the President they are carrying?" "Is it true that he was shot and will live?" "Oh, God, it can't be true!" "Where are they taking him?" "Who shot him?" "Was he stabbed or shot? I heard he was stabbed." "Was he shot bad or will he live?" "For God's sake, is there no chance for him?"

Packing Tenth Street straight across from the front door of Ford's Theatre is a crowd so massed that there is no hope of a path through for those carrying the President's body unless something is done. The same captain who had managed clearance inside the theatre comes to Leale: "Surgeon, give me your commands and I will see that they are obeyed." Leale asks the captain to clear a passage to the nearest house opposite. The captain draws a sword, commands the people to make an opening; they move back, and the procession begins its slow crossing. Several times they stop while Dr. Leale removes the newly gathered blood clots on the head wound. A barrier of men forms to keep back the crowds on each side of an open space leading to the house. Now comes the report that this house is closed. At the next house, Mr. Peterson's, No. 453 Tenth Street, Dr. Leale sees a man standing at the door with a lighted candle, beckoning them to come in. "This we did," ran Leale's account, "not having been interrupted in the slightest by the throngs in the street; but a number of the excited populace followed us into the house."

There they laid their stricken Friend of Man in the rented room of William Clark, a boarder in the house of William Peterson—on a plain wooden bed—at about 10:45 o'clock, somewhat less perhaps than a half-hour after the moment the trigger of the little eight-ounce derringer was pulled.

In a lingo of the common people, in a matter-of-fact speech not lacking salt and savor of truth and fact, one of the four Allegheny County, Pennsylvania, men in this mournful journey from the Ford's Theatre box to the room in the Peterson house, later told his story of that evening. This account

The Peterson house, opposite Ford's Theatre

had an authentic air and a queer finality. The four men had enlisted at Pittsburgh in February of '64 and had been present with their company every day from March of that year and on. The story of Jacob J. Soles, a Pennsylvania coal-digger:

"Bill Sample, Jabe Griffiths and John Corey and myself, all of Company C, Independent Artillery, went to Ford's Theatre at about 7:30 or 8 o'clock.

Lincoln was shot some time later—I can't give the hour accurately; I know the play had gone on for some time after we came in.

"We four were up in the balcony; we were on the same side of the balcony that Mr. Lincoln's box was on; we were back in toward the back of the theatre, about fifteen feet from the box where he was shot.

"We didn't know at first when we heard the pistol going off that it was in there, but they cried for help and we heard this woman crying and we four broke forward and rushed to the box, and we helped him down to the building where he was placed, in a little brick building standing across the street from Ford's Theatre.

"We four fellows carried him to the stairway in the theatre, then two others fell in and helped carry him. As we carried him out of the theatre, he was carried out flat, with his feet foremost; I was down at his feet with one of the fellows, and two men at his head, and the middle of him was sagging until the two others took him in the middle and we six carried him out.

"We carried Lincoln out of the theatre and we had him out on the street about five minutes until we found a place to put him, and then they hollered out that is where he would be put. A young man directed us to the house, a young man that was not in soldier's clothes; he told us to take him to the brick house. We put him in a room on the first floor; we went back through a long hallway to about the middle of the building; there was a bed in that room and we laid him on the bed.

"When we took him into the room we had to get out. The guard put them all out. They wouldn't let anybody in without it was a doctor or something. The street was jammed. You had to push a road through wherever you wanted to get to. We waited around until the doctors came out and said it was fatal and then we pulled for camp."

The body of the Friend of Man lies on its back in the center of the humble walnut bed. Now Dr. Leale holds the face upward to keep the head from rolling to either side. The long knee elevation troubles Leale. He orders the foot of the bed removed. Dr. Taft and Dr. King report it is a fixture. Leale requests it be broken. This it seems cannot be done with any satisfaction. Leale then has the body moved so it lies diagonally across the bed. Propped with extra pillows, the body is gently slanted with a rest for head and shoulders, finally in a position of repose.

On white sheets lies the unconscious patient still in frock coat and long leather boots. Under the white sheets is a cornhusk mattress resting on rope lacings.

The room fills with anxious people. Leale calls an officer, directs him to open a window, and to order all except the doctors and friends to leave the room.

After a short rest for the patient Leale decides to make a thorough physical examination to see if there are other wounds. He requests all except surgeons to leave the room. The captain reports that all have left but Mrs. Lincoln, with whom he does not feel authorized to speak. Leale makes his wish known to Mrs. Lincoln and she leaves immediately.

They undress the patient, search the body from head to foot, finding no other wound. The lower extremities are cold. Leale sends a hospital steward for hot water and hot blankets. These are put in use. He sends for a large sinapism (mustard plaster). This is applied over the solar plexus and to every inch of the entire anterior surface of the body.

The breath comes hard; pulse 44, feeble; the left pupil much contracted, the right widely dilated; both eyes totally insensible to light. The President is completely unconscious, an occasional sigh escaping with the labored breath.

Leale stands aside thinking what best to do next. He tells army officers to send messengers to the White House for the President's son Robert, also for Surgeon General Joseph K. Barnes, Surgeon D. Willard Bliss, in charge at Armory Square Hospital, the President's family physician Dr. Robert K. Stone, and each member of the President's Cabinet. On second thought he sends for Mrs. Lincoln's pastor, the Reverend Dr. Phineas D. Gurley.

"While we were watching and letting Nature do her part," ran Leale's account, "Dr. Taft came to me with brandy and water and asked permission to give some to the President. I objected, stating as my reason that it would produce strangulation. Dr. Taft left the room, and again came to me stating that it was the opinion of others that it might do good. I replied, 'I will grant the request, if you will please at first try by pouring only a very small quantity into the President's mouth.' This Dr. Taft very carefully did; the liquid ran into the President's larynx, producing laryngeal obstruction and unpleasant symptoms, which took me about half a minute to overcome, but no lasting harm was done."

In a near-by room Mrs. Lincoln has the company of Miss Harris, of several women who have arrived, and of the Reverend Dr. Gurley. Major Rathbone has fainted from loss of blood and is taken home. At intervals Mrs. Lincoln is notified she may visit her husband. "Whenever she sat down at the bed-side," wrote Surgeon Taft in his notebook of the evening, "clean napkins were laid over the crimson stains on the pillow where the brain tissue and life blood of the dying President was oozing away."

Once she cried to him, "Live! you must live!" and again, "Bring Tad—he will speak to Tad—he loves him so."

Dr. Robert K. Stone, the Lincoln family physician, arrives, followed soon by Surgeon General Joseph K. Barnes and his assistant Dr. Charles H. Crane, who take charge. Dr. Leale reports to his chief what he has done, officially detailing his diagnosis, stating that whenever a blood clot is allowed to form over the wound the breathing becomes greatly embarrassed. The Surgeon General approves the plan of treatment and it is continued—with the exception that brandy is again given, is of no benefit, and is not tried again.

At 11:30 the surgeons note a twitching of the left side of the face which continues some fifteen or twenty minutes, with the mouth pulled slightly to the left side. At 1 A.M. spasmodic contractions of the forearms occur, the muscles of the chest become fixed, causing the breath to be held during the spasm, which in turn is relieved by a sudden expulsive expiration.

At 2 A.M. Dr. Barnes tries to locate the bullet with an ordinary silver probe, meeting an obstruction at about two inches deep. Then Dr. Barnes uses a long Nélaton probe. It passes the obstruction several inches farther, contacts a hard substance at first supposed to be the bullet. As the white porcelain bulb of the probe, on withdrawal, has no indications of lead, the surgeons generally agree the obstruction is another piece of loose bone. A second time the Nélaton probe enters, and the Surgeon General supposes the bullet to be distinctly felt. The probe is now withdrawn and further exploration for the bullet is considered of no avail.

Now there is waiting for the end to come. The end may be kept off a little by continuous removal of the blood clot at the wound opening. Aside from this the surgeons count the pulse and respiration—and wait helpless before iron circumstance.

The room is fifteen feet long by nine wide, entered from the hallway by a door having a large pane of glass, covered with a curtain on the inside. A Brussels carpet is on the floor. The wallpaper is brown figured with white. Around are a few chairs, a plain bureau, a small wood stove, a washstand with pitcher and bowl. Immediately above the bed is a picture of an Italian woman, a little boy clinging to her as she plays a guitar for some rough soldiers on the porch of a wayside inn. Beyond hangs an engraving of Rosa Bonheur's "The Horse Fair."

Here there is waiting for the end to come.

Outdoors a vagrant white moon, over which dark clouds had earlier rolled and unrolled their smokelike shadows, is now long hidden and lost behind a cold gray sky, an even monotone of a sky.

In the White House Robert Lincoln and John Hay sit gossiping pleasantly, Nicolay off and away at the Charleston Fort Sumter flag-raising. The doors burst open and several voices at once tell them the news. They run downstairs, take a carriage, cannot quite believe the news. Slowly their carriage plows a path through the gathering thousands of people around Tenth Street. They go into the Peterson house. Dr. Stone gravely and tenderly tells Robert the worst: there is no hope. He chokes. The tears run down his face. After a time he recovers and does his best during hours of the night at comforting his mother.

As Robert Lincoln and John Hay were driving away from the White House a friend had rushed up to them with a second piece of startling news, as hard to believe as the first. He told them that Mr. Seward and most of the Cabinet had been murdered. The evening was getting fantastic, the world unreal. Yet what they soon learn to be fact and reality is uncanny and amazing enough.

At about the same hour and minute of the clock that the President was shot in Ford's Theatre a giant of a young man rode on a big one-eyed bay horse to the door of the Seward house on Lafayette Square, got off his horse, rang the doorbell, said he was a messenger from the attending physician and had a package of medicine that must be personally delivered to the sickroom of the Secretary of State. The servant at the door tried to stop the young man, who entered and went up the stairs. Fred Seward heard them disputing, came into the hal! to stop the noise; his restless father needed restorative sleep. At the head of the stairs he tells the young giant he will see that the medicine is delivered. At this the square-built, broad-shouldered young man seems about ready to yield and go—then he suddenly turns in a furious rush on Fred Seward, beats young Seward on the head with the pistol, tearing the scalp, fracturing the skull, and battering the pistol to pieces.

Though handicapped and seemingly crushed, young Seward grapples with the intruder, and in their scuffling the two of them come to the Secretary's room and fall together through the door. There Fred Seward fades out and for days knows nothing, in a stupor of unconsciousness. The Secretary's daughter and a soldier-nurse, Sergeant George T. Robinson, spring from their chairs. The murder-bent young giant knocks them right and left, gives Robinson a knife thrust, then rushes to the bed where the Secretary of State has lain nearly two weeks with a steel frame about the head and face, recovering from a fractured jaw. He stabs over and again at the throat of the sick man, delivers three ugly gashes in the cheek and neck. The steel frame foils a death gash. And the quick wit or odd luck of the victim still further foils him; the Secretary of State rolls off between the bed and the wall.

Sergeant Robinson by this time has made a comeback from his knife wound, gets a back hold on the intending killer, pulling him away from the bed. He whirls with cat speed, stabs Robinson twice over the shoulder, Robinson nervily keeping his hold. Now the second son of the Secretary, Augustus Seward, enters in his shirt and drawers, roused from bed by his sister's screams. He sees two men in a death grapple, at first thinks his father has gone delirious and is wrestling with Sergeant Robinson. On looking more sharply and seeing the difference in size between the two struggling forms, he now thinks the Sergeant has gone crazy and is trying to murder his father. His third guess is the correct one. He leaps on the giant intruder, slowly forcing him out of the sickroom door, while so doing getting one stab after another about the head and face.

Now the stranger in the house breaks away, hurls himself down the stairs, slashes an attendant on the way, is out of the front door unhurt, leaps into saddle and rides out Vermont Avenue toward an eastern suburb. Behind him he has left a quiet home transformed into a battlefield hospital, five persons bleeding from ghastly wounds, failing of death for any of them. Behind him too he has left a bloodstained knife, the pistol he battered to pieces over the head of Fred Seward—and his slouch felt hat. These are clews. They may bring him to the gallows. He worries about a hat. Soon thousands of furious soldiers and citizens will be hunting a hatless man and if they find one asking him first of all, "Where is your hat?"

This horror affair at Lafayette Square bordering on the White House grounds, on the heels of the story of the President being shot, is the basis for the wildfire rumor that nearly all the Cabinet members have been assassinated.

Senator Sumner is seated in comfort chatting pleasantly in the home of Senator Conness when a young man rushes in with cries: "Mr. Lincoln is assassinated in the theater. Mr. Seward is murdered in his bed. There's murder in the streets!"

"Young man," soberly urges Sumner, "be moderate in your statements— what *has* happened? Tell us!" The youth sticks to his story—lacking details.

Sumner puts on his cape overcoat, walks to the White House, finds a sentinel slowly pacing his beat. "Has Mr. Lincoln returned?" he asks. The sentinel: "No, and we have heard nothing from him." From the guard at the door Sumner hears the same. He finds a hack, is driven to Tenth Street above E, makes inquiries, is stopped by guards at the door of the Peterson house, says, "I *will* go in"—and his face and manner pass him. To the room where death waits and the Pale Horse is nearly ready he goes—and loyally and quietly watches and waits, occasionally with moist eyes, himself knowing what it is to be struck heavily from behind unaware in pain and darkness.

Two friends of Chase have dropped in to tell the Chief Justice the President has been shot at the theatre. He hopes they are mistaken and so writes in his diary. Two more callers one by one confirm the early rumors, adding that Secretary Seward has been assassinated. "My first impulse," Chase writes in his diary for April 14, "was to rise immediately and go to the President, whom I could not yet believe to have been fatally wounded; but reflecting that I could not possibly be of any service, and should probably be in the way of those who could, I resolved to wait for morning and further intelligence." Outside are guards sent to keep him from harm. From a front window he sees them pacing to and fro.

Secretary Welles is just falling asleep about 10:30 when his wife calls him. His messenger James Smith has arrived, excited, saying the President has been shot and Secretary Seward assassinated. Welles cannot believe that two assassins could have timed their separate murders so closely. He gets up and puts on his clothes, however, and refusing to obey the pleadings of Mrs. Welles that he must not go out, he starts with James Smith for the Seward house. Crossing Fifteenth Street, he sees under the lamp on the corner by St. John's Church four or five men in a huddle, "in earnest consultation." He has walked about half across the street when the corner lamp goes out just after the huddle of men scatter. In this sudden darkness Welles is "disconcerted." Anything can happen this night. The idea flashes on him that the moon will soon be out. "I proceeded on, not having lost five steps."

Through lines of soldiers and clusters of citizens gathered before the Seward house Welles makes his way. Inside the house he finds the lower hall and office crowded. Nearly all the foreign legations are there. They ask him what there is to the horrible rumors afloat. Welles says he himself is seeking the certain answer. The servants are relieved to see the Secretary of the Navy. They lead him upstairs, and standing at the foot of the sick-room bed, he sees the white sheets and blankets red and blood-soaked, Secretary Seward on his back, a cloth over the head down to the eyes, the mouth open, the lower jaw dropping down. Welles and the doctor whisper a few questions and answers. "Secretary Stanton, who came after but almost simultaneously with me," wrote Welles, "made inquiries in a louder tone till admonished by a word from one of the physicians." They go into another front room and see where the Acting Secretary of State Fred Seward lies unconscious and still. Welles's next paragraph in his diary carries some of the chaos and tension of the night:

"As we descended the stairs, I asked Stanton what he had heard in regard to the President that was reliable. He said the President was shot at Ford's Theatre, that he had seen a man who was present and witnessed the occurrence. I said I would go immediately to the White House. Stanton told me the President was not there but was at the theatre. 'Then,' said I, 'let us go immediately there.' He said that was his intention, and asked me, if I had not a carriage, to go with him. In the lower hall we met General Meigs, whom he requested to take charge of the house, and to clear out all who did not belong there. General Meigs begged Stanton not to go down to 10th Street; others also remonstrated against our going. Stanton, I thought, hesitated. Hurrying forward, I remarked that I should go immediately, and I thought it his duty also. He said he should certainly go, but the remonstrants increased and gathered round him. I said we were wasting time, and, pressing through the crowd, entered the carriage and urged Stanton, who was detained by others after he had placed his foot on the step. I was impatient. Stanton, as soon as he had seated himself, turned around, rose partly, and said the carriage was not his. I said that was no objection. He invited Meigs to go with us, and Judge Cartter of the Supreme Court mounted with the driver. At this moment Major Eckert rode up on horseback beside the carriage and protested vehemently against Stanton's going to 10th Street; said he had just come from there, that there were thousands of people of all sorts there, and he considered it very unsafe for the Secretary of War to expose himself. I replied that I knew not where he would be more safe, and that the duty of both of us was to attend the President immediately. Stanton concurred. Meigs called to some soldiers to go with us, and there was one on each side of the carriage. The streets were full of people. Not only the sidewalk but the carriage-way was to some extent occupied, all or nearly all hurrying towards 10th Street. When we entered that street we found it pretty closely packed."

At the bedside of "the giant sufferer" Welles's outstanding impressions were: "He had been stripped of his clothes. His large arms, which were occasionally exposed, were of a size which one would scarce have expected from his spare appearance. His slow, full respiration lifted the clothes with each breath that he took. His features were calm and striking. I had never seen them appear to better advantage than for the first hour, perhaps, that I was there. After that, his right eye began to swell and that part of his face became discolored."

One by one the other Cabinet members arrived till all were in the Peterson house except Seward.

Vice-President Andrew Johnson came for a brief visit. He had been picked for assassination this night, it was learned later, the conspirator chosen for the job having faltered at the last moment. Major James O'Beirne, commander of the provost guard, calling on Johnson at the Kirkwood Hotel, had insisted on sending a detachment of troops. Johnson, considering himself a plebeian, wanted no armed escort. He buttoned his coat, pulled his hat well over his face, told former Governor Leonard J. Farwell of Wisconsin to lead the way and O'Beirne to accompany him. They walked along packed and fear-ridden sidewalks to Tenth Street, threading their way to the one house and its death room.

The panic, the fear, the sense of storm, over Washington that night made an air familiar to Johnson. It was like being home in Nashville, Tennessee. Of his speech and controlling thought on this night that meant heavy destiny for him there seemed to be no record. That as always he feared no man nor any physical doom, that he could walk with death and defy it, was as evident in Washington this night as so many times in Nashville amid what he termed her "furnaces of treason."

At one o'clock in the morning, wrote the *New York Herald* man, "Senator Sumner was seated on the right of the President's couch, near the head, holding the right hand of the President in his own. He was sobbing like a woman, with his head bowed down almost on the pillow of the bed on which the President was lying."

Nerves were wearing away, faces haggard. Secretary Usher seemed to be the only one mentioned as having slept in that house that night. Dr. Leale continued the one expedient of keeping the wound opening free from blood clot. The surgeons directed or performed every necessary act that came to mind. They were supposed to be coldly practical, with no emotion to interfere with clear thinking, yet there were moments Surgeon Taft noted when "there was scarcely a dry eye in the room." To Taft it was "the saddest and most pathetic death-bed scene I ever witnessed." To Dr. Leale it was vastly more than one more surgical case. From a distance he had loved the President. He had heard the President's speech from the White House window on the night of April 11. He had gone to Ford's Theatre chiefly to have a look at a public man he admired as a heroic character. So he was softly moved to a procedure he later described: "Knowledge that frequently just before departure recognition and reason return to those who have been unconscious caused me for several hours to hold his right hand firmly within my grasp to let him in his blindness know, if possible, that he was in touch with humanity and had a friend."

The one man dominant in the house was Edwin McMasters Stanton. He seemed to have lived for this night, for the exercise of the faculties on which he prided himself, for the required energy he could summon for such an emergency, for the particular resources of grasp and command which he believed he possessed above others, they yielding to him as though perhaps no one else could better serve as Acting President with dictatorial powers.

Over Washington ran wild rumors that a new uprising of the Confederacy was breaking, a city guerrilla warfare—that secretly armed secessionists were to swarm from their hiding-places, take strategic points, and make a last desperate stand for the Confederate cause.

Key men of the Union League went the rounds giving on door panels the alarm to service—"two short, sharp raps thrice repeated"—sending members on the run to headquarters ready for duty. The day men of the police force had been called to help the night squads.

The long roll of drums at the White House barracks with the swift gallop and cobblestone clatter of the President's bodyguard riding to Tenth Street was but one of several dramatic acts that gave color to any wild rumors.

"Stanton," wrote one of his friends, "instantly assumed charge of everything near and remote, civil and military, and began issuing orders in that autocratic manner so supremely necessary to the occasion and so perfectly true to his methods, giving, during that strained and terrible night, an exhibition of the great qualities which had been potential in saving the nation." He ordered troops to keep clear the spaces around the house, to let no one enter the house except high government officers and persons on special business. He sent for the District of Columbia Chief Justice David K. Cartter, who arrived soon and in an adjoining room began taking testimony, with a shorthand reporter present, of persons who might have evidence bearing on the high crime. To Charles A. Dana, Assistant Secretary of War, who could write shorthand, Stanton dictated telegrams to all parts of the country.

"The extent of the conspiracy was, of course, unknown," later wrote Dana. From so horrible a beginning what might come next? The timing of two assassins and their escapes led to many guesses on how far the bloody work was to go. Continued Dana: "The safety of Washington must be looked after. Commanders all over the country had to be ordered to take extra precautions. The people must be notified of the tragedy. The assassins must be captured. The coolness and clearheadedness of Mr. Stanton under those circumstances were most remarkable."

Stanton sent for several army officers to act as aides; directed General Thomas M. Vincent (assistant adjutant general) to take charge of affairs in the Peterson house; telegraphed to General Grant at Philadelphia that Lincoln had been shot and to return at once to Washington; issued orders, oral and written, to the police and military authorities of the District to be prepared for emergencies; telegraphed to Chief Kennedy of New York to send on his best detectives immediately; ordered Colonel La Favette C. Baker to return from New York to search for the assassins; soothed and cheered Mrs. Lincoln; advised Grant (at 11:30) at Philadelphia to watch every person approaching him and have a detached locomotive precede his train on its way to Washington; ordered President Garrett to use the utmost speed of the Baltimore & Ohio Railway to bring Grant to the capital; wrote and dispatched a note to Chief Justice Chase, saying the President could not live and to be ready to administer the oath of office to Vice-President Johnson; notified the Vice-President that the President was dying; and sent to the country and the people bulletin after bulletin concerning the tragedy and the President's condition.

At about 1:30 in the morning, being convinced that the President had but a few hours longer to live, Stanton wrote to Vice-President Johnson a formal notification of the death of the President. This would be at hand to be dispatched to the Vice-President immediately after the last breath of the President. He took this to an adjoining room, handed the paper to General Vincent with orders to make a fair copy of it. Mrs. Lincoln had come into the room. She sprang forward with a hysterical scream. "Is he dead? Oh, is he dead?" General Vincent saw her as "almost insane with sudden agony, moaning and sobbing. . . . Mr. Stanton attempted to soothe her, but he was full of business, and knew, moreover, that in a few hours at most she must be a widow."

Thus, wrote a friend of Stanton, "he continued throughout the night, acting as president, secretary of war, secretary of state, commander-in-chief, comforter, and dictator. No one thought of questioning his authority nor hesitated to carry out his orders." For these hours, said Congressman Henry L. Dawes, "the Government had no other head than Stanton." Dr. Leale believed Stanton's ability and presence of mind "undoubtedly controlled millions of excited people" this night. Of one moment when Stanton's nerve came near a breaking-point Dr. Leale said:

"During the night Mrs. Lincoln came frequently from the adjoining room accompanied by a lady friend. At one time Mrs. Lincoln exclaimed, sobbing bitterly, 'Oh! that my little Taddy might see his father before he died!' This was decided not advisable. As Mrs. Lincoln sat on a chair by the side of the bed with her face to her husband's his breathing became very stertorous and the loud, unnatural noise frightened her in her exhausted, agonized condition. She sprang up suddenly with a piercing cry and fell fainting to the floor. Secretary Stanton hearing her cry came in from the adjoining room and with raised arms called out loudly, 'Take that woman out and do not let her in again.' Mrs. Lincoln was helped up kindly and assisted in a fainting condition from the room. Secretary Stanton's order was obeyed."

The night outside stayed dark, cloudy, and damp. The death room was small, overcrowded, its air stale. "The surgeons and members of the Cabinet were as many as should have been in the room," wrote Welles, "but there were many more, and the hall and other rooms in the front or main house were full."

As daylight began to slant through the windows, with its white clarity making the yellow gas jets and lamplights look garish and outdone, it became evident the President was sinking. Noted Leale: "At several times his pulse could not be counted. Two or three feeble pulsations being noticed, followed by an intermission when not the slightest movements of the artery could be felt. The inspirations became very prolonged and labored, accompanied by a guttural sound. The respirations ceased for some time and several anxiously looked at their watches until the profound silence was disturbed by a prolonged inspiration, which was followed by a sonorous expiration." Surgeon General Barnes, seated near the head of the bed, occasionally held his finger over the carotid artery to note its pulsation. Dr. Stone sat on the edge of the foot of the bed. Dr. Leale held the President's right hand, with an extended forefinger on the pulse.

At 5 A.M. the oozing from the wound ceased entirely and the breathing became stertorous and labored. On the haggard faces of the silent ones circled about it was written more than once they thought the end had come.

From eleven at night until six in the morning Welles had "remained in the room . . . without sitting or leaving it." At six o'clock he went out of the house, tasted a deep breath of fresh air, looked up at a gloomy sky, and took a fifteen-minute walk. Every few rods were huddles and bunches of people, all anxious, all wanting to know what of the night, some of them having stood waiting all night and into the morning.

One or more would step out from each of these groups and ask Welles, bearded and fatherly-looking, about the President. "Is there no hope?"

He was impressed, reading "intense grief" on every face at his answer that the President could survive but a short time. "The colored people especially—and there were at this time more of them, perhaps, than of whites—were overwhelmed with grief."

A cold rain began falling. Out of a monotonous sky inexorably gray a cold rain began falling. The sky deemed such a cold rain altogether fitting and proper.

In the Peterson house Welles seated himself in the back parlor, where Cartter and Speed had been taking testimony. "Stanton, and Speed, and Usher were there, the latter asleep on the bed."

Now it was said the end was near. The breathing would cease entirely for a minute and then resume after a convulsive effort.

A little before seven Welles went into the room where a warm Friend of Man was going cold, moving into the final chill that all men at the last must know.

"His wife soon after made her last visit to him. The death-struggle had begun. Robert, his son, stood with several others at the head of the bed. He bore himself well, but on two occasions gave way to overpowering grief and sobbed aloud, turning his head and leaning on the shoulder of Senator Sumner."

The last breath was drawn at 21 minutes and 55 seconds past 7 A.M. and the last heart beat flickered at 22 minutes and 10 seconds past the hour on

Saturday, April 15, 1865. Dr. Barnes's finger was over the carotid artery, Dr. Leale's finger was on the right wrist pulse, and Dr. Taft's hand was over the cardium when the great heart made its final contraction.

The Pale Horse had come.

To a deep river, to a far country, to a by-and-by whence no man returns, had gone the child of Nancy Hanks and Tom Lincoln, the wilderness boy who found far lights and tall rainbows to live by, whose name even before he died had become a legend inwoven with men's struggle for freedom the world over.

The voice of Phineas D. Gurley: "Let us pray." Kneeling at the bedside, his sonorous tones shook with submission to the Everlasting, to the Heavenly Father, with pleading that the dead man's country and family be comforted.

The widow was told. She came in and threw herself with uncontrollable moaning on the dead body. . . . When later she went away the cry broke from her, "O my God, and I have given my husband to die!"

Over the drawn face muscles Dr. Leale moved a smoothing hand, took two coins from his pocket, placed them over the eyelids, and drew a white sheet over the face.

Over the worn features had come, wrote John Hay, "a look of unspeakable peace."

Stanton, it was said afterward and by his wish became legend beyond recall, pronounced the words: "Now he belongs to the ages."

During the twenty minutes preceding death, noted Colonel A. F. Rockwell, who was present, Stanton stood motionless leaning his chin on his left hand, his right hand holding his hat and supporting his left elbow, the tears falling continually. "There was one impressive incident," continued Rockwell, "which involves an interesting query: When the death of the President was announced (by the surgeons), Mr. Stanton slowly and with apparent deliberation straightened out his right arm, placed his hat for an instant on his head and then as deliberately returned it to its original position." Both as an executive and as a pantomimist Stanton was baffling.

The Cabinet, with Seward and McCulloch absent, met in the back parlor, arranged to notify the Vice-President and the Chief Justice of the Supreme Court, and to meet again at noon in the room of the Secretary of the Treasury and take action with the newly sworn-in President toward "preserving and promoting the public tranquillity."

The young surgeon, the good Dr. Leale, who all through the night had stood to his armpits in a vortex and a pit of desolation, had done all that could be done and was leaving the fated house where Mr. Peterson with a lighted candle had beckoned him in nine hours ago—it seemed nine years—nine hundred years.

"I left the house in deep meditation," ran his story. "In my lonely walk I was aroused from my reveries by the cold drizzling rain dropping on my bare head, my hat I had left in my seat in the theatre. My clothing was stained with blood, I had not once been seated since I first sprang to the President's aid; I was cold, weary and sad."

His eyes happened to fall on his wrists and the detachable cuffs. They had been laundered stiff and immaculately white. Now they were limp, wet, blood-soaked. He decided he would keep the cuffs as long as he lived. To him they were "stained with the martyr's blood."

Now there was a tincture of deep violet given to the Gettysburg phrases: "We cannot consecrate—we cannot hallow—this ground."

Now there was a snow-white fabric crossed with sunset vermilion around the words written to the Boston widow woman:

"The solemn pride that must be yours to have laid so costly a sacrifice upon the altar of freedom."

CHAPTER 74

SHOCK—THE ASSASSIN—A STRICKEN PEOPLE

ON Easter Sunday, April 16, it did not go unnoticed that "sweet fields stood dressed in living green"; trees and leaves had their natural sap of breath and speech; white flowers lifted their apparitions, "each cup a pulpit and each bell a book." Yellow-spotted over lawn and pasture ran the democratic and somewhat riotous dandelion. The ivory-pale garden lily nodded as kin or acquaintance to the hardier bush lilac, purple and burgeoning. Serene as an unfailing tradition too was the redbud, the blood-color blossom of the Judas tree.

On this Easter Sunday, April 16, William H. Seward, Secretary of State, lay in bed with his many wounds. So far shattered was he that his physician feared the shock of the latest news events on him. In the hushed room where all made quiet for him no one had told him. They tiptoed and spoke in whispers, and told him nothing. The treetops of Lafayette Square were leafing out with bright green. He asked to have a better look at the treetops. They wheeled his bed around for a wider view.

His eyes roved the sky and the fresh foliage. Then suddenly he asked himself what he was seeing. Over on the flagstaff of the War Department building—what did his eyes see for sure? Yes, there was the Stars and Stripes, the old Union banner—*at half-mast!* A little longer he gazed on this flag at half-mast. Then he turned to the male nurse, the army sergeant, in the room:

"The President is dead!"

The nurse stammered and tried to say No. Seward insisted—and went on: "If he had been alive, he would have been the first to call on me. But he has not been here. Nor has he sent to know how I am. And there is the flag at half-mast."

Then he said no more—and great tears rolled down the steel-framed face, down the gashed cheeks into the lint bandages of the dagger wounds that came to him in the same hour that his friend received a lead ball in the brain.

HARPER'S WEEKLY.   [APRIL 15, 1865.

FROM OUR SPECIAL WAR CORRESPONDENT.

"CITY POINT, VA., *April* —, 8.30 A.M.
" All .seems well with us."—A. LINCOLN.

Harper's Weekly gives its readers its kindly final cartoon drawn while its subject was alive

On the Saturday morning between Good Friday and Easter Sunday Noah Brooks in his room on New York Avenue near the State Department building lay abed with a cold. He had stayed indoors, played cards, and gone to bed early the night before. Now in the early dawn he could hear the landlord Mr. Gardner outside the door crying, "Wake, wake, Mr. Brooks! I have dreadful news."

Out of bed sprang Brooks, turned the key in the door, heard the trembling and woebegone landlord tell of the President, the Secretary of State, and other men of the Government murdered. Brooks crept back into bed, lay cold a while shivering with horror. From a bed in another corner of the room he heard the loud weeping of his fellow roomer. They dressed and went out into the cold rain, finding the streets alive and darkened by people going they knew not where for sure, "men, women and children . . . everybody was in tears," pale tender blossoms of faces streaming with tears, and again furnace faces, hard-bitten faces of deep smoldering anger. Men and women strangers to each other spoke freely asking what had been done, what could be done.

The tolling of the bells began in Washington. Likewise in New York, Boston, Chicago, Springfield, Peoria, metropolitan centers and crossroads villages, the day had tolling bells hour on hour, flags at half-mast, the gay bunting, red-white-and-blue festoons brought down and crape or any fold of black put out and hung up for sign of sorrow.

"Wandering aimlessly up F Street toward Ford's Theater," wrote Noah Brooks, "we met a tragical procession. A group of army officers walked bareheaded, and behind them, carried tenderly by a company of soldiers, was the bier of the dead President, covered with the flag of the Union, and accompanied by an escort of soldiers."

In silence the onlookers stood on the sidewalks, heads uncovered, watching the little procession move to the sound only of measured soldier tread— and the tolling bells—taking the body back to the White House home it had left twelve hours before.

Out on the Illinois prairie of Coles County they went to a farmhouse and told the news to an old woman. Quiet and composed she was, the usage of the earth in her. She answered them:

"I knowed when he went away he'd never come back alive."

This was the stepmother, Sally Bush Lincoln, prepared for her sorrow which came that day.

Edwin Booth, the world's foremost Shakespearian actor, lay abed in Boston on the morning of April 15 when a servant came in and told him that his brother, John Wilkes Booth, had shot and killed President Lincoln. And as Edwin Booth related it to Joseph Jefferson, his mind "accepted the fact at once," for he thought to himself that his brother "was capable of just such a wild and foolish action." Edwin Booth added: "It was just as if I was struck on the forehead by a hammer." To General Grant's secretary, his old friend Adam Badeau, whom he addressed as "Ad," Edwin Booth on Sunday, April 16, wrote, "Abraham Lincoln was my President for, in pure admiration of his noble career and his Christian principles, I did what I never did before—I *voted* and *for* HIM!" On the previous Friday night, when his brother in Washington enacted a terrorist role, Edwin Booth in the part of one Sir Edward Mortimer was exclaiming, "Where is my honor now?" and again, "Mountains of shame are piled upon me!"

Edwin Forrest, a tragedian holding jealousy of Edwin Booth, awoke on the morning of April 15 to his costar John McCullough bursting into the

Four photographs of John Wilkes Booth

From the Barrett collection

Mary E. Jenkins Surratt

George A. Atzerodt

Lewis Paine

David E. Herold

John Harrison Surratt, Jr.

Edward Spangler

Samuel Bland Arnold

Michael O'Laughlin

room with the news that their fellow actor J. Wilkes Booth had shot President Lincoln.

"But I don't believe it," added McCullough.

"I do," ventured Forrest, no longer drowsing on his pillow. "All the goddam Booths are crazy."

The man-hunters and the fugitive John Wilkes Booth were second in national interest only to the death of Lincoln and the pity and strangeness of it. And side by side, day by day, ran the chronicle of the other fugitive Jefferson Davis and the man-hunters seeking to run him down.

Davis was known. But who was this Booth? What was he like? And where had he come from? In what kind of a green-poison pool of brain and personality had the amazing and hideous crime arisen? Out of a mediocre fame and a second-rate reputation as a mimic he had now wrapped the letters of his name with a weird infamy synonymous with Enemy of Mankind. His name on a thousand occasions was to go unspoken with loathing for the unspeakable and untouchable: a pitiless, dripping, carnivorous, slathered, subhuman and antihuman beast mingling snake and tiger; the unmentionable; the American Judas. And was he this? Yes—in his hours of brainstorm. His own Southern heroes almost universally repudiated him as a madman or a snake, one who fought foul. And he was that—a lunatic—a diabolically cunning athlete, swordsman, dead shot, horseman, and actor with an unstrung imagination, a mind deranged, a brain that was a haunted house of monsters of vanity, of vampires and bats of hallucination.

Now his face and name were published with a War Department promise of $50,000 for his capture dead or alive. A man twenty-six years of age, lithe and sinewy of body—having however a broken leg—intense of speech and behavior, inclined to be dashing and theatrical—such a person was sought by the Federal Secret Service, by State authorities and city police, by professional and amateur detectives, by cavalry and infantry in an organized pursuit, by a million and more men who doubted whether they could keep from killing him if they laid eyes and hands on him. "Height 5 feet 8 inches," ran one War Department description of him telegraphed nationwide, "weight 160 pounds; compact built, hair jet black, inclined to curl, medium length, parted behind; eyes black, and heavy dark eye-brows; wears a large seal ring on little finger; when talking inclines his head forward; looks down."

On a big wooded farm twenty-five miles from Baltimore J. Wilkes Booth (he omitted the John and used the J. in his signatures and announcements) was one of ten children born on that place to Mr. and Mrs. Junius Brutus Booth. To that farm had come from England the grandfather of J. Wilkes Booth, named Richard Booth, son of a silversmith in Bloomsbury, London. And this Richard Booth in his younger days had run away from home to seek from the agent of the American revolutionary colonies in Paris a commission in their army. Taken prisoner and returned to England, Richard Booth's law practice had suffered because he was antiroyalist and a radical

$25,000 REWARD

Will be paid for the apprehension of David C. Harold, another of Booth's accomplices.

LIBERAL REWARDS will be paid for any information that shall conduce to the arrest of either of the above-named criminals, or their accomplices.

All persons harboring or secreting the said persons, or either of them, or aiding or assisting their concealment or escape, will be treated as accomplices in the murder of the President and the attempted assassination of the Secretary of State, and shall be subject to trial before a Military Commission and the punishment of DEATH.

Let the stain of innocent blood be removed from the land by the arrest and punishment of the murderers.

All good citizens are exhorted to aid public justice on this occasion. Every man should consider his own conscience charged with this solemn duty, and rest neither night nor day until it be accomplished.

EDWIN M. STANTON, Secretary of War.

DESCRIPTIONS.—BOOTH is Five Feet 7 or 8 inches high, slender build, high forehead, black hair. black eyes, and wears a heavy black moustache.

ATZERODT is Five Feet 6 or 7 inches high, has dark short curly hair, and a short thick black moustache. He had a light goatee, and his whiskers were much thinner on the side of his face. He has a dark skin, and very dark eyes. He was dressed in a suit of greyish dark color, and wore a gray sack coat and a black kossuth hat. He had common coarse boots, with pants outside of them, and wore spurs.

HAROLD is a little chunky man, quite a youth, and wears a very thin moustache.

Portions of a War Department circular. From the Barrett collection.

War Department, Washington, April 20, 1865.

 # $100,000 REWARD!

THE MURDERER

Of our late beloved President, Abraham Lincoln,

IS STILL AT LARGE.

$50,000 REWARD

Will be paid by this Department for his apprehension, in addition to any reward offered by Municipal Authorities or State Executives.

$25,000 REWARD

Will be paid for the apprehension of JOHN H. SURRATT, one of Booth's Accomplices.

$25,000 REWARD

Will be paid for the apprehension of David C. Harold, another of Booth's accomplices.

LIBERAL REWARDS will be paid for any information that shall conduce to the arrest of either of the above-named criminals, or their accomplices.

All persons harboring or secreting the said persons, or either of them, or aiding or assisting their concealment or escape, will be treated as accomplices in the murder of the President and the attempted assassination of the Secretary of State, and shall be subject to trial before a Military Commission and the punishment of DEATH.

Let the stain of innocent blood be removed from the land by the arrest and punishment of the murderers.

All good citizens are exhorted to aid public justice on this occasion. Every man should consider his own conscience charged with this solemn duty, and rest neither night nor day until it be accomplished.

EDWIN M. STANTON, Secretary of War.

DESCRIPTIONS.—BOOTH is Five Feet 7 or 8 inches high, slender build, high forehead, black hair, black eyes, and wears a heavy black moustache.

JOHN H. SURRAT is about 5 feet, 9 inches. Hair rather thin and dark; eyes rather light; no beard. Would weigh 145 or 150 pounds. Complexion rather pale and clear, with color in his cheeks. Wore light clothes of fine quality. Shoulders square; cheek bones rather prominent; chin narrow; ears projecting at the top; forehead rather low and square, but broad. Parts his hair on the right side; neck rather long. His lips are firmly set. A slim man.

DAVID C. HAROLD is five feet six inches high, hair dark, eyes dark, eyebrows rather heavy, full face, nose short, hand short and fleshy, feet small, in-step high, round bodied, naturally quick and active, slightly closes his eyes when looking at a person.

NOTICE.—In addition to the above, State and other authorities have offered rewards amounting to almost one hundred thousand dollars, making an aggregate of about TWO HUNDRED THOUSAND DOLLARS.

From the Lincoln Library of the University of Chicago

republican. Richard Booth named his eldest son Junius Brutus, holding the assassin of imperial Julius Caesar to be a liberator of mankind. In their family household a favorite topic was the right of every people to self-government.

The son Junius Brutus, after moderate recognition as an actor in England, married, and in 1821 sailed with his bride for America. His playing tours took him to all parts of his newly adopted country. From the turmoil and excitement of these tours he always returned to the peace of his farm and the understanding affection of his family. From him the sons and daughters heard of his monotheism and his favored books, Shakespeare, the Bible, the Koran, the Talmud; of his never eating meat, holding all animal life sacred; of his tears over wild pigeons slaughtered for sale in an Ohio town where he had paid for a bushel of dead birds and bought a graveyard lot and hired the Unitarian clergyman J. Freeman Clarke to conduct the burial ceremonies; of his stern ruling that on his farm neither domestic nor wild animals were to be killed, "from the partridge to the black snake and wild boar." In one of his letters he advised his sons: "A robber of life can never give back what he has wantonly and sacrilegiously taken from beings perhaps innocent and equally capable of enjoying pleasure or suffering torture with himself. The ideas of Pythagoras I have adopted, and as respects our accountability to animals hereafter, nothing that man can preach can make me turn to the contrary. 'Every death its own avenger breeds.'" Hogs and sheep were raised on the farm, but the eating of meat forbidden. A pony named Peacock lay dying; it had sailed from England with Booth and his bride on their honeymoon voyage. He ordered feather beds from the house to be put under the pony. For its burial he had it wrapped in a white sheet, and having invited his neighbors to attend the last rites over "a beloved friend," he himself pronounced the funeral sermon.

Once during an Ohio River flood Junius Brutus Booth saw on a boat adrift mid-river a horse tied by a halter. To anyone who would get to the boat and cut the halter so that the horse could swim ashore Booth offered $20. Someone earned his reward and saved the horse's life. Many odd and whimsical incidents were reported of Booth's love of animals. He was a tragedian offstage, with somber broodings over the fate of mankind and its cruelty to itself. To the Unitarian clergyman who spoke burial service for his dead birds he wrote a note of thanks for "your prompt and benevolent attention to my request," continuing: "Although I am convinced your ideas and mine thoroughly coincide as to the real cause of man's degradation, yet I fear human means to redeem him are now fruitless. The Fire must burn and Prometheus endure his agony. The Pestilence of Asia must come again, ere the savage will be taught humanity. May you escape. God bless you, sir." He named one daughter Asia "in remembrance of that country where God first walked with man." Offstage he spoke and wrote in tones as though he might be on the stage—and vice versa. On the stage he enacted the quivering reality of agonized man—and carried the manner with him into everyday life.

Junius Brutus Booth seemed to be a man filled with tender and sublime compassion for human and all other forms of life—a compassion that often shook his controls and ran over into the pathetic, the ridiculous, and even the comic. When he died in 1852 his feet had wandered before all shrines and altars and paid homage. He was brought up an Episcopalian, the Masons buried him in a Baptist vault, he made it a custom to keep some of the sacred days of the Koran, Catholic priests claimed him for one of their own because of his familiarity with their faith, and in synagogues he had been taken for a Jew when he joined fluently in their worship in their own tongue. Also when he died the scholarly lawyer and playgoer Rufus Choate remarked, "Then there are no more actors." Soon after his arrival in America in 1821 both critics and the playgoing public gave him approval. Until his death he stood foremost of tragedians on the American stage, twice returning to England, where he met acclaim. He was widely accepted as a figure in American cultural life, the supreme interpreter of Shakespeare, a man of intense and commanding solemnity. "Singularly flexible and melodious, susceptible of the most exquisite pathos," ran one description of his voice by a critic who added that he was, "unquestionably, one of the greatest actors that ever lived."

The shining prestige of Junius Brutus Booth had blotch and shadow. He drank hard and often. And in moments, moods and periods, he was definitely insane. To enumerate the cases and instances of his being drunk would be to name scores of cities where he put on a debauch and everybody had regrets over a great actor making a fool of himself. On occasion managers and attendants tried to keep him away from liquor to make sure he would keep his date with his audience. Once when they locked him in a dressing-room he bribed a boy to bring a bottle to the door and through a straw inserted in the keyhole he drank his fill.

Sometimes he failed to meet his audience because of drink. Or again it was because of what his daughter Asia termed "those slight aberrations of mind which mark that exquisite turning point between genius and madness." These, wrote Asia, "seemed to increase in strength and frequency with maturer years." Suddenly it would happen that the manager and fellow actors could not locate the star; he would be found wandering in far-off streets or knee-deep in woodland snowdrifts. In several instances he so used his sword that he terrorized an opponent on the stage; such opponents were sure he tried to kill them. Occasionally friends intervened; sometimes a manager, knowing Booth to be in this mood, had him barred from the stage. Under the headline "Mr. Booth" the *New York Commercial Advocate* in 1824 chronicled:

We regret to learn that this distinguished actor was seized with a violent fit of insanity on Saturday. On Friday night he played Othello, and, in some passages, it is said to have been inimitably fine, while in others, it was thought by some he was turning the character of the Moor into burlesque. In the dying scene, we are informed, he even excelled himself. But, before the drop of the curtain, he turned over facing the audience, raised his head upon his hand, and said, "There, what do you think of that!" These circumstances were looked upon as very strange at the moment; but no further notice was taken of it at the time.

About eleven o'clock on Saturday, he was in the entrance of the theatre, conversing with Mr. Woodhull, when, suddenly, but with an air of calmness, he said to Woodhull, "I must cut somebody's throat today, and whom shall I take? Shall it be Wallack, or yourself, or who?" Woodhull asked him what he meant. "Why, I mean what I say," replied Booth. Woodhull then observed that he was grasping a dagger under his coat; and, at the very moment Wallack passed along. Booth made a pass at him, but, as Woodhull called him at the same instant, by turning round, the blow missed its object. Wallack then rushed into the street, and Booth after him; and Woodhull after him. Booth gained upon Wallack, and, just as he was making a plunge at his back, Wallack providentially stumbled and fell, and Booth passed over him. He was then seized, disarmed, and secured.

In the evening he was taken to the house of a friend where he was treated with every kindness and attention. He has become tranquil and it is to be hoped that he will soon recover from his painful indisposition. (Miss Johnson, in Desdemona, certainly ran a risk of being murdered by the jealous Moor in good earnest, and may felicitate herself upon her escape.)

On another occasion, when someone in the gallery interrupted the stage lines he was speaking, Booth turned his fierce dark eyes toward the heckler and let go the awesome warning: "Beware, I am the headsman! I am the executioner!"—which brought silence so the play could go on. Once in his cups in Philadelphia, it was told among fellow actors, he made a furious bareback ride on a horse, galloping the main streets, "clinging to the horse's tail, with his legs locked about the animal's neck." On a boat to New Orleans two preachers, distributing tracts and interfering with the usual amusements, roused Booth's dislike. And as Joseph Cowell, the comedian, told it, Booth when all were asleep placed his pocketbook with money in it under the mattress of one preacher, and another sum of money with papers easily described in the pocket of the other. Early in the morning before the clergymen were up, Booth set up a loud wailing over the loss of his valuables. The captain ordered a search, everybody being willing, and when the lost property was found, there was of course general astonishment—also general agreement that the two clergymen should be whipped and put off the boat in the wilderness. Booth felt this was going too far. He explained the little joke he had played. Then the passengers turned on him. For a time it seemed he would be whipped. The excitement let down with explanations that "everybody knew Mr. Booth was an oddity," and "at times supposed to be insane."

With the passing years drink ravaged his nerves and the spells of "singular phase" came oftener. Once when he was due to appear before an audience he was found manning the hand pumps of a fire brigade; he liked running to fires. Again he was found in New York standing in a pawnshop window wearing a pawn ticket; he had pawned himself for drink money, went and had his drink, and returned to be "redeemed." He spent money befriending a horse thief on trial in Louisville, Kentucky, the skull of his hanged friend being delivered at a later time to his home and used by his son

Edwin as Hamlet meditating "Alas, poor Yorick! I knew him, Horatio." On a southbound ship in 1838 passing near the identical spot in the Atlantic where his actor friend William Conway had leaped overboard to death, Junius Brutus Booth too threw himself into the sea with the cry, "I have a message for Conway"—being duly and with difficulty rescued by matter-of-fact sailors. In the same year in a barroom rehearsal of *Othello* he warned his manager, Thomas Flynn, "Villain, be sure thou prove my love a wanton," and warming farther into reality, he swung at Flynn with an andiron, receiving in return a blow from an iron poker that broke his nose, that permanently marred the regular mold of his face and somewhat nasalized his sonorous voice.

In time Junius Brutus Booth, America's sensational and incomparable tragedian, came to sense the oncoming seizures of insanity and would make for home, where a rare and faithful wife nursed him through dark tortures. The daughter Asia wrote of these attacks being looked on in their home "with awe and reverence."

In the year 1838, when Abraham Lincoln had lived twenty-nine years and become a member of the Illinois Legislature, Mary Anne Booth on the Belair farm near Baltimore bore her husband Junius Brutus Booth on May 10 their ninth child, a son the father named John Wilkes. A famous agitator, an exile and a jailbird who became Lord Mayor of London, a careerist of checkered exploits, a free lance and a friend of the American Revolution, the stubborn and mocking John Wilkes of London, England, had long been a hero of the Booth clan. Junius Brutus hoped the child would grow to enlighten the cause of freedom as he believed John Wilkes had. As he gazed at the newcome baby it was one year before Abraham Lincoln, shaping his mind toward a habit of inquiry and speculation, was saying in a candle-lighted political discussion in the House of Representatives in Springfield: "Let me ask how is it that we know anything—that any event will occur, that any combination of circumstances will produce a certain result—except by the analogies of past experience? What has once happened will invariably happen again when the same circumstances which combined to produce it shall again combine in the same way. We all feel that we know that a blast of wind would extinguish the flame of the candle that stands by me. How do we know it? We have never seen this flame thus extinguished. We know it because we have seen through all our lives that a blast of wind extinguishes the flame of a candle whenever it is thrown fully upon it. Again, we all feel to know that we have to die. How? We have never died yet. We know it because we know, or at least think we know, that of all the beings, just like ourselves, who have been coming into the world for six thousand years, not one is now living who was here two hundred years ago."

Possibly some farther reach of this particular speculation in philosophy was flitting through the mind of Abraham Lincoln at the instant when finally twenty-six years later he and the child born in Maryland in 1838 met—though the meeting was not face to face.

Mary Anne Holmes Booth, the wife of Junius Brutus Booth, gave love and thoughtful care to all her children. Both as the wife of a half-mad celebrity and genius and as the mother of ten boys and girls she was an unusual woman. She might have weakened under her load. She might have cried aloud, but if she did no one heard her. When finally there arrived the worst fate that could have been handed her, and the boy she called her "fondest" went indefensibly wrong, she accepted it as the fulfillment of a vision she had when her ninth child was six months old—and quietly sank out of life with a heavy heartbreak.

Not on the mother nor on the boy's upbringing could anyone say definitely that in comparison with others here or there the boy John Wilkes Booth had not had a fair chance. He had room to play, a 200-acre wooded farm, an oak-floored bedroom facing the east and the sunrise, a hard mattress and a straw pillow, on the walls deer antlers, swords, pistols, daggers, a rusty blunderbus, a bookcase holding Bulwer, Marryat, Byron, Shakespeare, histories of Greece and Rome, small red-covered volumes of Longfellow, Whittier, Milton, N. P. Willis, Poe, and Felicia Hemans. His brother Edwin saw him as "a good-hearted, harmless, though wild-brained boy . . . a rattle-pated fellow, filled with Quixotic notions" who "would charge on horseback through the woods [on the Maryland farm], 'spouting' heroic speeches." A favorite chum, his sister Asia, who loved his blemishes and overlooked or bore with his faults, saw him as a reader, a student, a dreamer of fame, a gentle amateur botanist and geologist, having charm of mind and manner. She saw "father's finely shaped head and beautiful face" in brother Wilkes, while "he had the black hair and large hazel eyes of his mother." She valued his "perfectly shaped hands" and read no vanity or freak of ego in his act when "across the back of one hand he had clumsily marked, when a little boy, his initials in India ink." Extraordinary physical vitality swayed him. "Life is so short—and the world is so beautiful—just to *breathe* is delicious," he would exclaim to her on a day of fine weather, Asia noting: "In the woods he would throw himself face downward, and nestle his nose close into the earth, taking long sniffs of the 'earth's healthy breath' he called it. . . . He loved to nibble at sweet roots and twigs, so that I called him a rabbit." Lightning bugs he told her were "bearers of sacred torches." Once he brought her a katydid, and when she asked to have it for her insect collection he kissed it and let it go with "Katy shall be free and shall sing tonight out in the sycamores." They read books together outdoors, Plutarch's *Lives*, Hawthorne. He recited from Shakespeare's *Julius Caesar* while she held the book and prompted. They sang together, or he played the flute to her piano accompaniment. She saw him ride away to secret meetings of a boy's Know-Nothing society. She saw him once put on a girl's petticoat and bonnet, walk past a group of workmen and win the respectful salutes they would give a well-behaved young girl. She saw him tame Cola, a beautiful colt, black without a white spot or hair, having a long silken mane and tail which she used to braid in tiny plaits. At Wilkes's saying "No" Cola would stamp and paw, at "Yes" would neigh and bow, at other commands would lie down as dead or would follow the master who often kissed him on the forehead. And the sister Asia remembered that one day Wilkes had a vicious-looking cut on one cheek and someone asked him how he got it. With quivering lips and running tears he choked out: "Cola bit me! I could have stood for anything but that, I love the creature so—a kick or any fit of temper might be accounted for, but for a pet horse to turn and bite is *vicious*." That some horsemen would have insisted on Cola's version of the affair seemed not to occur to Asia nor her bitten brother.

Though both Asia and Edwin described their brother as "gentle and loving," there was no lack of violence in his boyhood. Asia saw Wilkes and his brother Joseph come to the house one day with swollen faces, and blackened, bloodshot eyes nearly closed. Hornets had done it, the boys said glibly —a year later telling the truth that they had quarreled and fought, pounded and welted each other's faces till they found they were equally matched and decided to hide their disgrace on arriving home by laying it on the hornets. Once when a share-cropper, rebuked for overworking the horses, had called Wilkes's mother vile names, he had clubbed the share-cropper over the head and shoulders. A magistrate the next day heard witnesses and bound the Booth family over to keep the peace.

To a Quaker school in a near-by Quaker settlement at Cockeysville went the little boy Wilkes while his father was still alive. At the term end Asia sat on a bench among Quakeresses in snow-white linen listening to an outdoor program on the school grounds. Her brother had just finished giving the passionate and desperate lines of Shylock, had smiled, blushed, and bowed to applause, when a Quakeress beside Asia said pleasantly: "What is his name? He is a comely youth. Does thee think we are as merciful to the Hebrews as we should be? They are a benighted race, and we are permitted to enjoy so many privileges and blessings denied to them."

Just then Asia felt a tugging at her dress sleeve and heard Wilkes hoarsely: "Get away from thee and thou, and meet me over there in the hollow—I've something to tell." She slipped away to the hollow. They sat on the ground, his head leaning against her knees as he unfolded a paper from his pocket and read to her the words spoken to him a few days before when he had crossed with money the palm of a gypsy.

For many years Asia was to keep this paper whereon her brother had written the strange tattlings of a drab dark-eyed fortuneteller. He read to her the forecast:

"Ah, you've a bad hand; the lines all cris-cras. It's full enough of sorrow —full of trouble—trouble in plenty, everywhere I look. You'll break hearts, they'll be nothing to you. You'll die young, and leave many to mourn you, many to love you too, but you'll be rich, generous, and free with your money. You're born under an unlucky star. You've got in your hand a thundering crowd of enemies—not one friend—you'll make a bad end, and have plenty to love you afterwards. You'll have a fast life—short, but a grand one. Now, young sir, I've never seen a worse hand, and I wish I hadn't seen it, but every word I've told is true by the signs. You'd best turn a missionary or a priest and try to escape it."

The brother slowly refolded the paper. He had asked the gypsy if it was in the stars or in his hand how he could escape the fate foretold, whether for so evil a dose she expected him to cross her palm. "She took her money though, and said that she was glad she was not a young girl, or she'd follow me through the world for my handsome face." Then the brother laughed —and often again to his sister he laughed over this foretelling of his fate— she noticing that just as often he would "sadly" come back to the rambling haunting words of the old gypsy. Asia believed too that superstition natural to his blood was "kept alive by early association with the negroes, whose fund of ghost stories, legends, and ill omens never knew exhaustion."

To Asia this linked definitely with the mother, when he was six months old, having " 'a vision,' in answer to a fervent prayer, in which she imagined the foreshadowing of his fate," this being painfully repeated "by a 'dream' when he had attained manhood." Between 1838 and 1854 Asia heard of this dream from her mother so often that in June of the latter year she wrote verses titled "The Mother's Vision," one reading:

> Tiny, innocent white baby-hand,
> What force, what power is at your command,
> For evil, or good? Be slow or be sure,
> Firm to resist, to pursue, to endure—
> My God, let me see what this hand shall do
> In the silent years we are tending to;
>   In my hungering Love,
>
> I implore to know on this ghostly night
> Whether 'twill labour for wrong, or right,
> For—or against Thee?

If they were not deep and measureless, they were involved and tortuous— these Booths. They carried weights of woe—or meshes of doom and foreboding—the father and mother, Asia, Wilkes, and Edwin, who once wrote a close friend who had lost a child: "I cannot grieve at death. It seems to me the greatest boon the Almighty has granted us." In his mother's autograph album Edwin wrote:

> Nor I nor any man that but man is
> With nothing shall be pleased, till he be eased
> With being nothing.

The born comedian of warm mirth Joseph Jefferson saw the Booths as romantics and brooders, writing of his friend Edwin's unvarying melancholy that it was a permanent tone, a vital part of his nature, and adding, "The element of mirth was denied to the Booth family, their very name spelled tragedy."

Once when a schoolmate Jesse Wharton spoke of a sudden river current that had sucked under and nearly drowned Wilkes Booth, Asia heard her brother say, "No, Jess, I am not to drown, hang, or burn, although my sister yonder has believed I am a predestined martyr of some sort, ever since the time when she sat the whole night through reading *Fox's Book of Martyrs*."

Over the father's dark spells and grand whims, over Edwin's impenetrable melancholy, over the failings of others of the family, the mother and Asia had no such brooding near to anguish as they gave the boy and youth Wilkes. He was less to be trusted. He lacked moorings. They saw him shallow in the quality of reverence running deep in his father and in his brother Edwin, that he was too easily satisfied with his own facility, that for all his dash and confidence he had wayward doubts of himself. They knew it was said "Women spoiled him," that he did what he pleased and took what he wanted and kept his secrets and had a pride about his secrets and his management of them. They saw vanity grow in him—vague, dark personal motives beyond reading and to be feared, projects and purposes vast with sick desire, dizzy with ego and mocked inverted ambitions. Schemes came to his mind so colossal that they tormented him with challenges of whether he had the passion and daring to work them out. Once to Asia he spoke of having read *The Pilgrim's Progress*, how Bunyan made abstractions concrete, and illustrating with himself: "When I want to do something that I know is wrong, or that I haven't time for, no surer way of being rid of the temptation that [sic] just to pretend it a *reality*, in form and life; and then I lay my demon."

Not so vague, more revealing, was the confession John Wilkes Booth made to classmates of the finishing school at Catonsville, St. Timothy's Hall, where he received baptism and prepared for confirmation according to the Episcopal Church, where he wore the steel-gray uniform of an artillery cadet, where he had joined in a rebellion against the food served, the entire student body camping in near-by woods for several days till their grievances were heard. A Marylander classmate of Wilkes Booth, credited by Asia Booth as significant and worth hearing in what he could remember of her brother, wrote as follows:

Morris Oram always looked forward to the law as his profession, and in stating his views for the future his ambition was to be a greater orator than Daniel Webster, and a more profound lawyer than Reverdy Johnson, while Booth thought only of being a man admired by all people. He asserted that he would do something that would hand his name down to posterity never to be forgotten, even after he had been dead a thousand years. Booth and Oram had red clay pipes, with reed stems about a yard long, and when they with their pipes lay on the ground, these daily conversations were always in order. Our opinions of the future were freely discussed. I recollect when we asked Booth how he expected to acquire such greatness and notoriety as he was constantly talking of, one of his answers was: "Well, boys, I'll tell you what I mean. You have read about the Seven Wonders of the World? Well, we'll take the Statue of Rhodes for example. Suppose that statue was now standing, and I should by some means overthrow it? My name would descend to posterity and never be forgotten, for it would be in all the histories of the times, and be read thousands of years after we are dead, and no matter how smart and good men we may be, we would never get our names in so many histories."—On another occasion when the same subject was discussed, I recollect he said, "I wish there was an arch or statue at the mouth of the Mediterranean Sea across the Straits of Gibraltar, with one side resting on the rock of Gibraltar and the other on an equally prominent rock on the coast of Africa. I would leave everything and never rest until I had devised some means to throw it over into the sea. Then look out for history, English, French, Spanish, and all Europe, Asia and Africa would resound with the name of John Booth. I tell you it would be the greatest feat ever executed by one man."

While speaking, his whole soul appeared to contemplate with satisfaction the future he had drawn.

Oram said, "Billy, suppose the falling statue took you down with it, what good would all your glory then do you?"

His answer was: "I should die with the satisfaction of knowing I had done something never before accomplished by any other man, and something no other man would probably ever do."

Four years after his father died, when he was seventeen, John Wilkes Booth played a minor role in *Richard III* in Baltimore. Two years later in Philadelphia he played falteringly in Sheridan Knowles's *The Wife* and Hugo's *Lucrezia Borgia,* the critics being so kind as to say he was "promising." Then in Richmond in 1858 he saw his name on the playbills of a stock company and drew earnings of $20 a week. His mother wrote to another son at this time: "John is doing well at Richmond. He is very anxious to get on faster. When he has a run of bad parts he writes home in despair." In the same year the brother Edwin was writing of John, "I don't think he will startle the world . . . but he is improving fast and looks beautiful on the *platform.*"

Here in Richmond he suddenly dropped his stage acting for a role in real-life drama. To the hanging of John Brown went J. Wilkes Booth as a lieutenant in the Richmond Grays, a dandy unit of the Virginia State militia —to the Shenandoah to see Old John hang by the neck till he was dead. He may have heard of Old John saying the whole drama was foreordained, God having set the stage and arranged the lines for everyone beforehand ages ago. He may have read Lincoln's commentary in faraway Kansas on the lawless death-dealing violence of John Brown's effort: "That affair, in its philosophy, corresponds with the many attempts, related in history, at the assassination of kings and emperors. An enthusiast broods over the oppression of a people till he fancies himself commissioned by Heaven to liberate them. He ventures the attempt, which ends in little else than his own execution." This view, according to Asia Booth, her brother could not hold. Though he hated John Brown's cause, he was fascinated and spellbound by the dramatic, lone-handed audacity of Old Osawatomie. "He acknowledged him [John Brown] a hero when he saw him die, and felt a throb of anguish," wrote Asia, quoting her brother as saying of Brown, "He was a brave old man; his heart must have broken when he felt himself deserted." With those words he gave her to keep what he said was the spear of old John Brown, with "Major Washington to J. Wilkes Booth" inked in large letters on the handle.

Often Booth was to refer to the event of Brown's hanging and that he was there with the Richmond Grays. Though the Richmond Grays smelled no smoke at Harpers Ferry, Booth often openly and falsely boasted in speech and once in writing that he had taken a hand in the capture of Brown. He was identifying himself with the Southern cause, and his first stage successes came in Southern cities. As the Southern States moved into secession he moved North as a player. In New York he stepped forth in his father's favorite vehicle *Richard III*, the *New York Herald* saying, "Youth may be an excuse for his errors, but it is no excuse for presenting them to a metropolitan audience." William Winter saw the young star's acting as "raw, crude and much given to boisterous declamation." He delighted in leaps and bounds while acting, exhibited his sinewy agility at moving his body from one spot to another without breaking his neck, carried this business so far that one of his best friends termed his needless jumps "extraordinary and outrageous." In the scene in *Macbeth* where he entered the den of the witches, according to his manager John T. Ford, "Booth would not content himself with the usual steps to reach the stage, but had a ledge of rocks some ten or twelve feet high erected, down which he sprang on the stage." The *Baltimore Sun* critic ticketed Wilkes Booth "the gymnastic actor." Impulsive as a colt, "his heels in the air nearly as often as his head," said a manager, "but wait a year or two till he gets used to harness and quiets down a bit, and then you will see as great an actor as America can produce." William Winter added to his earlier severe criticism his estimate that the talents of the youth, if joined to hard work and study, might carry him high; "with members of the dramatic profession he was a favorite." Yet there were fellow actors, such as E. L. Tilton, knocked into an orchestra pit while fencing with Wilkes Booth, with whom Booth was no favorite. Some had been cut in mimic duels; he was as overly earnest in occasional swordplay as his father had been.

At least twice Wilkes Booth accidentally stabbed himself while playing before an audience. At about the same spot on the stage of Ford's Theatre where he broke a leg bone leaping from a box on April 14, 1865, he was a few years before enacting Romeo. "He so gave himself up to emotion in the cell of Friar Laurence," wrote the actor W. J. Ferguson, an onlooker, "that when he threw himself down at the line, 'taking the measure of an unmade grave,' he wounded himself on the point of the dagger he wore suspended from his girdle." In the week of February, 1861, when Lincoln passed through Albany, New York, on his way to inauguration, Wilkes Booth was laid up for two days with a stab wound which, had its course been slightly different, would have brought death. He was playing Pescara in *The Apostate*, the only time that play had been put on in Albany since his father gave it. "While playing the last act, in falling, the actor's dagger fell first and he struck upon it, the point entering the right arm-pit, inflicting a muscular wound, one or two inches in depth, from which the blood flowed freely."

Over a piece of scenery more than five feet high, wrote Ferguson, he saw Wilkes Booth jump "with little effort." These unexpected feats were accepted as part of a "dashing buoyancy" natural to him, though, noted Ferguson, who found him "a marvelously clever and amusing demigod," he "may have been touched with some hereditary insanity," and was "quite probably not in full mental control of himself." His verve, fire, and skill deeply moved Ferguson and others. "I saw him, after a rehearsal," wrote Ferguson of Booth the swordsman, "take on two men at once with the foils and disarm them both within a few seconds. In this encounter Charles Wheatley [sic] was the last to lose his foil. It flew upward from his hand, and into the box on the auditor's right side of the balcony, where later the victor in the bout was to commit his great crime." A prompter was slow in signaling to musicians in the wings for a flourish of trumpets. Ferguson saw Booth pick up a wooden wedge, about six inches long and three or four inches thick at the wide part, used for holding scenery wings plumb. And Booth aimed this missile at a point just a fraction of an inch above the prompter's head, landing it with so perfect an accuracy that the terrorized prompter sank to the floor in fright and frantically waved the required signal to the musicians. "Booth strode from the stage quite as if nothing out of the ordinary had happened." Once in *The Taming of the Shrew* Booth was required to give a tongue-lashing to other players and in the course of it swung a ham right and left over the cheeks of the players. As he had previously put lampblack on the underside of the ham, the result was that he blacked their faces—an unexpected prank the audience enjoyed. In a billiard-hall quarrel Ferguson saw Booth, swiftly and without anyone but Ferguson seeing him, throw a heavy book that hit a man in the back. The man turned, accused an innocent party, and started a free-for-all fight. The lights went out and Booth made his getaway, having had one more of his practical jokes. Ferguson lived, as he noted, to find that "behind all the roguery and dash, brilliance and artistry of the man of my boyish hero worship, were craftiness and evil intention."

In April of '61, when Booth played with a stock company in Albany, the leading lady, Miss Henrietta Irving, rushed into his room at Stanwix Hall and with a dirk tried to stab him, landing only a light cut on his face. Then she retired to her own room and stabbed herself, though not seriously. "Women spoiled him" was a repeated saying in Booth's circle. After an appearance as Romeo admirers trooped to the stage door for another look, possibly a word with him. Clara Morris, beginning her career, saw him as distinctly not leading "the godly, sober, and righteous life enjoined upon us all," saw him tearing away the signatures from the bottoms of letters filled with "amatory flattery." They were newly arrived letters, and before reading them he indulged some fancy of protecting the names from any others who might come on the letters, saying to Miss Morris, "They are harmless now, little one; their sting lies in the tail." Girls in restaurants always gave him extra attention, averred Miss Morris, adding, "Women naturally loved him," and giving the description: "He had an ivory pallor that contrasted with his raven hair. And his eyes had heavy lids which gave him an Oriental touch of mystery." A trifle short for heroic roles, noted Charles Wyndham, "he made up for the lack by his extraordinary presence and magnetism. . . . He was the idol of women. They would rave of him, his voice, his hair, his eyes. Small wonder, for he was fascinating." John T. Ford, who had managed engagements of both Junius Brutus and Edwin Booth, during the war years also handled the rise of J. Wilkes Booth toward stardom. On the morning of April 14, 1865, said Ford, Booth came walking along Tenth Street toward Ford's Theatre, faultlessly dressed in a suit of dark clothes and a tall silk hat. "He wore a pair of gloves of a subdued color, had a light overcoat slung over his arm, and carried a cane. My brother Harry, standing in front of the theater with some other gentlemen, first saw him, and turning to his companions, said: 'Here comes the handsomest man in the United States.' "

As J. Wilkes Booth played Hamlet, the Danish prince was unmistakably mad throughout, observed Charles Wyndham, in contrast with Edwin Booth's more poised and reflective character. "Edwin's conception of the part was that of uneven and unbalanced genius, and wonderfully he portrayed it. But John Wilkes leaned toward the other view of the character, as was in keeping with the bent of his own mind. His Hamlet was insane, his interpretation fiery, convincing, and artistic."

Such in degree was the youth who from his twenty-second to his twenty-sixth year, four years of war, had to choose between two ways of life that beckoned him. He could build a stage career—or he could fight for the Confederacy to which he was, in his own way, devoted. Possibly there was sincerity in his reply when asked by fellow actors why he didn't fight for the secessionists if he loved them so deeply: "I promised my mother I wouldn't." Or there was another explanation to the effect that he saw himself as a lone grand actor who must wait his time and show the world his own dramatic way of saving the Confederacy.

To Asia in her Philadelphia home he said once that he was passing quinine and drugs to persons who smuggled them south in "horse collars and so forth." On this occasion he swore, "So help me holy God! my soul, life, and possessions are for the South." She blurted the accusing question: "Why not go fight for her then? Every Marylander worthy the name is fighting her battles." This he was slow answering, sitting "with his thin face hard-set," and then: "I have only an arm to give; my brains are worth twenty men, my money worth an hundred. I have free pass everywhere, my profession, my name, is my passport; my knowledge of drugs is valuable, my beloved precious money—oh, never beloved till now!—is the means, one of the means, by which I serve the South."

From '61 continuously as he traveled the North he spoke as openly as was convenient for the Confederate cause. In Albany the theatre treasurer found him at breakfast one morning and explained that he would ruin his engagement there and put himself in personal danger if he went on talking secession. "Is not this a democratic city?" asked Booth. The reply: "Democratic? yes—but disunion, no!" After which Booth quieted in his talk, though sullen and sour about being gagged. During a Chicago run at McVickers

Theatre in May of '63, when the *Chicago Times* nearly every day had editorials and purported news stories which if half true would have justified any assassin in ridding the world of the alleged monster in the White House, Booth was heard to remark, "What a glorious opportunity there is for a man to immortalize himself by killing Lincoln!" It was taken in that hour as rather harmless bluster, to which the son of Junius Brutus Booth was more strictly entitled than the *Chicago Times* to its false news items and incitatory editorials.

Five months later in Hartford, Connecticut, Booth had printed on hand-bills announcing his performance of *Richard III* two quotations from the play, slightly altering and italicizing Shakespeare's text for his own peculiar ends. The mutilated quotation, overstressed by italics, read:

> *Let's muster men;* my council is my shield;
> We must be brief when *traitors brave the field!*
> (Act IV—Scene 3)

This was a maliciously mischievous violation of the Shakespeare lines in the true text, unitalicized, the first line reading when correct:

> Go, muster men; my counsel is my shield.

The line was mutilated with some deliberate intent to embody a proposal instead of a command. The substitution of the word "council" for "counsel" indicated a hope that some organization might come into existence for combat with the italicized "traitors" of the second line.

A second couplet on this handbill held a lurking though indefinite motive to bring death to those at whom the line pointed, reading:

> Let them not live to taste this land's increase,
> That would with treason wound this fair land's peace!
> (Act V—Scene 4)

There was only one John Wilkes Booth, "sad, mad, bad John Wilkes Booth," said the actor Sir Charles Wyndham, in telling of Booth in a railway coach sitting opposite his brother-in-law John Sleeper Clarke, actor and manager. Clarke mentions some piece of war news. Booth frowns, drums on the window sill with his fingers. Clarke mentions Jeff Davis as not much of a President for a country. And according to Wyndham: "As the words were uttered, Booth sprang up and hurled himself upon Clarke in a wild tempest of fury, catching him by the throat. Other passengers tried to interfere, but Booth held his hold, to all appearances bent upon strangling his brother-in-law. He flung Clarke from side to side with maniac strength while his grip tightened. His face was drawn and twisted with rage. Slowly his anger left him and his hold relaxed, none too soon for Clarke. Clarke hardly knew what had happened and looked at his assailant in amazement, gasping for breath. Booth stood over him with a dramatic gesture. 'Never, if you value your life,' he said tensely, 'never speak to me in that way again of a man and a cause I hold sacred.' Clarke passed the matter off as a harmless temporary aberration. . . . No one pretended to have an understanding of the strange man. It was just another queer prank such as his father used to play."

In '64 Booth seemed to have a deepening sense of guilt over keeping himself in safety and comfort while the war raged and the Southern cause sank lower and seemed riding to a tragic collapse. What could he do about it? His broodings took two directions. He would perform a deed saving the Southern cause while at the same time he gave the world a breath-taking dramatic performance. In August of '64 he won two recruits to "the enterprise," as they termed it. Samuel Arnold and Michael O'Laughlin, two former schoolmates of Booth at St. Timothy's Hall, after two years in the Confederate Army, considered themselves "engaged" with Booth as leader. The "enterprise," worked out in their talks, designed the kidnapping—they more often called it "capture" or "abduction"—of President Lincoln. Having gotten their prisoner out of Washington down to Richmond, they would exchange him for enough Confederate prisoners to win the war.

Booth went to the Pennsylvania oil regions, sold his stockholdings for gold, traveled to Canada, reaching Montreal in October. There he consulted with Confederates of the secret service which had fomented various violent affairs on the border and the Great Lakes, leaving Canada, so it seemed, under the definite impression that he would better play a lone hand without help, approval, or funds from the Richmond Government. At the Bank of Montreal he paid $300 in gold for a bill of exchange drawn on the bank's London agents, payable to his order, for £61, remarking that he was going to run the blockade and wanted to make sure that if taken prisoner his captors could not use the money. He also deposited $550 and opened an account. Stopping in New York, he agreed with his two brothers that they would on November 25 play *Julius Caesar* in that city for the benefit of a Shakespeare statue fund. He reached home in Maryland in time to vote against Lincoln for President and to hear next day, the news to him gloomy, that his native State had given a majority for Lincoln, who was to continue four years more as President—if he lived.

The personal hate of Booth for Lincoln, a scorn which he believed to be that of a fine-haired patrician for a plebeian mongrel, sharpened his motive and whetted it. He hoped not merely to remove a government head and shatter a symbol, but furthermore to realize the wild frenzy of killing a man he detested beyond speech—this stood forth in his spoken thoughts to his sister Asia in her Philadelphia home shortly before the November election returning Lincoln to the White House. "He could come and go at our house unquestioned and unobserved," wrote Asia. "He often slept in his clothes on the couch downstairs, having on his long riding boots. Strange men called at late hours, some whose voices I knew, but who would not answer to their names; and others who were perfectly strange to me; they never came farther than the inner sill, and spoke in whispers." One night he came excited, haggard, and worn, murmuring, "Oh God, grant me to see the end!" She begged him not to go South again. "Why, where *should*

I go then?" he asked, and began singing a wild parody, each verse ending "In 1865 when Lincoln shall be king." She answered that would never come to pass and he whispered fiercely, "No, by God's mercy, never *that!*" and springing to his feet moaned and wailed a speech she noted:

"That Sectional Candidate should never have been President, the votes were *doubled* to seat him, he was smuggled through Maryland to the White House. . . . This man's appearance, his pedigree, his coarse low jokes and anecdotes, his vulgar similes, and his frivolity, are a disgrace to the seat he holds. Other brains rule the country. *He* is made the tool of the North, to crush out, or try to crush out slavery, by robbery, rapine, slaughter and bought armies. He is walking in the footprints of old John Brown, but no more fit to stand with that rugged old hero—Great God! no. John Brown was a man inspired, the grandest character of this century! *He* is Bonaparte in one great move, that is, by overturning this blind Republic and making himself a king. This man's re-election which will follow his success, I tell you—will be a reign! The subjects—bastard subjects—of other countries, apostates, are eager to overturn this government. You'll see—you'll see—that *re-election* means *succession*. His kin and friends are in every place of office already. Trust the songs of the people—they are the bards, the troubadors. Who make these songs if not the people? 'Vox populi' for ever! These false-hearted, unloyal foreigners it is, who would glory in the downfall of the Republic—and that by a half-breed too, a man springing from the ashes of old Assanothime Brown, a false president yearning for kingly succession as hotly as ever did Ariston."

Only what happened later made this soliloquy worth a casual moment of study; with the drool of an ordinary lunatic it mixed the most ordinary maudlin chatter of three barroom Copperheads who had taken more than two drinks. "I had listened so patiently to these wild tirades," wrote Asia, "which were the very fever of his distracted brain and tortured heart, that I was powerless to check or soothe." On the night of this particular tirade, on leaving he kissed her, many times, saying "God bless you," wishing well her child to come in five months, infinitely tender toward the sister who perhaps understood and loved the quieter side of him better than any other person. She felt that "his was a developed character in boyhood," that he changed little as he matured. "Contrasting his deeds with his peaceful domestic qualities, there seems to have been the impetus of a desperate fate impelling him." From her brother Junius Brutus in New York in February of '65 she had a letter saying John had become acquainted with "the Deaf and Dumb poetess Miss Reading" and was "practising his fingers to talk with her." Also on this visit "John sat up all Mondays [sic] night" writing a Valentine Day poem for a Miss Hale and a long letter to her, keeping Junius awake as late as half-past three in the morning, "useing [sic] me as a dictionary," wrote Junius.

Most of the time until April 15, 1865, Booth lived in Washington, checking in and out of his National Hotel quarters, taking many trips on errands whose purpose he kept secret. He studied Lincoln's ways and habits, particularly as a theatregoer. At both Grover's Theatre and Ford's Booth was at home, receiving his mail at Ford's, John T. Ford having managed his early starring engagements. The entries and exits of these theatres knew him, every door, corner, hall, lobby, passageway, familiar to him. To the stock actors, stage hands, front-office employees, he was a distinguished figure whose nod they valued.

In the third week of November he rode over Maryland and Virginia south of Washington, bought a horse, studied the lay of the land so he could know its roads, paths, and hiding-places by day or night. From this he hurried away to New York to play on November 25 the role of Mark Antony in *Julius Caesar*, with his brothers Edwin as Brutus and Junius as Cassius. Then back to Washington and "the enterprise," pausing briefly in Philadelphia for a visit with his sister Asia and her husband John Sleeper Clarke, the comedian. To Asia, in whom he had every trust, he gave an envelope later found to contain some United States bonds and oil stock certificates—and a letter. More than any other document perhaps this letter gave the key to J. Wilkes Booth, his scrambled brain, his vanity and self-importance, his level of ideas and reasoning about that of an eighth-grade schoolboy, his ham-actor habit of speech and phrase, his desire to show the South that he was a Confederate hero even though they no longer loved him or cared about him. He referred in passing to his plan for making "a prisoner of this man, to whom she [the South] owes so much of her misery." He exhibited himself in a self-portrait by which he would have the world know him. If and when he achieved the kidnapping of Lincoln— or died in the attempt—this was to stand as his avowal and explanation of it. The letter read:

My Dear Sir: ——, ——, 1864.

You may use this as you think best. But as *some* may wish to know *when, who* and *why*, and as I do not know *how* to direct it, I give it (in the words of your master):—

"*To whom it may concern.*"

Right or wrong, God judge me, not man. For be my motive good or bad, of one thing I am sure, the lasting condemnation of the North.

I love peace more than life. Have loved the Union beyond expression. For four years have I waited, hoped, and prayed for the dark clouds to break, and for a restoration of our former sunshine. To wait longer would be a crime. All hope for peace is dead. My prayers have proved as idle as my hopes. God's will be done. I go to see and share the bitter end.

I have ever held that the South were right. The very nomination of Abraham Lincoln, four years ago, spoke plainly war—war upon Southern rights and institutions. His election proved it. "Await an overt act." Yes; till you are bound and plundered. What folly! The South were wise. Who thinks of argument or patience when the finger of his enemy presses on the trigger? In a *foreign war*, I, too, could say, "Country, right or wrong." But in a struggle *such as ours* (where the brother tries to pierce the brother's heart), for God's sake choose the right. When a country like this spurns *justice* from her side, she forfeits the allegiance of every honest freeman, and should leave him, untrammelled by any fealty soever, to act as his conscience may approve.

People of the North, to hate tyranny, to love liberty and justice, to strike at wrong and oppression, was the teaching of our fathers. The study of our early history will not let me forget it, and may it never.

This country was formed for the *white*, not for the black man. And, looking upon *African slavery* from the same stand-point held by the noble framers of our Constitution, I, for one, have ever considered *it* one of the greatest blessings (both for themselves and us) that God ever bestowed upon a favored nation. Witness heretofore our wealth and power; witness their elevation and enlightenment above their race elsewhere I have lived among it most of my life, and have seen *less* harsh treatment from master to man than I have beheld in the North from father to son. Yet, Heaven knows, *no one* would be more willing to do *more* for the negro race than I, could I but see a way to *still better their* condition.

But Lincoln's policy is only preparing the way for their total annihilation. The South *are not, nor have they been, fighting* for the continuance of slavery. The first battle of Bull Run did away with that idea. Their causes *since* for *war* have been as *noble* and *greater far than those that urged our fathers on. Even* should we allow they were wrong at the beginning of this contest, *cruelty and injustice* have made the wrong become the *right*, and they stand *now* (before the wonder and admiration of the world) as a noble band of patriotic heroes. Hereafter, reading of *their deeds*, Thermopylae will be forgotten.

When I aided in the capture and execution of John Brown (who was a murderer on our western border, and who was fairly *tried* and *convicted*, before an impartial judge and jury, of treason, and who, by-the-way, has since been made a god), I was proud of my little share in the transaction, for I deemed it my duty, and that I was helping our common country to perform an act of justice. But what was a crime in poor John Brown is now considered (by themselves) as the greatest and only virtue of the whole Republican party. Strange transmigration! *Vice* to become a *virtue* simply because *more* indulge in it!

I thought then, *as now*, that the abolitionists *were the only traitors* in the land, and that the entire party deserved the same fate as poor old Brown; not because they wish to abolish slavery, but on account of the means they have ever endeavored to use to effect that abolition. If Brown were living, I doubt whether he *himself* would set slavery against the Union. Most, or many in the North do, and openly, curse the Union if the South are to return and retain a *single right* guaranteed to them by every tie which we once *revered as sacred*. The South can make no choice. It is either extermination or slavery for *themselves* (worse than death) to draw from. I know *my* choice.

I have also studied hard to discover upon what grounds the right of a State to secede has been denied, when our very name, United States, and the Declaration of Independence, *both* provide for secession. But there is no time for words. I write in haste. I know how foolish I shall be deemed for undertaking such a step as this, where, on the one side, I have many friends and every thing to make me happy, where my profession *alone* has gained me an income of *more than* twenty thousand dollars a year, and where my great personal ambition in my profession has such a great field for labor. On the other hand, the South has never bestowed upon me one kind word; a place now where I have no friends, except beneath the sod; a place where I must either become a private soldier or a beggar. To give up all of the *former* for the *latter*, besides my mother and sisters, whom I love so dearly (although they so widely differ with me in opinion), seems insane; but God is my judge. I love *justice* more than I do a country that disowns it; more than fame and wealth;

more (Heaven pardon me if wrong), more than a happy home. I have never been upon a battle-field; but oh! my countrymen, could you all but see the *reality* or effects of this horrid war as I have seen them (in *every State,* save *Virginia*), I know you would think like me, and would pray the Almighty to create in the Northern mind a sense of *right* and *justice* (even should it possess no seasoning of mercy), and that he would dry up this sea of blood between us, which is daily growing wider. Alas! poor country, is she to meet her threatened doom? Four years ago I would have given a thousand lives to see her remain (as I had always known her) powerful and unbroken. And even now I would hold my life as naught to see her what she was. Oh! my friends, if the fearful scenes of the past four years had never been enacted, or if what has been had been but a frightful dream, from which we could now awake, with what overflowing hearts could we bless our God and pray for his continued favor! How I have loved the *old flag* can never now be known. A few years since, and the entire world could boast of *none* so pure and spotless. But I have of late been seeing and hearing of the *bloody deeds* of which she has *been made the emblem,* and would shudder to think how changed she had grown. Oh! how I have longed to see her break from the mist of blood and death that circles round her folds, spoiling her beauty and tarnishing her honor. But no, day by day has she been dragged deeper and deeper into cruelty and oppression, till now (in my eyes) her once bright red stripes look like *bloody gashes* on the face of heaven. I look now upon my early admiration of her glories as a dream. My love (as things stand to-day) is for the South alone. Nor do I deem it a dishonor in attempting to make for her a prisoner of this man, to whom she owes so much of misery. If success attend me, I go penniless to her side. They say she has found *that* "last ditch" which the North have so long derided and been endeavoring to force her in, forgetting they are our brothers, and that it is impolitic to goad an enemy to madness. Should I reach her in safety, and find it true, I will proudly beg permission to triumph or die in that same "ditch" by her side.

A Confederate doing duty upon his own responsibility.

J. Wilkes Booth

Thus the full text of a document which continually insisted "Here is the heroic portrait of myself by which posterity will remember me." It gave little trace of the shaken frame, flashing eyes, imperious voice, of Booth sweeping away opposition when hurling his points at the less dramatic, less sophisticated, players he picked up one by one for desperate deeds to be done under his planning. The letter indicated a "master mind," of a sort, holding sway over a little band of schemers and hopers meeting in a boardinghouse on H Street between Sixth and Seventh in Washington. They included a drugstore clerk, twenty years of age, living with his widowed mother and seven sisters near the navy-yard bridge; good-natured, loyal, fanatically devoted to Booth, he was David E. Herold, out of work and seeking a job when Booth found him. Another was a hump-shouldered, straggly-bearded fellow, dark, sly, fierce of looks though a coward in a pinch; he was of German descent, a carriage-maker at Port Tobacco, Virginia, where during the war by night he had ferried parties bound to and from Richmond. Booth's promises of gold brought him in—George A. Atzerodt. Then there was a tall, broad-shouldered athlete joining ox and tiger in his frame, twenty years old, a veteran of Antietam and Chancellorsville, wounded at Gettysburg, taken prisoner and detailed to serve as a hospital nurse, escaping and rejoining the Confederate Army; two of his brothers killed at Murfreesboro; the son of a Baptist preacher in Florida, as a boy of sixteen with A. P. Hill's corps of Lee's army he had seen and shared in the earliest frightful slaughters of the war. In January of '65 this youth after nearly four years of hard fighting at bloody salients had despaired of the Confederacy and deserted, happening in Baltimore when he was homeless, penniless, in rags, without money to buy food, to meet Booth, listening fascinated to Booth's plans for yet saving the Southern cause, finding sympathy, praise, new clothes and money. This was the man known as Lewis Paine (Lewis Thornton Powell), whose entry into the Seward home about the same moment that Booth entered Lincoln's box in Ford's Theatre had resulted in five persons stabbed and the Secretary of State narrowly missing a death wound. The keeper of the boardinghouse where Booth met Paine and the others to arrange their plans was the widow of a Confederate informer and dispatch-carrier who had kept a tavern ten miles from Washington. She was Mary E. Surratt.

These four, Herold, Atzerodt, Paine, and Mrs. Surratt, had few imaginings of what grisly fate lay ahead for all of them and what mockery of justice was to be dealt one of them—that all four were to be hanged by the neck till they were dead—that Mrs. Surratt was to enter the annals of American history as the first woman to be hanged by the neck and given execution of death sentence by the United States Government.

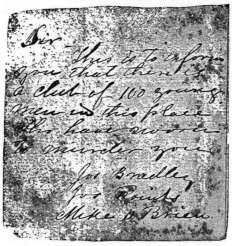

One of the many death-threat notices received by Lincoln. Original in the Barrett collection.

Daily Mrs. Surratt saw her boarders acquainting themselves with weapons, holding vague whispered conversations, telling her nothing definitely, intimating they would save the sinking Southern cause. The air had a touch of terror. Daily she crossed herself and more often hurried to church to pray.

Early in '65 their schemes aimed solely at seizing Lincoln and carrying him away to a hide-out to be held while negotiations went on to exchange the Yankee President for an army of Confederate soldiers in Northern prisons. Several outsiders came into "the enterprise" on Booth's representations, which were correct, that the proposed abduction was not a crime and was strictly included within acts of legitimate warfare. Precisely such an abduction, it became known later, was proposed to the Government at Richmond in '63 and failed of approval on the ground that there might, under the circumstances of risk involved, be a temptation to kill the abducted President, which act would be sure to rouse stormy public feeling. The human spirit of the H Street boardinghouse had arisen amid forces sketched by Lincoln in October of '63: "Actual war coming, blood grows hot, and blood is spilled. Thought is forced from old channels into confusion. Deception breeds and thrives. Confidence dies and universal suspicion reigns. Each man feels an impulse to kill his neighbor, lest he be first killed by him. Revenge and retaliation follow. And all this, as before said, may be among honest men only; but this is not all. Every foul bird comes abroad and every dirty reptile rises up. These add crime to confusion."

Had Lincoln been asked to point to some one instance of a foul bird, one illustrative specimen of a dirty reptile, he could have produced such an exhibit as the letter signed with the name of Pete Muggins, undoubtedly an alias. Other exhibits employed the obscene and lewd. This one hymned its hate with blasphemy, ran on into babbling and raving, suggested froth on the furious lips wishing death. This one read:

Old Abe Lincoln   Fillmore, La. November 25th, 1860

God damn your god damned old Hellfired god damned soul to hell god damn you and goddam your god damned family's god damned hellfired god damned soul to hell and god damnation god damn them and god damn your god damn friends to hell. God damn their god damned souls to damnation. God damn them and god dam their god damn families to eternal god damnation god damn souls to hell god damn them and God Almighty God damn Old Hamlin to[o] to hell God damn his God damned soul all over everywhere double damn his God damned soul to hell.

Now you God damned old Abolition son of a bitch God damn you I want you to send me God damn you about one dozen good offices Good God Almighty God damn your God damned soul and three or four pretty Gals God damn you

And by so doing God damn you you

Will Oblige

Pete Muggins

This was the breed of haters sought by Booth for his schemes. The first requisite was a hate so deep that only violence in the deed could gratify it. Of this human impulse Lincoln noted that it added crime to confusion.

For six months, in the words of Booth, they worked "to capture" the

President. Mrs. Surratt's son John H., Jr., at first opposed and then gave way to Booth's eloquence. Young Surratt had "done some hard riding" between Richmond and Washington, had, as he said later, carried dispatches "in the heels of his boots or between the planks of his buggy." Young Surratt served a cause he believed sacred and romantic. "It was a fascinating life . . . it seemed to me as if I could not do too much or run too great a risk." Just old enough to vote, six feet high, slender but powerful, blond with eyes sunken under a bulging forehead, he knew his footing more surely than the others. He quit his job as an Adams Express Company clerk to join Booth. With him came one Louis J. Weichmann, a wavering,

An extreme malediction received by Lincoln at Springfield. Original in the Barrett collection.

suspicious, and careful young man who had been Surratt's chum for two years at college when Surratt studied for the priesthood. Weichmann had been a schoolteacher in Washington, later getting a clerkship in the office of the commissary general of prisoners. Also there were the two former Maryland schoolmates of Booth, Samuel Arnold and Michael O'Laughlin. Arnold was a farm hand who hated farm work, rather lazy, a student of books with an unmanageable vocabulary. O'Laughlin was a Baltimore livery-stable worker, fairly good at handling horses and better yet at carrying

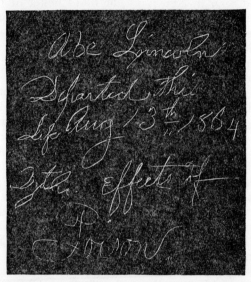

An inscription on a windowpane in Meadville, Pennsylvania, coincided with a visit of Booth there attending to his oil-stock investments. The scrawl read: "Abe Lincoln Departed this Life Aug 13th 1864 By the effects of Poison."

liquor. The crew filled the seven bedrooms of Mrs. Surratt's boardinghouse. Some of them subsisted on money furnished by Booth, and all except Weichmann were led and lighted by Booth's stratagems and wildfire eloquence over the glory awaiting them all for their service to the Confederacy.

A rather pleasant and ordinary American boardinghouse and no den of treason at all was Mrs. Surratt's home, considered aside from its whispered and furtive conferences. On February 6 of '65 John Surratt wrote to a cousin in New York, Miss Belle Seaman, a letter giving some of the human atmosphere with three young women and several boarders in an evening gathering after supper: "I have just taken a peep into the parlor. Would you like to know what I saw there? Well, ma was sitting on the sofa, nodding first to one chair and then to another, next the piano. Anna [the seventeen-year-old sister of John Surratt] is sitting in a corner, dreaming, I expect, of J. W. Booth. Well, who is J. W. Booth? *She* can answer the question. But hark! The doorbell rings and Mr. J. W. Booth is announced. And listen to the scamperings. Such brushing and fixing."

As though at least one fellow actor should be in the coming drama, as though the stage should be represented by one more than himself, Booth for many weeks kept after Samuel Knapp Chester, playing in a stock company at the Winter Garden in New York. They had been intimate friends six years or more and Booth ran the limit of his charms, threats, and persuasions in trying to get Chester to join him. In November of '64, when Booth played in *Julius Caesar* in New York, he told Chester he had a big speculation in oil. "I met him on Broadway," ran Chester's account, "as he was talking with some friends. They were joking with him about his oil speculations. After he left them, he told me that he had a better speculation than that on hand, and one they wouldn't laugh at. Some time after that I met him again and he asked me how I would like to go with him. I told him I was without means, and therefore could not. He said that didn't matter; that he always liked me, and would furnish the means. He then returned to Washington, from which place I received several letters from him. He told me he was speculating in farms in lower Maryland and Virginia; still telling me that he was sure to coin money, and that I must go in with him."

A few weeks later Booth calls at Chester's home, 45 Grove Street, asks Chester to go for a walk. They go to a saloon named The House of Lords on Houston Street, eat and drink for an hour, walk to another saloon under the Revere House, take a few more drinks, then go for a walk up Broadway. Occasionally Booth mentions his "speculation." If Chester asks what is the speculation, Booth says he will tell him by-and-by. They come to the corner of Bleecker Street. Chester turns off, saying good night. Booth asks him to walk farther. They walk up Fourth Street, Booth saying it is not so full of people as Broadway and he wants to tell Chester about the speculation. They walk to where they are practically alone.

"He stopped," testified Chester, "and told me that he was in a large conspiracy to capture the heads of the Government, including the President, and to take them to Richmond. I asked him if that was the speculation he wished me to go into. He said it was. I told him I could not do it; that it was an impossibility; and asked him to think of my family. He said he had two or three thousand dollars that he could leave them. He urged the matter, and talked with me, I suppose, half an hour; but I still refused to give my assent. Then he said to me, 'You will at least not betray me,' and added, 'You dare not.' He said he could implicate me in the affair anyhow. The party he said were sworn together, and if I attempted to betray them, I would be hunted down through life. He urged me further, saying I had better go in. I told him 'No,' and bade him good-night, and went home."

Shortly after this, in January, a letter from Booth says the plan is sure to win and he must come on to Washington, Chester replying it is impossible. By return mail comes another letter from Booth, enclosing $50 and saying Chester must come on to Washington. Before Chester answers

Booth shows up in New York and asks Chester to take a walk with him. As they walk Booth says he has been trying to get another actor, John Matthews, to join him, but Matthews took fright and said he wouldn't join. Matthews showed such fright, says Booth to Chester, that he would not have cared if he had "sacrificed" Matthews. Chester tells Booth he doesn't think it is right to speak in that manner. Booth says No, Matthews is a coward and not fit to live. Booth goes on to urge Chester to join, saying Chester must, there is plenty of money in the affair and if Chester joins he will never want for money as long as he lives. The President and other heads of the Government came often to the theatre when Forrest played, from fifty to one hundred persons were engaged in the plan, and they wished merely that Chester should open the back door of the theatre at a signal. Chester says he must consider his family and hopes Booth will not mention the affair again. Booth says he can ruin Chester in the acting profession if he does not go. Chester again begs him not to mention the affair.

At this point it seems Booth decided he could not win Chester. "When he found I would not go, he said he honored my mother and respected my wife, and he was sorry he had mentioned this affair to me; but told me to make my mind easy and he would trouble me no more. I then returned him the money he had sent me. He told me he would not allow me to do so, but that he was so very short of funds." Thus in one case were instanced the methods and persistence of Booth, with characteristic exaggeration, misrepresentation, and flamboyance. From his own profession he tried to enlist two and got none. His final move in the case of Chester was to urge Ford to lure Chester to Washington by the offer of an engagement.

To Chester, to Matthews, and to John H. Surratt, it seemed, Booth described his plan by which in a crowded theatre they would swarm in upon the President, overpower him and truss him with ropes, and in a house by prearrangement thrown into darkness the captive would be lowered to the stage, carried to a waiting wagon, and conveyed out of Washington cross-country to Richmond. When it was rumored the President was to occupy a box in Ford's Theatre on January 18 to see Edwin Forrest in the part of Jack Cade, Booth got his forces into action and made his personal preparations for what he expected to be the event of his life, "the enterprise," the abduction. He went to Philadelphia and received from Asia the long self-portrait letter he had written in November. Writing his bold signature "J. Wilkes Booth" on it, he put it back in the envelope, resealed it, returned it to Asia, and went back to Washington.

Surratt had traveled rapidly down roads well known to him, arranging here and there for relays of horses and provisions, arriving at Port Tobacco, where he and Atzerodt scoured the shores for boats to accommodate a party of ten or twelve who were scheduled to cross the wide Potomac on the night of January 18 with a captive. After a night of hard riding Surratt arrived in Washington on January 16 to report that the preparations on the route to Richmond were made.

An elaborate trap was set, ready and waiting. The lights were to go out. The President was to be seized, bound, thrown to the stage, hustled through a rear door to a wagon.

The attempt would have been made except for one fact and condition— the President did not on the appointed and expected evening of January 18 attend Ford's Theatre.

His pride shaken, his stars smutched, his standing not so good as it had been with his minions, Booth stayed away from Washington nearly a month, spending part of the time at the New York home of his brother Edwin. There as usual he spoke for the Confederate cause, though never revealing to his brother any slightest inkling of his desperate "speculation." With Surratt and Weichmann, however, on the evening of March 3 Wilkes Booth watched the closing night session of Congress. The next day he stood close to the central figure of the inauguration, saying to Chester weeks later amid drinks at a table in the House of Lords in New York, as his hand struck the table for emphasis, "What an excellent chance I had to kill the President, if I had wished, on inauguration day!" On the night of March 4 he was again in the parlor of the H Street boardinghouse. Surratt was there, having been on a horse all day watching the inaugural parade and picking up news.

On at least one day Booth prowled the White House grounds with Paine. And if later statements of Paine to Major Thomas T. Eckert were correct, Booth directly suggested to the powerful young panther from Florida that he should go into the White House, send in his card, enter Lincoln's office like any one of many petitioners—and then and there shoot the President. Booth seemed to have taunted Paine with lacking nerve in this. Yet again on Booth's suggestion Paine lurked among bushes in front of the White House conservatory. After a light rain had come a freeze with a crust of ice crackling under footsteps. Lincoln walked by in company with Eckert, and Paine heard Lincoln say, "Major, spread out, spread out, or we shall break through the ice." Paine in the bushes heard Lincoln telling Eckert of Illinois days once when neighbors returning from mill with their meal bags were crossing the frozen Sangamon River and as the ice cracked when they were part way over someone called the warning, "Spread out, spread out, or we shall break through the ice."

To Paine, it appeared, Booth spoke of killing the President. To the others his plans aimed at abduction. One March night he arranged for Surratt and Paine, with two ladies boarding at the H Street house, to occupy the box at Ford's used by the President. Between acts Booth came to the box. They examined doors, locks, the passageway, and became familiar with what Booth hoped was to be a scene of their operations. Soon after at the Lichau House on Pennsylvania Avenue between Sixth and Four-and-a-Half streets, Booth, Arnold, O'Laughlin, Surratt, Atzerodt, Herold, and Paine held a stormy session. Booth stood out for the spectacular method of abducting the President from the box of a crowded theatre. Others had doubts. Arnold led in voicing opposition, saying no one could foresee when the President would attend, and a capture in the suburbs would be safer

and surer, reminding Booth that the President was expected soon to attend
a theatrical performance at or near the Soldiers' Home. "If the thing was
not done in a week," Arnold would withdraw. Booth flashed with anger
and said Arnold had spoken enough to deserve shooting. Arnold quietly
made the point, "Two can play at that game." The majority leaned to
Arnold. They agreed to meet the following evening at Ford's Theatre,
where Booth was to play his noted role of Pescara. There they did meet,
all excepting Paine, who was kept in hiding from provost guards who might
inquire why he was violating a Confederate deserter's pledge to stay north
of Washington. They watched friends and admirers of Booth applauding
his appearance after long absence from the stage. They heard him pass the
word to them that the next Monday was the day for the big attempt.

On this Monday, apparently March 20, announcement had been made
that the President would attend a performance of *Still Waters Run Deep*
at the Soldiers' Home, some three miles from the White House. In a piece
of woodland near by, designated by Booth, they were to rendezvous. They
rode out two by two, Arnold and O'Laughlin, Atzerodt and Paine, Booth
and Surratt. Herold had been sent ahead to wait for them at the town of
Surrattsville, with ropes, rifles, ammunition, repair tools. The ropes were to
stretch across roads and delay pursuers until Port Tobacco, thirty-six miles
south of Washington, could be reached. There Atzerodt was to be at hand
with a boat. Arnold and O'Laughlin were to act as lookouts and stop interference. The carriage was to be surrounded. Surratt was to mount and take
the reins. Paine was to lock his gigantic arms around the victim and render
him helpless. Booth was to command and to serve any emergency. Across a
bridge into Maryland—on down through a few towns they knew well—
over the Potomac in Atzerodt's ferry—and they would have the Commander in Chief of the Union armies a prisoner near Richmond in enemy
hands—and a performed exploit that would daze the world with its finesse
and audacity.

Thus the scheme. Early in the afternoon they hear the wheels of the
President's carriage. They sit their horses in feverish anxiety. It is their
high hour. The world is to hear of them. The carriage comes nearer. It
draws near enough for them to see inside. Someone is there inside. They
look closer. They see the face is *not* that of the gaunt, woebegone Abraham
Lincoln. They are foiled again. Arnold and O'Laughlin ride for their homes
in Maryland. Surratt and Atzerodt ride to tell Herold they have failed.
Surratt about six o'clock enters his mother's boardinghouse on H Street
brandishing a small four-barreled revolver, answering Weichmann's query
why he is so excited, "I will shoot anyone that comes into this room; my
prospect is gone, my hopes are blighted." In ten more minutes Paine enters,
excited, pistol in hand. Fifteen minutes pass and the leader strides in, walking
frantically around the room three or four times, suddenly recognizing
Weichmann and saying, "I did not see you." Surratt, Paine, Booth, go upstairs to a third-story back room, and after a half-hour leave the house.
Paine goes to Baltimore, Booth to New York. Surratt leaves for Richmond

and disappears forever from Booth's plans to save the Confederacy by the device of abduction. Arnold too disappears from Booth's orbit, his vanishing marked by a letter to Booth March 27 inquiring, "Why not, for the present, desist for various reasons?" Arnold requires money and pleads: "I am as you well know, in need. I am, you may say, in rags; whereas today I ought to be well clothed." With no reproaches the farm hand appeals to the noted actor as between two scholars and gentlemen: "Do not in anger peruse this: weigh all I have said; and as a rational man and a *friend*, you cannot censure or upbraid my conduct. I sincerely trust this, nor aught else that shall or may occur, will ever be an obstacle to obliterate our former friendship and attachment."

And this same week Booth's mother addressed a letter to him at Ford's Theatre. She is alone and he does not come to her. She has heard enough about him to trouble her. She writes him as "My Dear Boy," is glad he has sent her a letter, is sad at being parted from him, and seems to sense something vaguely portentous. "I have never doubted your love and devotion to me; in fact I always gave you praise for being the fondest of all my boys, but since you leave me to grief I must doubt it. I am no Roman mother [meaning she had no sons to sacrifice for any country]. I love my dear ones before country or anything else. Heaven guard you, is my constant prayer."

From New York Booth returns to Washington on March 25. For the time all plans are off because the President on March 23 left for City Point and the army fronts. On April 1 Booth goes to New York. To Chester on April 7 he voices despair, admits funds are low and he is selling off his horses. He regrets not having killed the President on inauguration day, telling Chester, "I was on the stand as close to him nearly as I am to you." He leaves New York for the last time, arrives in Washington April 8. Two days later Washington is ablaze with flags and the North howling joy over the surrender of Lee's army. Paine, Atzerodt, and Herold are left to Booth, awaiting his wish and whim. On the evening of April 11 he is with Paine on the White House lawn near the window where the President speaks. He is shaken with rage at the President's saying the elective franchise, the ballot, should be given to the colored man, "the very intelligent, and . . . those who serve our cause as soldiers." He urges Paine to shoot the speaker, Paine protesting the risk is too great. The two walk away, Booth muttering, "That is the last speech he will ever make."

Events had swept away all doubts for Booth as to his course. Abduction now would serve no end. For what could an abducted President be exchanged? Now he could let loose the impulse to kill which had so definitely moved him. Now he must shape himself as an Avenger. The Roman avenger Brutus, the patriotic Swiss slayer of a tyrant, William Tell, both were in his mind. He expected to make it a famed and laureled trio: Brutus, Tell, and Booth. He would be the whirlwind dark angel of retribution and justice—this was the fond wish. Never for a moment in the piled and ramified materials of evidence was there an indication that he examined his own heart and studied himself on the question of what was driving him on and whether he was first of all an actor. No slightest phrase ever escaped him, it would seem, to indicate that for an instant he examined himself for key motives, saying: "Perhaps my mind is playing me with trick mirrors and I am seeing myself with monstrous distortions uncorrected. Can a mind have these false imaginings leading it on as though he should step off a roof to a floor of fog, believing the fog is still the roof? Or am I like a man on the top of a tall building daring himself to leap to death and finally being taunted by himself and by a crowd below that he is afraid to leap—finally leaping to his doom for the sake of proving to himself and the crowd that he can flirt with death and like it?"

Until this week, believed his sister Asia, who perhaps understood him through a deeper love than he had ever searched himself with, he was sane. "If Wilkes Booth was mad," she wrote, "his mind lost its balance between the fall of Richmond, and the terrific end."

In an inside coat pocket he carried the photographs of four actresses, rather beautiful women as the pictures rendered their faces, Fay Brown, Effie Germon, Alice Gray, Helen Western—and a fifth woman, half-smiling, later identified merely as "a Washington society woman." Whether any of them affected his motives in the slightest, whether any of them swayed him by taunt or pleasure or gift, whether any of them had intimacy of word and mind with him so as to know the seething concentrated purpose that swept aside all other passions—the later record revealed nothing. The main derivation was that out of many women whose faces he might have cared to look on there were five whose photographs he carried in an inner coat pocket.

Time for women, time for pleasuring himself with them, this he found, on an Aquidneck Hotel register on April 3 signing for Room No. 3 for

From the hotel register page. Original in the Barrett collection.

"J. W. Booth & Lady"—on March 5 of '65 signing his name to a verse he wrote on an envelope back:

> Now, in this hour that we part,
> I will ask to be forgotten *never*
> But in thy pure and guileless heart
> Consider me thy friend, dear Eva.

And the daughter of a United States Senator, her name protected during ensuing scandals, Eva joined her quoted lines on the same envelope back: "For of all sad words from tongue or pen—The saddest are these—It might have been," dating it "March 5th, 1865, In John's room—"

Now, in this hour, that we part,
I will ask to be forgotten never.
But in thy pure and guileless
Consider me thy friend, dear. Eva.

J. Wilkes Booth

" For of all sad words from
Tongue or pen.
The saddest are these—
It might have been "

March 5th 1865
In John's Room—

John Deery, the national champion billiard-player who kept billiard parlors and a bar in front of Grover's Theatre, during this week saw Booth often. What seemed out of the ordinary to Deery was "the amazing quantity of liquor Booth drank." Sometimes he called for a second glass of brandy and tossed it off when he had barely drained his first one. "During that week," said Deery, "he sometimes drank at my bar as much as a quart of brandy in the space of less than two hours of an evening. . . . It was more than a spree, I could see that, and yet Booth was not given to sprees." Later Deery was to judge of this "Booth was crazy, but he didn't show it." The theory was that any natural and inherited insanity dominating Booth this week was heightened and accentuated by liquor. "No man have I ever known who possessed a more winning personality," said Deery. "In his ways with his intimates he was as simple and affectionate as a child. John Wilkes Booth cast a spell over most men with whom he came in contact, and I believe all women without exception."

On April 12 Booth writes to a woman in New York who signs herself "Etta." She answers April 13, "Yes, Dear, I can heartily sympathize with you, for I too, have had the blues ever since the fall of Richmond, and like you, feel like doing something desperate." He has enlisted her in some phase of his projects and she lets him know "I have not yet had a favorable opportunity to do what *you* wished, and I so solemnly promised, and what, in my own heart, I feel ought to be done. I *remember* what happiness is in store for us if we succeed in our present undertakings." She informs him that "the means you gave me when we parted" is gone. She quotes, "Money makes the mare go" and assures him "I do as you desired and keep as secluded as a nun, which is not agreeable to me as you have found."

On April 14 Booth writes to his mother a letter dated "2 A.M." of that day. "Dearest Mother:" he begins. "I know you hardly expect a letter from me, and am sure you will hardly forgive me. But indeed I have had nothing to write about. Everything is dull; that is, has been till last night. [The illumination.] Everything was bright and splendid. More so in my eyes if it had been displayed in a nobler cause. But so goes the world. Might makes right. I only drop you these few lines to let you know I am well, and to say I have not heard from you. Excuse brevity; am in haste. Had one from Rose [his sister]. With best love to you all I am your affectionate son ever. John." That was all. To his mother, to his brother Edwin, to such intimate long-time friends as John T. Ford and John Deery, no inklings of a deed and a motive for which he is willing to pay his life, no hint of his interior self—lashed, driven, twisted to where he seemed at times two persons, one the player who is to enact an inconceivably tragic role 'for world gaze, the other a spectator fascinated and spellbound that he himself could see it all before the world saw it and himself not shrink back from it.

The word "assassin," several commentators were to note, took root from the word "hashish" or "hasheesh," an East Indian drug that inflates the self-importance of the one eating it.

Between eleven and twelve o'clock of Good Friday morning, April 14, Booth comes to Ford's Theatre for his mail, hears that a messenger from the White House has engaged a box for the President that evening. He goes into action, hires a bay mare for himself to be ready at four o'clock in the afternoon, orders a big one-eyed bay horse he bought in December to be hitched in the rear of Ford's for the use of Paine, who at this hour has the assignment of dispatching General Grant while Booth attends to the General's host. He calls on Mrs. Surratt just as she with Weichmann is leaving for Surrattsville, handing her a package holding a field glass to be delivered at a tavern there. To the empty Ford's Theatre he goes, seeing the two boxes thrown into one, the rocking chair brought for the President's corner of the box. (As Spangler, the stage carpenter, and John Peanuts, the chore boy, had arranged the box that afternoon and brought in the special rocking chair for the President, Spangler had grunted, "Damn the President," John Peanuts asking: "What are you damning the man for? A man that has not done any harm to you?" "Aw, he ought to be damned," rejoined Spangler, "for getting all those men shot in the war.") Booth inspects locks, bores a hole through the box door, digs a niche in a plastered brick wall for insertion of a bar to hold against the hallway door.

He leaves at four o'clock, rides his horse to Grover's Theatre, dismounts, hitches his horse, enters the office. There he writes a statement intended for publication next day in the *National Intelligencer* in explanation and defense of what is to happen in Ford's Theatre in the evening. He writes that he has for a long time devoted his money, time, and energies to the accomplishment of an end, but has been baffled; the moment has at length arrived when his plans must be changed; the world may censure him for what he is about to do, but he is sure that posterity will justify him. He signs the paper "Men who love their country better than gold or life. J. W. Booth, —— Paine, —— Atzerodt, —— Herold." He seals this in an envelope addressed to the editor of the *National Intelligencer*. On his horse riding up the avenue he sees John Matthews, the actor he had failed to enlist in the abduction scheme. He had put a postage stamp on the envelope and was going to mail it. Now he hands Matthews the envelope and asks him to deliver it personally in the morning unless in the meantime he sees Booth and hears otherwise. (He cannot know that in the later excitement of the evening Matthews will tear open the envelope, read its message, and lay it on a fire and watch every last fleck of it burn.)

While he talks with Matthews, officers of Lee's army pass by in a body as prisoners of war. Booth lays a theatrical hand on his forehead and gives a dramatic cry: "Great God! I have no longer a country!" Grant rides by in an open carriage, Booth perhaps in a moment of hurried wonderment trying to picture the meeting of Grant and Paine that night in a theatre box. Then he gives a good-by handshake to Matthews and gallops away. At the Kirkwood Hotel he stops to send up a card to the secretary of Vice-President Andrew Johnson. It reads: "Don't wish to disturb you. Are you at home?" He signs his name to this; a thousand interpretations are later to be put on it.

At seven in the evening Booth leaves his room at the National Hotel for the last time. In passing he asks the hotel clerk if he is going to Ford's Theatre this evening. The clerk hadn't thought about it. "There will be some fine acting there tonight," says Booth, and he moves on—there is work to do. News has come that General Grant has departed for Burlington, New Jersey. Booth hurries to the Herndon House and sees Paine. They arrange their timing: at the same hour and minute of the clock that night Paine is to go to the house of Seward and kill the Secretary of State and Booth to kill the President. Atzerodt, run the further plans, is to kill Vice-President Johnson. Herold is to guide Paine to the Seward home and then hurry to the support of Atzerodt. On the street Booth talks with Atzerodt, who has heard of the bowels and fighting nerve of Andy Johnson and now tells Booth he enlisted for abduction but not killing. Atzerodt begs and whimpers. Booth storms at him and curses him for a coward and a traitor. Furthermore, Booth reminds him he has gone too far to back out and if he does not hang for murder he may hang as an accomplice.

Atzerodt, armed with a revolver he knows he can never use, drifts away, never to see Booth again, though in his room at the Kirkwood Hotel on the floor above Vice-President Johnson's room he has the bankbook entrusted to him by Booth showing a credit of $455 with the Ontario Bank of Montreal. The horse Atzerodt hired that afternoon at one stable and left saddled and bridled at another stable, ready for his escape if he did what others expected of him, this horse he calls for, rides to the Kirkwood Hotel, but goes no nearer the man he is supposed to shoot than the ground-floor saloon. On his horse Atzerodt rides past Ford's Theatre. Riding past the Patent Office he throws away a bowie knife and its sheath. On his horse he rides till midnight, hearing tumult on the streets, going to the Pennsylvania House and hearing the wild news that the President and the Cabinet members are all murdered. Atzerodt returns the horse, rides a horsecar to the navy yard, begs permission to sleep in the store of a man he knows, wandering back to his hotel, wandering away early in the morning on foot headed toward his boyhood home twenty-two miles west of Washington, in Georgetown pawning his revolver for $10—a muddled and woe-struck wanderer, one of the only three men in the world who could have told the police beforehand to the hour and minute of Booth's intentions at Ford's Theatre that night.

At a stable near Ford's and close to ten o'clock Booth, Paine, and Herold get on their horses and part, Booth to go to Ford's, Herold to guide Paine to the Seward house. At the back door of Ford's Booth calls for Spangler to hold his horse, enters and goes down under the stage, out of a private door into an alley and therefrom to the street in front of the theatre. Spangler meantime calls the door boy John Peanuts to hold Booth's horse, Peanuts saying he has to tend his door, Spangler saying if anything goes wrong to lay the blame on him. Out front on the street Booth sees the President's carriage at the curb, a crowd of curiosity-seekers on the sidewalk, some of them waiting to have a look at the presidential party when it leaves the theatre. The play is more than half over and a stir of voices and laughter drifts out from the windows to the lighted and cheerful street.

Booth walks past the doorkeeper Buckingham with a pleasant smile and "You'll not want a ticket from *me?*" asks the time, and is pointed to the clock in the lobby. He requests a chew of tobacco from Buckingham, who draws a plug from which Booth takes a bite. Among many gentlemen of the time it is as customary a proceeding as gentlemen of a previous generation exchanging snuff; shining brass cuspidors are available and provided in the lobby. Buckingham introduces to some friends "the distinguished young actor Wilkes Booth." On the street an actor who is to sing a new patriotic song asks the time and the theatre costumer steps into the lobby and, looking at a large clock on the wall, calls out, "Ten minutes past ten." Booth opens a door from the lobby into the parquet, takes notes of the presidential box, whether there are any visitors, whether all is as serene as he hopes. He has seen *Our American Cousin* played and has calculated to fine points the strategic moment for his deed. Soon to come is that moment when only one actor will be out in front on the stage, only a woman and a boy in the wings. A laugh from the audience usually follows the exit of two ladies, a loud enough laugh perhaps to smother any unusual noises in a box.

Booth goes up the stairs leading to the dress circle, picks his way among chairs behind an outer row of seats, reaches the door of the passageway leading to the presidential box. He leans against the wall, takes a cool survey of the house. On the stage is only one actor. Booth knows him well, Harry Hawk, playing the character of Asa Trenchard, a supposedly salty American character as imagined by an English dramatist of the time. Mrs. Mountchessington has just left Asa alone with a rebuke that he was not "used to the manners of good society." Asa meditates alone over this: "Well, I guess I know enough to turn you inside out, old gal—you sockdologizing old mantrap."

Booth opens the door into the narrow hallway leading to the box, steps in, closes the door, fixes the bar in the mortised niche and against the door panel. On soft tiger feet he moves toward the box door, puts an eye to the hole bored through the door, sees his victim is precisely where he wishes and as he had planned. Softly he swings the door back and with his brass derringer pistol in the right hand and a long dagger in the other, he steps into the box.

Up till that instant any one of a million ordinary conceivable circumstances of fate could have intervened and made the next moment impossible. Yet not one of those potential circumstances arrived. What happened that next moment became world history—not because of him who did what was done, but because of the name, life, and works of the victim of the deed.

"Think no more of him as your brother," wrote Edwin Booth to Asia; "he is dead to us now, as soon he must be to all the world, but imagine the boy you loved to be in that better part of his spirit, in another world." And referring to a weeping nameless betrothed one, Edwin added, "I have had a heart-broken letter from the poor little girl to whom he had promised so much happiness."

The sheer technique of the assassin, his keen mathematical calculations beforehand, his swift and ruthless execution of those calculations, his dramatic assumption of the role of an Avenger laughing triumphantly over those who loved what he had killed—these were given praise, strange tribute, bitterly ironic plaudits, such as came from the Reverend Dr. E. N. Kirk, writing in a religious journal, the *Congregationalist:*

"Weep, brothers, weep! You have cause. It is right, it is manly. The murder was cruel. It searched for and found the spot where it might meet and wound a nation's heart. No common sacrifice would satisfy its morbid, fiendish appetite. It would not strike until it could bring to its foul divinity the libation of a nation's tears.

"Weep, brothers; confess to the success of the enterprise. The shot was well aimed. It brought us all down, down into the dust. Our hearts had all met in one man; and there they all received the fatal blow. It was cruel to hurt us so. We bow before the monster and confess his power. We acknowledge his skill. He understood his mission."

In New York the press chronicled the death by his own hand of a young Swede named Charles Johnson, who left behind him the written message "I want to join Abraham Lincoln." He had "brooded," ran the story, over an act beyond reason. Many others were brooding now, their reason shaken.

And the one man whose sworn duty it was to have intercepted the assassin—John F. Parker? There were charges brought against him by Superintendent A. C. Richards of the Metropolitan Police Force, "that Said Parker was detailed to attend and protect the President Mr. Lincoln, that while the President was at Ford's Theatre on the night of the 14th of April last, Said Parker allowed a man to enter the President's private Box and Shoot the President." But there was no trial on these charges, and it was not till three years later that Parker was to be dishonorably dismissed from the police force for sleeping on his beat.

Neither Stanton nor La Fayette C. Baker nor any member of Congress nor any newspaper metropolitan or rural, nor any accustomed guardian of public welfare, took any but momentary interest in the one guard sworn to a sacred duty who distinguished himself as a marvelous cipher, a more curious derelict than any during the war shot by a firing squad for desertion, cowardice in the face of the enemy, or sleeping at the post of duty. The watch guards of public welfare all had other fish to fry, and it was to be many years before the dereliction of John F. Parker, a nonentity and as such a curiously odd number, was to be duly assessed.

How did Parker take the news of Lincoln's assassination? It awoke some lethargy in his bones. Probably all night long he wandered half-dazed over the streets of Washington, stopping in saloons, gathering the news, wondering, bothering his head about what explanations he could make. At six o'clock in the morning, according to the police blotter, he brought to headquarters a woman of the streets he had arrested, her name Lizzie Williams. Parker had decided he would make it a matter of record that he was on the job as a police officer, that early in the morning he was on the job. So he brings in a forlorn, bedraggled streetwalker—against whom he proved no case, and Lizzie Williams was promptly discharged. This was his offering: instead of intercepting the killer of the President shortly after 10 P.M. he brings in to headquarters a battered and worn prostitute at 6 A.M. in a cold gray rain and the sky a noncommittal monotone.

The guard William H. Crook awoke in his home on the morning after Good Friday to hear the news, and his first thought was, "If I had been on duty at the theater, I would be dead now." His next thought was to wonder whether his fellow guard John F. Parker was dead. Years later he was to wonder why the negligence of the guard on duty had "never been divulged," writing: "So far as I know, it was not even investigated by the police department. Yet, had he [Parker] done his duty, President Lincoln would not have been murdered by Booth." Crook reasoned that a single guard at the box entrance could have made a struggle and an outcry that would have resulted in the disarming of Booth. "It makes me feel rather bitter," wrote Crook, "when I remember that the President had said, just a few hours before, that he knew he could trust all his guards. And then to think that in that one moment of test one of us should have utterly failed him! Parker knew that he had failed in duty. He looked like a convicted criminal the next day. He was never the same man afterward."

Crook believed that Lincoln had a vague inner warning of an attempt to be made on the night of April 14. He estimated Lincoln "a man of entire sanity," requiring a basis of reality for any dream that disturbed him. "But no one has ever sounded the spring of spiritual insight from which his nature was fed. To me it all means that he had, with his waking on that day, a strong prescience of coming change. As the day wore on the feeling darkened into an impression of coming evil. The suggestion of the crude violence we witnessed on the street pointed to the direction from which the evil should come. He was human; he shrank from it. But he was characterized by what some men call fatalism; others, devotion to duty; still others, religious faith. Therefore he went open-eyed to the place where he met, at last, the blind fanatic."

"If the sentinel over the President's box had been properly disciplined, the assassination would probably have been prevented," wrote J. W. Phelps to Sumner. Had Lincoln been more strict and concerned about his personal guard, the story would have been different. The incompetency in this particular affair, believed Phelps, was but one instance of the President "governed by personal peculiarities in his whole course of policy." Phelps shaped a verbal cartoon: "His [Lincoln's] goodness, benevolence, and magnanimity were as much out of place at the head of a people so truculently cunning as we are, as would be a human head upon a snake's body." From this Phelps proceeded to scathing judgments of the Government and its army, in tone matching what General William Tecumseh Sherman wrote this spring: "Washington is as corrupt as Hell, made so by the looseness and extravagance of the war. I will avoid it as a pest house."

In company with Senator Ben Wade went Congressman Henry Laurens Dawes to greet in the Kirkwood House the newly sworn-in President Andrew Johnson. And Wade's greeting, as Congressman Dawes told it to his daughter Anna, ran: "Mr Johnson, I thank God that you are here. Lincoln had too much of the milk of human kindness to deal with these damned rebels. Now they will be dealt with according to their deserts."

This feeling ran through a caucus of the Republican-party radicals meeting that day to consider, as Congressman George Julian phrased it, "a line of policy less conciliatory than that of Mr. Lincoln." Julian reported his observation: "While everybody was shocked at his murder, the feeling was nearly universal that the accession of Johnson to the Presidency would prove a godsend to the country." Several letters to Johnson this week carried this view. One from Senator B. Gratz Brown of Missouri almost jubilated. "Sad as was the atrocity which deprived us of a President whose heart was all kindness . . . I yet believe that God in his Providence has called you to complete the work of rebuilding this nation that it might be stamped with the idea of radical democracy in all its parts." A letter of T. Fiske to President Johnson April 20 actually did jubilate: "In the good Providence of the Almighty Ruler of events, you have been placed at the most exalted situation in the world. The people of this great nation will now 'thank God and take courage,' believing, as they must, that the days of criminal clemency to traitors are over; that milk-and-water and the oath of allegiance, will not longer be relied on, as sovereign remedies for treason and rebellion."

From the Judge Advocate's office, at headquarters of the Department of the South, Hilton Head, South Carolina, John C. Gray, Jr., wrote to John C. Ropes of how the news of the assassination had come like a thunderclap and overshadowed all other thought. "At first I did not know whether to attribute it to Jeff Davis or Ben Butler, the probability being about equal, but now I fancy neither of them had anything to do with it. . . . However that may be, it cannot fail terribly to embitter the feelings on both sides, the honest belief of Lincoln's friends that their enemies, domestic or rebel, instigated and approved the deed, and the indignation of those opposed to him who had nothing to do with the murder at the false accusations, will both be sources of evil. Yet I do not fear the action or feeling of the people so much, they will talk loudly, but the actions of a democracy, notwithstanding all said to the contrary, are generally only too merciful, but I do fear the terrible power that is given to the ultra radicals to work evil to the country."

Of the new President little was known, and, continued Gray to Ropes: "He may turn out more of a man than we hope. Henry Ward Beecher told an officer on the dock [at Charleston] a few hours after the news was announced of Lincoln's death, that Johnson's little finger was stronger than Lincoln's loins, and though I have heard nothing so bad myself, I can see that a good many think that Mr. Lincoln would have been too lenient with the rebels."

At a meeting of leading citizens on April 15 in the New York Customs House in New York City, William Pitt Fessenden, now the newly elected United States Senator from Maine, gave a reminiscence of Lincoln and coupled with it a gory promise. Fessenden stood with Lincoln one day in the office of the Secretary of State and seeing the President looking weary and worn, he said, "Mr. President, the people of the United States are praying that God will spare your life to see the end of this rebellion." And he recalled Lincoln's reply: "Mr. Fessenden, it may be that I shall not live to see it, and sometimes I think I shall not; but if I were taken away there are those who would perform my duties better." And Fessenden, believing now that the rebel government had taken a hand in the murder of Lincoln, the moderate and usually considerate Fessenden, distinctly not one of the radicals, seethed over a lunatic act, and gave his pledge: "*We will hang Jeff Davis!*" Thus publicly a scrupulous statesman was giving voice to what the *New York Herald* termed "an ominous muttering in the streets."

The single event of an assassination swept away a thousand foundations carefully laid and protected by the living Lincoln. A long series of delicate roots of human relationships that the living Lincoln had nursed and guarded were torn up in a night. Booth had so distinctly proclaimed himself an authorized Avenger of the South, and official statements and press stories implied so directly that the assassination had connections with the Jeff Davis Government, that now the word "reconciliation" had lost value. The cry of revenge in a day became a vogue and a rage.

No other organ had more consistently gone along with Lincoln in his policy of goodwill toward the South than the *New York Herald*. While Lincoln lay dying the *Herald's* April 15 issue came out with an editorial advising against hanging or the death penalty for Jeff Davis, urging rather: "Let him die like Benedict Arnold, in foreign lands, or go, like Judas, and hang himself." The *Herald* had for long disagreed with the now widely quoted demand of Andrew Johnson with reference to traitors: "Their reward should be the halter and the gallows." But on Easter Sunday, April 16, the *Herald* changed its tone in drift with a deep undertow moving the country, saying editorially: "The assassins struck at the best friends in the government to the prostrate rebels of the South. The policy of these men was forgiveness and conciliation to the fullest admissible extent; and the public mind everywhere was strongly inclined in the same direction. But the dark and shocking events of a single night have wrought in a few hours a fearful reaction. There is an ominous muttering in the streets; a general feeling is abroad that the lives of the wretched assassin or assassins in this horrid business will not meet the requirements of justice, and that justice should now take its course against treason and traitors wherever found."

One question was held pertinent: What from year to year during the war did Wilkes Booth meet that might generate a motive and play on it and shape it with finality? He saw and heard hundreds of men of the educated and privileged classes indulging in an almost unrestricted freedom of speech. Did he see and hear them speak, write, and publish much else than that one man had by his own wish and will brought on the war? Did they tell him anything else of import than that this one man had by his own whim and determination carried the war on through four devastating, howling, bitter years of agony? At whom other than this one man did they point the finger of blame for the origin and continuance of the war?

Had Wilkes Booth never for a moment listened to Southern voices about this one man—had he dismissed the cries of radicals that this one man was a faltering administrator, a trickster, a huckster, and a vain usurper—had he been indifferent to the educated and privileged orators and writers who pictured this one man as a buffoon and a charlatan if not a monster—had Booth merely permitted himself to be guided by such newspapers as the *New York World*, the *Detroit Free Press*, and the *Chicago Times*—then he would have felt himself correct and justified to go forth with a brass pocket pistol and stake his own life on the chance of sending a merciless bullet through the head of this one man. For on the head of this one man Lincoln had been charged not one but a thousand infamies any one of which could easily light the mind of a vain and cunning fool with a motive to annihilate with one shot the many fiends and monsters alleged to exist in this one man. The deed had a prepared scene.

In part the motive was conditioned in war, in a hurricane of hates and passions, where reason to many had become fantasy. While the fury and anguish brought out serene and majestic human truths, it also set going a vast array of human delusions and hallucinations. Amid the boiling rages and seething bewilderments Wilkes Booth moved from city to city, witnessing a national drama more wild, dark, and mysterious than all the plays of Shakespeare. Over and again he heard the questions put directly or indirectly: What was one more killing of a man in a land already strewn with corpses and cripples and famished skeletons in prisons? When was human life counted cheaper? Where was human dignity when served red on dripping bayonets or hacked and mangled by shot and shell, with profits and fortunes reaped from the strife by nonparticipating buzzards, and homes and landscapes indecently burned and ravaged? The *New York Herald* on Easter Sunday, April 16, dwelt on one public agency as no factor of enlightenment, no sobering influence at all. It said directly that newspaper editors shared in the guilt of leading an assassin toward his bloody work. An editorial headed "The Rebel Press North and South" said:

"There was an outcry in every house in the land yesterday—'The President is murdered.' From one member of the family to the other, from room to room, and up and down every stairway, this awful piece of news was repeated, and stunned and paralyzed everyone. And it was a natural tribute to the position held by this great man in the hearts of the people that if it had been the dearest member of each of those households that had been stricken down the sudden horror and anguish could hardly have been greater.

"But the blow has fallen, and whence did it come? From Richmond, no one doubts; yet wherever the idea was conceived, or the plan framed, it is as clear as day that the real origin of this dreadful act is to be found in the fiendish and malignant spirit developed and fostered by the rebel press North and South.

"That press has, in the most devilish manner, urged men to the commission of this very deed. They who jeered at the first attempt to assassinate Mr. Lincoln, in 1861, and said that it was gotten up to bring odium upon the South; they who coolly advertised that for one hundred thousand dollars Mr. Lincoln and Mr. Seward could both be killed before the 4th of March; they who thought the attempt to burn this city a very good joke—excellent food for laughter—and they who specifically incited to this murder by their invocation to the dagger of Brutus—they are indeed the real authors of this horrible crime."

In like tone was a diary entry of Adam Gurowski, in Washington on the night of April 14 giving his first reaction to the news of that night: "All over the rebel region, the press for years incited to Lincoln's murder. For years a part of the Northern press, which was and is the gospel of the Northern Copperheads, slavers, and traitors, pointed to Lincoln as a tyrant, and to Seward as his henchman. Murder and slaughter by infuriated wretches are now the fruits of those stimulating teachings."

Party spirit and its mouthpieces, the press, the politicians and orators, came in for blame from *Harper's Weekly*. Directly and indirectly, openly and cunningly, the passions of men were set on fire by "the assertion that Mr. Lincoln was responsible for the war, that he had opened all the yawning graves and tumbled the victims in." To carry their points the political opponents of Mr. Lincoln continuously said that he had superseded the laws and made himself an autocrat. "If any dangerous plot has been exposed, these organs of public opinion had sneered at it as an invention of the Administration. If bloody riots and massacres occurred, they were extenuated and called 'risings of the people,' as if in justifiable vengeance, and as if the oppression of the Government had brought them upon itself." On the Administration of Abraham Lincoln were laid "the basest conceivable crimes" of tyrant and despot. "Is it surprising that somebody should have believed all this, that somebody should have said, if there is a tyranny it can not be very criminal to slay the tyrant, and that working himself up to the due frenzy he should strike the blow?" *Harper's* inquired. Then it deduced: "The lesson is terrible. Let us hope that even party spirit may be tempered by the result of its natural consequence."

Yet even while there were men, mouthpieces, and organs who spoke of crying down passion, of soberly remembering the phrases "with malice toward none, with charity for all," a deep slow-moving tide of newly aroused hate was setting in motion toward the South, a snarling, restless hate connecting with the bloody malice of Wilkes Booth and the shadowy, inexplicable backgrounds of his deed. Mrs. Chesnut saw this tide rolling toward her people, writing in her diary: "Lincoln, old Abe Lincoln, has been killed. . . . Why? By whom? It is simply maddening. . . . I know this foul murder will bring upon us worse miseries." An element of the South which fought fairly by a clean code shrank in horror at the deed of Booth, the *Meridian* (Mississippi) *Clarion* saying: "We hope that the crime was not perpetrated by a Southerner, whom its very barbarity would disgrace. . . . We deem the independence of the South eminently desirable, but never dreamed that it was to be achieved by assassins. Providence rarely rewards crimes against which humanity revolts."

"A soldier is not, as many think, wholly devoid of feeling," wrote Private Jenkin Lloyd Jones of the 6th Wisconsin Battery at Chattanooga, in a diary entry April 15. "A gloom was cast upon everyone, silently hoping for a contradiction [of the news]. All regarded the loss of him as of a near and dear relative. Terrible were the oaths and imprecations uttered through clenched teeth against the perpetrators."

"I learned with pained heart of the assassination," wrote an Iowa chaplain. "Oh how many brave men & soldiers have I saw weep this day & when I met Judge H. C. Caldwell we wept together the Cannon was fired every thirty minutes all this day."

Sherman on his way to a conference with the Confederate General Joseph E. Johnston had a decoded telegram handed him by an operator. It was from Stanton and began: "President Lincoln was murdered about 10 o'clock last night." Sherman pledged the operator to say nothing to anyone of the telegram. When Sherman and Johnston sat alone in a small farmhouse,

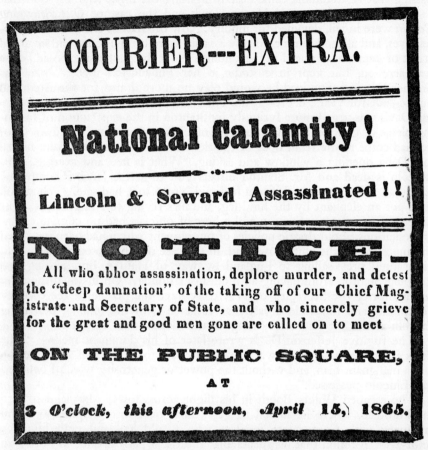

Top and bottom portions of a handbill newspaper extra issued in St. Louis. From the Barrett collection.

Sherman handed over the telegram. Johnston read. On his forehead slowly came sweat "in large drops," as Sherman watched him, Sherman remembering so clearly and for so long a time afterward how one of the greatest of Confederate captains said that "Mr. Lincoln was the best friend they had" and the assassination was "the greatest possible calamity to the South." In the surrender terms they were to sign, Sherman's motive, according to his keenest interpreter, probably ranged around a thought: "Lincoln is dead. I will make his kind of a peace."

When later the dread news was given to Sherman's army, there were curses and cries for vengeance among the troops. Many were ready to burn the city of Raleigh to the ground. Logan made speeches against it, other officers intervened, and discipline prevailed, though all agreed a horror sur-passing that at Columbia came near to lighting the night sky.

Now Laura Keene and Harry Hawk and the cast of *Our American Cousin* were in jail, detained for inquiry. Now the friends and acquaintances, relatives, and alleged kinsmen of the assassin were by the scores either under arrest or kept under guard in their homes. Now the gentle sister Asia Booth was arrested, but kept in custody in her Philadelphia home. Now the brother Edwin announced he would play no more drama for the American public—not for years, if ever again. Now the pursuit of the fugitive Jeffer-son Davis was urged more furiously by Stanton in the expectation of fasten-ing blame or guilt on high Confederate officials as conspirators. Now a colo-nel had come to the front door of Charles A. Dana's house early of a morn-ing, Dana opening a window and asking, "What is it?" and hearing, "Mr. Lincoln is dead and Mr. Stanton directs you to arrest Jacob Thompson." Less than a day previous Lincoln had said No to this, had said, "When you have got an elephant by the hind leg, and he's trying to run away, it's best to let him run." Now Stanton and a host of officials had no compunctions, no hesitations, about drastic policies of punishment which had been tempered and modified by the chief now dead. In the case of Thompson, Stanton lost, his wanted prey sailing to England by way of Halifax. But nothing was stopping Stanton from having an inquisitor's holiday. On his own initiative and authority the Secretary of War daily gave the people of the country viewpoints and impressions vastly at variance with the tone of the living Lincoln at the last Cabinet meeting on the morning of April 14.

The fugitive Jefferson Davis wrote later of his dominant feeling: "The news [of the assassination] was to me very sad, for I felt that Mr. Johnson was a malignant man, and without the power or generosity which I believed Mr. Lincoln possessed."

The escaped Wilkes Booth in his flight across lower Maryland toward the Potomac, where he hoped to get a boat over into Virginia and find sanctuary with Confederate loyalists who would hail and exalt him—the actor-assassin found that his spectacular theatrical performance in Ford's on the night of April 14 was not appreciated as he had expected. He met among Confederate loyalists suspicious eyes, questioning tones, looks and faces im-plying: "What sort of a slimy rat are you? Who can trust the likes of you?" In scraps of news that came to his hiding-places, as he winced at the pains of a leg bone broken by a mute, inanimate flag, he heard and read of a feel-ing deep over the South that he had wronged her and prepared the way for woe and folly and hard hearts. He could read and hear of such specific items as were summarized in a *Harper's Weekly* paragraph captioned "Mourning in Richmond":

"Roger A. Pryor stated in Petersburg that he believed Mr. Lincoln indis-pensable to the restoration of peace, and regretted his death more than any military mishap of the South. He and the Mayor placed themselves at the head of a movement for a town meeting to deplore the loss on both private and public grounds. General Lee at first refused to hear the details of the murder. A Mr. Suite and another gentleman waited upon him on Sunday night with the particulars. He said that when he dispossessed himself of the command of the rebel forces he kept in mind President Lincoln's benignity, and surrendered as much to the latter's goodness as to Grant's artillery. The General said that he regretted Mr. Lincoln's death as much as any man in the North, and believed him to be the epitome of magnanimity and good faith."

The Confederate brigadier general and former United States Senator from Texas, Louis Wigfall, who had killed eight men in duels wherein each man he shot dead had at least a sporting chance—Wigfall refused to credit Booth for marksmanship. Heading toward Texas and stopping in Atlanta, Wigfall in a room with several other Confederate officers heard the news of the assassination brought in. An impressive silence came. After some moments Wigfall spoke: "Gentlemen, I am damned sorry for this. It is the greatest misfortune that could have befallen the South at this time. I knew Abe Lincoln, and, with all his faults, he had a kind heart." Then Wigfall cursed Lincoln's successor—who had for months been crying for a rope around Wigfall's neck.

The wide anger of the people was like the face of the sea in an ominous moment, as the author of *Moby Dick*, Herman Melville, read the hour. Under the title of his poem "The Martyr" Melville noted: "Indicative of the Passion of the People on the 15th of April, 1865."

> Good Friday was the day
>   Of the prodigy and crime,
> When they killed him in his pity,
>   When they killed him in his prime. . . .
> . . . they killed him in his kindness,
> In their madness in their blindness,
> And they killed him from behind . . .
>
> He lieth in his blood—
>   The father in his face;
> They have killed him, the Forgiver—
>   The Avenger takes his place. . . .
>
> There is sobbing of the strong,
>   And a pall upon the land;
> But the People in their weeping
>   Bare the iron hand:
> Beware the People weeping
>   When they bare the iron hand.

In verses titled "Pardon" and footnoted "to Wilkes Booth," Julia Ward Howe wrote that "Harshly the red dawn arose on a deed of his doing . . . harsher days he wore out in the bitter pursuing." And under the title

"Crown His Blood-Stained Pillow" she gave six stanzas for the victim, "this passive hand," "this heart, high-fated," with the bidding:

In the greenest meadow	"Our First Hero, living,
That the prairies show,	Made his country free;
Let his marble shadow	Heed the Second's giving,
Give all men to know:	Death for Liberty."

Instead of a tyrant slayer the assassin was the murderer of a good friend of the South—this Booth may have read in the *Baltimore American* with its news of his home city draped and suffused with mourning. Or the *Richmond Whig* for April 17 may have come into his hands, saying: "The time, manner, and circumstances of President Lincoln's death render it the most appalling, the most deplorable calamity which has ever befallen the people of the United States. . . . Just as everything was happily conspiring to a restoration of tranquility, under the benignant and magnanimous policy of Mr. Lincoln, comes this terrible blow. God grant that it may not rekindle excitement or inflame passion again." The secrecy and stealth of the assassin, the "insane and malignant" method of the deed, made Southern men too heavy-hearted to talk about it.

Nor if a copy had come into Booth's hands of his favorite newspaper when in Chicago, the *Times*, would he have gleaned any comfort at reading that the future "just beginning to yield a glorious light, is again enveloped in utter night." This foremost of Western Copperhead journals had begun to soften its heart as it saw Lincoln moving into a policy it wanted for the South. The newspaper once suppressed by General Burnside, and later on at a nod from Lincoln being permitted to resume its scathing attacks on him, said on April 17: "Since the 4th of March last a higher estimate has been put upon Mr. Lincoln's life, and more voices have ascended to Heaven that it might be spared, than ever before. Since that time all men have realized something of the magnitude of the concerns involved in his lease of existence, and have shuddered at the thought of the possibility of his death." The *Times* hoped that the rebel leaders had not crowned their record with "an unpardonable sin," hoped further the crime would be found "the work of insanity only," which would be "more at the credit of human nature."

On human faces, in a foreboding air, in sudden tattlings of his own imps of thought, Booth came to know the awfulness of what his old friend, the *Chicago Times*, reasoned out for its readers on April 19. Nowhere in the civilized world could he find asylum if he should escape from America. "The assassin of a ruler strikes at all rulers; he is like a pirate whom all nations have an interest in destroying." In no foreign country could he show his true face or let his name be known. "At the moment he struck down Mr. Lincoln he also struck himself from existence. There can be no more a J. Wilkes Booth in any country. If caught he will be hanged. If he escapes he must dwell in a solitude. He has the brand of Cain upon his brow . . . an outcast."

In Richmond and other Southern cities Stanton had ordered that the press withhold publication of the news of Lincoln's assassination. By the word-of-mouth grapevine, by letters and the underground whisper, by leaks from the Union armies, the news did reach many places. And hope went down. Fear grew. The air had a stink of suspicion and mistrust. The former War Department clerk in Richmond, J. B. Jones, wrote a final entry:

"April 17th. Bright and clear. I add a few lines to my Diary. It was whispered, yesterday, that President Lincoln had been assassinated! I met Gen. Duff Green, in the afternoon, who assured me there could be no doubt about it. Still, supposing it might be an April hoax, I inquired at the headquarters of Gen. Ord, and was told it was true. I cautioned those I met to manifest no *feeling*, as the occurrence might be a calamity for the South; and possibly the Federal soldiers, supposing the deed to have been done by a Southern man, might become uncontrollable and perpetrate deeds of horror on the unarmed people. . . . President Lincoln was killed by Booth (Jno. Wilkes), an actor. I suppose his purpose is to live in history as the slayer of a tyrant; thinking to make the leading character in a tragedy, and have his performance acted by others on the stage."

Yet Booth had not entirely miscalculated. There was a small extremist minority element North and South who exulted over his deed. In front of the New York post office on April 15 a man saluted someone, "Did you hear of Abe's last joke?" In a few minutes he was encircled by raging men beating his head and crying "Hang him!" "Kill him!" "Hang the bastard up!" Police rescuers took a volley of bricks and stones. A young Englishman, Peter Britton, having had a few drinks (chronicled the *New York Herald*), walked Vandewater Street snarling oaths at Lincoln, saying, "I came a good ways to see the --- -- - ----- buried." Rescued by police from an excited crowd and taken before Justice Dowling, Britton was sentenced to six months in prison at hard labor. An old acquaintance of Wilkes Booth, Thomas J. Jackson, treasurer of the Winter Garden Theatre, on complaints of witnesses that they heard him say he was glad the President had been killed, was taken to police headquarters to await action by General Dix. Policeman John Brady, also chronicled the *Herald*, quit the force and handed over his shield and club to Captain Caffrey of the 15th precinct, fearing to meet before the police trial board the charge that his captain heard him say to another officer, "I am glad the President was killed; the damned old son of a b---h should have had his head blown off long ago; he had distracted the country long enough." Police Sergeant Walsh of the 6th precinct, at the corner of Chatham and Pearl streets threw a knockout blow to the mouth of one George Wells on hearing the words from that mouth: "Old Abe, the son of a bitch, is dead, and he ought to have been killed long ago." Justice Dowling sent Wells to prison for six months, giving the same sentence to a stage-driver named John Gallagher on the testimony of Officer MacWaters of the 26th precinct that he heard Gallagher say, "It served Abe Lincoln right; he ought to have been shot long ago; it would have stopped this war." In company with Gallagher and Wells went a man named William Fanning, rescued by police from a crowd that hoped to hang him for "opprobrious, insulting and abusive language concerning the President." A man of name unknown at a newspaper stand in the Bowery, on reading the assassination particulars, freely and loosely cursed out Lincoln and his works, suddenly finding himself knocked down and kicked in the face, managing to regain his feet and after a run of several blocks eluding his pursuers by dodging into a crowded Christie Street tenement house.

New York, the major draft-riot city, saw more of this tumult than other places. From coast to coast, however, there was a Copperhead minority to whom Booth was a hero. The *Troy* (New York) *Times* itemized: "At Saratoga Rev. Dr. Beecher expelled from his seminary a young lady pupil for remarking that the murder of Lincoln made Saturday the happiest day of her life. The Doctor says that no person with such sentiments shall sleep under his roof. A workman named Neil was expelled from the arsenal on Saturday for rejoicing. The other employés 'hustled him out.' " The *New York Herald* described a Poughkeepsie scene of April 15: "A large crowd of people are passing up Main Street, escorting a well known rebel sympathizer, whom they are compelling to carry the American flag. Stopping in front of the Eastman College, they compelled him to give three cheers for a flag which floated at half-mast. No violence was used but the mob seemed determined." Also in Poughkeepsie a woman named Frisbie "exulted in public over the assassination of the President," finding her house surrounded by several hundred infuriated people. A young man named Denton tried to interfere, "was immediately throttled," and with the woman was jailed. "This being accomplished the populace quietly dispersed. The city is draped in mourning, and the gloom is general."

A dispatch from Augusta, Maine, told of two women on the train from Skowhegan who "expressed themselves in an offensive manner, exulting over the deed of murder," on request of the train conductor being quietly delivered to a squad of soldiers, who lodged them in the Augusta jail to keep company with several men held for the same sort of talk. One of the men was about to get rough handling from a group of soldiers when the police intervened. The *Lowell* (Massachusetts) *Courier* told of an excited crowd in front of the office of Otis Wright, Superintendent of the Lowell Horse Railroad, demanding that Mr. Wright be given up to them, trying to rush upstairs, being halted by ranks of police and the mayor, who said Mr. Wright would make an explanation. Mr. Wright came out with a Union flag in his hand. The crowd roared they didn't want to hear him. Finally the mayor got him a hearing and he denied that he had made any statement as charged. "A gentleman stepped forward and stated that Mr. Wright said to him, when informed of the President's death, 'Who's fool enough to kill the damned old fool?' The crowd then gave Mr. Wright half an hour to leave the city, and ere that time he was on his way to the New Hampshire line."

At Swampscott, Massachusetts, dispatches recited that one George Stone "said in public it was the best news we had received for four years, and gave three cheers." Citizens and soldiers tarred and feathered Stone, dragged him through the town in a boat, made him hold the American flag over his head. "Upon promising to buy an American flag and keep it up during mourning for the President, at half mast, he was set at liberty." At East Braintree one Elijah Arnold was forced to come out on his front porch, wave the American flag, and give three cheers for the Union. In Fall River, said the telegraph, one Leonard Wood, "a notorious copperhead secesh sympathizer," was heard to declare at the bulletin boards telling of the assassination that it was "the best news he had heard for forty years." He was beaten, kicked, forced to go in a store and get an American flag, unfurl it, and salute it with three cheers. Going then to his own liquor store, he locked himself in and when the crowd came to break in the doors, he was saved by police, who took him to jail escorted by hooting hundreds who later returned to his place of business, stove in the doors, and wrecked the premises.

In most of these cases the offender rash with his mouth spoke his first personal reaction to the news of the assassination, without stopping to think of his community's reaction. The Lincoln-haters at first had no notion of how crushed with grief, how exquisitely sensitive, were an overwhelming number of Lincoln loyalists. "Some villains are fools—so great fools that they parade their villainy before the world," said the *Cleveland Leader*. "Certain traitors in Cleveland on Saturday [April 15] were crazy enough to express their joy at the murder of the President, and received therefore some very rough treatment. J. J. Husband, the well known architect, was in high glee over the news, remarking to one man, 'You have had your day of rejoicing, now I have mine,' to another, 'This is a good day for me,' and to a third, 'Lincoln's death is a damned small loss.' It seems that afterwards he became sensible of the danger he had incurred by these remarks, for he came sneaking to the newspaper offices to deny that he had made them." A mob ran Husband from his office to the roof, there catching him, throwing him through a skylight into his office, and from there kicking him down the stairs. "The mob would perhaps have pounded him to death had he not been rescued by prominent citizens. Locked in a Court House room, he broke out and, we understand, has since left town. He can never show his face in Cleveland again. His name has already been chipped from the place on the Court House where it was cut as the architect."

In another case, recited the *Cleveland Leader*, one James Griffith of Hamilton, Butler County, Ohio, was getting a shave in the Weddell House barber shop when he heard news of the assassination, the words rolling from his rash mouth, "Lincoln was a d----d son of a b---h and ought to have been shot long ago." The words spread, a mob gathered and started for him. A few more orderly citizens tried to take him to jail for safety, but the mob got at him and pounded him badly before he landed behind the bars. "Another traitor, expressing his joy on Ontario Street Saturday morning, was knocked stiff by a little fellow half his size. Other men of Southern sympathies knew enough to keep closely at home Saturday. Cleveland is an unhealthy place for rebels."

In San Francisco, said the telegraph on April 15, "several treasonable brawlers were saved by the police from being lynched." A mob went from one to another office of four "copperhead organs," and "emptied their contents into the street amid the applause of an immense crowd." Police arrived too late to prevent this violence. "Other Democratic newspaper offices are threatened."

In Chicago on Madison Street and Canal Street men and boys sent rocks crashing through the big glass windows of several saloons. In each of these places the Copperhead saloonkeeper had hung in the front window a large portrait of the more or less eminent Shakespearian actor, J. Wilkes Booth.

All of these were minor incidents—not quite events.

The total of them could be canceled, in the national accounting, by the incident of the Confederate Major Charles F. Baker of the Cherokee Volunteer Cavalry, at Cairo on his way to New Orleans for exchange, writing a letter published in the *Cairo War Eagle*. He wished "the vengeance of heaven" on the assassin and made it known in writing that if the Confederate authorities were implicated, "I am as far on my way south as I wish to go."

The North which had now established a Union of States was in grief. Everywhere the eye might turn hung the signs of this grief.

The sermons, the editorials, the talk in streets, houses, saloons, railroad cars and streetcars, the black bunting and the crape—these were attempts to say something that could not be said.

Silence counted.

Men tried to talk about it and the words failed and they came back to silence.

To say nothing was best.

Lincoln was dead.

Was there anything more to say?

Yes, they would go through the motions of grief and they would take their part in a national funeral and a ceremony of humiliation and abasement and tears.

But words were no help.

Lincoln was dead.

Nothing more than that could be said.

He was gone.

He would never speak again to the American people.

A great friend of man had suddenly vanished.

Nothing could be done about it.

Death is terribly final.

When you die and you are dead that is the end, and no speeches, no decorations, no trimmings will help. Death is the end.

There can be an immortality and a living on and a remembering, flowers and symbols and forget-me-nots, immortelles and white lilies and red roses —and these are beautiful and profound.

Yet death is a fact closing other facts and sealing them for all time.

Silence, grief, and quiet resolves, these only were left for those who admired and loved and felt themselves close to a living presence that was one of them.

The testimonies were vast that when the news came that he had been killed, that he was dead, that he had gone from them and would never speak again—there was shock, they were stunned, there was nothing to say, they could sit silent and weep.

The tears came—and nothing to say.

When they said "It is terrible" or "God help us!" or "It is too bad" or "Great God, how sad!" it was not as though they were talking to others but rather as though they were moaning to themselves and knowing very well no words were any use.

Thousands on thousands would remember as long as they lived the exact place where they had been standing or seated or lying down when the news came to them, recalling precisely in details and particulars where they were and what doing when the dread news arrived.

"President Lincoln is dead" or "President Lincoln is assassinated" were the four words with which so often the news was given in cities, at cross-roads, on farms—four smiting words.

Hundreds of thousands there were who had been the foundation and groundwork of what he had done.

They had given what he asked.

When he called for sons, fathers, husbands, brothers, these had been given—solemnly but willingly—without the draft—without coercion—willingly in a faith and belief that joined his, some for the sacred and mystic Union of States, some for that Union and furthermore the uprooting and destruction of slavery.

These people—the basic Lincoln loyalist legion—these had no words, they had only grief—sorrow beyond words.

"A stricken people came to their altars."

They were paralyzed with grief.

They were dazed, amazed, numbed—they required first of all silence for conference with their lonely hearts.

Men turned pale, shook hands slow and long, parted saying nothing.

Or if they spoke a few words they broke off as though aware it was hardly a time for words.

The national flag alone didn't seem right—it belonged for this hour with a black border, or a piece of crape festooning it.

For days the Stars and Stripes must be an emblem of anguish.

Solemn woe on faces—no hint of a smile—quiet mirthless faces—this was the order of the day.

Some spoke of the green spring grass so bright and the high sun blazing —how they wore shadows of twilight at noon.

The chatter of hopping and happy birds was forgiven as a sacrilege of the nonhuman world.

Whatever was sensitively and humanly aware wore crape, seen or unseen

The victory flag raised at Fort Sumter, it was noted, had come down to half-mast.

"No, it cannot be, it is too sad, too terrible to be true," said men and women hoping for comfort from such wailing.

Some asked why it had to come amid the glad guns and booming joy bells of the end of the war—why should they be woe-struck while they rejoiced?

And why should the day of the doom be Good Friday—"in coincidence with the Passion of Our Lord"?

To this they added their passing thought that if the slain one could have returned to waking consciousness one moment he would have said, "Forgive him—he knew not what he did."

The news came on the nation's head and heart, said one, "as a hammer with fire."

Another mentioned those "whose flesh quivered as from pincers tearing."

In Boston, said one, the story ticked off the telegraph at midnight was at first rejected, later staring out from grim newspaper lines making the reader's brain reel, passing along in husky voices, leaping from face to face, shaping as a fact in the black borders and crape hung over the festive flags of the day before, a hush of gloom coming over streets, shops, stores, depots —then finally the desperate fact wailing from steeple to steeple of church bells and groaning from the mouths of loud hoarse cannon.

Far out on the rolling prairie of the Iowa frontier, a farmer rode a fast horse and shouted from the saddle, first to this neighbor and then the next, "Lincoln is shot!" or "Lincoln is dead—shot in a theatre!"

That was all. The rider was gone. They had heard him. They stood in their foot tracks, amazed, dumbstruck, sadly waited for further news, some saying, "What will the country do now?"

On an early morning streetcar in Philadelphia a good Quaker unrolled a morning newspaper, stared at it, and broke out: "My God! what is this? Lincoln is assassinated!"

In the gray dawn on this streetcar men cupped their faces in their hands and on the straw-covered floor fell hot tears.

The driver of the streetcar came in to make sure of what he heard.

Then the driver went out and took the bells off his horses.

And he drove on with his car filled with mourners, some silent, some sobbing.

Newsboys at their stands cried no headlines, handed the damp sheets from the press to the buyers, one boy noticed as he brushed with his dirty hand the tears from his dirty cheeks.

In thousands of stores the merchant told the clerks they would close for the day; in many schools the sobbing teacher could only tell the children, "Go home, there will be no school today."

The father, the children, coming home unexpected, the mother asked what was wrong and heard "Mama, they've killed the President" or "Our President is dead."

Then the family hunted up crape or black cloth for the front doorway.

"Even the operators in gold," chronicled the *New York Herald* of April 16, "were shocked to such an extent that when the board met yesterday morning, and the sad intelligence was communicated to the members, they were utterly unable to transact the usual business and a motion to adjourn was unanimously adopted."

In the little village of Durham, North Carolina, just before the news arrived there, an old Negro keeping a shanty barbershop for Union Army patrons told his first customer, as his hand shook while holding the razor, that he wouldn't shave anyone this day, and being asked why: "Somethin's happen to Marse Linkum—I don' know jes wut it is—but somethin's gone wrong with Marse Linkum."

In Charleston, South Carolina, one old black woman walked a street looking straight ahead, wringing her hands and crying: "O Lawd! O Lawd! Marse Sam's dead! O Lawd! Uncle Sam's dead!"

The national capital took on a breathing bosom of mourning, one seeing it as "an immense black and white flower, with leaves and petals spreading grandly and in perfect keeping, with every point of the compass," an overwhelmingly somber harmony never before seen.

In Danville, Illinois, a white-faced editor came in with a telegram, without a word passed it to the printers, who read it, laid down their typesetter "sticks," and without a word took from wall nails their coats and hats, put them on, and walked out into the street.

In Boston a thousand or more men found themselves on the Common, marching in a silent procession, two by two, not a word spoken, just walking, just seeing each other's faces, saying nothing, marching an hour or so and then slowly scattering, having reached some form of consolation in being together, seeing each other in mute grief.

In a home at Huntington, Long Island, a mother and grown son heard the news early in the morning, sat at breakfast and ate nothing, sat at other meals during the day and ate nothing, silently passed newspaper extras to each other during the day and said little, the son deciding that as long as he lived he would on April 14 have sprigs of lilac in his room and keep it as a holy day.

Four years now since they had seen him take his oath of office, when they wondered what he would be like as a national Chief Magistrate.

And time had gone by and he had proved himself.

In the cost and slaughter of the Peninsula campaign, when he said that sending troops to McClellan was like "shoveling fleas in a barnyard," he had managed to keep hope alive while others were ready to quit.

They knew his thought lay close to the soldiers, as in his saying to a general when the platoons of the Army of the Potomac passed in review at Chancellorsville—"What is to become of these boys when the war is over?"

They knew his heart groaned over that stream of boys and men moving south and ever south for four long years, that he lived with a multitude of phantom youths who had called him by nicknames and pet words, that he walked with death and became its familiar, that he had no fear over joining "the bivouac of the dead," that in the shadowland to which he had now crossed had gone many comrades, Kearny and Reynolds and Sedgwick and Wadsworth and Mansfield and Private Scott and brave men he had commissioned and even deserters he had pardoned, that Ellsworth and Baker and others over whom he had wept were among the shadows.

They had not heard of his murmuring to the woman who wrote *Uncle Tom's Cabin*, "I shan't last long after it's over," though his face carried the weariness.

They could believe that a Pennsylvania Congressman told him of Northern enemies who threatened to go to Washington and hang him to a lamppost and his replying that he had considered "the violent preliminaries" to such a scene.

They knew he was in danger, though he had never let them know that his hat was shot off his head one night near the Soldiers' Home.

They had heard and believed and liked it that he said to one applicant, "I haven't any influence with this Administration," and to another, "I don't amount to pig tracks over in the War Department."

They had found a tone scriptural and portentous in his way of saying that the Mississippi River could not peacefully be shared out for ownership among a dozen States, that the generations pass but the earth remaineth and the issue of the Union could not be put off to another day and time.

They could well believe he had told a Hoosier Congressman, "Don't it seem strange to you, that I, who could never so much as cut off the head of a chicken, should be elected, or selected, into the midst of all this blood?"

Some saw him as a ship captain grave, serene, unfailing, through a series of storms that composed the one main endless storm of four years.

Language was inadequate, but into the quivering and tensed brain of the one man Lincoln had mentioned as a possible assassin came a serene gift of speech—and Adam Gurowski wrote in his diary of April 15: "The pilot of the Government welters in his blood. This murder, this oozing blood, almost sanctify Lincoln. His end atones for all the short-comings for which he was blamed and condemned by earnest and unyielding patriots. Grand and noble will Lincoln stand in the world's history. No crying injustice, not a single inhuman or perverse action stain Lincoln's name; and whatever sacrifices his vacillations may have cost the people, those vacillations will now be forgiven. His hand and his blood sealed the terrific struggle. His end will live in history and in the people's grateful, warm, and generous memory. The murderer's bullet opens to him immortality. To-day the regrets and the blessings of mourning humanity surround his funeral pile."

Amid slaughters too bloody and stupid to report to the country, amid vile babblings and a heavy sustained pressure of foolish counsels, he had gone on without one of the major mistakes that could have lost everything.

In a furnace and a huggermugger of blood and muck he had proved himself.

He was one of them.

He was of the people, by the people, and for the people.

When his decisions had gone wrong, more often than not it was because of the American scene and conditions, where any man's guess was as good as another's.

Over and again when the sky hung black and everything was dark he had spoken, and what he had said was what they, as they studied it, believed should be said.

Week by week he had slowly become their neighbor, their close friend, the man of understanding who was worth following even when they could not be sure where he was leading them.

The boy on the fighting fronts with McClellan, Burnside, Hooker, Pope, Thomas, Grant, Sherman, Sheridan—the son, brother, father, husband—he was fighting for the cause proclaimed by Father Abraham, by Old Abe, by President Lincoln.

Now Father Abraham was gone.

Ole Abe—there would be no more stories about him, alive there in the White House in Washington.

President Lincoln—his announcements and proclamations, his letters and speeches—it was all finished and over.

They had saved the newspapers or they had clipped from the paper such pieces as the Gettysburg speech and the letter to Mrs. Bixby and the second inaugural.

Now the newspapers had black borders, night's crape darkness, on the front-page columns.

Now there was a memory to keep.

That was left—the life he had lived—the meanings and the lights of that life.

This could not be taken away.

Neither a one-shot brass derringer nor the heaviest artillery on earth could shoot away and blot out into darkness the kept picture, the saved speeches, the remembrances and keepsakes—the shape and the tone of this tall prophet of the American dream and its hope of the Family of Man around the earth.

Farmers in southern Illinois said the brown thrush no longer sang.

They were to say that in the year to come the brown thrush never once sang.

One Illinois boy going to town, holding his father's hand, having heard the church and town-hall bells all day, having seen only dark sorrow on all faces, looked up at the sky and found it strange the night stars were all out.

Lincoln was dead—and yet as always the stars moved alive over the night dome.

Like a vast sunset of flame and changing gold ending a day and punctuating a period of time their faraway friend at Washington had vanished into the overhead planets and the same constellations of mist that had taken that long roll call of soldiers no longer answering "Present" as the company sergeant called the names.

There are houses into which Death enters as something personal and real only when someone dear in that house lies cold and still in the corruptions of flesh.

Not till then do they know Death as actual, vast, invincible, having an ethereal white beauty before which people bow while listening to an almost inaudible music.

Thus Death became present in a million and more American households when the news of April 14 winged its way across the continent.

A man they had come to know as personal, real, and cherished entered their thoughts with an actuality as though he might be lying dead near the doorsills of their own house.

This was so.

In cities, at crossroads villages, at far-off lonely farms and homesteads, it was so.

For the Lincoln loyalist legion, that basic element of the people who had upheld Lincoln's arms and for whom he was the living voice of the nation, it was so.

They had come to say as individuals those words of the assassin's brother, "Abraham Lincoln is *my* President."

For him more than any other spokesman they had accepted burdens, taxes, toil, weariness, monotony, matching their faith and hope with his.

For them now Death was in their houses—cold, still, personal—a friend and a kinsman of all men—gone.

And there was nothing to say.

The grief was beyond words.

They sought for words that might help and assuage.

"The land mourneth, every family apart," ran one Easter Sunday text.

"He is risen; he is not here" was quoted, and "Because I live, ye shall live also."

"Thy way is in the sea, and thy path in the great waters, and thy footsteps are not known" had a fitting music.

Also "The steps of a good man are ordered by the Lord: and He delighteth in his way."

For the travail of the hour was "The joy of our heart is ceased; our dance is turned into mourning."

Ominous was the note "His wounds cry out."

For those prostrated was the solace "All the inhabitants of the earth are reputed as nothing."

These served as sermon and editorial texts and allusions.

Scores of ministers quoted, not knowing how he had favored its quaint flavor, "His eye was not dim, nor his natural force abated."

Likewise he would have been pleased at the use of the verse "The Lord . . . made them to suck honey out of the rock, and oil out of the flinty rock."

Over doorways, in store windows, on arches spanning streets, ran the legend "And the Lord blessed Abraham in all things."

Also "The workman dies, but the work goes on" and its variant, "God buries his workmen, but carries on his work."

On one arch of crape and white over Broadway in New York ran the sentence "The great person, the great man, is the miracle of history."

Often from Matthew 9:15 was the verse intoned on Easter Sunday: "And Jesus said unto them, Can the children of the bridechamber mourn, as long as the bridegroom is with them? but the days will come, when the bridegroom shall be taken from them, and then shall they fast."

CHAPTER 75

A TREE IS BEST MEASURED WHEN IT'S DOWN

ON the Saturday following Good Friday thousands of sermons were laid away as of no use for Easter Sunday. A new sermon had to be written or extemporized after the news arrived on Saturday forenoon or afternoon that the President was dead. The pastor who failed to deal with the national grief heard from his flock. The *Boston Herald* instanced the Reverend Mr. Massey of Bellingham, Massachusetts, who preached by exchange in Medway village, "never deigning to mention the death of our good President," wherefore "a resolution was passed by the congregation, pointedly condemning his course, and giving him fifteen minutes to leave town; he left instanter."

In great stone cathedrals of the cities, in modest frame churches of small towns, in little cabin churches at country crossroads, in hospital chapels and in at least one State prison, on navy ships and in outdoor army-camp services, there were Easter Sunday sermons memorializing the dead President.

The outpouring from thousands of pulpits from coast to coast rather uniformly dwelt with varied emphasis and feeling on the same themes: the shock of the news coming in the midst of jubilation over the war ending; the day of the crime being Good Friday among Christians and the Fort Sumter anniversary to patriots; the President slain in a theatre and the slayer an actor and a monster not to be named; the hand of Providence in the event and the design of the Almighty inscrutable; death comes to each and all, wherefore lead the good life enjoined by the Scriptures; the President's martyrdom enshrines him with world immortals; the Republic will nevertheless go forward.

A large minority of the Protestant ministers made reference to the President meeting death in a playhouse and directly or by inference spoke their regret. Some were full and explicit about this, not condemning, but reluctantly voicing what was in mind and heart, as did the Reverend Justin Dewey Fulton in Tremont Temple in Boston:

"We remember, with sorrow, the place of his death. He did not die on Mount Nebo, with his eye full of heaven. He was shot in a theatre. We are sorry for that. It was a poor place to die in. It would not be selected by any of you as the spot from which you would desire to proceed to the bar of God. If ever any man had an excuse to attend a theatre, he had. The cares of office were heavy upon him. His brain reeled. His frame grew weak. He longed for a change. He desired to get away from the crowd, from the cares and responsibilities of office. Washington's closet would have been preferable. In conversing with a friend, he said, 'Some think I do wrong to go to the opera and the theatre; but it rests me. I love to be alone, and yet to be with the people. I want to get this burden off; to change the current of my thoughts. A hearty laugh relieves me; and I seem better able after it to bear my cross.' This was his excuse. Upon it we will not pronounce a judgment. This we will say: we are all sorry our best loved died there. But take the truth with its shadow."

It was to be six weeks later that the Reverend Dr. Phineas D. Gurley in the New York Avenue Presbyterian Church in Washington, facing the pew on which Lincoln paid rent and of which Lincoln had often been the occupant, would fully reveal an aversion and a deep abhorrence that could not have been properly spoken on Easter Sunday. The feeling that existed widely in church circles then, but was in the main repressed immediately after the assassination—this was voiced in a sincerity beyond questioning in Dr. Gurley's words:

"It will always be a matter of deep regret to thousands that our lamented President fell in the theatre; that the dastardly assassin found him, shot him there. Multitudes of his best friends—I mean his *Christian* friends—would have preferred that he should have fallen in almost any other place. Had he been murdered in his bed, or in his office, or on the street, or on the steps of the Capitol, the tidings of his death would not have struck the Christian heart of the country quite so painfully; for the feeling of that heart is that the theatre is one of the last places to which a good man should go, and among the *very* last in which his friends would wish him to die. Little or nothing has been said upon this subject in the pulpit or by the religious press; but it is one of the cases in which silence is more expressive than words."

Then came a confession of hate and loathing, one of the fiercest maledictions ever pronounced on the theatre and the theatrical tribe. Parts of it undoubtedly Lincoln had heard from Dr. Gurley in the pulpit or as a White House visitor—and had nevertheless continued going to dramatic performances, sometimes hand in hand with Tad. Dr. Gurley however spoke for a formidable and significant mass of church people in saying:

"For my own part, I have always regarded the theatre as in the main a school of vice and corruption—the illumined and decorated gateway through which thousands are constantly passing into the embrace of gaiety and folly,

intemperance and ·lewdness, infamy and ruin. I have always hated and.
avoided it, and taught my children to avoid it, on account of its characte**r**
and influence, its associations and accompaniments, its misleading, corrupt,
ing, and demoralizing tendencies; but henceforth it will be more odious to
me than ever before. May it be odious to you. I . . . lift my voice against it,.
and exhort you to number it from this day forth among the polluting, peril-
ous, and prohibited places where you and your children must never be
found. And as for yonder building stained with the blood of him for whom
the nation mourns to-day, let Aceldama be written upon its walls, and let
it stand for years to come as it now stands, silent, gloomy, forlorn, more
like a sepulchre than a place of amusement, saying to all the passers-by,
'Here the greatest crime of the age was committed, and committed by one
who was addicted to tragedy and had made the stage his home.' "

Such "heavy onslaught" upon actors, said the *Chicago Times*, was un-
called-for. The fact that Booth was an actor had no bearing whatever upon
his profession, the case being "the very first on record in which any actor
has been guilty of any crime of magnitude." The writer of the editorial, it
was plain, liked actors and enjoyed going to plays, saying: "From their
much traveling, actors become cosmopolitan; they do not sympathize with
factions or parties; and we suppose the fact that actors are not all abolitionists has given rise to the present attack."

The Reverend A. L. Stone of the Park Street Church in Boston believed
he spoke for "many of us" the feeling "that we could have wished for him
whom we mourn a different scene for the last hour." Yet Mr. Stone saw
too that Lincoln found "scarcely festal walls" in the theatre, rather "refuge
for one who had no retirement of home from the incessant calls and weary-
ing importunities of aspirants for place and office." One Reverend Dr.
Duffield of Detroit, however, rivaled Dr. Gurley in imprecations: "Would
that Mr. Lincoln had fallen elsewhere than at the very gates of Hell—in the
theater to which, through persuasion, he reluctantly went. How awful and
severe the rebuke which God has administered to the nation for pampering
such demoralizing places of resort. The blood of Abraham Lincoln can
never be effaced from the stage." If death was decreed for the President,
the Reverend L. M. Glover in Jacksonville, Illinois, would have rather it occurred "in the street, in the council chamber, in the national museum or
even the sanctuary of God." Mr. Glover refused to accept, however, the
dictum of those whom he had heard declare that the President "being in a
theater, had been out of God's jurisdiction and had forfeited the divine
protection."

That Lincoln, without being an affiliated churchman, had by a natural
reverence, without affectation, won his way to many hearts of the clergy
was evident in pulpit tributes paid him. The Reverend Mr. Fulton mingled
his praise with a reminiscence:

"He was one of the people. Well do some of us remember standing
upon the steps of the White House, as he came forth from the Presidential
mansion. He bowed to us in passing. Our hearts were touched by his care-

worn, anxious face. Passing into the grounds, on his way to the War Office, he stopped to give a greeting to a couple of pet goats that waited for his recognition. While thus engaged, one of the party stepped up and said, 'Mr. Lincoln, will you allow me to introduce to you two Massachusetts women.' He drew himself up to his full height, swept his hand over his face, and said, 'Yes, bring them along.' We came, and were introduced. He chatted pleasantly until we grew frightened, and begged him not to allow us to intrude upon his time. We felt, it was said, that it would be a great pleasure to shake hands with our honored Chief Magistrate, here, beneath God's open heaven, and on this green grass. 'Ah!' said he, waiting a moment, 'such a privilege is worth contending for,' and then, assuring us of his pleasure to greet the people, he passed on to his laborious tasks. Well has it been said, 'No one who approached him, whether as minister or messenger, felt impelled either to stoop or strut in his presence.' "

Another Boston sermon had its text from II Samuel 19:2: "And the victory that day was turned into mourning unto all the people." From this the Reverend Samuel K. Lothrop began in the tone of the day: "Brethren, but one theme can command your attention today. . . . I feel almost incompetent to direct your thoughts this morning, as I have scarcely been able for the last twenty-four hours to collect and guide my own. Language is impotent." Many made such acknowledgment. Mr. Lothrop gave a reminiscence: "I remember, in the only interview I ever had with him, in the autumn of 1861, at Washington, in company with twenty or thirty other persons, each of whom had his special purpose in the visit, and went up in his turn to present it, that I was at first amused, not to say offended, at what seemed an undignified levity, and a marvellous facility in conveying or enforcing his answers to the various requests presented, by telling some story, the logic of whose application to the case in point was unmistakably clear. During this part of the interview I was led to wonder where was the power? how had this man so impressed himself upon the people of the country, as to be elevated to the position he occupied? That wonder ceased, that inquiry was answered, before I left the presence. A lady made application for the release of her brother, who had been arrested for disloyalty by the major-general commanding in the vicinity of Frederick, Maryland. The President declined to interfere, on the ground that he knew nothing of the circumstances but what she had told him, and that the arrest and detention were, necessarily, within the discretionary power of the major-general commanding in the district. Considerable conversation ensued, and some tears were shed; and, at length, the President consented to indorse upon her petition, which was to be forwarded to the major-general, that he had no objection to the release, provided the general thought it compatible with the public safety. As he gave her back the petition, with this indorsement, he said, and I think I remember very nearly his exact words: 'Madam, I desire to say that there is no man who feels a deeper or more tender sympathy than I do, with all cases of individual sorrow, anxiety, and grief like yours, which these unhappy troubles occasion; but I see not how I can prevent or relieve them. I am here to administer this Government, to uphold the Constitution, to maintain the Union of the United States. That is my oath; before God and man, I must, I mean to the best of my ability, to keep that oath; and, however much my personal feelings may sympathize with individual sorrows and anxieties, I must not yield to them. They must all give way before the great public exigencies of the country!' I shall never forget the simple majesty, the grandeur and force with which these few sentences were uttered, or their effect. In a moment the room was as still as death. The little audience that had, just before, been laughing at his stories, were awed and impressed, thrilled through and through by these few solemn and earnest words. They were a revelation of the man. They made me feel that there was a power in him that gave him a right to be where he was."

The assassin, noted the Reverend George L. Chaney of Boston, was "a cool lunatic suicide." The Reverend Cyrus A. Bartol saw him as a madman depraved by the slavery institution. "The barbarism of slavery, that demon whispered in the actor's ear! That dragon fired his passion, and nerved his arm!" Mr. Bartol thought *"Sic semper tyrannis"* nothing short of "a marvelous cry" for a murderer "as he slew the softest-hearted of men, the mildest among all he was set over, mild as May, whose fault, if he had one, was that he was not sufficiently stern with the vileness he could not comprehend." The Reverend A. A. Miner saw the assassin as a product of Baltimore. "Unhappy city that gave the assassin birth! The home of disorder, the nursery of rioters . . . pity, oh, pity unhappy Baltimore!" The Reverend John E. Todd was sure "the infuriated and probably drunken actor" would not escape. "He may take the wings of the morning and fly to the uttermost parts of the sea; he may make his bed in hell; but he will not escape." The Reverend Sidney Dean in Providence, Rhode Island, pointed to the first Judas as merely a betrayer who took his price of money, let others do the deed of death, at once having enough remorse and good sense to go hang himself. "This second Judas, worse than his namesake, himself committed the murder. The second Judas we trust will be hanged in the sight of the world, whose air he poisons in inhaling, by the hands of a pure justice, and we trust all his blood-stained employers will be hanged with him."

Over and again were the parallels drawn of Lincoln and Christ in blood of atonement dying for mankind, and of Lincoln having his Judas no less than Christ. "The last and costliest offering which God demanded has been taken," said the Reverend C. B. Crane of the South Baptist Church of Hartford, Connecticut, clarifying further: "It is no blasphemy against the Son of God and the Saviour of men that we declare the fitness of the slaying of the second Father of our Republic on the anniversary of the day on which He was slain. Jesus Christ died for the world, Abraham Lincoln died for his country." To this was added counsel for the immediate hour: "As the tragedy of the cross has startled tens of thousands of sinners into a recognition of their sins, while it expressed the inflexibility of God's law and authority, so we may hope that the tragedy of last Friday night will startle the multitude of rebels, North as well as South, into a recognition of their crime, stiffen the government, which might otherwise bend, into requisite rigidness, and hasten the consummation of peace for which we devoutly pray."

In scores of sermons was sounded the note of doom for the Southern leaders, for those who incarnated what the Reverend E. B. Webb of Boston termed "the same hell-born spirit that dastardly takes the life of our beloved President." Too long had "a driveling, morbid, perverted sense of justice" been permitted under the shadow of the Capitol at Washington. "The idea, to me, of placing the leaders of this diabolical rebellion in a position where they might come again red-handed into the councils of the nation, is revolting and sacrilegious. It makes me shudder. And yet I think there was an *indecent* leniency beginning to manifest itself towards them, which would have allowed to these men, by and by, votes and honors and lionizing." Thus Mr. Webb in his Easter Sunday sermon shuddered in horror at the animating spirit of Lincoln in the Louisiana speech of April 11 and the final counsels with the Cabinet on April 14. From this Mr. Webb passed into eulogies of the new President Andrew Johnson and his hope and expectation that Johnson would live up to his pledge to try, convict, and hang the secessionist leaders. Nevertheless the first half of Mr. Webb's sermon proliferated with praise of Lincoln. Of the President whose leniency he considered "indecent," "revolting," "sacrilegious," he said: "Were I to select some one thing by which to characterize Abraham Lincoln, I should name his profound apprehension and appreciation of the popular instinct; that instinct which is true to the right as the needle to the pole, in all storms, and on every sea. He believed in God; he believed God was to be recognized in this war."

The Southern "mis-leaders," said the Reverend John E. Todd in his Easter Sunday sermon, "are men to be hunted down like wild beasts, and sent to the prison and the gallows; secession is not to be vanquished by leniency and kindness, but is to be stamped out with the iron heel." Having praised the dead President's purity of motive, his patience and self-control, his personal honesty, his sagacity which won the people to his policies and methods, his "remarkable kindness toward the colored race," and his management of the emancipation issue, his "virtues such as would have adorned a king," Mr. Todd named his "grave faults." They were "over-leniency and generosity, deliberation and patience—faults which would have been excellences in less desperate times, and which even in these times have probably been our salvation." The motive of God in ordaining the President's death at this time was hidden and inscrutable. "This awful crime perhaps was needed to bring the people to some desired point; perhaps He had a work to be done fitter for some other hands than those which have done so much noble work, and are now forever still. . . . For President Lincoln *himself*, perhaps there was no better time to pass away. He fell in the very height of his glory . . . a death becoming a Christian patriot—a glorious death to die . . . perhaps finding not only his headstone worn with the kisses of his own race, but the sods of his grave sprinkled with the tears of eyes that used to weep in the house of bondage."

Many sermons and editorials drew a parallel between Lincoln and Moses on Mount Pisgah, each taken away after the hard desert journey—and the Promised Land in sight. The Reverend J. M. Manning of Boston quoted the text "I have caused thee to see it with thine eyes, but thou shalt not go over thither." Mr. Manning pointed to the calm figure of Abraham Lincoln, while some were wildly urging him to take the archives and flee, as a rock "tranquil amid the raging billows." Mr. Manning when he considered that Mr. Lincoln "disliked the sight of blood," that Mr. Lincoln "was melted by tears," that Mr. Lincoln was "made soft as woman by the tones of pleading wretchedness," said he would not attempt to scan the counsels of the Most High, though he must confess: "Perhaps it is better for us that we should be orphans today, than that he whom we loved to call 'Father' should have been spared. His paternal heart, had it still throbbed in life, might have proved too tender for the stern work we are yet to do." To this was added the meditation: "Perhaps God is giving us our grand opportunity to show to an incredulous world, that we are indeed a government by the people. Had not our beloved President been taken from us, had he lived until we were clearly out of all our troubles, it might have been pleaded that his personal wisdom carried us through. Not so now."

Why did Providence permit the hand of the assassin to go unstopped in its course? Thus inquired the Reverend Chandler Robbins of Boston, saying: "You must discover that secret before you begin to question His wisdom. Who can tell us that greater evil would not have accrued from the arrest, than from the execution of that satanic deed?—greater evil to him whom we lament, to the people to whom he was so unselfishly devoted, to the cause dearer to him than life?" This had an Easter reverence and a delicacy of approach not evident in the sermon of the Reverend W. S. Studley of Boston, who cried for multiple hangings of Southern traitors, quoted the new President's demand, "the halter to intelligent, influential traitors," and declared from the pulpit: "In dealing with traitors, Andrew Johnson's little finger will be thicker than Abraham Lincoln's loins. If the *old* president chastised them with whips, the *new* president will chastise them with scorpions."

Like many speakers, the Reverend James Reed of Boston read aloud the full text of Lincoln's second inaugural. He appraised Lincoln's work. "The memory of it will live forever. A greater work is seldom performed by a single man. Generations yet unborn will rise up and call him blessed." Mr. Reed surmised, "It may be that he who was the best leader in time of war is not best fitted for the new exigencies which are arising," and included the cryptic "Certain it is that our President would not have been taken away, if he had not finished his appointed work."

In Trinity Church of New York City the Reverend Dr. Francis Vinton pointed to Samuel, who, "knowing his stern mission from God, took Agag and hewed him in pieces for the Lord," and admonished, "In this stern spirit should the leaders of the rebellion be dealt with." Scarcely veiling his political views and personal wishes, Dr. Vinton construed the latest inscrutable events: "President Lincoln had arrived at the end of his mission. On the very day not only of our Lord's crucifixion, but the day on which the raising of the flag over Sumter typified the resurrection of the nation, God had said to him, 'Well done, thou good and faithful servant, enter thou into the joy of thy Lord.' It may be that President Lincoln was unfitted, by the natural gentleness and humanity of his disposition, to execute the stern justice of Christ's viceregent. And so let us say, 'God's will be done.'"

In scores of sermons before large congregations of the well-to-do and influential, radicals who had opposed the living Lincoln's policy of leniency and pardon took advantage of the outcry and passion aroused by the dead Lincoln's assassin—and pressed the need for trials and hangings of Southern leaders. In the Protestant churches of Boston such clergymen were in a large majority of the pulpits. In other cities and communities, however, the clergy in the main humbly held themselves to spiritual ministration and kept out of politics. The latter was the course of the Reverend Edward Everett Hale in his Unitarian Church in Boston, dwelling on the Good Friday midnight kiss of Judas, of how the world has never known precisely what was the fate of Judas and "whether he were finished villain or fanatic fool: Satan chooses such accomplices . . . to kill the world's best friend." The martyr bespoke "On earth peace, and good will among men." Mr. Hale intimated that in the passions of the hour, including his own, it behooved good men to think twice and speak slow with political advice, saying: "I dare not trust myself to speak a word regarding this simple, godly, good, great man. . . . To speak of him I must seek some other hour." Mr. Hale saw the Republic as eternal, ready to live through successive assassinations, ending his sermon, "Fear not, little flock; it is your Father's good pleasure to give you the kingdom."

In like tone with the living Lincoln were many of the sermons in Roman Catholic churches and in Hebrew synagogues. "We pray," said Archbishop McCloskey in St. Patrick's Cathedral, New York, "that the sentiments of mercy and clemency and conciliation that so filled the heart of the beloved President whom we have just lost will still actuate and guide the breast of him who, in this critical and trying hour, is called to fill his place."

Henry Ward Beecher, the most accomplished artist of them all if stump oratory was required from the pulpit, threw himself with a wild-flowing vitality into the occasion. Nothing now of that remark of his in Charleston a few days earlier that Johnson's little finger was stronger than Lincoln's loins. The nation, in grief over the unburied one whose funeral procession was yet to move, wanted consolation, psalms of praise for the dead, and dirges of woe for the sorrowing. Beecher's Easter Sunday congregation in Plymouth Church, Brooklyn, filled all pews and added chairs in the aisles, the platform, the standing-room. When he opened the hymn-book and swept his eyes over the audience as the pipe organ sent its chords through open windows to hundreds outside who had failed to get in, he noticed that scores had climbed up on the window sills to stand and listen. To one outsider "the great white church was like a hive, with the swarming bees hanging in clusters upon the outside." It was an hour for oratory and Beecher had his manuscript ready, trusting to no impromptus in this highly emotional moment. As the wind blew freshly from the windows, he reminded the audience that a handkerchief laid on the head would prevent the sensitive from catching cold. Then opening his Bible, he read the story of Moses going up to Pisgah and began his sermon on Lincoln.

"He was a man from the common people, that never forgot his kind," said Beecher. "Every virtuous household in the land felt as if its first-born were gone. Men were bereaved, and walked for days as if a corpse lay unburied in their dwellings. There was nothing else to think of. They could speak of nothing but that; and of that they could speak only falteringly. All business was laid aside. Pleasure forgot to smile. The city . . . ceased to roar. . . . Even avarice stood still. . . . Rear to his name monuments, found charitable institutions, and write his name above their lintels; but no monument will ever equal the universal, spontaneous, and sublime sorrow that in a moment swept down lines and parties, and covered up animosities, and in an hour brought a divided people into unity of grief and indivisible fellowship of anguish."

Skillfully for his purposes the orator Beecher laid entire blame on the slavery institution for the assassination, pointing to the murderer as one suckled and nursed in the slave system, a logical outgrowth of its cruel and boisterous passions. "Slavery wastes its victims, and destroys the masters. . . . It corrupts manhood in its very centre and elements. Communities in which it exists are not to be trusted. They are rotten. . . . The honour that grows up in the midst of slavery is not honour, but a bastard quality." The rebellion, the war, the assassination, all resulted from "that disease of slavery which is a deadly poison to soul and body." Never, said the speaker, would men forget that the slavery institution with its "mischiefs and monsters" had martyred one American President. "Never! while time lasts, while heaven lasts, while hell rocks and groans."

From the crashing, fighting blare of this diatribe he moved into a soft and tenderly keyed passage ending with a dramatic oath. "Even he who now sleeps, has, by this event, been clothed with a new influence. Dead, he speaks to men who now willingly hear what before they refused to listen to. Now his simple and weighty words will be gathered like those of Washington, and your children, and your children's children, shall be taught to ponder the simplicity and deep wisdom of utterances which, in their time, passed, in party heat, as idle words. Men will receive a new impulse of patriotism for his sake and will guard with zeal the whole country which he loved so well.

"I charge you, on the altar of his memory, to be more faithful to the country for which he has perished. They will, as they follow his hearse, swear a new hatred to that slavery against which he warred, and which, in vanquishing him, has made him a martyr and a conqueror. I charge you, by the memory of this martyr, to hate slavery with an unappeasable hatred. They will admire and imitate the firmness of this man, his inflexible conscience for the right; and yet his gentleness, as tender as a woman's, his moderation of spirit, which not all the heat of party could inflame nor all the jars and disturbances of his country shake out of place. I charge you to emulate his justice, his moderation, and his mercy."

The orator wished his voice could go across the country and reach "that twilight million to whom his name was as the name of an angel of God." Wailing would rise in places where no minister could try to comfort. From the South one could hear the weeping of the "long-wronged, dusky children."

The most often reprinted passage from sermons of this Easter Sunday was Beecher's closing. He pictured a coffined martyr moving in triumphal march, with cities and states as pallbearers, bells and cannon beating the hours. He intoned his dead march for an immortal:

"Pass on, thou that has overcome! Your sorrows, oh people, are his peace! Your bells, and bands, and muffled drums, sound triumph in his ear. Wail and weep here; God made it echo joy and triumph there. Pass on!

"Four years ago, oh, Illinois, we took from your midst an untried man, and from among the people. We return him to you a mighty conqueror. Not thine any more, but the nation's; not ours, but the world's.

"Give him place, oh, ye prairies! In the midst of this great continent his dust shall rest, a sacred treasure to myriads who shall pilgrim to that shrine to kindle anew their zeal and patriotism.

"Ye winds that move over the mighty places of the West, chant his requiem! Ye people, behold a martyr whose blood, as so many articulate words, pleads for fidelity, for law, for liberty!"

Not equal to Beecher's dithyrambic ode and psalm was Miss Anna Dickinson in her Academy of Music speech in Philadelphia. Nor did she have his sense of events and issues. Since January of '64 she had repeatedly spoken of Lincoln as a trickster and a truckler, making it a point of pride that though she supported his party in the campaign of '64, she never mentioned him. Now she praised him as having "all the noble qualities of an honorable and high-minded man," as "the open and determined opponent of the slave power, and enemy to the man-stealer." She was certain now that "in the future his greatness will be dwelt upon." Now too she repudiated his greatness, unaware she was so doing. In the name of "inflexible justice" and "outraged law" Miss Dickinson cried for punishment of the Southern leaders. "Their crimes have rendered them unworthy of the respect of honest men. Hanging should be their deserts." Where few or none in the North had gone beyond naming Jefferson Davis as suitable for the gallows, Miss Dickinson included General Robert E. Lee. She spoke of Lincoln's assassin and added, "Of the two, Lee is a viler murderer." Much else she said in her flights and ravings. She wanted the wisdom and integrity of Wendell Phillips. In the tumult he was saying nothing. He too could

have stepped forth with his silver tongue and his Anglo-Saxon short words
and moved the pools of public emotion. But he didn't. He kept quiet. He
was no hypocrite. The event was involved. He would say nothing. Or
rather he would have one brief comment. Granted that Lincoln was a great
oak. "We watered him," said Wendell Phillips, the agitator.

The press from day to day gave its readers the news facts as they developed. In language, viewpoint, and feeling the news stories mourned with

Specimen of newspaper front-page mourning in the *Bangor* (Maine) *Times*. From the
author's collection.

the readers. In black-border crape typography, in editorial comment and
letters and poetical effusions, the newspapers went along with the grief of
the public. The weekly periodicals, the monthly magazines, these too wore
crape and spoke sorrow in the national mood that lasted weeks.

"The military measures of the country received their character from
the political policy," read part of the obituary biography of the *New York
Herald* on April 16, "and the war changed character, the armies changed
hands, as the nation under the skillful leadership of Mr. Lincoln gradually
advanced to the support of those more radical measures which he found
it necessary to inaugurate as the country became deeper and deeper involved." His emancipation policy, at first meeting strong opposition, later
"fully proved" itself, its wisdom accepted finally by "the action of the rebel
leaders in adopting the very same policy."

The *New York Herald*, which had at first so bitterly fought the abolitionists and the Emancipation Proclamation, spoke for a powerful fraction
of the North in now saying that until this policy went into force "the
Government was, as then asserted by its enemies in arms and the opposition
party at the North, without a system of policy other than the determination to restore the Union." A vast tangle of history was reduced to four
sentences, shaded with careful finality: "The first two years of Mr. Lincoln's
administration were devoted to educating the people of the North to the
support of his [emancipation] measure to that end [of restoring the Union].
From the moment of its firm establishment there has been no departure
from it. Upon it all other measures, military and political, have hinged,
and to it all have adapted themselves. The war has been prosecuted with the
view of the extinction of slavery, as the surest and quickest means of re-
establishing the Union."

On one occasion and another, continued this appraisal, Mr. Lincoln,
from his first inaugural on, had consistently moved toward Union through
emancipation. "The skill with which he educated the nation [including
naturally the *New York Herald*] to as full a belief in the necessity of the
second measure of his policy as it had always held in that of the first,
proves him to have been a wise and able far-seeing statesman. . . .

"In Mr. Lincoln," the *Herald* was certain, "the Southern people have
lost their best friend, and the rebel leaders one of their wisest and bitterest
enemies. . . . The apparent conciliations granted to the people of Virginia
were not undeserved kindnesses to the rebel leaders. Without relieving a
single rebel officer of any penalty which he might owe for crime Mr.
Lincoln's conciliatory measures were calculated to make it the interest of
every private soldier of their armies to abandon them to their fate."

This issue of the *Herald* with its remarkable extended biographical
sketch and its thorough news coverage in Washington sold out fifteen
minutes after its arrival. The price for an obtainable copy in Washington
the next day was $10. •

Under the heading "The Great Crime—Abraham Lincoln's Place in
History" the *Herald* on the next day, April 17, published a shrewd and
nevertheless moving and lavish estimate and portrayal. "In this moment of
benumbing regret and overwhelming excitement" not much should be said
till some calmer hour of "the insane ferocity of a bad and mad vagabond,
educated up to this height of crime by the teachings of our 'copperhead'
oracles." Bitter fruits to the South and to all Southern sympathizers would
follow "inevitably as the thunder storm following the lightning flash."
Then came a paragraph like thousands of this hour in American, English,
and Continental newspapers, taking Lincoln's measure as a never-before-
seen actor on the stage of international history:

"Whatever judgment may have been formed by those who were opposed
to him as to the calibre of our deceased Chief Magistrate, or the place he is
destined to occupy in history, all men of undisturbed observation must
have recognized in Mr. Lincoln a quaintness, originality, courage, honesty,

magnanimity and popular force of character such as have never heretofore, in the annals of the human family, had the advantage of so eminent a stage for their display. He was essentially a mixed product of the agricultural, forensic and frontier life of this continent—as indigenous to our soil as the cranberry crop, and as American in his fibre as the granite foundations of the Appalachian range. He may not have been, and perhaps was not, our most perfect product in any one branch of mental or moral education; but, taking him for all in all, the very noblest impulses, peculiarities and aspirations of our whole people—what may be called our continental idiosyncrasies—were more collectively and vividly reproduced in his genial and yet unswerving nature than in that of any other public man of whom our chronicles bear record."

He was a new figure. All other nations of the human family would study him "as the type man of a new dynasty of nation-rulers," holding that "the best and strongest rule for every intelligent people is a government to be created by the popular will, and choosing for itself the representative instrument who is to carry out its purposes." Gravely the *Herald*, naturally conservative though responsive to both property rights and human movements, considered this and noted: "The triumph of the democratic principle over the aristocratic in our recent contest is an assurance that time has revolved this old earth on which we live into a new and perhaps happier—perhaps sadder—era."

Lincoln was baffling, found the *Herald*. The more one gazed on him, the less easy it became to reckon what would be the end of his teachings. Those who believed they had him solved must first understand that he was democracy beyond Cromwell or Napoleon, that he was so completely modern that his like was not to be found in the past, in "the heroic antique." The old-time warriors and lawmakers wore purple, togas, crowns, wreaths. A new kind of historian, said the *Herald*, would be required "to comprehend the genius of a character so externally uncouth, so pathetically simple, so unfathomably penetrating, so irresolute and yet so irresistible, so bizarre, grotesque, droll, wise and perfectly beneficent as the great original thinker and statesman for whose death the whole land, even in the midst of victories unparalleled, is today draped in mourning." The hard going and involved difficulties for any and all who in the future should try to write truly, honestly, decently, adequately, about Abraham Lincoln, were sketched by the *Herald*:

"It will require an altogether new breed and school of historians to begin doing justice to this type-man of the world's last political evangel. No ponderously eloquent George Bancroft can properly rehearse those inimitable stories by which, in the light form of allegory, our martyred President has so frequently and so wisely decided the knottiest controversies of his Cabinet; nor can even the genius of a Washington Irving or Edward Everett in some future age elocutionize into the formal dignity of a Greek statue the kindly but powerful face of Mr. Lincoln, seamed in circles by humorous thoughts and furrowed crosswise by mighty anxieties.

It will take a new school of historians to do justice to this eccentric addition to the world's gallery of heroes; for while other men as interesting and original may have held equal power previously in other countries, it is only in the present age of steam, telegraphs and prying newspaper reporters that a subject so eminent, both by genius and position, could have been placed under the eternal microscope of critical examination."

Significant it was that the *Herald* should join with the Reverend Mr. Vinton, the Reverend Mr. Studley, and the other clergymen who feared what might have happened to Abraham Lincoln's fame and reputation had he lived on for the work of Southern reconstruction. By the circumstance of death with martyrdom the seal of immortality was stamped on his fame, noted the *Herald*, adding: "Nor is it any longer in the power of changing fortune to take away from him, *as might have happened had he lived* [Italics added], one of the most solid, brilliant and stainless reputations of which in the world's annals any record can be found—its only peer existing in the memory of George Washington."

George William Curtis in an unsigned editorial in *Harper's Weekly* was sure that those who knew Lincoln personally now felt "that the deep, furrowed sadness of his face seemed to forecast his fate." The nation had lost him, but it was something that he had lived to see daybreak. In his death it was not a party that lost a head but a country that mourned a father. "The most malignant party opposition in our history crumbled before his spotless fidelity." No personal tradition would be more cherished nor any name be longer and more tenderly beloved. "He loved liberty too sincerely for passion or declamation." The marvels of his life story, thought Curtis, would have to take account of these points:

"He saw farther and deeper than others because he saw that in the troubled time upon which he was cast little could be wholly seen. Experience so vindicated his patriotic sagacity that he acquired a curious ascendency in the public confidence; so that if good men differed from his opinion they were inclined to doubt their own. Principle was fixed as a star, but policy must be swayed by the current. While many would have dared the fierce fury of the gale and have sunk the ship at once, he knew that there was a time to stretch every inch of canvas and a time to lay to. He was not afraid of 'drifting.' In statesmanship prudence counts for more than daring. Thus it happened that some who urged him at the beginning of the war to the boldest measures, and excused what they called his practical faithlessness by his probable weakness, lived to feel the marrow of their bones melt with fear, and to beg him to solicit terms that would have destroyed the nation. But wiser than passion, more faithful than fury, serene in his devotion to the equal rights of men without which he knew there could henceforth be no peace in this country, he tranquilly persisted, enduring the impatience of what seemed to some his painful delays and to others his lawless haste; and so, trusting God and his own true heart, he fulfilled his great task so well that he died more tenderly lamented than any ruler in history."

In many of the estimates and tributes spoken or written in the immediate days of mourning there was a warm, vivid color. The words came as though they might have been the same a few days before when the man was alive. Often too came the admission, direct or a little hidden and furtive, that slowly the man had grown and taken on new lights and shadings with every year of his tests and trials, that behind his massive, scrawny exterior he lived subtly and intricately with the dark, quivering themes of humanity, freedom, and democracy.

An old plain proverb known to woodsmen with axes was fitting: "A tree is best measured when it's down." Likewise a suave epigram from the accomplished and highly civilized Francis Bacon: "There is no excellent beauty that hath not some strangeness in the proportion."

Beyond any doubt, said leading men and journals, there never had been on earth a man whose death brought in all countries such quick, deep human interest, such genuine sorrow, such wide-flung discussion and commentary. Often came the statement that over the world the whole civilized Family of Man shared in regrets or grief for the loss of a common hero who belonged to humanity everywhere, a spokesman to be consulted in future world affairs, a prophet too plain and salty to lay claim to being a prophet.

The story of the living and actual Lincoln had come to an end. Now began the vast epic tale of the authentic Lincoln tradition mingled with legend, myth, folklore. Believers and atheists, those of fixed doctrine or the freethinkers—both were to argue he was theirs. Letters and pamphlets were to picture him as Freemason or Spiritualist, as Protestant or Catholic or Jew or having Negro blood in his veins. The teetotalers were to claim properly he was theirs because he never drank alcoholic liquors; the saloon crowd amid the sawdust and the spittoons were to say his stories alone put him in their class. Some had no hesitation about one sweeping and beautiful claim: "He was humanity."

Lost in the huge and swelling choral acclaim were the few who agreed with the imperialist and Tory organ of London, England, the *Standard*, saying on April 21: "He was not a hero while he lived, and therefore his cruel murder does not make him a martyr." Of little weight now was the London *Times* in its mild April acknowledgment of "his homely kindness of feeling" which kept him "in a course of clemency," in its decisive recognition that "in all America, there was, perhaps, not one man who less deserved to be the victim of this revolution, than he who has just fallen." Yet also in April it must needs retract earlier, insistent judgment: "It would be unjust not to acknowledge that Mr. Lincoln was a man who could not under any circumstances have been easily replaced." What could this directly mean except that the *Times* of London required a slow, involved triple negative instead of an easy and simple affirmation of its contrition over having misread and slandered Mr. Lincoln? And who cared that the frustrated *Times* tried to be pleasant without knowing how in such mumblings as "He was a prominent figure in a great historical picture, and, as far as we can judge, was prepared to play a most noble part"? Of more import than the continued muddling and arrogance of the *Times* was the simple confession of the *Pall Mall Gazette:* "He was our best friend. He never lent himself to the purposes of that foolish and wicked minority which tried to set enmity between America and England. He never said or wrote an unfriendly word about us."

Among the people of England, the masses whose sentiment kept the Government from recognizing the Southern Confederacy, the mourning was genuine. In the House of Commons were calls of protest and denial when Sir George Grey said that a majority of the people of England had sympathized with the North. But there were no murmurs at his praise of Lincoln. And there were cheers when he said that Queen Victoria had written to Mrs. Lincoln with her own hand, "as a widow to a widow." Disraeli, with

Britannia lays her wreaths and mourns with Columbia, with the Negro, this being Sir John Tenniel's offer of apology and regret for the tone of his series of cartoons in *Punch*

a sense of events and speaking for the Conservatives, said: "There is in the character of the victim, and even in the accessories of his last moments, something so homely and innocent, that it takes the question, as it were, out of all the pomp of history and the ceremonial of diplomacy; it touches the heart of nations and appeals to the domestic sentiment of mankind." Bright and Cobden spoke publicly of their personal loss. The *Spectator,* having constantly reported the war and interpreted Lincoln with rare accuracy for a contemporary, offered verses by John Nichol, six of them reading:

A golden morn—a dawn of better things—
  The olive-branch—clasping of hands again—
A noble lesson read to conquering kings—
  A sky that tempests had not scoured in vain. . . .

The pilot of his people through the strife,
  With his strong purpose turning scorn to praise,
E'en at the close of battle reft of life,
  And fair inheritance of quiet days.

Defeat and triumph found him calm and just,
  He showed how clemency should temper power,
And dying left to future times in trust
  The memory of his brief victorious hour. . . .

May these endure and, as his work, attest
  The glory of his honest heart and hand,—
The simplest, and the bravest, and the best,—
  The Moses and the Cromwell of his land.

Too late the pioneers of modern spite,
  Awestricken by the universal gloom,
See his name lustrous in Death's sable night,
  And offer tardy tribute at his tomb.

But we who have been with him all the while,
  Who knew his worth, and loved him long ago,
Rejoice that in the circuit of our isle
  There is no room at last for Lincoln's foe.

The letter to Mrs. Lincoln signed by Victoria Regina was deeply personal, woman to woman, the Queen saying: "No one can better appreciate than I can, who am myself *utterly broken-hearted* by the loss of my own beloved husband, who was the *light* of my life, my stay—*my all*—what your suffering must be; and I earnestly pray that you may be supported by Him to whom alone the sorely stricken can look for comfort."

The House of Lords joined in an official address of sympathy to the American people, the discussion of it having reserve and polite modulations. In *Punch*, the humorous weekly which during four years had continuously satirized and slandered Lincoln, came verses by Tom Taylor, author of *Our American Cousin*. The verses apologized; they had wronged Lincoln and were deeply sorry. Two of them read:

Beside this corpse, that bears for winding-sheet
  The Stars and Stripes he lived to rear anew,
Between the mourners at his head and feet,
  Say, scurril-jester, is there room for *you?*

> Yes, he had lived to shame me from my sneer,
> To lame my pencil, and confute my pen—
> To make me own this hind of princes peer,
> This rail-splitter a true-born king of men.

In England and on the Continent, all forms of labor organizations, trade-unions, fraternal and mutual-benefit societies, socialist and communist bodies, spoke their words of sympathy and loss in resolutions and declarations, in addresses spread over their journals. They could never forget, said many of these, the American statesman of power and authority who had said "Capital is the fruit of labor, and could never have existed if labor had not first existed"; "Working-men are the basis of all governments"; "Labor is prior to, and independent of, capital"; "The strongest bond of human sympathy, outside of the family relation, should be one uniting all working people, of all nations, and tongues, and kindreds"; "I feel that the time is coming when the sun shall shine, the rain fall, on no man who shall go forth to unrequited toil"; "Thank God we live in a country where workingmen have the right to strike."

In the French Senate and Chamber of Deputies imperialists and republicans joined in formal expressions of grief while the Emperor and Empress sent a message of condolence to Mrs. Lincoln. A massive gold medal, bought with 2-cent subscriptions from masses of people, was brought to the American Minister by a committee of liberals. It was for Mrs. Lincoln, with their message, "Tell her the heart of France is in that little box." Of perhaps larger meaning, looking toward the future, was the march of a thousand young students of the Latin Quarter at the Pont San Michel, the bridge over the Seine. A barricade of police stopped the parade, ordered it dispersed, and arrested the leaders. A band of thirty however got together and marched to the Legation of the United States and presented Minister Bigelow with an address by inference thrusting at the dictator Louis Napoleon and declarations abrupt and pointed:

"In President Lincoln we mourn a fellow citizen. There are no longer any countries shut up in narrow frontiers. Our country is everywhere where there are neither masters nor slaves—wherever people live in liberty or fight for it. We are fellow citizens of John Brown, of Abraham Lincoln and of William H. Seward.

"To us young men, to whom belongs the future, is requisite a grand energy to found a true democracy. We cast our eyes to the other side of the ocean to learn how a people which has known how to make itself free knows how to preserve its freedom.

"He who has just been struck down was a citizen of that republic where the great men are—not the conquerors who violate right and the sovereignty of peoples, but the founders and the guardians of their independence, like Washington and Lincoln. Probity, simplicity, energy in the struggle, moderation in victory, respect for liberty always and everywhere—these were the qualities of the elect of the American people. To strike such men is to strike the law itself."

In Germany many bunds and vereins, workingmen's clubs, co-operative societies, labor journals, spoke their loss. Through Bismarck came the regrets of the King of Prussia. In the Landstag were sentiments given such as one from Wilhelm Löwe: "The man who never wished to be more nor less than the most faithful servant of his people, will find his own glorious place in the pages of history. In the deepest reverence I bow my head before this modest greatness." In Austria one parliamentary deputy noted a human memory taking on "supernatural proportions," Lincoln becoming "a myth, a type of the ideal democracy." In Sweden flags were ordered at half-mast on the ships in harbor at Göteborg and there were expressions such as the *Nya Daglig Allehanda* of Stockholm saying: "It is a beautiful death, and Lincoln forever will be surrounded by the rays of impeccable glory. The time for impartial judgment will not come for many years."

In the harbor of Stockholm flags hung at half-mast on all ships. Excitement and sorrow rooted partly in Swedish sentiment over the victory of the *Monitor*, designed by John Ericsson and carrying guns invented by Admiral John Adolph Dahlgren. A song of many verses that was to become a folk ballad arose reciting the shock and grief over "the killing of Abraham Lincoln." One observer wrote: "Our men clenched their fists in vain fury and our blue-eyed women shed many tears in memory of the remarkable man."

In the harbors of Norwegian cities also flags were at half-mast. Thousands in that country had blood relations in Wisconsin and Minnesota regiments. Young Henrik Ibsen in a flowing turbulent poem, "The Murder of Abraham Lincoln," challenged Europe's right to mourn over the passing of the foremost son of democracy in the Western world. Rulers were accused by Ibsen of "vows forgotten and words untrue," of "treaties ye tear and despoil," of "perjured oaths" that "have fertilized history's soil." From the American continent the words and decisions of Lincoln had reached Ibsen, and he felt called on to repudiate and blame those he deemed insincere mourners over the martyr Lincoln.

In the Orient, China, Japan, and Siam framed resolutions of condolence. At a religious meeting of Negroes of the Sea Islands one voiced a wish that he might see Lincoln and heard from an old silver-head: "No man see Linkum. Linkum walk lak Jesus walk—no man see Linkum."

To the four corners of the earth began the spread of the Lincoln story and legend. He was wanted. What he seemed to mean was reached for. Hunger and love told men to search him. Travelers on any continent came to expect in humble homes the picture of Lincoln, readiness to talk about him. Of the hundreds of incidents in this field none stood more fascinating than one from Leo Tolstoy of Yasnaya Polyana, Russia, saying: "If one would know the greatness of Lincoln one should listen to the stories which are told about him in other parts of the world. I have been in wild places where one hears the name of America uttered with such mystery as if it were some heaven or hell. I have heard various tribes of barbarians discussing the New World, but I heard this only in connection with the name

Lincoln. Lincoln as the wonderful hero of America is known by the most primitive nations of Asia."

Traveling in the Caucasus, Tolstoy happened to be the guest of a Circassian tribal chief, a devout Mussulman who lived in the mountains far from civilized life, with vague and childish understanding of the outside world. He received Tolstoy with the best of food and drink, after the meal asking his guest to tell him about the outside world, listening with no particular interest till Tolstoy spoke of great statesmen and great generals. Then the tribal chief called in neighbors and sons to listen, wild-looking riders, sons of the wilderness seated on the floor and looking up with a hunger for knowledge. Tolstoy talked about Russian czars and their victories, about foreign rulers and generals. As to Napoleon they wanted more details, asked how his hands looked, how tall he was, who made his guns and pistols, the color of Napoleon's horse. Tolstoy did his best, but could hardly satisfy them when he had told all he knew about Napoleon. Then the chief, a tall, gray-bearded rider, smelling of leather and horses and the earth itself, arose and said very gravely:

"But you have not told us a syllable about the greatest general and greatest ruler of the world. We want to know something about him. He was a hero. He spoke with a voice of thunder, he laughed like the sunrise and his deeds were strong as the rock and as sweet as the fragrance of roses. The angels appeared to his mother and predicted that the son whom she would conceive would become the greatest the stars had ever seen. He was so great that he even forgave the crimes of his greatest enemies and shook brotherly hands with those who had plotted against his life. His name was Lincoln and the country in which he lived is called America, which is so far away that if a youth should journey to reach it he would be an old man when he arrived. Tell us of that man."

Others shouted, "Tell us, please!" and promised Tolstoy they would pick the best horse in stock and give him as a present.

Tolstoy saw their faces shining, eyes burning. He saw rough mountaineer tribesmen thirsting to hear about Abraham Lincoln. He told them of Lincoln as a wise man, a ruler who came from poverty and the plainest of common people. They asked questions. Nine out of ten Tolstoy couldn't answer. They wanted to know all about Lincoln's habits, about Lincoln's influence on the people, how tall he was and how heavy a load he could lift. And they were astonished to hear that Lincoln wasn't much to look at when riding a horse.

"Tell us why he was killed," said one. Tolstoy did his best, gave them every last item he had about Lincoln. They were lighted over what he told them, spoke "wild thanks," and the next morning when Tolstoy was leaving the chief brought him a fine Arabian horse as a present for the marvelous story.

One rider went along with Tolstoy to the next town, where Tolstoy hoped to get a picture to send back for the tribe. He managed to find a large photograph of Lincoln. He handed this to the tribesman, who took it with a grave face and hands a little shaky, studied it several minutes like a man in prayer, his eyes filled with tears. Tolstoy asked why he had become so sad. The answer:

"I am sad because I feel sorry that he had to die by the hand of a villain. Don't you find, judging from his picture, that his eyes are full of tears and that his lips are sad with secret sorrow?"

To Tolstoy the incident proved that in far places over the earth the name of Lincoln was worshiped and the personality of Lincoln had become a world folk legend. Tolstoy believed Lincoln no great general like Napoleon or Washington, nor as skilled a statesman as Frederick the Great and others. Then, ran the inquiry, why should Lincoln overshadow all other national heroes? He was supreme, reasoned Tolstoy, through "peculiar moral powers and greatness of character." Many hardships and much experience brought him to the realization "that the greatest human achievement is love." And making this specific: "He was what Beethoven was in music, Dante in poetry, Raphael in painting and Christ in the philosophy of life. He aspired to be divine and he was."

On a highway of mistakes he walked true to one main motive, the benefit of mankind. "He was one," continued Tolstoy, "who wanted to be great through his smallness. If he had failed to become President, he would be no doubt just as great, but only God could appreciate it. The judgment of the world is usually wrong in the beginning and it takes centuries to correct it. But in the case of Lincoln, the world was right from the start. Sooner or later Lincoln would have been seen to be a great man, even though he had never been an American President. But it would have taken a great generation to place him where he belongs."

Any form of heroism is doomed to be forgotten unless rooted in four abstractions made concrete in behavior. These Tolstoy would name: humanity, truth, justice, pity. The greatness of Aristotle or Kant he saw as insignificant compared with the greatness of Buddha, Moses, and Christ. "The greatness of Napoleon, Caesar or Washington is moonlight by the sun of Lincoln. His example is universal and will last thousands of years. Washington was a typical American, Napoleon was a typical Frenchman, but Lincoln was a humanitarian as broad as the world. He was bigger than his country—bigger than all the Presidents put together."

Of all great national heroes and statesmen of history Tolstoy would say "Lincoln is the only real giant." He named many of these heroes to find them lesser than Lincoln "in depth of feeling and in certain moral power." Deep mystic shadows and a dazzling bright aura gathered around Lincoln's memory for the famous Russian who put his seal and blessing on it with ecstatic prophecy. "Lincoln was a man of whom a nation has a right to be proud. He was a Christ in miniature, a saint of humanity whose name will live thousands of years in the legends of future generations. We are still too near his greatness, and so can hardly appreciate his divine power; but after a few centuries more our posterity will find him considerably bigger than we do. His genius is still too strong and powerful for the common understanding, just as the sun is too hot when its light beams directly on us."

The question raised and dealt with by thousands of American clergymen on Easter Sunday of '65 struck Tolstoy too. Was Lincoln's death not foreordained by a divine wisdom and was it not better for the nation and for his greatness that he died just in that way and at that particular moment? Tolstoy would answer: "We know so little about that divine law which we call fate that no one can answer. Christ had a presentiment of his death, and there are also indications that Lincoln had strange dreams and presentiments of something tragic. If that was really the fact, can we conceive that human will could have prevented the outcome of the universal or divine will? I doubt it. I doubt also that Lincoln could have done more to prove his greatness than he did. I am convinced that we are but instruments in the hands of an unknown power and that we have to follow its bidding to the end. We have a certain apparent independence according to our moral character, wherein we may benefit our fellows, but in all eternal and universal questions we follow blindly a divine predestination. According to that eternal law, the greatest of national heroes had to die, but an immortal glory still shines on his deeds."

Another interpretation of divine interposition came from Ralph Waldo Emerson, speaking on April 19 before neighbors and fellow townsmen in Concord, Massachusetts. He saw a serene Providence ruling the fate of nations. "It makes its own instruments, creates the man for the time, trains him in poverty, inspires his genius, and arms him for his task." From this proceeded the inquiry: "What if it should turn out, in the unfolding of the web, that he [Lincoln] had reached the term; that this heroic deliverer could no longer serve us; that the rebellion had touched its natural conclusion, and what remained to be done required new and uncommitted hands,— a new spirit born out of the ashes of the war; and that Heaven, wishing to show the world a completed benefactor, shall make him serve his country even more by his death than his life?"

Emerson from his New England point of lookout believed in effect that Lincoln in his policy of conciliation, pardon, no trials or hangings of rebels on treason charges, misread Heaven and the Divine Will. (Yet Lincoln no less than Emerson tried to scan the counsels of the Most High. It was plain in Lincoln's once telling a visitor that he didn't care so much whether the Lord was on his side; he wished rather he could be sure that he was on the Lord's side.) What Emerson now feared was that Lincoln had guessed wrong as to the desires of Providence and therefore had been removed from his place as President. Where Tolstoy and many pulpit speakers held that God had inscrutable purposes in permitting the hand of the assassin to kill the President, Emerson and those of his viewpoint believed they could read more precisely what God intended and the motive of Heaven was not after all entirely inscrutable. Ben Wade's slant at Lincoln as having "too much of the milk of human kindness" Emerson rendered in two sentences not altogether cryptic: " 'The kindness of kings consists in justice and strength.'

Easy good-nature has been the dangerous foible of the Republic." To Emerson the key fault of Lincoln was that: easy good nature.

In the deep, unimpeachable sincerity that ran through everything Emerson said and did, he gave to his neighbors and fellow townsmen that day of April 19 his meditations on the end of Lincoln's life. The gloom of the calamity had traveled over sea and land, from country to country, "like the shadow of an uncalculated eclipse over the planet." Old as was history, Emerson doubted whether any one death had ever caused so much pain to mankind. "And this, not so much because nations are by modern arts brought so closely together, as because of the mysterious hopes and fears which, in the present day, are connected with the name and institutions of America."

On the Saturday after Good Friday "everyone was struck dumb, and saw at first only deep below deep, as he meditated on the ghastly blow." When now the funeral coffin of the President would move westward "we might well be silent, and suffer the awful voices of the time to thunder to us." Yet the first despair was brief; the man was not so to be mourned. Was he not the most active and hopeful of men? And his work had not perished. "Acclamations of praise for the task he had accomplished burst out into a song of triumph, which even tears for his death cannot keep down."

Thoroughly American, never having crossed the sea, "never spoiled by English insularity or French dissipation," with no aping of foreigners, no frivolous accomplishments, Lincoln through Emerson's prism was "a quite native, aboriginal man, as an acorn from the oak." On modest foundations was laid the broad structure of his fame. Slow, by prepared steps, he came to his place. With surprise and disappointment, "coldly and sadly" had Emerson and his friends five years ago heard of Seward losing the presidential nomination to Lincoln. "But it turned out not to be chance. . . . They did not begin to know the riches of his worth." They became aware of the President having no shine, no superiority, no vices, a strong sense of duty. It began to dawn on them he had "what farmers call a long head" and furthermore he could work hard, "had prodigious faculty of performance; worked easily," was cheerful and persistent at his office labor, "and liked nothing so well."

They became further aware of his "vast good-nature, which made him tolerant and accessible to all; fair-minded, leaning to the claim of the petitioner; affable, and not sensible to the affliction which the innumerable visits paid to him when President would have brought to anyone else." Of his compassion for a whole freed race thrown on his hands had come the incident of the poor Negro crying Marse Linkum was "eberywhere." His "broad good-humor" and "jocular talk" was a rich gift that "enabled him to keep his secret; to meet every kind of man and every rank in society; to take off the edge of the severest decisions; to mask his own purpose and sound his companion; and to catch with true instinct the temper of every company he addressed."

Curious it was that Emerson and Dr. Vinton of New York and several of the Boston clergymen should give such high and unreserved praise to Lincoln's instinct for knowing what the people and the country wanted, while they nevertheless refused to endorse the policy of conciliation and pardon which Lincoln was sure would have the sanction of the people and the country. Were these men who distrusted this policy of leniency, as Lincoln had once said to Wendell Phillips and Moncure D. Conway, members of "a movement" and giving their "movement" a higher valuation and a heavier weight than the rest of the country attached to it?

Emerson's praise rang truer than that of others in movements. He mentioned how Lincoln's offhand jests "by the very acceptance and adoption they find in the mouths of millions, turn out to be the wisdom of the hour." Emerson was certain "if this man had ruled in a period of less facility of printing, he would have become mythological in a very few years, like Aesop or Pilpay, or one of the Seven Wise Masters, by his fables and proverbs." Many passages in his letters, messages, and speeches had a weight and penetration "hidden now by the very closeness of their application to the moment," though destined to wide fame. "What pregnant definitions; what unerring common sense; what foresight; and, on great occasion, what lofty, and more than national, what humane tone!"

Lincoln, in Emerson's analysis, grew according to need, wrought incessantly with all his might and all his honesty, "laboring to find what the people wanted, and how to obtain that." The times allowed no state secrets; in the national ferment such multitudes had to be trusted that no secret could be kept. Every door was ajar. And as problems grew so did the President's comprehension of them. "It cannot be said there is any exaggeration of his worth. If ever a man was fairly tested, he was." In the whirlwind of the war he was "no holiday magistrate, no fair-weather sailor; the new pilot was hurried to the helm in a tornado." In four years of battle days his endurance, fertility of resources, his magnanimity, sore tried, were never found wanting. "By his courage, his justice, his even temper, his fertile counsels, his humanity, he stood a heroic figure in the centre of a heroic epoch. He is the true history of the American people in his time. Step by step he walked before them; slow with their slowness, quickening his march by theirs, the true representative of this continent; an entirely public man; father of his country, the pulse of twenty millions throbbing in his heart, the thought of their minds articulated by his tongue."

Thus Emerson, one among first of American seers and poets, sketched his national hero, coming finally to say, however, that perhaps this heroic deliverer "could no longer serve us," that what remained to be done "required new and uncommitted hands." Yet here too in closing he kept a depth of love for his Lincoln, seeing the assassination with its terror and ruin "already burning into glory around him." Suppose Lincoln had lived on. "Far happier this fate than to have lived to be wished away; to have watched the decay of his own faculties [as softly and with dark pathos later happened to Emerson]; to have seen,—perhaps even he,—the proverbial ingratitude of statesmen; to have seen mean men preferred. Had he not lived long enough to

keep the greatest promise that ever man made to his fellow-men,—the practical abolition of slavery? He had seen . . . the main army of the rebellion
lay down its arms. He had conquered the public opinion of Canada, England
and France. Only Washington can compare with him in fortune."

The suave diplomat John Bigelow believed that in ordinary peacetime
conditions Lincoln would have been a very ordinary President and of little
distinction. In a wild crisis calling for a man deep in moral issues, the nation
found Lincoln "even as the son of Kish found a crown while searching for
his father's asses." He walked by faith and not by sight. "He did not rely
upon his own compass, but followed a cloud by day and a fire by night,
which he had learned to trust implicitly." He was not strictly a statesman,
nor an educated man. His greatness was peculiar. "He was so modest by
nature that he was perfectly content to walk behind any man who wished
to walk before him. . . . St. Paul hardly endured more indignities and buf-
fetings without complaint."

Out of Bigelow's wide familiarity with statesmen, politicians, and men
of affairs he wrote of Lincoln: "I do not know that history has made a
record of the attainment of any corresponding eminence by any other man
who so habitually, so constitutionally, did to others as he would have them
do to him. Without any pretensions to religious excellence, from the time
he was first brought under the observation of the nation, he seemed, like
Milton, to have walked 'as ever in his great Taskmaster's eye.' "

Hidden among the pages of an obscure periodical, the *Friend of Progress*,
was an appraisal that mixed information, conjecture, and darkly tender con-
templations. This was from the pen of Octavius Brooks Frothingham, pastor
of the Third Congregational Unitarian Society in New York City. He saw
Lincoln as far spent, so worn by the war he had carried on his shoulders
that it would have been expecting too great a marvel to believe that he
would not have suffered cruelly had he lived another four years. Now a
nation held the man a saint. And why? Partly perhaps because of a great
crime timed to a moment so peculiar that it had a touch of superstition and
awe. "The North, which had already poured out such rivers of blood in
expiation of its guilty acquiescence in wrong, cannot be released till it has
made one crowning offering more—its own first-born child and chosen
leader. The man whose election was the cause of the war, becomes its victim. The President who had dealt so tenderly with Northern traitors, had
forgiven them, had treated with them, had almost cherished them, is stung
to death at last by the serpent he would insist on taking to his bosom."

The people were sorrowing now not because of the crime but because
they had lost a friend they loved simply as a man. "His belongings were
nothing; dignities would not stick to him. The White House was the place
where he lived—nothing more. The Presidency was his business for the time
being—that was all. His personal qualities protruded from his official skin,
as the angular lines of his figure did from his court dress—as the bones of
his great hands did from his kid gloves. The costumer, official or other, could

make nothing of him. He was a character—not a doll. The decorators tried their hands on him in vain."

Had he used dramatics and sought the hosannas of the crowd, had he played for grandeur and magnificence, "had he been such a person as that, the country would have gone wild over the tragedy of his death." Now however "the country does not go wild over him; it silently weeps for him; it does not celebrate him as a demigod—it mourns for him as a friend. It gives him no noisy place in the hall of the heroes—it gives him a dear and still one in the chamber of the heart. . . . Ordinary human nature was honored in him, and so ordinary human nature weeps for him."

Mr. Frothingham could only be quietly amazed over the sad, serious humility of Lincoln delivering his second inaugural, with its curious words when victory was in sight for his armies. Frothingham quoted: "Both sides have been disappointed." "We must go on." "With malice towards none; with charity for all." No bombast, no exultation, no boasting. "The sentences are uttered as if under the shadow of destiny, and the man who utters them—the Commander-in-Chief of all those triumphant armies, the President of the Great Republic, the newly elected ruler by the people's overwhelming vote, the most conspicuous potentate in Christendom—at that moment stands like the publican of the gospel, saying, with downcast eyes, before all the nation and before all the world, yet alone with the Eternal, 'God be merciful to me a sinner.' "

Never claiming to be more than a servant of the people, "he was a follower, not a leader." To read the people's wish, to fall in with their drift and will, was his ambition. "He let the people work through him; and in his own esteem held a high place enough when he acted as an organ and an instrument. Such humility almost passes understanding—it runs into self-forgetfulness; it borders even on saintliness. In all history I know no parallel to it. And how it is exalted now! what a memorial it has! how touchingly implied in all the mottoes inscribed on banners and badges and house fronts!"

Mr. Frothingham had never watched Lincoln at close range. He had no anecdotes of what he had seen of Lincoln and heard from him directly. He was one of many who studied the man from far off—and yet came honestly to believe that he knew the real man as one who had been near and breathing. For Mr. Frothingham meditated now as if some bosom companion had been swept away and he was saying to himself as though sure he knew the real Lincoln: "To me there seems a grace almost surpassing in the quiet, unwearied, infinite patience which this good man—not exhibited, for he exhibited nothing—but lived on. There was a touch of real saintliness in that. For consider he had no enthusiasms; no transporting dreams; no visions enchanting the soul. He hoped little, expected nothing. A man of low temperament and sad nature, he worked and waited, waited and worked, bearing all things, enduring all things, but neither believing all things nor all things happening; bearing and enduring oh how much! even from his friends.

What a history was written on that care-worn and furrowed face—of suffering accepted, sorrow entertained, emotions buried, and duty done!"

The newsman Horace White carried farther the expression of his associate John Locke Scripps that Lincoln had "an exquisite sense of justice,"
White writing: "More than intellectual gifts, more than good-fellowship,
did the sense of justice give him his hold on others. That was a magnetic
field whose influences could not be escaped. He carried it as unconsciously
as he carried his hair. The Athenians would never have ostracized him—
indeed, they would never have called him the Just. They would have taken
him as they took the bees on Hymettus—as one naturally searching after
sweet things."

Striving for a sense of measure White gave his opinion: "The popular
judgment of Mr. Lincoln is, in the main, correct and unshakable. I say in
the main, because there is in this judgment a tendency to apotheosis which,
while pardonable, is not historical, and will not last."

The jester, the quipster Robert Henry Newell (Orpheus C. Kerr) wrote
in tears and utter solemnity verses titled "The Martyr President," in the
opening lines touching the same theme of sacrifice and martyrdom that so
many others attempted:

> 'Twas needed—the name of a Martyr sublime,
> To vindicate God in this terrible time;
> 'Twas fitting the thunder of Heaven should roll,
> Ere cannon exultant had deafened the soul
> To what in all ages the Maker had taught,
> The pardon of sin is with suffering bought;
> 'Twas fitting the lightning of Heaven should fall
> On him, the supreme and beloved of us all,
> Ere, blest in his living to guide us and save,
> Our honor forgot what was due to the Slave.
> For still with the South must we share in the guilt
> That stabs us at last to the murderous hilt;
> And still to the loyal the horror belongs
> Of aiding the chief of humanity's wrongs.

Lincoln had stood as the national Fate, amid violence that was the shortest cut to a common Union of destiny for the States. Thus the Brazilian
Minister Joaquín Nabuco, saying, "I construe to myself that War as one
of those illusions of life, in which men seem to move of their own free will,
while they are really playing a tragedy composed by a Providence intent on
saving their nation." Lincoln, as the leading player in the drama, "saw distinctly that the South was not a nationality, and that it could not think of
being one, except during the hallucination of the crisis." In the velocities of
modern change, the year 2000 would be governed by currents of political
thought impossible to read. "But, whether the spirit of authority, or that of
freedom, increases, Lincoln's legend will ever appear more luminous in the
amalgamation of centuries, because he supremely incarnated both those
spirits."

No music more strange and mystical than that of the poet Walt Whitman followed the hovering blue-smoke mist of Lincoln's death. Whitman envisioned a ship that had weathered in a fearful trip every storm and rack of the sea. Into port she is ready to come with her keel, shouting crowds at the wharf, bells of welcome calling. And yet—on the deck are bleeding drops of red where the Captain lies cold and dead. And the grief of hammering heartbeats goes on:

> O Captain! my Captain! rise up and hear the bells;
> Rise up—for you the flag is hung—for you the bugle trills,
> For you bouquets and ribbon'd wreaths—for you the shores a-crowding,
> For you they call, the swaying mass, their eager faces turning;
>> Here Captain! dear father!
>>> This arm beneath your head!
>>>> It is some dream that on the deck,
>>>> You've fallen cold and dead.
>
> My Captain does not answer, his lips are pale and still,
> My father does not feel my arm, he has no pulse nor will,
> The ship is anchor'd safe and sound, its voyage closed and done,
> From fearful trip the victor ship comes in with object won;
>> Exult O shores, and ring O bells!
>>> But I with mournful tread,
>>>> Walk the deck my Captain lies,
>>>> Fallen cold and dead.

From his Long Island home where with his mother he had heard the news in Quaker quiet, Whitman went to Washington. From his one favorite chum, Pete Doyle, a streetcar driver who had a seat in the gallery of Ford's Theatre on the night of April 14, Whitman heard details of what he termed "the foulest crime in history known in any land or age." For days he walked alone brooding, sat silent contemplating, in his bones the beginning of a psalm:

O how shall I warble myself for the dead one there I loved?
And how shall I deck my song for the large sweet soul that has gone?
And what shall my perfume be for the grave of him I love?

Sea-winds blown from east and west,
Blown from the Eastern sea and blown from the Western sea, till there on the
    prairies meeting,
These and with these and the breath of my chant,
I'll perfume the grave of him I love.

Walt Whitman would have blossoms and green branches piled on the coffin—armfuls of roses fresh as the morning—in loaded arms sprigs of lilac just off the bushes—brought and poured on the coffin. He would study sea-blown cities and moving harbor ships, the changing lights of the Ohio River shores and the flashing bosom of the wide Missouri, far-spreading prairies covered with grass and corn—he would bring these to the coffin in his psalm. He would consider the miracle of light so gentle and soft-born from the most excellent sun so calm and haughty—evening and the welcome of night and the stars—these too he would carry along in a threnody of praise to death—lovely and soothing death—the sure-enwinding arms of cool-enfolding death. He had listened to a hermit thrush singing in solemn shadowy cedars and still ghostly pines—under the evening star a carol of death with praise of its serene arrival and its husky whispering to the huge and thoughtful night. This too he would bring to the coffin as his offertory and benediction, his chant of sane and sacred death. He gave it the title "When Lilacs Last in the Dooryard Bloom'd," in a closing line inscribing it "for the sweetest, wisest soul of all my days and lands—and this for his dear sake." Among its sixteen passages were the lines:

When lilacs last in the dooryard bloom'd,
And the great star early droop'd in the western sky in the night,
I mourn'd, and yet shall mourn with ever-returning spring.

Ever-returning spring, trinity sure to me you bring,
Lilac blooming perennial and drooping star in the west,
And thought of him I love. . . .

Coffin that passes through lanes and streets,
Through day and night with the great cloud darkening the land,
With the pomp of the inloop'd flags with the cities draped in black,
With the show of the States themselves as of crape-veil'd women standing,
With processions long and winding and the flambeaus of the night,
With the countless torches lit, with the silent sea of faces and the unbared heads,
With the waiting depot, the arriving coffin, and the sombre faces,
With dirges through the night, with the thousand voices rising strong and solemn,
With all the mournful voices of the dirges pour'd around the coffin,
The dim-lit churches and the shuddering organs—where amid these you journey,
With the tolling, tolling bells' perpetual clang,
Here, coffin that slowly passes,
I give you my sprig of lilac.

For Whitman, Lincoln was a great voice and a sublime doer in the field of democracy. He regarded both Lincoln and himself as foretellers of a New Time for the common man and woman. One of his verses saluted "Reconciliation" as the "word over all, beautiful as the sky." Of the four bloody years his line ran: "Beautiful that war and all its deeds of carnage must in time be utterly lost." He had written, for whatever it might mean to anyone: "My enemy is dead, a man as divine as myself is dead." And he compressed both melancholy and solace in his line "The hands of the sisters Death and Night incessantly softly wash again, and ever again, this soil'd world."

In thousands of commentaries that were to pile higher and higher, Lincoln stood as the incarnation of two practical results—Emancipation and Union. Tragedy was to go on and human misery to be seen widespread. Yet it was agreed two causes directed by Lincoln had won the war. Gone was the old property status of the Negro. Gone was the doctrine of Secession and States' Rights. These two.

Black men could now move from where they were miserable to where they were equally miserable—now it was lawful for them to move—they were not under the law classified as livestock and chattels. Now too the Negro who wished to read could do so; no longer was it a crime for him to be found reading a book; nor was it now any longer a crime to teach a Negro to read. The illiterate, propertyless Negro was to be before the law and the Federal Government an equal of the illiterate, propertyless white— and many sardonics were involved. And in spite of its many absurd and contradictory phases the Negro had a human dignity and chances and openings not known to him before—rainbows of hope instead of the auction block and the black-snake whip.

Decreed beyond any but far imagining of its going asunder was Lincoln's mystic dream of the Union of States, achieved. Beyond all the hate or corruption or mocking fantasies of democracy that might live as an aftermath of the war were assurances of long-time conditions for healing, for rebuilding, for new growths. The decision was absolute, hammered on terrible anvils. The Union stood—an amalgamated and almost an awful fact.

Now too, as Lincoln had pledged, a whole mesh of trammels and clamps on Western migration were to be cut loose. The homesteaders held back by the Southern landed proprietors could go. And the Pacific railways could go; the jealousies suffocating them were out. With almost explosive force the industrial, financial, and transportation systems of the North could be let loose, free to go. The war had done that. Incidental costs might be staggering, but the very onrush of them was to testify that they had been under restraint. Now they could go—with all their benefits and exploitations, their mistakes from which they must later learn to cease and desist.

Now also, as a result flowing from the war, the United States was to take its place among nations counted World Powers. The instinct of the Tories and the imperialists of the British Empire that they, if the North won its war for the Union, would have a rival was correct. And as a World Power the expectation was it would be a voice of the teachings of Washington, Jefferson, Jackson—and Lincoln—speaking for republican government, for democracy, for institutions "of the people, by the people, for the people." Though there might come betrayals and false pretenses, the war had put some manner of seal on human rights and dignity in contrast with property rights—and even the very definitions of property.

In a storm of steel and blood, without compensation and rather with shrill crying of vengeance, with the melancholy and merciless crying out loud that always accompanies revolution, property values of some $3,000,-000,000 had gone up in smoke, had joined the fabrics of all shadows. In sacrifice and moaning one property category had been struck off into emptiness and nothing. At terrific human cost there had been a redefinition of one species of property.

The delicately shaded passages of the second inaugural wept over the cost of doing by violence what might have been done by reason. Yet look-ing back it was seen that violence and not reason was ordained. With all its paradoxes and perfect though cruel sincerities, with all its garrulous pre-tenses and windy prophecies, the war testified to the awfulness of pent-up forces too long unreasonably held back. Of what avail the wisdom of the wise who could not foresee a House Divided and prepare it against storm that threatened final hopeless wreck and ruin? Of what service either the eminently practical men or the robed and assured professional and learned classes if human advance must be at such cost of suffering?

Out of the smoke and stench, out of the music and violet dreams of the war, Lincoln stood perhaps taller than any other of the many great heroes. This was in the mind of many. None threw a longer shadow than he. And to him the great hero was The People. He could not say too often that he was merely their instrument.

These were meditations and impressions of the American people in days following April 14 of 1865.

CHAPTER 76

VAST PAGEANT, THEN GREAT QUIET

THERE was a funeral.

It took long to pass its many given points.

Many millions of people saw it and personally moved in it and were part of its procession.

The line of march ran seventeen hundred miles.

As a dead march nothing like it had ever been attempted before.

Like the beginning and the end of the Lincoln Administration, it had no precedents to go by.

It was garish, vulgar, massive, bewildering, chaotic.

Also it was simple, final, majestic, august.

In spite of some of its mawkish excess of show and various maudlin pro-ceedings, it gave solemn unforgettable moments to millions of people who had counted him great, warm and lovable.

The people, the masses, nameless and anonymous numbers of persons not listed nor published among those present—these redeemed it.

They gave it the dignity and authority of a sun darkened by a vast bird migration.

They shaped it into a drama awful in the sense of having naïve awe and tears without shame.

They gave it the color and heave of the sea which is the mother of tears.

They lent to it the color of the land and the earth which is the bread-giver of life and the quiet tomb of the Family of Man.

Yes, there was a funeral.

From his White House in Washington—where it began—they carried his coffin and followed it nights and days for twelve days.

By night bonfires and torches lighted the right of way for a slow-going railroad train.

By day troops with reversed arms, muffled drums, multitudinous feet seeking the pivotal box with the silver handles.

By day bells tolling, bells sobbing the requiem, the salute guns, cannon rumbling their inarticulate thunder.

To Baltimore, Harrisburg, Philadelphia, New York, they journeyed with the draped casket to meet overly ornate catafalques.

To Albany, Utica, Syracuse, moved the funeral cortege always met by marchers and throngs.

To Cleveland, Columbus, Indianapolis, Chicago, they took the mute oblong box, met by a hearse for convoy to where tens of thousands should have their last look.

Then to Springfield, Illinois, the old home town, the Sangamon near by, the New Salem hilltop near by, for the final rest of cherished dust.

Thus the route and the ceremonial rites in epitome.

The weather was April and May but the smoke and haze was October and the feeling of the hour silent snow on the January earth of a hard winter.

The ground lay white with apple blossoms this April week. The redbird whistled. Through black branches shone blue sky. Ships put out from port with white sails catching the wind. Farmers spoke to their horses and turned furrows till sundown on the cornfield. Boys drew circles in cinder paths and played marbles. Lilac bushes took on surprises of sweet, light purple. In many a back yard the potato-planting was over. In this house was a wedding, in that one a newborn baby, in another a girl with a new betrothal ring. Life went on. Everywhere life went on.

In the East Room of the White House lay the body of a man, embalmed and prepared for a journey. Sweet roses, early magnolias, and the balmiest of lilies were strewn for an effect as though the flowers had begun to bloom even from his coffin. On a platform under a canopy of folds and loops of black silk and crape rested the coffin. Six feet six was the coffin in length, one foot and a half across the shoulders. The wood was mahogany, lined with lead, covered with black broadcloth, at the sides four massive silver handles. Tassels, shamrock leaves, silver stars and silver cords could be seen on facings and edges. A shield with a silver plate had the inscription:

ABRAHAM LINCOLN
SIXTEENTH PRESIDENT OF THE UNITED STATES
BORN FEB. 12, 1809
DIED APRIL 15, 1865

On a pillow of white silk lay the head, on plaited satin rested the body, dressed in the black suit in which the first inaugural was delivered, with its references to "fellow citizens," to "my dissatisfied countrymen," to "better angels," as though even among angels there are the worse and the better. The chandeliers at each end of the East Room drooped with black alpaca. The eight grand mirrors of the room spoke sorrow with night-shade silk gauze. The doors, the windows too, drooped with black alpaca.

It was Tuesday, April 18, and outside surged the largest mass of people that ever thronged the White House lawn. In two columns they filed through the East Room, moving along the two sides of the coffin, many pale and limping soldiers out of the convalescent wards of the hospitals, many women and children sobbing and weeping aloud as they passed pausing only the slightest moment for a look. Those counting estimated twenty-five thousand. If it had been a hundred thousand or ten thousand the impression of any beholder would have been much the same.

EAST.

Admit the Bearer to the

EXECUTIVE MANSION,

On WEDNESDAY, the

19th of April, 1865.

Card of admission. From the Barrett collection.

On Wednesday, April 19, arrived sixty clergymen, the Cabinet members, the Supreme Court Justices, important officials from coast to coast, foreign Ministers spangled in color and costume, General Grant with white sash across his breast, Admiral Farragut as a model of composure and quiet valor, the new President Andrew Johnson—six hundred dignitaries in all—crowded and squeezed amid the chandeliers and eight grand mirrors of the East Room. Mrs. Lincoln was still too distracted to be present. Robert Lincoln had come—and Tad with a drawn, tear-swollen face—it was not easy for them to be there.

To responsive, imaginative little Tad it was perhaps dreamlike, a living nightmare softened by festoons of black silk, by an illusion of black moonlight falling into a room where the tongue of no one could possibly compete with the loud, persistent, pervasive silence of one tongue stilled behind the shut lips amid the plaited white satin.

"Hear my prayer, O Lord . . . I am a stranger with thee, and a sojourner, as all my fathers were," intoned the Reverend Dr. C. H. Hall, rector of the Church of the Epiphany. "For a thousand years in thy sight are but as yesterday. . . . As soon as thou scatterest them they are even as a sleep; and fade away suddenly like the grass. In the morning it is green, and groweth up; but in the evening it is cut down, dried up, and withered."

The great poem of Anglo-Saxon speech comprised in the fifteenth chapter of the first Epistle of St. Paul to the Corinthians made the Lesson for the day. Man is cut down as a flower. He fleeth as a shadow. Yet death may be swallowed up in victory. . . . "Thou knowest, Lord, the secrets of our hearts; shut not thy merciful ears to our prayers."

Bishop Matthew Simpson of the Methodist Episcopal Church offered prayer that smitten hearts might endure, might not be called upon for further sacrifices, that the widow and children be comforted. "We bless Thee that no tumult has arisen, and in peace and harmony our Government moves onward; and that Thou hast shown that our Republican Government is the strongest upon the face of the earth. . . . Hear us while we unite in praying with Thy Church in all lands and ages. . . . Around the remains of our beloved President may we covenant together by every possible means to give ourselves to our country's service until every vestige of this rebellion shall have been wiped out, and until slavery, its cause, shall be forever eradicated." Then the Lord's Prayer . . . Thy will be done on earth, as it is in Heaven. Give us this day our daily bread. And forgive us our debts, as we forgive our debtors . . . deliver us from evil . . . Amen.

A bitter cup from the hand of a chastening Divine Father had been given the mourning nation, said the Reverend Dr. Phineas D. Gurley of the New York Avenue Presbyterian Church in the funeral address. "His way is in the sea, and His path in the great waters; and his footsteps are not known. . . . We bow, we weep, we worship." The cruel assassin had brought mysterious affliction. "We will wait for His interpretation . . . He may purify us more in the furnace of trial, but He will not consume us." The people had in the late President a loving confidence. No man since Washington was so deeply enshrined in the hearts of the people. He deserved it, merited it, by his acts, by the whole tone of his life. He leaned on God, remembering that "God is in history."

Dr. Gurley recalled his leaving Springfield, saying to old and tried friends, "I leave you with this request: *pray for me*," and added, "They did pray for him; and millions of others prayed for him; nor did they pray in vain." Dr. Gurley sketched the familiar outlines of the life, said it would

enter "the register of the ages . . . triumph over the injuries of time," sur-
viving busts and statues, which are frail and perishable.

The closing invocation was spoken by a Baptist clergyman, chaplain of
the United States Senate, the Reverend Dr. E. H. Gray. He beheld a nation
prostrate and in sackcloth over the remains of an illustrious and beloved
chief, asked compassion for hearts wrung with agony, asked blessings for
those of the Government who must now sustain the Government. And the
final ceremonial words spoken in the White House over the mute form of
the author of the second inaugural and the Louisiana reconstruction speech
of April 11 were as follows: "O God, let treason, that has deluged our land
with blood, and devastated our country, and bereaved our homes, and filled
them with widows and orphans, and has at length culminated in the assassination of the nation's chosen ruler—God of justice, and avenger of the nation's
wrong, let the work of treason cease, and let the guilty author of this horrible crime be arrested and brought to justice. O hear the cry, and the
prayer, and the tears now rising from a nation's crushed and smitten heart,
and deliver us from the power of all our enemies, and send speedy peace
unto all our borders, through Jesus Christ our Lord. Amen."

The services were over. The pallbearers took the silver handles. The
bong of big bells on cathedrals struck and the little bells of lesser steeples
chimed in, as across the spring sunshine came the tolling of all the church
bells of Washington and Georgetown, and Alexandria across the river.
Counting the minutes with their salutes came the hoarse boom of fort guns
encircling the national capital and several batteries sent into the city.

Out of the great front door of the Executive Mansion for the last time
went the mortal shape of Abraham Lincoln, sixteenth President of the
United States. Six gray horses stood waiting with a black hearse fourteen
feet long, seven feet wide, mounted eight feet from the ground. It moved
under escort of regimental bands playing a dead march, cavalry, artillery,
navy and marine detachments, infantry and drum corps with reversed arms
and muffled drums. On the one-mile route to the Capitol pavements and
curbs were packed with onlookers, who also filled every roof, window,
doorway, balcony, and stairway. Sixty thousand spectators watched a parade
of forty thousand mourners.

Marshal Ward Hill Lamon and aides headed the civic procession, which
included nearly all the high men of the Government, followed by department and bureau employees, State delegations, municipal officers, visiting
firemen of the Perseverance Hose Company of Philadelphia, three hundred
convalescents from Finley Hospital, representations from the Union League,
the Mount Vernon Association, the Fenian Brotherhood, the Sons of Tem-
perance, German glee clubs, a Catholic delegation of two hundred and fifty
students and teachers from Gonzaga College, three hundred Italians of the
39th New York regiment carrying the national flags of Italy and the United
States, several thousand "persons of African descent," as termed in the
Emancipation Proclamation, their banner reading "We mourn our loss." A
varied, kaleidoscopic, and human America followed a lost leader.

From his sickbed, sore with his dagger wounds, Secretary Seward gazed from the window with mingled grief and thanks. In a group of marching Treasury bureau officials he could see a flag with a gash torn in it. This had caught the assassin's foot and broken his leg. Immediately behind the hearse Seward could see two grooms leading a horse, surmising this was the horse that had most often carried the body now in the hearse.

At Seventh Street a regiment of colored troops just arrived from the front, by a mistaken maneuver, wheeled about and found itself at the head and forefront of the procession, winning admiration by their marching order and skill in the manual of arms. At Fifteenth Street one of the horses of President Johnson's carriage began rearing for a runaway and the President and his companion Preston King alighted and took seats in another carriage. Neither these nor any other incidents hindered the smooth flow of a procession that stretched for miles, moving into Pennsylvania Avenue as a long breathing link of living persons connecting and welding the unity of the White House and the Capitol.

In the rotunda of the Capitol, under the great white dome that had come to its finished construction while the war raged, twelve sergeants of the Veteran Reserve Corps carried the coffin to a huge catafalque. The honorary pallbearers ranged themselves in a circle. Generals, admirals, the President, the Cabinet, stood some ten feet from the coffin. Dr. Gurley spoke a brief service. Lincoln's bodyguard, with an added company and officers, formed a cordon around the coffin. The building was cleared.

In silence during night watches the body of Lincoln lay with eyes never opening to see far above him the arches of the great dome that for him symbolized the Union. When in front of this building he had spoken his first inaugural, the parts and pieces of that dome lay scattered on the ground around him. He had seen them lifted up and woven and mortised and completed for his second inaugural. Then he stood vertical and looked up. Now he lay horizontal with eyelids beyond opening. In the night watches while the guard mount changed, whispering, quiet on soft feet, into midnight and past into daybreak, midway between House and Senate chambers, midway between those seats and aisles of heartbreak and passion, he lay a horizontal clay tabernacle.

In the morning of Thursday, April 20, at ten o'clock the doors opened in special consideration for wounded soldiers from the hospitals, weak and battered men, some with empty sleeves, others on crutches, to file by. Afterward came the public, at times three thousand to the hour, before midnight twenty-five thousand persons. Many had seen him in the life, in buildings, on streets, in a carriage, on a horse, breathing and speaking before an audience. Now they looked at him, some in agreement and some not with the *New York World* reporter who wrote: "Death has fastened into his frozen face all the character and idiosyncrasy of life. He has not changed one line of his grave, grotesque countenance, nor smoothed out a single feature. The hue is rather bloodless and leaden, but he was always sallow. . . . Whatever energy or humor or tender gravity marked the living face is hardened into pulseless outline. . . . The white satin around it reflects sufficient light upon the face to show that death is really there."

The same reporter, George Alfred Townsend, described the embalmer as having by a customary process drained the blood from the body by the jugular vein, "and through a cutting made on the inside of the thigh the empty blood vessels were charged with a chemical preparation which soon hardened to the consistency of stone." Scalp and brain had been removed, blood emptied from the chest. "All that we see of Abraham Lincoln, so cunningly contemplated in this splendid coffin, is a mere shell, an effigy, a sculpture. He lies in a sleep, but it is the sleep of marble. All that made this flesh vital, sentient and affectionate, is gone forever." This was the factual and informative news version of what Dr. Gurley in his prayer of the day before had set forth more utterly: "For what is our life? It is even a vapor that appeareth for a little time and then vanisheth away. . . . We commit its decaying remains to their kindred element, earth to earth, ashes to ashes, dust to dust."

Some who gazed on the face remembered the poem he so often recited for them, that old-rose-and-lavender keepsake of a poem. For him it had a musk of smell and a dusk of light, a weatherworn stain of hard walnut with a sunset smoke loitering and elusive in the faded grain of the wood. Before he went to Congress, before the Mexican War, he said these verses. Years later when President he said them. They carried for him a music in the air now:

> The leaves of the oak and the willow shall fade,
> Be scattered around, and together be laid;
> As the young and the old, the low and the high,
> Shall crumble to dust and together shall lie. . . .
>
> The saint who enjoyed the communion of Heaven,
> The sinner who dared to remain unforgiven,
> The wise and the foolish, the guilty and just,
> Have quietly mingled their bones in the dust. . . .
>
> 'Tis the wink of an eye; 'tis the draught of a breath
> From the blossom of health to the paleness of death,
> From the gilded saloon to the bier and the shroud;
> O, why should the spirit of mortal be proud?

Friday morning, April 21, just six days after the death in the Peterson house on Tenth Street, President Johnson, General Grant, Stanton and other Cabinet members, saw the coffin placed aboard a special burial car at the Washington depot—joined by another and smaller casket, that of the son Willie, which had been disinterred and was to have burial in Springfield, Illinois, near his father. Railroad-yard engine bells tolled and a far-stretching crowd stood with uncovered heads as the train of seven cars—with a scout pilot engine ahead to test the roadway—moved out of Washington for Baltimore,

This was the start of a funeral journey that was to take the lifeless body on a seventeen-hundred-mile route which practically included the same points and stops that the living form had made four years and two months before on the way to the first inauguration. Aboard the coaches were five men who had made that earlier journey: Colonel Ward Hill Lamon, Justice David Davis, General David Hunter, John G. Nicolay, and John Hay. A committee of Senate and House members included Washburne, Yates, and Arnold of Illinois, Harlan of Iowa, and Julian of Indiana. Mrs. Lincoln, Robert, and Tad were to undergo an ordeal; with them was her kinsman Ninian W. Edwards. The Illinois delegation aboard included Lincoln's first law partner John T. Stuart and such Sucker State familiars as Lyman Trumbull, William Bross, Jesse K. Dubois, Shelby M. Cullom, and General John A. McClernand. Among State governors aboard were Oglesby of Illinois, Morton of Indiana, Brough of Ohio, Stone of Iowa.

Baltimore wore mourning everywhere and paid reverence. In the rotunda of the Exchange Building tens of thousands came to the coffin. The civic procession, the human outpouring, was unmistakable. More than surface changes had come to Maryland in the four furnace years.

As the funeral train moved slowly over Pennsylvania soil those aboard saw they were sharing in no mere official function, no conventional affair that the common people looked at from afar. At lonely country crossroads were people and faces, horsemen, farmers with their wives and children, standing where they had stood for hours before, waiting, performing the last little possible act of ceremony and attention and love—with solemn faces and uncovered heads standing and gazing as the burial car passed. In villages and small towns stood waiting crowds, sometimes with a little silver cornet band, often with flowers in hope the train might stop and they could leave camellias, roses, lilies-of-the-valley, wreaths of color and perfume, on a coffin. At York in a short stop six ladies came aboard and laid a three-foot wreath of red and white roses on the coffin.

Through heavy rains at Harrisburg came thirty thousand in the night and morning to see the coffin in circles of white flowering almond. At noon of Saturday, April 22, Philadelphia was reached, via Lancaster, where at a railroad bridge, on a rock, stood an old man alone with his thoughts, perhaps the loneliest man in the United States. He lifted his hat. No one could read what he meant by lifting his hat. It was Thad Stevens. And on the edge of the vast crowd at Lancaster sat a quiet old man in a carriage; this was Lincoln's predecessor, James Buchanan.

In Philadelphia a half-million people were on hand for the funeral train. In Independence Hall, where the Declaration of Independence was signed, stood the coffin, at its head the Liberty Bell and near by the chair in which John Hancock once sat. Outside was devotion, curiosity, hysteria. The line of mourners ran three miles. "A young lady had her arm broken," said the *New York Herald*, "and a young child, involved in the crush, is said to have been killed. Many females fainted with exhaustion, and had to be carried off by their friends." Through two windows the double column entered and passed by the casket, a third of a million people. A venerable Negro woman, her face indented and majestic as a relief map of the continent of Asia, laid evergreens on the coffin and with hot tears filling the dents and furrows, cried, "Oh, Abraham Lincoln, are you dead? are you dead?" She could not be sure.

At Newark, New Jersey, on the morning of April 24 the train moved slowly amid acres of people, a square mile of them. "The city turned out *en masse*," wrote reporters. At Jersey City was a like scene. There the depot

A silhouette wrought on buttons, medallions, rosettes, banners, posters, cards, badges. From the Lincoln Library of the University of Chicago.

at one end had the motto "A Nation's Heart Was Struck" and at the other end "Be Still, and Know That I Am God." A German chorus of seventy male voices sang "*Integer Vitae*." Chauncey M. Depew, secretary of state for New York, in behalf of the unavoidably absent Governor Reuben E. Fenton, for the Empire State formally received the body from Governor Parker of New Jersey. Ten stalwart sergeants carried the casket to a hearse which moved through street crowds to the ferry house. The paint was fresh on a legend here reading "George Washington, the Father: Abraham Lincoln, the Saviour, of His Country." The ferryboat *Jersey City* moved across the Hudson River, her pilothouse and cabins in crape, flags at half-mast. As she neared the wharf at Desbrosses Street, the German choral society gave a funeral ode from the first book of Horace.

Beyond the wharf as far as the eye could see stood waiting masses of people. A large force of police kept a wide space cleared. The Seventh Regiment National Guard formed a hollow square into which moved the funeral cortege. The procession marched to the City Hall through streets packed to capacity. The crowd gaze centered on the plate-glass hearse, topped with eight tall plumes of black and white feathers, draped with the American flag, drawn by six gray horses each led by a groom in black.

New York had prepared for this day and the next. A special committee and a unanimous Common Council had ordered all public buildings closed, had recommended that all citizens "close their respective places of business for the same period," that on all ships and on all public buildings flags fly at half-mast, that furthermore all public buildings be draped in mourning thirty days, "to testify their sorrow for the death, and their respect for the memory, of the illustrious deceased." Long was the list of members of the Committee of Citizens in charge of the obsequies, carrying many high names in business, finance, law, politics, science, history, in the financial and merchandising capital, the cultural center, of the country.

Never before, so everyone agreed, had New York put on such garb and completely changed its look so that it seemed another city. On the marble and brownstone fronts, in the ramshackle tenements of "those who live from hand to mouth," came out crape or black folds or drapery or black muslin, rosettes, sable emblems, what the news reporters termed "the habiliments of mourning." In store fronts and home windows were busts of Lincoln and little paper monuments resembling marble. Medals and plaques of bronze and copper were common, his face outlined on each. On street arches and over doorways, in store and house windows, were mottoes and quotations, insignia, rhymes. All were of good intention. Some had pointed value. "We Shall Not Look upon His Like Again" said one Broadway store. "The Nation Mourns" read the wide banner over the City Hall main doorway. "A Continent Weeps" said a house front on Nassau Street. Under a Lincoln portrait at his home, 48 Madison Street, the Aldermen's clerk Walsh had inscribed "God's Noblest Work, an Honest Man." Fox's Old Bowery Theatre amid black and white streamers announced "We Mourn the Loss of an Honest Man." The Bowery Savings Bank considered one word in antique script sufficient: "Lincoln." Briefer yet was Cooper Union Institute with its personal memories: "A. L." Easily conventional were the frequent "Gone But Not Forgotten" or "*Requiescat in Pace.*" Merely pious and divested of the personal was "In God We Trust," taken from a recent coin issue. Directly simple was "Our Chief Has Fallen." Darkly suggestive was "Death to Assassins." Possibly some Quaker inscribed the one over the Army and Navy Clothing Office: "Thou Art Gone and Friend and Foe Alike Appreciate Thee Now." On a black pedestal holding a bust of Lincoln in the store front of Knabe & Company, agents of a Baltimore house, was a gnarled and profound sentence reading:

"There was in this man something that could create, subvert or reform, an understanding spirit, and an eloquence to summon mankind to society, or to break the bonds of slavery asunder, and to rule the wilderness of free minds with unbounded authority—something that could establish and overwhelm an empire, and strike a blow in the world that should resound through the universe."

In the Customs House were elaborate drapings over pillars and panels, with folds of black and white encircling the busts of Washington, Jackson, Clay, Scott, and Webster. An official was asked why the bold relief bust of President Lincoln had no like signs. He answered: "No drapery or sorrow-suggesting emblems are needed around such a statue. The thoughts occasioned by the mere view of that face are sufficiently saddening, without the assistance of any mournful symbols."

From near noon of Monday, April 24, to noon of the next day the remains of Abraham Lincoln, the clay tabernacle horizontal amid white satin, lay in the City Hall. A vast outpouring of people hour by hour passed by to see this effigy and remembrance of his face and form. They came for many and varied reasons.

Hundreds who had helped wreck, burn, and loot this city, killing scores of policemen and Negroes in the draft and race riots of year before last—these came now with curiosity, secret triumph, hate and contempt, a story traveling Manhattan that one entered a saloon hangout of their breed, saying, "I went down to the City Hall to see with my own eyes and be sure he was dead."

Some could not have told precisely why they were drawn by a spell that held them to wait five and six hours till they had slowly moved on to where they had their look at the victim of a sudden appalling tragedy touched with the supernatural.

An overwhelming many came as an act of faith and attestation; they had come to love him and follow him; his many plain words and ways and stories told about him had reached them; he had become terribly real and beautifully alive to them; they must see this final shape and dust of him. The few women who sought to kiss his face and who were hurriedly moved on by the guards—each might have had some sufficient reason; all of the boys at Malvern Hill and Gettysburg had mothers.

Up a winding stairway of a rotunda went the double column of people, to arrive at the top where stood the coffin, then down the other side. Below on the main floor singing societies in changing shifts gave classic chorals of grief and dolor. In the evening, when the workingmen and workingwomen had come away from the shops and factories, it was noticed the lines were longer, the pressure toward the City Hall doorway heavier. At midnight the numbers were greatest. Yet at dawn and into daybreak there was no end, no letting up, of the flow of the lines of men, women, and children who wished to pass the coffin. Estimates were that an average of about eighty persons passed in a minute, that is, forty on either side. This would allow as a total not far from a hundred and twenty thousand people in grief —or curiosity.

At noon on Tuesday, April 25, a procession moved from the City Hall. It followed a giant canopied hearse drawn by sixteen black horses. From Broad to Fourteenth Street and then to Fifth Avenue wound the route— and up Fifth Avenue to Thirty-fourth Street and thence to Ninth Avenue and the Hudson River Railroad depot. Nearly every race, nationality, religion, political faith, and human phase and interest of America was repre-

Lying in state in the City Hall of New York—a *Harper's Weekly* sketch

sented among those who marched. Near a hundred thousand, possibly more, rode or walked in the procession. The troops in Union Army blue alone numbered twenty thousand. The panoramic show took hours. It was massive, bizarre, spectacular, dazzling—yet somber. A hundred thousand strangers had come to New York to see it. The sidewalk, street, curb, and window spectators ran perhaps to a million. At the procession's end came a delegation of two thousand Negroes, some wearing the Union Army service blue. There had been mutterings from a draft- and race-riot element that they would "never let the damned niggers march." This would have interested the man in the hearse, could he have heard it. It was customary and expected. From Assistant Secretary of War Charles A. Dana at Washington came a telegram to General Dix that the Secretary of War desired "no discrimination respecting color." And it was so ordered. Heading the Negroes was a banner reading on one side "Abraham Lincoln, Our Emancipator," on the reverse side "To Millions of Bondmen Liberty He Gave." At the Union Square exercises following the parade the Roman Catholic Archbishop McCloskey pronounced the benediction, Rabbi Isaacs of the Jewish Synagogue read from their scriptures, the Reverend Stephen H. Tyng of St. George's Church offered a prayer, the historian George Bancroft delivered an oration, the Reverend Dr. Osgood read an ode by William Cullen Bryant, the Reverend J. P. Thompson intoned Lincoln's second inaugural. Evening had come. New York, the metropolis, had spoken. The funeral train with a locomotive named *Union* was moving up the Hudson River on its westward journey.

"New York never before saw such a day," wrote a *New York Herald* commentator seeking to give tomorrow's readers the gist and lesson of the hour. "Rome in the palmiest days of its power never witnessed such a triumphal march as New York yesterday formed and looked upon. When four years ago Abraham Lincoln passed through the city to be armed with authority as the nation's leader, Broadway sufficed to contain the crowd which, with varied sentiments, cheered, and scoffed, and scowled him a doubtful welcome. When yesterday the same people, inspired with a common, universal sorrow, sadly followed his body, crowned with more glorious honors as the nation's savior, the same wide street held hardly a fraction of them. Then he was going to be crowned chief magistrate of a divided people and disrupted nation on the eve of a great, bloody and uncertain war. Yesterday he was the great martyr of a nation united under his guidance and that of God, by the successful close of that gloomy war. Then he passed through almost unknown, and the crowd that followed his coach with cheers were actuated by curiosity as much as admiration. Yesterday it was different; yesterday witnessed the real triumphal march of Abraham Lincoln; for he had conquered the prejudices of all hordes and classes, and the hearts of the people who honored him beat with love and veneration of the man. Better for his fame that it should come thus late than too soon. This test of his success and his greatness can never be doubted or disputed."

To the Reverend Octavius Brooks Frothingham the day in New York City had a lesson for all time and for all hearts. He found it momentous "to see how the people thought of this man who never thought of himself—how they heaped honor upon him who claimed none; how they called him martyr and saint who would have sunk into the ground had such names been bestowed on him when living; how they crowded and stood all night out of doors to get a sight of his dead pale face, who hid his face from the admiring crowd whenever he could."

George William Curtis walked the streets of Manhattan in a "misty spring moonlight" and wrote to a friend of what so many of the Lincoln loyalists were thinking and feeling. "As I think of the man we all loved and honored, I feel that I cannot honor too much, or praise too highly the people that he so truly represented. So spotless he was, so patient, so tender—it is a selfish, sad delight to me now, as when I looked upon his coffin, that his patience had made me patient, and that I never doubted his heart, or head, or hand. At the only interview I ever had with him, he shook my hand paternally at parting, and said, 'Don't be troubled. I guess we shall get through.'" Curtis mentioned three portraits on a mantel in his room, his own brother, Theodore Winthrop, Robert Gould Shaw. "They are all dead —the brave darlings—and now I put the head of the dear Chief among them."

The accusation was insinuated, or rather directly spoken, in various quarters that the body of Lincoln was being hawked about and vulgarly displayed in the interest of the Republican party and its radical wing. The very response of the people carried a reply to this. In the tumult of politics and in the crush of crowds he had had so much of his life, what was there of these few days before his burial not in accord? They wanted to see him as silent dust. What was the harm? In life he had met just about everyone who had sent word they wished to see him. So why not now again when he was beyond any and all harm? Those men with hats off along the railroad tracks at midnight and dawn, tears down the faces of many of them— why not? He would have wanted it. It went with his living and actual face and voice.

The vast and tireless outpourings of humanity at Washington and on through New York, the long lines of people waiting many hours in a tensed silence for the privileged fraction of a second when they could pass by a coffin and take a hurried glance at one memorable face, the spectacle of the rich and the poor, capitalists, wage-earners, the able-bodied and the lame and the crippled, an immense human family participating—this impressed the country. Those who might have had doubts about participating decided to be at least onlookers. The event was for an hour. It could never happen again. A deep interest grew into excitement. Here and there it verged into hysteria and delirium.

An epidemic of verse seized thousands. They sent their rhymed lines to the *New York Herald*, which publicly notified them that if it were all printed there would be no space for news, wherefore none at all would be

printed. The *Chicago Tribune* editorially notified them it "suffered" from
this "severe attack of poetry," that three days brought one hundred and
sixty pieces beginning either "Toll, toll, ye mourning bells" or "Mourn,
mourn, ye tolling bells."

Up the Hudson River east bank on the night of April 25 chugged the
locomotive named *Union*, with its train of seven cars. On every mile of
the route to Albany those on the train could see bonfires and torches,
could hear bells and cannon and guns, could see forms of people and white
sorry faces. "Yonkers Mourns with the Nation" read one craped flag, women
near by waving their handkerchiefs while tears ran down their cheeks. At
the little station of Irvington with its draped inscriptions—"The Honored
Dead" and "We Mourn the Nation's Loss"—were seven thousand persons.
At Tarrytown American flags arched over the railroad track, and under a
flowered dome of flags and black velvet stood twenty-four young women
gowned in white. At Sing Sing the burial car with its coffin again passed
through a tall arch of flags crossed with black velvet. Amid long dark ranks
of people stood a woman personating the Goddess of Liberty, white-robed
with a chaplet of evergreens about her neck, near her the legend "He Died
for Truth, Justice and Mercy." At Peekskill, encircled with roses and
tasseled red-white-and-blue, was a tall portrait of Lincoln. Firemen and a
company of Highland Grays with drooped flags marched before a large
crowd. At Garrison's Landing, opposite the West Point military academy,
were assembled the academy staff and professors—and a thousand precise
and caped cadets. At Cold Spring again was a young woman in the semblance of the Goddess of Liberty, her face black-veiled, at her right a kneeling boy soldier, at her left a sailor boy kneeling. Fishkill evergreened its
motto "In God We Trust," crowded both sides of the track; across the
Hudson River General George Washington's revolutionary headquarters
had flags with mourning signs. Here too were delegations from Newburgh,
New Paltz, and other parts of the apple country immediately across the
river. At Poughkeepsie the throng stretched far from the depot and railroad tracks, men with uncovered heads, hundreds of women and children
with miniature mourning flags, a thousand pupils and a cornet band from
the National Business College, gun booms counting each of the fifteen
minutes which the train stopped. A committee of women, with permission
granted, entered the funeral car and laid a wreath of roses on the coffin. At
each station farther en route to Albany were crowds, at Strasburg an ingenious circle of light, at Rhinebeck and Barrytown torch formations, at
Tivoli lighted lamps, at Catskill huge bonfires and United States vessels on
the river with flags at half-mast, at Hudson minute guns and two hotels
with all windows illuminated and black-draped.

Soldiers and firemen escorted the hearse across the river, moved through
immense crowds holding many from Vermont and Massachusetts, marched
up the steep hill to the Assembly chamber of the State capitol. As elsewhere, every public building, store front, factory, and shop had its flags
and mourning signs, likewise nearly every home, whether mansion or

shanty. On business and private houses were mottoes: "All Joy Is Darkened; the Mirth of the Land Is Gone, And the Mourners Go about the Streets"; "And the Victory That Day Was Turned into Mourning unto All the People"; "The Martyr to Liberty"; and one which Shakespeare had spoken over the daggered Brutus, met frequently in each city:

> His life was gentle, and the elements
> So mix'd in him that Nature might stand up
> And say to all the world, "This was a man!"

Past midnight of April 25 into the morning hours of April 26 the columns of mourners passed the coffin. It was a few days more than four years since Lincoln had spoken in this same room, a weary man facing chaos, saying against clamor and ridicule, "When the time comes, I shall speak," saying, "It is true that, while I hold myself, without mock modesty, the humblest of all individuals that have ever been elevated to the presidency, I have a more difficult task to perform than any one of them." Then he was alive, breathing. So was the actor J. Wilkes Booth, then performing in an Albany theatre near by. Now on this morning of April 26 neither of the two was alive and breathing.

For on this morning of April 26, hunted like a wild beast and cornered like a rat and dealt with as though he were truly no more than a rat, J. Wilkes Booth met his end. Near Bowling Green, Virginia, in a burning barn set afire from the outside, a bullet drove through his neck bone "perforating both sides of the collar," and he was dragged away from reaching flames and laid under a tree. Water was given him. He revived, to murmur from parched lips, "Tell my mother—I died—for my country." He was carried to a house veranda, there muttering, "I thought I did for the best." He lingered for a time. A doctor came. Wilkes Booth asked that his hands might be raised so that he could look at them. So it was told. And as he looked on his hands, he mumbled hoarsely, "Useless! useless!" And those were his last words.

In his pockets were found photographs of five women—and a diary in pencil. Under date of April 13-14, as though to make a record for posterity, he had written: "Until today nothing was ever thought of sacrificing to our country's wrongs. For six months we had worked to capture; but our cause being almost lost, something great and decisive must be done. But its failure was owing to others, who did not strike for their country with a heart. I struck boldly, and not as the papers say. I walked with a firm step through a thousand of his friends, and was stopped, but pushed on. A colonel [meaning Major Rathbone] was at his side. I shouted 'Sic semper!' before I fired [evidently wishing to convey the impression that he gave his victim warning]. In jumping, broke my leg. I passed all his pickets, rode sixty miles that night with the bone of my leg tearing the flesh at every jump. I can never repent it, though we hated to kill. Our country owed all her troubles to him, and God simply made me the instrument of his punishment. . . . I care not what becomes of me. I have no desire to outlive my country."

Of his week of writhing and misery since the murder and his flight, Booth had written: "After being hunted like a dog through swamps, woods, and last night being chased by gun-boats until I was forced to return, wet, cold, and starving, with every man's hand against me, I am here in deep despair. And why? For doing what Brutus was honored for, what made Tell a hero. And yet I, for striking down a greater tyrant than they ever knew, am looked upon as a common cut-throat." This plainly shook and tore his vast pride and ego worse than anything else. He had expected praise and applause. "Now behold the cold hand they extend to me. God can not pardon me if I have done wrong. Yet I can not see my wrong, except in serving a degenerate people." So far had he come in his despair. Those for whom he had killed saw him as no hero in his killing. And his word for them was "a degenerate people." A touch of sanity and chastening ran through a few sentences. "So ends all. For my country [though he had been too pettily egregious, vain, and personal ever to enlist for service under the Confederate flag] I have given up all that makes life sweet and holy; brought misery upon my family, and am sure there is no pardon in the Heaven for me. . . . I think I have done well, though I am abandoned, with the curse of Cain." Again however the chastening of a week of suffering and torture had not gone deep. He was still an actor playing to the large convex and concave mirrors of his self-esteem, writing: "God's will be done. I have too great a soul to die like a criminal. I bless the entire world; have never hated or wronged anyone."

One sentence of the diary had implications. Stanton was to withhold the diary from publication for many months. Then only under peculiar political pressure it was to be brought forth in the first impeachment trial of a President of the United States. This sentence read: "Tonight I will try the river, with the intent to cross, though I have a greater desire and almost a mind to return to Washington and in a measure clear my name, which I feel I can do." Whatever this meant that might be lucid and cogent, it was eventually and generally taken as one more strange flash of the cunning and malice that operated unexpectedly in J. Wilkes Booth. In the finish he was to be buried in the Booth family lot in a Baltimore cemetery, accepted and identified by those who knew him longest and best—though myths and fantasies were to arise around his name, life, and body. Into the War Department archives in Washington would go his diary and keepsakes, a bullet, and the little vest-pocket brass derringer pistol, so tiny it would fit into a man's covered hand and not be seen.

So John Wilkes Booth was a corpse cold and corruptible and the words of the old gypsy woman had come true, hard words that he could not shake off: "Ah, you've a bad hand; the lines all cris-cras. . . . You'll break hearts, they'll be nothing to you. You'll die young. . . . You'll have a fast life—short, but a grand one. Now, young sir, I've never seen a worse hand, and I wish I hadn't seen it."

Yes, for the passing hour Booth was a corpse around whose death revolved dispute, wrangling, and greedy hopes over the sharing of the $50,000 reward offered for him dead or alive.

And four thousand persons an hour passed by the open coffin of Lincoln in Albany, sixty thousand swarmed the streets where they moved in procession to the funeral train. And across the Empire State that day and night it was a mural monotone of mourning, the Erie Canal zone in sober grief with evergreens, flowers, sable emblems. By now it was not impressive that the St. Cecilia Society in Buffalo should intone the dirge "Rest, Spirit, Rest," and lay a harp of white flowers at the head of the coffin—nor that the ladies of the Unitarian Church placed an anchor of white camellias at the foot. Yet the mass effect of the intentions and devout hopes of so many who wished to pour out love joined to grief—the evidence there so often on men's faces that if called on they would serve in relays to carry that important coffin on their shoulders from the seaboard to the Great Lakes and the Sangamon River—the endless multitudinous effect became colossal. Thirty-six young ladies, gowned in white with black shoulder scarfs and the flag of their country, approached the dazzling when seen for the first time. But when seen and noted the twentieth, thirtieth, fortieth time, they took on a ritualist solemnity smoldering and portentous, a mingling of anger, sorrow, devotion, tenacity. Involved was the basis of the stubborn passion that had carried on four years of the bloodiest war known to mankind.

The human past and future participated. At Buffalo Millard Fillmore, one of the three living ex-Presidents of the United States, attended the funeral, which also was witnessed by a youth named Grover Cleveland.

In Ohio was a personal matter that would have interested the animate Lincoln. There had been reports published that the face in the coffin was shrunken and decayed to such an extent that perhaps good taste should forbid further exposure of it to public gaze. It was known that the embalmer on the train had several times by his craft wrought improvement. However this might be, there came from Toledo an old friend and a valued comforter of Lincoln, one David R. Locke, who had a reputation as a funnyman and had written many satirical pieces under the pen name of Petroleum V. Nasby. He wrote with no trace of jest or folly:

"I saw him, or what was mortal of him, on the mournful progress to his last resting-place, in his coffin. The face was the same as in life. Death had not changed the kindly countenance in any line. There was upon it the same sad look that it had worn always, though not so intensely sad as it had been in life. It was as if the spirit had come back to the poor clay, reshaped the wonderfully sweet face, and given it an expression of gladness that he had finally gone 'where the wicked cease from troubling, and the weary are at rest.' The face had an expression of absolute content, of relief, at throwing off a burden such as few men have been called upon to bear— a burden which few men could have borne. I had seen the same expression on his living face only a few times, when, after a great calamity, he had come to a great victory. It was the look of a worn man suddenly relieved. Wilkes

"On Fame's eternal camping ground"—Apotheosis

Cartes de visite from the Barrett collection

Obsequies in San Francisco

From a stereograph presented to the author in 1930 by Harold C. Holmes of Oakland, California

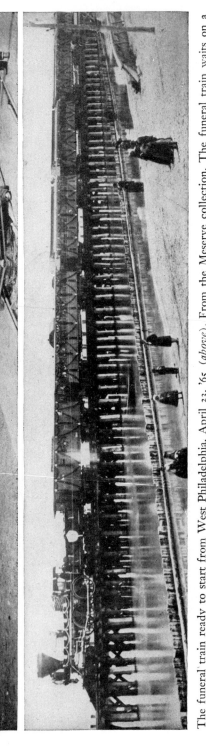

The funeral train ready to start from West Philadelphia, April 23, '65 (above). From the Meserve collection. The funeral train waits on a Lake Michigan pier during ceremonies of May 2, '65 in Chicago (below). From the Illinois State Historical Society.

The funeral cortege entering the Court House, Chicago, on May 3, '65

From the Chicago Historical Society

The outpouring of people around the Court House, Chicago, May 3, '65

From the Chicago Historical Society

The cortege entering the New York City Hall April 25, '65

From the Meserve collection

Booth did Abraham Lincoln the greatest service man could possibly do for him—he gave him peace."

On several railroad divisions of the journey the same locomotive pulled the train and handling it were the same railroad men as four years before. From Erie to Cleveland it was the same engine, the *William Jones*, and the same train conductor, E. D. Page. The engineer of 1861, William Congden, was dead, but his fireman George Martin had the throttle. The division superintendent, Henry Nottingham, as before had complete management.

Cleveland, Columbus & Cincinnati R. R.

SPECIAL TIME SCHEDULE

FOR THE TRAIN CONVEYING THE

REMAINS OF ABRAHAM LINCOLN, LATE PRESIDENT OF THE U. S., AND ESCORT,

FROM WASHINGTON, D. C., TO SPRINGFIELD, ILL.

Cleveland to Columbus, Saturday, April 29th, 1865.

Leave Cleveland	12.00	Midnight.
Berea	12.43	A. M.
Olmsted	12.51	"
Columbia	1.02	"
Grafton	1.23	"
La Grange	1.37	"
Wellington	2.00	"
Rochester	2.17	"
New London	2.36	"
Greenwich	2.59	"
Shiloh	3.19	"
Shelby	3.39	"
Crestline	4.07	"
Galion	4.23	"
Iberia	4.41	"
Gilead	5.05	"
Cardington	5.20	"
Ashley	5.43	"
Eden	5.55	"
Berlin	6.19	"
Lewis Centre	6.32	"
Orange	6.37	"
Worthington	6.56	"
Arrive Columbus	7.30	A. M

This Train will have exclusive right to the Road against all other Trains. A Pilot Locomotive will be run ten minutes in advance of the above Schedule time.

E. S. FLINT, Superintendent.

From the Lincoln Library of the University of Chicago

At Cleveland the Committee on Location of Remains had decided no available building would accommodate the crowds, wherefore the Committee on Arrangements had a pagoda put up in the city park, with open sides through which two columns could pass the coffin. "The floor was so inclined that on entering the building the visitors were able to see the remains and keep them in sight until nearly leaving the building." A high bank above the shore of Lake Erie was black with people as the train drew into the Union Depot. From there another engine took it to the Euclid Street station, and it was chronicled: "As the train came up the Lake Shore track a very beautiful incident took place. Miss Fields of Wilson Street had erected an arch of evergreens on the bank of the Lake near the track, and as the train passed appeared in the arch as the Goddess of Liberty in mourning." In charge of the military, which escorted the hearse drawn by six white horses wearing crape rosettes and silver stars, was Major General Joseph (Fighting Joe) Hooker.

A slow rain began falling and seemed in accord. Along Euclid Avenue to the park moved a procession of more than six thousand. A crowd that stretched for blocks near the city park gave way in order, making a path. Over the coffin Bishop Charles Pettit McIlvaine read from the Episcopal burial service. "We brought nothing into the world, and it is certain we can carry nothing out. The Lord gave, and the Lord taketh away; blessed be the Name of the Lord. . . . Man, that is born of woman, hath but a short time to live, and is full of misery. . . . Of whom may we seek for succour, but of Thee, O Lord?" The rain fell heavier and seemed in tune with the dirges of the bands. Nine thousand an hour passed the coffin the first four hours, the number diminishing in late afternoon and mounting higher in the evening and night. At ten o'clock when the park gates were shut it was said that more than one million pilgrims from northern Ohio had paid their homage. From Detroit had come five hundred with two brass bands. From Meadville, Pennsylvania, had come two hundred marshaled by Captain Derickson and some of his boys who had served with Lincoln's White House bodyguard.

A lashing wind drove torrents of rain as the night procession moved escorting the hearse through crowded streets to the depot. This side of the Alleghenies the grief seemed sharper and the weight of woe heavier. Everywhere was sorrow shown, wrote the *New York Times* correspondent, "and the feeling seems, if possible, to deepen, as we move westward." There was press mention of the prairie bosom waiting to take him, the prairie sod that had nursed him being ready with moist, sweet dews—gentle prairie flowers preparing to weave over him a perpetual chaplet.

From Cleveland to Crestline the rain kept on in torrents. Nevertheless at all towns and crossroads were the mourners, with uncovered heads, with torches and flags crossed with black, with here and there bonfires set blazing by veterans skilled in the bivouac. At Cardington the station had its white banner reading "He Sleeps in the Blessings of the Poor, Whose Fetters God Commanded Him to Break."

Along the railroad track in the morning five miles out from Columbus stood an old woman alone as the slow train came by, her gray hairs disheveled, tears coursing down her furrowed cheeks. In her right hand she held out a black mourning scarf. With her left hand she stretched imploringly toward the rain-and-storm-bedraggled funeral car, reaching and waving toward it her handful of wild flowers, her bouquet and token.

In the rotunda of Ohio's capitol, on a mound of green moss with white flower dots, rested the coffin on April 28, while eight thousand persons passed by each hour from half-past nine in the morning till four o'clock in the afternoon. The doors were shut and Ohio notables, with those from the funeral train, heard a prayer, a hymn, then an oration by J. E. Stevenson on "a Western farmer's son, self-made" who headed a great war. The orator saw it as epic in action. "The people trusted in God and him. There never were braver men than the Union soldiers, in Grecian phalanx, nor Roman legion, nor braver ever bent the Saxon bow or bore the barbarian battle-axe, or set the lance in rest. None braver ever followed the Crescent and the Cross, or fought with Napoleon, or Wellington, or Washington." Lincoln performed greatly—supported by a great people. Peace and prosperity would yet roll along the railways, blossom on the Great Lakes and whiten the seas, "while over and above all shall rise and swell the great dome of his fame."

In the changing red-gold of a rolling prairie sunset, to the slow exultation of brasses rendering "Old Hundred" and the muffled booming of minute guns, the coffin was carried out of the rotunda and taken to the funeral train.

It was now two weeks since the evening hour that Abraham Lincoln cheery and alive had left the White House in Washington to attend a performance of *Our American Cousin* in Ford's Theatre.

The slow night run from Columbus to Indianapolis saw from the car windows a countryside of people thronging to the route of the coffin. At Pleasant Valley were bonfires. A news dispatch from aboard the train, dated at New Milford, 9:19 P.M., said: "Bonfire here, around which are assembled some 400 or 500 people, who wave flags and handkerchiefs slowly. About twenty miles from this place a farmer and his family were standing in a field by a bonfire and waving a flag." And at New Paris, 2:41 A.M.: "Great bonfires light up the skies. A crowd is gathered about who stand with uncovered heads." Nearly every town had its arch of evergreen, flags, and black drapings. At Urbana ten young women strewed roses on the coffin, one of them breaking down in uncontrollable tears. At Piqua were ten thousand at midnight; at Richmond, Indiana, ten thousand again at three o'clock in the morning, women laying wreaths on the two coffins of the father and his son Willie. Also at Richmond were Governor Oliver P. Morton, United States Senator Thomas A. Hendricks, and a committee of more than a hundred public officials, military officers, clergymen, priests, editors. They officially took charge of the train for its stay in the Hoosier State.

Tolling bells and falling rain at Indianapolis saw the coffin borne into the State House for a Sabbath to be remembered. From Cincinnati, Ohio, and Covington, Kentucky, had come the City Councils. From Kentucky had come her Governor Bramlette and others. Pilgrims arrived from the southern counties where the boy Lincoln had learned to read and write, had walked many miles seeking books to read. Again was the inscription where all might read: "He Sleeps in the Blessing of the Poor, Whose Fetters God Commanded Him to Break," and another: "To Live in Hearts We Leave Behind Is Not to Die." In all churches the sermons were on the life of the one-time Hoosier boy. A venerable veteran of forty years' Sunday-school service, Colonel James Blake, marshaled five thousand Sunday-school children for marches to the State House. One hundred and fifty persons a minute passed the coffin, an estimated total of one hundred thousand.

At ten o'clock the doors closed, the marshals, the guard of honor, and the eight sergeants who bore the coffin took charge. The undertaker replaced the lid. Indiana had had its farewell glances. The hearse moved through a line of armed troops and torchbearers. The line ran from the State House to the west end of the Union Depot. In the civic and military escort were United States Senator Henry Lane and Congressmen Orth, Stillwell, and Farquhar. Amid acres of people, the men with heads uncovered, the coffin was put aboard a train made ready by the Lafayette Railroad Company.

On the slow night run to Chicago it was as in Ohio, thousands in Lafayette standing mute and daybreak not yet, thousands more at Michigan City, where the train stopped under a succession of arches and evergreen and flowers, mottoes reading "The Purposes of the Almighty Are Perfect, and Must Prevail"; "Our Guiding Star Has Fallen"; "Though Dead He Yet Speaketh." Sixteen young women in white waists and black skirts sang the Doxology. Thirty-six young women, one for each State in the Union, stood costumed in white with black scarfs on a flowered platform, holding flags; almost hidden in the folds of the national flag was one grave center lassie who represented the Genius of America. A niece of Speaker Colfax and fifteen other women entered the funeral car and laid wreaths on the coffin. A Chicago committee of one hundred were on hand and took charge of affairs.

Now over flat lands ran the slow train, between it and the blue levels of Lake Michigan the long slopes of pine-crept dunes and here and there the transient, wind-shaped piles of sand that tomorrow would be something else again.

The day was Monday, May 1, but in effect the Chicago obsequies had begun the day before when Speaker Colfax delivered in Bryant Hall a formal funeral oration and a panegyric of Father Abraham as a Man of Mercy beyond any mortal in history—and the assassination one of "utterly unpalliated infamy." To his portrait of Lincoln as the most forgiving of men Colfax joined allegations of Confederate atrocities: they had at Bull Run buried Union soldiers face downward and carved their bones into trinkets;

they had wickedly and systematically starved Union prisoners to death. For Colfax the war was not over. He was for his own purposes still fomenting war hate and metaphorically waving a bloody shirt of incitation. On and on he piled his materials to show Lincoln the humane pardoner—while in a minor tone building a case for passionate revenge on the South, and dwelling but briefly on his part in politics of the hour: "Andrew Johnson, to whom the public confidence was so quickly and worthily transferred, is cast in a sterner mold than him whose place he fills." The very bewilderment of Colfax's smooth and flowing contradictions could only add to whatever grief there was; in that sense he acquitted himself. And all could be in accord with the final quoted line: "from the top of Fame's ladder he stepped to the sky."

In the changed tone of the *Chicago Times* could be read the fact, not so peculiar after all, that among those who would gaze into the Lincoln coffin with a sincere grief this day would be at least a remnant of Copperheads who had once mocked at him and fought him. The *Times* hoped the country might be "happily disappointed" in Mr. Lincoln's successor, "a man in whom nobody feels confidence." And in the mercurial shifts of human issues, the *Times* set forth its reasons why every Copperhead could decently wear crape: "There are not on this day mourners more sincere than the democracy of the Northern States. Widely as they have differed with Mr. Lincoln—greatly as their confidence in him had been shaken—they saw in the indications of the last few days of his life that he might command their support in the close of the war, as he did in the beginning. These indications inspired them with hope, and confidence, and joy, which are now dashed to the ground. The democracy may well mourn the death of Abraham Lincoln."

This changed tone of the *Chicago Times* and part of its following was resented in some quarters. The *Illinois State Journal* at Springfield reprinted from the *Chicago Tribune* remarks of the Reverend R. M. Hatfield before the Young Men's Christian Association in Chicago. Following a eulogy of President Lincoln Mr. Hatfield said "that the men who had misrepresented, abused and vilified the President while he lived, should at least stop praising him now that he is dead. It's all of mercy these men have a right to expect, that they are allowed to live . . . they have not the decency to go out and hang themselves, like Judas."

From the *Cincinnati Commercial*, a Republican newspaper, the *Chicago Times* reprinted an editorial taking notice that the "profound regret" over Lincoln's death expressed in newspapers that had opposed him seemed genuine, and there was "no reason to believe their words of sorrow hypocritical, their grief the mask of malice." A touch of Lincolnian sober balance, in contrast with the lurid excesses of Colfax and others, ran through this editorial headed "The Democratic Press and the Late President," addressing itself to Republicans and saying: "Surely, while the nation mourns around the coffin of Abraham Lincoln, the lessons of the solemn hour should not be those of black vengeance, but of charity. Let us, if possible, think more highly, more kindly of each other than heretofore, and endeavor to appreciate the good we have before it is gone from us." The writer saw the country drifting too far from the spirit of the second inaugural and counseled: "Let us not belittle our cause, or lose the dignity that becomes national bereavement, or disparage the memory of the illustrious dead we mourn, by going to either extreme of the popular passion of last week or of this. Let us take care neither to gush with forgiveness for rebels before they have repented and done works meet for repentance, nor to involve the innocent with the guilty in the punishment of crimes."

Announcement of special passenger trains. From the Lincoln Library of the University of Chicago.

By railway train, by wagon or buggy and on horseback, something like a hundred thousand people had come into Chicago from all points of the Northwest—the region that had heard the Lincoln-Douglas debates, that had shifted the national political balance of power, that had marched its State delegations into Chicago and the Wigwam of the National Republican Convention in 1860 and with unheard-of shouting swung the nomination for President to their dark horse Abraham Lincoln. Here the War President had had less trouble over the draft quotas than in any other region. Here the vision of the Union of States with railways from coast to coast, with the Mississippi River flowing unvexed to the sea, with two oceans for national borders, with the curve of a continent for its land arc—here that vision lay deep and Lincoln had built on it. Here were thousands who had met him and talked with him as between friends and neighbors in the years far back when mention of him for President was a joke that he too laughed at. And since then what had not happened?

Over the south door of the Cook County courthouse an inscription outside read "Illinois Clasps to Her Bosom Her Slain, but Glorified Son" and inside "He Was Sustained by Our Prayers, and Returns Embalmed by Our

Tears." Over the north door the inscription outside read "The Beauty of Israel Is Slain upon Thy High Places" and inside "The Altar of Freedom Has Borne No Nobler Sacrifice."

The vocal attempts at solemn grief often failed and were overdone. But there was a silent grief—broken only by sobs, by choked snufflings, by low wailings, by almost inaudible moans—a loss lacking words and afraid of words. There was too a curious dumb sorrow, perhaps deeper than any other. The dry eyes, the face hard-set, the voice low and even—and far under a knocking and a knocking—and for a long time there would be no comfort— and always there would be a loss and an empty corner of which the less said the better. And this dumb sorrow dug itself in and made itself part of their lives, whether or no they had ever met the living Lincoln. It was a light to be carried. And this light could never go out. It burned for always. The shadows around it were the real Lincoln, the mortal of bowels and clay and ringing laughter. The light itself was the Lincoln ideal, what he at his best wanted to be—and his dream of freedom for all men.

Slowly at Twelfth Street and Michigan Avenue the funeral train came to a stop. Under a huge reception arch of side arches, columns, and Gothic windows in the lake-shore park near by, the eight sergeants carried the coffin and laid it on a dais. The pallbearers and guard of honor made their formation around it. Throughout brasses and drums gave a march written for the occasion, "The Lincoln Requiem." Thirty-six high-school girls moved forward, in snow-white gowns, crape sashes, black-velvet bands with a single star over the forehead, some with sunny ringlets dropping to their shoulders, others with neat braids down the back. Over the bier two by two they strewed immortelles and garlands of red and white roses.

Then a procession of fifty thousand people, witnessed by double as many, escorted the hearse to the courthouse. As in Manhattan and in Washington, there were in this procession the elements of all races, religions, nationalities, and classes composing America. Not hitherto, however, had any Confederate soldiers marched—though here was a regiment of Confederate prisoners of war who had taken the oath of allegiance and aligned themselves for Union service. In the line of march and looking on, sharing something common, were native-born Yankees and Mayflower descendants, Sons and Daughters of the Revolution, Jews, Negroes, Catholics, Germans, Irishmen, Dutchmen, Swedes, Norwegians, Danes—the so-called "big bugs" and the so-called "ragtag and bobtail" for once in a common front.

A drizzle of rain fell on what the press styled the Queen City of the Lakes. The unpaved streets and those cobblestoned were slushy with a slippery mud. Occasionally planks or supporting two-by-fours of the wooden sidewalks crashed with spectators. Women fainted and two-horse ambulances came. Barkeepers were busy. So were pickpockets. The police-station cells were filled. Considering the extent of the swarming human crush, however, the day was orderly, even sedate. The news-writers gave it all they had, one of them reporting as though it happened—and it may have—that when the funeral train drew to its stop at Twelfth and Michigan, "The waters of

Lake Michigan, long ruffled by the storm, suddenly calmed from their angry roar into solemn silence as if they, too, felt that silence was an imperative necessity of the mournful occasion."

All night long Monday, through all the night hours and through the day hours of Tuesday, the columns moved in and out the courthouse. When the doors closed, it was estimated one hundred and twenty-five thousand people had taken their last glance at the Man from Illinois.

A German chorus of three hundred voices chanted and a thousand men with blazing torches escorted the coffin from the courthouse to the depot and the funeral car for the slow night run to Springfield on the Alton Railroad.

At Joliet were midnight torches, evergreen arches, twelve thousand people. Every town and village, many a crossroads and lonely farm, spoke its mournful salutation across the hours of night and early morning. Here and there an arch or a depot doorway had the short flash "Come Home." At the town of Lincoln was an arch, and a portrait inscribed "With Malice toward None; with Charity for All."

The burial vault at Springfield

Then at last to Springfield came the coffin that had traveled seventeen hundred miles, that had been seen by more than seven million people—and the rigid face on which more than one million five hundred thousand people had gazed a moment or longer. The estimated figures were given. They were curious, incidental, not important—though such a final pilgrimage had never before moved with such somber human outpourings on so vast a national landscape.

In the State capitol, in the hall of the lower house of which he had been a member and where he had spoken his prophet warnings of the House

Three photographs by Gardner made about April 10, '65. Lincoln returned from City Point on the evening of April 9 and the sitting for Gardner is believed to have been one or two days thereafter. The plates registered a man worn almost haggard by four years of storm—yet his face shining over the war's end and his hope of reconciliation and "remolding society," as he phrased it, in the years of peace to come. These pictures and the frontispiece of this volume represent the Lincoln seen by men in the last week of his life.

The assemblage at the Lincoln home, Springfield, on May 4, '65

Photograph from the Barrett collection

Divided, stood the casket. Now passed those who had known him long. They were part of the seventy-five thousand who passed. They were awed, subdued, shaken, stony, strange. They came from Salem, Petersburg, Clary's Grove, Alton, Charleston, Mattoon, the old Eighth Circuit towns and villages. There were clients for whom he had won or lost, lawyers who had tried cases with him and against, neighbors who had seen him milk a cow and curry his horse, friends who had heard his stories around a hot stove and listened to his surmises on politics and religion. "We," wrote Bill Herndon, "who had known the illustrious dead in other days, and before the nation lay its claim upon him, moved sadly through and looked for the last time on the silent, upturned face of our departed friend."

All day long and through the night the unbroken line moved, the home town having its farewell.

On May 4 of this year 1865 Anno Domini a procession moved with its hearse from the State capitol to Oak Ridge Cemetery. There on green banks and hillsides flowing away from a burial vault the crowded thousands of listeners and watchers heard prayers and hymns, heard Bishop Matthew Simpson in a rounded, moving oration, heard the second inaugural read aloud.

Evergreen carpeted the stone floor of the vault. On the coffin set in a receptacle of black walnut they arranged flowers carefully and precisely, they poured flowers as symbols, they lavished heaps of fresh flowers as though there could never be enough to tell either their hearts or his.

And the night came with great quiet.

And there was rest.

The prairie years, the war years, were over.

INDEX

INDEX

This index is planned to include the following:

Names of persons. Every name each time it is mentioned except those of some with last name only and unidentifiable names in quotations and illustrations. *Exceptions:* "Administration of," "friend of," "to father, mother, wife, of," "staff of," only occasionally entered. If *CSA* or *CSN* is not used, the officer or official is *USA*. Names of fictitious persons in stories told are not indexed, but will be found in the list under "Stories."

Names of business firms. Only the more important.

Names of battles. Only when first named as taking place. A date following the name indicates a battle.

Names of places. Only when significant.

Note: Inclusive paging does not always mean continued reference, but often only frequent mention.

657-59; II. 4, 141, 341, 523; III. 487; IV. 138; treaties with, I. 579, 654-55; II. 480; Ministers to, I. 92, 282; II. 453 (*see also* Adams, Charles Francis, Sr.); on A. L., cartoons, 513; III. 245; A. L. on, 332; IV. 145

English, James E., *MC*, III. 4, 172; IV. 12

Englishmen: in the *USA*, I. 511; II. 608; III. 614; in the war, I. 216; II. 89

Era, London, II. 515

Ericsson, John, I. 483-84; IV. 375; wife of, I. 483; pors., 488-89

Essex Statesman, N. J., on A. L., III. 197-98

Etheridge, Emerson, *MC*, II. 501-02; IV. 123

Etowah River, Ga., ('64), III. 153

Euclid, A. L. on, III. 408

Eugénie, empress of France, IV. 374

Europe: and the *CSA*, I. 580, 588; and emigration, 43; and cotton, 12; and the war, 47, 581

Evans, William, Forbes to, II. 459

Evarts, William M., *Sen.*, I. 218, 232, 452; III. 588, 590

Everett, Edward, I. 28, 117, 362, 431; II. 453-55, 465-75; III. 280; IV. 100, 212, 369; wife of, II. 453; death of, IV. 115; on A. L., I. 48; II. 453-54; III. 664-65; A. L. on, II. 454; IV. 115; por., II. 468

Everett, Maj. Nicholls, I. 521

Ewell, Gen. Richard S., *CSA*, I. 530, 555; II. 342, 439; captured, IV. 185

Ewing, Thomas, Sr., I. 644, 649; II. 115, 598; III. 156, 602

Ewing, Gen. Thomas, Jr., II. 401

Fahnestock, Harris C. ("Fahny"), III. 122

Fair Oaks, Va. *See* Seven Pines.

Fairfax, Adm. Donald MacNeill, I. 359-60

Fairfax Court-House, Va., ('61), I. 301

Fairfield (Ia.) *Constitution and Union*, plant destroyed, III. 57

Fairs. *See* Sanitary Commission.

Family of men, A. L. speaks of the, I. 4?

Fanning, William, curses A. L., IV. 347-48

Farlin, J. W., contractor, III. 276

Farnam, Henry, I. 159-60; wife of, 159

Farnsworth, Gen. Addison, II. 40-41

Farnsworth, Gen. John F., I. 32; II. 41; III. 172, 305, 660

Farquhar, John H., *MC*, IV. 408

Farragut, Adm. David G., I. 511; II. 71, 108, 436, 437, 526; III. 12, 65-66, 203, 237; IV. 29, 87, 96, 389; takes New Orleans, I. 475, 655; takes Mobile, III. 192 (with illus.), 229; por., I. 361

Farwell, Leonard J., IV. 293

Father Abraham, Reading, Pa., III. 393

Fayetteville, N. C., ('65), IV. 138

Federalist, The, III. 131

Feeks, J. F., publisher, III. 267-68

Fellows, J. Q. A., III. 11

Felton, Samuel M., I. 66, 67

Fenton, Reuben E., *MC*, later *Governor of New York*, I. 413-14; III. 172, 217, 249, 569, 629; IV. 133-34, 395; por., III. 19

Ferguson, William J., actor, IV. 281-82; on Wilkes Booth, 313-14

Ferrandini (Fernandina), C., conspirator, I. 66-67, 71

Ferrer de Couto, José, II. 511-12

Ferry, Jedediah B. (?), ballot inspector, III. 288

Fessenden, Gen. Francis, III. 116, 121

Fessenden, Gen. James D., III. 116, 121

Fessenden, Lt. Samuel, killed, III. 116, 121

Fessenden, William Pitt, *Sen.*, later *Sec. of the Treas.*, I. 173, 313-14, 387, 434, 440, 637-51; II. 41, 348, 540, 556; III. 92-94, 115, 132-33, 174, 214-16, 275-76, 369-70, 562, 567, 573, 582, 588, 646-47, 656-57; IV. 12, 47, 61; apptd *Sec. of the Treas.*, III. 115-23, 254; resigns, IV. 107; and Chase, III. 595-96; and A. L., I. 387; on A. L., I.

voted by Congress, 538, (conferred by A. L.), 545-46, (illus.) 546; and the Hampton Roads conference, IV. 34-38, 62-65; plot to assassinate, 333-34; notified of Lincoln's assassination, 294-95; and Gen. Blair, III. 23-35; Mrs. Chesnut on, II. 535, 537, 544-45; and Thomas, III. 635-38; A. L. and, I. 598, 610; II. 120-21, 394, 406, 417, 455, 537-44, 546-54, 576; III. 60-66, 144-52, 209, 275, 504-05, 610, 616, 630, 635, 656; IV. 63-65, 110, 113, 121-22, 131, 139-63, 167, 171, 182, 185, 198, 215, 234-37; on A. L., II. 121; IV. 153-54; A. L. on, I. 462-63, 478; II. 55, 119-20, 358, 431, 537-38, 552; III. 43, 46-47, 52, 59, 62, 67, 98, 306-07, 631, 639, 659; IV. 133, 137, 220, 227, 271; and the Presidency, II. 536-39, 570, 594; III. 49, 59, 70, 72, 75-76, 83-84, 100-01, 109, 203, 217-18, (A. L. on), 49, 287; pun on, IV. 84; illus. (letter), 168; (signature), 202; pors., II. 548; III. 50; IV. 52. *See also* Rawlins, Gen. John A., and Grant; Sherman, Gen. William Tecumseh, and Grant.

Grant County (Wis.) *Herald*, on A. L., III. 212

Grant's Petersburg Progress, IV. 170

"Grass will grow in the streets," I. 89-90

Grau, Maurice, II. 318

Graves, Thomas T., and A. L., IV. 178-80

Gray, Alice, actress, IV. 331

Gray, Asa, and A. L., I. 364; on A. L., III. 104

Gray, Rev. Edgar H., at A. L.'s funeral, IV. 391

Gray, Maj. John C., Jr., I. 626; III. 179, 185; IV. 24, 339

Gray, Dr. John P., III. 488

Great Britain. *See* England.

Greece, ref. to ancient, I. 6, 257; II. 127, 135, 148, 467, 492; III. 130; IV. 383, 407

Greeley, Horace, I. 51, 55, 62, 65, 92, 159, 177, 179, 351-55, 372-73, 423, 440, 604; II. 47, 116, 213-14, 230, 282, 360, 493, 504, 532,

594, 607, 619, 636-37, 653; III. 16, 24-25, 113, 146-47, 205, 212, 215, 245, 259, 425, 564; IV. 130, 134, 241, 254-56; word por. of, I. 402-08; wife and children of, 407; peace attempts of, II. 66-67; III. 165, 167 (*see also* Niagara peace conference); and the Presidency, II. 569; IV. 255; and the Postmaster-Generalship, II. 464; III. 249; IV. 110, 254-55; on A. Johnson, III. 95; A. L. and, I. 54, 401-03, 559-60, 564; II. 298, 309, 584-85; III. 420-21; letters to A. L., I. 305-06, 564-67; II. 306, 386, 552; III. 157-58, 162, 210-11, (illus.) 159; IV. 216, 254-55, (illus.), I. 565; III. 157-59; opposes A. L.'s re-election, II. 195-96, 421, 643-45; III. 102-03, 203, 376, 421; supports A. L. in '64, 221, 237; on A. L., I. 143, 403, 408; II. 8, 47, 195-96, 331-32, 569-70, 585, 645-46; III. 7, 237-38, 421; IV. 255; A. L. on, II. 256, 584, 644; III. 136, 162-63; on Seward, I. 143; III. 161, 421; illus. (signature), I. 405; cartoons, 306; II. 101; por., 117. *See also New York Tribune.*

Green, Gen. Duff, *CSA*, II. 394; IV. 347; and A. L., IV. 181-82

Green, Dr. Horace, I. 511-12

Green, James S., *Sen.*, I. 16-17

Greenbacks, I. 651-53; II. 191-93, 194, 494; III. 124, 268, 312, 339, 387, 397, 599, 639; IV. 52

Greencastle, Pa., ('63), II. 338-39

Greene, J. Wesley, II. 130-32

Greene, Gen. Nathanael, IV. 185

Greene, Lt. S. Dana, *USN*, I. 481-83

Greene, William G., II. 431; III. 331

Greenhow, Rose M. O'Neale (Mrs. Robert), I. 326-27, 472

Greensboro (N. C.) *Patriot*, I. 8

Greenville (Ohio) *Democrat*, plant destroyed, III. 58

Greenwood, Grace (Sara J. C. Lippincott), on A. L., II. 286-87, 292-93; por., III. 339

223; Tyler to, I. 137; Sumner to, 347; II. 75; III. 595; IV. 70, 225

Lieutenant General (rank): revival of, urged, I. 638; revived, II. 539-40; Grant apptd, 540-41

Lighthouses, lightships, seized, I. 7

Limburg, Roest van, Dutch Minister, II. 69

Lincoln, Abraham, *16th Pres. USA*, chronology of these volumes:

VOL. I

The American scene in '61, 3-34; South Carolina secedes, 5; Lincoln journeys to Washington, speaking en route, 35-84; his election certified, 44-45; against his wishes, he avoids Baltimore and an assassination plot, 66-84; the false story of his disguise, 81-84; the '61 Peace Convention meets, 85-90; forming his Cabinet, 91-92; conferences with friend and foe, 92-120; an analysis of Charles Sumner, 99-114; Lincoln takes the oath as President, 120-40; the first inaugural, 125-35; the President names his Cabinet, 140-62; he deals with office-seekers, 162-79; he faces the problem of reinforcing Fort Sumter, 185-206; Sumter falls, 207-10; the first call for troops, 211; Lincoln and Stephen Douglas confer as colleagues, 213-14; the Uprising of the North and determination in the South, 215-35; Robert E. Lee resigns from the U. S. Army to take command of the Virginian forces, 223; the blockade and letters of marque, 227; the Confederacy organized, with Jefferson Davis as President, 237-40; Ellsworth killed, 264-67; Stephen Douglas dies, 268-69; Butler a cause of trouble, 278; a message on habeas corpus, 281; the July message to Congress, 295-99; First Bull Run, 300-04; Lincoln's plan after the battle, 309; McClellan heads the Army of the Potomac, 315; but he delays, 315-25; Ball's Bluff, 324; Edward Dickinson Baker killed, 324-25; Lincoln visits Gen-

eral Banks, 329-30; Missouri trouble, Frémont, 333-51; James Gordon Bennett and the *Herald*, 352-56; the Trent Affair, 359-69; "One war at a time," 365; more office-seekers, 369-76; the December, '61, message, 377-82; the death warrant for a slave-trader, 384-86; the Committee on the Conduct of the War is appointed, 388; Thaddeus Stevens, 392-400; Greeley and his *Tribune*, 401-08; McClellan still delays, 413-22; Lincoln sums up the situation in October, '62, 424-25; Cameron and contracts, 426-35; Cameron resigns, and Stanton becomes Secretary of War, 437-38; Lincoln's message on the Cameron contracts, 452-53; Willie Lincoln dies, 456; Donelson, "unconditional and immediate surrender," Ulysses S. Grant, 462-68; McClellan continues to delay, 468-75; Butler goes to New Orleans, 471; New Orleans taken, 475-76; Shiloh and Pittsburg Landing, 476-78; the *Monitor* and the *Merrimac*, 481-83; Lincoln goes to Fortress Monroe, 486-89; McClellan still fails to act, 489-503; the Seven Days' battles, 492-95; Lincoln visits Harrison's Landing and McClellan gives him a letter, 495-97; Halleck General in Chief, 498; the second call for troops, the draft, 505; "We are coming, Father Abraham," 507; the President signs the Homestead Bill, 510; the Army of Virginia formed (Pope in command), 515; Robert E. Lee, 516-24; Malvern Hill, 525-26; Second Bull Run, 532-33; Phil Kearny killed, 534; Pope relieved of command, 536; McClellan is still delaying, 537-44; Lincoln suggests his resigning, 543-44; Antietam, 550-54; the involved slavery question, 555-57; Hunter's emancipation proclamation, 561; Lincoln writes Greeley on slavery and the Union, 567; a committee of Negroes calls on him, 574-76; he signs the Confiscation Act, 579; again he suggests resigning, 580-81; the prelim-

Martin, George, R.R. engineer, IV. 405

Martin, Henri, II. 510

Martín, José Maria, sentenced to death, II. 64

Martin, Rev. William, *CSA,* IV. 84

Marvin, James M., *MC,* III. 172

Marx, Karl, I. 380; II. 4-5; to A. L., III. 579-80; on A. L., II. 5

Maryland, I. 70-71, 227, 231, 259, 261, 279, 296, 348, 378, 506, 549, 584, 586; II. 99, 102, 336, 346, 412, 414, 451, 482-83; III. 35-36, 92, 220, 275, 430; emancipation in, 126, 400, 456, 563, 572; IV. 14; delegation from, III. 572; Legislature, I. 273-76, 330; II. 645; III. 255, 594

Mason, James M., *CSA,* I. 359-69; III. 290, 396; por., I. 330

Mason, Jeremiah, I. 114; IV. 76

Massachusetts, I. 28, 111; III. 84, 92-94, 180-81, 563; delegations from, I. 185; 6th regiment, 228-29, 235, 275; Legislature, 624; II. 566-67; Sumner on, IV. 78; A. L. on, III. 449

Massanutton Mountain, Va., ('64), III. 296

Massey, Rev. Mr., dismissed from his church, IV. 357

Matthews, John, actor, IV. 327, 334

Matthews, W. T., painter, por. of A. L., II. 21

Maury, Com. Matthew F., *CSA,* II. 141

Maximilian, emperor of Mexico, I. 655; II. 395-96; III. 13; IV. 30-31, 110. *See also* France and Mexico.

Maxwell, Robert A., crank, II. 425-26

May, Rev. Samuel J., Jr., I. 3; III. 75; on A. L., II. 414-15

Maynard, Horace, *MC,* I. 13-14, 20; II. 178, 429; III. 79-80, 84, 95; por., 275

Mays, William J., private, III. 39-40

Mazzini, Giuseppe, II. 384

Mazzoleni, Francesco, II. 318

Meade, Gen. George A., II. 91, 94-95, 98, 102-03, 121, 339-58, 380, 427, 436-43, 446, 455, 460, 462, 472, 514-15, 521, 545, 551, 553; III. 47, 50, 52-64, 155-56, 219, 287, 293-94, 476, 478, 498, 518-19; IV. 36, 46, 123, 142-45, 148, 203-05, 215; word por. of, I. 334; heads the Army of the Potomac, II. 102-03, 336; removal urged, 545; wife of, III. 210; IV. 143, (letters to, included in other headings); C. A. Dana on, III. 63; on Grant, II. 545; III. 220; on A. L., 210, 335-36; A. L. on, II. 334, 354-55; III. 517; pors., I. frontispiece; II. 372

Meade, Lt. Robert L., *USN,* II. 30

Meade, Robert W., II. 30

Meagher, Gen. Thomas F., I. 629; II. 515; III. 75

Meconkey, Mrs. Sarah B., A. L. to, III. 46

Medary, Sam, II. 3, 134, 165; III. 583; on A. L., II. 527; III. 390-91. *See also Crisis.*

Medill, Joseph, I. 60, 149, 351, 571, 637, 651; II. 31, 190-91, 520, 532; III. 187-88; on Grant, II. 536; on A. L., 536, 571-72; IV. 218. *See also Chicago Tribune.*

Medill, Maj. William H., killed, II. 290

Meek, Rev. J. B., II. 223

Meigs, Capt., I. 197-99

Meigs, Quartermaster Gen. Montgomery C., I. 425, 430, 438, 480, 533-34; II. 55; III. 276, 356, 364; and A. L.'s death, IV. 292

Meissonier, Jean L. E., I. 183; II. 609

"Melton," (Melton Prior), III. 343-45

Melville, Herman, I. 375; III. 299; on A. L., I. 375; IV. 345

Memminger, Christopher Gustavus, *Sec. of Treas., CSA,* I. 201, 239-40; por., 297

Memphis, Tenn., A. L. on, I. 309

Memphis (Tenn.) *Appeal,* on A. L., I. 329

Memphis (Tenn.) *Avalanche,* I. 568

Memphis (Tenn.) *Bulletin,* II. 181

Menken, Adah Isaacs, (Dolores Adíos Fuertes; Mrs. A. I., Mrs. J. C. Heenan,

Shakespeare, William, frequent ref. from, II. 122 to IV. 341; quoted, II. 122-24, 314; III. 47, 389, 446-47, 667; IV. 195, 402; A. L. and, I. 61; II. 122-24, 217, 309, 314-17, 547; III. 47, 61, 309, 445-47; IV. 194-95, 213, 244-45, 280; A. L. sees plays by, III. 443, 446-47; cartoon, II. 9

Shannon, Thomas B., *MC*, III. 172, 331

Sharpe, Col. George H., III. 644

Sharpsburg, Md. *See* Antietam.

Shaw, Francis G., to A. L., II. 505

Shaw, Col. Robert Gould, II. 180; IV. 400; killed, II. 443; ref. to, 505

Shaw, W. B., III. 426

Shawneetown (Ill.) *Democrat*, II. 109

Sheldon, Lt., I. 472

Shellabarger, Samuel, *MC*, II. 60; III. 275, 569; IV. 270; por., III. 147

Shenandoah Valley, I. 260, 301, 304, 308, 490, 491, 527-30, 550, 552; II. 102, 339, 441, 551; III. 51, 84, 138, 150-52, 235-37, 287, 293, 297-98, 415, 455, 672; IV. 136, 146, 248

Shephard, Julia A., saw A. L. shot, IV. 280, 282

Shepherd, Annie P., and Frank, private, III. 453

Shepley, Gen. George F., IV. 180, 225-26

Sheridan, Gen. Philip H., II. 6, 478-79, 515, 550; III. 49, 51, 63, 150-52, 156, 233-37, 242, 287-88, 293, 296-99, 383, 521, 573, 637, 639, 672; IV. 29, 136, 146-48, 157, 160, 164-66, 182, 185, 197-99, 205, 215, 355; ride of, 297-99, (poems on) 298-99; A. L. on, II. 550; III. 287, 298; Sherman on, 619; por., IV. 52

Sherman, Ellen (Eleanor) Ewing (Mrs. W. T.), sees A. L., I. 411-12

Sherman, Francis C., I. 612

Sherman, Gen. Francis T., I. 612

Sherman, John, *Sen.*, I. 17, 171-72, 314, 333, 478, 637, 639; II. 290, 556, 604; III.

115, 174, 629; IV. 65, 156-57, 161, 216; and Chase, III. 593-94; on Grant, II. 547-48; on A. L., I. 639; IV. 26, 56; A. L. on, II. 301, 588

Sherman, Gen. William Tecumseh, I. 3-4, 20-21, 301, 303, 316, 328, 415, 425, 509; II. 112-13, 187, 388, 427, 431-32, 462, 479, 509, 545, 551, 552, 560, 586, 592, 610; III. 16-17, 23-27, 31, 37, 43, 63, 121, 128, 152-53, 167, 175, 177-79, 184, 192, 222, 237, 256-57, 283, 293, 299, 303, 457, 472, 481, 569, 636, 641; IV. 14, 18-19, 21, 28-29, 85, 112, 116, 137-38, 159, 168, 197, 205, 209, 218, 249, 253, 265, 355; word por. of, II. 115-16; "insane," I, 329, 411; II. 116; IV. 138; his wife protests his treatment, I. 411-12; at Shiloh, 476-77; takes and occupies Atlanta, III. 299, 614-15, 618, 645-46, 672; march to the sea, 619-35, (ref. to), 644-45, 672; IV. 20, 137-38; and Georgia Governor, III. 609-10; takes and occupies Savannah, 634-35, 639, 671-72; IV. 23-24; in South Carolina, 81-85; and the Presidency, III. 147, 203, 237; and the '64 election, 281-83; hears of A. L.'s assassination, IV. 342-43; army of, III. 619-20, 630-31; IV. 81-82, 138-39, 158, ("lost"; Grant on) III. 628; ("lost"; A. L. on) 629-31; and Grant, I. 478; II. 109, 114-15, 121, 391, 536-37, 541-42, 545-48; III. 13-14, 45, 50-51, 145-47, 152, 154-56, 186, 217, 615-31, 619, 638, 640, 658-59; IV. 26, 144, 156-57, 167; A. L. and, I. 171-73, 289-90, 307-08; II. 114, 389-91, 413; III. 50, 154-55, 179-80, 229-30, 521, 617, 634-35; IV. 113, 158-60, 215, 235-36; on A. L., III. 283; A. L. on, 630-31; IV. 80-81, 137, (illus. message) III. 632; Nasby on, IV. 61; soldiers on, III. 473; Southerners on, 621-22; IV. 139; and Thomas, III. 637; on Washington, D. C., IV. 339; por., III. 605

"Sherman hairpins," III. 622, and illus.

Shields, Gen. James. I. 334, 637; II. 240; III.